Getting Classroom Management RIGHT

Guided Discipline and Personalized Support in Secondary Schools

IN THE PARTNERS IN LEARNING SERIES

Engaging SCHOOLS

Connect • Collaborate • Learn

Getting Classroom Management RIGHT: Guided Discipline and Personalized
Support in Secondary Schools
In the Partners in Learning Series
By Carol Miller Lieber
© 2009 Educators for Social Responsibility

Engaging Schools
23 Garden Street
Cambridge, MA 02138
www.engagingschools.org

Cover design by John Barnett/Four Eyes Design
Book production by Erin Dawson

10 9 8 7 6
Printed in the United States of America

ISBN 13: 978-0-615-28123-0
ISBN 10: 0-615-28123-0

ACKNOWLEDGMENTS

The two new books in the Partners in Learning Series, *Making Learning REAL* and *Getting Classroom Management RIGHT*, represent a lifetime of work in education and twenty years of developing programs and facilitating professional development for the Cambridge, Massachusetts-based Engaging Schools (formerly Educators for Social Responsibility).

This effort would not have been possible without the support of many people. On a personal note, I would like to thank my mother and late father who nurtured, and at times tolerated, a fiercely independent, curious, and idealistic kid who didn't lose her vision as a grown-up. Professionally, I would like to thank Engaging Schools' executive director, Larry Dieringer, who has been a valued thought partner in this process, providing the organizational leadership and support so necessary for the development of new programs and publications.

Over the years, many colleagues have been true partners with me in this work and have served me well as friendly critics and critical friends. In particular, I would like to thank Rachel Poliner, Jennifer Allen, Connie Cuttle, Sherrie Gammage, and Doug Breunlin. I am indebted to Audra Longert and Denise Wolk, my editors, who both have an amazing capacity to fire up my passion while keeping me on track and focused. They don't miss a thing!

There are others who inspire my urgency to write: Thomas Jefferson, whose writings inform my identity as a teacher-citizen; John Dewey, whose work serves as the anchor for my professional practice and compelled me to cofound a progressive secondary school in 1973; Martin Luther King Jr., whose invitation to join the struggle for equity and opportunity changed a young woman's life; Nel Noddings, whose brave and utterly reasonable stance about what's good for children and what's wrong with current reform sheds light in a dark educational moment; and Linda Darling-Hammond, whose life as a teacher educator, researcher, and activist is a model for all educational writers.

Finally, I want to thank all of the school leaders, resident principals, teachers, and students I meet and work with every day here in Chicago, in New York, and across the country. Their needs, requests, and feedback keep pushing me and my Engaging Schools colleagues to make our work better.

CONTENTS

PREFACE TO NEW BOOKS in the PARTNERS IN LEARNING SERIES .ix
INTRODUCTION 1

CHAPTER 1: Classroom Management and Discipline 19
   The Punishment Approach 20
   The Do-Nothing Approach 21
   The Guided Discipline Approach 21
   Identifying the Problem and Guided Discipline Response 25
      Six Problem Types in the Classroom 26
      Match the Right Response to the Problem. 28
      Matching the Right Response to a Specific Unwanted Behavior 29
      Matching the Right Response to a Specific Learning Gap 34
   What Students Need to Know 35
   Frequently Used Terms 36

CHAPTER 2: 13 Guided Discipline Scenarios 43
   Scenario 1. 44
   Scenario 2. 45
   Scenario 3. 47
   Scenario 4. 48
   Scenario 5. 50
   Scenario 6. 51
   Scenario 7. 52
   Scenario 8. 53
   Scenario 9. 54
   Scenario 10. 56
   Scenario 11. 59
   Scenario 12. 60
   Scenario 13. 62

CHAPTER 3: Step 1: Know Yourself, Know Your Students, and Know Your School 63
Know Yourself. 63
      Know where your power and authority come from. 64
      Know if you are more authoritarian or authoritative 66
      Know your teaching stance. 67
      Know your goals for discipline and personalized support 69
      Know your nos, needs, and nonnegotiables 71
      Know how with-it you are 71
      Know how to define disrespect. 72
      Know how to depersonalize bad behavior 73
      Know how to avoid communication roadblocks. 76

Know your communication style 78
Know how to listen responsively. 80
Know how to manage your anger 81
Know how to handle conflict in the classroom 81
Know your conflict style. 84
Know how to recover 85
Know how to diagnose your own practice accurately 86
Know the teacher roles you want to strengthen. 87
Know Your Students 89
Know how to diagnose the underlying reasons for unwanted behaviors 91
Know key essentials of adolescent development. 92
Know key qualities and attributes of a developed student. 95
Know Your School. 96
Know your school's discipline policies and referral systems 96
Know colleagues and administrators whom you can count on for help
and assistance 97

CHAPTER 4: Step 2: Create Group Norms, Procedures, and Learning Protocols 99
Create Group Norms 99
Establish positive group guidelines and agreements 101
Discuss the issue of respect 104
Generate a list of rights and responsibilities 114
Explain your approach to discipline 114
Create Group Procedures. 116
Be clear about the reasons for procedures and be consistent in enforcing them. 117
Model, teach, practice, and assess the procedures you expect 119
Create Group Learning Protocols. 134
Use group learning protocols to build intellectual, metacognitive, social
and emotional competencies 135
Use group problem-solving protocols to help students manage conflict
and negotiate learning 136

CHAPTER 5: Step 3: Support Individuals and the Group 141
Support Students' Social and Emotional Development. 141
Model, teach, practice, and assess life skills 141
Teach Students How to Manage their Emotions 147
Teach the conflict escalator 151
Teach the differences between aggressive, passive, and assertive behavior 151
Provide scripts that encourage students to say and do the right thing 155
Provide Personalized Support and Recognition 158
Make personal connections with every student. 158
Provide immediate and meaningful feedback and encouragement 158
Provide personalized support for students who are struggling. 161
Create opportunities for students to link personal effort to their successes. 164
Recognize individual accomplishments in and out of the classroom 166

Provide Group Support and Recognition 168

Build and maintain a cohesive group 168

Strengthen your group facilitation skills 169

Monitor and assess group participation 171

Create classroom routines and rituals that involve every student 172

Recognize and celebrate the group's efforts and accomplishments 172

Use group incentives, random reinforcement, and intermittent rewards 173

CHAPTER 6: Step 4: Invite Student Engagement, Cooperation, and Self-Correction 177

Set the Stage for Engagement and Cooperation: Five Essential Everyday Practices 178

1. Get the group's attention 178

2. Give clear instructions 180

3. Insist on silence when silence is required 181

4. Use proximity and physical prompts first when students are off task 182

5. Design well-paced, student-centered lessons 184

Help Students Get Ready to Learn and Focus 188

Help students settle in at the beginning of class 188

Help students wake up, energize, and recharge the mind and body 189

Do a quick check-in to read the group before a lesson begins 191

Set goals to get ready to learn 192

Avoid Pitfalls that Derail Discussion 193

Prepare students to participate responsibly in discussion 193

Redirect unproductive group talk behaviors 194

Defuse, disarm, and deflate provocative behavior 195

Address Students' Negative Speech and Unacceptable Language 196

Review norms and consequences related to public speech 197

Interrupt negative speech using multiple strategies 198

Intervene immediately when students' speech is beyond correction 203

Invite Students to Cooperate and Self-Correct 204

Intervene when students are confused or stuck 204

Redirect students when they look bored or disengaged 205

When students are doing the wrong thing or doing it at the wrong time 207

Use Problem Solving and Logical Consequences when Self-Correction Isn't Enough . . . 207

Offer students chances to solve problems and make choices 207

Insist on problem solving and negotiation rather than complaints 208

Put the responsibility on the student when an unwanted behavior persists 209

Use logical consequences to correct minor problematic behaviors 209

Defuse Feelings of Anger, Frustration, and Discouragement 211

Help defuse students' anger and frustration 211

Let students know what they can do to cool down 213

Communicate your support and confidence when students feel discouraged 214

**Plan, Organize, Document, and Track Guided Discipline Supports
and Interventions** 215

Implement guided discipline supports and interventions every week 215

Track and document what you do and what your students do 216

CHAPTER 7: Step 5: Develop Accountable Consequences and Supportive Interventions . . . 221

  Address Persistent Unwanted Behaviors from Day 1 221

    Prioritize problem behaviors you want to be ready for 223

    Establish three levels of consequences and supportive interventions 226

    Discuss the difference between punishment and accountable consequences 229

    Diagnose problem behaviors accurately 230

  Defuse and De-escalate Potential Confrontations and Power Struggles 232

    Don't give students the opportunity to argue and "lawyer up" 233

    Name the consequence, exit, and deal with it later 233

  When the Group Messes Up 234

    Help the group get unstuck 235

    Create an intervention plan when the whole group is messing up 237

    Teach desired target behaviors that replace unwanted behaviors 239

  Make One-on-One Conferencing a Daily Practice 241

    Use one-on-one conferences to link problem behaviors to desired
    target behaviors 242

    Use one-on-one conferences to show concern when students are upset
    or personally distressed 243

    More conferencing tips when students are upset 244

    Use one-on-one conferences to find out more about unmotivated and
    resistant students 244

    Use one-on-one conferences to listen to "frequent fliers" 245

  **Use Behavior Report Forms, Problem-Solving Protocols, Conduct Cards,
  and Learning Contracts** 247

  Make a Plan when a Class Is "Off the Hook" 249

    Take time to reflect on the situation 249

    Choose a few strategies to get back on track 250

  Communicate with Parents in a Variety of Ways 253

  Problem Solve with Your Colleagues 255

APPENDIX A: Conference Forms and Problem-Solving Protocols 257

APPENDIX B: A Guide for Reflection, Practice, and Planning 279

APPENDIX C: Learning Protocols for Professional Development 335

  Prereading Protocols 337

  While-You-Read Protocols 346

  Small and Large Group Dialogue Protocols 354

  Products / Presentations / Report Outs 356

  Assessment / Feedback / Planning / Closings / Final Thoughts 363

INDEX 370

PREFACE TO NEW BOOKS
in the PARTNERS IN LEARNING SERIES:

Making Learning REAL: Reaching and Engaging All Learners in Secondary Classrooms

Getting Classroom Management RIGHT: Guided Discipline and Personalized Support in Secondary Schools

Why publish two new books instead of a second edition?

We have been gratified by educators' positive responses to the first edition of *Partners in Learning* and have welcomed feedback from teachers, principals, education professors, and professional developers since the book's publication in 2002. Instead of releasing a second edition, Engaging Schools has decided to produce two separate books in the Partners in Learning Series:

Making Learning REAL: Reaching and Engaging All Learners in Secondary Classrooms
and
Getting Classroom Management RIGHT: Guided Discipline and Personalized Support in Secondary Schools.

Producing the two new books has provided us the opportunity to incorporate readers' suggestions, add new material that teachers have requested, and make the original content and formatting more user-friendly. Moreover, the new publications enable Engaging Schools to turn the spotlight on two equally important areas of classroom practice that are particularly relevant for educators engaged in reform efforts aimed at ensuring that all students experience success in school, achieve at high levels, and graduate ready for college and career.

A decade of supporting hundreds of middle and high schools in their redesign and school improvement initiatives has affirmed our deep commitment to the principles and practices that form the framework for books in the Partners in Learning Series. Three lessons learned from our school change work have stood out for us at Engaging Schools:

Changing school structures without changing classroom practice is not enough. Merely adding new structures like advisory systems, block schedules, scaffolded academic interventions, freshman academies, and grade-level teaming without changing the practices and relationships within these containers is unlikely to produce the student outcomes that everyone wants. Supporting teachers to change what they actually do in the classroom and how they relate to students remains the most difficult challenge in the reform process. The two fundamental goals for these new publications is to provide new knowledge and "know-how" that build beliefs and a strong commitment to change classroom practice and to offer a wide array of explicit "how-tos" that enable teachers to do it.

▶ **Changing the quality of instructional practice without attention to personalizing learning and the classroom environment is not enough.** The standards movement and federal mandates of "No Child Left Behind" have put every school on notice to increase academic achievement and reduce the inequality of outcomes among different groups of students. Yet high school dropout and failure rates have hardly budged in recent years, suggesting that the ramping up of instruction and testing will not by itself produce different results—especially for underserved, underperforming students. Many studies have shown, however, that student achievement increases when high expectations and rigorous student work are complemented by efforts to personalize learning, provide higher levels of student support in the classroom, and strengthen positive relationships between and among students and teachers.

> Efforts to respond to the wide range of adolescent students' needs are often approached as add-on components, disconnected from academic achievement, rigorous curriculum, and high teacher expectations for student success. Current calls for reform emphasize the interdependent relationship between personalized learning communities and academic achievement, viewing both as essential to enabling ALL students to meet high standards and create productive futures for themselves. (National High School Alliance 2003)

> Personalized learning is emerging as a response to two notable features of the current high school experience: student apathy and dropping out. Many students see high school as an impersonal experience, forced upon them by an uncaring world at the very moment in their lives when they begin to imagine their independence and yearn for opportunities to expand and express their own talents. (DiMartino, Clarke, and Wolk 2003)

From Lee and Burkam's comprehensive study of school dropouts, their "most important finding" highlights the impact of student-teacher relationships on students' decisions to stay in school or leave. More than half of students who dropped out claimed that poor relationships with their teachers were a major reason for leaving school. Students who left school characterized many of their teachers as not getting along with students, not interested in their success or failure in school, not caring about them, and not willing to provide extra help when asked. When relationships between students and teachers were perceived as positive, students were much more likely to graduate from high school (Lee and Burkham 2003).

Although much has been written about efforts to personalize the school environment and curriculum, far less has been written about actual techniques for putting personalization into practice. *Making Learning REAL: Reaching and Engaging All Learners in Secondary Classrooms* speaks directly to teachers' requests for concrete tools, strategies, and activities that will personalize their classroom practice; help build better relationships with all of their students; and increase student engagement, effort, and motivation.

▶ **Changing the quality of instruction without attention to improving classroom management and discipline is not enough.** Too many veteran and new teachers cite classroom discipline as a primary reason for leaving the profession. An ASCD teacher poll conducted in December 2008 revealed that the number-one topic about which teachers wanted more information was classroom management and discipline.

> Classroom management skills affect the quantity and quality of the teaching profession. Contrary to popular belief, there is not a shortage of certified teachers in America but rather a shortage of those certified to teach who are willing to either enter or remain in the classroom. The primary reasons why new teachers never enter or quickly leave the profession are based on their inability to manage their classrooms. (Evertson and Weinstein 2006)

Since the implementation of the No Child Left Behind law, a single-minded emphasis on instructional leadership, instructional coaching, and content-specific pedagogy may have come at too high a cost. Particularly in urban schools, we encounter teachers who feel overwhelmed and inadequately prepared to manage a supportive and high-functioning learning environment. We believe that effective teachers need to get three things right:

1. High-quality instruction and high-challenge, highly engaging, and meaningful learning

2. Effective classroom management, discipline, and personalized student support

3. Effective interpersonal, facilitation, and group process skills to develop positive, supportive relationships with each student and build a high-functioning, high-performing group of learners

Contrary to current mythology, high-quality instruction and learning are NOT substitutes for #2 and #3. If you can't manage a classroom or negotiate and navigate student relationships with competence and care, quality instruction just isn't going to happen. Making matters even more problematic, research indicates that urban teachers, in particular, report that they receive little or no support when they seek administrators' help with classroom management issues.

Teachers want and need a comprehensive vision of classroom management that will enable them to organize and manage their classrooms for optimal learning; prevent most disruptive behaviors; diagnose and respond to problematic behaviors efficiently; and provide the right kinds of consequences and supportive interventions that will help reluctant and resistant students to turn their behavior around. Equally important, teachers want to feel confident that they can create a safe, welcoming, and supportive learning environment while maintaining order and respect at the same time. No small task! Thus, *Getting Classroom Management RIGHT: Guided Discipline and Personalized Support in Secondary Schools* is devoted entirely to classroom management, discipline, and personalized support.

What's new and different about *Making Learning REAL: Reaching and Engaging All Learners in Secondary Classrooms*

Making Learning REAL is now formatted into three sections.

Section 1: Readings Linking Theory and Research to Core Practices

All of the readings associated with the seven core classroom practices are now located in Chapters 1 through 4 for easy access. Chapter 5 describes how to integrate another critical practice—modeling, teaching, practicing, and assessing life skills—into daily classroom life. Chapter 6 compares a REAL classroom to a more traditional classroom to illustrate how these two settings look, sound, and feel for both students and the teacher.

Chapter 1: Personalize Relationships and Learning in the Classroom
Chapter 2: Cocreate a Respectful, Responsible, High-Performing Learning Community
Chapter 3: Meet Adolescents' Developmental and Cultural Needs through High Expectations and Personalized Support
Chapter 4: Meet Adolescents' Developmental and Cultural Needs by Affirming Diversity in the Classroom
Chapter 5: Modeling, Teaching, Practicing, and Assessing Life Skills
Chapter 6: Putting the Practices to Work: A Tale of Two Classrooms

Section 2: Getting Started

Chapters 7 through 10 provide a coherent guide to preparing for the new school year, the first day of class, and the first month of school. The final chapter in this section describes the challenges and opportunities associated with changing classroom practices and offers suggestions for individual and collaborative approaches to professional development.

Chapter 7:   Before the School Year Begins
Chapter 8:   The First Day of Class
Chapter 9:   The First Month
Chapter 10: The Challenges of Changing Classroom Practices

Section 3: The Core Practices

Chapters 11 through 17 present all of the specific strategies and activities associated with each of the core practices for personalizing secondary classrooms and reaching and engaging all learners. Each chapter is devoted to one practice.

Chapter 11: Practice 1—Develop Positive Relationships between and among Students and Teachers
Chapter 12: Practice 2—Emphasize Personalized, Student-Centered Learning
Chapter 13: Practice 3—Integrate Multiple Ways of Knowing and Learning
Chapter 14: Practice 4—Establish Clear Norms, Boundaries, and Procedures
Chapter 15: Practice 5—Build a Cohesive Community of Learners
Chapter 16: Practice 6—Provide High Expectations and High Personalized Support
Chapter 17: Practice 7—Affirm Diversity in Your Classroom

Our ongoing work with faculty, leadership teams, and student support staff over the last six years has prompted other significant changes and additions to the book, including:

- A revised and expanded introduction that provides an up-to-date portrait of adolescents in the United States and explores the challenges and dilemmas good teachers face under the mandates of No Child Left Behind

- Sample posters throughout the book that illustrate guiding principles, procedures, and protocols

- Tabs on the right-hand side of certain pages to make it easier to find specific sections and chapters

- A personalization primer in Chapter 1

- More information about adolescent development and the teenage brain in Chapter 3

- More professional development ideas in Chapter 10 that describe how educators have used Partners in Learning in various settings to improve classroom practice

- More strategies for designing and managing student-centered lessons and project-based and independent learning experiences in Chapter 12

- More strategies for differentiating instruction in Chapter 13

- A personal conferencing primer that describes a range of academic and behavioral conferencing opportunities and provides an array of associated question prompts

- An appendix that includes more than fifty professional development protocols that accompany readings and key topics. They include (1) prereading protocols; (2) while-you-read protocols; (3) small- and large-group dialogue protocols; (4) products, presentations, and report-outs; and (5) planning, closings, and final thoughts.

What's new and different about *Getting Classroom Management RIGHT: Guided Discipline and Personalized Support in Secondary Schools?*

Getting Classroom Management RIGHT is a complete revision and expansion of material presented in Chapter 5: Thinking about Discipline in a Partners in Learning Classroom from the first edition of *Partners in Learning*. The expanded content reflects what we've learned through our facilitation of more than a hundred Guided Discipline and Personalized Support institutes across the country over the last five years. The new book also includes more research and evidence-based practices that support our approach to classroom management and discipline. In particular, we show how the explicit practices, strategies, and interventions that inform Guided Discipline and Personalized Support are aligned with the three-tiered framework of Response to Intervention (RTI) and Positive Behavior Support (PBS), a national model for meeting the academic and behavioral needs of three distinct groups of students who inhabit any school. A brief summary of each chapter follows:

- Chapter 1 explores three approaches to classroom management and discipline including Engaging Schools' approach, Guided Discipline and Personalized Support; offers sample responses to six familiar problem types; and closes with a glossary of key terms used throughout the book

- Chapter 2 includes 13 disciplinary case studies that examine the costs and benefits of punitive, do-nothing, and guided discipline responses to typical unwanted behaviors in the classroom

- Chapter 3 introduces Step 1 of the Guided Discipline and Personalized Support approach—Know Yourself, Know Your Students, and Know Your School

- Chapter 4 introduces Step 2 of the Guided Discipline and Personalized Support approach—Create Group Norms, Procedures, and Learning Protocols

- Chapter 5 introduces Step 3 of the Guided Discipline and Personalized Support approach—Support Individuals and the Group

- Chapter 6 introduces Step 4 of the Guided Discipline and Personalized Support approach—Invite Student Engagement, Cooperation, and Self-Correction

- Chapter 7 introduces Step 5 of the Guided Discipline and Personalized Support approach—Develop Accountable Consequences and Supportive Interventions

In addition, three appendixes contain:

- More than 15 behavior report forms, problem-solving protocols, conduct cards, and learning contracts that can be used in conjunction with teacher-student conferencing, case conferencing with other faculty, and more intensive interventions.

- A set of reflection questions, guided practices, and planning tools that can accompany professional development opportunites using *Getting Classroom Management RIGHT.*

- More than fifty professional development protocols that accompany readings and key topics. These include (1) prereading protocols; (2) while-you-read protocols; (3) small- and large-group dialogue protocols; (4) products, presentations, and report-outs; and (5) planning, closings, and final thoughts.

Our team at Engaging Schools continues to be inspired by the students and educators we meet. We rededicate these new publications to every teacher who, in difficult times, has been willing to stand up for the kind of challenging, relevant, and personalized education that every adolescent deserves.

Sources:

Allensworth, E. and Easton, J. (2006) *What matters for staying on-track and graduating in Chicago public schools.* Chicago, IL: Consortium on Chicago School Research at the University of Chicago. Accessed online at http://ccsr.uchicago.edu/publications/07%20What%20Matters%20Final.pdf

Breaking Ranks II: Strategies for leading high school reform. (2004) and *Breaking ranks in the middle* (2006) Reston, VA: NASSP.

The Big Picture Company. http://www. Bigpicture.org

Costa, A., and Garmston, R. (1998) "Cognitive coaching: Mediating growth toward holonomy." Chapter 5, pp. 52–60. In Strunk, J., Edwards, J., Rogers, S., & Swords, S., (Editors). *The pleasant view experience.* Golden, CO: Jefferson County Public Schools.

DiMartino, J., Clarke, J., and Wolk, D. (2003) *Personalized learning: Preparing high school students to create their futures.* Lanham, MD: Scarecrow Education Press.

Evans, R. (1996) *The human side of school change.* Chapter 6, pp. 91–118, "Understanding reluctant faculty." San Franscisco: Jossy-Bass.

Evertson, C. M., and Weinstein, C. S. (Editors) (2006) *Handbook of classroom management: Research, practice, and contemporary issues.* Philadelphia: Lawrence Erlbaum Associates.

Lee, V., and Burkam, D. (2003) "Dropping out of high school: The role of school organization and structure." *American Educational Research Journal,* 40 (2), 353–393. DOI: 10.3102/00028312040002353. University of Michigan.

Lee, V., Smith, J., Perry, T., & Smylie, M. (1999) *Social support, academic press, and student achievement: A view from the middle grades in Chicago.* Chicago: Consortium of Chicago School Research at the University of Chicago. Accessed online at http://ccsr.uchicago.edu/content/ publications.php?pub_id=55

National High School Alliance. (2003) "Personalization and social supports: Site visit protocol and discussion guide." Accessed online at http://www.hsalliance.org/call_action/Protocols/ProtocolPersonalization.pdf

Payne, C. (2008) *So much reform, so little change: The persistence of failure in urban schools.* Cambridge, MA: Harvard University Press.

Stevens, W. D. (2008) *If small is not enough...the characteristics of successful small high schools in Chicago.* Chicago: Consortium on Chicago School Research at the University of Chicago.

INTRODUCTION

We believe that effective teachers need to get three things right:

1. High-quality instruction and high-challenge, highly engaging, and meaningful learning

2. Effective classroom management, discipline, and personalized student support

3. Effective interpersonal, facilitation, and group process skills to develop positive, support-ive relationships with each student and build a high-functioning, high-performing group of learners

Contrary to current mythology, high-quality instruction and learning are not substitutes for items 2 and 3. If you can't manage a classroom or navigate student relationships with competence and care, quality instruction just isn't going to happen. The goal of this book is to offer secondary school teachers the tools, skills, and understandings that will enable them to create productive learning environments where students feel respected and cared for and are motivated to become more self-disciplined and responsible learners.

How Is This Book Different from Other Classroom Management Resources?

Getting Classroom Management RIGHT focuses on adolescent learners only

In Engaging Schools' work with middle and high schools, teachers, principals, and professional development staff continue to cite classroom management as a primary concern. At the heart of this concern is the desire for resources that are specifically designed for faculty who work with adolescents. In our search for developmentally appropriate resources, we found too many books, programs, and models that were originally created for K–6 classrooms and then altered only slightly for use in secondary schools. We also reviewed too many programs that offer a K–12, one-size-fits-all approach to all things disciplinary. Seven-year-olds and seventeen-year-olds are not interchange-able. *Getting Classroom Management RIGHT* was written explicitly with adolescents in mind. Key characteristics of secondary schooling inform the writing of this book:

- The constant mobility of middle and high school students, who move from teacher to teacher and class to class, generates a set of challenges that simply do not exist in self-contained elementary classrooms. Simply put, middle and high school teachers don't have all day to get classroom management right. While elementary school teachers have the entire day, every day, to develop an effective set of supports, consequences, and interventions for one classroom of 30 children, secondary teachers see, on average, 140 students daily during five or six different periods of instruction. Thus, intentional efforts to build student rapport and establish timely and efficient procedures, routines, and management practices take on even more significance in secondary classrooms.

- Adolescents (particularly between ages 12 and 15) are far more likely than younger children to challenge adult authority, break rules, question school policies, and behave aggressively toward peers and adults. Rudeness, provocative speech, and noncompliance are, indeed, normal adolescent behaviors. Yet responding to these typical behaviors requires a vast and nuanced array of teacher strategies in order to redirect students' behavior quickly and defuse rather than escalate potential confrontations. This teacher skill set is a must-have because of the profound role that respect plays in adolescent-adult relationships. The perception of being respected or disrespected is, for many students, the most influential factor that determines their willingness or resistance to engage in learning and meet classroom behavioral expectations. Consequently, secondary teachers need a fine-tuned, adolescent-appropriate storehouse of effective scripts and prompts that will invite students' engagement, cooperation, and self-correction.

- Developing greater personal efficacy is a major task of adolescence. I've never met a teacher who did not want students to become more responsible for their learning and their behavior. Nonetheless, a secondary teacher's disciplinary repertoire seldom goes beyond punitive responses that range from critical or sarcastic retorts to detention, a referral to the dean, or tossing a student out of class. Crafting accountable consequences and supportive interventions for middle and high school students is a challenging proposition. Rare is the teacher who has developed a disciplinary plan that actually encourages students to take responsibility for correcting their behavior, make amends or make it right, repair the harm they caused, or restore their good standing. Secondary teachers want and need more effective practices that will support student accountability, self-discipline, and self-management.

Getting Classroom Management RIGHT focuses on teacher attitudes, qualities, and skill sets that support effective classroom management and discipline

Researchers share broad agreement about the attitudes, qualities, and skill sets that characterize effective teachers and classroom managers (Evertson and Weinstein 2006). The research tells us how good teachers present themselves to students, what good teachers do, and how good teachers communicate with and manage individuals and the group. Yet this knowledge base rarely informs teachers' assessment of their own strengths and growing edges. In *Getting Classroom*

Management RIGHT, teacher awareness is Step 1 of Engaging Schools' approach to guided discipline and personalized support. We have culled the effective teacher research base in order to spotlight some of the more important attitudes, qualities, and skills that set apart successful teachers from their struggling colleagues.

Getting Classroom Management RIGHT focuses on prevention first

Secondary teacher training reinforces, as it should, the twin goals of becoming a content specialist and becoming an expert at teaching one's specialized content to young people. However, this single-minded focus can easily generate a litany of erroneous mantras that don't serve teachers or students particularly well in secondary classrooms:

> *I teach subjects, not children.*
>
> *It's my job to teach and your job to learn.*
>
> *I'm not here to "discipline" you.*
>
> *You should have learned that in fourth grade.*
>
> *I don't have time to teach students social skills and habits of learning.*
>
> *All this stuff about setting up a classroom for success is just another version of coddling teenagers.*

Secondary teachers tend to undervalue intentional efforts to organize their classrooms for learning in ways that promote personal, social, and group efficacy and prevent most problematic behaviors. Instead, many teachers mistakenly focus most of their attention on responding to unwanted behaviors after they have already occurred. Classroom management research is very clear about one thing: disciplinary actions can only restore order. Classroom management—how you organize and manage your class for student success—is how you create order (Evertson and Weinstein 2006).

Getting Classroom Management RIGHT addresses teachers' desires for more effective responses and intervention strategies for a wide range of unwanted classroom behaviors. However, four of the five steps of the Guided Discipline and Personalized Support approach emphasize the prevention side of the continuum—how to create a well-managed, high-performing classroom.

GUIDED DISCIPLINE AND PERSONALIZED SUPPORT

Step 1:	Step 2:	Step 3:	Step 4:	Step 5:
Know Yourself, Know Your Students, Know Your School	Create Group Norms, Procedures, and Learning Protocols	Support Individuals and the Group	Invite Student Engagement, Cooperation, and Self-Correction	Develop Accountable Consequences and Supportive Interventions

← - →

PREVENTION   **INTERVENTION**

Research that Supports Engaging Schools' Five Steps to Guided Discipline and Personalized Support

The five steps of the Guided Discipline and Personalized Support approach are informed by the last 20 years of classroom management research. Evertson and Weinstein's *Handbook of Classroom Management: Research, Practice, and Contemporary Issues*, a 1,300-page research compendium published in 2006, posits four key principles that should drive classroom management practices:

1. Positive teacher-student relationships are the very core of effective classroom management

2. Classroom management is a personal (efficacy and self-management), social (interpersonal and intergroup efficacy), and moral (conduct and character) curriculum and set of processes and practices that must be modeled, taught, practiced, and assessed.

3. An emphasis on external reward and punishment strategies is not optimal for promoting academic, social, and emotional growth and self-regulated behavior.

4. To create orderly, productive environments, teachers must take into account student characteristics such as age, developmental level, race, ethnicity, cultural background, socioeconomic status, and ableness.

(Evertson, C. M., and Weinstein, C. S., Editors. (2006) *Handbook of classroom management: Research, practice, and contemporary issues.* Chapter 1, "Classroom management as a field of inquiry," pp. 3–13. Philadelphia: Lawrence Erlbaum Associates)

One contributing author sums up the editors' research conclusions in this way: "Teachers must (1) develop caring, supportive relationships with and among students; (2) organize and implement instruction in ways that optimize students' access to learning; (3) use group management methods that encourage students' engagement in academic tasks; (4) promote the development of students' social skills and self-regulation; and (5) use appropriate interventions to assist students with behavior problems." (Ibid. p. 1048)

These basic principles are at the core of Guided Discipline and Personalized Support. Our aim is to support teachers in developing and strengthening students' capacities to self-regulate, learn from and correct unwanted behaviors, make more responsible decisions, regularly practice prosocial behaviors, and demonstrate productive habits of learning and self-discipline in the classroom. In the pages that follow, each of the five steps is accompanied by key topics and research references that inform explicit teacher practices associated with each step.

Five Steps of Guided Discipline and Personalized Support

P R E V E N T I O N

I. KNOW YOURSELF, KNOW YOUR STUDENTS, KNOW YOUR SCHOOL

Know Yourself

— Know where your power zones and approaches to authority come from

— Know if you are more authoritarian or authoritative

— Know your teaching stance

— Know your goals for discipline and personalized support

— Know your nos, needs, and nonnegotiables

— Know how with-it you are

— Know how to define disrespect

— Know how to depersonalize bad behavior

— Know how to avoid communication roadblocks

— Know your communication style

— Know how to listen responsively

— Know how to manage your anger

— Know how to handle conflict in the classroom

— Know your conflict style

— Know how to recover

— Know how to diagnose your own practice accurately

— Know which of your teacher roles to strengthen

Know Your Students

— Know how to diagnose the underlying needs of unwanted behaviors

— Know key essentials of adolescent development

— Know key qualities and attributes of a developed student

Know Your School

— Know your school's discipline policies

— Know colleagues and administrations whom you can count on for help and assistance

PREVENTION

The Research

Adolescents respond more cooperatively and positively when teachers use their power authoritatively; provide clear expectations; and communicate to students in ways that feel respectful, attentive, helpful, flexible, and understanding. From Evertson, C. M., and Weinstein, C. S. Editors. (2006) *Handbook of classroom management: Research, practice, and contemporary issues:* Doyle, W. Chapter 5: "Ecological approaches to classroom management," pp. 97–126; Morine-Dershimer, Chapter 6: "Classroom management and classroom discourse," pp. 127–156; Woolfolk Hoy, A., and Weinstein, C., Chapter 8: "Student-teacher perspectives on classroom management," pp. 181–219; Emmer, E. and Gerwels, M. C., Chapter 15: "Classroom management in middle and high school classrooms," pp. 407–438.

Effective classroom managers exhibit the quality of with-it-ness, which is the capacity to intervene early before off-task behaviors become disruptive and to respond to low-impact problem behaviors immediately without undue drama. Kounin, J. S. (1970) *Discipline and group management in classrooms.* New York: Holt, Reinhart, and Winston.

Teacher self-diagnosis and the capacity to reflect on teaching behaviors that may, in fact, trigger or exacerbate unwanted student behaviors is a critical step toward improving teacher practice. Saphier, J., Haley-Speca, M. A., and Gower, R. (2007) *The Skillful Teacher.* Acton, MA: Research for Better Teaching.

Development of conflict management skills and a clear understanding of conflict management styles can reduce the frequency and intensity of conflicts in the classroom. Jones, T. Project Director of the Conflict Resolution Education in Teacher Education (CRETE) Temple University, Philadelphia; Jones, T. S. (2004) "Conflict resolution education: The field, the findings, and the future." *Conflict Resolution Quarterly,* 22(1/2), 233–267; Jones, T. S., and Kmitta, D. (Editions) (2000) *Does it work? The case for conflict resolution education in our nation's schools.* Washington, DC: Conflict Resolution Education Network; Jones, T. S., and Sanford, R. (2003) "Building the container: The impact of CRE on classroom climate." *Conflict Resolution Quarterly,* 21(1), 115–128.

Emotional objectivity and the capacity to depersonalize students' verbal reactions and problematic behavior are critical aspects of a teacher's mindset that separate effective from ineffective classroom managers. Marzano, R. J. (2003) *Classroom management that works.* Alexandria, VA: ASCD. Chapter 5.

Particularly for underserved, underperforming adolescents, students of color, and students who live in poverty, the quality of the student-teacher relationship and a teacher's commitment to know each student individually will often determine a student's willingness to learn and cooperate in the classroom. From Evertson, C. M., and Weinstein, C. S. Editors. (2006) *Handbook of classroom management: Research, practice, and contemporary issues:* Doyle, W., Chapter 5: "Ecological approaches to classroom management," pp. 97–126; Morine-Dershimer, Chapter 6: "Classroom management and classroom discourse," pp. 127–156; Woolfolk Hoy, A., and Weinstein, C., Chapter 8: "Student-teacher perspectives on classroom management," pp. 181–219; Gay, G., Chapter 13: "Connections between classroom management and culturally responsive teaching," pp. 343–371; Emmer, E., and Gerwels, M. C., Chapter 15: "Classroom management in middle and high school classrooms," pp. 407–438; Milner, H. R., Chapter 18, "Classroom

PREVENTION

management in urban classrooms," pp. 491–522; Pianta, R., Chapter 26: "Classroom management and relationships between children and teachers," pp. 685–710.

Darling-Hammond, L., LePage, P., Hammerness, K., and Duffy, H. (Editors). (2007) *"Preparing teachers for a changing world: What teachers should learn and be able to do."* San Francisco: Jossey-Bass.

Knowing students well and understanding their developmental needs are essential tools for providing high-quality academic, social, and behavioral supports to different students. Adelman, H., and Taylor, L. (2006) *The school leader's guide to student learning supports: New directions for addressing barriers to learning.* Chapter 4: "Controlling behavior at the expense of motivating learning," pp. 55–75. Thousand Oaks, CA: Corwin Press.

Accurate diagnosis of the underlying goals of unwanted behavior is often a first step to helping students replace an unwanted behavior with the desired target behavior. Saphier, J., Haley-Speca, M.A., and Gower, R. (2007) *The skillful teacher.* Acton, MA: Research for Better Teaching.

From Evertson, C. M., and Weinstein, C. S. Editors. (2006) *Handbook of classroom management: Research, practice, and contemporary issues:* Chapter 15: "Classroom management in middle and high school classrooms," pp. 412–413.

O'Neill, R. E., Horner, R. H., Albin, R. W., Sprague, J. R., Storey, K., and Newton, J. S. (1997) *Functional assessment and program development for problem behavior.* Pacific Grove, CA: Brooks/Cole.

Dreikurs, R., Grunwald, B., and Pepper, F. (1982) *Maintaining sanity in the classroom: Classroom management techniques.* New York: Harper & Row.

2. CREATE GROUP NORMS, PROCEDURES, AND LEARNING PROTOCOLS

— Establish positive group guidelines and agreements

— Discuss the issue of respect

— Generate a list of rights and responsibilities

— Explain your approach to discipline

— Keep a behavioral log book for the class

— Be clear about the reasons for procedures and be consistent in enforcing them

— Model, teach, practice, and assess the procedures you expect

— Use group learning protocols to build intellectual, metacognitive, social, and emotional competencies.

— Use group problem-solving protocols to help students manage conflict and negotiate learning

The Research

Effective teachers hold and communicate high expectations for student learning and behavior, teach behavioral norms and routines, and establish clear procedures to guide classroom transitions, stewardship of the classroom environment, the use of different learning strategies, and the completion and quality of student work.

Brophy, J. (1986) "Classroom Management Techniques." *Education and Urban Society*, (18/2), 182–194.

Evertson, C. M. (1989) "Classroom organization and management." In M. C. Reynolds (Edition), *Knowledge base for the beginning teacher.* Oxford, UK: Pergamon Press.

Ornstein, A. C., and Levine, D. U. (1981) "Teacher Behavior Research: Overview and Outlook." *Phi Delta Kappa. Kappan*, (62/8), 592–596.

Effective teachers spend time teaching students the specific habits and processes associated with productive use of group learning protocols. From Evertson, C. M., and Weinstein, C. S. Editors. (2006) *Handbook of classroom management: Research, practice, and contemporary issues:* Lotan, R., Chapter 19: "Managing group work in the heterogeneous classroom," pp. 525–540; Johnson, D., and Johnson, R., Chapter 30: "Conflict resolution, peer mediation, and peacemaking," pp. 803–832.

Jones, T., and Compton, R. (2003) *Kids working it out: Stories and strategies for making peace in our schools.* San Francisco: Jossey-Bass.

Gottfredson, D. C. (1989) "Developing effective organizations to reduce school disorder." In Moles, O. C. (Editor), *Strategies to reduce student misbehavior.* Washington, DC: Office of Educational Research and Improvement, 87–104. (ED 311 698).

3. SUPPORT INDIVIDUALS AND THE GROUP

— Model, teach, practice, and assess life skills

— Teach students how to manage their emotions

— Teach the conflict escalator

— Teach the differences between aggressive, passive, and assertive behavior

— Provide scripts that encourage students to say and do the right thing

— Make personal connections with every student

— Provide immediate and meaningful feedback and encouragement

— Provide personalized support for students who are struggling

— Create opportunities for students to link personal effort to their successes

— Recognize individual accomplishments in and out of the classroom

PREVENTION

— Build and maintain a cohesive group

— Strengthen your group facilitation skills

— Monitor and assess group participation

— Create classroom routines and rituals that involve every student

— Recognize and celebrate the group's efforts and accomplishments

— Use group incentives, random reinforcement, and intermittent rewards

The Research

Direct modeling, teaching, practice, and assessment of social and emotional competencies increases students' capacity to self-regulate and function effectively as individuals and within a group in the classroom. From Evertson, C. M., and Weinstein, C. S. Editors. (2006) *Handbook of classroom management: Research, practice, and contemporary issues:* McCaslin, M., et al., Chapter 9: "Self-regulated learning and classroom management: Theory, research, and implications for classroom practice," pp. 253–252; Elias, M., and Schwab, Y., Chapter 12: "From compliance to responsibility: Social and emotional learning and classroom management," pp. 309–342; Nucci, L., Chapter 27: "Classroom management for moral and social development," pp. 711–733.

Effective teachers are intentional about building high-functioning, high-performing groups of learners in addition to supporting the academic, social, and emotional development of individual students. From Evertson, C. M., and Weinstein, C. S. Editors. (2006) *Handbook of classroom management: Research, practice, and contemporary issues:* Watson, M., and Battitich, V., Chapter 10: "Building and sustaining caring communities," pp. 253–280; Emmer, E., and Gerwels, M. C., Chapter 15: "Classroom management in middle and high school classrooms," pp. 407–438; Pianta, R., Chapter 26: "Classroom management and relationships between children and teachers," pp. 685–710.

Providing high levels of academic, social, and behavioral support reduces student barriers to learning and increases students' capacity to focus and engage. From Evertson, C. M., and Weinstein, C. S. Editors. (2006) *Handbook of classroom management: Research, practice, and contemporary issues:* Woolfolk Hoy, A., and Weinstein, C., Chapter 8: "Student-teacher perspectives on classroom management," pp. 181–219.

Adelman, H., and Taylor, L. (2006) *The implementation guide to student learning supports in the classroom and school-wide,* Part II: "Learning supports in the classroom", pp. 79–177. Thousand Oaks, CA: Corwin Press.

Albert, L. (1996) *Cooperative discipline.* Port Angeles, WA: American Guidance Services Publishing.

INTERVENTION

4. INVITE STUDENT ENGAGEMENT, COOPERATION, AND SELF-CORRECTION

— Get the group's attention

— Give clear instructions

— Insist on silence when silence is required

— Use proximity and physical prompts first when students are off task

— Design well-paced, student-centered lessons

— Expand your teaching toolbox to engage all learners

— Help students settle in at the beginning of class

— Help students wake up, energize, and recharge the mind and body

— Do a quick check-in to read the group

— Set goals to get ready to learn

— Prepare students to participate responsibly in discussion

— Redirect unproductive group talk behaviors

— Defuse, disarm, and deflate provocative behavior

— Set norms and consequences related to public speech

— Interrupt negative speech using multiple strategies

— Intervene immediately when students' speech is beyond correction

— Redirect students when they are confused or stuck

— Redirect students when they look bored or disengaged

— Offer students chances to solve problems and make choices

— Insist on problem-solving and negotiation rather than complaints

— Put the responsibility on the student when an unwanted behavior persists

— Use logical consequences for minor problematic behaviors

— Help defuse students' anger and frustration

— Let students know what they can do to cool down

— Communicate your support and confidence when students feel discouraged

— Implement Guided Discipline supports and interventions every week

— Track and document what you do and what your students do

INTERVENTION

The Research

Effective activity management, pacing, and prompting reduce problematic behaviors and increase students' engagement in learning. From Evertson, C. M., and Weinstein, C. S. Editors. (2006) *Handbook of classroom management: Research, practice, and contemporary issues:* Doyle, W., Chapter 5: "Ecological approaches to classroom management," pp. 97–126; Emmer, E., and Gerwels, M. C., Chapter 15: "Classroom management in middle and high school classrooms," pp. 422–427.

How teachers talk to young people shapes a student's response and determines the degree to which students will cooperate and self-correct. From Evertson, C. M., and Weinstein, C. S. Editors. (2006) *Handbook of classroom management: Research, practice, and contemporary issues:* Woolfolk Hoy, A., and Weinstein, C., Chapter 8: "Student-teacher perspectives on classroom management," pp. 181–219; Gay, G., Chapter 13: "Connections between classroom management and culturally responsive teaching," pp. 343–371; Milner, H. R., Chapter 18, "Classroom management in urban classrooms," pp. 491–522.

Adelman, H., and Taylor, L. (2006) *The school leader's guide to student learning supports: New directions for addressing barriers to learning,* Chapter 4: "Controlling behavior at the expense of motivating learning," pp. 55–75. Thousand Oaks, CA: Corwin Press.

Saphier, J., Haley-Speca, M. A., and Gower, R. (2007) *The skillful teacher.* Acton, MA: Research for Better Teaching.

5. DEVELOP ACCOUNTABLE CONSEQUENCES AND SUPPORTIVE INTERVENTIONS

— Prioritize problem behaviors that you want to be ready for

— Establish three levels of consequences and supportive interventions

— Discuss the difference between punishment and accountable consequences

— Diagnose problem behaviors accurately

— Don't give students the opportunity to argue and "lawyer up"

— Name the consequence, exit, and deal with it later

— De-escalate power struggles calmly and quickly

— Help the group get unstuck

— Create an intervention plan when the whole group is messing up

— Teach desired target behaviors that replace unwanted behaviors

— Use one-on-one conferences to address problem behaviors

— Use one-on-one conferences when students are upset or personally distressed

— Use one-on-one conferences when students are unmotivated and resistant

INTERVENTION

— Use one-on-one conferences for "frequent fliers"

— Use behavior report forms, problem-solving protocols, conduct cards, and learning contracts

— Make a plan when a class is "off the hook"

— Communicate with parents in a variety of ways

— Problem solve with your colleagues

The Research

Teachers need to defuse or interrupt serious behavior disruptions and confrontations immediately in order to restore order and safety in the classroom. From Evertson, C. M., and Weinstein, C. S. Editors. (2006) *Handbook of classroom management: Research, practice, and contemporary issues:* Emmer, E., and Gerwels, M. C., Chapter 15: "Classroom management in middle and high school classrooms," pp. 427–431.

Accountable consequences and supportive interventions in the classroom should include opportunities for students to self-reflect, learn desired target behaviors, conference with teachers and parents, problem solve, restore one's good standing, and develop a plan or contract that supports and monitors student's progress and improvement.

Adelman, H., and Taylor, L. (2006) *The school leader's guide to student learning supports: New directions for addressing barriers to learning,* Chapter 4: "Controlling behavior at the expense of motivating learning," pp. 55–75 and Chapter 12: "Student support and behavior problems," pp. 233–244. Thousand Oaks, CA: Corwin Press.

From Evertson, C. M., and Weinstein, C. S. Editors. (2006) *Handbook of classroom management: Research, practice, and contemporary issues:* McCaslin, M., et al., Chapter 9: "Self-regulated learning and classroom management: Theory, research, and implications for classroom practice," pp. 253–252; Elias, M., and Schwab, Y., Chapter 12: "From compliance to responsibility: Social and emotional learning and classroom management," pp. 309–342; Nucci, L., Chapter 27: "Classroom management and moral and social development," pp. 711–731.

OSEP Technical Assistance Center on Positive Behavioral Interventions and Supports. www.pbis.org

RTI Action Network. www.rtinetwork.org

Stutzman, L., and Mullet, J. (2005) *The little book of restorative discipline for schools: Teaching responsibility; creating caring climates.* Intercourse, PA: Good Books.

Links to Response to Intervention (RTI) and Positive Behavior Supports (PBS)

The Guided Discipline and Personalized Support approach complements the frameworks of Response to Intervention (RTI) and Positive Behavior Supports (PBS), a national research-based model that calls for a three-tiered approach to early identification and support for students with different learning and behavior needs (RTI Action Network [www.rtinetwork.org]; OSEP Technical Assistance Center on Positive Behavioral Interventions and Supports [www.pbis.org]). In the PBS framework, Tier 1 serves all students in the school by establishing universal expectations, schoolwide practices, prevention programs, and student development initiatives intended to encourage, teach, and reward prosocial student behaviors. Tier 2 (targeted to about 15 percent of students) and Tier 3 (targeted to fewer than 5 percent of students) incorporate streamlined and uniform referral systems, supports, and interventions of increasing intensity that are matched to students' behavioral and mental health needs.

Thinking about classroom management and discipline from this perspective invites teachers to develop Tier 1 and Tier 2 consequences, supports, and interventions, and utilize schoolwide referral protocols to address the needs and challenges of three different groups of students:

- Tier 1 foundational classroom management expectations, procedures, positive supports, consequences, interventions, and deliberate teaching of life skills are aimed at all students and will work effectively for at least 80 percent of students most of the time.

- Tier 2 classroom management and disciplinary protocols are aimed at some students (about 15 percent) who need more targeted supports and interventions to get back on track. Sometimes these interventions are carried out by the teacher, sometimes they are carried out by the teacher in cooperation with other school staff and administrators, and sometimes they are carried out by assistant principals, deans, student support staff, and mental health professionals.

- Tier 3 schoolwide referral protocols are aimed at a few high-needs students (5 percent or fewer) who require even more intensive and individualized supports and interventions that teachers cannot or should not provide. Services for these students are usually provided by counselors, social workers, psychologists, case managers, and other trained mental health professionals.

Like Engaging Schools' approach to classroom management, PBS emphasizes prevention. Direct modeling, teaching, practice, demonstration, and assessment of prosocial behaviors and social and emotional competen-cies are critical components of classroom management that foster the development of high-functioning individuals and a high-performing group of learners. However, particularly for secondary teachers, the PBS model does not include a detailed array of prevention-focused teacher practices or teacher-driven supports, consequences, and interventions that should be part of any secondary teacher's toolbox.

Guided Discipline and Personalized Support helps to fill in the gaps so that teachers can begin thinking systemically about how to provide the right supports and interventions for different groups of students. The first two charts that follow illustrate schoolwide implementation of RTI and PBS. The third chart illustrates how the five steps of Guided Discipline and Personalized Support align with the RTI/PBS model.

Three Tiers of Academic Learning Supports and Interventions (Schoolwide Version)

Different students need different amounts and different kinds of time, attention, and support to learn successfully and behave responsibly.

TIER 3 (about 5%)

Intensive and individualized learning supports and interventions for a few students who experience severe learning gaps

Intensive Interventions for a FEW Students

- Special education placement
- Individualized tutoring
- Diagnostic testing and other individualized academic services
- Change of course, schedule, or teacher

TIER 2 (about 15%)

Immediate targeted supports and interventions for ANY students who are not achieving (facilitated by teacher, advisor, or learning support team) that are systemically applied and monitored

Learning Supports and Interventions for SOME Students

- Required AVID, Quest course, or skills clinic to improve learning, study, homework, and text reading skills
- Required tutoring, study groups, guided study hall, or Saturday school
- Grade level team, advisory, or learning support team case conferencing
- Student placed on weekly progress reports or learning contract
- Student-parent-teacher conference, student-teacher-counselor conference, or student-advisor conference
- Required workout session with teacher or required "Homework Hall"
- Initial teacher phone call to parent at first diagnosis of learning gaps

TIER 1 (about 80%)

Coherent, predictable learning supports and close monitoring of ALL students' academic progress

Learning Supports for ALL Students

Classroom Supports
- Before- and after-school faculty office hours
- Initial conference w/ student to address learning gaps
- Immediate response/diagnosis when student isn't learning
- In-class regular academic conferencing with every student
- Formative assessment for learning to adjust instruction
- Differentiated, personalized instruction
- Classroom protocols for completion of quality work
- Quarterly student goal-setting in each course
- Common learning expectations and standards

Schoolwide Supports
- Open tutoring periods / Invitational "Homework Hall"
- Established protocols for identification of and interventions for students earning low grades or declining grades
- Late bus
- Online grade access
- Common grading practices within and/or across departments
- Integrated study skill focus in 9th grade courses and advisory
- All faculty expect, insist, and support ALL students to complete significant pieces of quality work in every course every grading period

Based on the work of RTI Action Network (www.rtinetwork.org); OSEP Technical Assistance Center on Positive Behavioral Interventions and Supports (www.pbis.org); Center for Mental Health in Schools, UCLA (www.smhp.psych.ucla.edu); Osher, D., Dwyer, K. and Jackson, S. (2003) Safe, supportive, and successful schools. Frederick, CO: Sopris West; Lewis, T., and Sugai, G. (1999) Safe schools: School-wide discipline practices. Arlington, VA: Council for Exceptional Children; and Educators for Social Responsibility.

Three Tiers of Behavioral and Mental Health Supports and Interventions (Schoolwide Version)

Different students need different amounts and kinds of time, attention, and support to learn successfully and behave responsibly.

TIER 3 (about 5%)

Intensive and individualized behavioral and mental health supports and interventions for a few students who are experiencing severe behavioral difficulties or psychological distress

Intensive Interventions for a FEW Students

- Referral for outside mental health services
- Individual and family counseling
- Individualized diagnostic protocols for severely troubled students

TIER 2 (about 15%)

Immediate targeted behavioral supports and interventions for students engaged in chronic or egregious unwanted behaviors that are systemically applied and monitored

Behavior Supports and Interventions for SOME Students

- Identification of students experiencing severe challenges/crises
- Required "replacement behavior" counseling session in small groups
- Case conferencing with advisor or student intervention team
- Student placed on conduct card / Checks in daily w/ adult mentor
- Referral to dean or AP / Schoolwide accountable consequences /"Owed time"
- Parent phone call, student-parent-teacher conference, mediated conference with advisor or counselor and weekly conduct card if unwanted behaviors continue
- Initial student-teacher conference, "workout session", and/or behavior contract when unwanted behaviors persist or source of problematic behaviors isn't clear

TIER 1 (about 80%)

Behavioral expectations, rules, procedures, supports, and prevention strategies for ALL students

Behavior and Mental Health Supports for ALL Students

Classroom Supports

- Immediate consequences and interventions to redirect minor problematic behaviors
- Effective teacher talk that invites cooperation and self-correction
- Accurate diagnosis of problematic behaviors
- Teacher self-diagnosis of ineffective classroom practices
- Modeling, teaching, practice, and assessment of life skills/habits of learning
- Attention to building high performing community of learners
- Attention to building positive, supportive relationships with students
- Explicit classroom behavioral expectations and procedures

Schoolwide Supports

- Student/faculty voice influences school policies
- Referral protocols and accountable consequences are explicit, consistent, and predictable
- All adults share supervision of public space
- All faculty agree on a few rules and procedures that they will enforce the same way every time with every student
- All adults actively contribute to building a safe and respectful culture
- Positive social behaviors are modeled, taught, recognized, and rewarded
- Core values and behavioral expectations are explicitly communicated

Based on the work of RTI Action Network (www.rtinetwork.org); OSEP Technical Assistance Center on Positive Behavioral Interventions and Supports (www.pbis.org); Center for Mental Health in Schools, UCLA (www.smhp.psych.ucla.edu); Osher, D., Dwyer, K. and Jackson, S. (2003) *Safe, supportive, and successful schools*. Frederick, CO: Sopris West; Lewis, T., and Sugai, G. (1999) *Safe schools: School-wide discipline practices*. Arlington, VA: Council for Exceptional Children; and Educators for Social Responsibility.

Three Tiers of Behavioral Supports and Interventions (For Classroom Teachers)

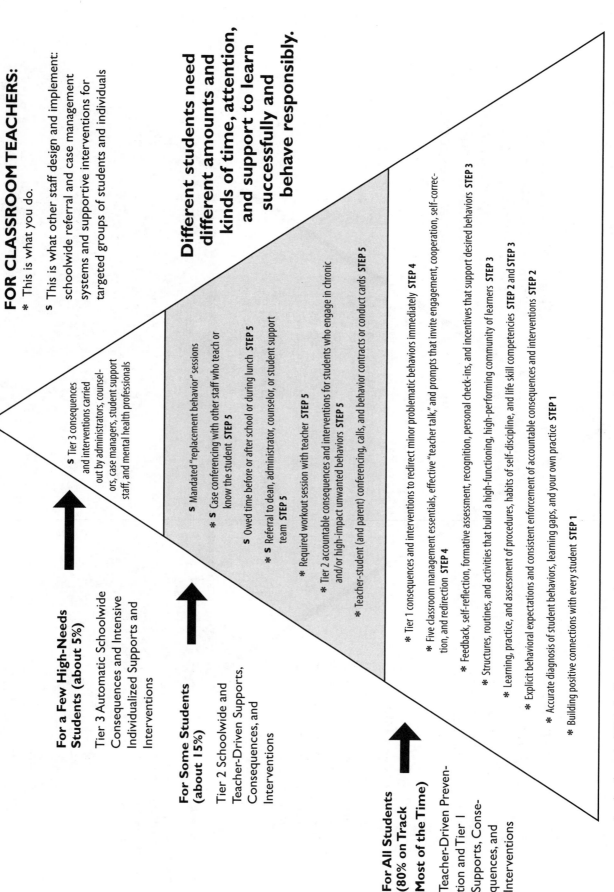

FOR CLASSROOM TEACHERS:

* This is what you do.

s This is what other staff design and implement: schoolwide referral and case management systems and supportive interventions for targeted groups of students and individuals

Different students need different amounts and kinds of time, attention, and support to learn successfully and behave responsibly.

For a Few High-Needs Students (about 5%)

Tier 3 Automatic Schoolwide Consequences and Intensive Individualized Supports and Interventions

s Tier 3 consequences and interventions carried out by administrators, counselors, case managers, student support staff, and mental health professionals

For Some Students (about 15%)

Tier 2 Schoolwide and Teacher-Driven Supports, Consequences, and Interventions

s Mandated "replacement behavior" sessions

* s Case conferencing with other staff who teach or know the student STEP 5

s Owed time before or after school or during lunch STEP 5

* s Referral to dean, administrator, counselor, or student support team STEP 5

* Required workout session with teacher STEP 5

* Tier 2 accountable consequences and interventions for students who engage in chronic and/or high-impact unwanted behaviors STEP 5

* Teacher-student (and parent) conferencing, calls, and behavior contracts or conduct cards STEP 5

For All Students (80% on Track Most of the Time)

Teacher-Driven Prevention and Tier I Supports, Consequences, and Interventions

* Tier 1 consequences and interventions to redirect minor problematic behaviors immediately STEP 4

* Five classroom management essentials, effective "teacher talk," and prompts that invite engagement, cooperation, self-correction, and redirection STEP 4

* Feedback, self-reflection, formative assessment, recognition, personal check-ins, and incentives that support desired behaviors STEP 3

* Structures, routines, and activities that build a high-functioning, high-performing community of learners STEP 3

* Learning, practice, and assessment of procedures, habits of self-discipline, and life skill competencies STEP 2 and STEP 3

* Explicit behavioral expectations and consistent enforcement of accountable consequences and interventions STEP 2

* Accurate diagnosis of student behaviors, learning gaps, and your own practice STEP 1

* Building positive connections with every student STEP 1

Based on the work of RTI Action Network (www.rtinetwork.org); OSEP Technical Assistance Center on Positive Behavioral Interventions and Supports (www.pbis.org); Center for Mental Health in Schools, UCLA (www.smhp.psych.ucla.edu); Osher, D., Dwyer, K. and Jackson, S. (2003) *Safe, supportive, and successful schools.* Frederick, CO: Sopris West; Lewis, T., and Sugai, G. (1999) *Safe schools: School-wide discipline practices.* Arlington, VA: Council for Exceptional Children; and Educators for Social Responsibility.

How to Use *Getting Classroom Management RIGHT*

Although reading the book cover to cover is ideal, we know that this is an unlikely prospect. It is more likely that readers will use the table of contents to search out specific topics of high interest or urgent concern. With that in mind, we put together a list of frequently asked questions that are addressed in specific chapters:

What exactly is guided discipline? How is it different from a punitive or do-nothing approach to classroom discipline?	CHAPTER 1
What key terms would help me become familiar with the basics of Guided Discipline and Personalized Support?	CHAPTER 1
What are the types of problem behaviors I should be able to diagnose? And what are the most effective responses for addressing different problem types?	CHAPTER 1
How does a guided discipline approach look and sound in a typical classroom situation? Does the book have real examples that could give me a clearer picture?	CHAPTER 2
What are the qualities, teacher behaviors, and skills associated with teachers who are highly effective classroom managers?	CHAPTER 3
What should I know about adolescents that will help me meet the needs of a wide range of students in my classroom and promote students' healthy social and emotional development and personal efficacy?	CHAPTER 3 CHAPTER 5
How can I use the skills and wisdom of my colleagues and administrators effectively when I need help with students who are particularly difficult or challenging for me?	CHAPTER 3 CHAPTER 7
What explicit norms, procedures, and learning protocols should I put in place so that my classroom is organized for student success?	CHAPTER 4
How can I incorporate the teaching and practice of life skills and habits of learning into my daily lessons and classroom practice?	CHAPTER 5
What can I do specifically to build a high-performing community of learners?	CHAPTER 3 CHAPTER 5
What kinds of feedback, recognitions, and rewards work better than others?	CHAPTER 5
What are some essential classroom management practices that I have to get right in order to facilitate and deliver quality instruction?	CHAPTER 6
How can I get kids back on task in 30 seconds without making a fuss?	CHAPTER 6

What are real examples of effective responses to students who are off task or unfocused, angry or frustrated, bored or discouraged, provocative or confrontational?	CHAPTER 6
What are some tips for when to contact parents and what to say?	CHAPTER 6
What are some explicit examples of accountable consequences that I can put in place from Day 1 and use consistently throughout the year?	CHAPTER 7
What kinds of supportive interventions are most likely to help a student change his or her behavior and become more motivated to behave responsibly in class?	CHAPTER 7
How exactly can I use personal conferencing and behavior contracts effectively?	CHAPTER 7

REFERENCES:

Evertson, C. M., and Weinstein, C. S., Editors. (2006) *Handbook of classroom management: Research, practice, and contemporary issues.* Chapter 15, "Classroom management in middle and high school classrooms." Philadelphia: Lawrence Erlbaum Associates.

CHAPTER 1

Classroom Management and Discipline

According to the NEA, classroom discipline remains the #1 problem identified by teachers. In framing this discussion about classroom discipline, I have to own up that I'm a big fan of the word discipline and its many meanings. I like thinking about areas in my life where I feel self-disciplined, where I can easily access tried-and-true qualities, habits, and skills that will lead to a job well done and a personal sense of well-being. I love the idea of engaging in daily disciplines that become comforting routines. I grew up in a disciplined household—there were ways that we did things in our home—but I didn't get disciplined in the punitive sense very often. Rather, I was mostly shown and taught how to do something and then I was expected to learn how to do it for myself. The reward was in the doing and the internal satisfaction I felt from doing it. Disciplined practice of the smallest tasks gave me a sense of control, responsibility, and competence. I also love the notion of learning and practicing a discipline—whether it's practicing the craft of writing or refining my skills as a coach and facilitator or creating original artwork. And even though there are undisciplined corners of my life that I don't like to visit, I also know that making room for my undisciplined self can help me think outside of the box and have fun doing it.

Think about yourself for a minute.

- How would you describe yourself when you feel disciplined and undisciplined?

- How were you disciplined at home and at school?

- When you were growing up how did adults help you become responsible and learn self-discipline?

- What kinds of support motivate you to be disciplined in some areas of your life?

- When and how has practice helped you become more disciplined?

- How do you feel when you have a sense of self-control in your life?

- What happens when you don't?

Your personal responses to these questions can help jump-start your thinking about discipline.

I'd like to propose that the goal of effective classroom management and discipline is to help all students to become more self-disciplined—that is, to regulate and manage their behavior in ways that promote personal efficacy and accountability, social skillfulness, responsible decision making, and academic success.

There are three choices we can make when students get into behavioral or academic difficulties. We can choose to respond with threats, verbal assaults, and punishments. We can choose to ignore the problem and do nothing. Or we can engage in the practice of Guided Discipline and Personalized Support that helps students develop greater responsibility, self-management, and personal and social efficacy.

The Punishment Approach

Punitive actions are done *to* a student. The intention is to verbally, psychologically, or physically inflict sufficient discomfort, deprivation, unpleasantness, harm, or humiliation so that a student will avoid the same behavior in the future to avoid being punished. Punishment is "past oriented" and remains focused on "what you did." The desire to punish may also be prompted by a teacher's need to exercise control and power over the student. When we operate in punitive mode, the unspoken message is something like, "My will must dominate your will. You need to be put in your place for what you've said or done." When we're not using our best skills, it's also easy to personalize the situation and interpret a student's unwanted behaviors or unskillful responses as a very personal threat to our authority or an assault on our dignity and respect—we gravitate toward payback and punishment. It's as if we are thinking, "You chose to make my life unpleasant so I'm going to return the sting."

Among educational researchers, there is remarkable agreement that punishment by itself, without accountable consequences and guided instruction and support, doesn't change a student's behavior for the better. The fact that most punishments have no immediate connection to the student's specific misbehavior further contributes to their ineffectiveness. Consider, for example, typical punishments like detention, demerits, administrative referrals, and in-school suspension. These "catch-all" consequences involve students in "doing time"—not undoing the harm they caused or learning skills they need to make a better choice next time.

Punishment may extinguish a negative behavior briefly, but that's about it. A "punitive only" approach becomes problematic because it often intensifies students' feelings of anger, hostility, alienation, resentment, or defiance. Punishment feels adversarial to students and is likely to reinforce "us vs. them" thinking. Instead of improving or repairing the relationship between student and teacher, punishments tend to worsen the relationship, making it difficult for either person to feel motivated and positive about moving forward positively. The irony here is that punitive strategies work least effectively for the kids who get in the most trouble, academically or behaviorally.

In addition, many punishments are meted out by someone not directly involved in the specific situation in which the student misbehaved. Removal from class to speak with the dean won't do much to repair the adversarial confrontation between a student and teacher that may have provoked the classroom referral in the first place. Imagine yourself as a parent for a minute. Your child misbehaves and you immediately send him to Mrs. Jones. Your note to Mrs. Jones says, "Don't send my child back home until he's fixed and the problem's solved." How comfortable would you be relinquishing your responsibility for disciplining your child to the neighbor down the street?

This happens every day in secondary schools when teachers expect the dean or assistant principal to "do something" with the student that will eliminate problems in their classrooms.

It's also important to note how often secondary teachers use grades as a form of academic punishment in hopes of getting kids to shape up. Yet, punitive grading rarely improves achievement, especially for reluctant and resistant students and those who have already experienced repeated failures.

The Do-Nothing Approach

The do-nothing approach literally means that a teacher doesn't intervene and nothing is done to, done by, or done with a student to interrupt or change a behavior. Sometimes we do nothing out of fear of a confrontation or fear of being disliked. Some teachers are simply disinterested in monitoring and helping kids change their behavior; claiming that their job is to teach, not to discipline secondary students. Sometimes, we may feel uneasy about using our authority in some adversarial situations and sometimes we just feel stuck, not knowing how to respond. Taking purposeful action can also feel draining. Especially when we're tired or stressed, intervening with care and intention can feel like it requires too much time and energy.

The choice to do nothing can emerge from the best of intentions. We might convince ourselves that "if I'm low key and don't draw attention to negative behavior, students will gradually stop engaging in these behaviors." Or we might hope that kids get the message, "I won't mess with you if you don't mess with me." Or we might think that if we attend to the rest of the group and keep focused on the task at hand, students with problem behaviors will eventually figure out expected behavioral norms and right themselves on their own.

This is a risky proposition because the message we think we're sending might not be the message a student takes in. Students may assume that a teacher's reluctance to intervene with problem behaviors is a sign of weakness—some kids may interpret a "hands-off" approach as a free pass to do whatever they want, whenever they want. Other students might think that your avoidance means you don't care enough to notice—these students may opt out and become passive and detached from you and the class. The bottom line is that doing nothing may serve as a temporary holding pattern while you observe the behavior of a particular student. But a do-nothing approach to discipline is likely to create more problems and solve next to none.

The Guided Discipline Approach

Guided discipline is as much about instruction and support as it is about classroom management. As its heart, the word discipline has everything to do with instruction. Among its Latin origins are the words *discipulus*, which means "pupil or learner," and *disciplina*, which means "teaching, training, and instruction" in the broadest sense.

Guided discipline helps students become more self-disciplined. (Self-discipline involves the habits, attitudes, and practices that promote self-management, produce high performance, wide-ranging expertise, or a well-ordered life.) Guided discipline is a combination of instruction, practice and rehearsal, invitations and interventions, accountable consequences, and personalized support that help students learn and regularly demonstrate more skillful and appropriate behaviors, more responsible decision making, and more effective work habits that lead to personal efficacy and academic success.

Five strategies distinguish guided discipline from most other classroom management models.

1. Guided discipline encourages teachers to *model, teach, practice,* and *assess* the behaviors, procedures, and problem-solving protocols that students are expected to use every day.

2. Guided discipline helps teachers develop a repertoire of *physical, visual,* and *verbal prompts* and *invitations that support students' cooperation and self-correction* before unwanted behaviors become a serious distraction or disruption.

3. Guided discipline emphasizes *personal accountability* and *accountable consequences* rather than punishment. When unwanted behaviors persist, accountable consequences are done *by* a student with the support of an adult—the intention is to help students take responsibility for their behavior or academic problems, understand the effects of their behavior on themselves and others, and learn and practice behaviors that are more skillful, responsible, and productive. Consequences and interventions are viewed as natural outcomes of the choices students make and the skills they need to learn. Accountability is more than just saying, "I'm responsible for my behavior." Being truly accountable involves specific actions that a student takes to make things right again. Accountable consequences involve four steps:

    -   **I'm responsible for my behavior.** What did you choose to say or do? Why do you think you're here?

    -   **My behavior affects others.** How did your words or behavior impact your own learning, the teacher, other students, or the learning environment? (How do you think _____ felt when you _____? Why do you think this wasn't the best choice?)

    -   **I'm expected to carry out an accountable consequence.** What can you do to correct it, fix it, make amends or make it right, repair the harm you've done, or restore your good standing, a relationship, a sense of harmony and trust?

    -   **I'm expected to change my behavior.** What do you need to learn and practice to become more skillful and make a better choice? What kind of plan will help you change your behavior? What will you do differently the next time this situation arises? How can the teacher support you in this effort?

4.   Guided discipline uses *personal conferencing* as a critical structure for discussing and resolving student problems. Conferencing can take many forms—from the 30-second student check-in, to the extended conference with a student outside of class, to a parent conference by phone or face to face, to a multiparty conference with the student, a parent, and other staff or administrators.

5.   Guided discipline helps students *develop and strengthen life skills competencies and habits of learning*.

Guided discipline is present and future oriented. It focuses on what students can do in the moment to regain control, self-correct, learn from their mistakes, redirect their focus, and get back on track and a plan. It also focuses on the future by expecting students to learn and demonstrate more appropriate and positive behaviors and make a plan that will help them make better choices the next time.

The concept of guided discipline is informed by beliefs that all students are capable of reflecting on their mistakes and setbacks and they can set goals and develop new strategies that will help them change their behavior. Rather than butting heads as adversaries, guided discipline emphasizes collaborative problem solving and tends to improve and repair student-teacher relationships.

Teachers are more motivated to provide the kinds of ongoing coaching and personalized support that builds a more productive learning environment and a more cohesive, high-performing learning community. Students who experience Guided Discipline and Personalized Support are more likely to feel respected, trusted, cared for, and competent. These positive feelings are more likely to increase students' internal motivation and effort to improve their behavior and become more successful learners.

A guided discipline approach holds out the best prospect for helping students change their behavior for real. Although it requires more intentional and timely actions on your part, you will have far fewer disruptions and problematic behaviors and more motivated and self-disciplined learners. More importantly, every interaction with students provides an opportunity to strengthen positive relationships and build bonds of trust and mutual respect.

Summary of Three Approaches to Classroom Management

What's your goal? What strategies will help you achieve your goal?

Punishment	Do-Nothing	Guided Discipline
Punishment is done *to* a student. The teacher's intention is to inflict sufficient discomfort, disapproval, deprivation, hurt, or humiliation so student will stop engaging in unwanted behavior. Punishment without instruction or support is about payback for breaking the rule.	Nothing is done to interrupt or change unwanted behavior **Do-Nothing** is about avoidance and a teacher's reluctance to engage students—out of fear of confrontation; fear of being disliked; uneasiness about one's authority; disinterest in helping students change behavior; belief that nothing will work; or concern that effective interventions will take too much time or energy.	**Guided Discipline** is about supporting students to make more responsible choices, learn more skillful behaviors, and develop greater personal efficacy and accountability. It involves invitations to cooperate and self-correct, accountable consequences and interventions, and collaborative problem solving *done by* a student with the support of an adult.
Immediate Focus and Goal: Teacher exercises sufficient power, control, and authority over student to stop unwanted behavior.	***Immediate Focus and Goal:*** Teacher ignores unwanted behavior, attends to the needs of the rest of the class, and keeps focused on the task at hand.	***Immediate Focus and Goal:*** Teacher's first response is to help student cooperate, self-correct, regain control, refocus, and get back on track.
Orientation: Past. (It's about what student did.)	***Orientation:*** Present. (But the focus is on *other* students *not* the student engaged in unwanted behavior.)	***Orientation:*** Present and Future. (What can student do differently right now and what can student do differently in the future?)
Longer-term Goals: Hope that student is sufficiently repentant so student avoids unwanted behavior in the future.	***Longer-term Goals:*** Hope that students will figure out behavioral norms and right themselves on their own.	***Longer-term Goals:*** To help students take responsibility for their behavior or academic problems, understand the effects of their behavior, and learn and practice behaviors that are more skillful and responsible.
Effects on Student: Likely to intensify feelings of anger, resentment, hostility, alienation, and defiance resulting in low motivation to change.	***Effects on Student:*** Likely to encourage detachment and passivity or an inflated sense of power to act out, test limits, and challenge authority.	***Effects on Student:*** Likely to encourage feelings of respect, trust, competence, and being cared for resulting in greater motivation to change.
Effects on Relationship: Relationship between student and teacher is likely to worsen or remain adversarial.	***Effects on Relationship:*** The teacher and student remain unattached and unaccountable to each other.	***Effects on Relationship:*** The relationship between student and teacher is maintained and is likely to improve.

Identifying the Problem and Guided Discipline Response

Before you read the case studies in Chapter 2, it's helpful to become familiar with the language we use to describe different problem types and different kinds of responses, consequences, and interventions.

Identify the problem type

Before you can make the right choice about what to do NOW and what to do LATER, you need to diagnose the problem as accurately as you can. The chart on pages 26–34 identifies six problem types that cover a comprehensive array of unwanted behaviors and include examples of low-impact and high-impact behaviors for each problem type. Low-impact behaviors have a minimal or temporary effect on the individual, the adult, the group, or the learning environment, while high-impact behaviors can have a dramatically negative effect on the classroom culture and/or result in physical or psychological harm to students or adults. The problem types include:

1. **Procedural Infractions, Noncompletion, and Noncompliance** (from forgetting to follow a procedure occasionally to chronic noncompliance of classroom guidelines or chronic noncompletion of student work)

2. **Noncooperation and Nonparticipation** (from temporary loss of focus to inability to resolve interpersonal differences to deliberate attempts to sabotage the group)

3. **Impulse Control, Self-Management, and Personal Distress** (from occasional lapses in effectively managing behavior and feelings to severe out-of-control behavior or chronic discouragement and frustration)

4. **Student-to-Student Aggression** (from unfriendly responses toward peers to hitting and harassment)

5. **Student-to-Teacher Aggression** (from the occasional rude response to an adult to hostile threats and confrontations)

6. **Academic Learning Gaps and Barriers to Learning** (from not fully understanding a particular concept or skill set in a lesson to significant cognitive skill gaps that make it difficult to complete any work with proficiency)

1	**Procedural Infractions**

1. Doesn't bring necessary materials to class
2. Unprepared for class
3. Noncompletion or poor quality of assigned work
4. Noncompliance with classroom procedures

2	**Noncooperation and Nonparticipation**

5. No attempt to do assigned work in class
6. Loss of focus, confusion, or temporary frustration, anger, or disengagement
7. Initiating or joining in "sidebar" conversations
8. Playing around or goofing off with others
9. Nonparticipation in activities, withdrawal, or detachment
10. Inability to work cooperatively with others or resolve interpersonal differences
11. Deliberate acts and use of negative speech that sabotage the group or suck the energy out of the room

3	**Impulse Control, Self-Management, and Personal Distress**

12. Distracting or disruptive movement or noise
13. Interrupting others, blurting out inappropriate comments or always having to have the last word
14. Persistent whining or badgering
15. Inability to work silently when required or to work independently without bothering others
16. Inability to manage anger or deal with persistent discouragement and frustration effectively
17. Student is easily triggered, annoyed, or upset by others
18. Persistent acts that seek teacher's attention or call attention to oneself
19. Persistently rude, uncivil, or offensive speech, gesturing, or posturing during whole group learning
20. Leaving classroom without permission
21. Out-of-control emotional outbursts or rage that jeopardize safety, order, and other students' well-being
22. Misuse or destruction of property / vandalism / unsafe or unlawful use of materials and equipment
23. Lying, stealing, or plagiarism

4	**Student-to-Student Aggression**

24. Hostile, unfriendly, or disrespectful responses to peers
25. Deliberately annoying, provoking, or bothering peers
26. Cursing, yelling, or excessive use of criticism, blame, sarcasm, and accusations directed at a student
27. Teasing, taunting, put-downs, and name calling

- -

Consequences and interventions for the remaining behaviors in this category warrant removal from class and schoolwide consequences and interventions.

28. Pushing, shoving, and uninvited contact with another student
29. Verbal intimidation and threats
30. Physical intimidation / gang behaviors / bullying
31. Hitting, punching, kicking
32. Harassment (abusive, obscene, or offensive language, gestures, propositions, or behaviors intended to target or harm an individual or a group based on race, color, origins, gender, sexual identity, age, religion, class, or disability)

5	**Student-to-Teacher Aggression**

33. Rude, unfriendly, provocative, or disrespectful verbal responses, gestures, and posturing directed at an adult (This is the annoying stuff that you can't take personally, but you do want students to correct or stop quickly.)
34. Persistent demands, argumentative and adversarial speech, and "lawyering up"
35. Walking away when an adult is speaking with student
36. Refusal to make a choice or follow a directive after repeated requests or refusal to accept and carry out accountable consequences

- -

Consequences and interventions for the remaining behaviors in this category warrant removal from class and schoolwide consequences and interventions.

37. Acts of spite and revenge directed at an adult
38. Cursing that is specifically directed at an adult
39. Verbal threats, hostile and aggressive confrontations, or physical intimidation directed at an adult
40. Assault with intent to harm

6	**Academic Learning Gaps and Barriers to Learning**

(Problem behaviors are often a "cover" for academic inadequacies. Thus, identifying learning gaps is an essential aspect of good problem diagnosis. See page 34.)

When we discuss a guided discipline approach with teachers, one big question looms in the room: "So this sounds good in theory, but what exactly can I do when _____ does or
                                                                                          name of student
says _____?"
       specific behavior

The charts on pages 29–34 provide brief summaries of six sets of responses that are described in detail in Chapters 3 through 7. They include:

A.   **Procedural Solutions for Procedural Infractions**
     (If behavior persists, move to **D**)

B.   **Proximity, Prompts, and Invitations for Off-task Behaviors**
     (If behavior persists, move to **D**)

C.   **Check Ins and Conferences for Problems that Don't Have a Quick Fix**
     (If behavior persists, move to **D**)

D.   **Intensive Accountable Consequences and Interventions for High-Impact Behaviors or Chronic Unwanted Behaviors that Have Not Improved**

E.   **Immediate Enforcement, Intervention, and Follow-up of Schoolwide Consequences for Egregious Offenses**

F.   **Personalized Academic Supports and Interventions for Academic Learning Gaps**

Important Note:
Over 80 percent of problem behaviors can be addressed effectively using **A** and **B** responses. When you use these responses consistently and predictably, classroom disruptions will reduce dramatically. Another 15 percent to 20 percent of problem behaviors will always require one-to-one conferencing with a student (**C**) to get to the source of the problem behavior and make a plan to **stop** the unwanted behavior and **start** practicing the desired target behavior. **D** and **E** responses signal that a student is in serious trouble and will require more intensive interventions that often involve parents, deans, assistant principals, or counselors.

A	When **Procedural Infractions** look like...

- Student doesn't bring necessary materials to class
- Student is unprepared for class
- Noncompletion or poor quality of assigned work
- Noncompliance with classroom rules, norms, and procedures

Procedures involve specific expectations and routines that facilitate effective learning, responsible classroom behavior, and high performance of the group.

Procedural infractions are problems of self-efficacy—students haven't yet demonstrated personal responsibility and habits of learning consistently and effectively. Students need to know why specific procedures are in place, what they're expected to do, and what will happen when they don't follow a specific procedure.

YOU NEED	**Procedural Solutions** (If behavior becomes chronic, move to D)

- Call attention to the procedure (visually or verbally) and ask student what she/he should be doing
- Offer the opportunity for student to self-correct and follow the procedure (This means that "Yes, I'll do it next time," isn't good enough—student needs to engage in correction or "do-over" immediately or before the class ends.)
- Use guided instruction to re-teach procedure to individuals, a small group of students, or the whole class
- Arrange for rehearsal and practice at lunch, before or after school, or at your convenience during a prep period (This is the "workout session.")
- Use verbal and written feedback and coaching to support continued and regular practice of the procedure

B	## When **Off-task Behaviors** look like...

- Loss of focus, confusion, or temporary frustration, anger, or disengagement
- Initiating or joining in "sidebar" conversations
- Playing around or goofing off with others
- Distracting or disruptive movement or noise
- Interrupting others, blurting out inappropriate comments, or always having to have the last word
- Rude, unfriendly, provocative, or disrespectful verbal responses, gestures, and posturing directed at an adult (This is the annoying stuff that you can't take personally, but you do want students to correct or cease and desist quickly.)

YOU NEED

Proximity, Prompts, Invitations, and Logical Consequences
(If behavior becomes chronic, move to D)

Proximity, prompts, and invitations to cooperate and self-correct are the most effective responses to the off-task but typical behaviors that interfere with a student's own learning or the group's capacity to function and learn. The goal here is to redirect behavior quickly, say as little as possible, and return to what you were doing.

- First, use physical proximity and physical prompts to redirect behavior
- Incorporate and point to visual prompts in the classroom that serve as reminders
- Offer verbal prompts and invitations that encourage students to cooperate, self-correct, refocus, and get back on track
- Offer a choice or opportunity to solve the problem
- Record what a student is doing or saying exactly or tally the number of times a behavior occurs, so you can discuss it later with the student. When you begin to write, most students will stop.
- Use immediate logical consequences when it's possible and appropriate. For example:
  ▶ Persistent talking among the same two or three students during activities that require silence → *Students must move to extra chairs placed around the periphery of the classroom during the period OR students are assigned different seats at the beginning of the next class period for _____ days.*
  ▶ Persistent interruptions and noisemaking by an individual student during activities that require silence → *Student is assigned a different seat on the periphery of the classroom or behind your desk for _____ days and may be barred from speaking for _____ days.*
  ▶ Throwing trash on the floor or throwing paper in the room → *Student must clean up trash on the floor, arrange furniture, or tidy up the room at the end of class for _____ days.*
- When off-task behaviors persist, state consequences and offer "double or nothing" ("STOP _____ and START_____ and you're good to go. Choose to continue _____ and you owe me a workout session and an accountable consequence.")

PLEASE READ THIS!!!! When a student verbally refuses a directive repeatedly after multiple prompts and overt hostility and aggression intensify...the student has crossed the line from noncompliance to defiance. Now, the student is in big trouble. (Oppositional defiance is a serious offense in most school codes of conduct and usually warrants an immediate referral and more intensive interventions including classroom removal and suspension.)

- Write a referral, but don't submit it. If behavior STOPS immediately and for the remainder of the week, referral is torn up.

C	When **Problem Behaviors Don't Have a Quick Fix** and look like…

- No attempt to do assigned work
- Nonparticipation in activities, withdrawal, or detachment
- Inability to work cooperatively with others or resolve interpersonal differences
- Inability to work silently or independently without bothering others
- Inability to manage anger or deal with persistent discouragement and frustration effectively
- Student is easily triggered, annoyed, or upset by others
- Persistent acts that seek teacher's attention or call attention to oneself
- Persistent whining or badgering
- Hostile, unfriendly, or disrespectful responses to peers
- Deliberately annoying, provoking, or bothering peers
- Persistent demands, argumentative and adversarial speech, and "lawyering up"
- Walking away when an adult is speaking with student

YOU NEED

Check-Ins and Conferences to Find Out What's Up and Plan What to Do (If behavior persists, move to D)

When you don't know what's triggering a specific behavior or when unwanted behaviors involve impulse control, a student's struggle to manage feelings, poor relationships with peers, or inability to cope with tough situations, you need to personally check in with the student.

If you don't set aside time to speak personally with the student, NOTHING will change!!!!

Speak with a student privately during your classroom "walk-around," at the end of class, or outside of class.

- Share what you observed and use non-threatening openers. "So I've noticed in the last week that _____. What's up?"
- Hunch out what student might be feeling, and invite student to talk. "You sound really upset about _____."
- Listen and acknowledge student's feelings—let student talk!
- Convey support and understanding of what you heard
- Probe for sources of the problem and what student needs to move forward
- Identify the specific behavior that needs to stop or change and why
- Spell out desired replacement behaviors that need to start
- Explore strategies that will help student get back on track
- Develop a plan, contract, or conduct card and provide follow-up feedback and coaching
- Change what you say and do to prompt a change in what students say and do

D	# Chronic Unwanted Behaviors Have Not Improved or High-Impact Behaviors look like….

- Deliberate acts and use of negative speech that sabotage the group or suck the energy out of the room
- Persistently rude, uncivil, or offensive speech, gesturing, or posturing during whole group learning
- Cursing, yelling, or excessive use of criticism, blame, sarcasm, and accusations directed at a student
- Teasing, taunting, put-downs, and name calling
- Pushing, shoving, and uninvited contact with another student
- Repeated refusal to make a choice or follow a directive after repeated requests; refusal to accept and carry out accountable consequences
- Acts of spite and revenge directed at an adult

YOU NEED

More Intensive Accountable Consequences and Interventions

Chronic **A**, **B**, and **C** behaviors and high-impact behaviors require a conference and a plan **(C) PLUS** more intensive accountable consequences and interventions that can include:

- Write referral but don't submit it. If the behavior STOPS immediately and for the remainder of the week, the referral is torn up
- Immediate intervention to STOP the behavior or DEFUSE situation
- Classroom referral to dean or assistant principal, but no immediate removal from the classroom
- Immediate removal from the classroom to dean or assistant principal
- Written reflection and report forms
- Student calls parent in presence of teacher or teacher, dean or assistant principal call parent
- Teacher-student conference or mediation with dean or assistant principal
- Student-parent-teacher-dean conference to review intervention and/or behavior plan
- Corrective or restorative action or restitution done by student
- Restrictions, modifications, or loss of privileges
- Verbal or written apology
- Lunchtime or after-school workout or practice session with teacher
- Saturday school
- Team meeting to discuss possible turn-around strategies
- Referral to Guidance, Student Intervention Team, or Student Support Team
- Written entry in student's record
- Daily conduct card and feedback for two weeks
- Parent observation of student in classroom with debriefing

E	When **Egregious Offenses** look like…

- Leaving classroom without permission
- Out-of-control emotional outbursts or rage that jeopardize safety, order, and other students' well-being
- Misuse or destruction of property / Vandalism / Unsafe or unlawful use of resources
- Lying, stealing, or plagiarism
- Verbal intimidation and threats directed at peers
- Physical intimidation / Gang behaviors / Bullying
- Hitting, punching, kicking peers
- Harassment (abusive, obscene, or offensive language, gestures, propositions, or behaviors intended to target or harm individual or a group based on race, color, origins, gender, sexual identity, age, religion, class, or disability)
- Cursing that is specifically directed at an adult
- Verbal threats, hostile and aggressive confrontations, or physical intimidation directed at an adult
- Assault with intent to harm

YOU NEED

Immediate Enforcement, Intervention, and Follow-up of Schoolwide Consequences

Consequences for egregious offenses or chronic unwanted behaviors that haven't improved after **(D)**, usually involve enforcement of schoolwide protocols, consequences, and interventions that can include:

- Immediate intervention to STOP the behavior or DEFUSE situation
- Classroom referral to dean or assistant principal, but no immediate removal from the classroom
- Immediate removal from the classroom to dean or assistant principal
- Student calls parent in presence of dean or assistant principal, or dean or assistant principal, or principal calls parent
- Conference with student, teacher, and dean or assistant principal, or principal
- Daily conduct card and feedback for two weeks
- Student must return to school with parent the next day for conference and/or home visit
- Classroom observation by student support or guidance staff or administrator
- Student-teacher mediation or reconciliation or other restorative justice protocols
- Referral to Guidance, Early Intervention Team, or Student Support Team
- Counseling or behavior replacement sessions with guidance staff during or after school or on Saturday
- Pre-suspension conference
- In-school suspension or time-out room plus re-entry protocols
- Out-of-school suspension plus re-entry protocols

F	# When **Academic Learning Gaps or Barriers** look like...

Problem behaviors are often a "cover" for students' academic learning gaps. Here's a "starter list" of some of the more recognizable learning gaps and barriers:

- Discrete gaps in understanding and comprehension related to a specific skill set, lesson, learning unit, product, or project—"I just don't get it."
- Learning readiness issues—students don't have prior experience, knowledge, or skills to do what they are asked to do.
- Honest boredom for students who already understand or have mastered the learning content; lack of rigorous, intellectually challenging work.
- Feelings of inadequacy, lack of confidence, or little belief in one's capacity to complete task successfully.
- Low motivation (low satisfaction, interest, or value associated with goal or task) or low effort (specific actions student can take to increase achievement).
- Mild disabilities or "learning-to-learn" gaps related to student's metacognitive capacities to pay attention, set goals, follow instructions, manage time, plan and organize, and problem solve and persevere.
- The gap between the dominant method of instruction and the dominant or preferred way a student learns; lack of differentiated instruction and learning accommodations. (If you can't learn the way I teach, I can learn to teach the way you learn.)
- Unmet developmental needs that impede learning (safety, belonging, control, acceptance, respect, etc.) or intense emotional turmoil that can hijack students in ways that make it difficult to focus.
- The refusal to learn because of fears that learning and succeeding in school mean losing one's identity, betraying friends, or rejecting the world that one knows.
- Significant cognitive skill gaps that impact a student's capacity to complete any task proficiently.

YOU NEED

Personalized Academic Supports and Interventions

Mislabeling learning gaps as "discipline problems" or using punitive grading as the "catch-all" response for poor academic performance comes at the cost of not providing the kind of academic instruction, supports, and interventions that will enable students to become competent and successful learners.

When learning gaps and barriers persist, supports and interventions can include the following:

- Academic conference using a similar format to conference description in (C)
- Academic learning contracts
- Guided instruction, re-teaching, re-testing, practice, and rehearsal with you during class or on designated conference hours before, during, or after school
- Required homework hall, Saturday school, owed work time, or before- or after-school tutoring or study groups to complete work or improve academic skills
- Verbal and written feedback and coaching
- Personalized encouragement and regular check-ins
- Parental phone call, note, or conference
- Referrals to provide appropriate diagnosis, interventions, and services that address serious and/or chronic academic learning gaps

What Students Need to Know

As you review the charts and develop your own set of responses, consequences, and interventions for unwanted and unacceptable behaviors, think about how you will let students know, "Here's what will happen when…" Here are a few examples:

What you can expect when your behavior becomes a problem...

"If you're not following our classroom guidelines and procedures, you'll have a chance to correct yourself, do it over, or owe me time to learn how to do it and get it right."

"If you're fooling around or off task, I'll give you a physical, visual, or verbal prompt. Your job is to refocus and get back on track. If the behavior persists, you have a choice of 'double or nothing.' Stop what you're doing and you're good to go. Continue what you're doing and you owe me a workout session and an accountable consequence."

"If you keep talking during activities that require silence you will be asked to move to another seat."

"If you get in the habit of using uncivil, disrespectful, or negative speech, you will be asked to correct it."

"When unacceptable behaviors persist, you will owe me a workout session and an accountable consequence to restore your good standing and make it right."

"Any behavior that seriously jeopardizes the safety of anyone or severely disrupts the learning environment, warrants an immediate removal from class...That includes threatening, bullying, harassing, or cursing out your peers or me. I will notify the office or security, write an EXIT Referral, and someone will escort you to the dean for follow-up consequences and interventions."

"If you're having trouble with an assignment or task in class, you can count on me to check in with you and work with you to get back on track. If it's a serious academic problem, we'll need to conference, problem solve, and make a plan."

"If you're angry, frustrated, or upset, you will have choices for what you can do to calm yourself and regain your control and equilibrium. Later, we can talk and problem solve."

Frequently Used Terms

Here's a reference list of key terms and phrases used throughout the book.

Accountable consequences are **carried out by students** with adult support to correct and change unwanted and unacceptable behaviors. Consequences and interventions are viewed as outcomes of the choices that students make and the skills they need to learn; students must **owe time and/or effort** to account for their unwanted behavior by:

- carrying out **logical consequences** that match a specific infraction and are often used to address minor problematic behaviors immediately (i.e., talk time limits and constraints when students interrupt others or use negative speech; workout session when students fail to complete three or more key assignments; time owed when students are tardy; clean up tasks when students make a mess).

- carrying out **reflective consequences** through **student-teacher conferences** that involve written and verbal reflections, problem solving, or development of a behavior plan, conduct card, or contract to monitor and support desired changes in behavior.

- carrying out **corrective consequences** that support students to correct unwanted behavior in the moment; learn, practice, and rehearse desired target behaviors; or correct, revise, redo, and finish incomplete or below-standard work.

- carrying out **restorative consequences** that help repair harm done, mend relationships, restore one's good standing, or make things right (making an apology; engaging in acts of generosity and goodwill; participating in a community circle, mediation, or reconciliation conference; making financial restitution for damaged property; contributing service hours to the community to earn back one's standing).

- carrying out **schoolwide consequences** and interventions that involve parents, the dean or assistant principal, other faculty who teach the student, counselors, or the student support/early intervention team.

Chronic refers to unwanted behaviors that occur frequently over an extended period (over several days or weeks) without an observable change or improvement in a specific behavior.

Civility refers to the manners you use (please, thank you, I'm sorry, excuse me) and the courtesy, respect, politeness, and friendliness you show in your conversations and interactions with people you know and people you don't.

Consequence is an outcome of an event or an individual's behavior. Consequences can be *positive* or *negative* and have a *positive* or *negative* impact or result. In this book, consequences are both the result of your behavior and the choices you make *and* the specific actions you and students take to address unwanted and unacceptable behaviors.

Desired or "Replacement" Behaviors are behaviors that you expect students to learn and practice as part of an accountable consequence. Good problem diagnosis always includes concrete descriptions of both unwanted and desired behaviors.

Discipline refers to a system of rules of conduct or method of practice; or the trait of being well behaved; or to training, instruction, and practice necessary to improve a strength, talent, skill, or self-control.

Egregious refers to the severity and intensity of specific incidents and behaviors that put a complete halt to ordinary activity, involve severe acts of student aggression, or jeopardize the safety, order, or personal well-being of anyone in the classroom. Egregious behaviors often require immediate actions to stop and interrupt the behavior or defuse the situation, remove the student from the classroom, and submit a referral to the dean.

Frequent Fliers are the students who are collecting mileage every day and getting in trouble all of the time. These students often don't respond to the normal range of consequences or the kind of effective "teacher talk" and prompts that will help most students get back on track. Helping frequent fliers to turn around their behavior often requires daily monitoring, check-ins, and conduct cards; guidance sessions to learn replacement behaviors; greater involvement of parents and the school administration; and more intensive interventions involving social workers and community partners.

Guided Discipline is an approach to discipline that supports students to make more responsible choices, learn more skillful behaviors, and develop greater personal efficacy and accountability. It involves a combination of instruction, practice, and rehearsal, with invitations to cooperate and self-correct; accountable consequences and interventions; and collaborative problem solving.

High-Impact Unwanted Behaviors are behaviors that have a severely negative impact on the whole group and the classroom learning environment. These are often behaviors that jeopardize students' feelings of safety, violate students' dignity and well-being, seriously disrupt the learning environment, silence the group, or involve acts of aggression toward adults or peers.

Impulsive behaviors refer to student behaviors that occur quickly without control, planning, or consideration of the consequences. Impulsivity illustrates a short-circuited process: "FEEL, ACT, THINK (much later)." **Self-regulated behavior** reflects a different sequence of events: "FEEL, THINK, ACT." Students engage in deliberative self-monitoring, self-reflection, and self-talk before choosing an appropriate response or action that matches the particular situation.

Life Skills and Habits of Learning are also identified as social and emotional competencies; personal, interpersonal, and group efficacy; employability skills; and metacognitive/learning-to-learn skills. Teachers need to decide which of these specific skills and habits have the biggest impact on students' achievement and students' capacity to perform and function in the classroom community and then develop a plan for how they will model, teach, practice, and assess the behaviors and habits that they expect.

Personalized Support includes all of the things teachers do and say to help individual students develop the academic, social, and emotional competencies to succeed in their class. Supportive teacher behaviors include personal check-ins, personal coaching, re-teaching, tutoring, lunchtime or after-school "workouts," and behavior and learning contracts. All of these efforts will strengthen your relationship with the student and galvanize your commitment and resolve to "do what it takes" to help students improve their behavior and academic performance.

Prevention Initiatives build a positive, pro-social climate and culture; reinforce desired behaviors; and prevent and reduce unwanted and unacceptable behaviors. Prevention efforts involve clear statements about core values and beliefs, rights, and responsibilities; clear expectations about behavioral norms and procedures; intentional pro-social skill development; and special events, peer initiatives, rituals, incentives, and signage that affirm, support, and communicate: "This is the way we do school here. This is the way we treat each other. This is the way we work together."

Procedural Consequence: The corrective actions a student is expected to take when they commit a procedural infraction (see below). For example, "If you enter the classroom inappropriately, you will need to re-enter the classroom immediately in a civil and respectful way or practice entering the classroom appropriately at lunchtime or after school."

Procedural Infraction: When a student hasn't followed the procedure you've taught and students have practiced, it's time to have a conference.

Procedures are established methods and processes for completing the same task the same way time and time again. Examples: entering the classroom, handing in assignments, arriving to school and class on time, using computers and special equipment, getting lunch in the cafeteria line, etc. Good procedures support more on-task behaviors, reduce disruptions, and improve group performance and the quality of the learning experience.

Conferencing for Procedural Infractions
1. What procedure didn't I follow?
2. Instead, I chose to...
3. We have this procedure because...
4. How did this interfere with my learning or other students' learning?
5. Two things I can do that will help me follow this procedure:

Public Space includes all spaces inside or outside the school building except classrooms, labs, and other learning environments used for classroom instruction.

Public Space Incidents include a) minor infractions and unwanted behaviors in public space (horseplay, yelling down the hall, goofing around) that should be handled by the adult who witnessed the incident, and b) more egregious incidents (ones that jeopardize student and adult safety and order) need to be reported to deans and administrators immediately.

Public versus Private refers to behavioral expectations in public and private spaces. This is a critical concept for students to understand. Schools, for example, are public places where commonly accepted norms of behavior and standards of conduct are developed and aligned with those that people use to navigate successfully in public and in the work place. Many students have a tough time switching from private to public behaviors and an even tougher time keeping their "personal business" from becoming "public." Here are two rules of thumb that students need to learn:

- "If I can hear it, your personal conversation is no longer private. It has become part of the public domain. If what I hear is threatening, abusive, obscene, or offensive, you and I will have to deal with it."

- "If you choose to take your personal disputes and fighting words into public settings—whether it's in the classroom, the hallway, or the cafeteria—your private business becomes public record, and the school will have to deal with it."

Punitive Consequences (Punishments) are *done to the student* as a penalty for doing wrong. Punitive responses are intended to cause hurt, humiliation, deprivation, or discomfort. Punishments usually include *doing time* by way of detention or suspension. Punitive consequences are not accountable consequences because the student is not expected to do anything to correct the situation, repair the harm, restore her/his good standing, change the unwanted behavior to a desired one, make restitution, or make things right.

Refusal to Carry Out Accountable Consequences refers to a student's refusal to accept a consequence without a fuss or take the opportunity offered to make things right and get back on track. Learning how to accept correction, criticism, and reprimands without aggressive push-back is a critical skill for getting along, getting a job, and getting a life. When students respond to respectful requests and directives hostilely and aggressively, noncompliance can turn into defiance. Now, the student is in big trouble. (Oppositional defiance is a serious offense in most "school codes of conduct" and usually warrants an immediate referral and more intensive interventions that may include classroom removal and suspension.)

Repetitive Unwanted Behavior: An unwanted or unacceptable behavior that persists during a short time span (one or two class periods).

Responsibility versus Accountability are different. Responsibility is more internally driven. It's about doing what you say you will do and doing what you're expected to do. Accountability involves an obligation or willingness to accept and *account* for one's actions to others. Accountability means that when you mess up, don't complete a task successfully, make a bad choice, or don't behave in a responsible manner, you are expected to correct it, fix it, complete it, or make it right.

Restorative Justice Protocols are protocols that enable

a) individuals or a group who have been harmed or violated to air and share feelings, needs, and grievances;

b) conflicting parties to resolve differences and mend relationships;

c) students to erase their "bads" and earn back or restore privileges or their good standing;

d) students who have been suspended or committed serious offenses to re-enter the community and declare what they will do in words and actions to make things right.

Restorative justice protocols include class meetings, peer mediation, group mediation, student-teacher mediation, reconciliation conferences, peer jury, community circle, and suspension re-entry protocols.

Scaffolded Consequences and Interventions involve a continuum of responses to unwanted behaviors that moves from fairly uniform responses for the *occasional* infraction/violation to a broad array of more intense and comprehensive consequences and interventions when the same behavior is *repetitive* or becomes *chronic* or the *intensity, frequency,* or *severity* of cumulative behaviors and incidents continues to escalate.

Schoolwide Rules and Discipline Policies: These usually involve four different types of infractions and incidents and each requires a distinct array of scaffolded consequences and interventions. It is critical for all adults to agree on the rules and consequences that they will publicly support and consistently enforce the same way every time with every student.

1. **Attendance** (late arrival, tardy during the school day, unexcused and excused absences, cuts, and truancy)

2. **Schoolwide Procedural Infractions** (dress code and uniform violations, contraband possessions, not wearing ID badges, no hall pass, etc.)

3. **Public Space Incidents** (any disciplinary incidents that occur in public spaces inside and outside the building)

4. **Classroom Referrals and Removal** (clear expectations about what should be handled by the teacher; what behaviors warrant a referral to the dean, guidance office, grade-level team, or early intervention team; what behaviors warrant immediate removal from the classroom; what a referral needs to say; and the time frame for submitting referrals and receiving feedback about actions taken)

Self-Discipline refers to the skills, habits, attributes, and practices that promote self-management, regulation of emotions, impulse control, and personal efficacy. Self discipline produces high performance, quality craftmanship, wide-ranging expertise, and a well-ordered life.

Student-Teacher Conferences create shared responsibility and accountability for the student and the teacher and lets students know you're willing to take the time to listen, deal with the issue, find out more information, problem solve together, and make a plan. It can be a one minute check-in, a ten-minute planning conference, or an extended conference with a student and parents to address serious academic or behavior issues. Conferencing is usually the first step toward helping students take responsibility for their behavior.

- **The Adult** supports student to do what it takes to change behavior, get back on track, and stay out of trouble. **Questions for the Adult:** What are my goals in this intervention? What are the unmet needs driving the student's behavior (attention, power, the need for choice, inadequacy, revenge, etc.)? What's going on? What do I need to know? What can I do to help the student meet his/her needs, solve the problem, take responsibility, restore equilibrium, repair relationships, support a change in behavior, develop new skills, and get back on track?

- **The Student** takes responsibility for what he/she did/said and accepts the consequence, intervention, support, etc. **Questions for the Student:** What did I do? What was I supposed to be doing? Why am I here? What's not working? What do I need or want? What's one skill I can learn, one thing I can do to get back on track? What can I do differently next time? A useful opening question is, "So tell me why you think you're here."

Conferencing Questions for Off-task Behaviors

1. What happened? What did I do?
2. What was I supposed to be doing?
3. How do I feel about what happened?
4. Two ways I could have handled the situation differently:
5. Next time I feel this way, I could try...

Conferencing Questions for Unacceptable Speech

1. What did I say that was inappropriate of disrespectful?
2. What was bothering me?
3. How did my words impact other students, the teacher, the classroom?
4. It probably would have been better not to say this at all because... OR I could have said...
5. Next time I feel this way, I could say...

Supportive Interventions are developed and facilitated by adults to support desired changes in student behavior and healthy growth and development. They include: personal conferencing, counseling, and behavior and learning plans; instruction, coaching, practice, and rehearsal of "replacement" behaviors with students; specific interventions for "frequent fliers"; and an effective system of referrals, early interventions, "kid talk" protocols, information sharing, faculty feedback, and case management.

Workout Session replaces the term *detention* and describes the time students owe you during lunch or after school to conference about unwanted behaviors, make a plan or contract, learn new skills, practice or rehearse desired behaviors, tackle specific learning gaps, or complete, revise, or redo student work.

CHAPTER 2

13 Guided Discipline Scenarios

The thirteen scenarios in this chapter illustrate how punitive, do-nothing, and guided discipline approaches result in very different outcomes for the student, the teacher, and the group.

As you read each one, you might want to use a blank piece of paper to cover up the text below the brief scenario in the box. Read the scenario, and jot down your responses to these questions.

1. **How would you describe the problem type?**

    1. Procedural Infractions, Noncompletion, and Noncompliance

    2. Noncooperation and Nonparticipation

    3. Impulse Control, Self-management, Personal Distress

    4. Student-to-Student Aggression

    5. Student-to-Teacher Aggression

    6. Academic Learning Gaps and Barriers to Learning

2. **What set of responses, consequences, and interventions might be most effective in this situation?**

    A. Procedural Solutions for Procedural Infractions (If behavior persists, move to **D**)

    B. Proximity, Prompts, and Invitations for Off-task Behaviors (If behavior persists, move to **D**)

    C. Check-Ins and Conferences for Problems that Don't Have a Quick Fix (If behavior persists, move to **D**)

    D. Intensive Accountable Consequences and Interventions for High-Impact Behaviors or Chronic Unwanted Behaviors that Have Not Improved

    E. Immediate Enforcement, Intervention, and Follow-up of Schoolwide Consequences for Egregious Offenses

    F. Personalized Academic Supports and Interventions for Academic Learning Gaps

As you read the descriptions of the punishment, do-nothing, and guided discipline approaches in each scenario, you might ask yourself any of these questions for each scenario:

- In each approach, how do the interactions between the teacher and the student help or hurt their relationship? What are the dominant feelings that the teacher and student take away in each approach?

- In each approach, how does the teacher's response impact other students and the overall tone and climate in the classroom?

- What are the potential costs and risks of using the *punitive* approach?

- What are the potential costs and risks of using the *do-nothing* approach?

- What are the potential benefits for you, the student, and the class of using the *guided discipline* approach?

- How is the student expected to be responsible/accountable in the *guided discipline* approach? What is the student doing or learning that will help him/her to become more self-aware, more skillful, and more responsible next time?

SCENARIO #1

Two boys are talking loudly across the room to friends in another group during a cooperative learning activity.

What's The Problem? NONCOOPERATION AND NONPARTICIPATION. (#7 Initiating or join in "sidebar" conversation and #8 Playing around and goofing off with others)

The Punishment Approach: The teacher responds by demanding in a voice louder than theirs that they stop the sidebar conversations with other groups and get back to work. When the pair continues talking across the room, the teacher says in an even louder voice: "That's it. You've got a zero for the day and a detention after school." The two students quiet down, continue to grumble among themselves, and don't do a lick of work. They don't go to detention and no one realizes they were missing in action until two weeks later.

The Do-Nothing Approach: The teacher ignores the students and focuses her attention on the students who are on task. The boys' behavior is not disrupting the class as a whole, but the conversation continues to distract their friends from focusing on their group's task. In the meantime, the two boys are contributing nothing to the efforts of their own group.

The Guided Discipline and Personalized Support Approach:

Response? B: PROXIMITY, PROMPTS, AND INVITATIONS

The teacher moves over to the two students, gets their attention, and talks to them quietly near their group. The goal is to get students back on track, so the teacher says, "The cross-talk with other groups needs to stop now. I want to make sure you're clear about what to do. What's your task right now?" One student doesn't have a clue, so the teacher says, "Okay, check in with your group and then tell me two things you need to do during the rest of the period. Got it?" The student checks back in with the teacher and begins working. At the end of class, the teacher checks in again with both students and asks, "Tell me what you accomplished today and what's left to do tonight." The teacher gives them a smile and thumbs up and closes by saying, "So when you come in tomorrow, let me know what you're going to do to stay focused on the assignment. Are we good? Okay!"

SCENARIO 2

A very bright 9th grade boy named Eric has set new records for disorganization. He constantly loses important papers, his notebook is a mess, he hasn't turned in key assignments, and he leaves his assignment notebook at home. Thus he doesn't write down his assignments at school.

What's the Problem? PROCEDURAL INFRACTIONS (#1 Doesn't bring necessary materials to class and #4 Noncompliance with classroom rules, norms, and procedures)

The Punishment Approach: The teacher responds by telling Eric the procedures he isn't following:

- There are strict guidelines for organizing notes and notebooks. Notebooks are collected and graded every month. Eric has received two Fs.

- When students are missing important papers they need to make a copy from a classmate's copy. Eric has not done this so he doesn't have important information to complete a major assignment.

- If students hand in homework a day late they receive 50 percent credit. After that , it's a zero. Eric is racking up the zeros.

- As part of 9th grade study skills, students are required to keep assignment notebooks. The teacher randomly checks a few students' assignment notebooks every day. Eric has received two zeros.

Eric is sinking fast. The teacher's message to students is, "I am not your mother, and it's not my job to help you get organized. You're in high school, so you better figure out how to stay organized or your report card grade will suffer. It's your choice."

The Do-Nothing Approach: The teacher posts organizational procedures at the beginning of the year, but doesn't collect notebooks and doesn't check students' work except for major assignments, quizzes, and tests. Eric has managed to get a C− because of his test scores, but he is not likely to clean up his organizational problems anytime soon.

The Guided Discipline and Personalized Support Approach:

Response? A: PROCEDURAL SOLUTIONS

Here are the procedures Eric isn't following:

- There are a number of options for how students can codify their notes and organize their notebooks. Eric has chosen to do none of them. Notebooks are spot-checked on a daily basis and collected once every month. Eric has received two incompletes because he has not turned his notebook in. This is one of the reasons he's meeting with the teacher today.

- When students are missing important materials they can go to a file on the wall to retrieve an extra copy. Eric never remembers this option so when he finally gets around to looking for an extra copy the extras are all gone.

- Students have a week to finish up back-work for reduced credit or they are required to make arrangements to spend time during conference hour completing important assignments. Eric insists that he's done several missing assignments but he can't seem to find them. This is the other reason he is meeting with the teacher today. Students must stay after school during conference hour until they complete a minimal number of class and homework assignments satisfactorily.

- As part of 9th grade study skills, students are required to keep assignment notebooks. The teacher spot-checks to see if students are writing down their assignments and notices that Eric can't even find his assignment notebook.

The teacher knows this is a developmental issue for some students and she recognizes the importance of not letting it go completely. She's willing to fight some battles even though she's aware she won't win the organizational war by the time Eric finishes the 9th grade. Eric fills out his problem-solving report form and he and the teacher discuss next steps to deal with the big mess.

Here's what they came up with:

- Eric agrees to bring everything he possesses related to class to conference hour tomorrow. The goals are to see what he can find that hasn't been turned in and assess ways that he might track and organize his materials.

- Eric agrees to organize the last two weeks of his notebook. Going back further would be futile.

- Eric calls his Mom while the teacher is present, so his Mom knows the story. Eric, the teacher, and a parent agree to establish some supports and consequences at home to try and sustain the clean up effort.

- Eric agrees to get a different kind of assignment notebook that fits easily within his notebook.

- Eric agrees to check in on Tuesdays and Fridays with the teacher to see how the plan is working. Eric's Mom agrees to call the teacher on Friday afternoons to check in.

2

SCENARIO #3

A junior girl named Cherise has a loose mouth. She is swearing under her breath about the assignment in front of her and announces loud enough for you and the students around her to hear: "I'm not going to do this stupid ass homework. What a waste of time." This is the third time Cherise has made inappropriate remarks during the class period.

What's the Problem? NONCOOPERATION AND NONPARTICIPATION (#6 Loss of focus, confusion, or temporary frustration, anger, or disengagement.) IMPULSE CONTROL AND SELF-MANAGEMENT (#16 Inappropriate expression of anger and other emotions and #19 Persistently rude, uncivil, or offensive speech and gestures during whole group learning), and ACADEMIC LEARNING GAP involving reading challenges.

The Punishment Approach: The teacher looks up and says, "And you don't think you're a waste of my time right now? Think again." The student sees everyone else looking at her, slams her book down on the desk, and sits for the rest of the period in stony silence.

The Do-Nothing Approach: The teacher is in the middle of discussing the assignment with a small group of students and notices that almost everyone is involved in some stage of working on the assignment. The teacher ignores the comment. Cherise continues her low-grade mumbling and does nothing.

The Guided Discipline and Personalized Support Approach:

Response? B: Proximity, Prompts, and Invitations
C: Check-Ins and Conferences for Problems That Don't Have a Quick Fix
F: Personalized Academic Supports and Interventions for Academic Learning Gaps

The teacher has already intervened twice with Cherise about making negative remarks and sidebar comments today. The first time, the teacher asked Cherise to restate her complaint in a way that used less negative, more respectful language. The second time, the teacher says, "That's twice, Cherise, is it double or nothing?" Cherise knows her choice here is to give up the trash talk or owe twice the time if her negative remarks continue.

Now, the third incident has occurred. Cherise has a short fuse, so the teacher wants to avoid any public confrontation with her. The teacher wants to accomplish three things in the next ten seconds: 1) she wants the class to know she heard the comment; 2) she wants Cherise to know she heard it; and 3) she wants to remind Cherise of the accountable consequence when kids continue to making disrespectful remarks: "After three, it's you and me." So the walks over to Cherise and says quietly, "I heard that, Cherise. So what's it going to be? Twenty minutes at lunch or twenty minutes during conference hour after school? You know the routine." Cherise sulks, but grudgingly says, "Okay, fine, at lunch." Students in class know that when disrespectful language and remarks persist after two opportunities to self-correct or stop, students will need to meet with the teacher privately, fill out a problem solving report form, and reflect on their behavior and make a plan for what to do differently.

The teacher meets with Cherise at lunch and begins by saying, "It sure sounded like that assignment set you off. What was that about?" At this point Cherise bursts into tears, and confides how long it takes her to read and how frustrated she feels. She has no confidence that she will ever be able to do the work. They talk a bit more and the teacher asks if Cherise would be willing to meet with the reading specialist to learn some new strategies for recording and remembering what she reads. Cherise agrees to do this.

The teacher revisits the earlier outburst in class and gives Cherise a problem solving report form that students are required to fill out when they use disrespectful language. They go over the questions together and brainstorm some accountable consequences. Cherise agrees to tell the teacher about the reading strategies that she's trying out, so the teacher can use the same strategies in class. The teacher also agrees to speak with the reading specialist about other ideas that will support students with reading difficulties. The report form closes by asking, "When you feel like this the next time, what are two things you can do to make a better choice?" Cherise agrees to write down what's happening when she gets frustrated or upset and she agrees to speak with the teacher privately when she needs help. The teacher reassures Cherise that they will work on the reading problem together and suggests one strategy for Cherise to try tonight. Cherise leaves much less upset and more motivated to hang in there.

SCENARIO #4

Forty percent of your students received Ds and Fs on a major math test.

What's the Problem? ACADEMIC LEARNING GAP (A significant group of students consistently performs poorly in this class.)

The Punishment Approach: The teacher's response is "Next time, those of you who earned Ds and Fs might want to reconsider how you study the day before a test. Some of you have continued to perform on the pathetic side of the grade equation. I suggest you rethink your strategy. Academic warning slips go out tomorrow." Some students feel antagonized by these comments and write off the teacher and the class. Other kids just feel stupid.

The Do-Nothing Approach: The teacher accepts that a percentage of students will not succeed in this class. Therefore, she makes no attempt to deal with the academic slide downward of one group of students. If some students are motivated enough to talk to her about getting some help, she'll make the time. Consequently, failing students get even further behind and become more resistant and reluctant to put in any effort to learn and succeed in this class. The division between those who "get it" and those who don't creates a prickly atmosphere within the group.

The Guided Discipline and Personalized Support Approach:

Response? F: Personalized Academic Supports and Interventions for Academic Learning Gaps

The teacher is frustrated that the same group of students is consistently performing poorly. He says to his class, "Here's what I've observed over the last few weeks. There's a split between those of you who have a pretty good grasp of what we're doing and those of you who are having a tough time passing and doing well. My expectation is that all you can master most of these skills, so I don't like what's happening. Your failure to succeed is my failure too. So I'm going to press the pause button today so we can try and sort out what's going on. I want to give my undivided attention to this issue during the rest of the period. You're not bad students for doing poorly. But it's a bad situation if we don't deal with it."

Students who have consistently been earning As and Bs receive passes to go to the library. Their assignment is to make solution flowcharts for key problems on the test.

The teacher facilitates a class meeting with the rest of the students, asking them to discuss how they see the situation, identify what they think is blocking their success, pinpoint what they don't know how to do, brainstorm what they could do to help themselves, and agree on several strategies that they could try out in class, with a buddy, and by themselves. Each student writes a brief reflection and sets goals for the next two weeks.

The next day is an informal test correction session where students work in pairs correcting their tests. The teacher spends the period checking in with individual students and small groups. The A and B students who created solution flowcharts for key problems share their work with their peers. Students are expected to retake the test. There are two math tutoring sessions available after school to review their corrections and prep for the test and three options before school, after school, and during lunch to retake the test within the next five days.

Since the class is truly split down the middle, the teacher is also considering offering an independent learning unit to high-achieving students during the next week, so he can do some intense coaching and reteaching with the group that's failing.

SCENARIO 5

A number of students don't bring pencils and/or pens to class.

What's the problem? PROCEDURAL INFRACTIONS (#1 Doesn't bring necessary materials to class and #3 Noncompliance with classroom rules, norms, and procedures)

The Punishment Approach: The teacher says, "No pencil? Again?" The teacher is visibly annoyed and can't help shooting off a one-liner. "Well, no pencil, no grade—that's a 0 for the day."

The Do-Nothing Approach: It's just not in this teacher's repertoire to pay attention to who brings what to class.

The Guided Discipline and Personalized Support Approach:

Response? A: Procedural Solutions

Pencils are not the teacher's problem—it's a student problem. Providing free pencils isn't an option because it doesn't encourage personal responsibility and penalizing students for not bringing pencils shortchanges learning time. So during the first week of school, the teacher introduces a class meeting using the pencil problem as the topic. The teacher names the problem, shares what she needs, and asks students what they need to reach a good WIN-WIN solution.

The teacher wants a solution that ensures students have pencils when they forget and ensures that she doesn't have to spend precious time dealing with the pencil problem.

Students want a solution that ensures that they're not yelled at when they don't bring a pencil and that enables them to get a pencil if they need one.

Together they brainstorm at least three solutions:

1. Teacher takes collateral from student when they need to borrow a pencil from her stockpile.

2. Everyone agrees to lend other students pencils when they need one.

3. Everyone brings an extra pencil or pen to put in a box so there are always pens and pencils for students to borrow and put back in the box.

They discuss the pros and cons of each solution and how well each solution meets the needs of students and the teacher. The teacher takes a "straw poll" where each student gets to vote once for their preferred solution. The vast majority of students vote for #3 and that becomes the solution for the "pencil problem."

SCENARIO 6:

Three 9th grade girls in one of your classes are friends one minute and enemies the next. Before walking into your class, you hear them outside your door, engaged in an Oscar® winning screaming match, and it looks like it's about to escalate from swearing, shoving, and pushing to a physical fight.

What's the Problem? STUDENT-TO-STUDENT AGGRESSIVE BEHAVIORS (#26 Cursing and yelling and #28 Pushing, shoving, and uninvited contact)

The Punishment Approach: The teacher steps outside and is seething with anger at having to take time to escort the three of them to the dean's office. The girls spend the rest of the day in in-school suspension. ISS is monitored by a teaching assistant whose job is to ensure that students remain silent and do some schoolwork. The three girls spend most of their time writing and passing notes to each other when the ISS monitor isn't looking. Students return to class as if nothing ever happened and the teacher is still steamed up about the incident.

The Do-Nothing Approach: The commotion is outside the teacher's door. She's busy setting up a lab. It's not her problem. Another teacher in the hall intervenes.

The Guided Discipline and Personalized Support Approach:

Response? E: Immediate Enforcement, Intervention, and Follow-up of Schoolwide Consequences for Egregious Offenses

The teacher steps outside, gets their attention, and says, "Stop. You've created a commotion that's drawn a crowd and you look like you're ready to come to blows. We can't have this in the hallways. It's not safe. The three of you need to deal with this now." She writes a note and asks a student to give it to a security officer immediately. (The alternative is to ask one girl to remain in the hall next to the door, one girl to sit next to her desk, and one girl to stay with her while she uses the phone inside her classroom to call security or the dean.)

The security guard escorts the girls to the Problem Solving Place (PSP, in-school suspension room) where the PSP coach signs them in and invites them to sit down and take a few deep breaths. He points to the protocol on the wall that explains what students need to do, passes out the PSP report form, and students take a few minutes to fill out their PSP report form.

Then the PSP coach talks them through their responses. He also asks them to plot what happened on the conflict escalator so they can see how their words and behavior escalated to BIG TROUBLE. They name how their behavior affected others and why it was unsafe. The goal of the session is also for the girls to come to some kind of agreement that will reduce the chance of another public drama in the halls or in class. The girls talk about the reasons for their "drama queen" behaviors and agree on several specific actions they can take to avoid this in the future. 1) They won't travel together in the halls for at least a week. 2) They will sit in the front of the classroom, but not next to each other. 3) They agree to come to school early sometimes so they can socialize (they don't have the same lunch period together). The PSP coach engages them in role-plays where they replay the incident discussing what escalated the conflict and they role-play other responses they might have used to resolve their differences.

The girls choose a verbal apology to the teacher as their accountable consequence. They rehearse what they will say to the teacher and the PSP coach escorts the girls back to their teacher later in the day so they can apologize and tell her their plan. The PSP coach also arranges a series of one minute check-ins with the girls so they can tell him what they are doing to keep their agreements.

SCENARIO 7

Jose enters the classroom already angry about something and looks like he's about to blow.

What's the Problem? NONCOOPERATION AND NONPARTICIPATION (#6 Loss of focus, confusion, or temporary frustration, anger, or disengagement)

The Punishment Approach: Jose slams down his books on the desk and kicks the chair, creating a buzz in the room. The teacher comments, "You'd better collect your things NOW and try entering the room civilly this time." The teacher's comment only increases Jose's level of distress. He takes his books, slams the door on the way out, and keeps on going. Now Jose has a cut and a detention.

The Do-Nothing Approach: Jose slams down his books on the desk and kicks the chair, creating a buzz in the room. The teacher doesn't get involved in students' personal problems. He ignores Jose and moves to another area in the room, so the rest of the class redirects their attention away from Jose to the teacher.

The Guided Discipline and Personalized Support Approach:

Response? B: Proximity, Prompts, and Invitations

The teacher is at the door greeting students as they enter the room. He sees immediately that Jose is visibly upset and says quietly, "Jose, wait a sec. You look upset about something. Do you need a minute to collect yourself? Take the pass and get a drink. That work for you?" Jose looks down and mumbles, "Sure," takes the pass, and returns to class in a couple of minutes. The teacher has the good sense to consider that today might not be a productive work period for Jose. In the this situation, the teacher's best shot is to keep connected and say a few encouraging words that might help Jose get back on track for the remainder of the period. When students are working independently, the teacher strolls by Jose and asks, "You okay?" Jose says, "I'll be all right. Thanks." The teacher says, "I appreciate your effort to keep it together and focus on the assignment. If you want to talk later, let me know."

SCENARIO 8:

Nearly half of the students on your grade level team are not turning in homework consistently that is on time, complete, or proficient. This is true in your classes and it's also true for others on your team.

What's the Problem? ACADEMIC LEARNING GAPS and PROCEDURAL INFRACTIONS (#3 Students are not consistently following procedures for completing missing work or correcting shoddy work)

The Punishment Approach: The teacher's mantra is, "You play, you pay." If students don't request help and assistance, it's not given. When homework is not handed in on time, students receive 0s. End of story. The teacher wants no part of a shared homework policy and doesn't show up for the discussion at team meeting. "I've got my plan and it works for me."

The Do-Nothing Approach: Over time, the teacher gives less and less of her time and attention to the no homework "regulars." The teacher thinks requiring a homework hall is a good idea, but is not willing to volunteer once a month to monitor the after-school homework session.

The Guided Discipline and Personalized Support Approach:

Response? A: Procedural Solutions and C: Check-Ins and Conferences for Problems that Don't Have a Quick Fix

The team meets and first decides to create a homework survey that all students on the team fill out the next day. After they looked at the data they decide to take five actions.

1. The team will create a test and project schedule every month to ensure that big assignments don't stack up on the same day.

2. They agree to clarify different types of homework so students have a better idea of how homework is linked to in-class learning and how doing homework on time influences their understanding and performance. Homework tasks include: representing to learn (students choose different ways to record and represent what they read, viewed, heard, or discussed); skill practice (students practice a skill to demonstrate their understanding); going further (students choose what to read, research, or explore to learn more about the subject on their own); real world applications (students link what they're learning to people, issues, and problems in the real world); study and preparation (students use various strategies that provide evidence that they have studied for a test or prepared for a discussion, presentation, etc.); products (multistep projects and papers that require at least a week to complete); and reflections (journals, end of unit self-assessment, etc.).

3. They agree to develop a shared homework policy with accountable consequences. Since quality and completion are big issues, the team has set an expectation that all students

will complete at least 80 percent of their work. Ten points will be recorded for each assignment, product, project, or test not turned in, not completed proficiently, or not retaken or corrected. When students have accumulated 30 points they are required to attend homework hall until they complete their work. When students have accumulated 60 points they must attend a 3½ hour session of Saturday school. At this point all work will be counted and graded. The goal right now is to build a culture of completion. The school will pay a stipend to teachers who volunteer for homework hall and Saturday school.

4. The team writes a letter that is emailed and mailed home to all parents and arranges for a parent night to discuss homework policies and practices and how parents can support their students to meet the teams' homework expectations.

5. The team sets aside one planning period a week to discuss how the new policies are working and coordinate homework hall and Saturday school. They also agree to share the kinds of homework tasks they're assigning so that they can develop a rubric for quality assignments and think through how to personalize homework for students who don't need a lot of practice and students who need more practice than is assigned.

SCENARIO 9

Monica has a learning disability and struggles in all of her classes. As the year grinds on and her failures and personal defeats pile up, she has begun to ridicule other students, especially those whom she labels as the "smart ones." Monica feels like an outsider in class. Most students ignore her remarks, but a few are slinging zingers back as good as they get. This is an average, regular education class where it's already challenging to create a culture where civility and achievement are valued by every student.

What's the problem? STUDENT-TO-STUDENT AGGRESSIVE BEHAVIORS (#24 Hostile, unfriendly, or disrespectful responses to peers and #27 Teasing, taunting, put-downs, and name calling) and ACADEMIC LEARNING GAPS that make it difficult to accept the range of differences among students in her class and turn school into an ordeal that she has to survive everyday.

The Punishment Approach: The teacher has warned Monica about her name-calling and assigned Monica to a seat that is isolated from the rest of the group. When other students target Monica, the teacher comments in front of the whole group, "Now you know what it feels like. See what happens when you dish it out? It's going to come back and bite you." Monica storms out of the room and the teacher requests that Monica be sent to in-school suspension for a couple of days. He's told her he doesn't want her back in class until she cleans up her act. Monica is so angry that she cuts school for the next two days.

The Do-Nothing Approach: The teacher is so focused on content coverage and prepping students for the state proficiency test that he really doesn't attend to the inner world of adolescent angst in his own classroom. Furthermore, he doesn't see Monica as his responsibility; she has a special education facilitator who works with her in class occasionally and he asks the facilitator to step in and speak with her.

The Guided Discipline and Personalized Support Approach:

Response? D: Intensive Accountable Consequences and Interventions for High-Impact Behaviors or Chronic Unwanted Behaviors that Have Not Improved

The teacher's immediate concern is the poisonous dynamic between Monica and the rest of the group. Near the end of class, he comments on what he's observed during the last couple of days, revisits group guidelines about harassing speech, and asks the group to discuss why negative speech is one of his nonnegotiables. The teacher shares his disappointment with the group (a useful tactic when used very sparingly) and closes by saying, "We all have moments when we don't live up to our better selves and this is one of them. Let's put this episode behind us when class ends today. I have confidence that we can start at a better place tomorrow."

The teacher has already had conferences with Monica, but has decided that a classroom intervention won't be sufficient to address the multiple issues that Monica faces. He arranges for a meeting with Monica, her special education facilitator, the counselor, and one of her parents. The teacher doesn't want to facilitate the conference because he wants to share his observations and concerns. During the conference, Monica opens up in a different way than she has before. She feels isolated and different from everyone else in class and her only weapon against rejection is to take on the role of class critic and put-down artist. Her verbal assaults are a way of protecting herself from the inadequacies she experiences every day. With the help of the counselor, they develop a plan. Monica has agreed to:

- Meet with the counselor several more times to talk and practice some positive ways to respond to her classmates, so she doesn't feel so isolated

- Write down one thing each day that she finds interesting about class

- Read an excerpt from the *Facing History and Ourselves Resource Book* on prejudice and put-downs and discuss her reactions with the teacher

- Come in early once a week to rehearse the day's class so she will be prepared to fully participate

- Spend one day a week working in the after-school program at the neighboring elementary school

- Meet with the special education teacher to work on more "school smart" strategies she can use to re-imagine herself as a learner in this class

- Check in with the teacher weekly to review her target goals: no put-downs and at least one positive contribution per class

SCENARIO 10

During the remaining week of scheduling adjustments, you have been assigned five more students to your last period class. (You knew the gift of 19 students wasn't going to last!) This new group of students seems incapable of listening attentively to you or each other for more than a few seconds. Even when learning activities require silence, they are unable or unwilling to stop talking. The combination of Chatty Cathys and the Bickersons has changed the chemistry of the whole group—everyone seems a little more grumpy and talkative, and you're leaving the class exhausted and frustrated.

What's the Problem? NONCOOPERATION AND NONPARTICIPATION (#7 Initiating or joining in "sidebar" conversations and #8 Playing around and goofing off with others) and IMPULSE CONTROL AND SELF-MANAGEMENT (#13 Interrupting others or blurting out inappropriate comments and #15 Inability to work silently or independently without bothering others)

The Punishment Approach: The teacher assigns a zero participation grade to students who are talkative, although this action doesn't seem to improve students' behavior. In addition, the teacher has referred several of the new students to in-school suspension. In the students' absence, however, excessive talking continues. The teacher has become trapped into a cycle of yelling louder than the students to be heard, so the din is getting worse.

The Do-Nothing Approach: The teacher has given up. She posts assignments on the board every day and works with individuals and small groups of students while the rest of the class talks its way through the period.

The Guided Discipline and Personalized Support Approach:

Response? C: Check-Ins and Conferences for Problems that Don't Have a Quick Fix and D: Intensive Accountable Consequences and Interventions for High-Impact Behaviors or Chronic Unwanted Behaviors that Have Not Improved

Although the teacher and the group established norms and procedures at the beginning of the year, these expectations have not rubbed off on the new students. The teacher thought individual conferencing with the new students would be enough to bring them on board. But, after a week of worsening behavior, he steels himself to STOP, re-group, and re-teach earlier procedures. He follows through with these action steps:

1. He facilitates an abbreviated class meeting, knowing he won't have everyone's attention for more than ten minutes. He passes out note cards and asks students to write their responses to these questions: a) What's changed in the last week? b) What agreements and guidelines need to be revisited so we can get back to being a high-performing group? c) What's one thing you can do to get our class back on track? He reads some of the responses and shares his own observations, feelings, and concerns.

2. Slowing down now means making some hard choices about what work is assigned in class and out of class. The more time spent re-teaching and assessing procedures, the less time students will have for guided practice, small group study, and independent reading and writing time. The group will need to make some choices about in-class and home-work tasks.

3. The teacher does what he wishes he'd thought to do when the new students first entered class. He asks for five volunteers (through private, personal recruiting) to come in at lunch for a couple of days to buddy up with the new students who are required to attend at least two lunchtime sessions during the next week to talk and walk through some basic learning protocols. He will also rearrange seating in class so buddies can sit next to a new student for a couple of weeks.

4. He re-posts procedural charts on the walls, including these three.

I Will Only Give Instructions ONE TIME:

If students are talking when I give directions, I will stop in mid-sentence and wait for silence.

After I finish giving instructions, you have two minutes to check for understanding with other students.

Then I will take two or three questions if directions need to be clarified.

Silence Is Necessary When...

- I begin class and begin whole group instruction
- I'm giving directions.
- One of us (teacher or student) is presenting new material to the group or demonstrating how to do something.
- One of us is talking or reading to the whole group
- We are viewing a film or listening to a classroom guest
- I am lecturing (It will never be more than 15 minutes!)
- I am responding to students' questions during a whole group activity
- You are doing quick-writes before speaking in a small group or the whole group
- You are engaged in silent reading or writing activities
- You are taking paper and pencil tests and exams

When you're talking out of turn, not listening to others, or speaking during silent learning periods...

1. The first time I notice that you're not focused on the speaker or the task, I will give you a physical cue that means, "It's time to refocus."

2. If the talking continues during the same class, I may ask you to sit in a place where you will be less distracted and assign you a quick-write to record what you're hearing OR give you the choice of "Double or Nothing." (If you refocus for the rest of the period, you're good to go. If the talking persists, you owe me double the time in a workout during lunch or after school.)

3. If your talking out of turn becomes chronic, you owe me owe me a workout and you will need to call one of your parents and make them aware of the problem, so we can put a plan together to improve your listening habits.

5. The teacher re-thinks lessons for the next week to include even more tightly structured activities and more practice including:

- All learning activities will be limited to 15 MINUTES OR LESS. Each group listening or silent learning activity will alternate with an interactive learning protocol where students need to talk and work with each other in pairs or small groups to complete the task.

- Individual talk time will be limited to three times per class at 30 seconds a time.

- More one minute silent quick-writes will be used before students can speak.

- Students will practice re-stating other students' comments during several discussion opportunities.

6. The teacher will make more intentional efforts to assess "good group talk" behaviors. One strategy will be randomly selecting five students a day who will receive a grade for their behavior during silent learning as well as their listening and discussion skills: listening to others without interrupting, asking good questions, paraphrasing what others say, contributing thoughtful comments to discussion, etc. Students won't know what day they were assessed until the end of the week. This is a "use it or lose it" proposition: You either get an A added to your quarter grades or you get 10 points added to your "time owed" tally (100 points = 100-minute class offered after school twice a month).

SCENARIO 11

Kevin is a cynical yet charming, highly verbal student who turns ordinary requests, questions, and instructions into endless opportunities for "smart-alecky" remarks, legal arguments, and verbal jousting. Kevin is no fool, so his responses always fall short of abusive speech or insubordination. His words and tone, however, continuously cross the line to rudeness and incivility. Kevin's sense of entitlement (I can say anything I want because I'm smart) is reinforced by parents who always back him up.

What's the problem? STUDENT-TO-TEACHER AGGRESSIVE BEHAVIORS (#34 Persistent demands, arguing, and "lawyering up") and IMPULSE CONTROL AND SELF-MANAGEMENT (#19 Persistently rude, uncivil or offensive speech during whole group learning)

The Punishment Approach: The next time Kevin begins to argue (this time, it's about the instructions for an essay—Kevin wants to change the focus of the assignment), the teacher picks up the rope and argues back, confronting him publicly. Now there's an audience waiting to see who wins the battle of words. The teacher says, "Kevin, when you get your Masters in English Literature, you can choose the assignment. Until then, I decide." Kevin, always ready to have the last word, says to the classmate sitting next to him, "So do you think she bought her degree online?" At this point, the teacher's done and says, "Kevin, you're out of here. Maybe you need to figure out how you can get your high school diploma online so we don't have to put up with your smart remarks." Kevin earns a referral and a removal to the dean's office.

The Do-Nothing Approach: The teacher tries to avoid direct engagement with Kevin as much as possible.

The Guided Discipline and Personalized Support Approach:

Response? D: Intensive Accountable Consequences and Interventions for High-Impact Behaviors or Chronic Unwanted Behaviors that Have Not Improved

The teacher is pretty skillful at redirecting and interrupting Kevin's diatribes before they get out of hand. However, Kevin persists in turning ordinary encounters into a personal stage for showing off. The teacher has written down exactly what Kevin has said today and lets Kevin know that his behavior has earned a referral to the dean and other consequences. The dean, the teacher, and Kevin arrange a time to meet. The dean checks in with other teachers to see if Kevin's MO is the same in other classes and finds that his other teachers are experiencing similar frustrations with Kevin. The dean facilitates an informal mediation between Kevin and the teacher that provides space for the teacher to share why Kevin's speech is a big deal, and provides Kevin an opportunity to explain himself with the goal of working out an agreement to make amends and make a plan to change his behavior.

Kevin has agreed to:

- Call his parents in the presence of the dean and teacher to explain what he's done and why this incident will go in his permanent record. Kevin has to read back to his parents what he said in class.

- Read a chapter in Sarah Lawrence Lightfoot's book, *On Respect*, and write an essay on respect and civility in the classroom—how you give it and how you get it.

- Meet with the teacher during her conference hour to review behavioral expectations and identify three things Kevin will do to demonstrate more positive participation in class.

- Speak privately with his teachers about any questions related to instructions, assignments, and grades.

The dean has agreed to:

- Remove the incident report from his permanent record if teachers confirm that Kevin has stopped his adversarial, aggressive speech within the next two weeks and demonstrated more positive participation in class.

The teacher has agreed to:

- Speak with Kevin's parents weekly about his behavior in class for the next month.

- Review the difference between aggressive, assertive, and passive speech and behavior, discuss how Kevin's typical comments are perceived as aggressive responses, and rehearse how to communicate his thoughts and opinions more appropriately.

SCENARIO 12

You have two students in different classes who manifest polar opposites of the same problem—putting down and ridiculing other kids. Mario is a very bright boy who is much too quick to call kids stupid, and sighs and smirks when students don't "get it" as fast or as well as he does. The other boy, Greg, directs his sarcasm and ridicule toward anyone who acts "smart" or expresses any enthusiasm about what they are doing in class. In both classes their disrespectful behaviors have become chronic and they suck the positive energy out of the air. You are worried about the negative impact of their behavior on other students and the learning environment, and you are also worried about the negative attitude you are beginning to have toward them.

What's the Problem? NONCOOPERATION AND NONPARTICIPATION (#11 Deliberate acts and use of negative speech that sabotage the group and suck the energy out of the room) and STUDENT-TO-STUDENT AGGRESSION (#27 Teasing, taunting, put-downs, and name calling)

The Punishment Approach: With both boys, the teacher has warned them about their attitudes, called their parents, and sent them to the office; but nothing seems to be working. Now their hostility toward other kids has rubbed off, and the teacher is increasingly hostile toward them.

The teacher is aware that she is increasingly impatient, sarcastic, angry, and threatening with them—she finds herself tossing back zingers to these boys so they get a taste of what it feels like to be personally attacked. This is becoming a grudge match of who can deliver the most cutting verbal blow. The teacher has assigned several detentions to both boys and they have not shown up. Now they will be suspended.

The Do-Nothing Approach: The teacher has steeled herself to her students' rudeness and has moved students who were the targets of their comments to other seats. The teacher doesn't believe that she can do anything that will change their ingrained insensitivity. Real life is learning to toughen up and live with people you don't like or who bother you.

The Guided Discipline and Personalized Support Approach:

Response? D: Intensive Accountable Consequences and Interventions for High-Impact Behaviors or Chronic Unwanted Behaviors that Have Not Improved

The teacher has already had conferences and developed behavior plans with each boy, but has decided that a classroom intervention alone won't be sufficient. She arranges for separate meetings with each boy, a parent, the counselor, and herself. The teacher wants to proceed in this way so that she can be a full participant in the conversations with the boys and their parents. It turns out that each boy feels isolated and different from the other students in class; they both take on the same roles of critic and judge at home. For each of them, it appears that their verbal assaults on others are a way of protecting themselves. During each conference, they develop and sign behavior contracts that include the following:

Mario has agreed to:	**Greg has agreed to:**
• meet with the counselor two times to practice and rehearse other responses	• meet with the counselor two times to practice and rehearse other responses
• keep a learning log where he will write about positive contributions that he notices that others make in class and write about the ways he is encouraging and supporting other students to be successful in class	• keep a learning log where he will write about ways that he sees himself as smart in and out of class and write down what's going on when he feels frustrated in class
• spend one period a week doing peer tutoring instead of attending class	• spend one period a week helping out in a SPED PE class instead of attending class
The teacher has agreed to:	**The teacher has agreed to:**
• note the changes she has observed in Mario's behavior toward others	• note the changes she has observed in Greg's behavior toward others
• check in with Mario every day, assess his conduct card on Friday, and make a weekly phone call home to the parents	• check in with Greg every day, assess his conduct card on Friday, and make a weekly phone call home to the parents
	• develop an academic plan with Greg so that he can improve his performance in class

SCENARIO 13

Jared has been sleeping in class three out of the last five days, has missed a major exam, and has not turned in any completed work for two weeks.

What's the Problem? NONCOOPERATION AND NONPARTICIPATION (#5 No attempt to do assigned work), and (#9 Nonparticipation in activities, withdrawal, and detachment)

The Punishment Approach: The teacher has made it clear that students who sleep in class will receive a 0 for the day, a 0 on the test, and 0s for incomplete assignments. That's as far as the interaction goes.

The Do-Nothing Approach: The teacher assumes that Jared is preoccupied and lets it slide for right now. Although, the teacher is somewhat concerned, there are other students who need her attention. This student can't possibly pass this semester anyway; the student will repeat the course with another teacher next semester.

The Guided Discipline and Personalized Support Approach:

Response? C: Check-Ins and Conferences for Problems that Don't Have a Quick Fix

The teacher asks Jared to meet with her during lunch to talk. That teacher begins the conference by saying, "I see you sleeping in class and you haven't completed any work in a week. What's up?" The student pours out a story that involves a serious family crisis. The boy is reluctant to seek out any counseling at school and the teacher reassures the student that a commitment to speak with someone for fifteen minutes isn't a commitment for life. The teacher makes a deal with the student: She will speak with his guidance counselor next period and he will agree to go to guidance today and check in with her tomorrow. The teacher also submits an early intervention referral to the student support team in order to arrange a meeting with Jared's teachers and the student support team to exchange information and determine appropriate interventions.

CHAPTER 3

Step 1: Know Yourself, Know Your Students, and Know Your School

By assessing your strengths, your inner resources, and your predictable responses to problems in the classroom, you'll be better prepared for trouble ahead. The less thinking you have to do on a moment's notice, the more quickly and confidently you can respond before a behavior becomes disruptive. When you can anticipate what you will do, your stress level ratchets way down. When you're less stressed, it's much easier to access and use the most effective strategy to respond to a specific situation.

KNOW YOURSELF

Effective classroom management begins with knowing yourself well enough to be able to:

- Use your power and authority in ways that feel genuine and effective

- Use your physical presence and movement to prevent most unwanted behaviors

- Predict your reactions to various student behaviors and classroom situations

- Forecast strategies and approaches to use in situations that might be problematic

- Use your communication and conflict toolbox to build strong positive relationships with students

- Use your strengths to connect with students whom you find most challenging

- Change your behavior when you know your current approach isn't getting the results you want

- Assess aspects of classroom management and discipline that are not your strong suit and add new strategies to your toolbox

The next section includes critical information and insights that can help you become more confident as a teacher, more comfortable with your teacher persona, and more effective in challenging situations.

Know where your power and authority come from

Your power and authority create the opportunity to influence, inspire, guide, teach, coach, and shape the behavior of others. If you don't know where these qualities come from, it's hard to draw on your strengths, even harder to assess your limitations, and really hard to develop a bigger power zone that feels authentic and effective.

Does your power and authority come from…

- The personal relationships you develop with people?

- Your values, convictions, and ethical principles?

- Your content expertise?

- Your organizational expertise and know-how?

- Your reputation and experience?

- Your age?

- Your race, class, or gender?

- Your background or personal story?

- Your qualities of character?

- Your personal passion, charisma, and style?

- Your humor?

- Your physical presence, size, stature, or appearance?

- Your official position and formal status?

- Your capacity to threaten, punish, and exercise power over others?

Use this diagram to assess your power zones:

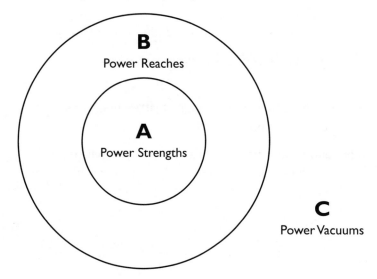

In the inner circle (A), jot down four or five teaching and disciplinary situations in which you feel most effective—that is, in which you've met your own goals and students have met goals that you and/or students have identified. For each situation, name the primary power source that enabled you to be effective. Circle the two power sources that feel most authentic, effective, and easy to access. These are your *power strengths*; keep refining and building these strengths.

In the (B) circle, jot down teaching and disciplinary situations in which you have felt ineffective or inadequate—that is, in which you haven't met your goals and students have met theirs. For each situation, name the power source you need to feel more effective, confident, and authentic. These are your *power reaches*. What will help you develop these power sources?

In the area outside the circles (C), name the power sources that will never be part of your personal power zone. These are your *power vacuums*. It's helpful to acknowledge your limitations and think about how you can use your power strengths to compensate for power vacuums.

More tips on using or losing your power and authority

What's the good news from discipline research? All teachers can increase their classroom effectiveness by developing and augmenting their organizational and management expertise and know-how. This is all about being completely prepared for class and ready for whatever walks in the door (Marzano 2003, p. 11). Particularly with adolescents, two sources of personal power will give you a positive edge:

- PERSONAL RELATIONSHIPS: Make use of personal contacts, informal conversation, conferencing, group gatherings, journal writing, surveys, feedback, and diagnostic assignments to know each student well (their abilities, strengths, learning profiles, needs and interests, and hopes and aspirations). Remember that reluctant, resistant, difficult, and underperforming students will work for you if your actions show that you want to know them, listen to them, and care about them.

- HUMOR: If humor is not a natural place you go, listen to students' humor and invite it into the room. In most classes you can count on at least one student to be your chief officer in charge of humor, who is ready and willing to share a funny joke, an amusing story, or a quirky take on the topic at hand when it's time to lighten up. If you don't have a personal funny bone, steal from others who do—use cartoons, anecdotes, and stories that you think will resonate with students. Just remember that humor is different from sarcasm, which almost always bites you back.

Every time you send a student "out" to get "fixed" by someone else, you're giving away some of your power and authority; you're giving up your influence over what will happen with the student or what sort of consequences the student is expected to carry out. On the other hand, you keep your power when you request a conference with the dean or assistant principal, the student, and possibly a parent to discuss serious behavioral issues and develop a plan for improvement. Others can support your efforts to help a student turn around, but it's you and the student who have to do the work. Leave discipline in the hands of others, and the student's behavior won't change in your classroom!

In the current era of punitive accountability at district and federal levels, you have more constraints and restrictions and less flexibility and control over the curriculum you teach and how you teach it. So it's crucial to focus on what you do control and what you can decide. You have the power to design and arrange your classroom container in ways that maximize your ability to manage and monitor individuals and the group; you're in charge of the hills you're willing to die on; you choose the structures and procedures that will help you organize learning effectively; you determine the kinds of choices students have; and you decide the strategies you will use to expect, insist, and support every student to behave responsively and complete quality work in your classroom. Use your power to change what you can!

Know if you are more authoritarian or authoritative

"Many behavioral problems ultimately boil down to a breakdown in teacher-student relationships: the causes of many classroom behaviors labeled and punished as rule infractions are, in fact, problems of students and teachers relating to each other interpersonally" (Marzano 2003, p. 42).

Authoritarian teaching

People who are authoritarian command obedience and demand respect. They tend to rely on their formal status and position as primary sources of their power and authority—in other words, "I'm the teacher; you're the student, and this is the way it's going to be." In authoritarian classrooms, students must usually conform to a narrow set of rules and behaviors with little room to be themselves. Authoritarian teachers need to feel that they are 100 percent in charge and in control. They have the final say in all matters, and students have virtually no input about what goes on in class. Classroom instruction tends to be teacher directed, and interactions with students tend to be more formal, distant, or adversarial. The idea of strong, personal student-teacher relationships is an alien concept to the authoritarian teacher.

Authoritarian teachers exhibit low to no tolerance for questions about rules, procedures, or processes. Student misbehavior, mistakes, and missteps are viewed as a violation of the teacher's authority; thus preferred punishments for offending students often involve threats, verbal attacks, zeroes in the grade book, or removal from class.

Behavior management researchers suggest that this type of extreme teacher dominance comes at a high price. The need for control overpowers the spirit of cooperation and the importance of developing positive relationships. What's more, pushing one's own goals and agenda exclusively tends to devalue the goals, needs, interests, and feelings of others.

We all know a teacher or two who can pull off this kind of instruction brilliantly with A-list students. These teachers often combine a quirky persona with unwavering academic standards and a vast knowledge bank that garners genuine respect from high-achieving kids who seek similar mastery and control. The authoritarian formula, however, backfires big time for most other kids.

Authoritative teaching

Authoritative teachers know they're in charge too. The difference isn't about giving up power or control; it's about how teachers use their power and authority. Authoritative teachers place equal value on assertive expectations and cooperation. Researchers agree that effective teachers and classroom managers exhibit clarity of purpose, a strong resolve to meet their goals, and a high commitment to providing academic and behavioral guidance. But they also show a deep commitment to meeting the needs of students, and they use the power of positive relationships to increase cooperation and motivation (Marzano 2003, pp. 42–46). Hence the handy phrase "I'm on your side and on your case!"

Authoritative teachers use their power to assert their right and responsibility to create a learning environment that is first and foremost a safe place for everyone. Being in charge means asserting that all students will be supported to learn and achieve and that everyone (including the teacher) deserves to be treated with dignity and respect. Purposeful action, persistence, and consistent follow-though are hallmarks of authoritative teaching.

Authoritative teachers model respect and trust rather than demanding it. They establish a community of "we" rather than "us vs. them," putting in place practices that invite teachers and students to become partners in the classroom. Sharing responsibility for learning shifts the emphasis from *my* classroom to *our* classroom, and from "what I'm teaching" to "what you're learning."

Authoritative teachers know the risks of demanding that adolescents do everything "my way." They are more likely to provide options for how students can meet important learning goals and academic expectations. Finally, authoritative teachers use their power and influence to solve problems rather than punish. Student accountability is linked to students' efforts to correct themselves and develop new skills and strategies that will help them become more capable and responsible.

Know your teaching stance

What values and principles do you stand for in the classroom? How do you present yourself to your students? What impression do you want them to have when they first meet you? At the end of the year, what do want them to remember about you?

Your teaching stance is the combination of attitudes, outlook, and demeanor that you wear most often and most visibly. Your stance communicates first principles, or the things that matter to you most. It is how you present yourself to your students, what you prize, and what you want to protect.

Some aspects of your teaching stance are like a second skin. Others are harder to come by, requiring time and practice before you can express that aspect of your teaching persona with authenticity and confidence. If you were to ask your students at the end of the year to write down five words or phrases that they think describe what you stand for, their responses would give you a pretty good sense of whether they took in what you tried to convey throughout the school year.

There isn't one right teaching stance, but there are some wrong ones, especially on the first day or during the first month of class. The question you need to ask is this: What is the most effective teaching stance that will help you put your best foot forward with a group of young people whom you may never have met before?

The dilemma is choosing what to play up and what to tone down on the first day. You do want to respond to students' first-day anxieties about what to expect, but you don't want your teaching persona to overwhelm students before they've had a chance to watch, listen, and settle in. Some qualities that you prize most about yourself as a teacher and a learner may need to take a backseat during the first week.

Sending the message that you care about your students on the first day sounds and feels phony to adolescents, but your actions during the first month will speak louder and more effectively than words. A culture of caring doesn't happen overnight; it develops over time through the sharing of critical events and experiences.

Most adolescents are justifiably cautious and a little subdued when they encounter new adults in their lives. They don't want to give away too much or appear too vulnerable, and they are rightly suspicious of adults who want to be "up close and personal" during a first encounter. (What you'll need to be ready for is the one kid who walks in as if he's known everyone, including you, for his entire lifetime.) A handy rule of thumb for meeting a group of adolescents for the first time is to avoid extremes. This is the one time when going all out for the middle ground is a good thing. Your first day is about creating the foundation for building the learning community that you and your students will become in the next month or so, and your teaching stance should reflect the attitudes, outlook, and demeanor that will help get you there.

A first-week teaching stance might look like this:

Respectful: You can do four things on Day One that let students know you want to be thought of as an adult who is respectful to young people: (1) prepare materials and create an attractive classroom space to tell students they are worthy of your time and effort; (2) show a sincere desire to learn all of their names as quickly as you can; (3) be attentive to their questions and concerns; and (4) display interest in getting to know them as individuals.

Serious, but with a Touch of Humor: Students will shut down if you present yourself as a stern taskmaster, but don't try to be an emcee on Comedy Central, either. Balance and timing are everything.

Friendly: Forget about the "Don't smile until Christmas" mantra. Nobody turns down a smile and a little warmth as a way of saying, "Welcome back." On the other hand, being overly familiar and too personal is about as effective as being cold and detached.

Invitational: You can't demand much of anything from adolescents without risking passive resistance. You can, however, invite students to cooperate and work with you. Use phrases like, *"I'd like us to___," "I have a request to make___," "For today, it would be helpful if everyone___," "For the next five minutes, I'd like you to___," "Because we need to___, I'm asking if everyone will___,"* and of course *"Please"* and *"Thank you."*

Knowledgeable: Have something in the room that indicates your passion for, curiosity about, and knowledge of the course content. Examples include an unusual object, a stack of books, an interesting piece of equipment, a compelling photograph, a provocative quotation, a list of puzzling terms that are specific to your content area, or a poster or article linked to your discipline or to people who practice your discipline in the work world.

Organized: Feeling flustered when you can't find what you need is the daytime version of your worst nightmare. Label, color-code, and box everything for different classes; make more than enough copies; keep a special tray for all the tools you need for the day; and don't use any electrical equipment if there's a chance it will go haywire.

Sequential: This is not the day to skip around randomly from one thing to another and hope that all will be revealed in the last five minutes. Students should be able to see the connections between the activities you complete on the first day.

Clear and Succinct: No long-winded speeches, no confusing instructions, no complex tasks—keep it simple.

Calm and Low-Key: If *quiet, uneventful,* and *smooth* are words that come to mind at the end of your first day, you're good to go.

Know your goals for discipline and personalized support

Why make a big deal about goals? Because goals should drive everything you do. Pick the wrong goal and you choose the wrong intervention. Choose the wrong intervention and you don't get the result you want, or you make the problem worse.

It's helpful to identify ongoing goals that you introduce at the beginning of the year and continue to revisit throughout the year. In disciplinary situations, it's crucial to separate immediate and long-term goals. *At the moment,* what's your immediate goal? What can you do to shift gears, defuse or redirect the student, or de-escalate the situation while sustaining the flow and positive energy of the lesson or learning activity? *Later,* what's your long-term goal to improve students' behavior or academic performance?

Take a look at the sample list of goals. Which ones are already part of your repertoire, and which would you add to your list?

What are your goals for effective discipline and student support?

Ongoing goals for everyone in class:

❏ I want to establish a set of positive behavioral norms and expectations that are clear to all students.

❏ I want students to learn and practice self-management, communication, and problem-solving skills that will help them become more self-disciplined, skillful, responsible, and academically successful.

❏ I want to create a supportive learning environment where everyone feels safe, welcomed, respected, and connected.

❏ I want to establish a classroom community of high-functioning, high-performing learners and leaders who take responsibility for creating a positive classroom climate and developing positive relationships with each other.

Immediate goals when students engage in unwanted behavior:

❏ I want to intervene effectively when students engage in behaviors that are unsafe, aggressive, or disruptive.

❏ I want to interrupt negative, aggressive, uncivil, and disrespectful speech and promote the use of more positive, assertive, civil, and respectful language.

❏ I want to defuse potential confrontations and power struggles quickly and calmly.

❏ I want to defuse students who are emotionally charged before they lose control.

❏ I want students to have immediate opportunities to self-correct and get back on track when they're off task and fooling around.

Long-term goals when students engage in unwanted behavior:

❏ I want to understand the sources of problematic behaviors so I can help students meet their underlying needs more effectively.

❏ I want students to have opportunities to learn from and reflect on their mistakes.

❏ When unwanted behaviors persist, I want students to be responsible for their behavior and carry out accountable consequences that feel fair, consistent, and supportive.

❏ I want to provide emotional support when students' upset feelings get in the way of their learning.

❏ I want to provide academic support when students are experiencing learning gaps and challenges.

As you read through the goals, ask yourself these questions:

- How would my use of classroom time change if I wanted to meet some of these other goals?

- What might be the learning benefits of spending more time developing students' habits of learning and discipline during the first two months of the school year?

Know your nos, needs, and nonnegotiables

The boundaries and limits you set will influence the classroom culture you and students create together. A big list of nos, needs, and nonnegotiables (the three Ns) will wear out their welcome fast in a room full of adolescents. Be choosy and try not to pick more than five. Students need to know exactly what your Ns are, why they matter to you, what they can do to avoid getting in trouble over the Ns, and what will happen when they cross the line.

For example, if one of your nonnegotiables relates to harassment of other students, you will need to communicate explicitly why this is a nonnegotiable, what harassment sounds like and looks like, and what you will do when you see it or hear it. Or if you're a neatnik and trash on the floor drives you over the edge, you will want to let students know that this is one of your needs and establish a regular procedure for kids to tidy up before class is over.

Know how with-it you are

The concept of with-it-ness originated with Jacob Kounin and refers, in his words, to a teacher's capacity "to be aware of what is happening in all parts of the classroom at all times." In Kounin's research, what separated effective from ineffective classroom managers was not their rules, procedures, or consequences (Kounin 1970). The big difference was a teacher's ability to scan the room while attending to other tasks, sense a potential problem immediately, identify the problem accurately, and intervene promptly before the unwanted behavior became disruptive.

Classroom Management That Works, Robert Marzano's meta-analysis of disciplinary research, similarly suggests that a teacher's "mental set" has a huge impact on reducing disciplinary problems (Marzano 2003). What teaching behaviors can help you become more with-it?

- Spend more time moving around than standing or sitting in one place.

- Ensure that students spend more time working in small groups or learning independently than listening to "the sage on the stage." It's a hundred times easier to assess problems; act immediately; and respond in a quiet, low-key, matter-of-fact manner when you're not in front of the whole group.

- Anticipate problems when the lesson content, skill instruction, or learning processes might feel daunting, boring, or frustrating for particular students or the whole group. Head off disaster by giving the class or individual students a heads-up before the lesson or developing special instructions, resources, or modifications that will encourage tentative students to engage fully in the lesson.

- Constantly make eye contact with different students throughout the class period.

- When you spot potential trouble or off-task behavior from an individual student or group, use eye contact, physical proximity, and other physical and visual prompts first.

- If nonverbal cues aren't enough, use the verbal prompts and invitations suggested in Chapter 6 ("Step 4: Invite Students Engagement, Cooperation, and Self-Correction").

Know how to define disrespect

We teachers make two big mistakes that get us in trouble:

(1)   We identify way too many behaviors as acts of disrespect.

(2)   We use vague language—words that can mean different things to different people—to describe most unwanted behaviors in the classroom. Vague descriptors don't provide you or the student with the specific information needed to diagnose and change the unwanted behavior.

Disrespect involves comments or actions directed at you (or others) personally that violate one's dignity and identity. Disrespectful actions generally occur between people within close proximity of each other most of the time. We think the other person has treated us badly or acknowledged us in a way that's inappropriate or off-limits. When we feel disrespected, we are likely to respond from an emotional state of anger rather than a rational state of mind from which we can use our skills to help students correct the behavior. Mild forms of disrespectful behavior call for insistence that the student correct his or her speech or perform an action again using a more respectful, civil, or courteous manner. Egregious forms of disrespect that involve abusive, vulgar, aggressive, threatening, hostile, or confrontational verbal and body language call for accountable consequences and may require an immediate referral for a more intensive intervention.

Noncooperation, noncompliance, nonparticipation and noncompletion are not the same as disrespect. These behaviors are not directed at you personally, and there are a hundred different reasons why students might not be fully engaged and on task at a particular point in time. As you become clearer about distinguishing between and describing specific unwanted behaviors, your responses are more likely to produce a desired change in the student's behavior and increased engagement in learning.

DISRESPECT	NONCOOPERATION and NONCOMPLIANCE	NONPARTICIPATION	NONCOMPLETION
Concrete Examples Student walks away when you are speaking to her or him personally Student says "F--- you" or uses other profanity that is directed at you Student repeatedly refuses to follow a directive after repeated requests using aggressive, hostile, and/or threatening words and body language (This is different from mumbling "I'm not going to do this stupid assignment!") Student continues to "lawyer up" and argue with you aggressively after you have said twice that you will discuss the problem with him or her privately at a later time Student attacks you personally, saying, "You are such a _____ "	**Concrete Examples** Student doesn't follow directions or procedures Student is talking while you or others are speaking Student doesn't do his or her share of the work in cooperative groups Student doesn't do homework assignment Student doesn't do class assignment Student says "I'm not going to do this" to no one in particular Student doesn't bring necessary materials to class Student rejects your coaching and encouragement Student slams books down and slams the door as he walks out the door without permission	**Concrete Examples** Student is absent Student doesn't participate in discussion Student falls asleep or has head down on table Student chooses not to participate in a group problem-solving exercise Student doesn't want to share during a gathering Student is daydreaming and glazed over	**Concrete Examples** Student doesn't complete homework or class assignments Student doesn't correct, edit, or redo work that doesn't meet an acceptable level of proficiency

The next section, Know How to Depersonalize Bad Behavior, offers more suggestions for dealing with adolescent disrespect effectively.

Know how to depersonalize bad behavior

We've all been there. Think about how it feels when…

- A student rejects your efforts to personally connect with him

- A student continues to produce little after several conferences and study sessions

- You've used your best skills to bring an academic problem to a student's attention, and the student responds by yelling, "Just leave me alone! I don't care if I get it right or not!"

- A student blows you off by walking away when you're still talking

- During independent work time, you cruise by a student who's rarely on task and notice that she's calm, focused, and actually writing, only to realize she's artfully covered an entire page with the sentence "I hate this class"

- A student finds just the right moment to ask an off-the-wall question that stops the flow of a lesson

- A student fires off an expletive meant for you and every other adult in the universe

Adolescent bad behavior is an unavoidable and normal occurrence for every adult who spends more than ten minutes with a group of teenagers, much less 40 hours a week. Yet if we take kids' verbal potshots, disrespect, or uncooperative behavior personally, we're in big trouble. When we approach students' academic and behavioral problems from a calm, collected place using our best professional skill set, we are less likely to lose control or use angry words to hurt back through sarcasm, insults, belittlement, or humiliation.

When kids are emotionally charged or behaviorally challenged, they need to count on us to be emotionally objective. Along with with-it-ness, emotional objectivity and the capacity to depersonalize students' verbal reactions and problematic behavior are two other aspects of a teacher's skill set that separate effective from ineffective classroom managers (Marzano 2003, Chapter 5). These are not easy goals to accomplish.

Teaching is, in many ways, the most personal of professions. Personal commitment and emotional connection to students are the very things that can help build positive relationships and increase students' attachment to learning. How do we square this apparent contradiction between developing personal relationships with students while depersonalizing our responses to their problematic behavior?

Here's one way to think about it.

Scenario One
You and your students are in the learning zone, and everyone's engaged. There's a positive and productive buzz from the kids, and you're in a positive mental state. This is the time to communicate your passion for teaching; your affection for the students; and your personal enthusiasm, encouragement, and support. (This is also the best time, incidentally, to teach procedures and protocols.) Your face is open and animated, you're smiling, your demeanor is friendly, and your humor and light touch are probably in good form. The positive mood and relaxed yet productive climate also make it easier for you to deal with minor infractions in ways that prompt immediate self-correction. You're at your personal and professional best, and so are the kids.

Scenario Two
An individual or group of students is looking for trouble or have already stepped in it. Your students are off task, inattentive, disruptive, or emotionally upset, and they're not meeting the goals that you've carefully constructed for the day's lesson. At this point you can't be very happy.

Response A *(The disaster version):* If you become personally offended and feel personally attacked by students' negative reactions, hostility, and unwanted behaviors, the focus is fixed on your personal feelings, and two things happen next. First, since you're probably feeling some combination of frustration, disappointment, anger, resentment, or powerlessness, you're stuck in a negative place—never a good starting point for responding to a tough situation. Second, when you're focused on your feelings, the situation becomes all about *you*, not about the *students*. Your personal need to release the emotional charge and express your anger and frustration overpowers a more rational and effective response.

At this point, it's nearly impossible to shift the focus from yourself to the students. Now you've lost the opportunity to zoom in on an individual student's behavior and handle the situation calmly and effectively. You're not at your professional best because you never got to use your professional skills.

Response B *(The good-to-go version):* You have worked hard at getting good at making the shift to a more professional, emotionally detached place when kids' negative reactions or unwanted behaviors might trigger your own emotional reaction. Here's a sequence (in slow motion) of what you might think, say, and do to make the shift to your discipline demeanor.

1. You need to decouple the student's behavior from anything to do with you; as Marzano has pointed out, "Misbehavior on the part of students usually has little to do with a specific teacher" (Marzano 2003, p. 72). Try imagining a reason for the unwanted behavior that's unrelated to disrespect or a personal attack. (You can think to yourself and say the following: *"This is not about me; it's not personal. This is probably happening because_____"* or *"_____must have happened to trigger this"* or *"I wonder if_____ might be the problem."*)

2. You know your kids, and you know that sometimes kids say stuff just to be provocative and get on your last nerve. (You can say to yourself, *"_____ is not the skillful person here; I am. I'm the one who has to make the shift."*)

3. You remind yourself not to be surprised when kids are upset or engage in unwanted behaviors. (You can say to yourself, *"Okay, you're doing your adolescent thing, so I need to do my professional thing."*)

4. Since you view students' academic, behavioral, and emotional problems as normal, you see problems as opportunities to interrupt unwanted behaviors and to guide, support, and instruct students in doing the right thing. You're not demanding extra money for combat pay; you see discipline as a vital aspect of your job. It's not your favorite thing about teaching, but you get enormous satisfaction from helping students improve their behavior. (You can say to yourself, *"This is worth my time and energy because I know it will get results. It's time to use my best professional skills and shift to my discipline demeanor."*)

5. The shift to your discipline demeanor means that you do the following:

- You diminish your animation. You neither smile nor show anger. Smiling is the worst thing to do when you're in discipline demeanor. It confuses students; they can't figure out whether you're serious or not. The second worst thing you can do is communicate negative emotions. Instead, it's time to put on your "flat face"—the face that broadcasts relaxed alertness but not much else. If you want kids to know that you mean it, that you're not fooling around, your face should be emotion free, with an unclenched jaw. This will help you breathe and enable you to relax the rest of your body (Jones 2007).

- You take a deep breath or two as you feel your way to a comfortable, relaxed, grounded posture—your shoulders relax, your knees are bent a little forward, your feet are about two feet apart, and your arms and hands are at your sides.

6. You've made the shift, so now you can focus on the student and the behavior. (You can ask yourself, *"What's the problem? What's my goal now? What's my goal later? What's the best strategy in this situation?"*)

7. You've done your quick assessment, and you're ready to respond. (You can ask yourself, *"What's the right physical move, visual cue, or verbal prompt?"*)

8. If you need to speak, you're ready to use a tone of voice that's steady, low key, and matter-of-fact.

In real time this sequence happens in a few seconds. Teachers who are really good at this spend time learning how to reframe student behavior, developing self-talk that works for them and rehearsing their physical moves, visual cues, and verbal prompts so that they're easily retrievable. Over time, the shift to the discipline demeanor becomes more intuitive and comfortable.

For more about physical prompts and the pivot to redirect off-task behavior, see Chapter 6 ("Step 4: Invite Student Engagement, Cooperation, and Self-Correction.")

Know how to avoid communication roadblocks

The language you use matters. In your interactions with students, try to filter out language that has the potential to shut down communication, cause silent withdrawal, or provoke greater resistance. With poor communication, conflict grows; with good communication, people grow. Watch out for the communication roadblocks in the chart that follows.

Five roadblocks to effective communication

Whys and badgering questions often feel like attacks. These questions put us on the defensive and put us in a corner where we shut down, lie, make excuses, and deny personal responsibility.	**Examples:** *Why didn't you do your homework? Why can't you behave yourself? Why are you doing this? Why can't you do what you're told? What's wrong with you? How many times do I have to tell you this?*
Threats create resentment and anger and provoke defiance. Kids will often challenge you to carry out the threat.	**Examples:** *One more time and you're out of here. You try that and see what happens! If you don't do this, you're in serious trouble. You better do this or else.*
Arbitrary demands and commands give students no way to choose to do the right thing or to save face. Rather, these responses corner kids, put them on the defensive, and create a power struggle.	**Examples:** *Just do it and quit whining. You heard what I said. Stop it. Get over here right now! Shut up and get to work.*
Moralizing and lecturing prompts kids to feel stupid, bad, guilty, and embarrassed. These responses do not teach young people how to become more skillful or motivate them to be more cooperative.	**Examples:** *Didn't anyone ever teach you to…? You should have learned that in fourth grade. You have no respect for yourself. I've never had a class this bad. Your conduct is appalling. Let me tell you what's wrong with you.*
Sarcasm and put-downs are intended to deliver a sting, demean the person, or discount the person's thoughts or feelings.	**Examples:** *What do you want? A gold medal for breathing? You're such a baby! Even an idiot can figure this out. I can see you put in a lot of effort—maybe five minutes? Don't we look happy. You're just not capable of doing this kind of work.*

3

Know your communication style

The quality of a teacher's communication impacts students' willingness to attend, engage, and cooperate. In other words, a teacher's relationship with students is the crucial starting point for effective classroom management. Extensive research conducted in elementary and secondary classrooms indicates that students perceive High Dominance (clarity of purpose and strong, supportive academic and behavioral guidance) and High Cooperation (concern for the needs and opinions of others and a strong desire to function as a member of a team) as the most important characteristics of strong, effective teachers (Marzano 2003; Wubbels and Levy 1993, 1997).

Optimal student-teacher relationships are associated with the four shaded attributes:

Student-Teacher Relations

Communication Styles	Indicators from a Student's Perspective
LEADERSHIP	Teacher explains things clearly. / Teacher knows everything that's going on in the classroom. / Teacher is in charge. / Teacher is fair.
HELPFUL AND FRIENDLY	Teacher helps us with our work. / Teacher has a sense of humor. / Teacher likes us.
UNDERSTANDING	Teacher is patient. / Teacher knows we're kids and make mistakes. / If we don't agree with the teacher, we can talk about it. / Teacher is flexible.
STUDENT RESPONSIBILITY, FREEDOM, AND CHOICE	We can decide some things in this class. / We have choices. / We can express ourselves in this class. / We have to correct our work.
UNCERTAIN	Teacher is hesitant. / Teacher doesn't know what to do when we fool around. / Teacher changes her mind all the time.
DISSATISFIED	Teacher thinks we can't do the work. / Teacher thinks we cheat.
ADMONISHING	Teacher is sarcastic. / Teacher yells at us. / Teacher gets angry quickly.
STRICT	Teacher is strict (rigid). / We're afraid of the teacher. / There's only the teacher's way of doing things.

COMMUNICATION STYLES ASSOCIATED WITH EFFECTIVE AND INEFFECTIVE TEACHERS

(**Extreme Dominance:** Relentless pursuit of purpose and aggressive need to control others without considering their needs and feelings)

DOMINANCE

Optimal Student-Teacher Relations— Two Most Effective Teacher Types

DOMINANT	COOPERATIVE
high Leadership	high Leadership
low Student Responsibility and Freedom	high Student Responsibility and Freedom
high Helpful	high Helpful
high Understanding	high Understanding
low Strictness	low Strictness
low Admonishment	low Admonishment

Combination of **High Dominance** (clarity of purpose and strong, supportive academic and behavioral guidance) AND **High Cooperation** (concern for the needs and opinions of others and a strong desire to function as members of a team)

OPPOSITION   COOPERATION

(**Extreme Opposition:** Active antagonism toward others and aggressive blocking of their goals and desires)

(**Extreme Cooperation:** Inability or lack of resolve to act without input and approval of others)

Poor Student-Teacher Relations—Three Ineffective Teacher Types

REPRESSIVE	UNCERTAIN/AGGRESSIVE	UNCERTAIN/TOLERANT
low Leadership	low Leadership	low Leadership
low Student Responsibility and Freedom	low Student Responsibility and Freedom	high Student Responsibility and Freedom
low Helpful	low Helpful	low Helpful
low Understanding	low Understanding	high Understanding
high Strictness	some Strictness	low Strictness
high Admonishment	high Uncertainty	high Uncertainty
high Dissatisfaction	some Admonishment	low Admonishment

SUBMISSION

(**Extreme Submission:** Lack of clarity and purpose; anything goes)

Know how to listen responsively

Responsive (active) listening increases a sense of connection with students and reduces potential conflicts and misunderstandings (see Chapter 15, "Make Group Talk Good Talk" in *Making Learning REAL*). However, your in-class modeling of effective listening habits will provide the best lesson. Keep these responsive listening tips in mind:

1. Demonstrate your full attention and interest through your body language and facial expression.

2. Before you assume, find out more information. *"What happened? How did you decide to_____? What else should I know? What triggered your reaction to that?"*

3. When you listen, convey interested silence and focus directly on the speaker.

4. Restate what people say so that they know they've been understood. *"So it sounds like _____. So you're hoping that _____."*

5. Use verbal encouragers that invite someone to continue speaking. *"Uh huh. Say more about that. I'm interested in what you have to say about _____."*

6. Check for accuracy of understanding and invite correction. *"Let me make sure I understand. You said that you_____. Did I get that about right?"*

7. Empathize by reflecting a speaker's feelings in ways that acknowledge the person's emotional state and the feelings he or she attaches to the issue being discussed. *"So most of you are frustrated that it's taking so much time to_____."*

8. Ask open-ended questions that give the speaker a chance to clarify his or her thinking and provide more information. *"What else should we know about _____? What's missing, misleading, or confusing? What might be the reasoning behind...? What supports your thinking about this? What would be an example of_____? Could you explain_____?"*

9. Summarize key ideas, solutions, and issues.

10. Move to problem solving only if the person is ready. *"Where would you like to go from here? What would a good solution look like? What might be the first step for resolving this?"*

11.   Remember PEARS:

PARAPHRASE the facts

ENCOURAGE the person to speak

ASK questions that help clarify the problem and foster self-awareness, self-reflection, and self-assessment

REFLECT feelings to defuse highly charged emotions like anger and frustration

SOLVE the problem if the person is ready to change and make a plan

(See Appendix B for more on PEARS)

Know how to manage your anger

Knowing what sets you off is a good thing. You have the advantage of preparing yourself for what to say and do when your anger trigger is pushed. Your actions let students know what you do when you're angry and invite them to find a constructive way to deal with their anger. When you do get upset, frustrated, or angry, how do you reduce these emotions? What will help you to stop, defuse the emotional charge that you feel, and get recentered so that you can think clearly about what to do next? For example, you might experience a situation in which you feel so upset that your best response is to stop what you are doing, take a few deep breaths, walk to the other side of the room, and say, *"I'm too angry to deal with this right now; we'll make time later to talk about this when I can hear you and you can hear me."*

When the whole class has really blown it behaviorally or academically, how do you want to communicate your negative feelings? Expressing your frustration, anger, and disappointment is a tricky thing. Do it too often and it sounds like a broken record to kids: "Blah, blah, blah...here she goes again." Think about picking your battles carefully. Expressing negative feelings has a different impact if you do it once every couple of months instead of several times a week. If you rehearse what you want to say and know how you want to involve students in addressing the issue, your message will have a greater impact on more students.

For more about managing anger, see Chapter 5 and 6.

Know how to handle conflict in the classroom

How we handle conflicts with students says a lot about the kind of teachers we want to be and the kinds of relationships we want to build. Students get more powerful messages from what adults actually do than from what they say or teach. As veteran researchers and school reform leaders Ted and Nancy Sizer remind us in *The Students Are Watching,* kids are acutely aware of how we conduct ourselves when conflicts and controversy flare up within the classroom and the school community (Sizer and Sizer, 2000). Healthy classrooms are places where teachers normalize conflict and address it with candor and care. Open acknowledgment of conflict and open dialogue form the foundation for collaborative problem solving in the classroom. Kids are learning lessons about conflict all the time from how we handle it ourselves.

Even if they've never heard the term, most kids are pretty quick at figuring out the dominant conflict styles of their teachers. They know the commanders in chief for whom "it's my way or the highway." They know the accommodators, who try to develop good relationships with them but never get around to dealing with real problems constructively. They know the avoiders, who ignore unacceptable behavior out of fear of confrontation or being disliked. And students know what's different about the teachers who act quickly to address the problem. These are the teachers they love and can count on—the ones who are clear about what's expected, treat them respectfully even when they mess up, and believe in their capacity to solve problems and improve their behavior.

For better or worse, our conflict management tools (or lack of them) reveal our own attitudes about conflict. When we become aware of a problem, is our stance threatening and defensive? Or is it observational and invitational? Do we encourage cooperation and self-correction, or do we go directly to criticizing, judging, or punishing the student, leaving no opportunity for students to reflect on their choices and try out a different strategy? Recognizing the connection between conflict management and classroom management is valuable for several reasons. Our capacities to manage our own emotions, defuse confrontational situations, and communicate positively during a conflict will shape how our students respond when they get into academic and behavioral difficulties. Students take their cues from us. The teacher who snaps, blames, or uses sarcasm when things go wrong unwittingly encourages students to do the same.

All conflicts share these common elements:

- Conflicts are normal, and they're neither bad nor good. How we choose to handle conflict, however, will produce positive or negative results.

- Conflicts involve a clash between each person's needs and goals in a specific situation in a specific moment in time. Our goals and needs change constantly.

- No one comes to a conflict empty-handed: we each bring a suitcase filled with a limited or plentiful set of skills; our prior experiences in similar situations; our perceptions, assumptions, and attitudes about the other person; and our current mood and emotional state.

- With students, everything we do or say will either escalate or de-escalate the situation. Our physical stance and movement, tone of voice, emotional intensity, and choice of words will move us a step up toward a major confrontation or a step down to a place where each of us can keep our respect and dignity intact. And our response will always shape what a student says and does next.

- Anger is the motor that drives the conflict escalator. Each step up the escalator gets more emotionally charged. The further up we go, the harder it is to get off the escalator.

The following diagram illustrates a typical adolescent encounter that can remain a non-incident or turn into a full-blown explosion. It all depends on the teacher's knowledge of the student, the teacher's primary goal at the moment, and the teacher's capacity to de-escalate and defuse.

CONFLICT ESCALATION AND DE-ESCALATION

Here's the situation:

As students are entering the classroom, the teacher confronts Michael and says "Michael, where are those two missing assignments?"

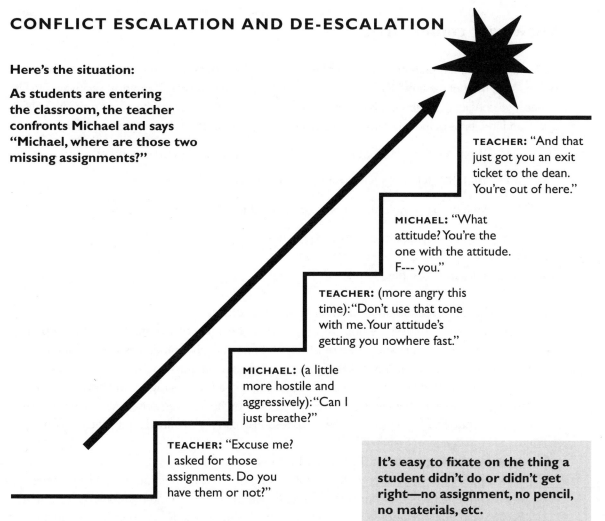

TEACHER: "And that just got you an exit ticket to the dean. You're out of here."

MICHAEL: "What attitude? You're the one with the attitude. F--- you."

TEACHER: (more angry this time): "Don't use that tone with me. Your attitude's getting you nowhere fast."

MICHAEL: (a little more hostile and aggressively): "Can I just breathe?"

TEACHER: "Excuse me? I asked for those assignments. Do you have them or not?"

MICHAEL: "Can I breathe?"

It's easy to fixate on the thing a student didn't do or didn't get right—no assignment, no pencil, no materials, etc.

The risk is "picking up the rope" and forcing a power struggle that teachers never win.

TEACHER: He knows this student is prickly, so he backs off NOW and says, "Absolutely. Get settled and we'll catch up later."

TEACHER: When students are working independently, he checks in with Michael privately to discuss the status of the assignments.

Know your conflict style

Each conflict style has potential uses and potential limitations, but sometimes we get stuck and rely on one style most of the time. There is no one style that's the right way to handle all conflicts. The art of effective conflict management is choosing the most effective style given the specific situation, your goals, and the status of the relationship. You need to ask four questions before making a choice.

- What are my goals both now and later? What's the desired outcome?

- Will this style help me meet my goals and get what I need?

- Will this style help the student get what she or he needs?

- Will this style help or harm the relationship?

Six conflict styles are presented here:

1. **Take charge, force, demand, protect yourself or others**
   "It's my way or else." We do not, cannot, or will not bargain or give in. We use this response when safety is an issue and/or we must respond immediately. Sometimes we are standing up for our rights and deeply held beliefs; sometimes we are pursuing what we want at the expense of another person. We may also be caught in a power struggle and not see a way to negotiate to get what we want. (This is a version of the fight response.) Although you may achieve your goal by using this style, your response can potentially damage the relationship.

2. **Accommodate, give in, let it go, smooth it over**
   "We'll do it your way." We yield to another's point of view, meeting the other person's needs while letting go of our own. We may give in to smooth the relationship, or it may be an issue that's just not very important to us. Using this style can help you maintain a shaky relationship, but it will not help you achieve your goals. Sometimes accommodation can be a first step before you are ready to tackle the problem.

3. **Avoid it, ignore it, drop it, or exit**
   "I'm outta here." We don't address the conflict, we withdraw from the situation, or we behave as though the situation were not happening. We leave it to others to deal with. (This is a version of the flight response.) Although avoidance can be a protective response in unsafe situations, it can also have negative repercussions because the problem never goes away.

4. **Postpone, pause, and reflect; return to the problem later**
   "Let me think about this. I'll get back to you later." As teachers, it's useful to remember that doing something later is not the same as doing nothing. Too often we regret our words and actions in the heat of the moment when postponing a decision or speaking with a student later would have produced a more constructive outcome.

5. **Seek out a trusted adult, a level-headed friend, a greater authority, or a mediator**
   "Help me out here." We turn to others whom we perceive as having more power, influence, authority, skills, or wisdom to resolve the conflict. If the people involved bring intense feelings to the situation, it can be helpful for a neutral third party to mediate the problem.

6. **Collaborate to solve problems**

"Let's work it out." We work together to get important needs met. We are invested in achieving our goals and finding solutions. People are partners rather than adversaries. We share points of view, identify common interests, and explore alternatives before agreeing on a mutually satisfying solution. Using a problem-solving style often gives us the best chance for achieving a goal and maintaining positive relationships. The stages of problem solving can include the following steps:

- Check it out: notice, observe, and ask questions before you decide what to do

- Listen and defuse angry feelings if the other person is upset

- Assert your feelings, interests, needs, and nos

- Identify common interests, goals, and possible solutions

- Negotiate *("Let's talk it out and reach a WIN-WIN solution that works for both of us.")*

As you think about your primary conflict styles, consider these questions:

- Does your primary conflict style work for you most of the time? How do you know?

- What style are you most likely to use when you feel stressed?

- Are you likely to use different conflict styles with different groups of students? Why do you think that happens?

- What style would you like to use more often or less often to become more effective with students who exhibit challenging behaviors?

Know how to recover

Every teacher loses it sometimes with a whole class or an individual student. Think about how you usually respond after an incident when your better self was missing in action. Whatever you choose to do in the classroom sends a strong message to students. If we say or do nothing, we are conveying a message that mistakes are so bad that it's better to cover them up than deal with them openly. Inadvertently, we are also asking students to pretend that the incident never happened or to believe that somehow, as if by magic, the conflict that created the incident has been resolved and everything's fine. Our silence can also imply that it's not important to take responsibility for things we do, however unintentional, that affect others negatively.

On the other hand, when we acknowledge our mistakes, admit when we think we've gone off track, or apologize when it's appropriate, students get the message from our own modeling that we all have the capacity to recover, self-correct, and right ourselves. Owning up in the class-room is not the same as going to confession. Brevity and a light touch go a long way toward clearing the air and moving on gracefully. You might want to try out a three-part message that enables you to (1) revisit the incident; (2) reflect on your behavior and take responsibility for what happened; and (3) commit to trying a different approach or response next time.

It might sound like this to an individual student:

"I thought about what I said to you yesterday. It was thoughtless. I wasn't thinking about how that might make you feel. I want to apologize to you, and I want you to know that I'm going to be a lot more conscious about the words I choose. I'd like to make a fresh start tomorrow. How about it?"

Or like this to the whole group:

"You know how I'm always insisting that we need to be accountable for our actions. Well, I need to be accountable for what happened yesterday. I behaved badly and turned into Wanda the Witch for a few minutes. The situation isn't nearly as dreadful as I made it out to be. And I'm sorry I used the word 'slackers' in my diatribe. I've tossed away my broom and I'm ready to work out a realistic timeline for what we need to do to get ready for the conference. Can we get started? Good."

Here are a few more openers:

- *"I went home and thought about what happened yesterday. I don't feel good about the role I played in making the situation worse."*

- *"I'm not happy with my behavior yesterday. I want you to know why I lost it at the end of the period."*

- *"About yesterday, I know I blew it when I..."*

- *"Just to set the record straight, I realize that what I said yesterday didn't come out the way I intended. My penchant for bluntness went too far. Let me try saying it again minus the 'foot in mouth' disease."*

- *"About our conference yesterday. I know I was impatient with you and shut you off before I really heard the whole story. I'm sorry about that. Can we try it again at lunch today?"*

Know how to diagnose your own practice accurately

Good problem diagnosis begins with critical self-reflection. Think about your own teaching behaviors and practices before you zoom in on your students. What might you be doing or not doing that contributes to students' inattention and classroom disruptions? Taking an uncompromising look at your own practice can help you teach to your strengths and prioritize one or two areas that you want to improve. *The Skillful Teacher,* a well-used guide for improving teacher effectiveness, identifies major gaps in teaching expertise that can contribute to student inattentiveness and classroom disruptions (adapted with permission from Saphier et al. 2008):

1. *Ineffective classroom management.* Is there clarity and consistency about academic and behavioral expectations, norms, routines, procedures, and consequences? Do you communicate your authority effectively?

2. *Lack of strong personal relationships and group cohesiveness.* How do you make personal contact with each student? How do you communicate your commitment to students' well-being and your confidence in students' capacity to be successful in your class? How do you establish purpose, trust, and respect so students will work with you and for you instead of against you?

3. *Inappropriate work for some or all.* Is the work too hard or too easy? Is the concept or topic too abstract without appropriate scaffolding and concrete learning contexts?

4. *Boring instruction.* Is there too much lecturing, too much redundancy, too many worksheets and overreliance on study guides, no variation in routines or learning activities, too much low-level questioning, or not much enthusiasm on your part?

5. *Confusing instruction.* Are goals and objectives clear? Are concepts presented in ways that students can understand and absorb? Are you using daily informal assessments and checks for understanding to determine what students have learned or not learned? Does the sequence of learning activities make sense to students?

6. *Not enough classroom organization and structure.* Is the classroom environment organized for productive and purposeful learning? Does the seating arrangement minimize distracting student interactions and give you easy access to every student? Is a structure for what to do and how to do it embedded in all learning activities?

7. *Lack of balanced pacing.* Are you intentional about chunking learning time into 5-minute to 20-minute doses? Do you shift and vary the mode of learning, grouping structures, and noise level throughout the period?

8. *Value and culture disconnects.* How do you build rapport and navigate relationships across racial, cultural, class, and gender differences among you and your students? Are there disconnects between what you value and what your students value? Are there habits, behavioral norms, or ways of speaking that are givens for you but may not be valued or understood similarly by students? Do you and your students have different or similar beliefs about how to earn respect, resolve conflicts, handle frustration, and respond to mistakes? How do you acknowledge these differences and assert the values and beliefs that inform your teaching without rejecting students' cultural identity?

Know the teacher roles you want to strengthen

Teacher preparation, mentoring, and supervision focus almost exclusively on the teacher's role as instructor, often at the expense of understanding the importance of other teacher roles. Take a look at "Beyond Instruction: Unpacking Other Key Teacher Roles" on the next page. Which of these roles (facilitator, advocate, listener, coach, and interventionist) are more familiar and comfortable for you? Is there any role that represents a "growing edge" that you want to improve? Are there any skill sets described that you want use more intentionally or more often?

BEYOND INSTRUCTION: UNPACKING OTHER KEY TEACHER ROLES

WITH THE GROUP

You're a Facilitator
who assists, guides, and enables the group to do its work effectively by…

- Modeling the spirit, presence, behaviors, and skills you expect of participants

- Reading the group and what it needs at the moment

- Spending more time observing, coaching, and listening to the group than the group spends watching and listening to you

- Making purpose transparent: Why are we doing what we're doing?

- Making observations transparent: Here's what I'm seeing and hearing.

- Asking questions that enable the group to focus, probe, reflect, and assess; encourage curiosity and insight; deepen understanding; and help the group apply what they have learned

- Redirecting and helping the group to get back on track

- Insisting on group accountability for working effectively together, achieving a goal, or completing a task

- Insisting on individual responsibility for learning

- Debriefing the group experience

WITH INDIVIDUAL STUDENTS…
"I'm on Your Side and on Your Case!"

You're an Advocate
"I believe in you."

- Words of encouragement

- Confidence in your capacity to meet learning expectations

- Support when you need it

- Mirroring your assets

You're a Listener
"Tell me more about _____."

- Discovering who students are, what they need, what they know, and what they can do

- Learning about each student's strengths, assets, talents, aspirations, and plans for the future

You're a Coach
"I will help you get it right."

- Explicit academic and behavioral expectations

- Giving immediate and concrete feedback to help students correct mistakes and get it right

- Guided instruction, reteaching, tutorials, and individual conferences

- Providing practice and rehearsal

- Sharing experiences and reflecting on lessons learned

- Pushing for quality and excellence

- Transparent assessment and record keeping

You're an Interventionist
"So let's take a look at what's happened and what you need to do."

- Straight talk and personalized academic and behavioral conferencing

- Workouts with students during lunch or after school

- Probing, planning, and problem solving

- Behavioral and learning contracts

- Student referrals for additional support services and intervention

KNOW YOUR STUDENTS

The better you know your students, the more effectively you can reach, teach, encourage, and support each individual.

Who are your students? Do most of them feel connected to school or alienated from school? Do they see school as a placeholder during the day? Is the boredom and the grind of school just part of being an American teenager? Do few, some, or most of your students assume that high school is the gateway to the rest of their lives? Or do you have a lot of students who have so little hope and confidence in their own future that school holds little relevance? Do most of your students feel that adults are on their side, or are they mistrustful of adult authority?

Young people's feelings about education, learning, and adult authority; their level of trust and respectfulness toward adults; and their sense of personal hope or disillusionment will all influence what it will take to develop effective classroom management and discipline strategies in your classroom. For kids who feel less connected, respected, and cared for, the words and tone you choose to communicate your expectations will resonate for the rest of the year.

For example, if your message about classroom discipline sounds like it's coming from the commander of the fifth army division, you risk further alienating those who are already looking for any excuse to shut down or act out. On the other hand, if you come across as a pushover without clear and consistent disciplinary goals and practices, these students will look for every opportunity to get by you, get over you, or do you in. The challenge here is to know your students well enough that you can begin to answer these three critical questions:

- What teacher behaviors will set your students off and result in off-task behaviors, confrontations and power struggles, noncompliance, hostility, or disengagement?

- What kinds of disciplinary strategies will work best for your frequent fliers, the students who experience the most behavioral difficulties? How do you make time to provide more coaching, monitoring, feedback, and positive attention to students who really need it?

- What kinds of teacher behaviors (encouragement, instruction, and support) will help your students become more self-disciplined and engage in more skillful behaviors more of the time?

Observing students carefully and learning from them what they need and want can eliminate some problems altogether, lessen student resistance, reduce adversarial situations, and strengthen student engagement. Consider whether any of these factors might be a source of student disruptions, inattentiveness, or resistance*.

- Students' need for fun, playfulness, and stimulation: How do you "game up" what students need to learn? How do you make room for humor and a light moment? How do you provide learning opportunities during which students can move around or work with high interest resources and materials?*

- Students' need for choice, ownership, and control: Do students have choices about what they can do, when they can do it, how they can do it, and with whom they can do it? One rule of thumb: never do for a student what you can teach a student to do for herself.*

- Students' need for personal relevance: How do you communicate an understanding that you know your students are kids, not adults? How do you make personal connections between the subject-matter content and students' own experiences? How do you incorporate real-world issues and learning applications into your curriculum?*

- Students in your classes, especially those who are reluctant and resistant, are silently asking you these two questions every day:

  ▸ What are you going to do for me so that I'm going to work for you?

  ▸ What are you going to do to make what you're teaching important and meaningful to me?

- Students' need for caring and trusting relationships with adults: So much of learning is influenced by the quality of the relationships you develop with your students. When students trust and respect you, when they know you care about them, when they know you will notice them and listen to them, when they like you and what you stand for, they will make a choice to learn from you. When you've made authentic connections with students, they are more likely to:

  ▸ Take academic and social risks because they believe you won't humiliate them

  ▸ Ask for help when they are confused or don't understand something because they believe you will listen and give them personal attention

  ▸ Be willing to show caring and respect for one another because you are modeling those same qualities

  ▸ Be more open about their own lives, thoughts, and feelings because they believe you will accept and value them

* Adapted with permission from Saphier et al. 2008.

Know how to diagnose the underlying reasons for unwanted behaviors

In many situations, particularly with students whom you might not know well, it's helpful to explore the underlying needs that might trigger a particular behavior. Sometimes the most effective response is to work with the student to identify a more appropriate behavior that meets the same need.

BEHAVIOR expresses student's need to...	1. Get Attention	2. Seek Power	3. Seek Revenge	4. Hide Inadequacy
Active Characteristics	Behaviors that distract students and teachers	Disruptive and confrontational behaviors	Physical and psychological attacks	Student loses control when pressure to win or succeed becomes too intense or overwhelming
Passive Characteristics	Behaviors that exhibit slow, slower, and slowest speed	Quiet noncompliance; student does his or her own thing	Student is sullen and withdrawn, refuses friendship	Procrastination, avoidance, and failure to complete task
How Society Encourages Misbehavior	Adults pay more attention to misbehavior than positive behavior; kids don't get enough positive attention	Society stresses equality in relationship rather than obedience, yet individual power is rewarded; kids get mixed messages about authority	Violence is an acceptable way to resolve conflict; violence as entertainment rewards force, coercion, and intimidation	Unreasonable pressure to perform produces the "I have to be perfect" syndrome and too much emphasis on competition
Silver Lining	Student wants relationship with teacher and students	Student exhibits leadership potential, assertiveness, and independent thinking	Student is trying to protect self from further hurt	Student may want to succeed if given reassurance and clear steps to make success possible
Principles of Prevention	Give lots of attention to appropriate and positive behaviors	Avoid and defuse direct confrontation. Create opportunities for students to use power positively	Build strong relationships. Teach student how to express feelings and manage anger. Always listen!	Develop a relationship with student through thick and thin. Use different instructional strategies. Help student connect with other students

Adapted with permission from Albert 1996.

Know key essentials of adolescent development

Knowing more about the developmental needs of your students is the basis for creating a classroom and curriculum that connect to who your students are, what they know, what motivates them, and how they learn.

Major developmental tasks

The four major tasks of adolescence are:

- *Establishing one's own identity.* Identity has two components: self-concept (the set of beliefs one has about one's attributes and assets) and self-esteem (how we evaluate our self-concept and how we feel about either our perceived self as a whole or a specific aspect of ourselves) (APA 1997, p. 15). Healthy identity also involves a balance between being with and identifying with others and being comfortable being alone and thinking and acting on one's own. (Pruitt 1999, p. 30).

- *Becoming more intimate with peers.* As students get older, they spend increasing amounts of time with friends and develop new forms of relationships based on sexual attraction. Peer groups serve as powerful re-enforcers that validate popularity, status, prestige, and acceptance (APA 1997, p. 21).

- *Developing a mature relationship with one's family.* Older adolescents tend to see themselves as the equals of their parents, and parents tend to recognize that the power balance in family relationships is shifting.

- *Achieving a growing sense of autonomy, control, and mastery in the world.*

Teens have a strong sense of fairness and are judgmental of adults and peers who do not do what they view as fair. Teens have a deep need for love and acceptance by parents and peers. Adults should be aware that such a need is often hidden in an effort to act mature.

What's normal?

It's normal for adolescents to

- *Argue for the sake of arguing.* Although this annoying habit gets on adults' last nerves, it is one of the ways that adolescents test out their reasoning abilities.

- *Jump to conclusions.* Logical thinking comes and goes. Trying to correct a student's faulty logic or arguing back will only corner a student and make the conversation even more adversarial. Listen, appreciate the point of view, share your perspective, but don't try to convince the student to change positions when the students' feelings are charged.

- *Constantly find fault with an adult's position.* A newfound capacity to think critically ignites the fire to find discrepancies and contradictions.

- *Be overly dramatic.* In most cases, this is a style of presenting oneself rather than a forecast of extreme action.

Self-Esteem and Self-Concept

Self-concept "refers to a student's perceptions of competence or adequacy in academic and non-academic domains" that they value as important. This includes the domains of academic achievement, social competence with peers, physical appearance, and athletic competence, among others. Self-esteem "is a student's overall evaluation of him- or herself, including feelings of general happiness and satisfaction." Self-concept and self-esteem are not developed by asking students to write down ten things they like about themselves. Perceptions and evaluation of personal competency and worthiness are not a "cause of high achievement, but appear to be a consequence of high achievement" (Manning 2007, p. 11). Thus, teachers can nurture students' healthy self-esteem and self-concept by incorporating these four elements into the classroom experience: (1) experiences of mastery in work that students value; (2) strong positive attachments to adults and peers; (3) opportunities for control, power, and choice in what and how students are learning; and (4) positive identity development that recognizes and supports students' racial, ethnic, and cultural diversity. Students who experience success and satisfaction in school and everyday life want to experience it again. They will keep doing the things that build confidence and generate continued success.

Resiliency

Resiliency is the capacity to bounce back from adversity, recover from loss and personal setbacks, and adjust to new challenges in ways that help people achieve positive outcomes and life chances. Resiliency in young people reflects the "self-righting tendencies that move children toward normal adult development under all but the most persistent adverse circumstances" (Benard 2004).

Four personal strengths foster resiliency:

(1) social competence;

(2) problem solving;

(3) autonomy (positive identity, internal locus of control, self-efficacy, and mastery); and

(4) sense of purpose (goal direction, achievement motivation, hope, and optimism).

Three protective factors (in schools, at home, and in the community) support development of these personal strengths:

(1) caring relationships;

(2) high expectations and consistent boundaries; and

(3) opportunities to participate and contribute.

As you think about discipline and classroom management, the concept of consistent boundaries is particularly important. Students want both choice and limits. When boundaries about how to behave and what's acceptable are absent or confusing, students may take on a stance called "hostile freedom." From a kid's perspective, hostile freedom sounds like this: "If you don't give me the boundaries I need so I can do the right thing, I'm going to do what I want and push you to the edge. You might think this will make me happy, but it really makes me kind of mad."

Metacognitive development

Metacognitive development refers to students' self-awareness as learners and their abilities to reflect on how and what they learn; to manage and direct their own learning; to assess their strengths and weaknesses; to think their way through problems; and to develop habits that support learning and personal efficacy. A meta-analysis of 28 factors that influence student learning in the classroom cites metacognitive processes as the second most important influence. (Classroom management is number one.) (Walberg and Haertel 2007).

Motivation

Motivation—the "natural capacity to direct energy in pursuit of a goal" (Wlodkowski and Ginsberg 1995, p. 22)—is an internal quality driven by a person's feelings, thoughts, beliefs, and experiences. Goal orientation and one's confidence in achieving a goal are huge internal motivators. Big goals that reflect one's future hopes and aspirations enable students to persist and persevere through high school and beyond. You can't motivate anyone but yourself, but you can create conditions that help students develop greater positive motivation.

Allen Mendler, author of the book *Motivating Students Who Don't Care*, suggests some key strategies that can support students' positive changes in motivation, attitude, and achievement over time.

- Emphasize *effort* (Ability + Effort = Achievement).

- Create *hope* by building each student's expectation of success and communicating your confidence in the student's ability to succeed.

- Respect a student's desire for power and focus of control (choice and voice).

- Make a *personal connection* with the student every day.

- *Find out more* about the student: his or her interests, family background, and learning profile. ("If you can't learn the way I teach, I can teach the way you learn.")

- *Identify learning gaps* and address them immediately.

- Express your *enthusiasm, encouragement,* and *support.* Unmotivated kids rarely experience someone who makes a positive fuss over them or what they're doing. Your cheerleading spirit can rub off. (Mendler 2000)

For more about student motivation, see Chapter 3, *Making Learning REAL.*

Know key qualities and attributes of a developed student

Think about how you nurture these qualities and attributes through your day-to-day teaching, coaching, and support to individual students.

Relational development

Developed students:

- Develop positive connections between and among adults and peers

- Communicate effectively with different groups in different settings

- Ask for help when needed and make use of school and community resources

- Seek out and cultivate social and professional networks

- Navigate the system successfully

- Make positive contributions to a group through teamwork and leadership

Cognitive Development

Developed students:

- Assess their skills, effort, and quality of work accurately

- Learn from their mistakes, setbacks, and failures

- Identify and build on their successes

- Make realistic plans and set short-term and long-term goals

- Engage in critical, creative, and logical problem solving

- Apply knowledge to real-world situations

- Manage their time effectively and prioritize tasks

Self-actualization

Developed students:

- Know and value their abilities, talents, interests, passions, and aspirations

- Possess confidence and healthy self-esteem

- Plan for a future after high school with a sense of hope and optimism

- Listen to their inner compass

- Strive to succeed

- See themselves as leaders

- Know how to present themselves in the world in multiple settings and contexts

Character development

Developed students:

- Have strong character, integrity, convictions, and resolve

- Take personal and social responsibility for their words and actions

- Give respect to get respect

- Are aware of others' needs and feelings

- Make healthy choices

- Accept and value differences and diversity

KNOW YOUR SCHOOL

Some schools are completely transparent when it comes to communicating expectations to teachers; in other schools, teachers are on their own. Know the kind of school you work in and adjust your expectations accordingly. Do make an effort to seek out all written policies related to discipline, student referrals, and the ladder of academic and behavioral interventions and supports.

Know your school's discipline policies and referral systems

Make sure that you and your students know the ins and outs of the school's student code of conduct and schoolwide rules and policies.

- Are there particular schoolwide rules and policies that have a direct impact on student behavior in your classroom? Be sure to review rules about food, dress codes, personal possessions, cheating, harassment, and so forth. Make sure students know how you will enforce schoolwide rules and procedures.

- Which schoolwide rules and policies are enforced consistently? Which ones are rarely enforced at all? What are you prepared to say to students when you enforce schoolwide rules that other teachers choose not to enforce?

- Do most of your students assume that rules will be enforced fairly and consistently at school? Or do they feel that it all depends on the student, the adult, or the situation? Find out what your students think.

- Is there a schoolwide late arrival and tardiness policy? Are attendance policies consistently enforced by all teachers? Do all students receive the same consequences? If the schoolwide tardiness policy is unevenly enforced without clear consequences and follow-through, you might want to create your own rules within the classroom. In the long run, implementing your own attendance policy can pay out better dividends than griping about a school policy over which you may have no control.

- Does the school have specific policies about what kinds of disciplinary problems teachers are expected to handle themselves? What's the referral process for students who engage in chronic or egregious unwanted behaviors? What infractions and violations warrant a written referral, an exit referral and removal from the classroom, or a referral to a counselor or student support team? When you refer students out of the classroom, how will you be informed about actions that were taken?

- How are you informed when a student is suspended? What's the re-entry policy for students? What are the school policies regarding makeup work?

- If you're in a school where compliance, orderliness, and adherence to adult authority are unspoken expectations for almost all students, you caught a lucky break. On the other hand, if you teach in a school with few schoolwide norms and ineffective enforcement of school rules, students will be testing you from day one. They want to see if you are up to the challenge of creating a disciplined classroom environment within a normless school culture. In this situation, your best strategy is to seek out other colleagues who teach the same students and, together, develop a set of rules and expectations that you all agree to enforce consistently.

Know colleagues and administrators whom you can count on for help and assistance

Teachers have the right to request support and clarity from administrators, counselors, and support staff. It's also helpful to have a couple of teacher colleagues in your corner. Who might be your go-to person in the following situations?

- The administrator who is most likely to provide crystal-clear explanations about enforcement and follow-through of schoolwide rules and consequences.

- The administrator who is the most effective mediator or conference convener. This is the person with whom you want to arrange conferences with a student or students and parents when unwanted behaviors persist or when the student has committed an egregious offense.

- The dean or assistant principal who can help round up kids for a lunchtime or after-school workout session so you can count on students actually showing up.

- A counselor or social worker who is willing to observe a challenging student in your classroom and later share observations and strategy suggestions.

- The counselor or social worker you think has the best therapeutic skill set to work with troubled students. You want to be able to refer students to someone in whom you have confidence, someone who will follow up with you and share appropriate information.

- A security or safety officer who can help you out in the following situations: (1) conducting a student to a dean or assistant principal when a student's behavior warrants immediate removal from the classroom; (2) confiscating personal electronics or personal possessions from students in situations where you feel uncomfortable doing this; or (3) restoring order and/or breaking up a fight or noisy crowd in your immediate vicinity. (Don't leave your classroom; send a note to the staff person to request assistance.)

- A teacher in a nearby classroom who can serve as your "buddy" and is willing to help you out in the following situations: (1) taking a student who needs a time-out for the remainder of the period; (2) alerting security or an administrator when a critical incident occurs in your classroom (send a student to alert your buddy); or (3) covering your class for a few minutes during their prep period if you need to handle an emergency situation with a student.

- A veteran teacher who has worked in the school for many years and who will happily tell you what's what and who's who so you can figure out what you need to know.

- A teacher who "walks on water" with failing, resistant, and difficult kids. This is the person whom you want to consult before you get into a standoff with hard-to-reach students.

REFERENCES:

Albert, L. (1996) *Cooperative Discipline*. Port Angeles, WA: American Guidance Services Publishing.

Benard, B. (2004) *Resiliency: What we have learned.* Los Angeles: WestEd.

Kounin, J. (1977) *Discipline and group management in classrooms.* Malabar, FL: Krieger Publishing Co.

Manning, M. (2007) "Self-concept and self-esteem in adolescents," *Principal Leadership* (February).

Marzano, R., Marzano, J., and Pickering, D. (2003) *Classroom management that works.* Alexandria, VA: ASCD.

Mendler, A. (2000) *Motivating students who don't care: Successful techniques for educators.* Bloomington, IN: Solution Tree.

Saphier, J., Haley-Speca, M. A., and Gower, R. (2007) *The Skillful Teacher.* Acton, MA: Research for Better Teaching.

Walberg, H., and Haertel, G. (1997) *Psychology and educational practice.* Berkley, CA: McCutchen Publishing.

Wlodkowski, R., and Ginsberg, M. "Culturally responsive teaching." *Educational Leadership*, 53(1) (September).

Wubbels, T., and Levy, J., Edition (1993) *Do you know what you look like? Interpersonal relationships in education.* London: Falmer Press.

Wubbels, T., Levy, J., and Brekelmans, M. (1997) "Paying attention to relationships." *Educational Leadership*, 54(7), 82–86.

CHAPTER 4

Step 2: Create Group Norms, Procedures, and Learning Protocols

Developing group norms and teaching basic procedures and routines in the beginning of the school year will save endless amounts of time off task; eliminate your need to nag; and reduce your students' levels of confusion, resistance, and helplessness. The bottom line? Unless the group can work on its own effectively, you have no chance to provide personalized instruction and support to individual students during class time. If students don't learn how to function as a group, you're stuck with thirty students who will be happy to wear you down with thirty different sets of demands for personal attention, private instruction, and preferential treatment during every minute of every class period. If this sounds too exhausting to even think about, you're right!

In this chapter, prevention is the name of the game. It's extremely important to remember that a teacher's responses to disciplinary problems can only restore order; they do not and cannot create order in the classroom. Effective classroom management "seeks to establish and maintain an orderly environment so students can engage in meaningful academic learning [and] it also aims to enhance students' social and moral growth" (Evertson and Weinstein 2006). Thus, front-loading the consistent implementation of norms, procedures, and group learning protocols is a critical step toward developing a high-functioning group of learners and preventing many typical classroom disruptions.

CREATE GROUP NORMS

Life Skill Connections (See pages 141–144)

13. Set large and small goals and make plans.

27. Cooperate, share, and work toward high performance within a group to achieve group goals.

28. Respect everyone's right to learn, to speak, and to be heard.

35. Use a variety of strategies to make decisions democratically.

Note: the full Life Skills list will appear in Chapter 5.

Creating norms for positive group behavior begins with what you do, not what students do. Your academic and behavioral goals and expectations give your students a picture of what this class will be like, what they are expected to learn, and how they are expected to behave. Using charts like the examples below can help you spell out your expectations.

Expectations:

- I'm counting on everyone to encourage and support each other.
- Working with each other collaboratively is a big deal with me. It's something we will spend a lot of time doing, and I expect everyone to get pretty good at it.
- You don't need to be friends with everyone, but I do expect you to be friendly with everyone.

Expectations:

- I expect all of you to pass this course. If you put in the effort, I can promise you will pass.
- All of you can be successful learners in this class. I know you have what it takes to do well.
- I expect all of us to treat each other with respect and consideration.
- I expect everyone to try to do your best and be your best.

Expectations:

- We all make mistakes and we can learn from them and right them.
- I know that there will be times when you may feel challenged and struggle a bit. We'll get through it.
- Sometimes you might make poor choices. And I'm confident that you can recover and get back on track.

Establish positive group guidelines and agreements

Positive group agreements and guidelines begin with students' contributions to the development of group norms. If you skip this process, students don't have a voice in making the classroom a good place to be. The cost? For adolescents, the absence of student input can diminish a sense of personal responsibility or group accountability.

Shifting the emphasis from "my rules that you follow" to "guidelines we agree to implement together" communicates mutual responsibility for establishing a positive classroom climate where everyone is a stakeholder. When we invoke tons of rules in the classroom, we may unintentionally pit the rule breakers against the rule keepers. Furthermore, rules tend to keep the focus on negative behaviors—catching kids doing the wrong thing becomes the goal.

In contrast, agreements that describe desirable behaviors that are observable, concrete, and positive invite everyone to recognize and encourage the regular use of these behaviors. In addition, group guidelines become a natural assessment and reflection tool. Teachers and students can engage in an ongoing process of reviewing how well agreements are kept and discussing how to modify agreements so they are more effective.

Group guidelines can make any learning process more meaningful. When students know how to approach a learning task and know what skills and behaviors will help them complete the task, more kids will be more successful. In addition to developing general classroom agreements, students can help develop specific guidelines for making an effective oral presentation; working effectively in teams; and discussing controversial issues, when students may bring strong feelings and disparate opinions to the dialogue.

At both levels, students engage in the authentic practice of conflict resolution skills: defining the problem; sharing perspectives and listening to all points of view; exploring what's negotiable and what's not; identifying mutual interests; brainstorming possible solutions; and reaching a mutually satisfactory agreement. Students can use this process later for class meetings and negotiating other classroom issues.

Suggested Instructions for Making Group Agreements

1. Say, "The first thing we're going to do today is make some agreements that we can live with as a whole group. I'd like you to help brainstorm some guidelines that reflect how you think we should work together, talk to each other, and treat each other."

2. Say, "Here are a couple of examples of the kinds of agreements we can make." Choose two or three examples from the list below to write on newsprint or chart paper.

    Sample List of Group Agreements

    *   Let people finish what they have to say before someone else speaks.

    *   Share the talk space. Give everyone a chance to speak.

- Take care of your own needs. If you have a question, ask it. If you need to say something, say it.

- Start on time.

- It's okay to make mistakes and self-correct.

- Use "I Statements." Speak from your own experience.

- Respect yourself and others.

- Listen carefully.

- Be honest and open.

- Be a willing participant.

- Help each other out.

- Check things out before you make assumptions.

- Have fun!

- Confidentiality.

- Don't make fun of what other people say or do.

3. Say, "What agreements would you like to add to the list that will make our time together productive and positive?" Another way to say this is, "What kinds of agreements can we make as a group that will make this class work for you, that will help you be your best?" Brainstorm for about ten minutes and write down all suggestions on the chart paper.

4. Use any of these questions to review the list: "Now look at the list. Are there any final suggestions? Any suggestions you'd rather leave out? Any that can be combined? Any words or phrases that you're unclear about? Any objections or concerns about any of the suggestions? Any words that you would like to replace?"

Key Points to Remember:

- Respect is a word that illustrates the problems with "global language," that is, language that is abstract and often means different thing to different people. It is essential that students name very concrete behaviors that show (through words or actions) how to treat someone with respect. Here are two ways you can encourage students to clarify what they mean when someone says, "We need to respect other people."

  - "What could someone do or say that would show you that you're being treated respectfully?"

  - "If I had a movie camera here in the classroom, what behaviors would I film that show you treating each other with respect?"

- If this is challenging to students, you might begin by generating specific behaviors that show disrespect and then identify what you would like someone to say or do instead.

- Take the time to work through the wording of agreements until everyone is fairly comfortable with the list. This process lets your students know that it's okay to discuss areas of difference and that it's valuable to reassess and modify "first thinking."

5. Check the list for "positive framing." This is the time to transform any statements that are negatively framed into statements that are positive and proactive. For example, in the sample agreements list above, #1 has been changed from "Don't interrupt," to "Let people finish what they have to say before someone else speaks."

6. Use a consensus process to reach agreement. Explain that consensus decision making means that everyone participates and has a say before reaching agreement on a decision that everyone can support. Remind students, "You have been using this process already. Now we've reached the final stage of consensus. Each of you needs to decide if you can live with and support this list of agreements for our class. It's important to remember that this list is not forever. We can revisit, discuss, and change these agreements if the group feels the need to do so. So I will ask two last questions."

    – "Are there any objections to the agreements as they stand right now? If you still have a strong concern or objection, it's important to bring it up now, and we can address it before we move on."

    – If there are no other objections at this time, move to the final question. "Are these agreements good enough for right now so that you can support them and use them during our time together? I will ask each of you to say, 'Yes' or 'No.'"

7. When everyone has said, "Yes," including you, you may want to suggest that everyone initials the group agreements that you have made.

8. Ask for a volunteer who is willing to rewrite the group agreements in large, clear print so that you can post them in the classroom.

Take a few minutes at the end of every week to revisit your agreements. Here are some questions you might ask:

- What have you noticed that indicates that we are keeping most of our agreements?

- Have you noticed anything that indicates that we are not keeping some of our agreements?

- Which ones are hardest for the group as a whole to keep? What can we do to help everyone get better at keeping this agreement?

- Is there anything at this time that you want to add, delete, or change?

- Would anyone like to share how these agreements have made this class a different experience for you?

More about Agreements

- Agreements work hand-in-hand with consequences and interventions you apply when students violate classroom boundaries or fail to follow procedures you have taught.

- Agreements in the classroom can't replace schoolwide rules that are universally enforced (i.e., if there is a schoolwide rule that no food or drink is allowed in classrooms, you can't make an agreement that supersedes the school rule).

- The practice of making classroom agreements is carried out on two levels: general guidelines for how students work together, learn together, and treat each other, and more specific guidelines for how to engage in a specific learning experience. General group guidelines involve all students in envisioning the kind of classroom in which students feel safe, respected, cared for, and motivated to learn.

Discuss the issue of respect

Giving and Getting Respect

Everyone needs to talk about respect as a foundation for building positive relationships in the classroom. Too often, not feeling respected is the trigger for fights, angry confrontations, grievances, and low morale among students and faculty. Versions of "You disrespected me" is the most common source of conflict between and among students and teachers. Respect is a global word that can mean something different to each person in the room. It is very helpful for you and students to identify specific, observable behaviors that individuals perceive as being respectful and disrespectful. One more thing—the "Golden Rule" is not enough in diverse learning communities where students come from many different family experiences and cultural and religious traditions. Yes, it's important to consider treating others as we would like to be treated; but it's just as important to treat others as they tell you they would like to be treated.

Respect begins with the belief that every person has value and deserves to be acknowledged with courtesy and treated with dignity. Respect means appreciating each other's uniqueness. It means accepting that differences in people's values, opinions, and perspectives are normal. Disagreeing with another person is not a sign of disrespect. A climate of mutual respect is supported by greeting people by name in a friendly matter, asking instead of demanding, focusing your attention on others when they are speaking, and listening to others without interrupting them.

Disrespect involves comments or actions that violate another person's dignity and identity. Actions of disrespect occur between people within close proximity of each other most of the time. We think the other person has treated us badly, insulted or embarrassed us, or acknowledged us in a way that's inappropriate, offensive, or off-limits.

The issues of respect and disrespect present a number of challenges in most schools:

- Students' and adults' definitions and understanding of RESPECT and DISRESPECT are often very different from each others'.

  How do we describe respectful and disrespectful behaviors, exactly, so we can clearly communicate the respectful behaviors we expect of students and faculty?

- From the perspective of many young people, "street cred" and daily survival outside of school may require a different code of respect—one where students feel that they must demand respect aggressively and use aggressive language, a hostile stance, or physical violence to respond to acts of disrespect.

  How do we communicate to students that schools are public places that require everyone to learn and practice a code of respect that gives students the power to navigate in multiple settings outside the world of their family, their peers, and the neighborhood?

- When we feel disrespected, we take it very personally—so we are likely to respond from a place of *anger*, become emotionally charged, and intensify the conflict. This is why it's so easy to "give back as good as we got."

  How do we model and teach students the skills to respond to disrespectful behaviors assertively without becoming overly hostile or aggressive?

- Finally, we all live in a world of media voices and images that normalize and glorify profanity, negative and confrontational speech, incivility, and disrespectful behaviors at home, in the work place, between men and women, between adolescents and adults, and among different racial, religious, and socioeconomic groups to name a few. For educators, cultivating a climate and culture of respect can feel like spitting in the ocean. Tackling the issues of respect beyond a superficial tune-up requires a campaign-like effort on many fronts that stays in the spotlight for a long time.

  As a teacher, how do you teach and practice respect on a daily basis?

Learning Carousel about Respect

Choose the questions below that you want to use and write one question on each piece of newsprint or chart paper. Post around the room. Divide students into groups of three. Make sure you have a posted question for each group of three students. So, for example, you would need ten posted questions for a group of 30 students. (You can repeat some of the same questions. Each trio will only respond to four or five questions altogether.) Explain to students that they will have two minutes to jot down their responses to the question on the chart paper in front of them. Ask trios to position themselves in front of one of the questions and write their responses to the question.

After two minutes ask trios to rotate to the next question and give groups two minutes to add their responses to what has already been written on the chart paper. Continue to rotate trios through two or three more questions.

When you have finished the rotations, give each student five sticker dots. Invite students to do a "gallery walk" and read all of the responses. Explain that their task is to place their dots on five comments that communicate important "Dos" and "Don'ts" for establishing a respectful classroom.

After everyone has finished the "gallery walk", place all of the "Don'ts" charts together (Questions #2, 4, and 6) and place all of the "Dos" charts together (Questions #1, 3, 5, 7, and 8). Then circle the 10 to 15 comments that received the most dots. Invite students to read the comments. Are there any surprises? Are there any themes that emerge? If a few comments received many more dots than most of the others, explore why these particular comments generated so much interest.

Post your "Dos" and "Don'ts" list as part of your classroom norms.

Further Inquiry: Do this exercise with all staff and students on the same team or within the same grade level. Invite a group of students and staff to review those data, looking for student and staff responses to the same question that are very similar to each other or very different from each other. Share your data with all staff and students on the team or in the same grade.

QUESTIONS ABOUT RESPECT

1. **Student-to-Student RESPECT**

   What do **students** do and say that shows **RESPECT** toward other **students**?

2. **Student-to-Student DISRESPECT**

   What do **students** do and say that shows **DISRESPECT** toward other **students**?

3. **Teacher-to-Student RESPECT**

   What do **teachers** do and say that shows **RESPECT** toward other **students**?

4. **Teacher-to-Student DISRESPECT**

   What do **teachers** do and say that shows **DISRESPECT** toward other **students**?

5. **Student-to-Teacher RESPECT**

   What do **students** do and say that shows **RESPECT** toward **teachers**?

6. **Student-to-Teacher DISRESPECT**

    What do **students** do and say that shows **DISRESPECT** toward **teachers**?

7. What are some ways students can disagree with a teacher and show respect
    at the same time?

8. How do teachers correct and discipline students and show respect at the same time?

Student Self-Reflection on Giving and Showing Respect

The survey on page 111 gives students an opportunity to think about the degree with which they show respect toward different people in different situations. Give students about five minutes.

When five minutes are up, ask students to pair up and share their survey responses with each other: You might want to share your own responses to these questions first to show students how you would respond. Take five minutes for the pair-share.

- In what two or three situations is it easiest for you to be respectful to everyone?

- In what two or three situations is it toughest for you to be respectful to everyone?

- Pick one situation where you know you should be more respectful than you are. What would you need to tell yourself to begin responding differently?

With the whole group, discuss two or three of the situations that you think will generate the most interest from your students or invite students to choose the two or three situations that they want to discuss further. For each specific situation, you might use any of these question prompts:

- Why act this way all of the time with everyone? How is this action a sign of respect?

- When you act this way all of the time, what does it say about you as a person?

- If all adults and students acted this way most of the time, how would school feel different?

- If it's tough to act this way all of the time, why is that? What gets in the way?

If you ask students to look at the array of situations as a whole, you might ask:

- In which situations do you think most students at school find it hard to be respectful? Why is that?

- What would help students to be more respectful in these situations?

Facilitating a Schoolwide Dialogue about Respect

This survey activity can serve as a catalyst for a deeper joint student-teacher dialogue about respect throughout the school. The survey **Student Perceptions of Teacher Respect** invites students to assess levels of teacher respect for students at school and the survey **Teacher Perceptions of Student Respect** invites teachers to assess levels of student respect at school.

Disseminate the survey to students and teachers and explain to both students and faculty that completion of the survey is the first step toward facilitating a schoolwide conversation about respect. Explain that everyone will have an opportunity to discuss the results of the survey and compare student and teacher responses in another session, after the data have been collated and summarized.

Identify a "working group" of students and staff who will help collate and summarize the data. Create an "easy to read" graphic depiction of the data summary for distribution to students and staff.

FURTHER ACTIVITIES:

Teachers and students might use the following process to discuss the data summary in a follow-up session:

- **Make observations about the student and teacher survey data:**

   What do you see? (I see…I observe…I notice—focus on the numbers!! "I see that 40 percent of teachers said_____." "I see that over half of students said_____.")

- **Make interpretations and speculations**

   I'm wondering why…
   I'm curious about…
   I'm puzzled by…
   I'm surprised about…
   It looks like _____
   It's bothers me to see_____

- **Record responses to these questions to submit to the working group for use in further discussions.**

   What do you think you know after examining the data?

   Are there one or two particular concerns that feel urgent to address? Why?
   How would school be different if the negatives turned positive?

   What else do you want to know? What other questions do you have?
   Who do you want to talk to in order to gather further data?

Invite the "working group" of students and teachers to review the written responses from the previous session and prioritize two or three issues that the school should tackle. Explore possible root causes of current perceptions.

Facilitate a series of "Lunch and Learn Dialogues" between students and teachers to discuss the urgent concerns and brainstorm what students can do and what adults can do to address the urgent concerns.

Role-Playing Disrespectful and Respectful Behaviors

Role-plays offer a great way to do three things:

- Introduce students to norms that communicate, "This is how we do school here. This is how we treat each other."

- Help students have a clearer understanding of words and actions that communicate respect and disrespect.

- Support students to practice and rehearse respectful responses in typical school day situations.

Role-playing a DISRESPECTFUL response FIRST creates a way for everyone to lighten up a bit (especially if an adult plays the disrespectful student) and also provides the audience with a chance to discuss the exact words and behaviors that communicate disrespect. Here's one protocol to use for any of the role-play situations below:

1. Read out the role-play situation.

2. Do a quick brainstorm of words and behaviors that would show disrespect in this situation.

3. Ask for two volunteers to role-play the scenario. Explain that disrespect is a form of aggression, so in the role-plays the person who is disrespectful is identified as the aggressor and the person on the receiving end of the disrespect is identified as the target.

4. After the students finish the role-play, first ask how the target felt about what happened. Then ask the audience exactly what they heard and saw that was disrespectful. Ask students how this response could lead to a verbal confrontation or physical fight.

5. Invite students to brainstorm alternative responses that show respect for the other person.

6. Then ask students to "rewind the tape" and role-play the situation in a way that shows a more respectful response.

7. After the second role-play ask the target what felt different about the situation this time.

ROLE PLAY SITUATIONS:

Situation #1:   You meet a new student in your class whom you've never seen before.

Situation #2:   You want help in class when you don't understand the directions.

Situation #3:   You want a student to move, who is sitting at a desk where you already put your stuff.

Situation #4:   Your teacher is asking you about an assignment that you haven't completed.

Situation #5:   You want to borrow something from a student or adult that's not yours.

Situation #6:   You disagree with another student's opinion in class.

Situation #7:   Your teacher asks you to move your seat after you have continued talking with your friend while your teacher is giving instructions.

Situation #8:   Your teacher greets you as you walk in the room.

Situation #9:   You think the current book you're reading in English is really boring. You can't figure out why it's required reading.

Situation #10:   You are discussing your progress report grade with your teacher, and you think the grade is unfair.

HANDOUT
Student Self-Reflection on Giving and Showing Respect

Rate yourself on how you show your respect for others in each situation.	I do this day in and day out with almost everyone	I do this on a good day with most people	This is tough for me to do with most people
1 I call people by the name they wish to be called.			
2 I greet people in a friendly manner when they say "hello" to me.			
3 I get along with others in my classes, even if they have different opinions or disagree with me.			
4 I consider others' needs and feelings before I act or respond.			
5 I treat others the way they want to be treated.			
6 When people are talking to me, I focus my attention on them and I listen with interest.			
7 I encourage people to have their say without interrupting them.			
8 I understand that honest mistakes, accidents, or misunderstandings are not the same as disrespect.			
9 I assume that everyone deserves to be treated decently.			
10 I say "please" and "thank you" as a normal courtesy.			
11 I can accept feedback, correction, and "No" from adults without putting up a fuss.			
12 I don't pressure others to do things they don't want to do.			
13 I try not to make assumptions or judgments about a person before I get to know them.			
14 I don't intentionally embarrass, humiliate, or insult people.			
15 I don't use or borrow other people's stuff without asking permission.			
16 When people want to be left alone or do something different, I'm okay with that.			
17 I don't use vulgar language or profanity in public places, including school.			
18 Even with unpleasant people, I make my best effort to courteous, take care of my business and move on.			
19 I accept adult authority and direction, even when it doesn't feel fair or reasonable.			
20 When others are disrespectful to me, I can handle the situation without becoming threatening, aggressive, or hostile.			

4

HANDOUT
Student Perceptions of Teacher Respect

Check the response that most accurately reflects your experiences at school.	All my teachers	Most of my teachers	Some of my teachers	A couple of my teachers	None of my teachers
1 Teachers know my name, pronounce it correctly, and call me by my name in class.					
2 Teachers welcome us into their classrooms and speak to us in a friendly manner.					
3 Teachers like us.					
4 Teachers notice me and want to get to know me—they appreciate my own uniqueness and affirm my background and cultural identity.					
5 Teachers teach us habits and skills that help us get along, listen to each other, cooperate in a group, and disagree respectfully.					
6 Teachers embarrass, humiliate, or insult students or allow students to embarrass, humiliate, or insult each other.					
7 Teachers understand that we all learn differently and need different kinds of help and support.					
8 Teachers see respect as a two-way street where each person gives respect to get respect.					
9 Teachers listen to me before they judge, punish, or yell at me.					
10 Teachers understand that we will mess up sometimes and they help us correct our mistakes and get back on track.					
11 Teachers assume that students have something to contribute; they value our thoughts, feelings, and opinions.					
12 Teachers use profanity, negative speech, and harsh criticism to get students to do what they want them to do.					

HANDOUT
Teacher Perceptions of Student Respect

Check the response that most accurately reflects your experiences at school.	All my students	Most of my students	Some of my students	Few or none of my students
1 Students call me by my proper name and speak to me in a friendly manner.				
2 Students are attentive and focused when I speak to them in a large group.				
3 Students are attentive and focused when I speak to them individually, one-on-one.				
4 Students get along with each other, even when they have different opinions and disagree.				
5 Students acknowledge and appreciate my efforts to make the classroom a good place to learn.				
6 Students embarrass, humiliate, or insult each other in class.				
7 Students see respect as a two-way street where each person gives respect to get respect.				
8 Students ask permission and make requests when they want to do something else or do something differently.				
9 Students get to know me before they make assumptions and judgments about me.				
10 Students accept feedback, correction, and "No" without putting up a fuss.				
11 Students assume that I have something of value to contribute to their learning and education.				
12 Students are aggressively argumentative and use profanity and negative speech to communicate their thoughts and ideas in class.				

4

Generate a list of rights and responsibilities

Identifying everyone's rights and responsibilities is another way to develop clear norms and encourage personal accountability. This exercise can be done as whole group, or you and students can generate the list of rights as a whole group and then each student can list personal responsibilities that are associated with each right. Here are a few examples.

Rights and Responsibilities	
We all have the right to...	**I have the responsibility to...**
Express our opinions	Listen to others even when I disagree
Feel safe in this class	Not to embarrass or make fun of others
Get help when we need it	Think it through on my own before I ask for help
Good teaching that keeps us active and interested	Put forth my best effort to learn and participate
Work that prepares me for college	Complete every part of the assignment
Be myself and be accepted for who I am, what I like, and what I believe, even if my identity, likes, and beliefs differ from those of most other people	Appreciate differences in others
Get help, encouragement, and support when I'm experiencing academic difficulties	Accept corrections and suggestions that will help me get back on track
Learn without disruptions and distractions	Work without bothering others
Work and learn in a clean, attractive environment	Do my fair share to keep the room clean

Explain your approach to discipline

Share your approach to discipline. Using Chapter 1 as a reference, you might want to post a set of key words and concepts that will help students learn the language of Guided Discipline and Personalized Support.

Explain what students can expect when they engage in unwanted behaviors occasionally or chronically. Refer to Chapter 1, pages 26–34 and Chapters 6 and 7 for more about problem types and accountable consequences. The following chart illustrates what you might put on a poster or a one-page handout for students and parents.

What you can expect when your behavior becomes a problem

When unwanted behaviors occur, *I will...*

1. Notice the behavior and give you a physical, visual, or verbal cue or prompt to help you refocus, self-correct, or get back on track.

2. Make observations about what I see and ask you or the group to assess the problem and solve it.

3. Give you verbal and written feedback and coaching.

4. Provide personalized support and check-ins.

5. Offer you a choice of "double or nothing" if the behavior persists. Stop what you're doing and you're good to go. Choose to continue _____ and you owe me twice the time.

When an unwanted behavior persists, *I will...*

1. Name the accountable consequence, expect you to carry it out, and support you to do it.

2. Ensure that your parent or guardian is contacted.

3. Discuss the problem with other colleagues or make a referral if necessary.

When an unwanted behavior persists, *you will...*

1. Write what you did in **THE LOG BOOK** or on a behavior report form.

2. Call your parent or guardian to explain the problem and the consequence.

3. Conference with me, the team, or your parent/guardian during your lunch or after school and make a plan to change your behavior.

4. Carry out accountable consequences and interventions that might include a corrective action, written or verbal apology, conduct card, or a workout session during lunch or after school.

5. Carry out additional interventions with the dean, assistant principal, counselor, or student support staff if necessary.

4

Keep a behavioral log book for the class

The log book is a behavior, habits, and performance log of "the good, the bad, and the ugly." It's the place where students in each class record kudos and accomplishments, mistakes and missteps. The act of recording what you did, both positive and negative, encourages ownership and accountability. One good guideline is insisting that students can write only from a personal perspective—what they did and said, what they're thinking and feeling—and that they can't blame others. However, they can say what's upsetting them, what they don't like, and what they'd like you to do differently.

The log book is also the place where you jot down notes that add details about specific incidents, provide specific feedback and encouragement, support students' efforts to change a behavior, and congratulate students on their successes.

Use a separate lined composition book for each class and ask students to write their names on the upper right-hand corner of the right-hand page and leave the next two pages blank. The log book keeps your documentation in one place and serves as a useful source of information for students, parents, principals, your team colleagues, and student support staff.

		Jason Smith
9/17		I wouldn't stop talking and yelled out.
9/17		Jason was using aggressive, hostile speech and back-talked 2 times in a way that disrupted the flow of class and the learning of others.
9/18		AC (Accountable Consequences) Called parent—conference w/ Jason—behavior report and plan
9/18		I can only talk 3 times a period If I get mad I can write notes to Ms. Wheeler & she'll write back to me.
		I can choose a 20-minute pass time to go to the library once a week if I interrupt less than 5 times and clean up my language
9/25		It's been a whole week, Jason, and you're on a roll: only 4 interruptions, so you earned your Library Pass! Nice work.

CREATE GROUP PROCEDURES

Life Skill Connections (See pages 141–144)

9. Exercise self-discipline and impulse control.

12. Focus and pay attention.

27. Cooperate, share, and work toward high performance within a group to achieve group goals.

We all use procedures, spoken and unspoken: how to enter class, how to clean up, what to do when students need help. Procedures enable you and students to develop an established method for completing the same task time and time again. Good procedures support more on-task behaviors, reduce disruptions, and can improve the quality of the learning experience and the quality of the academic product or performance. If you don't have procedures in place that let students know what behaviors are expected and what will happen when they come up "short" of your expectations, students are left without a compass with which to get back on track. Yet secondary school teachers often avoid putting procedures in place. Why?

First, we engage in "teaching is *telling*," so we don't actually take the time to model and teach and practice specific procedures we want students to use. We might mention a procedure once and then assume everyone knows what to do. Or we might reject teaching a procedure outright on the grounds that students should have learned it in 4th grade. But if we don't teach it, we can't hold students accountable for learning it.

Second, we rarely insist that the group practices a procedure until everyone gets it right. It's not good enough for half the kids to be on the same page while the other half haven't yet picked up the book! The whole class needs to engage in disciplined practice of procedures or you're back to the exhausting proposition of implementing thirty individual learning plans during every class period, every day.

Finally, we rarely assess students' use of procedures. Informal assessment involves observing students doing the procedure, providing feedback as they practice a procedure, and stopping to reteach procedures when they're not followed. Formal assessment can include evaluating students' proficiency at following procedures as part of their participation grade. Many new small schools include a "habits of work" section on their report cards for just this reason.

So why is it so hard to do what it takes to implement procedures effectively? The easy answer is that teachers don't want to take the time to ensure that all students have learned a procedure and use it every time it's expected. There may, however, be a bigger disincentive at work here: adolescents absolutely hate this stuff. They hate to practice; they hate thinking they're being treated like babies; they hate the very idea of uniformity and repetition if the suggestion comes from an adult and not from them. You've got to decide whether you're willing to weather the storm of moans and groans to get the results you want.

Be clear about the reasons for procedures and be consistent in enforcing them

Here are a few tips that can help you stand your ground and help students tolerate your insistence on getting it right.

- Students need to discuss sensible reasons for the procedure. What are the benefits for you, the group, and individual students? Ask students to discuss the impact on individuals, the group, and you if a procedure for _____ isn't in place. Spell out the classroom cost if everyone doesn't learn it and do it.

- Acknowledge that taking the time to learn and practice procedures is a pain. Reassure kids that no one will die and that the time it takes to learn is up to them. You might also say, "If we don't get the group stuff down, we can't get to the fun stuff, and I won't be able to give individual students personal attention and support."

- Sometimes it's helpful to link classroom procedures to workplace procedures. Ask students who work to name some of the repetitive tasks they had to learn on the job during their first few weeks of employment. You might also ask students to name the conflicts that arise when procedures aren't followed on the job.

- Use examples from the U.S. military, professional sports teams, or performance groups. These are all stellar models of training and instruction because of the emphasis on teamwork, repetition, practice, and group accountability.

- Create posters that provide visual reminders of important procedures.

- Do a walk-through of the same procedure at least twice during the same period.

- Do at least one more walk-through again in the same week.

- Give a quiz on basic procedures, create a review sheet that teams or home groups complete, or turn your procedure review into a team game.

- Give students a window of time by which you expect everyone to get it and do it without fussing.

- As you introduce new procedures, add them to your procedure checklist and continue to assess how the group is performing various procedures.

Procedure Checklist Class_____				How are we doing?		
Procedure	We're still practicing	Some people have it.	Most people have it.	Everyone's got it.	The group took a backslide.	The group's back on track.

- Finally, you have to be ready to implement accountable consequences when students still don't have the procedure down after the window for proficiency has closed. You will need to develop a script that communicates, "I mean it about the whole group getting it right." What you do depends on the number of students not following through.

If a significant group of kids aren't following through	You've got to STOP, use class time to practice, and charge the group for time and aggravation: no game or project time on Fridays, less in-class homework time, no bonus or choice questions on quizzes and tests, etc.
	You may also want to use incentives when everyone gets it right: immediate positive feedback, a snack, goofy prizes (pull two or three students' names), more in-class homework time, more bonus or choice questions, more time to pursue independent or group projects of students' choice, etc.
If fewer than five kids aren't following through	Kids need to know they owe you a procedure workout—they have to come in at lunch or during your conference hour for reteaching and practice. This gets really boring really fast.
	After a procedure workout, give students daily feedback on how they're doing.
	For some high-performing, generally cooperative kids who devalue this stuff and think it's petty, an immediate call to a parent will let them know it's not.
If an individual student engages in chronic procedural infractions, it's never about the procedure! It's about something else.	When kids commit endless procedural infractions, something else is going on besides the refusal to follow through. Your options might include personal conferencing with the student; a behavior plan; a meeting with your instructional team; a parent conference with you, the student, and perhaps a dean; and/or other interventions with guidance and student support staff.

Model, teach, practice, and assess the procedures you expect

Here are 35 sample procedures to model, teach, practice, and assess. The procedures are numbered so it's easy to refer to them as you prioritize the ones that matter the most to you. They are divided into four types:

1. Transition Procedures

2. Classroom Environment Procedures

3. Learning Procedures

4. Student Work Procedures

Consider inviting students to help you develop classroom procedures. Students are usually pretty quick to suggest the easiest way to do something in the least amount of time with the least amount of hassle.

Transition Procedures

1. **Entering the classroom**: Here's a sample list of guidelines to encourage students to enter the room in a quiet and orderly manner.

> # NOTICE TO ALL WHO ENTER:
> # This classroom is a learning environment and a public place....
>
> ⊘ **not your living room**
>   (what you do and say there is between you and your family),
>
> ⊘ **not the cafeteria**
>   (hanging out is not your reason for being here),
>
> ⊘ **not the bathroom**
>   (this is not the place for personal hygiene care from nails to hair),
>
> ⊘ **not the Fight Club** (no public brawling, cursing, or yelling),
>
> ⊘ **not PE or the playing field** (no contact sports),
>
> ⊘ **and this is not a party place**
>   (please keep your hands and the rest of you to yourself).
>
> # THANK YOU.

2. **Arrival after the late bell**: It's downright rude and disrespectful for students to assume that they can mosey into a classroom whenever they choose. If your school doesn't have an effective, enforceable policy about late arrival to class, you'll have to create your own. Some teachers use this system: When students are late, they must sign in on the tardy list that is posted right by the door. Every minute late equals 10 minutes of time owed. If students don't sign in or fill in the accurate arrival time, it's an automatic 5 minutes late and 50 minutes of time owed during lunch or your designated conference hours before or after school. After the third late arrival, students owe you 30 minutes. If late arrivals are chronic, contact a parent, make a written referral, and arrange for a conference with you, the student, the dean, and a parent. Some teachers tie lateness to a participation grade or the habits-of-learning section of student progress reports. Another way to tackle tardies is to provide incentives when everyone is on time and ready to go: bonus or choice questions on quizzes and exams; a group snack as a thank-you when everyone's on time for the whole week; competition among your classes for the longest perfect attendance record and/or no tardy record during a quarter or semester; wagers in which you make a goofy bet about what you will do if everyone is on time for x consecutive days.

3. **Beginning class, giving directions, or transitioning to whole group instruction**: Use the same physical, verbal, or audio cue every day. For example, stand in the same place every day; say the same thing every time; raise your hand as a cue for all students to freeze, focus, and raise their hands; or ring a chime.

4. **Ending class**: Use the same sign-off, sound, or closing statement every day, and emphasize that until students hear it, class isn't over.

Until you hear

"Thanks for being here,"

class isn't over.

5. **Exiting class at the end of the class period**: If you have large groups, you might want to alternate groups that leave first, second, third, etc.

BEFORE YOU EXIT

✔ Chairs under desks

✔ No trash on floor

✔ Materials put away

6. **Student Passes**: Explain when students may use a pass and when they can't. Some teachers attach a pass to a large object (like a plastic inflatable dinosaur, mummy, or crayon) that students aren't necessarily thrilled to carry around with them. Other teachers give each student a set of passes that they choose when to use during each quarter or trimester. In the latter case, to ensure that students don't trade or hoard passes, use a different color of paper each quarter for printing out student passes. Give students uncut pass sheets, have them write their names and the period or block on each pass, review for

accuracy, and hand them back. Then you can cut the sheets into cards and distribute a set to each student. (See the pass card samples that follow.)

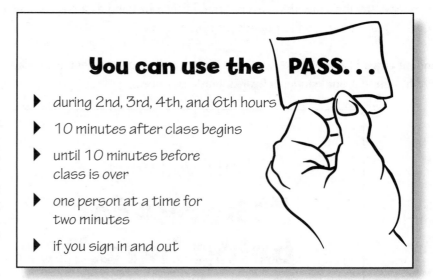

You can use the PASS. . .

▶ during 2nd, 3rd, 4th, and 6th hours

▶ 10 minutes after class begins

▶ until 10 minutes before class is over

▶ one person at a time for two minutes

▶ if you sign in and out

Bathroom Pass
Ms. Susan Smith, Room 207

Name _____

Period or Block _____

Date _____   Time _____

Bathroom Pass
Ms. Susan Smith, Room 207

Name _____

Period or Block _____

Date _____   Time _____

Media Center Pass
Ms. Susan Smith, Room 207

Name _____

Period or Block _____

Date _____   Time _____

Media Center Pass
Ms. Susan Smith, Room 207

Name _____

Period or Block _____

Date _____   Time _____

Guidance/Career/College
Ms. Susan Smith, Room 207

Name _____

Period or Block _____

Date _____   Time _____

Guidance/Career/College
Ms. Susan Smith, Room 207

Name _____

Period or Block _____

Date _____   Time _____

7. **When students must leave class for disciplinary reasons**: If your school doesn't have a schoolwide procedure, make up your own so everyone knows the drill. Whatever you do, don't send students out on their own and expect them to show up where they're supposed to be. Write an exit referral and (a) use the room phone to call a security staff member or administrator to escort the student to the designated place, (b) send another student with a note to find a security staff member or administrator to come and escort the student, or (c) see if your faculty "buddy" or another staff member will cover your class while you escort the student.

8. **Forming groups and circling up**: Practice dividing students into differently sized groups using a timer, and train students to form groups and rearrange furniture within 30 seconds to 2 minutes, depending on the task.

Classroom Environment Procedures

9. **Gum, food, or drinks in the classroom**: If your school strictly enforces rules about drinks, gum, and food, you need to show and tell students where it goes when they walk in the room and provide a trash can for stuff that shows up during class.

10. **Contraband items in the classroom (hats, hoodies, personal electronics, etc.)**: The easiest rule of thumb? If you don't see it and don't hear it, you don't know that students have it. If you see or hear it, they need to put it in the "save it for later" bin and pick it up when they leave class. If students have a chronic habit of bringing contraband items into the room, you can ask a security staff person to keep it in a safe place, and a parent or guardian will have to pick it up from the office at the end of the week. Have a stock of heavy envelopes on hand to tag and seal items.

11. **Moving furniture to accommodate special activities**: Assign certain students to take responsibility for moving furniture and equipment, or rotate the role over time.

12. **Cleaning up and putting away materials**: Students have to know the level of order and cleanliness you expect to see at the end of a class period, and you have to be consistent about enforcing your expectations. If your procedure requires that nothing is out of place and nothing is on the floor before students leave, you will need to set aside time before the bell rings to clean up. You may want to assign different students to take turns as classroom stewards during the year. Use two students at a time who will signal you with a thumbs-up when the room is good to go.

13. **Class-keeping and stewardship tasks**: Many teachers expect all students to make positive contributions to the learning community and assign or rotate students to take responsibility for various class-keeping and stewardship tasks. Think about designating a student, in advance, to be your TA (teaching assistant) for the day, assisting you with tasks like taking attendance; reading the agenda; making announcements; helping pass out papers and materials; reading a passage, brief reflection, or quotation at the beginning of class; and so on.

If your students work in home groups on a regular basis, identify a home chair for each group every week who is responsible for picking up and returning supplies and materials for all groups. Make materials distribution easy by creating a bin for each group that contains everyday supplies like tape, markers, notecards, sticky notes, etc.

Another way to support classroom stewardship is by creating a set of community contribution cards that students receive every quarter or trimester. Different tasks have different point values, and students can apply their points toward the participation portion of their progress report grade or use their points for participation in a weekly Friday lottery.

Community Contribution Chart

GOAL: Everyone contributes to the classroom community

Week _____

Weekly Tasks	Names of Students
TA (Teaching Assistant) for the Day	M _____ T _____ W _____ TH _____ F _____
Home Group Chairs for the Week	
Monday Reading or Gathering	
Plant Care	
Gofer for the Week	
Photographer/Documenter	
Cleanup Supervisor	
Lab or Project Prep	
Chart-maker	
Friday Closing	

Community Contribution Cards

TA (teaching assistant) for the day 25 pts. Name _____ Date _____	**Home group chair** 10 pts. Name _____ Date _____
Classroom cleanup 50 pts. Name _____ Date _____	**Bulletin boards** 25 pts. Name _____ Date _____
Equipment care for a week 25 pts. Name _____ Date _____	**Plant care for a week** 25 pts. Name _____ Date _____
Gofer for the week 25 pts. Name _____ Date _____	**Class meeting facilitation** 25 pts. Name _____ Date _____
Poster and chart-making 50 pts. Name _____ Date _____	**Friday closing** 25 pts. Name _____ Date _____
Lab or project preparation 25 pts. Name _____ Date _____	**Bring healthy snacks for class** 25 pts. Name _____ Date _____
Monday reading or gathering 25 pts. Name _____ Date _____	**Data input and newsprint transcription** 50 pts. Name _____ Date _____

14. **Borrowing books and other resources**: Whether students are using folders of articles about a specific topic or borrowing a book from your personal collection, it's worth the time to create a sign-out system. This can be as simple as a printed sheet on the wall that provides a place for students to write their names, identify the items, and write the date on which they borrowed them.

Learning Procedures

15. **Posting assignments**: Use a board or chart paper to post major assignments and deadlines. Use the same space for the same class every day.

16. **No textbooks or other essential tools and supplies**: This is a good issue for group problem solving. Brainstorm options and decide as a group on the best solution when students don't bring in required materials.

17. **No pens or pencils**: This is another opportunity for group problem solving. (See Scenario 5 in Chapter 2 for more ideas.)

18. **Key documents missing in action**: Whether the dog really did eat the project instructions or not, students need to know what to do when they've misplaced important papers. Many teachers keep a rolling file cart stocked with work folders that include copies of key materials from the previous two weeks, the current week, and the week coming up as well as a folder of essential documents that students refer to throughout the course. Assign each class a different color, and color-code your files. The key here is not to supply endless copies—make only five or six extras. When they're gone, students will need to rely on the kindness of their peers to borrow a document and make a copy of what they need.

19. **Distributing, collecting, or putting away papers, materials, and supplies**: Create a system for how books, instructions, readings, study guides, project materials, and supplies are to be distributed. Rotate who passes out and collects the stuff that students need to do their work. Draw names or come up with another creative way to ensure that every student has a turn.

20. **Activities that require silence**: Most adolescents hate quiet. If you expect students to work in silence most of the time, you risk never getting silence at all. The problem here is that kids can't really practice the discipline of sustained silence if any noise, however muffled, is always part of the mix. So serve up silent learning in small chunks, and build up to longer periods of sustained silence. Identify specific activities during which absolutely no noise is permitted, and discuss why silence is a reasonable and necessary expectation for these activities. (See Scenario 10 in Chapter 2 for more ideas.)

21. **Guidelines for being an attentive, respectful audience for peers, guests, and speakers**: Develop a set of guidelines that answer the question, "What specific behaviors demonstrate that the class is an attentive respectful audience?"

22. **Independent work time**: Spell out what students can and can't do, where they can and can't go, and when they can talk and when they can't during independent work time.

23. **Labs, shops, and studio classes**: Safety, distribution, and handling of materials, and cleanup procedures in labs, shops, and studios should be discussed and practiced *before* students actually engage in a comprehensive lab or project from beginning to end. During the first couple of weeks, it's also helpful to take the extra time to chunk hands-on experiences into small steps with the condition that no one can move to the next step until everyone has completed all procedures associated with the previous step.

Student Work Procedures

24. **Using assignment notebooks**: Support students' ongoing use of assignment notebooks (or alternative forms of recording assignments) by (a) conducting random spot checks, with everyone getting three checks per term; (b) allowing five minutes on Mondays for students to write in their assignments for the entire week; and (c) soliciting feedback by periodically asking students to think about several weeks' worth of assignments and respond to the following questions: What was hard? Easy? Really boring? What's the first or last assignment to get done? What work are they most proud of? What took less time or more time than they expected?

25. **When students have questions about current work**: Reassure students that you will try to address all questions during times reserved for questions. Be very clear about when students can ask questions and when they can't. For example, a brief question period works well after instructions are given, during a review, during independent work time, during small group time, or at the end of whole group instruction. You might also encourage students to post their questions on a "parking lot" chart so you can integrate students' questions during an appropriate time within a lesson. You also need to be clear about what kinds of questions you'll respond to and those that are a waste of time, redundant, or out of bounds. "Can I go to the bathroom?" or "Can I sharpen my pencil?" should never even be asked if you've already taught students what to do. "How long do we have to do this?" is redundant if you've already posted the number of minutes assigned for a specific task. "What's your favorite restaurant?" goes in the circular file unless you offer an open-mike Q and A at the end of class on Fridays if the group has earned Fun Friday points.

26. **When students are stuck or don't know what to do next**: Try the approach spelled out in the poster below. Be clear about how students can ask for help. Some teachers invite students to fold a piece of paper in half and create a HELP! sign that they place on their desks. This help card accomplishes four things: (1) it normalizes a request for help; (2) students don't have to flap their hands in the air to get help; (3) students don't have the option of whining their way to your attention ("Ms. Smith! I need you to come over here *now*!"); and (4) it's one more way to teach patience and perseverance. In situations that require individual help, coaching, and support, you can't be everywhere at once, and students need to learn how to wait their turn without seeking inappropriate attention and/ or distracting others.

If you're stuck, try...
"Three before me!"

1 Reread the instructions, problem, or document one more time.

2 Ask a nearby classmate or a home group buddy for help.

3 If you're still stuck, circle, mark, or sticky-note the place where you're stuck.

Then post your "Need Help" sign, and I'll check in with you.

---

27. **When students are unable to meet an important deadline**: Encourage students to speak with you privately before they're swamped. Invite them to come to you with an update of their work so far, what they still need to do, the problem with meeting the deadline, and a reasonable plan for when the work will be turned in.

28. **When students haven't completed work on time or with proficiency**: Whatever procedures you create about late, incomplete, or uncorrected work, try to navigate the tensions between completion and timeliness. If zeroes or half-credits kick in too soon, students who live in the land of late and undone have absolutely no incentive to correct, redo, or complete work to a proficiency level. A more effective early intervention system involves required attendance at homework hall; a workout session with you during lunch or after school; or Saturday school when students have accumulated a specific number of missing, incomplete, or uncorrected pieces of work.

29. **When *students* are absent from class**: Keep the protocol simple by providing a sign-in sheet for students who return from an absence and a standard place where students can retrieve the information and assignments they missed.

30. **When *you* are absent from class**: Make it easy for students to be productive, and make it possible for subs to have a decent day. Create a formulaic agenda that never varies for times when you're absent. This makes it easy for you to fill in specific details and provides a measure of predictability for students and the sub.

31. **Student record-keeping, reflection, and course portfolio organization**: Student achievement goes up when students are in charge of recording and reflecting on their own progress. Create templates that enable students to record their grades and reflect on their habits of learning on a weekly, quarterly, and semester basis. These self-assessment documents may include the following:

    - *Weekly Habits of Learning Log*: You choose, students choose, or you and students decide on four or five habits of learning that you will focus on for the entire quarter.

    - *Quarterly Learning Tasks and Progress Log*: This chart provides an easy way for students to document the work they do during the quarter and track their grades.

    - *Habits of Learning Daily Checklist*: Use this document when a few students or a whole class needs to assess their habits on a daily basis for a few weeks.

    Self-assessment charts can be placed in course folders in which students also keep journal entries, records of their goals, and a portfolio of their coursework. See sample charts on the following pages.

4

HANDOUT
Weekly Habits of Learning Log

Name _____ Course _____ Week # _____ / _____ Quarter From _____ to _____

Absent M = ___ T = ___ W = ___ Th = ___ F = ___   Tardies M = ___ T = ___ W = ___ Th = ___ F = ___

Rate Your Habits: (20% of your term grade)

4: I do it all the time without prompting and encourage others to do it;   **3:** I do it most of the time with little prompting;
2: I do it some of the time with some prompting;   **1:** I seldom do it and I always need prompting;   **0:** I refuse to do it

↗ Student's Assessment
→ Teacher's Assessment

Habits of Participation	Habits of Work	Habits of Discipline	Habits of Communication	Habits of Mind
1. I worked cooperatively with others and did my fair share of the work.	6. I followed directions and asked questions when I didn't understand.	11. I sustained my focus and paid attention even when work was boring or difficult.	16. I listened respectfully without interrupting or making sidebar talk.	21. I approached tasks with positive expectations and an open mind.
2. I put the goals of the group ahead of my own needs and issues and didn't let others distract me.	7. I brought all necessary materials to class and was ready and organized to learn.	12. I persisted in my effort until I "got it" and finished the task. I didn't give up.	17. I shared my thoughts and ideas in small and larger groups.	22. I accepted challenges, took academic risks, and pushed to excel.
3. I volunteered to take on leadership or more responsibility in a group.	8. I followed classroom guidelines, agreements, routines, and procedures.	13. I worked silently when it was required and worked independently without bothering others.	18. I explained, restated, questioned, and summarized what I heard, viewed, or read.	23. I took initiative to ask questions, ask for help, or probe for deeper understanding.
4. I was friendly, helpful, courteous, and good-humored with others.	9. I attempted each part of the question, task, assignment, or test.	14. I handled mistakes, setbacks, anger, and frustration constructively.	19. I used positive, nonaggressive language to express myself, ask for help, and get what I need.	24. I used evidence and data to inform and support my thinking.
5. I did something positive to make class a good place to learn.	10. I corrected, proofed, edited, revised, and completed all work.	15. I accepted help, feedback, correction, or consequences without putting up a fuss.	20. I accepted other viewpoints, and resolved differences or conflicts respectfully.	25. I expressed curiosity, enthusiasm, or personal interest in what I was learning.

What's one habit where you've made big improvements? _____ What's one habit where you need to make more of an effort? _____

What's something you learned, experienced, or accomplished that made you feel smart or proud this week? _____

What's left from this week that you need to complete, correct, revise, redo? _____

HANDOUT

Quarterly Learning Tasks and Progress Log

Name _____ Course _____ Quarter _____ From _____ to _____

Practice Work, Drafts, Editing, Revisions, Corrections (10% of your grade)	In-Class Labs, Discussion, Seminar, Demos, Presentations (10% of your grade)	Journals, Reflections, Notes, Evidence of Reading and Study (10% of your grade)	Habits of Learning (20% of your grade)	Major Written Tests, Projects, Products (50% of your grade)

HANDOUT

Habits of Learning Daily Checklist

Name _____ Course _____ Week # ___ / ___ Quarter _____ From _____ to _____

_____ Period

Habits of Learning ✔ = I did it 0 = I didn't do it.	M	T	W	Th	F
1. I arrived on time.					
2. I started the Do Now immediately and completed it.					
3. I brought all necessary materials to class; I was ready and organized to learn.					
4. I followed classroom guidelines and procedures.					
5. I worked silently when required and worked independently without bothering others.					
6. I participated in all assigned activities.					
7. I turned in all assigned work.					
8. I worked cooperatively with others and did my fair share of the work in a group.					
9. I used positive, nonaggressive language to express myself, ask for help, and get what I need.					
10. I did not allow other people's behavior to distract me from the task.					
11. I handled mistakes, setbacks, anger, and frustration constructively.					
12. I accepted help, feedback, correction, or consequences without putting up a fuss.					

32. **Grading student work**: Don't become a prisoner to grading every piece of paper that crosses your desk. If you do all of the grading, you're the one making all the judgments about quality and effort. Be clear about the role you expect students to play in assessing, reviewing, editing, and even grading their own work. Be clear as well about the different levels of scrutiny you will use to examine and assess student work.

Students should expect spot checks so you can see if they're on the right track. When students turn in work that provides evidence of practice, that's exactly what you're looking for. You're not going to spend precious hours reading every line and every word. The same is true when students are submitting draft outlines, work in progress, or notes and graphic representations of what they are reading and researching—you're looking for the quality of students' thinking, their use of specific skills or evidence of core understandings.

Save grading that requires your rigorous attention to detail for final tests and products. For your own sanity, schedule regular times during the term when you collect journals, notebooks, lab books, and so on, and stagger your collection and return dates for different classes. Give yourself a window of time for returning student work that is reasonable and timely. Keep your promises.

33. **In-class self-grading**: Have a special set of correction pencils (a bright color like lime, fuchsia, or turquoise) so it's very easy to spot-check and review students' corrections. After you do a couple of self-graded exercises and you notice that some students are not doing complete or accurate corrections, make time for a grading clinic while the remaining students are involved in independent work.

34. **Revisions and test corrections:** Make your expectations about revisions and test corrections explicit from day one. Here's one way to drive home the point that "you're not done until you finish the job." Let students know that permanent grades aren't recorded until and unless revisions, corrections, and complete work are turned in. This is a battle well worth picking.

REMEMBER...

You don't earn a grade until you have corrected, completed, or edited your work.

35. **Completing work with time to spare**: Invite the class to brainstorm four or five choices for what students can do when they finish timed work before others. Solicit interesting reading material from students, families, and friends to keep on hand. Offer two or three ongoing "sponge" or independent learning activities that students can be working on throughout the term.

If you have finished your work, you can...

▶ Read a book or magazine

▶ Work on homework

▶ Work on your independent project

▶ Write in your journal

▶ Close your eyes and daydream

CREATE GROUP LEARNING PROTOCOLS

Life Skill Connections (See pages 141–144)

23. Analyze the sources and dimensions of conflict, and utilize different styles to manage conflict.

24. Use win-win problem solving to resolve conflicts that meet the important goals and interests of the people involved.

27. Cooperate, share, and work toward high performance within a group to achieve group goals.

28. Respect everyone's right to learn, to speak, and to be heard.

29. Encourage and appreciate the contributions of others.

30. Engage in conscious acts of respect, caring, helpfulness, kindness, courtesy, and consideration.

33. Exercise effective leadership skills within a group.

34. "Read" the dynamics in a group; assess group skills accurately; identify problems; generate, evaluate, and implement informed solutions that meet the needs of the group.

35. Use a variety of strategies to make decisions democratically.

Group learning protocols are more complex than group procedures. Procedures are about completing a finite task in quick order the same way every time. Classroom norms are not in place unless and until every student uses procedures regularly and efficiently.

Group learning protocols describe a multistep process that facilitates effective learning in small and large groups. The content may vary, the amount of time set aside for the protocol may vary, but the process for a specific protocol stays the same. Cooperative learning protocols and Socratic seminar protocols are useful examples of group protocols (in contrast to, for example, text protocols, in which individual students might use a step-by-step process to engage with the text while they're reading). Group learning protocols require much more practice and skill than procedures, and students' capacities to become proficient will vary widely in any classroom.

Use group learning protocols to build intellectual, metacognitive, social and emotional competencies

Group learning protocols create power-packed learning experiences because students learn on multiple levels at the same time. Students utilize:

- their intellects to learn a skill, increase their knowledge and understanding, develop a product, or demonstrate a proficiency;

- metacognitive skills to think out loud and assess and choose the best learning strategies to accomplish the task;

- social skills to communicate and participate effectively in a group; and

- emotional competencies to monitor their behavior, manage their emotions, and use their emotions to fuel positive motivation and high performance.

Getting the most out of a good group learning protocol requires repeated practice, your coaching and feedback, and students' written and verbal self-assessment and group assessment about what they learned (content) and how they learned it (process).

Cooperative learning protocols

For every secondary school teacher who implements cooperative learning groups effectively, there are dozens who do it poorly. Think about what you already do to set up successful cooperative learning experiences. Then consider what you might do differently or more intentionally to boost the quality of student participation and student work. See *Making Learning REAL,* Chapter 13, Practice 3 for more ideas on cooperative group work.

Home group protocols

Home groups encourage students to take more responsibility for their own learning as they support and encourage their home group buddies. Home groups remove a lot of organization and management chores from your desk and place them in the hands of students. See *Making Learning REAL,* Chapter 15, Practice 5 for suggestions about how to form home groups and how to use them for learning, organizational, and management tasks.

Group talk protocols

Making Learning REAL includes over 25 protocols for structuring whole group and small group discussions and dialogues in ways that strengthen listening and speaking skills, increase student voice, and maximize what Lauren Resnick calls "accountable talk" (talk that deepens under-standing and is informed by evidence and prior knowledge). Choose three or four protocols that you teach, practice, and assess throughout the first several months of school. Don't introduce new group talk protocols until most students have mastered the ones you've already taught. (See *Making Learning REAL,* Chapter 15, Practice 5 for examples of group talk protocols.)

Small group and whole group read-alouds

Discuss when and why it makes sense to do small and large group read-alouds, and identify what makes reading aloud feel productive and comfortable as opposed to boring or embarrassing. If you expect all students to read aloud at some point in the course, reassure them that they can let you know when they're ready to read aloud. If you have a few students who are truly panicked about reading in front of others, create alternative read-aloud opportunities that are more private.

Use group problem-solving protocols to help students manage conflict and negotiate learning

Some group learning protocols have an additional classroom management function—they are used intentionally to make group decisions and solve problems, discuss hard-to-talk-about issues, and resolve conflicts and differences between you and the group or within the group.

Class meetings

Class meeting is a key protocol for teachers who invite student voice and choice into their classrooms. It's the ideal vehicle for discussing tough issues, engaging in group problem solving, and negotiating what students learn and how they learn it. (See *Making Learning REAL,* Chapter 15, Practice 5 for the nuts and bolts of facilitating effective class meetings.)

A, B, C, D, E problem solving

Take time to teach everyone A, B, C, D, E problem solving. This five-step process is used throughout the guide for individual, interpersonal, and group problem solving. To learn more about A, B, C, D, E problem solving, see *Making Learning REAL,* Chapter 15, Practice 5.

A, B, C, D, E Problem Solving

Assess the situation and ask, "What's the problem? How do you feel about the situation? What do you each need? What interests do we have in common?"

Brainstorm at least three possible solutions. Picture what the situation would look like if it were solved. Do this without criticizing or evaluating anything suggested.

Consider each **choice** carefully. How does each choice meet the needs and interests of everyone involved? What are the benefits of each choice? What are the negative constraints and limitations? Is the choice respectful, responsible, and reasonable? Cross out the choices that the group feels are the least effective.

Decide on the best choice and **do** it. Discuss the remaining choices and come to agreement on the best solution. Be mindful that the best choice might include a combination of several possible solutions.

Evaluate your decision after it has been implemented. What happened? Did it work? What evidence do you have that it worked effectively? Is there anything that would help the group implement the solution more effectively?

Three-minute problem solving

When two students are involved in an interpersonal conflict, offer students an option to resolve it in three minutes using this protocol:

1. What happened and why is it a problem?

2. What does each of you need to solve the problem or improve the situation?

3. What are two solutions you would both be willing to try to resolve the problem?

Check back with both of them in three minutes to hear their solutions. Ask them to choose the one that will work for both of them.

Mediation

Increasingly, we find teachers who want to use informal mediation when their own students are experiencing a protracted interpersonal conflict in the classroom. We also hear from teachers who want to teach a mediation protocol to their students. Below you'll find a brief snapshot of key negotiation and mediation skills as well as a mediation protocol Engaging Schools has used with middle and high school students throughout the United States. A couple of quick tips:

- Mediation is a voluntary process. You can't make anyone mediate.

- The mediator does not give advice or suggest solutions. The mediator functions as a neutral party who uses the protocol and excellent communication skills to ensure that both disputants get to express their feelings and needs, hear each other out, and take responsibility for reaching a mutually satisfactory solution.

Key Negotiation and Mediation Skills

- Listening for understanding / Nonverbal attending skills
- Restating / Paraphrasing
- Listening for and reflecting feelings / Defusing upset feelings
- Asking good questions to find out facts, feelings, perspectives, needs, and interests
- Identifying positions (what I want) and interests (the underlying needs, concerns, and interests behind the position—why do I want this?)
- Brainstorming and summarizing solutions
- Interrupting and reframing negative language
- Giving and receiving feedback
- Expressing wants and needs as "I" statements
- Giving encouragement

The 3 Rs of a Good Solution

Is it reasonable? (Is it fair? Are you both okay with this?)
Is it realistic? (When, where, how will you do this?)
Is it responsible? (Is it safe, legal, moral?)

The Mediation Protocol (S-T-A-R-T)

Set Up

1. Welcome students to the mediation.

2. Ask, "Are each of you here to work on the problem?"

3. Review ground rules as needed: (a) Treat each other with respect. (b) No name-calling. (c) Be as honest as you can. (d) Listen without interrupting each other. (e) Mediation is confidential, so what you say here stays here.

Tell Your Story

4. Ask student 1, "What happened?" **Restate.** Ask, "How do you feel and why?" Ask clarifying questions that show you're listening and draw out specifics. **Restate.**

5. Ask student 2, "What happened?" **Restate.** Ask, "How do you feel and why?" Ask clarifying questions that show you're listening and draw out specifics. **Restate.**

6. Ask each student to **Restate** how the other person feels and why

7. Ask both students, "Is there anything else you want to say?" Then **Summarize** the **WHOLE PROBLEM**, including key facts and feelings.

Assess Needs

8. Ask student 1, "What do you need to solve the problem or make things better?" **Restate.**

9. Ask student 2, "What do you need to solve the problem or make things better?" **Restate.**

10. Is there anything else you want to say or ask each other? **Summarize** what both people need.

Review Solutions and Choose the Best One

11. What are two or three solutions that will work for both of you? (Who does what, when, how, and where.) **If they get stuck, ask,** "Any other ideas? What would you tell someone else to do who had a similar problem? How would this solution work? Can you think of something else you could do? Can you say more about your idea?"

12. Choose the best solution and **summarize** what each person will do. Ask, "Is the problem solved?"

Think and Thank

13. Ask, "What can you each do differently next time if this happens again?" **Restate.**

14. If it's appropriate, remind students to let their friends know that the problem has been solved so that rumors won't spread.

15. Congratulate students on solving the problem successfully.

REFERENCES:

Desretta, M.A., and ESR (2005) *The Courage to be Yourself: True Stories by Teens About Cliques, Conflicts, and Overcoming Peer Pressure.* Minneapolis, MN: Free Spirit Publishing.

Evertson, C. M., and Weinstein, C. S., Editors. (2006) *Handbook of classroom management: Reseach, practice and contemporary issues.* Philadelphia: Lawrence Erlbaum Associates.

Polaco, P. (1998) *Thank You Mr. Falker.* New York: Philomel Books.

CHAPTER 5

Step 3: Support Individuals and the Group

Your efforts to help students develop and strengthen life skills will make it easier for them to accept responsibility for their actions and learn from their mistakes. Your personal connections and personalized support of each student will make it easier to handle tough situations or tough conversations when they arise. Your efforts to notice, recognize, celebrate, and reward positive behavior will encourage students to keep doing the right thing. Finally, when students feel connected to you and the group feels connected to each other, learning becomes fun and contagious. This is why we do what we do.

Positive behavior and a positive group culture don't sustain themselves without a big dose of what Linda Albert refers to as the five As: Acceptance, Attention, Appreciation, Affirmation, and Affection (Albert 1996). Think about routines and rituals you can do every week that help you personalize student support and maintain a positive, high-performing community of learners.

SUPPORT STUDENTS' SOCIAL AND EMOTIONAL DEVELOPMENT

Model, teach, practice, and assess life skills

Identify specific life skills that you want to introduce and practice during the first month. Focus on one or two at a time so that students can experience saturated practice and you can provide multiple opportunities for feedback. Every quarter, you might encourage students to identify one or two life skills that they want to develop and strengthen.

The Life Skills Checklist that follows outlines these competencies in three clusters:

1. Self-awareness, self-expression, and self-management (personal efficacy)

2. Interpersonal communication and problems (interpersonal efficacy)

3. Cooperation, group participation, and leadership (group efficacy)

The checklist provides a quick summary of skills and can be used to prioritize skills that you want to emphasize in your classroom. The checklist can also serve as a self-assessment tool for students to identify:

- Skills they use competently and routinely without prompting

- Skills they want to improve and use more often

- Skills they are not using currently that they want to learn and practice

LIFE SKILLS CHECKLIST

Life skills are the competencies that help you navigate and negotiate your way in the world.

- You need them to be successful students

- You need them to be responsible citizens

- You need them to be good life partners

- You need them to have fun with other people

- You need them to get a job and keep a job

- You need them to be a friend and keep a friend

- You need them to be good parents

- You need them when life deals you a bad hand

Assessing Life Skills

Try using a 0–4 scale for assessing life skills competencies.

(4)   I do it competently on a regular basis without prompting and encourage and support others to do it.

(3)   I do it competently most of the time with a little prompting.

(2)   I do it competently some of the time. I still need a lot of prompting and feedback.

(1)   This is still a growing edge for me. I hardly ever do it. I always need prompting and I need a lot more practice and feedback.

(0)   I won't do it and/or I don't know how to do it.

Cluster #1: Self-Awareness, Self-Management, Self-Expression (Personal Efficacy)

1. Recognize and name your own feelings.

2. Express feelings appropriately and assess the intensity of your feelings accurately (on a MAD scale of 1 to 10, I feel...).

3. Understand the cause of your feelings and the connection between your feelings and your behavior.

4. Manage your anger and upset feelings (know your cues, triggers, and reducers).

5. Know what you do that bothers others and accept responsibility when you mess up.

6. Reflect on your behavior; be able to learn from, self-correct, redirect, and change it when you need to.

7. Make responsible choices for yourself by analyzing situations accurately and predicting consequences of different behaviors.

8. Deal with stress and frustration effectively.

9. Exercise self-discipline and impulse control.

10. Say "NO," and follow through on your decisions not to engage in unwanted, unsafe, unethical, or unlawful behavior.

11. Seek help when you need it.

12. Focus and pay attention.

13. Set large and small goals and make plans.

14. Prioritize and "chunk" tasks, predict task completion time, and manage time effectively.

15. Activate hope, optimism, and positive motivation.

16. Work for high personal performance and cultivate your strengths and positive qualities.

17. Assess your skills, competencies, effort, and quality of work accurately.

5

Cluster #2: Communication and Problem Solving (Interpersonal Efficacy)

18. Exercise assertiveness; communicate your thoughts, feelings, and needs effectively to others.

19. Listen actively to demonstrate to others that they have been understood.

20. Give and receive feedback and encouragement.

21. "Read" and name others' emotions and nonverbal cues.

22. Empathize; understand and accept another person's feelings, perspectives, point of view.

23. Analyze the sources and dimensions of conflict and use different styles to manage conflict.

24. Use win-win problem solving to resolve conflicts that meet the important goals and interests of the people involved.

25. Develop, manage, and maintain healthy peer relationships.

26. Develop, manage, and maintain healthy relationships with adults.

Cluster #3: Cooperation, Group Participation, and Leadership Skills (Group Efficacy)

27. Cooperate, share, and work toward high performance within a group to achieve group goals.

28. Respect everyone's right to learn, to speak, and to be heard.

29. Encourage and appreciate the contribution of others.

30. Engage in conscious acts of respect, caring, helpfulness, kindness, courtesy, and consideration.

31. Recognize and appreciate similarities and differences in others.

32. Counter prejudice, harassment, privilege, and exclusion by becoming a good ally and acting on your ethical convictions.

33. Exercise effective leadership skills within a group.

34. "Read" dynamics in a group; assess group skills accurately; identify problems; generate, evaluate, and implement informed solutions that meet the needs of the group.

35. Use a variety of strategies to make decisions democratically.

Learning, Practicing, and Assessing Skills and Competencies

Learning and mastering any academic or behavioral skill requires multiple "hits" (6 to 8) and a sequence of steps. Here's what students need:

1. Give me a reason to learn this. (When we're not very clear about why a skill is important, we're less likely to engage students in the rest of the steps necessary for habitual and competent use of effective life skills.)

2. Show me how to do it; model it for me.

3. Let me practice it multiple times in multiple contexts.

4. Assess how I'm doing and give me feedback and coaching.

5. Let me practice some more so I can get really good at this and assess how I'm doing on my own.

6. Recognize and notice when I'm doing it regularly and skillfully.

7. Give me opportunities to demonstrate my competency.

8. Let me lead by modeling and encouraging others to use this skill.

Assessing Social Skill Proficiencies and Emotional Competencies:

④ I do it competently on a regular basis without prompting and encourage and support others to do it.

③ I do it competently most of the time with a little prompting.

② I do it competently some of the time. I still need a lot of prompting and feedback.

① This is still a growing edge for me. I hardly ever do it. I always need prompting and I need a lot more practice and feedback.

⓪ I won't do it and/or I don't know how to do it.

Identify the life skills that you want to model, teach, practice, and assess intentionally at the beginning of the school year:

Week 1 _____

Week 2 _____

Week 3 _____

Week 4 _____

Week 5 _____

Week 6 _____

John Schindler (2005) suggests the development of rubrics for assessing specific life skills competencies and other aspects of personal growth and development. Developing very clear targets for exemplary behavior does three things:

1. You can legitimately measure students' improvement in life skills competencies.

2. You're going to be more intentional about looking for what students are doing right and more likely to support students' efforts to improve their behavior.

3. Students experience the satisfaction of meeting real competencies. Personal mastery and efficacy are basic adolescent needs.

Here are three examples:

	Cooperation	Attitude/Motivation	Effort
Level 4	Cooperates consistently with the other group members; shares ideas and materials; takes turns talking and doing; does fair share of the work; takes initiative to ensure a quality product or performance; listens to others and acknowledges their thoughts and feelings; performs various roles in the group; encourages others to cooperate; monitors behavior of the group.	Approaches the task with a consistently positive expectation of success; exhibits perseverance and initiative; takes setbacks and challenges in stride; handles frustration effectively; seeks help when needed; says positive things about classmates and themselves; looks for ways to solve problems before blaming or quitting.	Consistently works for high personal performance; cultivates strengths and positive qualities; works smarter, not harder; sustains focus throughout class regardless of situation, activity, or the group's behavior; completes all tasks at a high level of accuracy and efficiency.
Level 3	Cooperates with other group members; shares ideas and materials; usually takes turns talking and doing; performs some roles effectively.	Approaches most tasks with positive expectation of success; exhibits perseverance and initiative occasionally; sometimes seeks help when needed; says positive things about themselves.	Makes best effort to work for high performance consistently; works hard most of the time; sustains focus throughout the class; completes most tasks at a proficient level of accuracy and quality.
Level 2	Cooperates most of the time and takes turns most of the time.	Approaches some tasks with positive expectation of success; exhibits perseverance and initiative occasionally; seeks help when needed occasionally.	Makes best effort some of the time; works hard some of the time; sustains focus for short periods of time; completes some tasks.
Level 1	Cooperates some of the time; sometimes distracts group from goal; disengaged from group some of the time.	Approaches tasks with positive expectation of success occasionally; occasional use of negative language to describe themselves, others, the class, and the work.	Makes honest effort and works hard once in a while; sustains focus for only moments at a time and completes few tasks.
Level 0	Refuses to cooperate; dominates, distracts, and blocks group from achieving goals.	Few or no positive expectations of success; chronic use of negative language to describe themselves, others, the class, or the work.	Refusal to work and put forth effort; unable to sustain focus to complete any tasks.

TEACH STUDENTS HOW TO MANAGE THEIR EMOTIONS

Life Skill Connections (See pages 141–144)

1. Recognize and name your own feelings.

2. Express feelings appropriately and assess the intensity of your feelings accurately ("On an anger scale of 1 to 10, I feel like a...").

3. Understand the cause of your feelings and the connection between your feelings and your behavior.

4. Manage your anger and upset feelings (know your cues, triggers, and reducers).

5. Know what you do that bothers others and accept responsibility when you mess up.

6. Reflect on your behavior; be able to learn from it, self-correct, redirect, and change when you need to.

7. Make responsible choices for yourself by analyzing situations accurately and predicting consequences of different behaviors.

8. Deal with stress and frustration effectively.

There are more feelings than mad, bored, or fine. Having an accurate vocabulary for describing feelings is a crucial step in dealing with them. When we're in a good place, we feel (name our feelings accurately), then think (reflect on what we're feeling, why we're feeling this way, and what we need or want to do), and finally act (respond in a way that meets our needs appropriately). This three-step sequence is an illustration of self-regulating behavior (FEEL-THINK-ACT). We can influence our emotions more than we might think. Feelings don't *make* us perform specific actions.

However, without the right words or the ability to express emotions, many people simply act without naming any feelings at all or reflecting on what to do. The result is impulsive behavior that can lead to big trouble (FEEL-ACT-THINK much later).

Feelings have different intensities and change over time. We don't have to act as if each circumstance is extreme and permanent. One important goal is to make appropriate matches between what we feel and what we do. (Compare how you might act when you feel somewhat irritated versus how you might act when you feel really furious.) All feelings are okay, although how a person responds will have positive or negative consequences for them and other people.

Another strategy for managing emotions is to imagine what it will take to shift from one feeling to another. In other words, a student could say to herself, "Right now, I'm feeling _____. I want to feel _____. To feel _____, I can _____." The ability to do this gives students powerful feelings of agency and control. With practice, this can become a strategy of choice.

Some feelings can conflict with other feelings, complicating their impact. It can be hard to navigate between competing emotions, such as feeling both attracted to and afraid of an experience, person, or task. With some self-awareness and self-management, people can make choices even when experiencing strong or conflicting emotions.

The handout "Feelings, Moods, and Attitudes" on page 149 is not strictly a list of emotions. Instead it includes a wider range of expressions that adolescents might use or find useful. Encourage students to add to the list. For students whose emotional vocabulary is composed mainly of curse words, particularly for anger, this can be a challenging and helpful exercise.

Then, review with students the seven steps for managing emotions, especially anger.

1. **Find the words** for your feelings and others' feelings. Go beyond using the words *mad* and *bored*. Don't settle for one word if you feel angry; there's probably another. Are you embarrassed and angry, sad and angry, hurt and angry? Learn the difference between thoughts and emotions. Learn words that describe the intensity of the emotion. Practice reading other people's emotions—but don't assume you know exactly what someone else is feeling.

2. **Know your anger cues**. How do you know that you're getting angry? What are the physical signs of anger? What happens to your body, your voice, your face, and your stance?

3. **Know your anger triggers and what happens when you get angry**. What behaviors are triggers for you? When you're feeling really angry, what *don't* you want someone to do or say? What response is likely to make you even more angry? Review the handout "When You Go Up Anger Mountain" to reflect on what happens when you get angry. When we're in a charged emotional state like anger, we tend to get hijacked and act without thinking. Until the anger is released, defused, or discharged, we're unable to shift to a thinking mode and transition to calmer, more relaxed state.

4. **Learn and practice reducers** that help you cool down, stay in charge, and release your feelings in a healthy way. When you're already angry, what can you do or say to yourself to feel calmer, more relaxed, and more in control of your emotions? What can someone else say or do that will help you?

5. **Take responsibility** for your behavior. Be aware of the things you do and say that other people might experience as anger triggers.

6. **Communicate**. Express your feelings so that others can hear what you have to say. Consider how you can say what you feel, what you need, or what's bothering you without attacking and accusing the other person. (See section on the differences between aggressive, passive, and assertive behavior on pages 151–154.)

7. **Reflect** on how you manage your emotions. Assess what's working and what's not. Congratulate yourself when you've handled a difficult situation effectively. Try out other strategies that might help you handle situations more constructively.

HANDOUT
Feelings, Moods, and Attitudes

accepted	depressed	grouchy	nervous	shocked
affectionate	desperate	guilty	obstinate	shut down
afraid	determined	happy	open	shy
agitated	disappointed	hateful	optimistic	silly
aggravated	disconcerted	heartbroken	overwhelmed	sorrowful
aggressive	discouraged	helpless	pained	spiteful
amazed	disgusted	hopeful	panicked	stubborn
ambivalent	disillusioned	horrified	paranoid	stuck
amused	disrespected	hostile	peaceful	sulky
angry	distracted	humiliated	peeved	supported
annoyed	down	hurt	perplexed	surprised
anxious	eager	hysterical	persecuted	suspicious
appreciative	ecstatic	impatient	pessimistic	sympathetic
argumentative	elated	independent	playful	tenacious
arrogant	embarrassed	indifferent	positive	tense
ashamed	empty	indignant	powerful	terrific
awestruck	energized	inferior	powerless	terrified
awkward	enraged	inspired	prepared	threatened
bad	enthusiastic	intimidated	proud	thrilled
belligerent	envious	irate	psyched	ticked off
bored	exasperated	irritated	puzzled	timid
brave	excited	jazzed	reflective	trusted
calm	excluded	jealous	refreshed	uncertain
cautious	fearful	jolly	regretful	uncomfortable
cheerful	fearless	joyful	rejected	uneasy
closed	focused	juiced	relieved	unsafe
comfortable	foolish	jumpy	remorseful	up
confident	frenzied	livid	repulsed	upset
confused	friendly	lonely	respected	vengeful
contemptuous	frightened	loved	righteous	victimized
content	frustrated	loving	sad	victorious
courageous	furious	mad	safe	vindictive
crabby	good	malicious	satisfied	warm
cranky	goofy	mellow	scared	wary
curious	grateful	mischievous	secure	weary
defeated	greedy	miserable	self-assured	weird
defensive	grief-stricken	mortified	self-conscious	wistful
delighted	grossed out	negative	self-pitying	worried

5

HANDOUT

When You Go Up Anger Mountain...

Your adrenaline keeps you climbing until you release your anger, lose control, or hurt others emotionally or physically.

TRIGGER

Your 8-second window

You have eight seconds before you start climbing! This is the time to step back, take a few deep breaths, count to 10, and then think about what you want to do.

You can't THINK when you're climbing anger mountain!

Know your CUES — — — ➔ How do I know that I'm getting angry? What happens in my body, to my voice, with my movements, or on my face?

Know your TRIGGERS — — — ➔ What sets me off? What makes me really mad? Frustrated? Upset?

Know your REDUCERS — — — ➔ What can I do that will help me cool down and regain control? What can others do to help me cool down and regain control?

Teach the conflict escalator

Life Skill Connections (See pages 141–144)

3. Understand the cause of your feelings and the connection between your feelings and your behavior.

Ensure that students know the language of conflict escalation presented on pages 81–83 in Chapter 3. This is a useful tool for discussing the step-by-step trajectory of specific conflicts and reflecting on what a student might have done or said to get off the escalator.

Teach the differences between aggressive, passive, and assertive behavior

Life Skill Connections (See pages 141–144)

18. Exercise assertiveness; communicate your thoughts, feelings, and needs effectively to others.

Students have the right to express their needs, interests, feelings, and opinions in class. And they also have the responsibility to do so in ways that don't hurt, insult, or disrespect others. Assertive speech enables people to take care of themselves *and* take care with other people. Students should learn that they can express themselves and stand up for themselves without being aggressive.

Sounds easy enough, but most students don't know the difference between aggressive and assertive speech and behavior. The handout on page 152 provides openers that help students use assertive language; the handout on page 153 helps clarify the differences between aggressive, passive, and assertive speech. Be mindful of any opportunities you have to model assertion, and offer explicit invitations for students to practice assertive speech.

5

HANDOUT

 **PASSIVE**

I ALLOW OTHERS TO TAKE ADVANTAGE OF ME BY CHOOSING NOT TO ACT OR NOT TO SAY WHAT I REALLY FEEL, NEED, WANT, OR THINK.

"Whatever…" "I don't care…"

"I guess so…" (silence, mumbling, or whining)

 **AGGRESSIVE**

I get what I need and want at the expense of others; I use rude, crude, mean, disrespectful, or abusive speech.

"That was so stupid." "You never ___"

"Why can't you _____" "You are such a _____" "Get out of my face!" "You @#%&*●❋!!"

Make the choice to be ASSERTIVE

▶ Name what you're thinking and feeling, what you need and want.
▶ Give others information that can help them understand your situation. Nobody can read your mind.
▶ Let others know when you're frustrated, angry, or upset so they don't have to guess your mood.
▶ Say what's bothering you and what you want to stop.
▶ Point out how someone's decision or action affects you.
▶ Say what you like and don't like.
▶ Ask for help when you need it.
▶ Make suggestions and state your preferences.
▶ Say "no" when you really need to.

HANDOUT
Find the Right Words to Be ASSERTIVE

From complaining, confusion, or helplessness to...

I need / I want / I'd like _____.

Help me understand _____.

I'd really like some help _____.

I'm feeling _____ about _____. Can we talk about this?

I'm confused. Can you tell me more about _____?

From blaming and attacking to...

I feel _____ when you _____ because _____.

It bothers me when _____. I'd like you to _____.

I don't like it when _____. I want you to _____.

I know you didn't mean any disrespect, but that's how it felt.

Please stop _____.

From speaking for or about others to...

I feel _____.

I see _____.

I think _____.

I noticed _____.

I wonder _____.

I imagine _____.

I'm not sure _____.

From denial and making excuses to...

Well, that didn't go well. What if we _____?

Okay, I messed up. I'd like to fix it.

From saying "yes" when you really mean "no" to...

That's not going to work for me. I need to take a pass this time.

I'm really not interested. You okay with that?

I need to say no for right now.

From just going along or saying nothing to...

I'd much rather _____ if that's okay with you.

For me, it would work better if _____.

Here's what I'd like to suggest...

From putting down someone else's idea to...

I see that differently.

It sounds like you think _____. I think _____.

I see your point and here's how I see the situation.

I guess we're agreeing to disagree on this one. Are we good?

HANDOUT

Aggressive, Passive, or Assertive: What's the Difference?

Aggressive	Passive	Assertive
I get what I want and need at the expense of others—by dominating or hurting others physically or emotionally.	I allow others to take advantage of me by choosing not to act and not expressing my feelings, needs, or thoughts.	I take care of myself by expressing my needs, thoughts, and feelings while showing respect and decency toward others.
Sounds like: You put down the other person, attack and accuse: "You're such a…"; "You always…"; "You never…" You blame, assume, stereotype; you're argumentative and interrupt a lot. Your voice is loud, dramatic, or hostile. Your language is often mean, negative, rude, abusive, or sarcastic.	**Sounds like:** You never really say what you feel, want, and need. "Whatever, it doesn't really matter to me"; "I guess so." You're silent or withhold information; you speak so softly others can't really hear you; you apologize a lot and blame others. You go along even if you really don't want to. You whine and wear people down.	**Sounds like:** You share your needs, requests, and opinions honestly and openly. "I need to …"; "I feel…when…because …" You listen attentively even if you disagree, and appreciate others' efforts to listen. You speak up. You take responsibility when you mess up. Your voice is even, calm, friendly. Your language is respectful, neutral, or positive.
Looks like: Getting in someone's face; eye-rolling; threatening, confrontational posture; invading someone's personal space; dramatic arm movements; pointing fingers.	**Looks like:** Shoulder shrugs; you look weighted down; you don't make eye contact; you look away, like you're trying to hide; you pout or frown; you look flustered.	**Looks like:** Relaxed; open expression and posture that invites conversation; matching how the other person is sitting or standing; side-by-side rather than eyeball-to-eyeball.
Payoffs: You get what you demand most of the time; you stay in control; others see you as powerful; you protect yourself.	**Payoffs:** You avoid confrontation or taking responsibility. You don't get blamed. Using the silent treatment, you can ruin someone's good time without being aggressive.	**Payoffs:** You keep your dignity and self-respect; you get your needs met more often; you maintain respect for others; you value others; you use your power positively.
Costs: Your behavior can be dangerous and destructive; you may alienate and use other people. People may not like you. You fear not being in control and then lose control when you don't get what you want. You put on a front for others and can isolate yourself.	**Costs:** You don't feel in control of your emotions very often; you get anxious, resentful, or angry a lot. Instead of expressing feelings, you seethe inside; you lose your self-respect; you give up being yourself. Other people walk over you. You don't have many real friends.	**Costs:** It takes time. You may experience more conflict, although you have more tools with which to handle it effectively. Even when you're sensitive to others' needs and feelings, they can still feel uncomfortable with your directness and reject what you're saying.

Provide scripts that encourage students to say and do the right thing

At some point you may encounter a whole class or a small group within a class who needs more explicit instruction, practice, and rehearsal to learn how to express themselves more appropriately. For many students, if they don't have the words, they are unable to try on the desired behavior. This is the time when "kid scripts" are a handy thing to have around. Pages 155–157 present some kid scripts that address typical problematic behaviors that get students in trouble. Kid scripts can be posted or made into cards that students can place in their notebooks, or that you can place on a student's desk as a reminder.

Check yourself before you...

▶ Make demands, argue, or "lawyer up."

▶ Walk away when an adult is talking to you.

▶ Refuse options after repeated requests.

▶ Refuse to follow through with consequences.

▶ Curse out or threaten an adult.

▶ Get in a fight or physical confrontation.

Make the choice to be FRIENDLY and POLITE

▶ Introduce yourself to people you don't know.

▶ Focus attention on the person speaking to you.

▶ Respond verbally when someone has acknowledged you.

▶ Work with different people.

▶ When you want it, need it, gotta have it—ask permission first, make a request, and say please.

▶ Show your appreciation for what others do.

▶ Ask if you can help.

▶ Be enthusiastic—it's catching!

5

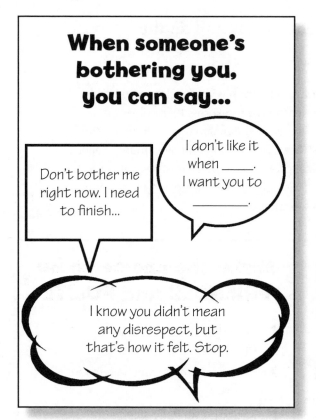

When you want to do something different, you can say...

I'd like to ask permission to _____. Is that okay?

He're what I'd rather do now. Is that possible?

This isn't working for me. Is it okay if I _____?

When you mess up, you can...

▶ Take responsiblity and say, "Here's what I did. I _____.

▶ Think about how your actions had a negative impact on others.

▶ Decide what you can do to make amends, correct the mistake, repair the harm, restore the good standing, or make it right.

▶ Decide what you can do differently next time.

When you get NO for an answer, get criticized, or reprimanded, you can...

▶ Accept the comment, say "okay," and let it go for now.

  • Think about what you might have done to trigger the remark. Is there anything you can do differently right now?

▶ If the comment feels really unfair or upsetting, keep calm, write me a note, or talk to me privately. Ask if we can discuss this...

  • later in class?
  • during lunch?
  • at _____.

When you're angry or upset, you can...

▶ Ask me privately for permission to "take five," get a pass, or get a drink.

▶ Close your eyes, touch your pulse, go to your "anchor" place, and take a few deep breaths.

▶ Write down what you're feeling, what you need, and what you can do to get it.

When you've finished your work, you can...

▶ Read a book or magazine.

▶ Do homework or work on your independent project.

▶ Daydream! Imagine your future!

▶ Relax, close your eyes. Check out for a few minutes.

5

PROVIDE PERSONALIZED SUPPORT AND RECOGNITION

An annoying reality of adolescence is that good behavior and a positive peer culture don't sustain themselves without a big dose of what Linda Albert refers to as the five As: ACCEPTANCE, ATTENTION, APPRECIATION, AFFIRMATION, and AFFECTION. If you were to set aside 15 minutes a week in each class to support and maintain the positive behaviors of individual students and the group, what would you choose to do? (Albert 1996)

Make personal connections with every student

The one thing you can do that will have the greatest positive impact on your relationships with students is finding a way to personally connect with each student every day. Yet when kids' needs are so different, it's difficult to ensure equitable doses of personal attention. One option? Develop a daily routine of one-minute check-ins with several students when students are working on the Do Now activity at the beginning of each class period. Keep your student list on a clipboard and challenge yourself to rotate through your student rosters every week. For more ideas, see *Making Learning REAL*, Chapters 11 and 16.

Provide immediate and meaningful feedback and encouragement

Life Skill Connections (See pages 141–144)

16.	Work for high personal performance and cultivate your strengths and positive qualities.
17.	Assess your skills, competencies, effort, and quality of work accurately.
20.	Give and receive feedback and encouragement.

Feedback is useless if it feels false or trivial. Academic and behavioral feedback to individual students or the group should focus on what you do or don't observe, see, and hear. Be intentional about giving concrete feedback when:

- Students are trying out new skills and behaviors.

- Students are working on or have completed a task that requires significant effort.

- Students take personal pride and satisfaction in something they've accomplished.

Always provide concrete feedback (whether it's written or verbal) as the prerequisite for correcting, editing, redoing, or completing a task or product to a proficiency level. Positive feedback is easy: identify specifically what's correct, on-target, accurate, exemplary, clear, coherent, or complete. Good corrective feedback is a bit more complicated because it must respond to both (1) the overall purpose of the task or assignment and (2) the details:

1. Indicate where students have gone off course, gotten lost, or missed the final destination altogether—whether it's a math or science problem, a written essay, an evidence-based argument, or a final product or presentation. Then provide specific questions and suggestions that can help the student get back on course.

2. Indicate specifically what's missing; what needs to be added, changed, replaced, or corrected; or what needs to be revised, redone, or completed.

Give encouraging feedback that describes what students have accomplished and link their accomplishment to the personal quality that they used to do it. Example: Your group showed real collaboration when you made sure everyone made a suggestion before you made your decision. (See page 160, Personal Assets and Qualities of Character). Below are suggestions for concrete reinforcement of positive behavior:

- Emphasize a specific life skill that you will observe and students will practice each week. Provide feedback on how the group and individual students are practicing the skill.

- When someone has had a bad day, write a note with words of encouragement and a reminder that they can start fresh tomorrow.

- Be particularly mindful of situations in which students have recovered and bounced back from personal setbacks. Encourage students to tell you what they have learned from these experiences.

- Notice when students do something out of character that reveals a different, more positive image of themselves.

- Write notes that show that you have noticed the effort students have made to practice desired behaviors and meet behavioral expectations in learning contracts.

For more about feedback and formative assessment for learning, see *Making Learning REAL*, Chapter 16.

5

HANDOUT
Personal Assets and Qualities of Character

Accurate / Accuracy
Adaptable / Adaptability
Ambitious / Ambition
Analytical / Analysis
Appreciative / Appreciation
Assertive / Assertion
Attentive / Attentiveness
Brave / Bravery
Careful / Carefulness
Caring / Care
Cautious / Caution
Collaborative / Collaboration
Committed / Commitment
Communicative / Communication
Compassionate / Compassion
Competent / Competency
Concerned / Concern
Confident / Confidence
Considerate / Consideration
Consistent / Consistency
Cooperative / Cooperation
Courageous / Courage
Creative / Creativity
Curious / Curiosity
Decisive / Decision maker
Dependable / Dependability
Detail-oriented
Determined / Determination
Effective / Efficacy
Efficient / Efficiency
Effort
Empathetic / Empathy
Encouraging / Encouragement
Energetic / Energy
Enthusiastic / Enthusiasm
Ethical / Ethics
Even-tempered

Fair / Fairness
Flexible / Flexibility
Focused / Focus
Forgiving / Forgiveness
Friendly / Friendship
Generous / Generosity
Gentle / Gentleness
Goal-oriented
Gritty / Grit
Hard-working
Helpful / Helpfulness
Honest / Honesty
Humorous / Humor
Idealistic / Idealism
Imaginative / Imagination
Inclusive / Inclusiveness
Independent / Independence
Industrious / Industriousness
Initiating / Initiative
Insightful / Insight
Intuitive
Kind / Kindness
Leader / Leadership
Logical / Logic
Loving
Loyal / Loyalty
Mature / Maturity
Observant
Open-minded / Openness
Optimistic / Optimism
Organized / Organization
Passion / Passionate
Patient / Patience
Perceptive / Perceptiveness
Persevering / Perseverance
Persistent / Persistence
Polite / Civility

Positive
Powerful / Power
Precise / Precision
Prepared / Preparation
Principled
Problem solver
Prudent / Prudence
Purposeful / Purpose
Reasonable
Reflective / Reflection
Reliable / Reliability
Resilient / Resiliency
Resourceful / Resourcefulness
Respectful / Respect
Responsible / Responsibility
Responsive / Responsiveness
Self-aware / Self-awareness
Self-control
Self-disciplined / Self-discipline
Self-motivated / Self-motivation
Self-regulating / Self-regulation
Sensitive / Sensitivity
Skeptical
Skillful
Spirited / Spirit
Steady / Steadiness
Strong
Studious
Supportive / Ally
Tactful / Tact
Thorough / Thoroughness
Thoughtful / Thoughtfulness
Tolerant / Tolerance
Trustworthy
Understanding
Warm / Warmth

Provide personalized support for students who are struggling

Life Skill Connections (See pages 141–144)

6. Reflect on your behavior; be able to learn from it, self-correct, redirect, and change when you need to.

7. Make responsible choices for yourself by analyzing situations accurately and predicting the consequences of different behaviors.

8. Deal with stress and frustration effectively.

11. Seek help when you need it.

13. Set large and small goals and make plans.

14. Prioritize and "chunk" tasks, predict task completion time, and manage time effectively.

15. Activate hope, optimism, and positive motivation.

16. Work for high personal performance and cultivate your strengths and positive qualities.

17. Assess your skills, competencies, effort, and quality of work accurately.

5

Practice 6: High Expectations and High Support in Chapter 16 of *Making Learning REAL* includes many suggestions and strategies for working with struggling students. In addition, try out these ideas:

- Create a set of quotes about people who have overcome great challenges and personal difficulties. Give a quote to a student when you want to acknowledge that she is having a rough time of it and share the fact that other people have overcome difficult circumstances and found meaning and success in their lives.

- Invite a student who needs a little boost of encouragement and support to eat lunch with you.

- Share your own experiences when you struggled to learn something.

- For students who have a particularly difficult time managing anger, controlling their impulses, or handling interpersonal conflict, invite them to write themselves a "congratulations" note when they handle a tough situation effectively.

- Read stories and vignettes about people who have turned their lives around, learned from painful mistakes, or overcome a major hurdle. Some favorites: *Thank You Mr. Falker* by Patricia Polacco (an inspiring story of the author's reading disabilities and negative school experience and Mr. Falker's commitment to help Ms. Polacco learn to read); *The Courage to Be Yourself* edited by Al Desetta (student authors share their stories about overcoming difficult circumstances); any of the *Chicken Soup for the Teenage Soul* books.

- Connect a struggling student with a former or current student who can share what she or he did to turn things around in this course.

- Set up one-minute daily check-ins before or after class with students who need to be on a short leash. These are the kids who need to know you are not going to stop noticing how they are doing. Before class begins, you might ask troubled or difficult students one or more of the following questions:

  ▶ What's one thing you're going to do today that will help you have a good day?

  ▶ What's one thing you'd like me to be able to say about your behavior at the end of class today?

  ▶ What's a goal to focus on that will help you stay on track?

  ▶ When other students bother you or try to get you off track, what will you do or say?

  ▶ If you get upset or frustrated during class, what can you do?

  ▶ What can you say to yourself if you get angry or upset in class?

After the class, you might ask them one or more of the following questions:

- What did you do today that made you proud of yourself?

- When were you most focused during class today?

- What's one thing you did today that helped you stay out of trouble?

- What's one thing you can do tonight that will help you prepare for tomorrow?

- What was tough or frustrating about class today? What might help make tomorrow go better?

Academic coaching, monitoring, tutoring, and remedial instruction during class time

If you intentionally balance whole group, small group, and independent learning activities throughout the week and spend more time observing students than they spend watching you, you'll be able to make time for individual and small group conferencing, coaching, and remedial instruction several days a week. Think about scheduling at least two or three 20- to 30-minute sessions a week that you can facilitate while other students are working independently or in small groups.

Academic intervention 1: When? _____ **How long?** _____

Students involved in the intervention _____

Other students will be _____

Description of the intervention _____

_____

_____

How will you know that the intervention is effective? _____

_____

_____

Academic intervention 2: When? _____ **How long?** _____

Students involved in the intervention _____

Other students will be _____

Description of the intervention _____

_____

_____

How will you know that the intervention is effective? _____

_____

_____

What's the right frequency for check-ins, monitoring, and feedback given students' wide range of learning profiles and levels of academic readiness?

Struggling students → EVERY STEP (Check in personally with individuals and small groups; keep monitoring, coaching, assessment, and feedback loops frequent and tight.)

Novice students → EVERY STEP (Incorporate more visual prompts; more student self-checks; and less frequent monitoring, feedback, and coaching from you.)

Proficient students → INTERMITTENT STEPS (Incorporate mostly visual prompts and student self-checks with much less monitoring and coaching from you. Encourage proficient students to make conference appointments to discuss their learning and advanced work.)

5

Create opportunities for students to link personal effort to their successes

Life Skill Connections (See pages 141–144)

16. Work for high personal performance and cultivate your strengths and positive qualities.

17. Assess your skills, competencies, effort, and quality of work accurately.

Many students don't know how to complete the equation *Ability + Effort = Achievement*. Pointing out how one's effort makes a difference in learning reminds students that achievement is not simply a result of fixed ability that you either have or you don't. (Smart people can always tell you exactly what they did to get a quality result.) Deconstructing the concept of effort is also a way to strengthen the metacognitive skill set that Mel Levine labels *instrumentation:* "planful" task and time management, prioritizing, and sequencing; patience and perseverance for incremental progress; and the ability to sustain goal-directed, progress-conscious efforts (Levine 2007).

Invite students to respond to this question: "Think about learning tasks where you have successfully achieved the goal or produced an "A"-quality product. Post the list of learning tasks and products. Then invite students to share one big thing that contributed to a successful result, and finally, identify specific strategies that provide evidence of effort. Here's a sample of what deconstructing effort looks like:

Deconstructing Effort

Task or Product	One Big Thing that contributed to your success	Specific Evidence that shows your effort
A unit test	Intensive study	• Highlighted important facts, concepts, and terms in my notes • Organized the important facts, concepts, and terms on notecards • Reread my study cards twice before I went to bed and twice in the morning
An argument or position paper	Proofread and edited before it was turned in	• Reviewed the directions and original essay question and circled key statements that helped to answer the question • Underlined specific details and evidence that helped make my argument • Circled what might be spelling and syntax errors • Asked a good writer (adult or student) to read it for errors
Reading a text that is particularly difficult	Used several reading strategies when I got stuck	• Wrote questions on post-its and placed them on the reading • Marked where I lost track so I could go back and reread • Reread difficult passages, captured the ideas on post-its, and placed them on the text • Looked for cue words that would help me understand the gist of the text
A science lab	Checked for accuracy and completeness	• Reread directions to ensure that I responded to every part of the lab • Recalculated all of the math equations • Reviewed the diagram to make sure that nothing was left out
Team project	Made a plan and timeline for completion	
Mock trial	Prepared for final argument	
Socratic seminar	Prepared questions and issues I wanted to discuss	
Speech	Rehearsed	

Carefully choose specific opportunities when students must provide evidence of effort *before* they do the task, test, or activity at hand. The first time, students may not really believe you mean it when you say, "I'll expect you to show me the evidence." Stand your ground, and don't allow students who can't provide evidence of effort to participate in the activity or take the test when everyone else does. However, those students are not off the hook—they will need to schedule a workout on their time during your lunch, your prep period, or before or after school to complete the work. If you follow through consistently, students will get the message that they are expected to identify and provide evidence of specific efforts associated with producing quality work. Here are some other ways to reinforce the importance of effort:

- Encourage students to keep a checklist of skills they are learning and mastering.

- Provide folders for students on which they can record their grades and assessments on a weekly basis.

- Encourage students to name specific behaviors that reveal a personal attribute that enabled them to accomplish a task.

- Ask students to review the list of personal efficacy life skills (pages 143–144) or habits of learning (page 130) and identify skills they have improved during the past quarter and skills they want to work on during the next quarter.

- Invite students to describe efforts that have helped them to accomplish something during the week that they didn't think they could have done a month ago.

- At the end of every grading period, have students write their parents a note that describes three things they feel they have accomplished or enjoyed learning during the quarter and the efforts that enabled them to be successful.

For more information on links between effort and achievement, see *Making Learning REAL*, Chapter 16.

Recognize individual accomplishments in and out of the classroom

Life Skill Connections (See pages 141–144)

16. Work for high personal performance and cultivate your strengths and positive qualities.

29. Encourage and appreciate the contributions of others.

Below are some ideas for ways to recognize individual student advances and successes:

- Celebrate important milestones and accomplishments of individual students, whether it's something that's happened at school or in their lives outside of school. You might ask students to write a personal milestone or accomplishment on a notecard and either submit the card to you or drop it in a Milestone Box. Then, throughout the week, read each milestone and invite students to guess the authors' names.

<table>
<tr>
<td>

????

Did you know that Michael Wells just received the Employee-of-the-Month award at his workplace?

CONGRATULATIONS!!

????

</td>
<td>

Kudos to SHANDRA on her appointment to the Office of Youth Development

</td>
</tr>
</table>

- Write personal recognition notes to individual students.

- Create Friday lottery tickets with a space for the student's name and a description of something they've done to contribute in a positive way to the learning environment: an act of kindness and generosity, or a notable accomplishment or improvement. Give the ticket to the student, and then the student can place it in the Friday lottery bowl. Near the end of Friday's class, pull out four or five tickets that students can turn in for a homework-free pass, 10 extra points on a quiz, homemade cookies or treats, a homemade lunch with you during the next week, cheap but cool stationery supplies, a handwritten or computer designed quotation, or other small prize. Your imagination is the only limit (Rubinstein 1999).

- Deliver "mystery whispers" a few times during a class period when you catch a student doing the right thing or you notice an important success or improvement in behavior. Whisper the good news in the student's ear. Whispering makes it private and a little secretive and mysterious (Curwin and Medler 1988).

- Remove the anxiety of "not getting it" the first or second or even third time around by inviting students to share their ah-ha moments when they do finally get it. Then celebrate with a chocolate for everyone in the group.

PROVIDE GROUP SUPPORT AND RECOGNITION

Build and maintain a cohesive group

Life Skill Connections (See pages 141–144)

27. Cooperate, share, and work toward high performance within a group to achieve group goals.

29. Encourage and appreciate the contributions of others.

30. Engage in conscious acts of respect, caring, helpfulness, kindness, courtesy, and consideration.

Thomas Sergiovanni, who has written extensively on school culture and school leadership, suggests four key elements that build cohesive groups and high-performing learning communities (Sergiovanni 1994).

1. **Vision, Purpose, and Intentionality**
    Do we give students compelling reasons for why we're doing what we're doing that make sense to them, not just to us or the local school board or department chair? How do we construct a vision of we, not just I? How can we go about developing a sense of shared goals that all of us value? How do we plan ahead, set the stage, seed the ground so students will do what we'd like them to do? If students come without the skills and attitudes we expected, what can we do to help them strengthen their academic and social competencies? What kinds of meaningful opportunities do we provide for students to feel positive about themselves as individual learners and as members of a group?

2. **Trust**
    Trust is all about the relationships we create with students and that students create among themselves. Trust emerges when relationships are supported and maintained through dependability, predictability, genuineness, honesty, competence, integrity, consistency, and personalization. A sense of trust deepens when we feel safe and know that if the boundaries of safety are broken, violations won't be ignored. What can kids count on from us time after time after time? What can kids count on from each other day in and day out?

3. **Respect**
    Respect begins by developing an appreciation for each other's uniqueness and what we each bring to the classroom. It's nurtured by cultural sensitivity and by teachers who welcome, notice, and learn about the diversity of their students and teach to students' differences. A respectful classroom is a place where students aren't embarrassed, insulted, belittled, or humiliated. A climate of mutual respect is supported through the courtesy of asking, inviting, and requesting, and by listening before judgment or punishment. Teachers model respectfulness by focusing on the issues, not by attacking the person. They are mindful of using a tone of voice and words that communicate that each person has dignity and each student has something important to contribute.

4. **Optimism**

   Optimism begins by holding a positive image of human beings as able and capable. We convey our optimism by valuing an individual's efforts, not just his or her ability. We hold high hopes in life for every student. From smiles to immediate feedback to personal conferencing, we let students know that we are confident in their capacities to learn, grow, and change. We believe that students can succeed, and we don't downplay small successes. (The lesson wasn't perfect, the students weren't perfect, and still it was successful!) In fact, we encourage students to see mistakes, missteps, and setbacks as opportunities to imagine different choices and possibilities. Above all, we do everything we can to let young people know they have the power within them to choose the kind of human beings they want to be in a future of their making.

Think about deliberate actions you can take every week to build and sustain these four elements of community. (For recommendations about specific activities, see *Making Learning REAL*, Chapter 15.)

Strengthen your group facilitation skills

Good facilitation involves reading the group, thinking on your feet, and adjusting the activity to maximize group participation and learning. In Engaging Schools' work in schools, we often ask groups of teachers to practice facilitating group activities with each other. It sounds simple to execute, and it never is. Teachers always note how challenging is it to grow into a facilitation style that feels natural and authentic. Included here is a set of guidelines and a set of debriefing questions for facilitating group activities. The more you practice, the easier it gets. Keep in mind that if you don't debrief group activities, students won't take away the purpose, meaning, and learning applications of the activity. From a student's perspective, it turns into a stupid activity that's a waste of time.

Guidelines for facilitating group activities

1. Tell students what they're going to do. (*"Now we're going to do an activity called _____."*)

2. Give directions for how students should arrange themselves for the activity (standing in a circle, sitting face-to-face in a circle of four, divided into two lines of students facing each other, etc.).

3. Share the purpose or goal of the activity and/or the big idea, problem, or concept to which it is linked.

4. Share some of the skills and attitudes that will make this activity a successful one. (*"I'd like everyone to participate with an open mind, use your creativity, and listen carefully to the instructions."*)

5. Give directions that are clear and specific.

6. Ask if there are any questions about the instructions. Then ask for a volunteer to repeat the instructions to make sure everyone got it.

7. Do the activity.

8. Debrief any activity using any of the following questions:

   • What did you like or not like?

   • What did you observe about your own participation or the participation of others?

   • What tools, skills, and attitudes helped the group to be successful? Helped the group complete the task or achieve the goal?

   • What did you learn about yourself or about the group?

   • Link what you learned or observed to situations at school or qualities and skills you need to be successful in school and life.

More debriefing and closing questions

1. In five words or less, what's the most important thing you learned today about yourself, about the group, or about the issue?

2. What's a banner headline of five words or less that would best summarize what we did, learned, or discussed during this experience?

3. What was this experience like for you?

4. What was one thing you liked the most about the activity? The least?

5. How can you use what you've learned in this activity?

6. As I began this activity, I felt... At the end of this activity, I felt...

7. One thing that surprised me was...

8. As we worked together, I kept thinking about...

9. Now I'm more aware of how important it is to...

10. I liked this activity because...

11. I would have changed this activity by...

12. One thing that was fun, challenging, or eye-opening was...

13. After participating in the activity I realized...

14. I found it really difficult to... I found it easy to...

15. This activity helped me to learn more about...

16. I want to remember this experience the next time I...

17. How did this activity work for you? What made this experience interesting or uninteresting? Hard or easy? Strange and different, or comfortable and familiar?

18. What's one thing you want to remember from today?

19. What's one thing you learned today that you can apply to your life?

20. How did your group make decisions or decide what strategy to use? Was everyone listened to and included in the decision? How do you know?

21. What did you observe about how your group worked together? What was easy to do? What was hard? What did your teammates do or say that helped your team be successful? Is there anything you could have done that would have helped your group to be more effective as a team?

22. How would you describe the role you played? How did it feel to be a leader or a follower? What would you personally do differently next time if you were involved in a similar activity?

23. Name one way each person in your group participated and/or contributed? Could you have completed this task by yourself? Why or why not?

24. Name three specific positive behaviors you noticed that helped your group meet your goal and complete the task.

Monitor and assess group participation

To work together effectively in groups, whether they be study groups, classrooms, groups of friends, or sports teams, people in the group need to exercise positive leadership, communication, and conflict resolution skills. We need to analyze the barriers to working together well, learn techniques to surmount them, and build a cohesive community of learners. For more ideas, see *Making Learning REAL*, Chapter 15.

Create classroom routines and rituals that involve every student

A feeling of belonging emerges in part from shared expectations and experiences: everybody gives and everybody gets. Sometimes we start relying on volunteers and giving students the choice of opting out too early and often. Inadvertently, this can create a classroom culture in which students take on permanent roles as either "doers" or "slackers." For more ideas, see *Making Learning REAL*, Chapter 15.

Recognize and celebrate the group's efforts and accomplishments

John Schindler (2005) has summarized the advantages of recognizing collective accomplishments:

- The group experiences the sense of winning as a team.

- Group members gain trust in the prospect that all individuals will do their part. Trust breeds acceptance and a feeling of emotional satisfaction and well-being.

- The focus of the recognition is on the behavior and accomplishments of the group, not the individual.

- The group feels a sense of pride and cohesion when their efforts are recognized, which heightens a sense of belonging.

Here's one way to chart how the group is doing:

The 100% Club—Everyone...

Week_____	M	T	W	Th	F
1. arrived on time					
2. completed Do Now without prompting					
3. completed homework					
4. brought all materials to class					
5. met goals in cooperative learning activity					
6. used positive language (no cursing)					
7. listened and participated during whole group time (no interruptions)					
8. passed a major test					
9. completed independent work					
10. remained silent during silent activities					

When the whole group meets specific behavioral expectations or meets a challenging academic goal, make a habit of doing these three things:

1. Acknowledge and appreciate occasions when the whole group met a behavioral expectation or academic challenge.

2. Recognize the effort it took.

3. Mention the benefits: *"When everyone _____ , it's so much easier to _____ ."* Or *"When everyone _____ , we have more time to _____ ."*

Use group incentives, random reinforcement, and intermittent rewards

Remember these guidelines for incentives, reinforcements, and rewards.

- Incentives and rewards should be low cost, with low stakes. Judgments about students' worthiness and academic merit should never be attached to a specific reward.

- Don't use if-then statements regarding rewards and incentives. (*"If you _____ , then you will receive _____ ."*) Don't trap students into working for rewards.

- Use rewards as a symbolic gesture of success, appreciation, and congratulations *after* the whole group has demonstrated the desired behavior or completed a challenging task proficiently. Name what students have done and:

  ‣ provide a treat or snack to the whole group

  ‣ draw random names from a basket for treats and trinkets

  ‣ do an activity that students have placed on the Fun Friday list of things they like to do

- Don't give rewards every time for the same learning activity—random, intermittent reinforcement works best because it's unexpected. It also brings fun and lightheartedness into the room.

- If there's a particular academic accomplishment or a behavioral goal that you want every student in the group to meet, make a goofy wager. Students love to see faculty act like fools if it's for a good cause, and they will often step up collectively to meet a big challenge. Here's a short list of wagers:

Classroom Wagers
No failures first semester and I will…shave my head!
No failures first semester and I will…prepare to run the 5K in your names.
No tardies for the month and I will…dye my hair blue for a week.
Every student earns proficiency on the quarterly project and I will…perform a dance and put it on YouTube.

- Post giant appreciation notes for the whole class. A few samples are shown below.

- Some schools have found that inviting students to earn school-distributed gold cards (literally a plastic card that comes with rewards and privileges) is a way to promote positive behaviors, a high-achieving academic culture, and school pride. Individual teachers, grade-level teams, or a whole school committee can develop criteria for earning a card and the privileges and rewards that come with it. The following example illustrates how students can earn a card in a specific course for use during the remainder of the semester and lists some of the benefits that come with the card.

Semester Gold Cards for Ms. _____'s Classes

How do you earn one?

- Present and on time every day for at least four weeks in a row
- No more than two disciplinary referrals
- 80% of major tests, products, and projects completed with proficiency
- 100 Gold Card classroom participation points
- Three tickets that provide evidence of your attendance at Homework Hall, Tutoring Tuesdays, AP Study Groups, Saturday School, Computer Lab, or Library Lab
- Scores of 3 or 4 on five habits of learning you choose
- Completion of 80% of your work on time
- Evidence of revising and correcting three important pieces of work that you put in your course portfolio
- Evidence that you have read a book or article on your own that is related to this course or the larger subject matter discipline

Gold Card Rewards and Privileges

- Certificate and letter to your parent/guardian
- Breakfast with principal
- End-of-quarter field trip or after-school event
- Independent project time in the library
- A reception with local personality _____
- You get to pick the music for independent work time
- Two tickets to _____
- A night out with other Gold Card members
- Two pass cards that you can submit instead of turning in journal entries, quizzes, or in-class or homework assignments
- A job shadow day away from school to explore the career or profession of your choice
- A $10 certificate for school tools and gear sold in the bookstore
- Raffle for a laptop computer
- Raffle for gift certificate to Staples
- Raffle for college savings bond

5

REFERENCES:

Albert, L. (1996) *Cooperative discipline*. Port Angeles, WA: American Guidance Services Publishing.

Classroom Management Resource Site. http://www.calstatela.edu/faculty/jshindl/cm/

Curwin, R., and Medler, A. (1988) *Discipline with dignity*. Alexandria, VA: ASCD.

Levine, M. (2007) "Unpacking the cognitive backpack." *Educational Leadership*, (April)

Rubinstein, G. (1999) *Reluctant disciplinarian*. Fort Collins, CO: Cottonwood Press, Inc.

Sergiovanni, T. (1994) *Strengthening the heartbeat: Leading and learning together in schools*. San Francisco: Jossey-Bass.

Schindler, J. (2005) *How to live 365 days a year*. Philadelphia, PA: Running Press.

CHAPTER 6

Step 4: Invite Student Engagement, Cooperation, and Self-Correction

This step is all about two essential components of effective classroom management: how you manage activities and pace lessons to maximize student engagement, and how you use "effective teacher talk" to invite cooperation and self-correction when problematic behaviors occur. Activity management begins with how you get students' attention; how you give instructions; how you make transitions from one activity to another; and how you use physical, visual, and verbal prompts to help students focus and get ready to learn (Evertson and Weinstein 2006, pp. 422–427). Effective teacher talk encompasses the verbal prompts you use to respond immediately to problematic behaviors in ways that invite cooperation and self-correction, help students get back on track, and prevent potential confrontations and power struggles.

No one can sustain focus a hundred percent of the time. When students' unwanted behaviors propel them into the no-learning zone, they are looking for a reason to keep you from teaching and other students from learning. The more quickly you prompt immediate self-correction, the less you need to rely on more time-consuming consequences and interventions later on. Invitations have a different feel from demands and threats. They communicate your intentions to activate students' attention, anticipation, and positive motivation and alert students to what they need to do in the moment.

By paying attention to early warning signals from individual students or the group, you can defuse a situation before it requires a more serious intervention. Jacob Kounin (1977) used the term "with-it-ness" to describe teachers who are acutely sensitive to the classroom environment. Teachers who develop this quality can pick up the first sign of potential trouble even as they continue their instruction.

The approach we use to respond to inattentiveness and potential disruptions makes all the difference. When you notice students who look bored, blue, disengaged, or distracted, when you see kids who are already off task and looking for trouble—the sum of your words, tone of voice, and body language will influence students' willingness to cooperate and work with you, or against you. And cooperation, after all, is the goal here.

If you rush to the scene in a squad car, you risk creating more commotion than the situation warrants. The student is caught in the flashing lights for everyone to see. High drama creates high anxiety, and when anxiety rises, students are unable to listen, think clearly, and shift gears. When you send in the sirens, kids will probably become more, not less, defensive and resistant. This is not a particularly winning formula for getting students back on track.

6

On the other hand, if you wander over to a distracted student during a casual classroom stroll, you can check out what's going on quietly, almost invisibly. When your approach is attentive, relaxed, and matter-of-fact, you're conveying that this is a check-in, not a catastrophe. For adolescents, the lower the stakes are, the more likely it is that they will give us a look and listen and respond cooperatively.

Invitations create a way for us to connect rather than criticize. Moreover, they build students' capacity to right themselves. By sharing observations, providing information, and soliciting a student's take on a situation, you communicate your confidence in students' ability to take responsibility for changing their behavior and making different choices. Students feel competent because they (not teachers) are making the choice about what to do; they experience the satisfaction of doing something for themselves. You feel good because you've avoided major interruptions and confrontations.

SET THE STAGE FOR ENGAGEMENT AND COOPERATION: FIVE ESSENTIAL EVERYDAY PRACTICES

Over the years, we have generated a short list of five essential practices that *must* be in place every day in order to teach effectively, manage activities and the group, and garner the cooperation and goodwill of your students. They are:

1. Get the group's attention and make transitions using physical, visual, and verbal prompts; location cues; physical arrangement of space and people; music, noisemakers, and timers.

2. Give clear instructions using verbal, visual, and written prompts; pair check-ins; demonstrations; paraphrasing; and short question-and-answer periods

3. Insist on silence when silence is required; whatever you do, do not talk over students!

4. Use physical proximity and prompts *first* when students are off task during whole group instruction

5. Design balanced, active, well-paced lessons in which you vary time chunks, learning activities, grouping structures, and noise levels

1. Get the group's attention

When you're ready to begin class…

-   Stand in the same place every day, or

-   Use the same signal every day, or

-   Say the same thing every day, or

-   If you are playing music, turn it off.

When you're transitioning from one activity or one process step to another…

- Get students to move themselves or move materials to shift the energy and focus. ("*Before we focus on the presentations, please put everything away except your feedback cards and move your chairs into a semicircle so we can all see the presenters.*")

- Use a timer, chime, hand signal, rain stick, thunder tube, or unusual word (for example, *sikiliza*, which is the Swahili word for "interested silence") as a cue for students to listen up as a whole group, switch partners, transition to the next activity, return to original groups, or put away materials.

- Cue students when it's time to get to work in groups or on their own. ("*Okay, go.*" Or "*Are you ready? Do it.*" Or "*Let's do it.*" Or "*Okay, folks. Time to use your smarts. Go for it.*" Or "*You're good to go.*")

- When you begin an activity, you might say, "*You have about x minutes to complete y.*" Or "*This should take about x minutes to do.*"

When you need to get everyone's attention in the middle of small group or independent work time, move to the same spot in the classroom and use a signal that indicates "Freeze, stop talking, stop what you're doing, and focus on me."

When learning time for a specific activity is nearly up:

- Note that the end time is near; observe the progress you see; and check whether students need two minutes, five minutes, or ten minutes to complete the task. Compromise on the number of minutes if students' need for more time varies or if the requested amount of time is markedly different from your time estimation for completion of the task.

- Near the end time, you can say "*Take two more minutes to finish up.*" Or "*Let the last person in your group finish speaking and STOP.*" Or "*Finish your work on the current question/problem and STOP.*"

- When time is up, you can say "*And now it's time to _____.*" Or "*And focus front please.*"

When reminders are in order, post important information in the room or on the door.

Chemistry

When you arrive tomorrow,

I will ask you to show me

<u>some evidence that you</u>

<u>studied for your test.</u>

American Studies

Don't forget to bring

your study cards to class

tomorrow for the test.

(10 bonus points!)

2. Give clear instructions

Always provide at least three different ways for students to process and understand instructions. Whenever you're working with a new group of students, keep tasks simple and instructions very brief for a few weeks. (*"Read _____ and write down _____ while you're reading."*) Otherwise you'll lose half the group before work time even begins. Always scan the room as you speak, making direct eye contact with students who have the most trouble listening. For more complex assignments, chunk directions into four parts and, pausing after each part:

1. Name the task and describe how the task links to the big picture of the lesson or unit, and why students are doing it. (*"Now that we have a clearer idea of the complexities of _____ , your job is to produce a two-minute newscast for* Youth News Today *that captures the problem and identifies possible solutions. This task will give you the opportunity to communicate your understanding of the issue and practice your presenting skills."*)

2. Explain step-by-step what you want students to do using simple but precise language. (*"First, you will create an entry line: 'From _____ , we have a report on _____.' Second, you will identify the problem and cite at least three pieces of evidence that illustrate why it's a problem. And third, you will share at least two possible solutions, noting their potential costs and benefits."*)

3. Explain how students will do it, what materials they will use, and how much time is allotted. (*"You will work with your current partner. You will have 20 minutes to prepare your newscast and a final three minutes to rehearse with your partner. Decide who is partner A and who is partner B. Use chapter _____ in your textbook and the handout entitled _____."*)

4. Explain what the final product, presentation, or report should look like or sound like at the end of work time. (*"When you come up front to present your newscast, partner A will say your entry line, partner B will report on the problem, and partner A will report on possible solutions."*)

If you use both verbal and posted or handed-out written instructions, make sure the wording is exactly the same as it was in the oral instructions. Written instructions may include a sample product, demonstration, or model of what to do, or a visual or graphic depiction of steps. To confirm student understanding, you may ask students to pair-share in order to paraphrase and clarify instructions; request an instruction summary from a random student; or allow a two-minute time period for questions after initial instructions.

The biggest mistake we make when giving directions? We repeat the original instructions over and over again the same way every time. Say it two, three, or five times, and students have no incentive to listen the first time. See the sample poster for one way to remind students how you will give directions.

> # I will only give directions ONCE!!!
>
> If students are talking when I give directions,
> I will STOP in mid-sentence and wait for silence.
>
> After I finish giving directions,
> you have one minute to check for
> understanding with a partner.
>
> Then I will take two questions
> if directions need to be clarified.

3. Insist on silence when silence is required

If you don't insist on silence when you are speaking to the whole group, you will slide into the awful habit of talking over students. This often begins unconsciously, and then suddenly you're aware that your voice is getting louder and harsher, more students are talking, and fewer and fewer students are actually listening. Don't go there!

You have to stand your ground on this one. Stop talking, still your body, take a relaxing breath, and wait until silence re-emerges. At this point, peer pressure among students usually kicks in, and the troops will rally to your attention. You can also do yourself a big favor by limiting directions, mini-lectures, summary points, and explanations to less than a couple of minutes or fewer than 50 words until the group has proven that they can sustain absolute silence for extended periods of time, day after day.

If you have two or three outliers who just don't get it, you will need to act quickly, firmly, and calmly. You might say, *"Deandre, stop talking now and we're good. Keep talking when I'm speaking and you owe me 20 minutes of silence during lunch or after school. It's your choice."* If a student's interruptions are chronic, follow through with other consequences that might include (1) more owed time for a longer workout session; (2) calling a parent; (3) a written referral describing the unwanted behavior and exactly what measures you have already taken; and/or (4) arranging for a conference that includes you, the student, the dean, and a parent.

If you don't make uninterrupted silence your line in the sand, you risk becoming trapped in a habitual loop of requesting silence, speaking louder and becoming more frustrated, demanding silence again, repeating yourself, and finally yelling at the group to "Shut up!" The bigger risk, however, is losing your authority during whole group instruction. Students will simply refuse to function as a cohesive group that expects itself to respond the same way, all at the same time.

6

Although this issue was previously discussed in the section on procedures (see Chapter 4, page 126), it's worth revisiting what to do when a learning activity requires absolute silence all around. Most adolescents hate quiet. If you expect students to work in silence most of the time, you risk never getting silence at all. The problem here is that kids can't really practice the discipline of sustained silence if any noise, however muffled, is always part of the mix. So serve up silent learning in very small chunks, and build up to longer periods of sustained silence. Be sure to identify specific activities during which absolutely no noise is permitted, and discuss why silence is a reasonable and necessary expectation for these activities. Below is a sample poster of silence guidelines.

Silence is Necessary When...

- I begin class and start whole group instruction
- I'm giving directions
- One of us (teacher or student) is presenting new material to the group or demonstrating how to do something
- One of us is reading or speaking to the whole group
- We are viewing a film or listening to a classroom guest
- I am lecturing (It will never be more than 15 minutes!)
- I am responding to students' questions during a whole group activity
- You are doing quick-writes before speaking in a small group or to the whole group
- You are engaged in silent reading or writing activities
- You are taking paper-and-pencil quizzes, tests, and exams

4. Use proximity and physical prompts first when students are off task

Take full advantage of your physical presence to work the classroom during whole group instruction. Try not to stand or sit in one place for more than three or four minutes. Arrange student seating in a way that makes it easy for you to scan the group, switch the direction of your focus, and move quickly from students within your immediate physical proximity to those further away. Make direct eye contact with students around the room as you change your location.

Use physical prompts first to help students refocus and get back on task. More often than not, the students who are talking and goofing off are not where you are, physically or cognitively. Use your facial expressions, physical stance, and physical movement to redirect behavior. It's helpful to remember that more than 75 percent of communication involves your personal demeanor, your facial gestures, your physical stance, and your tone of voice—not the specific words you say.

When you can physically cue students to refocus without speaking, you save time, energy, and potential hassles. However, this approach comes with a warning label: doing it right almost always leads to immediate self-correction for most students in most situations; doing it wrong can make the situation worse. It all depends on your discipline demeanor. (For more on discipline demeanor, see Chapter 3, pages 67–69.)

If your body language communicates seriousness of purpose and a relaxed, quiet strength, kids will respond positively to your invitational prompts without feeling cornered or threatened. If, however, your body language communicates anger or hostility, some students (usually the very same students you're trying to redirect) will push back. Fred Jones (2007) discusses the how-tos and benefits of physical prompts in great detail in his book *Tools for Teaching: Discipline, Instruction, Motivation*. Here's a snapshot of the "physical pivot" that will prompt redirection for most students.

1. Stop what you're doing. Say "excuse me" to the whole group or the students with whom you're working.

2. Shift to your discipline demeanor. Take a couple of deep breaths, put on your "flat face" (no affect or animation), and relax your body.

3. Shift your physical stance. Pivot your body toward the uncooperative student slowly, and square off so that your shoulders and your feet are directly facing that student. This only takes three or four seconds to do. Remember that slow, deliberate movements let your students know that you're relaxed, steady, and serious. Hurried, dramatic movement can communicate alarm, anxiety, or excitement. If you appear on edge, you've lost the opportunity for a low-stakes interaction. Low-stakes interactions always elicit more cooperation than a high-stakes move.

4. Say the student's name, make direct eye contact with him or her, and wait. Most students will stop what they're doing at this point and get back on task.

5. If your physical pivot isn't enough, you need to move. Change your physical proximity and take a few seconds to move within three or four feet of the student. Stand slightly to the side of the student, bend slightly forward, and make direct eye contact. Your proximity to the student will depend on your read of the student and the situation. Adolescents, in contrast to younger children, are much more prickly about what they perceive as an invasion of their personal space. You need to gauge the distance that produces positive redirection versus the distance that will provoke a student's hostility.

6. Say the student's name and give a direct prompt to the student that spells out exactly what the student is expected to do right now. ("_____, *you need to be working on _____.*" "*Page 73 in the text, bottom paragraph.*" "*Project direction guide, page 2.*")

7. Wait. Don't move away until the student is refocused and on task. Take another deep breath.

8. Say "thank you" and exit.

5. Design well-paced, student-centered lessons

Although pacing is one the most obvious elements of good instruction, it's not so easy to do in practice. We tend to talk too much and drag things out beyond the point of interest or attention span. Boredom and monotony are major contributors to inattentiveness and low-level disruptive behaviors. Well-paced lessons that incorporate high interest, student-centered learning strategies and challenging work will keep most students focused, on task, and engaged most of the time. Look at the chart on page 185 that illustrates five elements of well-paced, student-centered lessons. Then think back to a lesson you taught to one group of students in one course during the last week, and consider the following questions:

- How did you alternate short and long chunks of time and incorporate a wide array of learning strategies, grouping structures, noise levels, and instructional supports throughout each instructional period?

- Over the course of the lesson, did students spend more time listening to and watching you, or did you spend more time observing, coaching, conferencing, and listening to students as they worked on their own? This question asks you to think about the ratio of passive vs. active learning time during any instructional period.

Consider the benefits of increasing the amount of time during which students are directing their own learning and reducing the amount of passive, teacher-directed time when you're the "sage on the stage." The sample 75-minute workshop model at right shows a three-part lesson that includes (A) a teacher-directed overview; (B) student-centered work time; and (C) oral and written reflection, discussion, and feedback. When ,students are working on their own in groups or independently, you get to spend more time monitoring and assessing what students are actually learning; you reduce the incidents of students goofing off during whole group instruction; and you get more time to check in and conference with individual students.

SAMPLE WORKSHOP LESSON MODEL:

	(7)	**Do NOW or Gathering**
A	(10)	**Mini-Lesson** Connections / Teaching point / Directions 3 ways
	(15)	**Guided Practice** Try It out /Active engagement in learning task
	(3)	**Check for Understanding** / Link to follow-up tasks
B	(20)	**Independent Practice or Small Group Tasks** (Students are working and you are teaching by "walking around," coaching, conferencing, and working with small groups)
		Activities for Early Completers
		Assessment for Learning
C	(15)	**Reflection, Discussion, and Feedback** informed by high-level questions
	(5)	**Homework / Preview / Personal Check-ins**

FIVE ELEMENTS OF WELL-PACED, STUDENT-CENTERED LESSONS

Time Chunks	Learning Strategies	Grouping Structures	Noise Level
3 MIN	Reading, Research, Text-Based Protocols	Whole Group	Silence
5 MIN	Writing, Recording, and Representing to Learn	Small Group	Quiet Conversation
7 MIN	Viewing/Observing Listening and Lecture MINI-LESSON	Pairs	Team Work
10 MIN	Thinking and Reflecting	Independent Work	
15 MIN	Gatherings, Closings, and Brain-Body Energizers	Individual Conferencing, Coaching, and Check-ins	
20 MIN	Seminar and Structured Discussions	Small Group Tutorials and Reteaching	
30 MIN	Presenting and Performing		
	Labs, Projects, and Studios		
	Games and Team Challenges		
	Drawing and Charting		
	Guided Practice and Problem Solving		
	"Hands-On" and Experiential Learning		

✔ INSTRUCTIONAL SUPPORTS

Class keeping and planning

Helping students settle in and get ready to learn

Clear expectations and instructions

Physical, visual, and verbal prompts

Modeling and effective group facilitation

Signals for silence and getting students' attention

Smooth transitions from one activity to another

Reminders, clues, tips, and suggestions

Examples and explanations

"Real time" positive, corrective, and appreciative feedback and formative assessment for learning

Personal and group encouragement

Individual and group check-ins

Celebrations, recognitions, and incentives

6

Expand your teaching toolbox to engage all learners

The current group of curriculum specialists and instructional coaches believe that effective instruction rests solely on your capacity to deliver lessons that:

- begin with explicit aims and learning outcomes aligned to content standards;

- help students navigate through an anticipatory set, a mini-lesson, and guided practice;

- emphasize formative assessment to monitor student learning;

- and wrap up the lesson with review, closure, and homework.

What could possibly be objectionable about a lesson plan recipe that is used in almost every school in America? Yet relying on just one lesson type assumes that your job is to teach expert lessons, rather than becoming an expert at engaging students authentically and rigorously in the subject you love. Because many adolescents do not particularly like school to begin with, lesson planning that includes a more eclectic array of group processes and learning strategies will grab students' attention, build a sense of group cohesion, heighten their interest and curiosity, and engage their emotions as well as their intellect. Engagement increases when student interest goes up.

Researchers have differentiated between two types of student interest: personal and situational (Evertson and Weinstein 2006, pp. 419–420). Personal interest is a function of individual preferences and characteristics and the value that students place on the course content or the goal that they associate with the topic or task; it is most often connected to *what* students are learning. Situational interest, which is more about *how* students are learning, refers to "catch-and-hold" processes and strategies that emphasize group work, the use of technology, puzzles and games, hands-on activities, learning tasks that are perceived as fun, and opportunities for students to investigate topics on their own (Evertson and Weinstein 2006, p. 420). Other strategies that increase student engagement include personalizing learning and involving students in planning and decision-making related to the content and delivery of the course.

The learning and social needs of the group should shape the structure and pacing of your lessons, not the other way around. Discovering and capitalizing on each group's personality, preferences, and rhythm is what authentic teaching is all about. The next page presents a snapshot of group processes and learning strategies that align with the qualities and characteristics of adolescent learners and help prepare students to be ready for college, career, and life in the 21st century. As you design instructional units and develop weekly plans and individual lessons, think about how you might incorporate some of these suggestions to boost student engagement.

INSIDE THE TEACHING TOOLBOX: BUILDING PERSONAL AND SITUATIONAL INTEREST

Student Voice and Civil Dialogue

- Pair-shares and small group listening labs
- Class meetings and negotiated learning
- One-minute rants, raves, reviews, opinions
- Student-led activities
- Student surveys and feedback (what students like and what they don't)
- Opinion continuums, four corners, walkabouts, learning carousels, and concentric circles that get kids moving and talking

Self-Perpetuating Routines

- Group gatherings
- Group closings
- Goal setting, self-assessment, student-directed record keeping of academic progress
- Assignment notebook review and check-ins
- Journaling
- End-of-week, unit, or quarter learning reflections
- Progress report check-ins (mid-term and end-of-term)

Group Building Tools

- Explicit expectations
- Group guidelines and agreements
- Sit in a circle, oval, or square so everyone can see each other
- Know everyone's names
- Class keeping and group check-ins (How's it going?)
- Cooperative learning and collaborative problem solving
- Assessment of habits of learning and life skills
- Celebrations and recognition

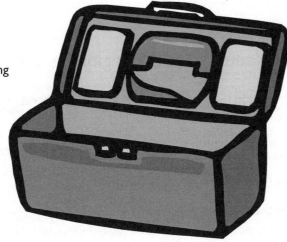

Game It Up!

Games are organized structures for learning that involve:

- A common goal or task
- A challenge or problem to solve
- Obstacles to overcome
- Playfulness
- Positive energy
- Rules
- Roles
- Cooperation and/or competition
- Strategic thinking strategies
- Social navigation and negotiation
- Interpersonal and group efficacy
- Emotional investment
- Group norming
- Reflection about what you experienced
- Links to real life

Making Learning Personally Relevant

- Give students options and choices
- Link learning to students' interests and real-world problems, issues, or applications
- Utilize experiential learning through fieldwork, labs, interviews, simulations, role-plays, mock trials, etc.
- Learn from a practitioner's perspective (Think like a _____ or imagine yourself as one.)
- Make the most of your personal relationship with the student (I'll learn and work for you because you care about me.)
- Emphasize authentic assessments for real audiences

Grabbing Students' Attention and Interest

- If you were in this situation, what would you do? How would you feel?
- Problematize anything and everything (Here's the problem. Here are the rules, constraints, and resources. Your job is to construct the best solution. Go!)
- You decide…You be the judge…
- Your group needs to agree on, choose, or design…
- Here's the situation. Yes or no? Right or wrong? Fair or unfair? Good choice or bad?

6

HELP STUDENTS GET READY TO LEARN AND FOCUS

Life Skill Connections (See pages 141–144)
12. Focus and pay attention.
15. Activate hope, optimism, and positive motivation.

The rush of one class after another, from one end of the building to another, means that secondary school students are making constant transitions as they leave where they've been, what they've been doing, who they've been with, and what they've been feeling. Think about how you can help students settle in, leave the past hour behind, reconnect with another group of people, and get ready to focus and learn. The suggestions here provide a variety of ways to begin class and sustain focus and energy throughout the instructional period. You will want to introduce some routines that stay the same every day, all year long. You may also want to vary others—everyone likes a little novelty. When a routine or ritual starts to wear thin, have another one ready to put in its place.

Help students settle in at the beginning of class

Help students transition from noisy to quiet, from high-speed movement to sitting still, from the previous experience to the here and now.

- Post announcements on the door that headline what students can expect today.

- Meet and greet students at the door.

- Post the Do Now activity in the same place everyday so students know what to do immediately upon arriving in your classroom.

- Some teachers have found it very useful to ring a small meditation chime and insist on absolute silence and physical stillness (no reading, writing, or any other activity) for one or two minutes to give students time to collect themselves and refocus. When the chime rings a second time, class begins. This sounds like a ritual that's just too weird for high school students. Yet the word from kids is a resounding *yes* to this brief respite from the noise of their lives. After the initial awkwardness, kids actually look forward to the quiet chance to focus.

- Try out different kinds of music at the beginning of class to find out what students like that may help them to settle in.

- Choose a student to serve as your TA (teacher assistant) for the day; he or she will assist you with routine tasks at the beginning of the period. (See procedure 13, Chapter 5.)

Help students wake up, energize, and recharge the mind and body

Human beings get bored pretty easily and need novelty and movement to get focused, sustain focus, and shift focus. Keep in mind that when we can't focus, we have no access to memory and thus cannot learn. Invite your students into this conversation by asking them two questions.

1. When classwork gets boring or you lose your focus, what's happening? What are you doing? What am I doing?

2. What kinds of things might help you keep focused, alert, and energized?

Neuroscience research has provided a compelling platform for exploring how teachers might manage and optimize students' emotional states more effectively in order to maximize learning. Eric Jensen, a pioneer in brain-based learning, describes seven target states that build readiness to learn at key points during instruction (Jensen 2003).

High Energy

"Yikes!"
Use to energize or create emotions

"Yahoo!
Use for celebrations, to reward behaviors, or to have fun

"I Got It!"
Use to deepen learning, build confidence, or strengthen understanding and recall

"Uh-Oh!"
Use to trigger healthy concern or create a vested interest in upcoming learning

"Huh?"
Use for getting attention, building curiosity, or generating confusion

"Ah-hh"
Use to improve focus, enhance comfort, and lessen sense of stress or threat

"Peace and Quiet"
Use to calm, turn thoughts inward, focus minds, and promote relaxation and reflection

Low Energy

When people sit for long periods of time, energy ebbs and focus fades. At least once every thirty minutes or so, get students out of their seats for at least one minute to move at least ten feet. This 30-1-10 strategy will raise heart rates and epinephrine levels and heighten student alertness, thus promoting an arousal state important for learning (specifically, the "Huh?" state associated with getting student attention, building student curiosity, or generating useful confusion). Here are four examples of ways to apply the 30-1-10 strategy:

1. **Partner Walk-Around:** Provide a focus question related to the content or topic of the lesson and ask students to find a partner and take a walk around the perimeter of the room as they discuss the focus question.

2. **Write and Post:** After a lecture, discussion, or text reading, give each student a large sticky note and ask them to write down one thing they just learned and then post it on the blackboard. This exercise has the added bonus of helping you get a quick read on what students learned or understood from the previous activity.

3. **Vote with Your Feet:** Pose a question related to your broader academic discipline or current topic of study and post four possible responses on the wall around the room. Ask students to select their response to the question, move to that part of the room, and discuss their reasons for choosing their preferred response with a partner in the same group or a partner from another group. (Examples: If you worked in print or broadcast journalism, which position would you apply for? As you think about world health, which disease would be your number one priority for research dollars? If you had lived in the 19th century, who would you most want to be?)

4. **Relay Review or Quiz:** Divide students into groups of four, and give each group ten index cards. Assign each group a different letter of the alphabet for identification, and create a placeholder spot on the chalk or whiteboard tray for each group to place its cards.

Give each group a quiz or review sheet with ten questions on it. Each group writes the number 1 and the answer to question 1 on the first index card, and one student from each group walks to the board and places the index card by the group's letter. The student goes back to their group, and the group answers question 2 and the second person takes card 2 to their place on the tray. Each group keeps rotating students who take the answer cards to the tray until all questions are completed or time is up.

Here are five resources full of strategies, activities, quick energizers, and brain-body exercises that promote learning readiness:

Teaching with the Brain in Mind, Revised 2nd Edition, Eric Jensen (2005)

Tools for Engagement: Managing Emotional States for Learner Success, Eric Jensen (2003)

Brain Compatible Strategies, Eric Jensen (2004)

Making the Brain Body Connection: A Playful Guide to Releasing Mental, Physical & Emotional Blocks to Success, Sharon Promislow (2005)

Brain Gym, Paul and Gail Dennison (1994)

Do a quick check-in to read the group before a lesson begins

All of the activities in this section provide quick ways for you to read the group and for students to share starting points before the lesson begins. Whether the format is a whole group go-around or partner-share, students realize immediately that they all bring different feelings, issues, and hopes into the room. When you acknowledge and accept the range of student responses, you're inviting students to walk in as themselves rather than insisting that they fake it or leave their real selves outside the door. Keep on hand copies of "Feelings, Moods, and Attitudes" on page 149 when students are doing exercises that involve naming feelings. You might want to create or invite a student to create a large chart of feeling words that you can post in your classroom.

Feelings Cards

1. Place blank 5" x 8" notecards and markers in a central location and invite students to take a notecard and write a word that describes what they are feeling at that moment. Allow two minutes to do this.

2. Invite everyone to raise their cards so others can see them. You might have students turn to their neighbor to share why they chose the words they did. You can also use these words to create a class list of feelings to post in a prominent place, and continue to expand the list.

3. Close by inviting everyone to empty their minds and take a deep breath, exhale, and focus.

Reading the Group One to Five

Ask students how they're feeling right now on a scale of one to five, in which five is a really good mood and you're ready for anything, and one is a bad mood and nothing's working out today. Ask students to say their numbers out loud all at once, or hold up one to five fingers, or write their numbers on notecards. After you get a quick read, you might say, *"So we're all over the place. Fours and fives? Keep us moving and energized. Ones, twos, and threes, let's hope you're feeling a little more upbeat by the end of class."* Or *"Hmmm…this is not a good sign. We've got our work cut out for us. We can shift how we work today—we can go quiet and on your own or make today more active and social. You decide."*

6

Feeling-go-rounds

Toss out one of these questions and invite students to answer with a one-word response:

- What musical instrument do you feel like today?

- What color describes how you feel at this moment?

- What place inside or outside a house describes what you feel like right now?

- What kind of weather describes how you are feeling today?

Baggage cards

When the group appears to be utterly preoccupied as they walk in or a particular student has major challenges making transitions, try passing out baggage cards. Students can write down the baggage on their minds that's hard to stop thinking about. By writing it down and placing their cards back in the basket, students are saying, "I can set this aside for the period, and it's okay to come back to it later." Tell students they can pick up their cards at the end of class.

Group gathering

Gatherings welcome and acknowledge the group and invite every voice into the room. Gatherings are essential for building a cohesive classroom community. Try to do at least one group gathering every week. See *Making Learning REAL,* Chapter 15 for more information and ideas for gatherings.

Set goals to get ready to learn

Use any of these prompts to encourage daily goal-setting. Ask students to turn to a partner and share their responses with each other. Or, if students keep journals, ask them to write down their responses.

- My goal for today is _____.

- Today, I hope I will be able to _____.

- Right now I feel _____. By the end of class, I want to feel _____. To get there I can _____.

- What am I doing right? What can I do better?

- Two things I can do today that will help me focus are _____.

- One thing I want to learn, accomplish, or do today is _____.

- To keep myself on track today, I want to avoid _____.

- What did I do well yesterday that I want to do again today?

- What's one thing I can do better today than yesterday?

AVOID PITFALLS THAT DERAIL DISCUSSION

Life Skill Connections (See pages 141–144)

18. Exercise assertiveness; communicate your thoughts, feelings, and needs effectively to others.

28. Respect everyone's right to learn, to speak, and to be heard.

29. Encourage and appreciate the contributions of others.

30. Engage in conscious acts of respect, caring, helpfulness, kindness, courtesy, and consideration.

31. Recognize and appreciate similarities and differences in others.

Making Learning REAL, Chapter 15, presents numerous strategies and protocols for making group talk good talk. This section, however, focuses on what you can do as the facilitator to prepare students to engage in civil discussion and to redirect unproductive group talk behaviors.

Prepare students to participate responsibly in discussion

Make a T-chart, soliciting from students the behaviors and language that shut down good conversation and behaviors that invite everyone to be fully present, to listen, and to express themselves openly and thoughtfully.

Making Group Talk Good Talk	
What do people say and do that shuts down good talk?	**What do people say and do that encourages everyone to focus, listen, and express themselves?**

Discuss the concept of filtering your thoughts before you speak. One teacher who wanted her students to understand the importance of thinking about what they want to say *before* saying it out loud suggested that her students ask themselves, "Do I really need to make this comment right now? Does it add to or subtract from the discussion?" Her students agreed that everyone would be comfortable saying the word "filter" when a student began to ramble or take over class discussion.

Redirect unproductive group talk behaviors

The following suggestions and prompts will help you redirect students who are off topic and restrain students who are likely to dominate the discussion and silence other students.

- Move within close proximity (two to four feet) of students who are engaging in sidebar talk. Make eye contact and speak directly to them as you continue facilitating the group discussion.

- When a student is rambling or off point, refocus attention by restating the relevant point or by directing questions to the group that are back on the subject; ask how the off-point topic relates to the main issue under discussion; or ask the student to summarize the main point.

- When a student makes the occasional juvenile, goofy, or off-the-wall remark that breaks the flow of the conversation, you've got to figure out how to acknowledge it quickly and move on (especially if the comment was truly funny and triggered lots of laughter). Waiting for repentance or an apology just keeps the spotlight on the student. Instead, use your light touch to shift the focus back to the topic. You might make a quick but low-key comment like *"That's just what I was thinking"* (or *"That's a fresh perspective!"* or *"I hadn't thought of that"*). Then shift and say, *"Now let's get back to _____."* Or you might say, *"Thanks for the comedy spot; now let's move on to _____."*

- For students who always have to have the last word or who want to speak ad nauseam, say *"That's an interesting point. Let's see what others have to say."* Or, *"Twenty seconds please."* Or, *"You've spoken twice already. I want to hear what others have to say."*

- Ask students who rarely pay attention to what others are saying to restate what the previous student said or invite them to ask a question to learn more about the previous speaker's perspective.

- For students who are argumentative or hostile to what other students say, you might say, *"You have the right to your opinion and the responsibility to say it civilly without being argumentative (or aggressive)."* Or, *"Can you try to summarize both points of view?"* Or, *"Can you restate that as a question?"*

- Finally, here's a conference tip for students who persistently argue in an aggressive manner. Students who argue often, often argue to win. Yet these are the same students who have no clue that their aggressive speaking style tends to turn people off. So instead of influencing the discussion, their remarks, however compelling, are discounted. Later on, when you can conference with the student privately, try exploring this line of questioning. *"So you made your point, but did it make a difference in the discussion? Are you aware of how other students react and respond when you begin to speak? Here's what I see. Is that the reaction you want? If you want to influence what others think, let's strategize some ways to tone down the hostility and aggressiveness so others can really hear what you want to say."*

Defuse, disarm, and deflate provocative behavior

Some adolescents will go out of their way to say and do things that are provocative just to see how you will react and what you will do. Think about the comments students say that are most likely to trigger a charged emotional reaction or "deer in the headlights" paralysis. These are situations in which you absolutely want to avoid turning a little nothing into a big deal confrontation. Instead, you want to develop effective responses that do two things. First, the response should communicate, *"You didn't get to me. I'm not going to fuss or fret over this."* Second, you want to end the encounter feeling relaxed, in charge, and ready to move on.

Saying the unexpected has an amazing capacity to defuse, disarm, and deflate the incendiary word bomb. No single approach will work in all situations with all students, so consider the following questions:

- Who's the student? Grumpy or good-natured? Clown or bully?

- How do you respond? Verbally or in a brief personal note?

- When do you respond? At the moment or later in the period?

- Where do you respond? With the whole group or in a more private moment?

With time, most teachers develop a repertoire of responses that feel authentic and effective. Using humor shows your capacity to see the world from kids' perspectives. But be careful to avoid trumping smart-mouth remarks with clever comebacks that cross the line to mocking sarcasm and ridicule. Try out these responses:

- **The deadpan stare**: Put on your face that says, *"I've seen it all and heard it all before."*

- **Hmm…**: *"I hadn't thought of that." "Let me think about that."*

- **Quick acknowledgment or agreement**: Resist the temptation to push back; simply agree with the student and move on. *"Uh huh." "I can see that." "You've got a point." "That's just what I was thinking."*

- **Exaggerated agreement**: When students question your capacity as a teacher or critique assignments by saying, *"This is stupid"* or *"You are so unfair,"* you might respond, *"Yup, I spent $80,000 getting degrees that help me create stupid assignments."* Or, *"You know I go home and spend the entire evening thinking up ways to make you miserable."* Or, *"You're right, I am completely annoying and unreasonable. Do I have that about right?"* The effectiveness of this kind of response depends on your delivery: yes to friendly and humorously, no to sarcastically or angrily.

- **Just a thought (especially effective in a note)**: *"Testing me as a teacher keeps me on top of my game. How about doing it once a week instead of every day?"*

- **Career jujitsu**: Transform the personal quality that's getting on your last nerve into a future career asset. *"I hope your ability to argue every point makes you a rich trial lawyer some day. For class, let's take it down a notch." "I truly admire your ability to _____. Next time, save it for _____."*

- **Poke fun at yourself**: *"This may be the worst lesson I've ever taught, and you all survived."*

ADDRESS STUDENTS' NEGATIVE SPEECH AND UNACCEPTABLE LANGUAGE

Before you even begin to tackle adolescents' negative speech, keep in mind that the language students use in class has a huge impact on classroom culture. Negative speech and unacceptable language are expressions of aggression and hostility. If you ignore them, other students will be silenced. They will never feel safe enough to express themselves. They will be reluctant to take intellectual risks for fear of ridicule. They will reject the idea of becoming a cohesive community of learners. This is a battle you have to fight.

Thinking about the range of negative speech and unacceptable language along a continuum will make it easier to decide how to respond. Expressions of negative speech and unacceptable language are not created equal. Does it occur in informal conversation or during whole group instruction? Is it directed specifically at another student or an adult? Does it involve speech that is uncivil, rude, vulgar, or simply negative? Sometimes students' speech is correctable at the moment of expression. At other times, it's more effective to address the incident later in private or arrange a conference with students whose speech is relentlessly uncivil. When students cross the line to obscene or harassing speech directed at a specific person, they need to know exactly what will happen (for example, immediate removal from the classroom and more serious schoolwide consequences). A sample continuum appears below:

Rude, uncivil, or unproductive speech during whole group instruction or discussion

Unfriendly speech and a hostile demeanor toward peers and adults that some students wear as a badge of honor

Use of curse words not directed at anyone in particular

Deliberate negative speech intended to derail or sabotage whole group instruction or small group work

Persistent provocative, argumentative, and adversarial speech directed at an adult

- -

When a student crosses this line, removal from class should be immediate, and other serious consequences must be implemented.

Obscene, abusive language directed at a particular student

Teasing, taunting, put-downs, and name-calling directed at a particular student

Bullying and harassment that targets an individual or a group

Cursing and hostile verbal confrontations directed at an adult

Review norms and consequences related to public speech

Be crystal clear about specific language that students cannot use and the norms of speech that you expect students to practice every day

The classroom is a public place and should reflect the norms of civil speech and the use of constructive language to communicate one's thoughts and feelings. You will need to spell out four things to students:

1. Be clear about words that are absolutely unacceptable to use in the classroom. You don't want to post this list, but you do want students to know what's on the list.

2. Be clear about what teasing, taunting, ridicule, and harassment sound like. (See *Making Learning REAL*, Chapter 17 for specific strategies and activities for preventing and interrupting harassment)

3. Stress the difference in words and tone between negative speech and constructive speech. Here's one effective strategy that teaches students how to turn negative comments into more constructive ones: Keep a running list of negative comments that you hear from the group. It's much better not to make this stuff up; students' own words generate juicier examples. Make a T-chart that looks like this:

Laundering Negative Language	
What does the negative version of the comment sound like?	**What does the constructive version sound like?**
Example: "This is a really stupid assignment."	"I don't understand why we're doing this assignment. Can you tell me again?"

Write a list of five to seven negative comments on the left-hand side. For each comment, ask the class to identify words that have a negative charge, words that might provoke or offend the listener, and words that convey gloom and doom or a negative outlook. You might also ask students to figure out the concern or issue being expressed. This exercise is not about discounting or dismissing the idea behind the words. The goal is to clean up the language so that the listener (whether a peer or the teacher) is more open and responsive to the need, concern, or idea being expressed. Then as a whole group, ask students to transform the negative comment, keeping the idea but replacing the negative words with language that is more neutral, positive, constructive, or hopeful. (You may also want to refer to Chapter 5, pages 151–154 on aggressive, passive, and assertive speech and behavior.)

4. Clarify the difference between public and private conversation. Very often, students will say in their defense, "I was only talking to my friend _____. It's not anybody else's business." Students don't understand that if everyone in the room (or hallway) can hear it, their words have become public speech. And public speech becomes the business of every adult in the building. You need to enforce the public conversation rule: *"If you want to keep your conversation private, don't talk loud enough for me or others to hear it. If I hear it, it becomes my job to deal with it."*

Review consequences for unacceptable speech

The chart that follows on page 199 presents a range of public speech infractions and suggested consequences from problematic in the left-hand column to the most egregious in the right-hand column. The numbers here align with the charts on pages 26–27.

Interrupt negative speech using multiple strategies

Remind yourself that you're the one with the skills in this situation, not the student. If you see yourself as the skillful teacher, your job is to respond in ways that help students become more aware of the impact of what they say and support students to learn to say things more respectfully and constructively. Intention is not the same as impact. Sometimes students are not fully aware of the negative impact of their language and posturing. Their intentions may in fact be sincere and well meaning, but their choice of words and tone has the opposite effect when you hear it. If you don't insist that students correct their speech, they'll never learn how to clean it up. With students who adopt a habit of speech that is constantly on the verge of rude, crude, or uncivil, you'll need to go beyond the immediate goal of interruption and correction, and set aside time to conference with the student and develop a plan for improving public talk.

Remember that student incivility reflects a larger uncivil culture. Adolescents didn't make the world they live in. Most teenagers do not yet possess a full command of language or the ability to switch their modes and codes of speech easily from one context to another. Add to the mix a popular culture that encourages people to use words as weapons. The media is saturated with wise-cracking kids talking back to adults who don't even flinch at the abusive language hurled in their direction. The harangue of invectives that kids hear on TV, in movies, and on CDs sounds perfectly normal to American teens. Every time we stop the conversation and insist that students clean up their language, we take a small step toward reclaiming a sense of civility in our schools and our lives.

What's the behavior?		
These are examples of negative speech that are correctable in the moment but probably require a written referral, conferencing, and other accountable consequences and interventions when behavior is habitual.	These are examples of negative speech that are unlikely to change without a conference with you and other accountable consequences and interventions.	These are all egregious violations of another person's dignity and warrant immediate consequences and interventions, including removal from the classroom.
19. Persistently rude, uncivil, provocative, or offensive speech, gesturing, or posturing during whole group learning 33. Rude, unfriendly, or disrespectful verbal responses, gestures, and posturing directed at an adult (This is the annoying stuff that you can't take personally, but you do want students to correct or cease and desist quickly.)	11. Deliberate acts and use of negative speech that sabotage the group or suck the energy out of the room 34. Persistent demands, argumentative and adversarial speech, and "lawyering up" 26. Cursing, yelling, or excessive use of criticism, blame, sarcasm, and accusations directed at specific students	27. Teasing, taunting, put-downs, and name-calling directed at specific students 32. Harassment (abusive, obscene, or offensive language, gestures, propositions, or behaviors intended to target or harm an individual or a group based on race, color, origins, gender, sexual identity, age, religion, class, or disability) 38. Cursing that is specifically directed at an adult
What's the consequence?		
• Offer verbal prompts that invite immediate self-correction • Record what a student is saying exactly or tally the number of times a negative speech incident occurs so you can discuss it later with the student (This is especially effective for negative speech and unacceptable language if students know they will need to restate what they said to you, an administrator, or a parent.) • When negative speech persists, state consequences and offer "double or nothing" ("*Stop _____ and start _____ and you're good to go. Choose to continue _____, and you owe me a workout session and an accountable consequence.*")	• Speak with a student privately during your classroom walk-around, at the end of class, or outside of class • Develop a plan, contract, or conduct card and provide follow-up feedback and coaching • Student calls parent in presence of teacher • Phone call or conference with parent and student • Restrictions on speaking during class • Verbal or written apology • Lunchtime or after-school workout that includes practice or rehearsal to express oneself more constructively • Classroom referral to dean or assistant principal, but no immediate removal from the classroom	• Immediate intervention to stop the behavior or defuse the situation • Immediate removal from the classroom to dean or assistant principal • Student calls parent in presence of dean or assistant principal, or dean, assistant principal, or principal calls parent • Conference with student, teacher, and dean, assistant principal, or principal • Daily conduct card and feedback for several weeks • Counseling or behavior replacement sessions with guidance staff • Pre-suspension conference • In-school suspension or time-out room plus re-entry protocols • Out-of-school suspension plus re-entry protocols

6

Insist on self-correction

Two questions should frame your responses to negative and unacceptable speech:

- *"What's the goal of my response?"*

- *"How much emotional charge do I want behind my words?"*

If you react to students' poor choice of language as if it's a personal attack on you or your values, your focus remains fixed on expressing your own distress. When anger drives your response, you're likely to slam down hard and use emotionally loaded language like "You're way out of line. What gives you the right to use that kind of language in here?" Or, "Where do you think you are—in the middle of a street fight?" Or, "You have no respect for yourself when you speak like that." Or, "Don't think you can get away with that kind of trash talk. You're out of here for the rest of the period."

The problem with this approach is that students hear your anger directed at them; they don't hear your insistence that they learn and practice more effective, more respectful ways of saying what they want to say. If you depersonalize the situation, you can use your energy to remain calm, focused, and matter-of-fact. Once you're in a good place, use your well-rehearsed scripts to interrupt negative speech and help students correct it. When you use neutral, less emotionally charged language, you increase the odds that the students will listen, reflect, and self-correct in a way that's more respectful and constructive.

Think about when and where you will insist that students correct their speech:

- Is it more effective to insist on correction in private or public?

- In what circumstances do you insist on immediate correction? When do you wait until a later opportunity in class? When do you address it with the student at the end of the class period?

- What incidents require a personal conference and practice to replace unacceptable speech with more appropriate and constructive language?

Here are some scripts to try out:

- *"When you use language like that I have a hard time listening. Try that one more time."*

- *"Wait a second. Try saying that again leaving out the loaded language."*

- *"Your words crossed the line of respect. Say that again in another way, please."*

- *"Here's another way you could say that to get your point across respectfully. Now try it again in your own words."*

- *"For me to make a serious effort to listen to you, I need you to make a serious effort to discuss your concern in a way that feels respectful. Can you do that? Let's rewind the tape and try it again."*

- *"Wow, that sounded pretty (hostile, blameful, rude, offensive). Is that what you wanted me to think? Tell me again what you want to say."*

- *"Here's what I heard. Is that what you really meant to say to me?"*

- *"When I hear words that feel so disrespectful, it's hard to even hear you out. Try saying it another way and this time I will try to listen."*

- *"Say that in another way, please."*

- *"You might want to check yourself about that. Try again."*

- *"Excuse me? Let's try that again."*

Some teachers involve the peer group in countering negative speech. The group decides on corrective measures, and students hold each other accountable. For example, the group might agree to say, "That's a negative hit" when they hear comments that are particularly negative. The offending student must then either restate the comments with the negatives laundered out or forfeit the right to speak for the rest of the period.

Reframe students' negative language

When students use negative language to express their opinions, try reframing their remarks in a way that draws out the concerns behind their remark and replaces negative speech with more neutral words and a more positive tone. When we do this, we are letting students know that we want to keep the conversation going, but not on negative terms. We are modeling more appropriate speech by reframing the student's statement, and we're encouraging students to clarify their thinking by asking them to say more precisely what they mean. Here are a few examples:

Student comment to teacher: Why do we have to read this stupid book about a bunch of religious crazy people?

Teacher response: *"So you wouldn't recommend* The Scarlet Letter *to your best friend, huh? Tell me how you think those characters in the book are different from us."*

Student comment in class discussion: "What an ignorant thing to say. Everybody knows that's not true."

Teacher response: *"Let's reframe that, shall we? What is it precisely about this statement that you disagree with?"*

Student comment: "This school sucks. People get suspended for no reason around here. It's just like a prison."

Teacher response: *"I can tell you're upset about this. What is it exactly about the suspension policy that bothers you the most?"*

6

Document negative speech incidents to discuss with the student later

For students who persistently use negative speech and unacceptable language, record exactly what they say, when it occurs, and the number of times it happens it on a clipboard you have handy at all times. There are many ways to use this documentation, and each option has huge benefits.

1. Sometimes just the act of recording students' negative speech will prevent or reduce its occurrence.

2. In a private moment, insist that the student read his or her comments back to you, or you read it back to the student. Just hearing their own words out loud can sometimes jolt students into checking themselves before they speak.

3. In a phone call with a parent, insist that the student read back what they said to the parent. If students know this is the usual protocol, most will think at least twice before saying it again.

4. Include your exact documentation on a written referral to make your case to the dean or assistant principal that the student's behavior warrants more intensive consequences and interventions.

5. Your documentation serves as starting point of a conference; the evidence for what needs to stop and why; the rationale for developing two-week conduct cards that you and the student use to monitor reduction in unwanted behaviors and an increase in the desired behaviors related to speech and self-expression. (See Appendix A: Conduct Card on page 264.)

6. You have ready-made content that the student can use to practice reworking unacceptable speech into more constructive statements during a workout session with you.

Restrict students who habitually use negative speech

Some teachers work out very specific speaking restrictions for students who have no filters to temper what they say, when they say it, where they say it, and how they say it. As the students' speech improves, restrictions are lifted. Restrictions might include (1) the five-second delay, in which the student needs to write it before he or she can say it; (2) limiting the number of a student's verbal responses during whole group time within a class period; (3) not calling on the student first in any situation where the group's comments or questions are solicited; (4) restricting opportunities when the student can speak publicly; and (5) insisting that the student speak with you privately, rather than publicly, about specific topics and issues.

Intervene immediately when students' speech is beyond correction

When students' words are so ugly, shocking, or hateful that they leave us speechless, this is the time to stop, shore up your convictions, and in a quiet and serious voice say something like, *"I don't ever want to hear that again. And here's why. Those words violate the dignity every person deserves and the right of all of us to feel safe and respected in this room. That is unacceptable for me."*

In these situations, the student must be removed from class immediately. Write an exit referral and phone or send a note to the dean or a security officer to escort the student to the office. What you do next may depend on how unsettled the class feels or whether a particular student or group has been targeted viciously. You might stop what you are doing, post some open-ended questions, and ask students to write in their journals while you speak with the person or group who was targeted. Or you might say, *"I want to think carefully about how we discuss this, so right now I want you to work silently on _____. Before class is over, we'll have a conversation about what just happened."*

The point is that you can't ignore speech that breaches students' trust in you to keep the classroom a safe place. Three things need to happen:

1. Students need to be able to express how they experienced what happened.

2. With the offending student, you will need to discuss how he or she restores his or her good standing in the classroom. Even though it's uncomfortable, you may want to talk with the offending student about what he or she will say to the group or what you will say to the group when the student returns to class.

3. You will need to discuss with the group how they will handle the offending student's re-entry in a way that doesn't make the offender a new target.

None of this is easy. However, your efforts to help the offender and the group make things right can have a powerful impact on students' sense of right and wrong and ethical responsibility.

6

INVITE STUDENTS TO COOPERATE AND SELF-CORRECT

Life Skill Connections (See pages 141–144)

5. Know what you do that bothers others and accept responsibility when you mess up.

6. Reflect on your behavior; be able to learn from it, self-correct, redirect, and change when you need to.

7. Make responsible choices for yourself by analyzing situations accurately and predicting consequences of different behaviors.

9. Exercise self-discipline and impulse control.

11. Seek help when you need it.

12. Focus and pay attention.

17. Assess your skills, competencies, effort, and quality of work accurately.

The following sections present suggestions for effective teacher talk for redirecting off-task behaviors when students are working independently or in small groups.

Intervene when students are confused or stuck

Encourage students to place a help sign on their desks when they've tried other strategies (such as "three before me") and still need your assistance. This avoids needless hand-raising and whining to get your attention. In most situations, a direct but brief prompt will work.

- *"What's your best guess about what to do next?"*

- *"Look at _____. Here's what you need to do."*

- *"Here's how you might tackle _____."*

- *"Here's what you need to do next."*

- *"Here's what you might want to think about and write down before you _____."*

- When you notice a student blanking out, say, *"So what's next?"*

When tasks are complex or it's not clear what the issue is, tell students what you see and check out their understanding of the task at hand.

- Say, "*I see that you _____. Tell me what you think the task is right now.*"

- Ask, "*How are you doing with this?*"

- Say, "*Show me where you are.*"

- Say, "*Tell me what you're working on right now.*"

- Say, "*I've noticed you're having a hard time getting started. Stop for a minute, and write down in your own words what you think the task is. Then name one thing that's getting in the way of doing it and one thing you can do to feel like you've accomplished something today.*"

- Describe what's left to do, and communicate your confidence in the student to do it.

- Ask the student to predict how long it will take to do a particular task or a specific part of the task.

When the group has lost focus or the energy in the room is at a low ebb:

- Say, "*Where are we right now?*" Or, "*Let's review what we've already done today.*" Or, "*What's left on the agenda for today?*"

- Do a two-minute exercise or warm-up that helps students relax and refocus.

- Chunk tasks into small steps so students can name what they have done and what they need to do.

- Use a timer and set a specific amount of time for each step.

Redirect students when they look bored or disengaged

As you're walking around the room when students are working in groups or on their own, take a minute to check in privately with students who look bored, glazed over, or disengaged. Don't expect to remedy AWOL behaviors in the moment. Your best strategy is to make a quick connection during class that communicates your awareness, curiosity, or concern. Then schedule a conference time for later, when you can explore the sources of the discontent and make a plan to break the cycle of disengagement.

- "*I see that you look _____. Can you give me a clue about what's going on?*"

- "*I can see that you're not _____. What's up?*"

- "*I can see you're not with us. Tell me what it's going to take to get you back.*"

- Instead of "*Yes, but,*" try saying "*Yes, and.*" "*Yes, you're bored and you need to finish this.*"

You might also describe what you think a student is feeling, and commiserate with him or her to bring the student back to the situation at hand. Say, *"I bet you're wishing you were _____. Sometimes I wish I could be _____. Right now, though, we're here. Can you get your focus back for the next half-hour? Then you're done."* Or, *"Can you hang in there for the rest of the period? I'd really appreciate that."* Or, *"I'm wondering whether you're thinking, 'I _____.' Is that about right? Let's set a time to conference and see what we can work out."*

You could also get the student out of an unproductive funk by asking him or her to do you a favor. Say, *"It would be great if you could help me _____. Can you help me out with that?"* When the student is finished with the task, ask, *"Are you good to go back and work on _____? Thank you."*

When students are reluctant to participate in a particular activity or work on a specific assignment, ask them to take one minute and write down an alternative way to complete a task or meet the goal or expectation. If we insist that there is only one way to do the task or that students must do it our way, we risk provoking further resistance.

When a student is spending a lot of time doing nothing, nagging and interrogation are not likely to inspire an immediate turnaround. Instead, try "fogging." Connect with the student about something important to him or her that is completely unrelated to the course or the task at hand. (*"Who do you think has the best shot in the Final Four? Hmm…I'm hoping they win too."*) Then move on. Come back to the student later in the period to arrange a time to talk. Particularly for resistant students, the personal connection needs to come before the academic intervention.

For students who continue to express lack of interest, dislike, or boredom with the course, it's hard to help them move out of the land of "not learning" without naming what is making this a bad experience for them. You might say, *"It looks like you're really stuck and can't find a way to make this class okay for you. So let's start where you are. Cover a page with everything you dislike about class. Then we'll talk and see if we find a way through this."* Later during a personal conference, you might ask, *"What do you need to make this class a place you want to be?"* or *"What can I do to make class work better for you?"* or *"What can I do to help you get back on track?"*

This strategy can produce three positive results. First, you're catching a student off guard because you're not asking her to pretend that everything's fine when it isn't. You're validating that a student's negative feelings are real. Second, you're telling the student, *"Just because you don't like class doesn't mean I can't like you."* You're communicating that it's worth your time to listen and try to understand what's going on. Third, this kind of quick exercise can provide useful information to plumb underlying resistance, and it gives the two of you a place to begin working on a plan.

When students are doing the wrong thing or doing it at the wrong time

Use as few words as possible to give them quick information about what they should or should not be doing at the moment.

- *"Here's the trash can for the gum."*

- *"This is not the right time to _____. You can do that _____."*

- *"Now would be a good time to _____."*

- *"Save that for later when we _____."*

- *"Look on the agenda on the board to see when we're going to _____."*

- *"Here's where you need to be now."*

- *"You'll have a chance to _____ during _____."*

USE PROBLEM SOLVING AND LOGICAL CONSEQUENCES WHEN SELF-CORRECTION ISN'T ENOUGH

Life Skill Connections (See pages 141–144)

7. Make responsible choices for yourself by analyzing situations accurately and predicting the consequences of different behaviors.

24. Use win-win problem solving to resolve conflicts that meet the important goals and interests of the people involved.

All of the strategies in this section expect and support students to be responsible for the choices and decisions they make.

Offer students chances to solve problems and make choices

Give students at least two choices that you can live with that are both doable and will meet the immediate goal. Mention what students can do in addition to or in place of what they can't do. Say:

- *"You're welcome to _____ or _____. You decide."*

- *"Feel free to _____ or _____. You decide."*

- *"Would you rather _____ or _____. You decide."*

- *"What would work best for you right now? _____ or _____?"*

- *"Tell me two choices you can make right now. Okay, what's your preference?"*

- *"If you choose to continue _____, what will happen next? Is there another choice you can make?"*

- *"When you finish _____, you may choose to _____ or _____."*

- *"We have two options: _____ or _____. You can choose."*

Another strategy is to directly ask the student to name the problem. Give her a minute to think about a solution, and say, *"I'll get back to you in a minute when you've made your choice."*

Insist on problem solving and negotiation rather than complaints

When students feel that something is unfair, don't get hooked into arguing or justifying your actions. Don't listen to complaints in the middle of a lesson, and don't listen to complaints that don't come with suggestions. Make it very clear that students have at least three appropriate ways to discuss issues that are bothering them:

1. Students can use a feedback and suggestion form and write down the issue and their suggestions for how to remedy the situation.

2. Students can arrange a time to discuss the issue with you during independent work time in class or during your conference hours before or after school. You need to teach the language you want students to use to start this conversation. For example, *"This deadline seems unfair. Can we talk about this?"* Or, *"I'd like to know why _____. Can we talk about this?"* Or, *"I'd like to ask if there's another way we can _____. Can we talk about this?"*

3. If the issue in question affects the group, students can request a class meeting to discuss it and solve the problem.

Students like making deals. Let students know that individuals and the group are invited to make offers and suggest trade-offs that might increase motivation and productivity. Keep deals simple: *"If you do _____, I'll do _____."* Or, *"I'll trade you _____ for _____."*

The most effective problem-solving prompt of all time is a single word. When you hear a complaint or concern, just say *"And?"* and stop. Give the student a minute to be more specific and make a responsible suggestion.

Put the responsibility on the student when an unwanted behavior persists

Continually remind students that they know the consequences and they own the choices they make.

- *"Right now would be a good time to check yourself and rethink your options. You can _____ or _____. You choose."*

- *"I've said what I needed to say. You're the one in charge of what happens next."*

- *"If you choose to continue _____, you know the consequence. It's your choice."*

- *"Which is it going to be? Solve it yourself now in the classroom or work with me after school?"*

- *"It looks like you're making a choice to _____. Do you really want to go there?"*

- *"What choice is going to keep you out of trouble right now?"*

- *"What choice will help you get back on track?"*

Use an I-message when you want a student to know how her or his behavior is affecting you or the class. *"I feel ____ when you ____ because ____."* If your statement doesn't produce an appropriate response, you might say, *"I've said what I wanted to say now, and I will make a time to talk about this with you later."* Or, *"I was hoping that telling you how I felt about this would make a difference in what you choose to do right now."*

Give students the option of "double or nothing." If the unwanted behavior stops for the rest of the period, the student doesn't owe you time on your conference hour. If the unwanted behavior persists, the student owes you twice the time during a lunch or after-school workout session. An alternative to double or nothing is writing a classroom referral but not submitting it. If the student stops the unwanted behavior and has a clean slate the rest of the week, the referral is torn up.

6

Use logical consequences to correct minor problematic behaviors

Logical consequences (Tier 1) are always directly related to a specific behavior. (You made the mess, now you clean it up.) They are particularly effective for garden-variety disruptions that are typical in any classroom. When physical and verbal prompts don't work and the behavior persists, enforce the same no-frills consequence every time. Students will learn the drill quickly. Just keep the consequence clear and simple; don't make kids guess what's going to happen. Logical consequences save time and aggravation because they leave no room for arguments or problem solving. They are what they are and offer students the opportunity to remedy mistakes without a big fuss.

Logical Consequences	
What's the incident?	**What's the logical consequence?**
Persistent talking among the same two or three students during activities that require silence.	Students are assigned different seats placed around the periphery of the classroom during the same period or students are assigned different seats at the beginning of the next class period for _____ days.
Persistent interruptions and noisemaking by an individual student during activities that require silence.	Student is assigned a different seat on the periphery of the classroom or behind your desk for _____ days and may be given speaking restrictions for _____ days.
Uncooperative behavior in inter-active group activities	Student must work alone during any small group activities and/or write down a verbatim transcript of large group interactive activities for _____ days or the next week.
Throwing trash on the floor or throwing paper in the room	Student must clean up trash on the floor, arrange furniture, or tidy up the room at the end of class for _____ days.
Persistent goofy, irrelevant, and inappropriate questions	Student must attend a workout session during lunch or after school and write answers to a page of ridiculous questions.
Defacing property; making a mess	Student must attend a workout session to clean all of the tables, chairs, and desks in the room.
Two students who are constantly bickering with each other	Each student owes you a written explanation of his or her side of the story and a mediation session to work out an agreement for keeping the peace between them during class.
When a student repeatedly verbally refuses a directive to carry out a logical conse-quence…in an aggressive hostile manner	Now the student is in big trouble. The student has crossed the line from noncompliance to defiance, which is a serious offense in most school codes of conduct and usually warrants an immediate referral and more intensive interven-tions including classroom removal and suspension.

DEFUSE FEELINGS OF ANGER, FRUSTRATION, AND DISCOURAGEMENT

Life Skill Connections (See pages 141–144)

1. Recognize and name your own feelings.

2. Express feelings appropriately and assess the intensity of your feelings accurately (on an anger scale of 1 to 10, I feel...).

3. Understand the cause of your feelings and the connection between your feelings and your behavior.

4. Manage your anger and upset feelings (know your cues, triggers, and reducers).

5 Know what you do that bothers others and accept responsibility when you mess up.

8. Deal with stress and frustration effectively.

15. Activate hope, optimism, and positive motivation.

18. Exercise assertiveness; communicate your thoughts, feelings, and needs effectively to others.

21. "Read" and name others' emotions and nonverbal cues.

When students are upset, the focus shifts from correction and problem solving to empathy and recovery. Remember, when people are emotionally charged (whether it's intense feelings of anger or frustration), they can't think rationally. This isn't the time to probe or push. You have two jobs here. First, try to defuse a student's feelings by listening and reflecting back what you hear and see. Second, provide strategies that can help students recover, regain their control and composure, and get back on track.

Help defuse students' anger and frustration

Noticing what you see and using calming words of support and encouragement offer the best approach for defusing a student's emotional charge and making a personal connection. Your invitation gives the student the opportunity to collect himself and refocus. Your choice of response will often depend on what the group is doing at the time. If students are involved in small group or independent work, you have a bigger window of time to check in, listen, and assess what might be a good next step.

- Use your instincts to try to figure out what's bothering a student, and name and accept the negative feelings. *"I can see you're frustrated with this. It's the last thing you want to be doing right now, isn't it? Take a minute and I'll check back to see where we can go from here."* Your quick exit at this point gives students some space. When people are upset they can't solve problems. Come back later to check in.

- For some students, it's better to ask directly what they can do for themselves to cool down. Say, *"I see you're upset. What can you do for yourself to feel more relaxed and in control?"*

- For students who walk into your classroom already steaming and ready to blow, take the student aside and say, *"You look like you're ready to blow. On a scale of one to ten, how upset are you? Take a minute to cool down. Give me a signal when you feel like you're down to a five."*

- When students are emotionally charged by a comment made in a classroom discussion, say, *"You had a really strong reaction to that comment. Let's hear how others feel about this."*

Here are other prompts that communicate the message, *"I noticed, I'm checking in, we all get upset sometimes."*

- *"Take a minute to get a drink, and when you get back to your seat, we'll start again."*

- *"I can see you're too upset to focus right now. Take a few minutes to stop, take a few breaths, and relax a bit. Let me know when you think you're ready to rejoin us. Does that work?"*

- *"Are you okay?"*

- *"How can I help?"*

- *"You look too upset to discuss this now. We'll talk about this later."*

- *"Why don't you stand up and stretch a minute?"*

- *"You look _____. Tell me more about what you're feeling."*

- *"Is there anything I did that prompted _____?"*

Let students know what they can do to cool down

Any of these strategies gives students the space to take five, recover, and regain control before they reconnect with the group.

- Encourage students to get in the habit of asking themselves, *"How do I feel right now? What can I do for myself to cool down? How would I like to feel in a few minutes? What will help me get there so I can reconnect?"*

- Invite students to use one of their passes to take a two-minute walk and get a drink.

- Identify a soft object or toy as the "chill thing." When students need a few minutes to collect themselves in class, they can place the object on their desks. The object signals *"Leave me alone for a few minutes. I need some space. Then I'll be okay."*

- Encourage students to use self-talk to help them settle and refocus. For example, *"I know I'm angry right now, but I don't want to blow it. Let me just relax for a minute, take some deep breaths, and get back to the task. I can deal with this later."*

- For some students, writing helps. Invite students to take a few minutes to write down what they're feeling and what they can do to feel differently.

- Ask students to picture an image of a favorite place that helps them feel relaxed and calm. *"Touch your pulse with one finger, and use this image as your 'anchor' to relax and breathe for a minute."*

- Write down what you want to say or do at a later time.

- Invite students to take a personal time-out in the rocker (or another special place in the classroom).

- If a student is at the point where she can't think and can't work and needs some space and quiet to collect herself, let her know she can use one of her passes to go to the library.

- If a student is at the point where he needs to talk to someone *right now*, ask him to speak with you privately or write you a quick note. Students may use one of their passes to go to the guidance/student support center.

- If a student is upset with you, you're probably upset with her. You probably both have regrets and a little hostility at this point. It may be time to arrange a conference and use a restorative justice protocol that focuses on mending the relationship before you can fix the problem.

6

Communicate your support and confidence when students feel discouraged

When students feel discouraged, they've moved beyond anger and frustration to a place where they're saying, "I can't do this," "I'm stupid," or "I give up." When students don't believe in their capacity to succeed, their motivation plummets to zero. What you do and say depends on what you observe. When discouragement is temporary and connected to a specific academic task, your responses need to communicate your confidence in students' capacity to work through it.

- *"I know this is difficult and I know you can do it."*

- *"I know and you know you can do this. Thanks for giving it a try."*

- *"You can handle this."*

- *"I'm confident you can do this."*

- *"I understand. I have times when I want to give up too. I know you can get through this."*

- *"You've been successful before. You can use those strengths and qualities to be successful again."*

- *"Remember when you _____. You really showed yourself that you could do it."*

- *"Let's just focus on one thing right now."*

- *"Let's work through this together."*

- *"Take a break from this right now. We'll pick it up tomorrow when it's fresh."*

On the other hand, when discouragement looks like a permanent condition for the student (in your class or in school generally), your work's cut out for you. Committing yourself to working with permanently discouraged students requires the mantra "Go slow to go fast." Discouraged students are especially vulnerable. When students feel vulnerable, they are less likely to trust any adult who comes near them. You probably want to speak with your team or a counselor, social worker, or intervention specialist to discuss possible strategies and interventions.

In the meantime, what do you do? In cases of severe discouragement, the relationship has to come first, and specific academic interventions and support come later. It may take weeks or even months to make a connection that can enable you and the student to get to the sources of discouragement and figure out a plan that can help her turn it around. Think about one thing you can do every single day that creates a personal connection with the student (a physical gesture or light touch, written or verbal words of support and encouragement, a small act of kindness and generosity). Whatever you choose to do should communicate these messages:

- I won't give up on you. I'm here to help and support you when you're ready.

- Even when you're discouraged, who you are matters to me.

- I'm glad you're still here and coming to class every day.

- These are things you've done that have made my day.

- I believe you can right yourself and get through this difficult time.

- I don't expect miracles. I'll give you some time and space to work on this.

PLAN, ORGANIZE, DOCUMENT, AND TRACK GUIDED DISCIPLINE SUPPORTS AND INTERVENTIONS

Implement guided discipline supports and interventions every week

You need to put in the time to get the results you want. Particularly during the first month of school, the more time you put in, the more satisfied you'll be with the degree to which students can discipline themselves and participate actively in creating a positive learning environment. Concentrating instruction about all things disciplinary in the first month of school will ensure that your discipline goals, behavioral expectations, procedures, and protocols are crystal clear to everyone.

One way to support your own intentional practice of implementing guided discipline and personalized student support is to set aside in-class and out-of-class time each week that is devoted specifically to disciplinary conferencing, interventions, and follow-up. If this becomes a weekly routine, it's not nearly so stressful to make that parent phone call or meet with a group of students for a workout or tutorial during planning periods or during conference hours before and after school.

Every week during out-of-class time, do the following:

- Make eight proactive calls to inform parents of behavior or academic problems; to discuss student conferences, discipline plans, problem-solving reports, or academic contracts; to discuss follow-up consequences; to update a student's progress; or to make arrangements for a parent-student-teacher conference.

- Use one lunch or planning period to conference with students and work with them on disciplinary plans, self-management strategies, problem-solving reports, and academic work.

- Schedule one after- and before-school conference hour to work with students on disciplinary plans, self-management strategies, problem-solving reports, and academic work.

- Make five sunshine calls to parents. The goal is to talk to every parent at some point during the semester, sharing something their child has done well and/or something you appreciate about their child.

6

- Review and assess academic and behavioral data, behavioral plans, and academic contracts that will shape group instruction, and student check-ins for the following week.

- Do 15 written feedback and appreciation notes to students and the whole class.

- Make time for two one-on-one sessions with students who really need an extra dose of connection, support, and encouragement.

Every week during in-class time, do the following:

- During the Do Now activity that students begin upon entering class, you can do two-minute check-ins with two students each day.

- Make sure every student gets positive comments twice a week (when you meet and greet at the door, when students are engaged in independent or group work, etc.).

- Open and/or close the week with a 10- to 15-minute activity that focuses on goal-setting, reflection, and behavioral and academic self-assessment.

- Do at least one gathering where everyone in the class gets an opportunity to be heard.

- Review discipline policies, procedures, and problem-solving protocols as needed.

- Integrate life skills and habits of learning into your lesson plans. For every lesson, identify behavioral goals and life skills student will practice.

- Facilitate brief class meetings to discuss whole class concerns or negotiate class-room decisions.

Track and document what you do and what your students do

Transparency works for both you and students. Organized documentation also increases the likelihood that you'll sustain the systems you create for more than a week!

- Keep a student conference log for each class. A sample log can be found on page 116.

- Keep a parent contact log for each class. A sample template can be found on page 218. See more about parent connections in Chapter 7.

- Keep a discipline/student support journal to record your plans and reflections during the year.

- Post data related to academic and behavioral goals students are working on. A sample chart is shown below.

Goal: Increase number or percentage of students who complete three homework assignments per week

Week	Number or Percentage of Students	
_____	_____	_____%
_____	_____	_____%
_____	_____	_____%
_____	_____	_____%
_____	_____	_____%
_____	_____	_____%

- Create a deck of student data cards for each class. Put each student's name and contact information on a 5" x 8" note card. Then punch a hole in the corner of each card and use a steel ring to hook your student deck together. Record notes, anecdotes, cues, strategies, and life skill goals that are specific to each student. This is an easy system for collecting useful information for conferences, check-ins, parent contacts, etc.

- Make your classroom practices transparent by posting:

  ▶ procedures and routines

  ▶ expectations (learning, student work, behavior)

  ▶ norms, agreements, and guidelines

  ▶ class meeting and decision-making guidelines

  ▶ activities that require silence

  ▶ cooperative learning expectations

  ▶ accountable consequences and interventions

- Use written conference and report forms and learning contracts.

- Use folders in which students record their weekly goals, progress, reflections, and self-assessments.

STUDENT CONFERENCE LOG Name of Student			
Procedural Infractions			
Uncooperative, Off-Task Behaviors			
Interpersonal Conflicts			
Boundary Violations			
Academic Learning Gaps			
Upset Feelings and Personal Distress			
Behavioral or Academic Contacts			
Mediation			
"Kid Talk" Protocol w/Team			
Classroom Referral & Request for Support			
Student Intervention/ Support Team Referral			
_____ _____			

PARENT CONTACT LOG Name of Student			
"Tell Me More" Calls			
Sunshine Calls or Notes			
Problem Calls			
6 a.m. Call			
Parent Signatures			
Parent Newsletter			
Student Newsletter			
Parent/ Homework Connection			
Parent Conference			
Parent- Student Conference			
Parent, Team, and/or Admin. Conference			
_____ _____			

REFERENCES:

Dennison, P., and Dennison, G., Editors. (1994) *Brain gym*. Teacher's revised edition. Ventura, CA: Edu-Kinesthetics.

Evertson, C. M., and Weinstein, C. S., Editors. (2006) *Handbook of classroom management*. Philadelphia, PA: Lawrence Erlbaum Associates.

Jensen, E. (2003) *Tools for engagement: Managing emotional states for learner success*. Thousand Oaks, CA: Corwin Press.

Jensen, E. (2004) *Brin compatible strategies*. Thousand Oaks, CA: Corwin Press.

Jensen, E. (2005) *Teaching with the brin in mind*. 2nd edition. Alexandria, VA: ASCD.

Jones, F. (2007) *Tools for teaching: Discipline, instruction, motivation*. Santa Cruz, CA: Fredric H. Jones and Associates.

Kounin, J. (1977) *Discipline and group management in classrooms*. Malabar, FL: Krieger Publishing.

Promislow, S. (2005) *Making the brain body connection: A playful guide to releasing mental, physical, & emotional blocks to success*. Vancouver, BC: Enhanced Learning and Integration, Inc.

6

CHAPTER 7:

Step 5: Develop Accountable Consequences and Supportive Interventions

More intensive accountable consequences and supportive interventions are needed when:

- Invitations to cooperate and self-correct don't work, and unwanted behaviors persist;

- Students are angry and confrontational; they're looking for a fight with you or another student;

- Students or the group engage in chronic unwanted behaviors that disrupt the learning environment;

- Students commit egregious acts of aggression;

- You and an individual student or group of students are experiencing a protracted conflict that generates anger and resistance, and ultimately results in hostile stand-offs or broken relationships;

- Students are involved in protracted interpersonal conflicts with peers;

- Students experience sustained emotional distress; or

- Students or the group experience sustained academic learning gaps.

To review, accountable consequences and interventions are done *by* a student with the support of an adult. The intention is to help students take responsibility for their behavior or academic problems, understand the effects of their behavior on themselves and others, correct the situation or repair the harm, and practice desired behaviors that are more skillful, responsible, and productive. Developing a full array of accountable consequences and interventions enables you to respond with immediacy and authority to a variety of problems without feeling put on the spot.

ADDRESS PERSISTENT UNWANTED BEHAVIORS FROM DAY ONE

Knowing what you're going to say and do *before* persistent unwanted behaviors occur will increase your comfort, conviction, and capacity to act. You won't spend time nagging or yelling because students know what to expect from you and know what's expected of them. Effective consequences and interventions have four things in common:

7

You are decisive
You are clear and direct
You are consistent
You follow through

Most of us weren't born with the gut instincts of a tiny group of teachers who make all things related to discipline look easy. However, repetitive use of the same consequences and interventions over time will help your disciplinary approach become more authentic and intuitive. Ultimately, there's nothing more satisfying than seeing your efforts pay off in improved student behavior.

Think Before You Intervene

Think about your goals when unwanted behaviors occur. In the moment, you want do whatever you can to help students self-correct, get back on track and on task, and sustain the flow and positive energy of the lesson or learning activity. Later, you can talk with students privately about the situation, solve problems, and make a plan.

Doing something later is not the same as doing nothing.

Keep these questions in mind before you choose to intervene with a student:

- What do I say and do now? What is my immediate goal?

- What do I say and do later? What kind of consequences or interventions will support the desired behavior or academic turnaround?

- What do I say and do now to maintain the relationship?

- How can I respond in a way that is as private as possible?

- How can I respond in a way that is more observational than critical or punitive, more low-key than dramatic, more assertive than aggressive?

- How do I create the physical and emotional space for the student to save face?

- Where am I and where is the student? (I don't want to do anything that will heighten the drama or draw more attention to the situation than it deserves.)

- What is the learning context? Is it...

  ▸ **ME and the WHOLE GROUP?** (I want to notice what's happening and move on so I don't disrupt the flow of the current learning activity or allow the unwanted behavior of one student to get in the way of the group's learning.)

  ▸ **ME and SOME STUDENTS?** (If I'm working with some students while other students are going off track, I can walk over to the other students, check in and observe the situation, and name the consequence.)

  ▸ **SMALL GROUP WORK?** (I can walk over to the group involved in the unwanted behavior and talk privately with them.)

  ▸ **INDEPENDENT WORK?** (I can walk over to the student or students involved in the unwanted behavior and talk privately with them.)

Bottom line? It's far more difficult to intervene effectively during whole group instruction. Think carefully about pacing each class period in ways that include whole group, small group, and independent learning time.

Prioritize problem behaviors you want to be ready for

Not all unwanted behaviors and incidents are alike. Anticipate the unwanted behaviors that are most likely to walk through your door, and be prepared to handle them effectively from day one. The unwanted behaviors described in Chapter 1 are also listed in this section on page 225. For most unwanted behaviors, plan out the following sequence of scaffolded responses:

1. When the unwanted behavior is occasional, what's the procedure or prompt that you use to redirect students and help them self-correct, refocus, and get back on track?

2. If the unwanted behavior persists, is there a logical consequence that goes into effect? (See section on logical consequences, Chapter 6.)

3. If there is not an immediate logical consequence, what's your "double or nothing" statement? ("*If you stop _____ and start _____ , you're good to go. If you choose to continue_____ , you owe me double the time in a workout session.*")

4. When students show up for the workout session, be clear about what you expect them to do and what other accountable consequences may kick in:

7

The Workout Session	Other Accountable Consequences
• Completion of behavior report forms • Written reflection or essay related to the behavior or incident • Personal conference to check in and find out what's up • Behavior plan, conduct card, or learning contract • Student calls parent in presence of teacher • Corrective or restorative actions to make things right and earn back one's good standing • Verbal or written apology • Session devoted to learning and practicing procedures or practicing and rehearsing desired behavior • Academic makeup session for tardies • Academic tutorial • Academic workout to revise, redo, and complete unsatisfactory work • Logical consequences associated with specific behaviors	• Phone call or conference with parent and student • Restrictions, modifications, or loss of privileges • Daily conduct card for several weeks that parent must sign and student must return • Team meeting to discuss possible turnaround strategies • Referral to guidance, early intervention team, or student support team • Written entry in student's record • Student-parent-teacher-dean conference to review intervention and/or behavior plan • Parent observation of student in classroom with debriefing • Classroom referral to dean or assistant principal, but no immediate removal from the classroom • Immediate removal from the classroom to dean or assistant principal • Student calls parent in presence of dean or assistant principal; or dean, assistant principal, or principal calls parent • Conference with student; teacher; and dean, assistant principal, or principal • Student-teacher mediation or other restorative justice protocols • Counseling or behavior replacement sessions with guidance staff during or after school or on Saturday • Pre-suspension conference

Prioritize the Problem Behaviors You Want to Be Ready For

1. Procedural Infractions, Noncompletion, and Noncompliance

1. Doesn't bring necessary materials to class
2. Unprepared for class
3. Noncompletion or poor quality of assigned work
4. Noncompliance with classroom or schoolwide norms and procedures

2. Noncooperation and Nonparticipation

5. No attempt to do assiged work
6. Loss of focus; confusion; or temporary frustration, anger, or disengagement
7. Initiating or joining in sidebar conversations
8. Playing around or goofing off with others
9. Nonparticipation in activities, withdrawal, or detachment
10. Inability to work cooperatively with others or resolve interpersonal differences
11. Deliberate acts and use of negative speech that sabotage the group or suck the energy out of the room

3. Impulse Control, Self-Management, and Personal Distress

12. Distracting or disruptive movement or noise
13. Interrupting others, blurting out inappropriate comments, or always having to have the last word
14. Persistent whining or badgering
15. Inability to work silently when required or work independently without bothering others
16. Inability to manage anger or deal with persistent discouragement and frustration effectively
17. Student is easily triggered, annoyed, or upset by others
18. Persistent acts that seek teacher's attention or call attention to oneself
19. Persistently rude, uncivil, or offensive speech, gesturing, or posturing during whole group learning
20. Leaving classroom without permission
21. Out-of-control emotional outbursts or rage that jeopardizes safety, order, and other students' well-being
22. Misuse or destruction of property; vandalism; unsafe or unlawful use of materials and equipment
23. Lying, stealing, or plagiarism

4. Student-to-Student Aggression

24. Hostile, unfriendly, or disrespectful responses to peers
25. Deliberately annoying, provoking, or bothering peers
26. Cursing; yelling; or excessive use of criticism, blame, sarcasm, and accusations directed at a student
27. Teasing, taunting, put-downs, and name calling

- -

Consequences and interventions for the remaining behaviors in this category should be covered by schoolwide rules, policies, and protocols.

28. Pushing, shoving, and uninvited contact with another student
29. Verbal intimidation and threats
30. Physical intimidation, gang behaviors, bullying
31. Hitting, punching, kicking
32. Harassment (abusive, obscene, or offensive language; gestures, propositions, or behaviors intended to target or harm an individual or a group based on race, color, origins, gender, sexual identity, age, religion, class, or disability)

5. Student-to-Teacher Aggression

33. Rude, unfriendly, provocative, or disrespectful verbal responses, gestures, and posturing directed at an adult (This is the annoying stuff that you can't take personally but you do want students to correct or stop quickly.)
34. Persistent demands, argumentative and adversarial speech, and "lawyering up"
35. Walking away when an adult is speaking with student
36. Refusal to make a choice or follow a directive after repeated requests or refusal to accept and carry out accountable consequences

- -

Consequences and interventions for the remaining behaviors in this category should be covered by schoolwide rules, policies, and protocols.

37. Acts of spite and revenge directed at an adult
38. Cursing that is specifically directed at an adult
39. Verbal threats, hostile and aggressive confrontations, or physical intimidation directed at an adult
40. Assault with intent to harm

7

Establish three levels of consequences and supportive interventions

As described in the introduction, more and more districts are incorporating a three-tiered PBS model (Positive Behavior Supports) into schoolwide discipline systems and classroom management practices. The list on this page and the chart on page 228 illustrate three levels of behavioral consequences, interventions, and supports.

Tier 1 Consequences and Supportive Interventions (Immediate teacher responses to interrupt and redirect minor problematic behaviors)

- Physical, visual, and verbal prompts to redirect behavior immediately

- Logical consequences that take immediate effect (change your seat, pick up trash at the end of class for the rest of the week, correct inappropriate language, etc.)

- Start- and end-of-class check-ins with students who need the additional support and encouragement

- Informal check-ins with every student every week or rotating miniconferences to assess every student's progress

- Offer a choice or opportunity to solve the problem

- Record what a student is doing or saying exactly, or tally the number of times a behavior occurs, so you can discuss it later with the student

- Sunshine phone calls and notes to students and parents

- Random, intermittent group incentives and recognitions

Tier 2 Consequences and Supportive Interventions (Teacher responses to chronic unwanted behaviors and problem behaviors that don't have a quick fix)

- Student-teacher conference with learning/behavior plan or conduct card/progress card

- Office hours or mandated workout sessions with teacher for individual or small group guided instruction, practice, or learning of replacement behaviors, or correction and completion of work

- Owed time for multiple tardies

- Follow-up feedback and coaching to practice desired target behavior with the student

- Time-out with buddy teacher for remainder of period, and follow-up conference

- Classroom referral to dean, guidance, student intervention team, SPED team, or academic support team

- Case conferencing with other staff who teach or know student

- Conference with student and dean, or student, dean, and parent, with follow-up learning/behavior contract

- Daily conduct card and feedback for several weeks involving check-ins with dean or assistant principal

- Student-teacher mediation, reconciliation, or other restorative justice protocols

Tier 3 Consequences and Supportive Interventions (Automatic schoolwide responses that directly involve the principal, dean, counselor, or other support staff, and follow-up with teacher)

- Immediate removal from the classroom to dean or assistant principal

- Student calls parent in presence of dean or assistant principal, or dean, assistant principal, or principal calls parent to arrange a pre-suspension conference

- Student must return to school with parent the next day and/or receive a home visit

- Classroom observation by student support or guidance staff, or administrator

- Counseling or behavior replacement sessions with guidance staff during or after school or on Saturday

- Parent required to observe child in the classroom

- In-school suspension or time-out room, plus re-entry protocols

- Out-of-school suspension plus re-entry protocols

7

Three Tiers of Behavioral Supports and Interventions (For Classroom Teachers)

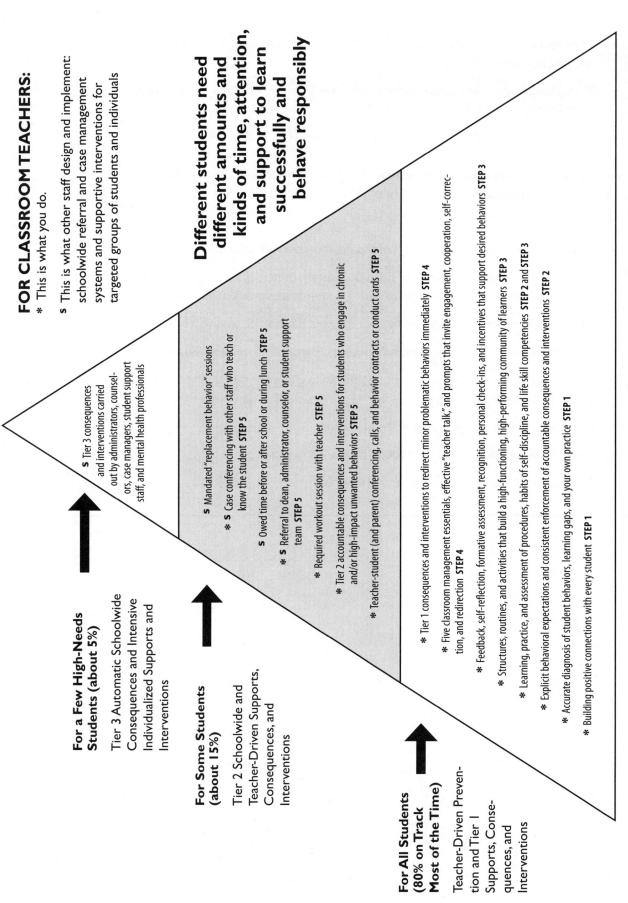

FOR CLASSROOM TEACHERS:

* This is what you do.

s This is what other staff design and implement: schoolwide referral and case management systems and supportive interventions for targeted groups of students and individuals

Different students need different amounts and kinds of time, attention, and support to learn successfully and behave responsibly

For a Few High-Needs Students (about 5%)

Tier 3 Automatic Schoolwide Consequences and Intensive Individualized Supports and Interventions

s Tier 3 consequences and interventions carried out by administrators, counselors, case managers, student support staff, and mental health professionals

For Some Students (about 15%)

Tier 2 Schoolwide and Teacher-Driven Supports, Consequences, and Interventions

s Mandated "replacement behavior" sessions

* s Case conferencing with other staff who teach or know the student **STEP 5**

s Owed time before or after school or during lunch **STEP 5**

* s Referral to dean, administrator, counselor, or student support team **STEP 5**

* Required workout session with teacher **STEP 5**

* Tier 2 accountable consequences and interventions for students who engage in chronic and/or high-impact unwanted behaviors **STEP 5**

* Teacher-student (and parent) conferencing, calls, and behavior contracts or conduct cards **STEP 5**

For All Students (80% on Track Most of the Time)

Teacher-Driven Prevention and Tier I Supports, Consequences, and Interventions

* Tier 1 consequences and interventions to redirect minor problematic behaviors immediately **STEP 4**

* Five classroom management essentials, effective "teacher talk," and prompts that invite engagement, cooperation, self-correction, and redirection **STEP 4**

* Feedback, self-reflection, formative assessment, recognition, personal check-ins, and incentives that support desired behaviors **STEP 3**

* Structures, routines, and activities that build a high-functioning, high-performing community of learners **STEP 3**

* Learning, practice, and assessment of procedures, habits of self-discipline, and life skill competencies **STEP 2** and **STEP 3**

* Explicit behavioral expectations and consistent enforcement of accountable consequences and interventions **STEP 2**

* Accurate diagnosis of student behaviors, learning gaps, and your own practice **STEP 1**

* Building positive connections with every student **STEP 1**

Based on the work of RTI Action Network (www.rtinetwork.org); OSEP Technical Assistance Center on Positive Behavioral Interventions and Supports (www.pbis.org); Center for Mental Health in Schools, UCLA (www.smhp.psych.ucla.edu); Osher, D., Dwyer, K. and Jackson, S. (2003) *Safe, supportive, and successful schools.* Frederick, CO: Sopris West; Lewis, T., and Sugai, G. (1999) *Safe schools: School-wide discipline practices.* Arlington, VA: Council for Exceptional Children; and Educators for Social Responsibility.

Discuss the difference between punishment and accountable consequences

Be sure to review the concept of accountable consequences with students. Students will learn what you're up to by witnessing your previous responses to the same behavior. They will be watching every day to see if you follow through consistently and really mean what you say. Stress that you expect students to take responsibility for their behavior by correcting mistakes or repairing the harm they caused. Explain that specific consequences will vary depending on the frequency and severity of the incident or unwanted behavior.

Accountable consequences promote shared accountability

The Adult takes responsibility to support the student to do what it takes to change behavior and sustain the new behavior over time.

Questions for the Adult

What are my goals in this intervention?

What else do I need to know?

What can I do to help the student meet his or her needs, solve the problem, take responsibility, restore equilibrium, repair relationships, learn and practice new skills, support a sustained change in behavior, and get back on track?

Students must first acknowledge the problem and then accept the responsibility to understand the effects of their behavior on themselves and others, and learn and practice behaviors that are more skillful, responsible, and productive. Consequences and interventions are viewed as natural outcomes of the choices students make and the skills they need to learn. Accountability is more than just saying, "I'm responsible for my actions." Being truly accountable involves specific actions that a student takes to make things right again. Accountable consequences involve four steps:

Questions for the Student

1. You're responsible for your behavior: *What did you choose to say or do? What do you think you said or did that made the teacher upset? Why do you think you're here? What were you supposed to be doing?*

2. Your behavior affects others: *How did your words or behavior impact your own learning, the teacher, other students, or the learning environment? How do you think _____ felt when you _____? Why do you think this wasn't the best choice?*

3. You're expected to carry out an accountable consequence: *What can you do to correct it; fix it; make amends or make it right; repair the harm you've done; or restore your good standing, a relationship, a sense of harmony, and trust?*

4. You're expected to change your behavior: *What's not working? What do you want to change? What kind of plan will help you change your behavior? What do you need to learn and practice to become more skillful and make a better choice? What will you do differently the next time this situation arises? What's one thing you can do to get back on track? How can the teacher support you in this effort?*

For consequences and interventions to work smoothly, students and parents need to be absolutely clear about why you're intervening and what will happen. When everyone knows that certain consequences and protocols are always going to be applied, students are less likely to put up a fuss and parents are more likely to support your efforts.

Diagnose problem behaviors accurately

When you misdiagnose the problem, you are less likely to choose the right goals or implement the most effective consequence or intervention. Review the suggested responses, consequences, and interventions that match different problem types and behaviors in Chapter 1.

Try using the Problem Diagnosis worksheet below to think through a problem and develop specific strategies for handling it. Four factors will influence how you tackle the problem.

1. The problem type

2. The frequency of the unwanted behavior

3. The severity of the behavior or specific incident

4. The number of students engaged in the unwanted behavior

Problem Diagnosis

Step 1: Name the Problem: What exactly is the problem? What have you observed?

Problem Type (Procedural infractions, noncompletion, and noncompliance; noncooperation and nonparticipation; lack of impulse control and self-management; student-student aggression; student-teacher aggression; academic learning gap?)	**Frequency** (Is the behavior occasional, repetitive, or chronic?)	**Severity** (Is it a garden-variety annoyance; a high-impact behavior that affects the whole group; or an egregious behavior that jeopardizes safety, respect, or dignity of individuals or the classroom community?)	**Number of Students Involved** (One student, two or three students, a handful, more than ten, the whole group?)

What's your goal now?

What's your goal (or goals) later?

Step 2: Group Norms, Procedures, and Learning Protocols: What can you do to prevent the unwanted behavior in the future?

Are there any procedures you need to put in place or any modifications to the learning environment that you need to make?

What are the desired target behaviors you want the student to learn and practice?

Step 3: Support Individuals and the Group:

How will you monitor and provide feedback on desired target behaviors?

What kinds of personal and group support, recognition, rewards, and incentives will encourage, motivate, and sustain the desired target behavior?

Step 4: Invite Students to Engage, Cooperate, and Self-Correct: What do you say and what do you do when it happens the first time? Is there a verbal or nonverbal cue that can help the student recover and correct?

7

Step 5: Develop Accountable Consequences and Supportive Interventions: What will you do when...

The unwanted behavior persists?

The unwanted behavior is chronic or egregious?

Is there any kind of external support or assistance you need from guidance counselors, administrators, or other colleagues in order to implement effective consequences and interventions?

What else do you need to know or find out?

DEFUSE AND DE-ESCALATE POTENTIAL CONFRONTATIONS AND POWER STRUGGLES

Life Skill Connections (See pages 141–144)

5. Know what you do that bothers others and accept responsibility when you mess up.

6. Reflect on your behavior; be able to learn from it, self-correct, redirect, and change when you need to.

7. Make responsible choices for yourself by analyzing situations accurately and predicting consequences of different behaviors.

Angry adolescents are their own worst enemies in the classroom. Kids can't think when they're in anger mode; their adrenaline overpowers any attempt to be reasonable and respectful. The toughest challenge for most teachers is defusing and de-escalating students' confrontational behavior when they're angry and hostile. Yet that's exactly what we need to do if we want kids to recover and regain a measure of calm and self-control.

When invitations to help students cooperate and self-correct don't work, use as few words as possible to defuse the situation, name the consequence, and make a quick exit. Remember, doing something later is *not the same* as doing nothing. You can always inform the student of a consequence at the end of class.

Try these strategies to de-escalate potential confrontations and power struggles, knowing that no strategy will work for every student. What you say to a boy with whom you have a solid relationship will differ from your approach to the girl in the corner who's angry all the time and waiting to pick a fight.

Don't give students the opportunity to argue and "lawyer up"

One of the worst things you can do is argue with an adolescent. You will never, ever win. You get upset. You lose focus. You waste time. Make a brief statement and then move on.

- When a student is geared up to argue with you, state both viewpoints. *"Here's how I see it, and here's how you see it. For the moment we're going to have to agree to disagree."*

- *"You have other opportunities to discuss this. Now is not the right time."*

- *"I'm not going to argue about this now."* Or, *"I'm through discussing this for now."* Or, *"I heard what you said and I need to think about it."*

- *"I'm not a lawyer, and class is not a courtroom. We're not going to trial over this."*

- *"I've given you the information you need."* Or, *"I think the procedure is pretty clear about this."* Move on, don't say anything else about the issue, and don't call on the student for the rest of the period.

- *"Let me think about that and I'll get back to you."*

- *"I've said what I needed to say. That's the end of the discussion for now."*

Name the consequence, exit, and deal with it later

When chronic or egregious unwanted behaviors require more deliberate consequences and interventions at a later time, quietly inform the student and move on. If you make a big deal out of it, most students are primed to make it a bigger deal. You will always lose.

- *"I noticed that (heard that) and we'll deal with it later."*

- *"I heard what you said, and we'll discuss the consequence at the end of class."*

- *"That violates the boundary of _____. We'll talk about the consequence later."*

De-escalate power struggles calmly and quickly

"Drop the rope" in power struggles, or try not to pick up the rope at all. Remind yourself that the goal right now is to de-escalate the situation by lowering the decibel level, defusing a student's emotional charge, diminishing the drama, and moving on.

- *"I know you think this is unfair, and I will talk with you about it later. Right now, I need you to _____. Can you do that?"*

- *"I know you're angry, so I'm not going to discuss this right now."*

- *"I can see how angry you are, and I don't want you to have to leave class. Here's the deal. Keep it contained for the rest of the period and we'll start over tomorrow."*

- Accept the feelings even as you stop the unacceptable behavior. *"I know you're upset about this and here's what you need to do right now."*

- *"I'm not going to get in a power struggle with you over this now."*

- For students who count on a pushback response, acknowledge their power and move on. *"You're right. I can't make you do this."*

- *"I've said what I needed to say. You're the one who's in charge of what happens next."*

- *"I want to keep your personal business personal. Let's find a minute at the end of class and hear each other out."*

WHEN THE GROUP MESSES UP

Life Skill Connections (See pages 141–144)

5. Know what you do that bothers others and accept responsibility when you mess up.

6. Reflect on your behavior; be able to learn from it, self-correct, redirect, and change when you need to.

7. Make responsible choices for yourself by analyzing situations accurately and predicting consequences of different behaviors.

24. Use win-win problem solving to resolve conflicts that meet the important goals and interests of the people involved.

33. Exercise effective leadership skills within a group.

34. "Read" dynamics in a group; assess group skills accurately; identify problems; generate, evaluate, and implement informed solutions that meet the needs of the group.

Help the group get unstuck

When the group is glazed over, squirrelly, or in a funk, slogging through the rest of the lesson just makes it worse. Stop! Name what you see and try one of these options:

- Invite everyone to get up, stretch, and walk around for a minute.

- Acknowledge that whatever you are currently doing in class is not working. *"Well, that didn't go very well."* Then announce that it's time to shift gears and try something else.

- Give the group a couple of options for what to do next. Take a quick vote (thumbs up or thumbs down), and do "the people's choice."

- Sometimes you have to just give in to the moment, let the goofiness run its course, or turn the annoyance on its head. One teacher, after one too many "accidental" cell phone interruptions, stopped and asked everyone to take out their cell phones and listen to the recorded sounds. It lightened up the moment, and then everyone got back to work.

Sometimes tensions within a group worsen simply because no one will actually say out loud what's bothering them about the behavior within the group. One way to break the logjam is to facilitate a series of brief class meetings (no more than ten or fifteen minutes each) to get the story out and move forward with a problem-solving focus and a new direction.

Class meeting 1

1. Ask individuals to take a note card and write down the comments or behaviors that feel irritating, upsetting, or hurtful to individuals or the group. You might suggest these starters: *"I don't like it when _____. It feels frustrating when _____. It bothers me when I see/hear _____."* Or these questions: *"What's getting in the way of making this class a good place to be? What behaviors bug you the most? What do you like doing most in this class? If you could do any project in class, what would you want to do?"*

2. Collect the cards and tell students you will share their feedback tomorrow.

Class meeting 2

1. Read some of the cards out loud in the back of the room where students can't see you but can only hear you. Read cards that capture the dominant themes and perspectives of the students.

2. After you've read students' comments, give students time to think and talk: *"How did it feel to hear these comments? What do these comments say about how we're doing as a community? Given what you've heard, what agreements should we revisit? Where do we go from here?"*

7

3. Use a "talking stick" that students can pass from one person to another when they speak.

Class meeting 3

1. Revise and renew your agreements and develop some group incentives to keep them. You might also invite the group to generate a list of projects and activities that students think will be fun.

2. Pass out another round of cards, asking each student to write down one thing that he or she can do to improve the situation or change the energy in the class.

3. Collect the cards.

(For more on setting class agreements, see *Making Learning REAL,* Chapter 14.)

Class meeting 4

1. Before the next class meeting, implement at least one of the students' suggestions to garner goodwill and develop trust that things can get better.

2. Then take a few minutes at the close of class or the next day to review new agreements and assess where you are. *"How are we doing? Where did we get it right? Where do we still have work to do? What will it take to stay in the groove?"*

Think about the role of public apologies in the group. Some schools and teachers develop a culture in which public apologies offer a powerful opportunity to recover, forgive, and restore one's good standing. Sometimes you can privately coach a few students who may feel a sense of relief when they own up to their mistakes. Here's one possible script: "I want to apologize for _____. My behavior made it difficult/frustrating/impossible for me/for the class to _____. I want to start over and I want to try to _____."

> There's nothing wrong with you
> that what's right with you can't fix.
> We can learn from our mistakes,
> recover, and start fresh.

Create an intervention plan when the whole group is messing up

When a group of students is engaging in the same behavior over several class periods, it's time to develop an intervention plan specifically for this group.

1. Take a few days to collect accurate data. How often is the behavior occurring, and how many students are involved in it?

2. Facilitate a class meeting to discuss the unwanted behavior and develop a plan to reduce it and increase the use of the desired target behavior. (See charts on pages 239–240.)

3. Implement your plan over two or three weeks.

4. Monitor, post, and chart the progress you see. Focus on the improvement, not the lapses.

5. You may want to provide some random re-enforcers just for fun.

    *   Put everyone's name in a basket and draw a name for treats or trinkets on days when no one has engaged in behaviors.

    *   At the end of the week, put in a basket the names of students who have not engaged in the unwanted behavior all week and draw a few names for treats or trinkets.

    *   Bring a snack for the whole class when the class has reduced incidents of the unwanted behavior by half.

    *   Be sure to make your data transparent so students can see how they're doing.

Goal: Increase amount of time the group can engage in silent independent work.

Week #		M	T	W	Th	F
	Number of Minutes					

7

When many students are engaging in the same unwanted behavior that gets in the way of...

- Learning effectively

- Relating to peers and adults positively

- Building a learning community that feels safe, welcoming, respectful, and connected

Name the Unwanted Behavior	**Name Desired Target Behavior**
_____	_____

| **Collect baseline data for a few days**
How often does the behavior occur? | **Record data for several weeks after intervention**
What's your goal for reducing the behavior?

From _____ to _____ per week
From _____ to _____ per day |

	Mon	Tues	Wed	Thurs	Fri	Mon	Tues	Wed	Thurs	Fri
Number of incidents										
Number of incidents										

Three ways to teach, practice, notice, encourage, and assess the desired target behavior:

Three ways to invite students to self-correct, cooperate, or get back on track:

Three ways to intervene effectively when the behavior persists:

Three ways that you will recognize, celebrate, and reward improved behavior:

Teach desired target behaviors that replace unwanted behaviors

What are some of the most common unwanted behaviors that get in the way of effective learning. What's the desired behavior you want to replace it? Below is a sample list generated by a team of teachers who identified the unwanted behaviors they wanted to reduce or eliminate and the desired target behaviors that they wanted students to use more regularly. The numbers here align with the chart on pages 26–27.

Unwanted Behaviors	Desired Target Behaviors What Do You Expect, Model, Teach, Practice, and Assess?
7. Initiating and joining in sidebar conversations; verbal disruptions; self-centered shouting out; not letting others have a chance to speak 13. Interrupting others, blurting out, always having to have the last word	*Responsive Listening* Teach responsive listening skills through pair-shares, listening labs, paraphrasing, and summarizing; taking turns to speak; encouraging others to comment by asking them questions; self-monitoring so students limit the number of times they speak during any one activity; students take charge of speakers' list
27. Teasing, taunting, and name-calling; put-downs that are viewed as part of mainstream culture, so it's OK and not a bad thing to say	*Respect; Supporting Students' Personal Dignity; Ally Behaviors that Interrupt Negative Speech Directed at Another Person* Supportive dialogue with students about creating a safe community where no one feels silenced or put down; model, discuss, teach, practice ally behaviors; self-monitoring so students catch themselves and clean up their language before they say it (think before you speak); self-correction when students do use negative or inappropriate language; students who are willing to encourage students to say something a different way or express their discomfort with put-down language
18. Persistent acts that seek teacher's attention; calculated disruptions to distract or become the center of attention	*Self-Discipline; Self-Management* Teach and assess habits of discipline, including capacity to focus, attend for sustained periods of time, and get back on track quickly when distracted
9. Nonparticipation in activities; withdrawal; detachment; apathy	*Meaningful Engagement and Participation* Demonstrate specific participation behaviors that show you're connected, interested, engaged
36. Refusal to accept and carry out accountable consequences; not accepting responsibility for one's words and actions; dishonesty and denial ("I didn't do it.")	*Acknowledgment of Actions; Acceptance of Consequences* Naming what you did; taking responsibility to come up with solutions; naming when you make mistakes; honest apologies; required workouts to follow through on consequences; tell students it's okay to own and admit mistakes; reflecting on accountable consequences begins with, "Here's what I did."

7

Unwanted Behaviors	Desired Target Behaviors What Do You Expect, Model, Teach, Practice, and Assess?
2. Unprepared for class	*Be Prepared* Clear expectations about being prepared; clear procedures when students are not prepared; implement clear accountable consequences, including workout sessions, when students are chronically unprepared for class; weekly/daily self-assessments of students' perceptions about feeling prepared for class
6. Loss of focus; agitated; temporary frustration 15. Inability to work silently or independently without bothering others	*Capacity to Focus, Attend, and Sustain Attention* Specific routines that help student settle in and get ready to learn; physical/proximity prompts; use a timer; build up sustained blocks of silent, independent work time; cues when silence is required
1. Doesn't bring necessary materials to class	*Bring all Materials Needed to Class* Generated student solutions to the problem of not bringing materials to class; students take responsibility for implementing solution; explicit procedures when students don't have needed materials
18. Persistent acts that seek teacher's attention or call attention to oneself; whining	*Assertive Speech and Behavior* Teach differences between aggressive, passive, and assertive speech and behavior; learn and use the language of requests; teach appropriate help-seeking behaviors, including "three before me"
3. Noncompletion or poor quality of assigned work; doing nothing when given time to complete assigned work	*Completing Quality Work that Meets a Standard of Proficiency* Invite student predictions on how long a task will take; "chunking" tasks and using a timer; visual prompts to review steps of an assignment or parts of a task; self-assessment related to work quality; accountable consequences, including required workouts when students turn in incomplete or shoddy work
33. Rude, unfriendly, provocative, or disrespectful verbal responses, gesturing, and posturing; talking back to adults 19. Persistently rude, uncivil, or offensive speech during whole group instruction 34. Aggressive speech (persistent demands, argumentative and adversarial speech)	*Constructive, Appropriate Speech* Modeling respectful speech to students; teaching differences between aggressive, passive, and assertive speech; teaching students how to disagree without being disagreeable; clear expectations governing nonacceptable speech; insistence on self-correction; recording and then discussing student's negative speech in personal conference; self-monitoring; strategies to stop and think before you speak (e.g., write it down before you say it, ask if it supports a respectful learning environment or shuts it down)

MAKE ONE-ON-ONE CONFERENCING A DAILY PRACTICE

Teacher-student conferencing (from one-minute check-ins to longer conferences for addressing more serious issues) serves many purposes. It's the ideal opportunity for discussing students' behavior, listening and problem solving when students are upset, discussing academic learning gaps, and completing problem-solving report forms, behavior plans, and academic contracts. If you don't set aside time to speak personally with students, nothing will change!

- **The Adult** supports the student to do what it takes to change behavior, get back on track, and stay out of trouble. **Questions for the Adult**: What are my goals in this intervention? What are the unmet needs driving the student's behavior (attention, power, the need for choice, inadequacy, revenge, etc.)? What's going on? What do I need to know? What can I do to help the student meet his or her needs, solve the problem, take responsibility, restore equilibrium, repair relationships, support a change in behavior, develop new skills, and get back on track? A useful opening statement is "So tell me why you think you're here."

- **The Student** takes responsibility for what he or she did or said and accepts the consequence, intervention, and support. **Questions for the Student**: What did I do? What was I supposed to be doing? Why am I here? What's not working? What do I need or want? What's one skill I can learn or one thing I can do to get back on track? What can I do differently next time?

When do you make time for conferencing?

It may seem impossible to schedule one-on-one conferences daily, but we strongly urge you to get creative and make the time. You can fit them in during class, when other students are engaged in silent reading and silent writing, small group work, independent work or sponge activities, homework time and guided practice at the end of the period, or study time for major tests and exams. Take two chairs and talk just outside the door. You can arrange to meet during your lunch or prep periods, during the student's lunch period (if you're available), during your weekly conference hours, or during workout sessions before and after school. And don't forget the power of conferencing with the student on the phone.

7

Use one-on-one conferences to link problem behaviors to desired target behaviors

When students owe you a workout session for persistent problem behaviors, the conference plays a critical role in making things right. Without a conference, you can't make a plan that names what the student will do to practice desired target behaviors and what you will do to support the desired change. Try using the conference forms and contracts contained in Appendix A as part of your conference protocols.

Conferences linked to problem behaviors

- **Make an observation or ask an open-ended low-threat question.** *"I've noticed that _____. So what's up?"* Or, *"You've not really been present for the last week—no homework, a poor test grade, no participation. Tell me what's going on?"* Or, *"I can tell that you're not thrilled to be in this class right now—talk to me about what's not working."* Or, *"You know the agreement we had about _____. Give yourself a grade on how you've been doing this week."* **Then stop and wait for the student to respond.**

- **Listen and acknowledge students' feelings. If the student is mad or upset, name the feelings that the student is expressing and restate what the student is saying.** *"I can see this has upset you a lot." "It sounds like you felt _____ when _____. So when _____ happened, you _____. Is that right?"* If the student has a hard time getting the words out, try to hunch out what he or she is feeling and thinking. *"So you're upset about _____ and now you feel _____. Is that the situation?"*

- **Convey support and understanding of what you've heard. Probe for sources of the problem and what the student needs. Remember, listening doesn't mean agreement!** Encourage the student to tell his or her story and say more about the situation. *"Tell me more about that. How do you feel about that? How was this different from _____?" "Is there anything else you can say that would help me understand the situation better?" "So what do you need for this class to be an okay place for you?" "What can I do to help you _____?"*

- **Share what needs to stop and why.** *"When you _____, here's how it feels for me." "When you _____, other students are unable to _____." "How does _____ get in the way of _____?" "So here's the deal..." "Let me explain why _____ has to stop... Now say it back to me." "So here's what you can't do and here's what you can do."*

- **Share what needs to start and why. Explore strategies that will help the student learn and practice target behaviors.** *"What might be a first step for fixing this?" "What are a couple of things you might do to get back on track?" "What is it going to take for you to _____?" "Okay, now here's what I'd like to see and hear during the rest of the week."*

- **Develop a behavior plan, a learning contract, or a conduct card.**

- **Provide follow-up feedback and coaching.** Change what you say and do to prompt a change in what students say and do.

Use one-on-one conferences to show concern when students are upset or personally distressed

You need your best communication skills when you notice a dramatic change in a student's mood or behavior or when a student's personal distress appears to be chronic. Arrange for a private conference with the student to show your concern and hear his or her story. Here's a sample protocol to try out.

Conferencing when students are upset

1. Make an observation or ask an open-ended low-threat question. "*I've noticed lately that _____. Is everything okay?*" "*Take a deep breath and take a minute to gather your thoughts. I'm here to listen.*" "*So is there anything I should know about what happened today?*" "*You really sounded (angry, frustrated, upset) earlier. Is that right?*" "*A lot's been happening. Say a little about what's going on for you.*"

2. Then **stop** and wait for the student to respond before you say anything else. Your first goal is to let the student know you want to listen. Keep your focus on the student.

3. Defuse upset feelings by naming the feelings the student is expressing and restating what the student is saying. "*I can see this has upset you a lot.*" "*It sounds like you felt _____ when _____.*" "*So when _____ happened, you _____. Is that right?*" If the student has a hard time getting the words out, try to hunch out what he or she is feeling and thinking. "*I can see you're upset about _____ and now you feel _____. Is that the situation?*"

4. Encourage the student to tell his or her story. "*What happened next?*" "*Tell me more.*" "*Can you say more about that?*" "*How do you feel about that?*" "*Is there anything else bothering you?*" "*What's stopping you from feeling okay right now?*" "*Is there anything else you can say that would help me understand the situation better?*"

5. Sometimes just listening to a student's story is enough. If a student does want to problem solve, you might ask, "*What do you need right now?*" or "*Where would you like to go from here?*" or "*What would a good solution look like?*" or "*What might be one step you can take toward working this out?*" or "*How would you like things to change?*" If it's appropriate, use A, B, C, D, E problem solving to move to the next step.

6. If the student's situation feels particularly serious or worrisome, invite the student to consider talking with the right person at school. You are NOT a counselor—you're the person who provides a safety net and a connection to others who are trained to help students with specific academic, behavioral, or mental health problems or crises that come up. "*Do you think this is a good time to talk to _____?*" Or, "*This sounds like something that's important to talk about with _____. Can you do that today? Is there anything I can do to help make that happen?*"

7

More conferencing tips when students are upset

When students bring a problem to you, tell them that you appreciate their willingness to talk about it. Say little and let the student talk it through. Listening doesn't mean agreement; listening confers respect and indicates your desire to understand the student. If you agreed to conference with a student, you agreed to hear what a student is thinking or feeling, whether you like hearing it or not. Listen first and listen attentively before you assume, judge, correct, or problem solve. Don't get defensive and take the student's upset feelings personally—you're the one using your skills to defuse charged feelings and empathize with the student's distress.

If a kid says something off-the-charts scary or troubling, you might say, *"What do you think my reaction is to hearing you say that?"* Or, *"Imagine you're me. What would you be thinking now?"* Or, *"What do you imagine I'm thinking right now?"* Or, *"How would your Mom react if she heard you say _____?"* The goal here is to help the student try and see the situation from another perspective.

Remember that when students are upset and emotionally charged, they can't think. You need to help students reach a calmer place and gain some equilibrium before they can problem solve. Try to identify unmet needs (power, belonging, safety, autonomy) or fears that might be the source of the distress or unwanted behaviors. When young people assume absolutes or overgeneralize, help them clarify their thinking and speak more precisely about their situation. You can respond by saying, *"Always? That never happens? Everyone does that? Are you sure that you're the only person who...? Are you sure that's the way it has to be?"*

With students who are really having a hard time, choose to work on one behavior or one problem at a time. Try to eliminate or limit any negative feedback. Ask the student what you as a teacher can do to help. Do a daily check-in with the students who need it. Give encouraging feedback when you see the student engaging in the desired behavior or notice when the student has a more upbeat mood.

If you think the student's emotional distress is a sign of more serious mental health problems that require immediate attention, submit an early intervention referral and talk with the student about possible counseling or other kinds of supports and interventions. See a sample early intervention referral form on page 277.

Use one-on-one conferences to find out more about unmotivated and resistant students

Try to discover what the student finds really boring and disengaging about school—what's the disconnect? Then probe a bit more to find out more about the student. For example, ask, *"Is there anything at school you like doing? What's something you want to spend time getting good at or learning how to do? What words would you use to describe yourself here at school? How would your friends describe you? Would teachers use the same words? What do you imagine other students are thinking when they see you_____? Tell me what you imagine your-self doing five years from now."* Try to tease out any personal goal or hopes the student has that can help him or her focus.

The first conference is not about getting the student to shape up. It's about showing your interest in who this student really is and what makes him or her tick. You want to close the first confer-ence with an appreciation to the student for being honest. End the conference by saying *"You've given me a lot to think about. Here's what I'd like you to think about: What can I do to make this class an okay place for you to be?"*

The second conference should be about looking for ways to make class bearable by attaching success in class to the student's effort and your encouragement and support. *"What feels like a fair and doable work expectation for next week?"* Talk it through so the student can say, *"I can do this because it will help me _____." "I'll try to make this work because _____." "I'll try this out for a week as long as you _____."*

It's important to note that the quality of the personal relationship with the teacher is the key factor that helps unmotivated kids turn themselves around. Reluctant and resistant learners don't start working because they suddenly find the subject fascinating or develop a five-year plan for graduation and college. These kids are likely to come to school with no goals and few hopes, so they work first for the teacher. Every small success and achievement matters. Students' personal satisfaction from experiencing a job well done can lay the groundwork for helping students link their personal goals, hopes, and interests to success in school and success in life.

Use one-on-one conferences to listen to "frequent fliers"

Flip the switch and don't talk about the behaviors that get frequent fliers in trouble time and again. Surprise them by using a first conference to listen and find out more. *"What's the day like for you here at school? What's the low point? High point? What words would you use to describe yourself here at school? How would your friends describe you? Would teach-ers use the same words? What do you imagine other students are thinking when they see you_____?"*

A first conference is not about a new behavior plan. It's about convincing students that you really want to hear their thoughts and perspectives about school and how they see themselves at school. You want to close the first conference with an appreciation to the student for being honest. End the conference by saying *"You've given me a lot to think about. Here's what I'd like you to think about: What can I do to make this class an okay place for you to be?"*

The second conference is a time to engage frequent fliers in a candid conversation about why everything people have tried doesn't work. *"Here's what we've tried. And here's what keeps happening. Talk about why these strategies aren't working. I really want to know. What am I missing here? What don't I know? What will it take for you to be okay here at school? What's getting in the way? What can I do to help?"*

The next step is looking for ways that the student can still be himself or herself without being disruptive or distracting in class. *"Let's make a deal—here's what I can do for you. What can you do for me? Let's try to work out a way for you to _____ and for me to support that. What feels fair and doable? Let's agree on one goal for next week."* Talk it through so the student can say, *"I can do this because it will help me _____."* *"I'll try to make this work because _____."* *"I'll try this out for a week if you_____."*

Use scaffolded consequences with frequent fliers

Disciplinary actions become ineffective—and frequent fliers are let off the hook—when we implement the same consequence over and over again for the same infraction by the same student. Scaffolded consequences raise the ante and communicate an increasing sense of urgency and seriousness to the student and the parent by:

- increasing the amount of time a student owes to correct it, fix it, or make it right

- increasing the degree of personal effort, discomfort, or inconvenience that is required in order for students to carry out a specific consequence

- increasing the degree of involvement, supervision, communication, face time, discomfort, or inconvenience for the parent as consequences and interventions scaffold upward

- involving other teachers, support staff, and/or administrators in behavioral conferences and contracts with student and parent

- increasing the levels of adult supervision and monitoring of the student through daily check-ins, conduct cards, and teacher feedback

- shortening the timeline for expected improvements in behavior

- placement of written documentation of incidents into the student's permanent file that will not be removed without dramatic improvement in behavior within a discrete time period

And when you're stuck or a student is stuck, try one or more of the following responses:

- *"I'm unwilling to try that because _____. Do you have another idea?"*

- *"That's a good idea. If you don't follow through, what feels like a fair consequence?"*

- *"I want to hear what you have to say and I want you to hear what I have to say. Can we try that?"*

- *"I'm not interested in fault finding or blaming. I'm interested in solutions."*

- *"It sounds like you're not ready to problem solve about this, so I will have to decide."*

USE BEHAVIOR REPORT FORMS, PROBLEM-SOLVING PROTOCOLS, CONDUCT CARDS, AND LEARNING CONTRACTS

Consider using these protocols and learning contracts in conjunction with student conferences and other interventions that may involve administrators or student support staff. Here is an index of the forms and protocols that are included in Appendix A:

What's the form?	When do you use it?
Procedural Infractions Page 259	When students engage in chronic procedural infractions
Uncooperative, Off-Task Behaviors Page 260	When students engage in egregious or chronic unwanted behaviors
Interpersonal Classroom Conflicts Page 261	When two students are experiencing a protracted conflict that has a negative impact on themselves and the classroom community
Boundary Violations Page 262	When students engage in egregious or chronic violations related to classroom safety, trust, respect, and civility
Rude, Uncivil, Disrespectful Speech Page 263	When students engage in egregious or chronic disrespectful speech
Daily Conduct Card (for at least two weeks and signed by parent) Page 264	When a student needs close monitoring and you and the student have agreed on the specific behaviors that need to stop and the desired target behaviors that the student will start using
Feedback and Suggestion Form Page 265	When students have an issue or problem with you, the group, or the class and want to speak with you about it
Personal Problem Solving Form Page 266	When students are experiencing personal distress and want to problem solve
Making It Right Between Us Page 267	When a student and teacher are upset and angry with each other and want to mend the relationship
The Fifteen-Minute Kid Talk Protocol Page 268	When a teacher collaborates with colleagues to focus on one student's problems and issues to develop shared strategies
Problem-Solving Place Intake Form Page 269	When a teacher needs to remove a student temporarily to defuse, reflect, and problem solve

7

What's the form?	When do you use it?
Problem-Solving Place Conference Form Page 270	What students discuss and rehearse in the problem-solving place before they return to class
Behavior/Learning Contract Page 271	When you and the student have made an agreement about what the student will do and what you will do within a specific window of time
Re-Entry Contract Page 272	When students are re-entering your class after an egregious incident or fight for which they were suspended
Faculty Feedback for Student Contracts Page 273	When a team and/or student support staff member works out a contract with the student for a specified number of weeks, this is the weekly feedback form that the student's teachers can use.
Academic Assessment Page 274	When students are experiencing a learning gap that's blocking their success in class, this is the first step in developing a learning contract.
Academic Learning Contract Page 275	When you and the student have made an agreement about what the student will do and what you will do within a specific window of time
Classroom Referral and Request for Support Page 276	This referral and/or request for support can be submitted and discussed with your team, the dean, or other administrators when unwanted behaviors merit an automatic referral or when unwanted behaviors persist after you have tried multiple strategies to address the behavior.
Student Intervention/Support Team Referral Page 277	When you notice unusual and persistent unexpected behaviors that may be signs of personal distress or mental health concerns

MAKE A PLAN WHEN A CLASS IS "OFF THE HOOK"

At some point in your teaching career, the class from hell will darken your door. When I was supervising student teachers, one of our master teachers was brought to her knees by a room full of kids who hated school, hated the subject, and didn't much like each other. The chemistry was so volatile, the atmosphere so toxic, that students couldn't function alone or in the group. Although my student teachers were secretly relieved when such a gifted teacher was haunted by their own worst nightmares, they were terrified at the prospect that this would happen to them! Thus, the dysfunctional class became the focus of our action-research project for the semester. The guiding questions and strategies we developed continue to resonate with teachers who find themselves in this truly awful predicament.

Take time to reflect on the situation

Imagine the worst-case scenario in the classroom. Name it, write it, imagine it as a movie. To fix it, you have to face it first. What are the kids doing, and what are you doing? What feels out of control?

Imagine a series of possible incidents that produced such a dysfunctional group. What are students unable to do? What combination of personalities and learner profiles seem to ignite the flames? Are there any incidents or chronic behaviors you ignored or let slide? What incidents propelled you and the group to this juncture? Are there any procedures, routines, or classroom agreements that might have prevented or contained some of the chaos?

What teacher behaviors do you want to avoid at all costs? These are the things you know will only make it worse, not better. The top ten: (1) giving up on the group and working with one student at a time; (2) turning your back on the group at the board; (3) sitting at your desk seething silently holding on to the desperate hope that this will pass; (4) crying; (5) deer-in-the-headlights paralysis, or just staring at the group speechlessly because you can't believe what you're witnessing; (6) demanding that the class cease and desist without any backup consequences; (7) making empty threats that are unenforceable, as in "I'm going to call every one of your parents tonight!" or, "The next person who _____ will be suspended for two weeks"; (8) yelling; (9) referring students to the dean or another administrator without a re-entry plan; and (10) any version of you-statements to the group that drip with sarcasm, criticism, and belittlement.

What do you need to do to get grounded, relaxed, and focused, so you can think clearly and act decisively? When you're upset, angry, and frustrated, you act impulsively. What's your version of a personal time-out that doesn't send the message that you can be pushed around?

What else do you need to know about the students? Find out all you can about students in the group. Ask a few students privately to name adults in the building whom they trust or like, and ask these staff members to share their perspectives and insights. Sometimes you'll find out information about particular students that can help you turn resisters into allies.

7

Who else can help you think this through? Sometimes it's impossible to move forward without bringing in reinforcements. Other people can't repair the relationship between you and the group, but they can offer the wisdom of experience and provide both visible and behind-the-scenes assistance that will support your action plan. Who might help you think this through? What assistance do you need from the dean or the assistant principal? Is there anyone on the guidance/student support team or elsewhere who can provide tips for working with a noncooperative group or dealing with oppositional defiance?

Choose a few strategies to get back on track

Regrettably, there's no magic formula for transforming a toxic group into a cohesive learning community. As you read through the strategies suggested here, think about the combination of strategies that's best for you, your students, and your school.

Don't do anything dramatically different *before* you've...

- Talked through the situation with colleagues you respect

- Mapped out a week-by-week plan of action that you can sustain for at least a month

- Secured the backup you need to make your plan happen

False starts and half-hearted attempts to restore order, trust, respect, and a sense of purpose almost always backfire.

Slow down, get quiet, and delay your response until the next day. Remember that taking a day to think about what to do is not the same as doing nothing.

Ask someone you trust to observe you and the class. Although doing this is often scary and can make you feel vulnerable, there's nothing like another set of eyes and ears to help you get a little distance and take a fresh look at what's going on. When you debrief the observation with your colleague, you might ask yourself these questions:

- What do I need to pay more attention to?

- Are there any particular points in the class period when more kids get off track or hit a wall?

- What signals am I communicating to students? Is there anything about my stance, my physical presence, my voice, or my demeanor that's getting in the way of being more effective and connected to the group?

- What can I try to *stop* doing?

- What can I *start* doing or doing more often?

Be prepared to enforce accountable consequences consistently. Clear your schedule for lunch and after-school workout sessions and be prepared with a list of tasks that students need to do to restore their good standing in class.

Implement enforceable and accountable consequences and interventions with the help of reinforcements. What cooperation do you need from administrators or support staff to enforce accountable consequences and interventions? For example, if one of your consequences is a lunchtime conference and work session for five students per day, request that the dean help you round up the troops. Or ask the principal to stop by on the day that you're developing a plan with your students. Or request that the dean arrange a conference with a student and parent and use an informal mediation process to develop a contract and follow-up plan. Or invite the school psychologist or social worker to observe one or two instigators and sit in with you when you conference with these students.

Keep the dominoes from falling. Focus your attention on a few key "players" who have the greatest impact and influence on the rest of the peer group.

- Meet with students individually or in small groups to develop contracts

- Request an immediate intervention for one or two students with the help of the support staff

- Sometimes an immediate serious consequence for one or two students sounds the alarm bell to others.

Don't broadcast what you're going to do by saying, "The next time I see_____, here's what's going to happen." Kids already know they've messed up, so make your move unannounced with the right student, and don't announce it to the group.

Rearrange the room and how you work it. Change seating arrangements; change a focal point; change where you stand to give instructions.

Keep classes simple but challenging. Easy "busy work" is a bad solution, but so are complicated lessons. Create interesting tasks that students can complete independently so you can coach your way around the room, checking in with students.

Change two routines or procedures that are easy for students to do successfully. Small victories matter. Look through the procedures on pages 119–135 and choose two that will move the group a few steps closer to functioning as a cohesive unit.

In extreme situations, provide alternative learning options when the group is split between those who are ready to learn and work and those who aren't. This is not the same as giving up on the group and, in defeat, consigning yourself to working with a few individuals—a strategy that will always backfire. The harsh reality is that you can't make students learn what you're teaching. It can take a while to capture the hearts and minds of extremely resistant learners. In the meantime, what can you do when a group of students is stuck in a not-learning stance?

7

Provide some clear alternative learning options that create a way for everyone to coexist with some degree of order and purpose. A not-learning group of students cannot be allowed to disrupt others' learning. Assign seats so that not-learning students are scattered around the room. Talk to students privately and individually, and spell out what students can't do and what they can do. *"Your choice not to work with the rest of us may cost you, but it cannot cost the class. You cannot disrupt the classroom lesson. Here's what you can do. You can choose to work on _____, read _____, or _____."*

Bring kids in on the solution.

- Meet with key students at lunch and do a reality check. *"What are you trying to tell me? What do we need to do to make this work?"*

- Sometimes candor works. *"It didn't take us a day to get here, and it won't take us a day to make things right. So we're going to start fresh today. I need your help to get back on track. Here's what I will do, and here's what you need to do."*

- *"My job is to see that you do your job."* Generate a list of actions that you and the group can take.

- Some kids respond well to the idea of negotiating. *"Let's make a deal. Here's what I can do for you. And here's what you can do for me."*

Track reductions in negative behaviors and increases in positive behaviors. Make your behavior goals for the next week completely transparent, and track what happens.

In the future, prepare yourself and your students for what to do when things go wrong.

- *"I'll make mistakes; you'll make mistakes; we might crash and burn for a day, but we can always recover."*

- Communicate to students that they're not going to wear you down or wear you out. Even if you have to fib a bit, tell students you've seen it and heard it all before, so nothing's going to surprise you very much.

- Be clear with yourself about the warning signs that forecast trouble ahead, and have your intervention plan ready. At the first signs of group dysfunction, be prepared to name it and deal with it immediately.

COMMUNICATE WITH PARENTS IN A VARIETY OF WAYS

When we think about connecting with students' parents, we usually don't think beyond the phone call or face-to-face conference. Here are some suggested scripts and other ways to keep in touch.

Communicate with parents in a variety of ways

First-Month "Tell Me More" Calls: Sometimes you teach a student who's new to you, and you don't have a clue about what makes him or her tick. Parents are thrilled when you phone and say, "*Hello, Ms. Jones. This is Mr. _____, and I'm Joe's _____ teacher. I'm glad he's in my class, and I'd I like to know Joe a little better. Is there anything you can tell me that will help me support Joe to be successful in this class?*"

Sunshine Calls: These can be a powerful connector between you, the parent, and the student. The goal here is to share with a parent something the child has done well and/or something you appreciate about the child. If it's impossible to get around to making a call to every parent, try to make sure you call the parents of students who don't get the spotlight, students who have made a turnaround, students whom you are 95 percent sure have never received a positive call home.

Sunshine Notes: These serve the same purpose and take much less time. Try to do a few every week.

Insist that the Student Call the Parent: Accountable consequences begin when the student takes responsibility to make the call home. Speak with the student first before the call and rehearse what the student is going to say. When students are anxious because "my mom will kill me or I'll be punished for life," reassure students that they are taking a big step by taking responsibility for what happened. During the call, the student explains what he or she did and what he or she needs to do now. Then you take the call from there for any further discussion or explanation.

Forewarned and Unannounced Problem Behavior Calls: You have several options for making problem phone calls.

- You can state your intention to the student and then call the parent.

- You can first conference with the student so you can share what the student intends to do to rectify the situation.

- You can make an unannounced phone call to a parent without informing the student. The element of surprise can make this strategy particularly effective.

Phone calls should never be more than ten minutes. Here's one script that produces positive results and leaves parents feeling heard and supported.

- Introduce yourself and say what course the student is taking with you. Ask the parent if it's a convenient time to talk for a few minutes.

- Say something that indicates that you know something about the student—a positive quality that she or he brings to the classroom, something he or she does well, something unusual that she or he knows about, etc.

- Get right to the point and state the problem simply. For example, you might say, "*I'm calling about an incident that happened yesterday. Here's what happened.*" Be clear about what needs to stop and what the student needs to start doing. You may need to explain how the behavior is affecting his or her child, other students, and the classroom environment.

7

Communicate with parents in a variety of ways *(continued)*

- Inform the parent of any other consequences.

- If the parent is upset, acknowledge their feelings and try to find a common concern or hope that you share about their daughter/son. *"Here's how I hope we can work together on this."*

- Share how much you would appreciate it if the parent would talk to their son/daughter about this. Reassure the parent that this is not the end of the world. You're calling now because you have confidence that the student can turn this situation around. Thank them for their support.

The 6 a.m. Wakeup Call: If you have had difficulty tracking down parents, try the 6 a.m. phone call. Apologize for calling early and explain the reason for the call. Use the "problem call" script, but add that you hope you don't have to call again tomorrow morning. This strategy provides an instant wakeup call to the student and can produce sudden changes in behavior that you've wanted to see for weeks.

The Call to a Parent's Workplace: This communicates a sense of urgency that is similar to that of the 6 a.m. wakeup call.

Daily Conduct Cards: If a student is on a daily conduct card for two weeks, inform the parent that he or she must sign the conduct card that a student brings home on Fridays. You may also want to arrange a follow-up call with the parent.

Parent Signatures: You might want parents to sign specific assignments, tests, and projects, or you may want students to choose three of their best pieces from class to send home and get signed.

Parent Newsletters: You may want to send home a course news summary every quarter that describes what students have been studying and doing in class and preview what's coming up.

Student-Produced Newsletters: At the end of the term, ask students to write a letter or create a brochure for their parents in which they assess their progress, describe what they learned, identify their best efforts, and note their goals for improvement.

Parent Conference Period: Let parents know a planning period (the same day every week) that you make available for phone calls regarding students' progress, behavior plans, and academic contracts. This period can also be used for face-to-face conferencing with parents.

Team Conferencing with Student and Parent: Include parents during re-entry conferences when student returns from an administrative referral, in-school or out-of-school suspension. (See the next section.)

Parent-Student Homework/Reflections: Create occasional homework assignments that involve students interviewing their parents about a specific topic or issue.

PROBLEM SOLVE WITH YOUR COLLEAGUES

Use a "kid talk" protocol to problem solve with other faculty who teach the same student

Either arrange a meeting with other colleagues who teach the student or meet with your team members during your common planning time. You might want to invite the student's dean, counselor, or social worker to the "staffing." Many faculties who work in small schools or academies, grade-level teams, or grade clusters set aside a weekly or biweekly time to staff two to four students per session. When teachers collaborate, they can share their lists of high-needs students and develop a list of frequent fliers, the kids who experience chronic academic and behavioral difficulties across classes and settings. A team staffing can be an important step in a student support team referral.

The "kid talk" protocol described on page 268 takes about 15 minutes. The time frame is intentionally brief; too often faculties waste precious time telling war stories about the referred student instead of probing for observations and insights that may help explain what's worked and what hasn't. Furthermore, if faculties get in the habit of taking 45 minutes to staff one student at a time, the protocol will only be used as a crisis measure rather than a proactive strategy for supporting students before the crisis. The purpose of the protocol is to generate a set of strategies and interventions that the group agrees to implement for a discrete window of time (between two to four weeks). Students need to know that they don't have all year to get it together, and teachers are more willing to monitor students closely when they know it's not going to last forever.

Submit a student referral or request for support to the dean or assistant principal

Many of our client schools use a version of the form on page 276 for teacher referrals and requests for support. Teachers describe the unwanted behaviors and identify the steps they have taken to support a change in the student's behavior. The dean or assistant principal should use the form to describe their interventions with the student and the accountable consequences that are done by the student. A copy of the form is returned to the referring teacher.

Refer students to mediation, counseling services, and student assistance programs

Try to become familiar with all of the special academic services and student assistance programs that are available in your school. Keep a folder of all these programs and services so that you can discuss options with students when it's appropriate.

Submit a student intervention/support team referral

When you notice unusual behaviors or dramatic changes in a student's behavior and performance, pass on your observations to the early intervention or student support team so that they can determine next steps and possible interventions for the student.

7

Change the in-school suspension room to the problem-solving place

Most students who visit the in-school suspension room in September keep collecting their ISS frequent flier miles during the rest of the year. Many middle and high schools are wising up and turning the in-school suspension room (where kids pretty much just kill time) into a program staffed by trained staff and aides who discuss the problem with the student, teach and practice alternative behaviors, and rehearse what they will say and do when they return to class. See a sample form on page 269 that describes a process many schools have used to reduce repeat referrals.

Arrange for a re-entry conference when a student returns from an administrative referral or in-school or out-of-school suspension

If students have committed violations that require automatic in-school suspension, out-of-school suspension, or other referrals to the dean, assistant principal, or student support team, consider the benefits of a re-entry conference. A re-entry conference creates a marker between what happened in the past and a fresh start. The student needs to communicate to you what will be different upon his or her return to the classroom. More specifically, students need to identify different choices they will make so the unwanted behaviors are not repeated. A re-entry conference also gives you the opportunity to review your expectations and discuss ways in which you will monitor student's behavior, check in to see how things are going, and develop cues or warning signals at the first sign of situations that could spell trouble. Re-entry conferences can help diminish adversarial feelings by communicating your confidence that a student can change while providing support to make it happen. (See the sample form on page 272.)

APPENDIX A

Conference Forms and Problem-Solving Protocols

HANDOUT
Procedural Infractions

1. What procedure didn't you follow?

2. Instead of following the procedure, I chose to...

4. Two things you can do that will help you follow the procedure.

3. We have this procedure because...

5. Two things the teacher can do to support your efforts.

Student's Name _____ Date _____

Teacher's Name _____ Date _____

Follow-up: _____

_____

HANDOUT
Uncooperative, Off-Task Behaviors

1. What happened?

What did you do?

2. What were you supposed to be doing?

3. What can you do to make amends—to correct it, make it right, repair relationships, restore your good standing?

4. What skills do you need to learn or practice?

How can you handle the situation differently next time?

5. Two things the teacher can do to support your efforts:

Student's Name _____ Date _____

Staff Person's Name _____ Date _____

Follow-up: _____

_____

HANDOUT
Interpersonal Classroom Conflicts   (Both students fill out the form.)

1. What's the conflict about? What happened?

How do you feel about what happened?

2. What words and body language escalated the conflict?

3. What do you need to resolve the conflict?

5. Two solutions that can improve the situation or solve the problem:

Are solutions fair, reasonable, respectful, and responsible?

4. Two ways you might have handled this situation differently:

OR

6. What's our agreement?

_____ will _____

_____

_____ will _____

_____

Student's Name _____ Date _____

Student's Name _____ Date _____

Follow-up: _____

_____

HANDOUT
Boundary Violations

1. What boundary did you violate?

SAFETY / TRUST / RESPECT

DIGNITY / CIVILITY

2. How did your actions have a negative impact on individuals or the community?

3. What could you have done or said instead?

4. What do you need to do to restore your good standing and to rebuild a sense of safety, trust, respect, or civility?

5. Two things the teacher can do to help you reconnect?

Student's Name _____ Date _____

Staff Person's Name_____ Date _____

Follow-up: _____

_____

HANDOUT
Rude, Uncivil, and Disrespectful Speech

1. What did you say that was rude, uncivil, or disrespectful?

How did your words have a negative impact on others?

2. It might have been better not to say this because…

Instead, you might have said…

4. Next time you feel this way, you could say…

3. What can you do to make amends—to correct it, make it right, repair relationships, restore your good standing?

5. Two things the teacher can do to support your efforts to clean up your speech.

Student's Name _____ Date _____

Teacher's Name _____ Date _____

Follow-up: _____

_____

Sample Daily Conduct Card

Student Joe Schmoe	Teacher Alicia Advocate	Period 6th

Week from FEB. 10 to FEB. 14 Conduct Card # 2	Course: ELA 9th

Please circle for each day:
0   No incidents
✔   One or two incidents where student self-corrected
✗   Several incidents with no self-correction

Please circle for each day:
3 – Consistently does it without prompting
2 – Does it with some prompting
1 – Rarely does it and always needs prompting
0 – Refuses to do it

Unwanted Behaviors	M	T	W	Th	F	Desired Behaviors	M	T	W	Th	F
STOP goofing off and instigating sidebar conversations during instructions, whole group, and independent work	0 ⓥ✗	⓪ ✔ ✗	0 ⓥ ✗	0 ✔ ⊗	⓪ ✔ ✗	**START** focusing on task immediately	3 ② 1 0	③ 2 1 0	3 ② 1 0	3 2 ① 0	3 ② 1 0
STOP gossiping about your personal and social business during class	⓪ ✔ ✗	⓪ ✔ ✗	0 ⓥ ✗	0 ✔ ⊗	⓪ ✔ ✗	**START** listening carefully to instructions and asking questions or seeking help if you don't understand	3 ② 1 0	3 ② 1 0	③ 2 1 0	3 2 ① 0	3 ② 1 0
STOP using curse words and negative or offensive speech	0 ⓥ ✗	⓪ ✔ ✗	⓪ ✔ ✗	0 ⓥ ✗	⓪ ✔ ✗	**START** accepting requests, direction, correction, and feedback without a fuss	3 2 ① 0	3 ② 1 0	3 ② 1 0	3 ② 1 0	3 ② 1 0

Strategies, cues, prompts, accommodations, and environmental alterations that Ms. Advocate will use to support the desired changes in your behavior:

- I will greet you when you come and give you a "heads up" for what to expect in class today.
- If you start goofing off, I will ask you to move to a designated desk. This is your chance to get back on track for the period. If you refuse, you are in BIG TROUBLE. This is oppositional defiance!
- I will give you quick feedback at the end of each period.

Teacher comment, signature, and date: Joe has made a positive turn around this week. It took lots of effort and self-control. Congrats!!!   *Ms. Advocate Dec. 14, 2009*

Parent comment, signature. date: *Thank you for the conduct card. I expect Joe to do what you tell him to do. Ms. Shirley Schmoe Dec. 17, 2009.*

HANDOUT
Feedback and Suggestion Form

What's the issue???

what the issue is about: (Please check ✔)

☐ the group   ☐ the teacher   ☐ what we're learning (content)...

☐ how we're learning it (process)   ☐ what you're expected to do (academic expectations)

☐ how you're expected to behave (behavioral expectations)

(I'm not liking... It feels unfair when... Some of us are having a hard time... It really bothers me when... I'd like to know why... I'm finding it really difficult to... There's got to be a better way to...)

_____

_____

This is an issue for me because _____

_____

What's your suggestion?

(Is there a better, easier, more interesting way to do something? Is there something you'd like to do more of/less of? Is there something you'd like me to do differently? Is there something you would like students to do differently? Is there another way to meet the same goal or expectation?)

_____

_____

My suggestion is fair/reasonable/responsible because _____

_____

_____

Student's Name _____ Date _____

Follow-up: _____

_____

HANDOUT
Personal Problem Solving Form

Assess the situation and **Ask,** "What's my problem?"

Brainstorm Solutions. Picture what the situation would look like if it were solved. Write down every idea whether you like it or not. Think of solutions your friends or parents might suggest.	Consider the pros and cons of each Choice. What are the benefits? How is it respectful, responsible, and reasonable? Will this choice help me get what I need? What are the negatives and limitations?	
	+	**–**
1.		
2.		
3.		
4.		

Decide on the best choice. How is this a better decision than other ideas?

Evaluate the decision after it's been implemented. How did it work? What did you learn?

Student's Name _____ Date _____

Teacher's Name _____ Date _____

HANDOUT
Making It Right Between Us

Student	Teacher
What's happened that's broken the relationship? What were your feelings when this happened?	What's happened that's broken the relationship? What were your feelings when this happened?
How has this conflict hurt or harmed me and/or the classroom community?	How has this conflict hurt or harmed me and/or the classroom community?
What can each of us do to make it right and mend our relationship? (What actions feel reasonable, respectful, and restorative?)	What can each of us do to make it right and mend our relationship? (What actions feel reasonable, respectful, and restorative?)
Before leaving, what do you want to say that closes the past and opens a new relationship between us?	Before leaving, what do you want to say that closes the past and opens a new relationship between us?

Student's Name _____ Date _____

Teacher's Name _____ Date _____

Follow-up Meeting: _____

_____

HANDOUT
The Fifteen-Minute "Kid Talk" Protocol

Name of Student _____ Grade _____

Name of Referring Teacher _____ Date _____

1. Introduce the student; name the specific unwanted behaviors; and name the strategies and interventions you've already tried. (2 minutes)	
2. Invite colleagues to ask you clarifying and probing questions. (3 minutes)	
3. Invite colleagues to share any additional observations, information, concerns, success stories, or strategies that they have found particularly successful with this student. (2 minutes)	
4. Discuss and decide on a set of strategies and interventions you will put in place for a specific window of time. (4 to 6 weeks) (6 minutes)	
5. Decide on any other "next steps" (a conference with student, parent, teachers, a behavior plan, a weekly behavior report that is sent home, or a referral to the early intervention/ student support team) (2 minutes)	

HANDOUT

Problem-Solving Place Intake Form

Date _____ Time _____ Class _____

Student's Name _____

Teacher's Name _____

Reason for referral _____

_____

_____

Briefly describe the incident and what triggered the unwanted behavior.

_____

_____

How often has the behavior occurred in the last two weeks?

_____

_____

What strategies and interventions have I tried already?

_____

_____

What change in behavior would you like to see when the student returns?

_____

_____

List any other information that would be helpful to know.

_____

_____

HANDOUT
Problem-Solving Place Conference Form
Getting the Story Out
What did you do that got you here? What happened? _____

_____

How are you feeling about what happened? _____

_____

Taking Responsibility
When you got in trouble, what were you supposed to be doing? _____

_____

How did your behavior affect others or the learning environment? _____

_____

How did your behavior get in the way of your own learning? _____

_____

Problem Solving
What could you have done instead that would have been a better choice? _____

_____

What two or three positive behaviors will help you get back on track?

_____

What can you do the next time you're in this situation? _____

_____

Rehearsal
What do you want to say to the teacher when you return to class? _____

_____

Getting Support and Keeping on Track
What can the teacher do to support your change in behavior? _____

_____

What else can you do for yourself to help stay on track? _____

_____

HANDOUT
Behavior/Learning Contract:

1. This is the problem I need to work on:

2. In the future, I need to avoid:

3. These are the skills and behaviors I need to learn/practice/do more often.

I need help…

4. During the next ____ weeks, I agree to:

5. My teacher agrees to:

6. If I meet my contract commitments, I will…

If I don't meet my contract commitments, I agree to…

Student's Name_____ Date _____

Staff Person's Name_____ Date _____

Follow-up: _____

_____

HANDOUT

Re-entry Contract

What can you do to earn your way back into the school and classroom community and restore your good standing?

_____

_____

How can you show others that the conflict or incident is over? _____

_____

_____

What academic goals will help you focus in class? _____

_____

_____

How can teachers support your turn-around? _____

_____

_____

You can't change anyone but yourself. What can you do to handle the conflict, reduce tensions, and keep the peace in class?

_____

_____

Name of student _____

Parent/Guardian _____

Teacher _____

HANDOUT
Faculty Feedback for Student Contracts

Name of Student _____

Time Frame of Contract: From _____ to _____

Staff member who is coordinating contract _____

Reasons for the contract: _____

_____

The following teachers will be giving feedback:

The student has agreed to: _____

_____

The student's teachers have agreed to: _____

_____

Specific behaviors to observe: (Please assign 0–4 to student's demonstration of each behavior each day.)
4 – Consistently does it without prompting and encourages others to do it
3 – Does it most of the time with little prompting
2 – Does it some of the time with prompting
1 – Does it on rare occasions and always needs prompting
0 – Refuses to do it

Week #_____: Dates: _____ to _____

Specific Behavior	Monday	Tuesday	Wednesday	Thursday	Friday

Please put your feedback form in _____'s mailbox each Friday afternoon during the contract.

HANDOUT
Academic Assessment

1. What's going on that tells you that you're in academic trouble?

How are you feeling about what's going on?

2. What's getting in the way of being more successful?

Where are you stuck?

3. Three things you can try to get back on track:

A

B

C

4. Two things the teacher can do to support your efforts:

A

B

Student's Name _____ Date _____

Staff Person's Name _____ Date _____

Follow-up: _____

_____

HANDOUT
Academic Learning Contract:

1. This is the problem I need to work on:

2. In the future, I need to avoid:

3. These are the skills and behaviors I need to learn/practice/do more often.

I need help…

4. During the next ____ weeks, I agree to:

6. If I meet my contract commitments, I will…

If I don't meet my contract commitments, I agree to…

5. My teacher agrees to:

Student's Name_____ Date _____

Staff Person's Name_____ Date _____

Follow-up: _____

_____

HANDOUT Classroom Referral and Request for Support

Student's Last Name _____ First Name _____ ID # _____ Grade _____

Date _____ Submitted by _____ Period/Time _____

Immediate Referral to Disciplinary Team: Check the box and describe the behavior and exactly what happened:

☐ Physical fighting   ☐ Left classroom without permission

☐ Chronic use of vulgar, offensive, obscene, abusive language and/or gestures   ☐ toward student   ☐ toward adult

☐ Hitting, shoving, pushing, threatening, intimidating, bullying, or harassing another student

☐ Cursing, threatening, pushing, shoving, hitting, or harassing an adult

☐ Severe destruction of classroom, student, or adult property

☐ Oppositional defiance or loss of control that makes others feel unsafe or significantly disrupts teaching and learning

☐ Behavior that jeopardizes personal or environmental safety

☐ Stealing, cheating, plagiarism, forgeries, extortion, gambling

☐ Sexual harassment

☐ Possession, use, or attempt to use, or transfer of any firearm, knife, razor blade, or other dangerous object.

☐ Possession, sale, distribution, or use of any alcoholic beverage, controlled substance, imitation controlled substance, marijuana, or tobacco on school property or at school-sponsored events

Details of Incident/Background _____

_____

Request for Support when student engages in chronic, repetitive, or egregious infractions of the same procedure or chronic, repetitive, or egregious incidents of unwanted, uncooperative, or off-task behavior

Describe specific behavior _____

_____

Level 1 corrective steps and interventions teacher took when behavior persisted:

☐ Offered choices/prompts to self-correct or problem solve   ☐ Corrective/restorative action/accountable consequence

☐ Conference with student or student and team   ☐ Phone call or letter home (1) _____ (2) _____
                                                                                          Date   Date

☐ Problem solving form/behavior plan   ☐ Before-, after-school, or lunch detention with teacher

☐ Modifications in instruction/task/environment   ☐ Written or verbal apology

☐ Parent/student/teacher/AA conference   ☐ Loss of points or privileges

Details _____

Actions taken after Referral or Request for Support:

☐ Student conference with teacher/team/dean/AA/principal	**Accountable Consequences**
☐ Phone call, letter, and/or conference with parent	☐ Verbal or written apology
☐ Before-, after-, or lunchtime detention	☐ Corrective/restorative action
☐ Entry in discipline file and notification to parent	_____
☐ TIME-OUT ROOM/PROBLEM-SOLVING PLACE	☐ Student calls parent in presence of dean or _____
Date _____ From _____ To _____	☐ Written essay, behavior report form/plan, reading response
☐ Learning modifications/restrictions/loss of privileges	☐ Mediation between student and teacher
_____	☐ Informal negotiation between teacher and student where dean serves as convener/facilitator
☐ Referral to counseling or student support team	☐ Learn and practice desired behavior during _____ sessions.
☐ Peer mediation	☐ Guidance/student support interventions or special programs
☐ Pre-suspension conference: Date _____	_____
☐ Suspension: Date _____	☐ Restitution or community service_____
☐ In-school suspension: Date _____	☐ Other_____
☐ School or district hearing _____	

Notes _____

Name of Staff Person who Processed Referral/Request _____ Date _____

H A N D O U T   Student Intervention/Support Team Referral

Student _____ Date form completed _____

Person making referral _____ Student grade level _____ Gender _____

Do you want the student to know you made the referral?   Yes   No

Has the student/family asked for: information about services?   Yes   No

                      an appointment to initiate help?   Yes   No

                      someone to contact them to offer help?   Yes   No

Please check area(s) of concern or the behaviors that are exhibited on a consistent/frequent basis:

BEHAVIOR

____ Abusive language/chronic profanity

____ Alcohol/drug abuse (suspected or known)

____ Argumentative; overly adversarial

____ Attention seeking (positive and/or negative)

____ Bizarre thoughts or behaviors (i.e., hearing voices, seeing things, eating inedible objects, rocking, head-banging, etc.)

____ Bullying/harassment

____ Coping with chronic illness

____ Cutting/scratching/hurting self

____ Depressed/extended periods of sadness

____ Eating problems

____ Excessive absences

____ Excessive tardiness

____ Excessive or uncontrollable crying

____ Falling asleep

____ Hostile/unapproachable/chronic challenges to authority

____ Identify development issues (adolescent, racial, cultural)

____ Impulsive behavior/unable to regulate emotions/control behavior

____ Inability to stay on task/complete assignments

____ Irritable/quick to anger/comes to school angry

____ Isolated/withdrawn

____ Lethargic/low energy

____ Negative peer influences/gang involvement

____ Physical assaults toward others/fighting

____ Preoccupation with death

____ Rejected by peers/excluded/chronic teasing

____ Self-esteem problems

____ Separation anxiety

____ Sexual identity issues

____ Sexually harasses others/explicit, vulgar behavior

____ Suffered sexual and/or physical assault

____ Talks about suicide

____ Threatening/intimidating remarks or comments

____ Worrying/over anxious/nervousness

____ Other _____

FAMILY

____ Mentions abuse (physical, sexual, emotional)*

____ Speaks angrily about parents/family

____ Suffered recent loss (including divorce of parents)

____ Other _____

APPEARANCE

____ Appearance/hygiene neglected

____ Bizarre, strange clothing, hair, appearance

____ Bloodshot eyes

____ Bruises*

____ Needle or burn marks

____ Weight loss/gain (dramatic/sudden)

____ Other _____

ACADEMIC

____ Significant reading/writing skill gaps

____ Significant mathematics skill gaps

____ Grades falling significantly

____ Skipping classes

____ Low motivation/effort/nonparticipation

____ Possible learning disability_____

_____

____ Other _____

*May need to be reported to Child Protective Services. See policies and procedures, or consult with principal/counselor.

Please rate the urgency of this request by circling the number that best corresponds to your assessment of the issue:

Mildly concerned   **Moderately urgent**   **Very urgent**

1   2   3   4   5   6   7   8   9   10

Please list any interventions previously taken and the results _____

_____

Specific comments, concerns, impressions, evidence _____

APPENDIX B

A Guide for Reflection, Practice, and Planning

Pages 282 to 333 serve as a guide for reflection, planning, and practice documents that can be used with *Getting Classroom Management RIGHT: Guided Discipline and Personalized Support in Secondary Schools* and *Making Learning REAL: Reaching and Engaging All Learners in Secondary Classrooms*

Documents, Page Number	Purpose / Directions	Text Reference
Reflections: ***Building a Community of Learners***, page 282	These questions can be used for journaling or small group dialogues at the beginning of a workshop series or course.	
Reflections: ***Urgent Issues and Questions***, page 283	Ask participants to post their responses to these questions on sticky notes, so you can keep them up for the duration of a workshop series or course.	
Reflections: ***Thinking about Discipline*** and ***Three Approaches to Classroom Management***, page 283	These questions can be used for written reflections during a workshop or course, small group dialogues, or homework.	*RIGHT* Chapter 1
Reflections: ***Know Yourself***, pages 284–285	These questions can be used for written reflections during a workshop or course, small group dialogues, or homework.	*RIGHT* Chapter 3
Reflections: ***Know Your Students***, page 285	These questions can be used for written reflections during a workshop or course, small group dialogues, or homework.	*RIGHT* Chapter 3
Classroom Management and Discipline Plan: ***Organize Your Classroom***, pages 286–287	Think carefully about how to arrange classroom space for various kinds of tasks and utilize the physical environment to communicate academic and behavioral goals, expectations, and reminders.	*RIGHT* Chapter 6
Classroom Management and Discipline Plan: ***Expectations and Norms***, page 288	Be intentional about developing specific academic and behavioral expectations and norms that become mantras for how you work and learn together in your classroom.	*RIGHT* Chapter 4
Classroom Management and Discipline Plan: ***Model, Teach, Practice, and Assess the Behaviors You Expect—Procedures***, pages 289–290	Identify specific procedures that you will implement in your classroom: 1) Transition Procedures; 2) Classroom Environment Procedures; 3) Learning Procedures; 4) Student Work Procedures. Think about how you will introduce and scaffold practice of each procedure during the first month of school.	*RIGHT* Chapter 4

Documents, Page Number	Purpose / Directions	Text Reference
Classroom Management and Discipline Plan: **Model, Teach, Practice, and Assess the Behaviors You Expect—Group Learning Protocols**, page 291	Think carefully about when and how you will introduce and then practice group learning protocols, group talk protocols, life skills, habits of learning, and other activities that help you build a high-performing community of learners. Prioritize the protocols, skills, and habits that are most important to teach and practice in the first month of school.	*REAL* Chapter 15
Model, Teach, Practice, and Assess the Behaviors You Expect—Group Talk Protocols, page 292		*REAL* Chapter 15
Building a Cohesive Community—Positive Behavior Supports, page 293		*REAL* Chapter 15
Positive Behavior Supports for Individuals, page 294		*RIGHT* Chapter 5
Classroom Management and Discipline Plan: **Academic Learning Supports for Individuals**, pages 295–296	Decide on the academic learning supports, accountable consequences, and interventions that will be "standard procedure" in your classroom when students don't learn or haven't completed important academic work proficiently.	*REAL* Chapter 12 and 16
Academic Accountable Consequences and Interventions, page 297		*RIGHT* Chapter 5
Classroom Management and Discipline Plan: **Classroom Management Essentials**, pages 298–299	Think about the physical, verbal, and visual prompts and cues you want to have in place from day one that enable students to do the right thing at the right time during whole group instruction.	*RIGHT* Chapter 6
Classroom Management and Discipline Plan: **Behavioral Accountable Consequences and Interventions**, pages 300–301	Decide on the set of scaffolded consequences that take effect when the same unwanted behavior persists 1) after repeated prompts to self-correct; 2) after a first round of logical consequences; or 3) if a student shows no improvement after a first round of accountable consequences. Your choice of consequences should reflect what you are willing to enforce every time with every kid.	*RIGHT* Chapter 1 and 7
Practice: **What's Punitive? What's Accountable?**, pages 302–303	Use as a small group exercise. Some schoolwide consequences will always be punitive—the challenge is to develop value-added accountable consequences that take effect alongside purely punitive consequence.	*RIGHT* Chapter 1 and 7
Practice: **You Decide**, page 304	Think through what incidents should be handled by teachers most of the time and what incidents warrant referrals or removal from class.	*RIGHT* Chapter 1 and 7
Practice: **Help! Fix This Referral**, page 305	In small groups, choose one or two referrals to rewrite using the criteria at the top of the page as a guide.	*RIGHT* Chapter 1 and 7

Documents, Page Number	Purpose / Directions	Text Reference
Practice: **PEARS—Responsive Listening**, page 306	Use these guidelines to engage in responsive listening practices.	*RIGHT* Chapter 3 and 5
Practice: **Back-to-Back Drawings**, page 307	This exercise enables participants to compare one-way vs. two-way communication.	*RIGHT* Chapter 3 and 5
Practice: **Constructive vs. Negative Speech**, pages 308–309	Cut statements into strips and pass out. People who have examples of positive speech move to one side of the room, and people who have examples of negative speech move to the other side of the room. Read statements and then pair up to transform negative statements using constructive language.	*RIGHT* Chapter 3 and 5
Practice: **Aggressive, Passive, and Assertive Speech and Behavior**, pages 310–311	These exercises can be used to practice identifying aggressive, passive, and assertive behaviors and speech.	*RIGHT* Chapter 3 and 5
Practice: **How Does Conflict Escalate?**, page 312	Use this graphic organizer to deconstruct conflicts by writing down specific speech and behaviors that escalate the conflict.	*RIGHT* Chapter 3 and 5
Practice: **Anger Iceberg**, page 313	Identify the primary emotions that may lie beneath the secondary emotion of anger that is expressed.	*RIGHT* Chapter 3 and 5
Practice: **Why Does Healthy Development Matter?**, page 314	These two illustrations show how a person's emotional state influences the capacities to think and learn.	*RIGHT* Chapter 3
Practice: **Conflict Management Styles**, page 315	Explore how the characteristics of various animals reflect each conflict style.	*RIGHT* Chapter 3 and 5
Practice: **Conflict Management Grids**, page 316	The conflict management grids and question prompts explore how different responses generate a range of outcomes.	*RIGHT* Chapter 3 and 5
Practice: **Positions and Interests**, page 317	Generate several needs, concerns, and interests that provide possible reasons for each stated position.	*RIGHT* Chapter 3 and 5
Practice: **One-Minute Problem Solving**, pages 317–318	Decide which response on page 40 is the best match for each problem situation described on page 39.	*RIGHT* Chapter 3 and 5
Practice: **Defusing Provocative Speech**, page 319	In the blanks #1–#4, write down specific provocative statements that trigger frustration and anger. Then work in pairs to construct "wrong way" and "right way" responses.	*RIGHT* Chapter 6 and 7
Practice: **Practicing Effective Teacher Talk**, page 320	Develop and perform "wrong way" and "right way" role-plays using sentence prompts and questions.	*RIGHT* Chapter 6 and 7
Practice: **Personal Conferencing**, pages 321–322	Any of these conferencing protocols can be used for practice role-plays. Be sure to provide a detailed snapshot of the particular student in the role-play.	*RIGHT* Chapter 5 and 7
Practice: **Facilitating Gatherings, Group Games, and Team Problem Solving**, pages 323–333	Divide participants into small groups and use sample gatherings, group games, and team problem-solving activities to rehearse and practice group facilitation and debriefing skills.	*REAL* Chapter 15 Use guidelines on pages 323–333

REFLECTIONS

Building a Community of Learners

1. How would you describe the kind of learner you want to be during these sessions?
2. What skills or habits do you consciously want to practice during these sessions?
3. What's your "growing edge" or "discomfort zone" as a learner or as a participant?
4. What behaviors or attitudes do you consciously want to minimize during these sessions?
5. How do you want others to see you as a group member?
6. What do you need from me and the group to be a high-performing member of this learning community?
6. What group norms will make these sessions feel productive and engaging? (How we work and learn together; talk to each other; treat each other)
7. What are the specific behaviors associated with global words that can mean something different to everyone in the room?

What does it look like?	What does it sound like?
Respect Engagement Tolerance	Respect Engagement Tolerance

Example: **ENGAGEMENT**

What is engagement? Engagement in learning involves:

- Cognitive behaviors (attention, effort, problem solving, the use of metacognitive strategies like goal-setting, reflection, and accurate processing of information)

- Intellectual behaviors (the use of higher order thinking skills to increase understanding, solve complex problems, create original work, and construct new knowledge)

- Observable behaviors (active participation in class, completion of high-quality work, demonstrating persistence and seeking assistance when tasks are difficult, taking challenging courses)

- Emotions (enthusiasm, interest, alertness, confidence, curiosity, pride, excitement, satisfaction)

Engagement in learning is a combination of:

I CAN	(students' perceptions of competence and control)
I WANT TO	(students' desires, goals, values, and interests)
I BELONG	(students' social connectedness)
I SHOULD	(students' identification with school learning expectations, norms, and core values)

REFLECTIONS

Urgent Issues and Questions You Want Addressed

Name two or three unwanted behaviors in your classroom that you want to tackle during these sessions.

What are your most pressing questions or concerns related to classroom management, discipline, and other student behavior challenges?

Thinking about Discipline

1. In what aspects of your life do you see yourself as disciplined? How would you describe yourself when you feel disciplined?
2. What motivates you to be self-disciplined?
3. What words and phrases do you associate with self-discipline?
4. When you were growing up how did adults help you become responsible and self-disciplined?
5. Jot down your goals and desired student outcomes for classroom discipline and management. *Revisit your goals and desired student outcomes later: What's changed? What's the same?*
6. What makes a response to unwanted behaviors effective? What's one of your most effective strategies for responding to unwanted behaviors in the classroom?
7. What disciplinary practices and responses would you like to use less often? Why?
8. What disciplinary practices and responses would you like to use more often? What would be the benefits for you and students?
9. What feelings do you associate with being self-disciplined?

Three Approaches to Classroom Management and Discipline

1. Identify three words or phrases that capture the characteristics of PUNISHMENT/ PUNITIVE CONSEQUENCES.
2. What are the risks of a "DO-NOTHING" approach to discipline?
3. Describe one or two ways that GUIDED DISCIPLINE differs from a PUNISHMENT approach?
4. When you are stressed, which approach to disciplinary problems are you most likely to use? Explain why this is likely to be your immediate response?
5. What distinguishes ACCOUNTABILITY from RESPONSIBILITY?
6. Name a PUNITIVE CONSEQUENCE and an ACCOUNTABLE CONSEQUENCE. What's the difference?
7. Are there any features of the guided discipline approach that are already part of your classroom management repertoire?
8. What aspects of guided discipline might be challenging to implement in your classroom?
9. What questions or confusions have emerged after these readings?

REFLECTIONS

Three Approaches to Classroom Management and Discipline *(cont.)*

10. What kinds of teacher behaviors will help your students become more self-disciplined and engage in more skillful behaviors more of the time?

11. What kinds of disciplinary strategies will work best for your frequent fliers—the students who experience the most behavioral difficulties? How do you make time to provide more coaching, monitoring, feedback, and positive attention to students who really need it?

Know Yourself

Reflecting on your teaching behaviors and communication style:

1. After reading #1 through #8 on pages 75–76, identify two that accurately describe issues that make it challenging for you to reach and teach every student effectively? What makes these two issues significant concerns for you?

2. Which two on pages 75–76, don't feel like challenges at all? How do you know that you are successful at avoiding these problems?

3. What's the difference between *authoritarian* and *authoritative*? Your table needs to discuss the reading, pages 66–67, and reach consensus on a definition, slogan, or mantra for each word. What are the distinguishing differences between these two ideas? Post their definitions on a wall.

4. What do you want to communicate to students the first day of class? How would you describe your first day teaching stance?

5. What are your "NOS", your needs, and your non negotiables that you want students to know? What's NOT on the table for you and students to co-construct? What are behaviors that totally cross the line in your classroom—behaviors that you are willing to interrupt and address every time it happens?

6. What are the accountable consequences? What do kids know will happen when they engage in behaviors that break the boundaries of safety or severely violate a person's dignity and well-being?

Dealing with anger:

7. Cues: How do you know when you're angry? What do you experience physically? What's going on with your body, your voice, your posture, etc.?

8. Triggers: What are your triggers? What do kids do that will set you off? Do kids know your cues and triggers?

9. Responses to anger that don't work: When you are already "IN ANGRY", what do you not want someone to say or do? What kinds of responses are NOT helpful?

10. Reducers that do work: What are your anger reducers? What can you do (or say to yourself) that will help you regain control and get your equilibrium back? What can someone else say or do that helps you become calmer?

REFLECTIONS

Know Yourself

Thinking about conflict styles:

11. Talk about the conflict styles you tend to use most often in the classroom? In what situations are they most effective? Least effective?
12. What's one conflict style you would like to be more intentional about using in the classroom? What would be the benefits for you? For students?
13. What's one conflict style you would like to use less often in the classroom? What would be the benefits for you? For students?
14. When is POSTPONE an effective response?

Cultural Sharing:

15. Share something about your family's origins, where your people live and have lived; or other aspects of your background that illuminate who your family is and what your family is about.
16. Name two or three values or beliefs from your family that still drive who you are today and one family belief or value you've chosen to let go of.
17. We all belong to groups by birth (race, gender, sexual orientation, physical abilities/disabilities); by family background (class, culture, religion, socioeconomic status; education attainment, home location); and by choice (work groups, political groups, recreation, sports, and hobby groups and affiliations, etc.). Share some of the groups you belong to by choice.
18. Choose the lens of race, ethnicity, class, gender, sexual orientation, or religion for this question: As a member of this group, a) what's something you're proud of? And b) What's one thing you never want to hear others say about this group?

Know Your Students

1. What do you want to know about your kids, as teens and as learners?
2. What activities, journal prompts, gatherings, learning tasks, and conference opportunities will help you do this?
3. What do you do in the classroom that creates conditions that promote positive self-esteem?
4. What teacher behaviors will set your students off and result in off-task behaviors, confrontations and power struggles, noncompliance, hostility, or disengagement?
5. What strategies will you use to learn every student's name?
6. What strategies will you use to ensure that students learn each other's names?
7. What classroom and school conditions impede development of healthy self-esteem?

CLASSROOM MANAGEMENT AND DISCIPLINE PLAN

Organize Your Classroom

Student Seating

What different classroom seating arrangements will ensure that…

- you can move easily to every student quickly when they are working independently

- students can easily work with one partner

- students can arrange the space to work in groups of three and four

- students can arrange the space for group discussions where everyone can see each other's faces

CLASSROOM MANAGEMENT AND DISCIPLINE PLAN

Organize Your Classroom

Signage

What posters and signs will you post in your room to communicate learning goals and expectations, core skills, tools for learning, important norms and procedures?

_____

_____

_____

_____

Walls for Teaching and Organizing

Type of Information	Where will you place it?
Daily agenda	
Calendar of important activities, due dates, and reminders	
Assignments	
Notes and work-in-progress on chart paper or large newsprint for each class section	
Essential questions for the year and the current learning unit	
Career connections to your discipline	
Student news and photos	

CLASSROOM MANAGEMENT AND DISCIPLINE PLAN

Expectations and Norms

Behavioral Expectations (See page 100)

Based on what you know about your students, your school, and yourself—what are your behavioral expectations?

Academic Expectations (See page 100)

Based on what you know about your students, your school, and yourself—what are your academic expectations?

Group Norms (See pages 101–104)

How and when will you develop group norms for the classroom?

Respect (See pages 104–113)

How and when will you facilitate a conversation about respect?

CLASSROOM MANAGEMENT AND DISCIPLINE PLAN

Model, Teach, Practice, and Assess the Behaviors You Expect

Transition Procedures (See pages 120–123)

What's the procedure? Why insist that all students learn to do it?	When and how will you **introduce** and **teach** it?	What kinds of **practice** will students do?	How will you **assess** students' use of the procedure?

Classroom Environment Procedures (See pages 123–126)

What's the procedure? Why insist that all students learn to do it?	When and how will you **introduce** and **teach** it?	What kinds of **practice** will students do?	How will you **assess** students' use of the procedure?

CLASSROOM MANAGEMENT AND DISCIPLINE PLAN

Model, Teach, Practice, and Assess the Behaviors You Expect

Learning Procedures (See pages 126–127)

What's the procedure? Why insist that all students learn to do it?	When and how will you **introduce** and **teach** it?	What kinds of **practice** will students do?	How will you **assess** students' use of the procedure?

Student Work Procedures (See pages 127–135)

What's the procedure? Why insist that all students learn to do it?	When and how will you **introduce** and **teach** it?	What kinds of **practice** will students do?	How will you **assess** students' use of the procedure?

CLASSROOM MANAGEMENT AND DISCIPLINE PLAN

Model, Teach, Practice, and Assess the Behaviors You Expect

Group Learning Protocols (See *Making Learning REAL,* Chapter 15)

Which protocols do you want to use frequently?	When and how will you **introduce** and **teach** it?	What kinds of **practice** will students do?	How will you **assess** students' use of the protocol?
☐ Gatherings and Closings			
☐ Pair-Share-Record			
☐ Cooperative Learning Pairs (One task/Same info to both students)			
☐ Cooperative Learning Three's and Four's (One task/Same info to all students)			
☐ Cooperative Learning Three's and Four's (Jig-Saw/Different info to each student)			
☐ Carousel and Walk-Abouts			
☐ Whole Group Games			
☐ Team Problem-Solving Games/Exercises			
☐ Problem-Solving Class Meeting			
☐ Home Groups			

CLASSROOM MANAGEMENT AND DISCIPLINE PLAN

Model, Teach, Practice, and Assess the Behaviors You Expect

Group Talk Protocols (See *Making Learning REAL,* Chapter 15)

Which protocols do you want to use frequently?	When and how will you **introduce** and **teach** it?	What kinds of **practice** will students do?	How will you **assess** students' use of the protocol?
☐ Turn and Talk and Pair Walk-Arounds			
☐ Listening Lab			
☐ Opinion Continuum			
☐ Four Corners			
☐ Rubric Driven Group Discussion			
☐ Text-Based Seminar			

CLASSROOM MANAGEMENT AND DISCIPLINE PLAN

Building a Cohesive Group—Positive Behavior Supports

Gatherings (See *Making Learning REAL,* Chapter 15)
What kinds of gatherings will you facilitate during the first month of school that will encourage student voice and enable you to find out more about who's in the room?

Closings (See *Making Learning REAL,* Chapter 15)
What kinds of closings will you facilitate on Fridays that will help the group to reflect on the past week (highlights, personal and group benchmarks, appreciations, assessment of learning and participation, etc.)?

Games, Exercises, and Activities that Build Teamwork, Leadership, Group Collaboration and Problem-Solving Skills (See *Making Learning REAL,* Chapter 15)
What kinds of games, exercises, and activities will you incorporate into your first several learning units that require students to learn and practice teamwork, leadership, group collaboration and problem-solving skills?

Group Rituals, Recognitions, and Celebrations (See page 172)
What kinds of group rituals, recognitions, and celebrations will you and students create to build a sense of belonging and acceptance?

Incentives (See pages 173–175)
What kinds of low-stakes, random, intermittent incentives might you use to support students doing the right thing?

CLASSROOM MANAGEMENT AND DISCIPLINE PLAN

Positive Behavior Supports for Individuals

Life Skills: What life skills will you emphasize during the first semester of the year? (See pages 141–145)

Which life skills? Why insist that all students demonstrate this skill?	When and how will you **introduce** and **teach** it?	What kinds of **practice** will students do?	How will you **assess** students' use of the procedure?

Habits of Learning: What habits of learning will you emphasize during the first semester of the year? (See pages 130–132)

Which habits of learning? Why insist that all students demonstrate this habit?	When and how will you **introduce** and **teach** it?	What kinds of **practice** will students do?	How will you **assess** students' use of the procedure?

CLASSROOM MANAGEMENT AND DISCIPLINE PLAN

Academic Learning Supports for Individual Students

Recording and Charting Students' Academic Progress and Responsibilities (See *Making Learning REAL,* Chapter 12)

How will students record and chart their academic progress and responsibilities from week to week? What tools will students have to do this?

☐ Student work folder

☐ Weekly or biweekly progress chart or graph on which students record what they have completed, what has not been completed, what needs to be revised or redone, and what grades they have earned

☐ Assignment notebook or weekly assignment sheet

☐ Monitoring and tracking. How do you record anecdotal information for each student?

☐ What gets publicly displayed?

Assessing Students' Academic Progress (See *Making Learning REAL,* Chapter 12)

What tools and strategies will you and students use to assess students' academic progress and learning gaps?

☐ Goal-setting at beginning of every term or semester

☐ Student written self-assessments and reflection journals at least once a week

☐ Informal conferencing while students are engaged in guided practice, independent work, or small group work

☐ Formative assessment strategies and tools

☐ Formal academic assessment conferences with all students at key points in the school year

☐ As-needed conferences for students with learning gaps

☐ Clear procedures and protocols in place for students

CLASSROOM MANAGEMENT AND DISCIPLINE PLAN

Academic Learning Supports for Individual Students

Expectations and Procedures for Completing High-Quality Work (See *Making Learning REAL,* Chapter 16)
How do you expect, insist, and support all students to complete multiple samples of high-quality work every grading period?

☐ **100% Completion with Quality:** Major products, projects, or presentations that every student must complete proficiently during the first semester:

_____

_____

☐ **Must Revise:** Work that students must revise, redo, or complete before earning a grade:

_____

_____

☐ **Homework Policy:** 1) Does it insist that students complete all assignments? 2) Does it provide enough credit for late assignments so students are motivated to complete it? 3) Does it have a window of time for completion, so students can't leave all missing or incomplete assignments to the last week before grades are submitted?

_____

_____

☐ **Cleanup Days:** Do you set aside a cleanup day every month to ensure that class time is available for students to check in with you about particular assignments, organize notebooks, review their portfolio of work, get clear on work that needs to completed, and receive notification of required academic workouts and homework hall?

Dates:_____

☐ **Office Hours:** Do you have office hours at least one day before school, one day after school, and at least one lunch period?

_____

☐ **Homework Hall:** Is there a weekly or biweekly homework hall for students who seek voluntary help and students who are required to attend?

_____

CLASSROOM MANAGEMENT AND DISCIPLINE PLAN

Academic Accountable Consequences and Interventions

Effective interventions: 1) are predictably enforced; 2) identify concrete tasks that students do and concrete skills and habits that students use; and 3) include follow-up feedback and coaching

Academic Learning Gap Conferences (See pages 34 and 275)

Intervention takes effect when student _____

Follow-up and feedback _____

Academic Learning Contracts or Weekly Progress Reports (See pages 34 and 116)

Intervention takes effect when student _____

Follow-up and feedback _____

Parent Phone Call (See pages 253–254)

Intervention takes effect when student _____

Follow-up and feedback _____

Parent-Student-Teacher Conference (See page 254)

Intervention takes effect when student _____

Follow-up and feedback _____

Case Conference with Student's Counselor and Other Faculty Who Teach Student
(See page 255–256)

Intervention takes effect when student _____

Follow-up and feedback _____

Required Homework Hall or Academic Workouts: (See page 224)

Intervention takes effect when student _____

Follow-up and feedback _____

CLASSROOM MANAGEMENT AND DISCIPLINE PLAN

Classroom Management Essentials

Getting Students' Attention and Making Transitions (See page 178–179)

What's your desired target behavior for students?

What's your cue or prompt to get it?

If all students are not with you after the first cue or prompt, then what will you do?

What will be the accountable consequences for individuals or a small group of students who repeatedly cannot or will not engage in the desired target behavior?

Giving Clear Instructions (See page 180)

What's your desired target behavior for students?

What's your cue or prompt to get it?

If all students are not with you after the first cue or prompt, then what will you do?

What will be the accountable consequences for individuals or a small group of students who repeatedly cannot or will not engage in the desired target behavior?

CLASSROOM MANAGEMENT AND DISCIPLINE PLAN

Classroom Management Essentials

Insisting on and Getting Silence, When Silence Is Required (See pages 181–182)

What's your desired target behavior for students?

What's your cue or prompt to get it?

If all students are not with you after the first cue or prompt, then what will you do?

What will be the accountable consequences for individuals or a small group of students who repeatedly cannot or will not engage in the desired target behavior?

Using Physical Proximity and Prompts at the First Sign of Off-Task Behaviors (See pages 182–183)

What's your desired target behavior for students?

What's your cue or prompt to get it?

If the student(s) is not with you after the first cue or prompt, then what will you do?

What will be the accountable consequences for individuals or a small group of students who repeatedly cannot or will not engage in the desired target behavior?

CLASSROOM MANAGEMENT AND DISCIPLINE PLAN

Behavioral Accountable Consequences and Interventions

Behavioral Nonnegotiables

When I see or hear...	You can expect me to...	And you will need to...

Preparing for Unwanted Behaviors that Walk in Your Room

Think about the most frequent unwanted behaviors you want to be ready for—what will be your first response when redirection, self-correction, or quick problem solving isn't enough?

Unwanted behavior / Desired target behavior	Is there an appropriate logical consequence that takes effect when redirection doesn't work?	What consequences take effect when unwanted behavior is persistent? (What will you do? What must student do?)

CLASSROOM MANAGEMENT AND DISCIPLINE PLAN

Behavioral Accountable Consequences and Interventions

Scaffolded Consequences for Frequent Fliers (See pages 245–246)

When students show no improvement after the first intervention, you need to increase the intensity of the intervention. A common mistake is repeating the same consequence over and over. What is your standard sequence of consequences when a first intervention isn't enough? Keep in mind that one standard sequence of accountable consequences doesn't rule out implementing other additional consequences that might be an appropriate match for some particular behaviors or incidents—like a written apology, a student-teacher mediation, or anger management sessions with a counselor.

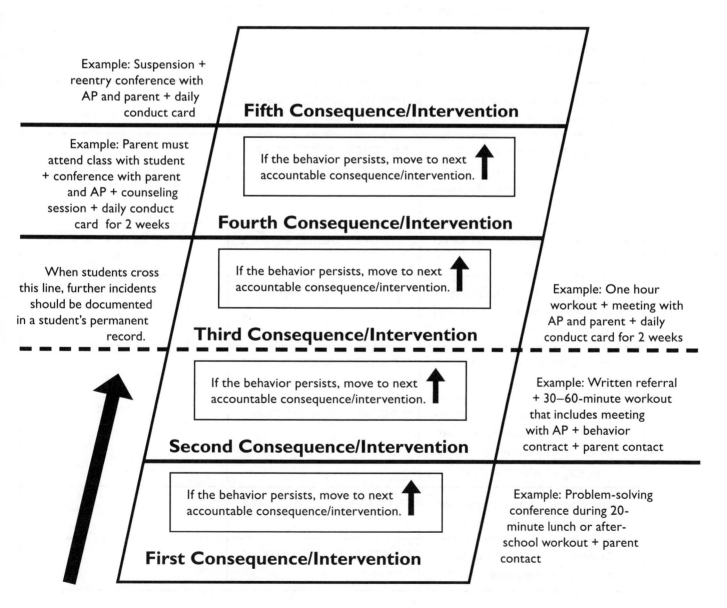

Example: Suspension + reentry conference with AP and parent + daily conduct card

Fifth Consequence/Intervention

If the behavior persists, move to next accountable consequence/intervention.

Example: Parent must attend class with student + conference with parent and AP + counseling session + daily conduct card for 2 weeks

Fourth Consequence/Intervention

If the behavior persists, move to next accountable consequence/intervention.

When students cross this line, further incidents should be documented in a student's permanent record.

Third Consequence/Intervention

Example: One hour workout + meeting with AP and parent + daily conduct card for 2 weeks

If the behavior persists, move to next accountable consequence/intervention.

Second Consequence/Intervention

Example: Written referral + 30–60-minute workout that includes meeting with AP + behavior contract + parent contact

If the behavior persists, move to next accountable consequence/intervention.

First Consequence/Intervention

Example: Problem-solving conference during 20-minute lunch or after-school workout + parent contact

PRACTICE

What's Punitive? What's Accountable?

CONSEQUENCE	What kind of consequence is it?	If PUNITIVE, what would you add or change to make it ACCOUNTABLE?
1. Ten-day suspension for fighting	PUNITIVE ACCOUNTABLE	
2. Student must wear a rental shirt when s/he arrives at school not in uniform	PUNITIVE ACCOUNTABLE	
3. Conference with teacher, student, parent, and dean to develop a weekly conduct card for chronic unwanted behaviors	PUNITIVE ACCOUNTABLE	
4. Student receives a 0 for incomplete assignment	PUNITIVE ACCOUNTABLE	
5. Student AND parent must sign in on time for five days in a row when student is chronically late for school	PUNITIVE ACCOUNTABLE	
6. Student receives detention for no ID badge	PUNITIVE ACCOUNTABLE	
7. Students gets a "cut" erased by completing a week of school with no tardies or late arrivals	PUNITIVE ACCOUNTABLE	
8. Student receives detention for three tardies	PUNITIVE ACCOUNTABLE	
9. Student with chronic confrontational, angry behavior is required to attend three sessions on anger management with counselor	PUNITIVE ACCOUNTABLE	
10. Student doesn't have a pencil and is removed from the classroom	PUNITIVE ACCOUNTABLE	
11. Student cuts 4th period three times and is suspended	PUNITIVE ACCOUNTABLE	

12. Student who engages in repetitive sidebar talking is tossed and sent to dean	PUNITIVE ACCOUNTABLE	
13. Students who damaged property in a science room participate in a peace circle with their parents, the head custodian, the principal, and science teacher so offenders can hear and respond to those affected by their actions and develop a plan to restore their good standing and make things right	PUNITIVE ACCOUNTABLE	
14. Student who cannot function in a cooperative group is sent to the dean	PUNITIVE ACCOUNTABLE	
15. Student who is missing three important assignments is assigned to mandated "homework hall" after school	PUNITIVE ACCOUNTABLE	
16. Student who threw trash on the floor must pick up trash at end of period for the rest of the week	PUNITIVE ACCOUNTABLE	
17. Student receives detention for not wearing a hat	PUNITIVE ACCOUNTABLE	
18. Student is removed to dean's office for throwing paper	PUNITIVE ACCOUNTABLE	
19. Student who doesn't follow classroom procedures must attend a lunchtime "workout" with teacher for practice	PUNITIVE ACCOUNTABLE	
20. Student receives suspension for defacing school property	PUNITIVE ACCOUNTABLE	
21.		
22.		
23.		
24.		

PRACTICE

You Decide

Most of the time...
What should be handled by the teacher and the student? (Put a ✱)
What warrants a written referral to the dean, but no removal? (Put a ✔)
What warrants a referral to the counselor/social worker? (Put a **C**)
What warrants a referral and immediate removal from classroom? (Put a ❗)

___ 1. Student doesn't bring necessary materials to class	___ 2. Student doesn't cooperate in small group work	___ 3. Student doesn't participate in classroom discussion
___ 4. One student is deliberately annoying another student	___ 5. Student is talking while you or others are speaking	___ 6. Student rejects your coaching and encouragement
___ 7. Physical fight between students	___ 8. Student throws objects across the classroom	___ 9. Student mumbles to her/himself, "I'm not going to do this"
___ 10. Pushing, shoving, and touching other students when contact is uninvited	___ 11. Student verbally attacks another student personally, saying, "You are such a _____"	___ 12. Student doesn't do their share of the work in cooperative groups
___ 13. Student continues to argue with you aggressively after you have said twice that you will discuss this personally in private at a later time	___ 14. Student engages in emotional outbursts/out-of-control behavior that jeopardizes classroom safety and order and student well-being	___ 15. When unwanted behavior persists, student repeatedly refuses teacher's request or directive using aggressive, confrontational, hostile or threatening words/body language
___ 16. Student tags desks or classroom equipment	___ 17. A group of students are playing around and goofing off in their small groups	___ 18. Student doesn't correct, edit, redo work, so it doesn't meet an acceptable level of proficiency
___ 19. Student verbally harasses individual student or targeted group	___ 20. Confrontation in which student is yelling and cursing out the teacher	___ 21. Inappropriate use of technology, text messaging, video games
___ 22. Student makes excessive noises and engages in disruptive movement in the classroom on a regular basis	___ 23. Student persistently uses rude, uncivil, or offensive speech and gestures during whole group learning	___ 24. Student tends to respond to most students in a hostile, unfriendly, and disrespectful manner
___ 25. Teasing, taunting, put-downs, and name calling	___ 26. Student walks away when you are speaking personally to her/him about _____	___ 27. Student verbally threatens a teacher and says, "You are a _____"
___ 28. Student doesn't complete homework or class assignments to a proficiency level	___ 29. Student slams books down and slams the door as he walks out the door without permission	___ 30. Student exhibits passive-aggressive body language (teeth sucking, eye rolling, etc.)
___ 31. Student walks away when an adult is speaking with her/him	___ 32. Student sleeps in class several times a week	___ 33. Student is daydreaming and glazed over
___ 34. Student constantly cries and seeks your attention	___ 35. Student makes no attempt to do assigned work	___ 36. Student doesn't follow directions or procedures

PRACTICE

Help! Fix This Referral

Good referrals meet the following criteria. They describe:

- the exact unwanted behavior

- the circumstances during which the unwanted behavior occurred

- note the frequency, duration, and/or severity of the behavior

- note the exact language that was unacceptable

- note if aggressive behavior or speech was directed at a specific person

- note any suggested interventions (especially any intervention in which you would like to be involved)

- note how you intervened BEFORE the incident

Rewrite one of the referrals so it becomes a clear, legitimate referral:

1. "Henry was cursing during class."

2. "Kiesha was disrespectful."

3. "Jose was lazy and obnoxious."

4. "Anna was using foul language."

5. "Kim has no interest in being in class today."

6. "Han Su refuses to do the work."

7. "Tye was talking excessively during class."

8. "Lisia was loud and rude."

9. "Omar was uncooperative."

> **Avoid using the four Ds:**
> Disruptive
> Disrespectful
> Distracting
> Disobedient

PRACTICE

PEARS—Responsive Listening

"The first step toward violence is the refusal to listen."

"Listening doesn't mean agreement. Listening indicates your respect for the other person and you interest in hearing what the person has to say."

When is it easy to listen? When is it hard to listen?

Here are some guidelines for responsive listening. Just remember PEARS.

Paraphrase the facts:
- "You're saying that _____."
- "So you had trouble with _____."
- "You want me to know that _____".
- "So when_____happened, you _____."

Encourage the student to speak:
- Focus your whole attention on the student in interested silence.
- Lean in slightly; keep your arms relaxed and still; encourage the speaker by nodding.
- "Tell me what happened."
- "I want to hear your side of the story."
- "So tell me more."
- "Say that in another way so I can better understand exactly what you need."

Ask questions that help students clarify the problem and foster self-awareness, self-reflection, and self-assessment:
- "What exactly happened when _____?"
- "How did you feel when_____?"
- "What else should I know about _____?"
- "What do you think is getting in the way of _____?"
- "What do you need so you can _____?"
- "Where there any other choices you might have made?"
- "What do you think your Mom would say about_____?"

Reflect feelings and defuse highly charged emotions like anger and frustration:
- "So you're feeling angry about_____."
- "I can see you're upset about_____."
- "Wow! You sound really excited about_____."
- "So you felt _____when _____."
- "It must have been difficult for you to _____."

Invite student to Solve the problem if student is ready to take charge and make a plan:
- "What do you need right now to be okay for the rest of the day?
- "Where would you like to go from here?"
- "What would a good solution/good plan look like?
- "What might be a first step to resolving this?"
- "What could you do or say to work this out?"

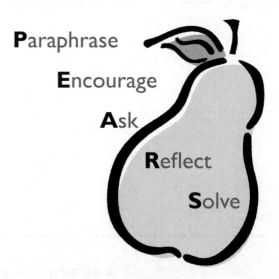

PRACTICE

Back-to-Back Drawings

A) Ask a volunteer to stand facing an opposite wall from the place where you or a student creates a simple drawing of shapes and lines. Then give verbal directions to the student who is drawing that will enable her to make an exact copy of the drawing. Do this the first time with the rule that the person drawing cannot speak or ask questions. Then do it a second time where the person drawing can speak and ask questions. **OR**

B) Create drawings like the samples below and copy them. Ask students to find partners and sit back to back. Give each partner a different drawing. Partner A gives directions for how to make an exact copy of their drawing while the other student draws. Partner B (the drawer) can't talk or ask questions. Give students five minutes. Compare the original and copy of the drawing. Then switch roles, so Partner B gives directions and Partner A is the drawer. This time Partner A can talk and ask questions. After five minutes, tell students to stop and compare drawings. Was it easier to draw accurately the second time? Why?

PRACTICE

Constructive vs. Negative Speech

Who died and put you in charge?

You are such an idiot. A five year old could do this.

I'm too upset to talk about this now. Let's talk later.

Just forget it. You can't do it anyway.

I'm confused. Tell me again why you're mad.

So what did you expect? A miracle?

Just get over it. You're being a baby.

If you really loved me, you'd do it.

I don't have to take your crap. You're not worth it.

I know some of this is on me. Let's try and fix it.

I could use your help here.

I'm not sure this is the right thing to do. Let's talk it over.

Don't you ever do that again or you'll be sorry.

Don't be a wuss. Everyone else is doing it.

Here's why I feel embarrassed about this.

What a fool. You never know when to stop.

This is all your fault.

Hey, you stole my pencil.

How many times do I have to tell you this?

What's wrong with you?

What if we tried doing it this way?

I can see you point. Here's how I see it.

What do you need to feel okay about this?

I didn't mean any disrespect. I'm sorry I said it that way.

This is not helping. Let's stop and come back to it later.

You're really mad at me. What can I do to make it right?

I want to hear your side of the story. What happened?

Let me explain why this is important to me.

You have a lousy attitude that will get you nowhere.

You're right. I didn't think about that.

Thanks for listening to my side of the story.

I told you so. You never listen to me.

Wait a minute. Is this worth risking our friendship?

You never do what you're supposed to do.

This was an accident. Let me help you clean it up.

PRACTICE

Aggressive, Passive, and Assertive Speech and Behavior

Divide group into trios, and give each trio a white board or three signs that say, AGGRESSIVE, PASSIVE, and ASSERTIVE. Call out random behaviors below and give trios ten seconds to decide and respond.

- You deliberately annoy, provoke, or bother someone to get a reaction.

- You listen before you make your case.

- You embarrass the other person and call him/her stupid.

- You explain your nonnegotiables.

- You constantly interrupt others and you have to have the last word in any conversation.

- You say what you don't like and exit.

- You make demands and constantly argue.

- You whine and complain but don't do anything to change the situation.

- You explain your preference and why you want it.

- You don't stand up for yourself.

- You walk away from someone who is speaking to you.

- You get in someone's face, you roll your eyes, you suck your teeth, you give them a hostile look.

- You don't express your opinion or tell people what's bothering you.

- You ask for help when you need it.

- You say, "Whatever," and then get mad when it's not your way.

- You give someone the "silent treatment."

- You acknowledge a disagreement without attacking the other person.

- You assume that the other person wants to harm you or do you in.

- You deny that anything's wrong when a problem exists.

- You choose to problem solve with the other person.

- You let the other person know what's bothering you and say what you need.

- You do what your friend is doing even though you don't really want to.

- You scream and curse at the other person to get them to do what you want.

- You say "yes" when you really mean "no."

- You suffer in silence.

- You blame and accuse the person before you have all of the facts.

- You say "no thanks" and exit.

- You apologize when you did something that bothered someone else.

- You yell and curse to get your way.

For each situation, describe what a person might say and do that illustrates an aggressive, passive, and assertive response.

AGGRESSIVE	PASSIVE	ASSERTIVE
"I get what I want and need at the expense of others—by dominating or hurting others physically or emotionally."	"I allow others to take advantage of me by not choosing to act and not expressing my feelings, needs, or thoughts to others."	"I take care of myself by expressing my needs, thoughts, and feelings in a strong way, while showing respect to the other person."

1. Student is upset about failing at mid-term and meets with teacher. What does student say and do?

2. Student A is making fun of student B. What does student C say and do?

3. Student doesn't understand what to do to complete the science lab. What does student say and do?

4. Teacher is frustrated with the sidebar talking during the discussion. What does teacher say and do?

5. Student A disagrees with student B's comment in a discussion. What does student A say and do?

6. Student A pokes a pencil in student B's back (sitting in desk in front). What does student B say and do?

PRACTICE

How Does Conflict Escalate?

			Feelings	Words
		Feelings	Words	
	Feelings	Words		
				Body Language/ Behavior
Feelings	Words		Body Language/ Behavior	
		Body Language/ Behavior		
Words	Body Language/ Behavior			
Body Language/ Behavior				

PRACTICE

Anger Iceberg

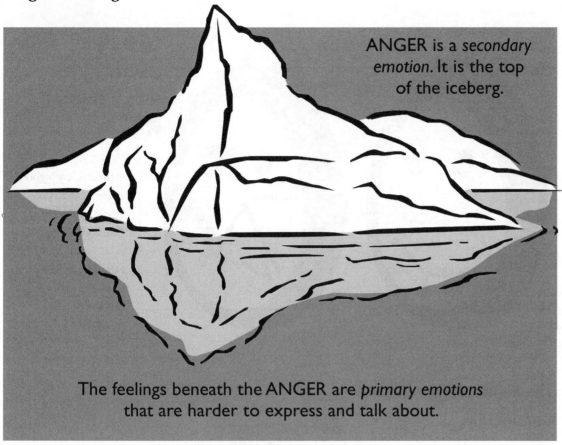

ANGER is a *secondary emotion.* It is the top of the iceberg.

The feelings beneath the ANGER are *primary emotions* that are harder to express and talk about.

People get angry when they are harassed or threatened because they feel _____.

People get angry when they don't have friends because they feel _____.

People get angry when they do poorly in school because they feel _____.

Children get angry when parents get divorced because they feel _____.

People get angry when they are criticized in front of others because they feel _____.

When person A breaks up with person B, person B is likely to feel _____.

People get angry when they are unemployed because they feel _____.

People get angry when there's neighborhood gang violence because they feel _____.

People get angry when someone close them dies because they feel _____.

PRACTICE

Why does healthy emotional development matter?

Imagine Two EGG People....

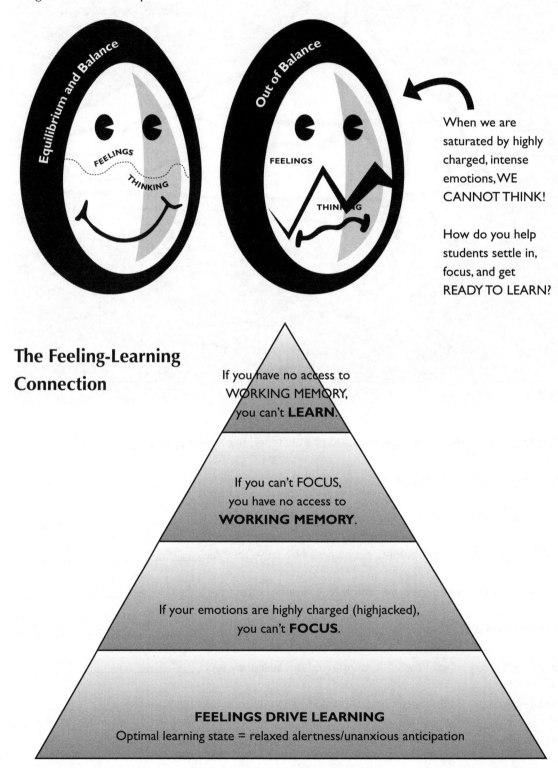

Equilibrium and Balance

FEELINGS

THINKING

Out of Balance

FEELINGS

THINKING

When we are saturated by highly charged, intense emotions, WE CANNOT THINK!

How do you help students settle in, focus, and get READY TO LEARN?

The Feeling-Learning Connection

If you have no access to WORKING MEMORY, you can't **LEARN**.

If you can't FOCUS, you have no access to **WORKING MEMORY**.

If your emotions are highly charged (highjacked), you can't **FOCUS**.

FEELINGS DRIVE LEARNING

Optimal learning state = relaxed alertness/unanxious anticipation

PRACTICE

Conflict Management Styles

FIGHT Force, direct, and demand; "My way or the highway"; use your power at others' expense; take charge when safety and security are at stake; engage in acts of peaceful nonviolence to confront injustice.

PROBLEM SOLVE Define the problem; share feelings and perspectives; listen responsively; identify NOs, needs, and wants; talk it out, negotiate, and come up with a solution that works for both people.

APPEAL TO A THIRD PARTY Help me out here; I'd like to talk it through before I decide; let's get a mediator to help us resolve this.

AVOID Avoid it, ignore it, deny it, or exit for safety.

POSTPONE Save it for later; "Let me think about it"; "I'll get back to you when it's a better time to talk."

ACCOMMODATE Let it go; give in; smooth it over; you want it more than me—that's okay.

PRACTICE

Conflict Management Grids

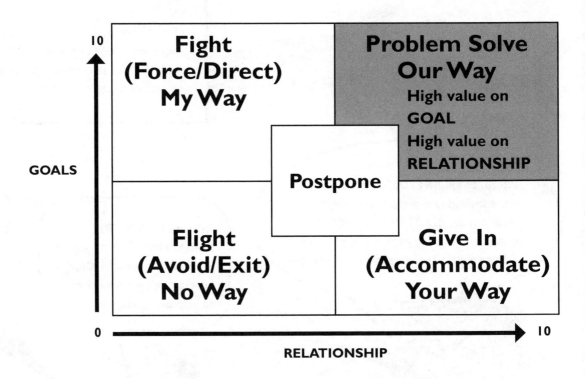

Win or Lose Outcome Grid	Person or Group A's wants and needs are met	Person or Group A's wants and needs are NOT met
Person or Group B's wants and needs are met	**A Wins** **B Wins**	**A Loses** **B Wins**
Person or Group B's wants and needs are NOT met	**A Wins** **B Loses**	**A Loses** **B Loses**

1. A few students rarely have pens or pencils for class (**A**) and the teacher is extremely frustrated (**B**).

2. Michael (**A**) calls Cho Min (**B**) a name in the hall. Cho Min is hurt and mad.

3. Tonya (**A**) and Marita (**B**) have been best friends since elementary school. Marita wants to hang out with new friends in high school and that makes Tonya mad.

4. Ricky (**A**) and Keith (**B**) got into a physical fight at school.

PRACTICE

Positions and Interests

Here are the positions. What are the underlying needs and interests?

1. Every student should go to a four-year college.
2. A student received a two-week suspension for fighting.
3. You must do the outline for your report exactly this way.
4. Standardized tests are the only valid measure for assessing student achievement.
5. All students must complete the same assessment at the end of the learning unit.
6. If your homework isn't completed on time, you get a zero.

One-Minute Problem Solving

Which conflict tool would you use in each situation?

A. The kid behind you in class keeps rapping his pencil on your chair.
B. Your mom is yelling at you because you haven't done your job of cleaning up the living room.
C. One of your friends uses racial and ethnic slurs in her conversation all of the time. You are embarrassed when other kids hear her saying this stuff.
D. Your curfew is midnight, but the cast party for the play in which you performed doesn't begin until 11 p.m.
E. The classroom smart mouth makes fun of you because you like school and get good grades.
F. Your friend who picks you up every morning has been late twice this week. You got to school ten minutes late and couldn't take a test yesterday.
G. Your friend is crying in the bathroom after a big fight with her father who hit her.
H. Your teacher is upset with you because you haven't handed in the last three assignments.
I. Someone has taken your textbook off the desk and now class is about to begin.
J. You really want to go see a different movie than your friend has suggested.
K. You and your friend are arguing about whether drugs should be legalized.
L. Your mom doesn't want you to work more than 15 hours a week, but you need to work at least 20 hours so you can buy_____.
M. You shared your friend A's secret with friend B, and now friend A is really mad.
N. You notice a shy girl who is being a harassed by a group of boys. She's afraid to say anything.
O. You're not sure if it's a good idea to go to your friend's house after school because you have a big project due tomorrow.
P. You accidentally knocked someone's books on the floor.

PRACTICE

The Conflict Toolbox

Handling conflicts skillfully means choosing the best tool for the situation you're in.

YOU ALWAYS HAVE CHOICES!

1. Ignore it and move on.

2. Make a sincere apology.

3. Use surprise or humor.

4. Just say "NO."

5. Check it out, ask questions, and seek more information.

6. Postpone a decision until later.

7. Make a request or state a preference.

8. Agree to disagree.

9. Say how you feel and think or what you need.

10. Talk it out and problem solve.

11. Seek help or advice.

12. Listen and defuse upset feelings.

13. Take responsibility and fix it.

14. Say what's bothering you and what you want to stop.

15. Accept the criticism or comments without a fuss and discuss the problem later.

PRACTICE

Defusing Provocative Speech

#1:_____

_____

_____

What's your GOAL? **Redirecting, Reframing, Correcting, Fogging, and/or Defusing Negative and Provocative Speech**

Wrong responses?

Effective responses?

#2:_____

_____

_____

What's your GOAL? **Redirecting, Reframing, Correcting, Fogging, and/or Defusing Negative and Provocative Speech**

Wrong responses?

Effective responses?

#3:_____

_____

_____

What's your GOAL? **Redirecting, Reframing, Correcting, Fogging, and/or Defusing Negative and Provocative Speech**

Wrong responses?

Effective responses?

#4:_____

_____

_____

What's your GOAL? **Redirecting, Reframing, Correcting, Fogging, and/or Defusing Negative and Provocative Speech**

Wrong responses?

Effective responses?

PRACTICE

Practicing Effective Teacher Talk

Choose one of the "effective teacher talk" sections on pages 177–187. Read the responses in this section. Your group needs to:

1. Decide on a classroom situation/problem behavior that calls for an effective response from the section you read. For example, if you choose the section, **Offer chances to problem solve and make a choice**, on pages 207–208, you might role-play a situation where two students are repeatedly talking during silent independent work time. (Use the chart on page 199 for other ideas.)

2. What's the immediate goal of your response?

3. What's the desired target behavior you want from the student?

4. If there is a long-term goal that requires a student conference, what is it?

5. What's the response from the section that you want to use the role play.

Create a role-play using a classroom setting with a teacher and a group of students. Rehearse your role-play with two different endings (wrong way/right way):

- The teacher responds to the situation in a way that actually escalates the conflict, creates more drama, or results in a power struggle. (wrong way)
- The teacher responds to the situation in a way that defuses the conflict, enables the student to self-correct, redirects the students, or helps the student get back on track. (right way)

Players: When you're ready, say "Action." When you're done say, "Curtain."
Audience: Watch and listen carefully so that you can provide feedback:
Role-Play #1: Identify the teacher's words, body language, and actions that escalated the conflict.
Role-Play #2:
- Identify the teacher's words, body language, and actions that effectively defused the conflict or redirected the student.
- Share any other responses that might have been effective in this situation.
- Be prepared to identify the benefits of the teacher's response in role-play #2 (for the teacher, the students involved, and the rest of the class).

PRACTICE

Personal Conferencing

---

1. Informal Check-ins

In what situations with which students would you make this a classroom practice?

Sample teacher prompts and tips:

- How's it going today?
- How has your week been so far?
- What are you looking forward to this week/weekend?
- What's getting easier to do? What's still hard?
- What's something new and good going on in your life?
- What can do you to have a good day today?
- What's a goal for class that will help you stay on track?

---

2. Learning Gap Conferences

In what situations with which students would you make this a classroom practice?

Sample teacher prompts and tips:

- What's going on that tells you that things aren't going so well in class?
- How are you feeling about class right now? Where do you feel stuck?
- I'm concerned about _____. What's your thinking about this?
- What's getting in the way of being successful in this class? What would it take to make this class work for you?
- Where are you stuck? What's easy? What's hard?
- What should I know that might help me understand how to help?
- Here's what I see. Does that sound about right to you?
- What are three things you might to do to turn it around in class?
- What can I do to support your efforts to get back on track?

---

3. Learner Profile Conference

In what situations with which students would you make this a classroom practice?

Sample teacher prompts and tips:

- How would you describe yourself as a learner? What's easy to learn? What's hard to learn? What subject area interests you the most?
- What are you interested in? What's your passion? What do you really want to learn about, become an expert at doing? What personal talents might you want to develop and strengthen?
- What kinds of courses and subjects do you like least? Most?
- In what instances does learning feel real and important to you?
- When you think about this class, what tasks and topics capture your interest? What's boring or difficult?
- What do you imagine yourself doing ten years from now? What are your hopes and dreams?
- How is school helping you get where you want to go?

PRACTICE

Personal Conferencing

4. When the same unwanted behavior persists over time…

In what situations with which students would you make this a classroom practice?

Sample teacher prompts and tips:

- What is the unwanted behavior?_____
- Share what you observed and use nonthreatening openers. "So I've noticed in the last week that _____. What's up?" OR, "So what's going on this week. You seem out of sorts." OR, "This hasn't been your best week, huh."
- Listen and acknowledge student's feelings—let student talk!
- Convey support and understanding of what you heard.
- Probe for sources of the problem and what the student needs in order to move forward.
- Identify the specific behavior that needs to stop or change and why.
- _____
- Spell out desired target behaviors that need to start _____
- Explore at least two or three strategies that will help the student get back on track.
- _____
- Develop a plan, contract, or conduct card and provide follow-up feedback and coaching.

5. When nothing you've tried has worked so far for "frequent fliers"…

In what situations with which students would you make this a classroom practice?

Sample teacher prompts and tips:

- Surprise "frequent fliers" by using a first conference just to listen and find out more. "What's the day like for you here at school? What's the low point? High point? What words would you use to describe yourself here at school? How would your friends describe you? Would teachers use the same words? What do you imagine other students are thinking when they see you_____?"
- A first conference is not about a new behavior plan. It's about convincing students that you really want to hear their thoughts and perspectives about school and how they see themselves at school. You want to close the first conference with an appreciation to the student for being honest. End the conference by saying: "You've given me a lot to think about. Here's what I'd like you to think about—what can I do to help make this class okay for you."

6. When a student requests a conference…

In what situations with which students would you make this a classroom practice?

Sample teacher prompts and tips:

- Arrange when you can meet with the student during lunch, your prep or conference period, or before or after school.
- Thank the student for requesting conference time.
- Say, "I'm glad you felt comfortable enough to talk to me. I need to know a little more about how I can help. I can either listen or help you problem solve. What feels most helpful right now?"
- Use responsive listening skills described in the PEARS document on pages 81 and 306.
- Hear what the student is saying without being judgmental or taking sides. Be mindful that some students want to draw a teacher into their reality.

PRACTICE

Facilitating Gatherings, Group Games, and Team Problem Solving

Go-Rounds

Ask students to sit in an arrangement where they can all see each other. Introduce the Go-Round topic in the form of a statement or question. Students then take turns responding, going around the room. A person always has the right to pass when it's his or her turn to speak. After most students have spoken, you can go back to those who passed to see if they want to say something now. Topics should be ones that all students can comment on without feeling embarrassed or defensive.

If you don't feel you have enough time for everyone to speak during one advisory period, introduce variations where some, but not all, students will get the opportunity to speak. However you choose to mix it up, be sure that everyone gets a chance to speak at some point during the week.

- Set the timer for five to seven minutes and invite anyone who wants to share to speak to the statement or question
- Invite half the group to speak on one day and the other half to speak on the next day
- Invite students to speak to the statement or question on the basis of a specific category: everyone who's wearing glasses; everyone who ate breakfast this morning; everyone who's wearing black; girls only or boys only; anyone whose last name ends in F through P, etc.
- Limit responses to the first ten students who volunteer

1. A boring thing in my life right now is…
2. An exciting thing in my life right now is…
3. A bad thing about being a teenager is…
4. A good thing about being a teenager is…
5. Favorite music group / TV show / Website / Athlete / Radio station / Food / Flavor / Smell / Movie / Clothes/designer / Personal possession
6. What's one place you would like to visit in your lifetime? Why do you want to go there?
7. If you had to eat the same meal every day for a month, what would it be?
8. What's one thing you would like to change about your neighborhood that would make it a better place to live?
9. If you were a TV reporter right now, what story would you want to investigate?
10. If you were a scientist, what problem would you most like to explore and solve?
11. What century would you most like to live in if you were not growing up in the twenty-first century?
12. If you were given $500 today, what would you do with it?
13. What movie is worth watching 20 times?
14. What three toys should every child get to play with? Why?
15. A sports figure, musician, or artist who embodies perfection in pursuit of her/his craft or discipline

PRACTICE

Facilitating Gatherings, Group Games, and Team Problem Solving

Name and Motion

1. Have everyone in the group stand in a circle, including the facilitator.
2. The facilitator models the activity, saying his/her name, what they love to do, and then making a sign/mime/ motion that represents the activity.
3. One by one, go around the room and have each participant state their name, share something they love to do, and make a sign/mime/motion that represents the activity. **BUT** each person must repeat everyone's name/activity/sign before they say theirs.
4. Debrief by asking a couple of students to name everyone in the group in less than a minute.

Name Card Match (Speed Names)

Give one 5" x 8" note card to each student and ask everyone to write one word that begins with the first letter (or sound) of their first name that reflects something about themselves (e.g., Chris-creative, Cindy-smiling). Have students form a circle and ask everyone to say their name, the word, and the connection they have to the word they chose.

Then ask everyone to toss their cards into the circle. Using a timer, ask for two volunteers to see how fast they can return the correct cards to the people who wrote them. Do this a number of times to see if successive advisees can beat the previous time.

The M&M's Game

1. Start by passing around the bag of candy to each student. Do not give them any more instructions than, "Take as many or as few as you want. Make sure that everyone gets some."
2. When everyone has their candy, explain the rules.
3. For each piece of candy they took, they have to say one interesting fact about themselves.
4. Start at one end of the room and go to the other until everyone has taken a turn.

Whip

A whip is a positive, incomplete statement that is completed in turn by each person in a circle. It goes quickly, with each person responding with *one word or a short phrase*. Some possible whips are:
- Something you're good at that ends with "-ing"
- If you could trade places for one week with anyone currently living, who would it be?
- What's something you wish someone would invent?

PRACTICE

Facilitating Gatherings, Group Games, and Team Problem Solving

Warp Speed

Materials: You need five or six soft toys/balls/bean bags to toss in a circle.

1. Participants stand in a circle.
2. Person #1 says the name of a person in the circle and then tosses the first object (underhanded) to Person #2. Each participant must ALWAYS say the name of the person FIRST before tossing the ball to that person.
3. Person #2 says the name of Person #3 and then tosses the object to Person #3.
4. People continue tossing the object to others, making sure that no one gets the object more than once.
5. Now a pattern has been established. Practice one more time using only one object and tossing the object in the SAME ORDER as the first round.
6. Try to toss it faster on each successive round.
7. After several rounds, introduce another soft object into the game and then another and another. There will be lots of laughter and sometimes people will drop the ball—encourage people to just pick it up and keep going. See how many objects you can "juggle" at once.

Debriefing:
- Did it get easier with more practice?
- What helped the group to accomplish this task?
- How did you react when you or someone else made a mistake? Was it okay to make a mistake? Why or why not?
- How does this experience connect with skills and attitudes you need to be successful at school?

You Like...I Like...

This is an activity that meets two goals: 1) hearing everyone's names repeatedly; and 2) finding out something interesting about each person. Call out a question that invites students to name two things they like or like to do. Going around the circle, each person must repeat the names of the five previous students and what they like. For example, if the question is, "What are your two favorite things to wear?" and the first person who speaks says, "I like to wear jeans and hoop earrings," the next person would say, "Marisa likes to wear jeans and hoop earrings, and I like to wear patched overalls and leather jackets." Continue around the circle until everyone has had a turn to both share and repeat what five others liked.

Example questions:
What are your two favorite things to do on a snow day?
What are your two favorite places to visit?
What are your two favorite foods?
What are two possessions you couldn't live without?

PRACTICE

Facilitating Gatherings, Group Games, and Team Problem Solving

Are You More Like...?

Ask all participants to stand up in the center of the classroom. Explain that they will be asked to decide if they are more like one object/idea or another on the continuum, with the left side of the room representing one object/idea and the right side of the room representing the other object/idea.

Sample question: "Are you more like a dog or a cat?" Left side, if you're more like a dog and right side, if you're more like a cat.

From the left to the right of the classroom, participants should stand where they feel they belong on the continuum. Students who place themselves in middle of the continuum communicate that they either share the values or meanings of both objects/ideas or of neither of them. Once participants have located themselves in the appropriate place on the continuum, ask them to:

1. Look were they are in relation to others
2. Think about why they chose to stand where they have
3. Consider what their location on the line says about each of them

Next, if you feel the group is ready, ask participants to explain why they chose to stand where they have. Why is each person more like one animal than the other or somewhere in between? Ideally, this will help participants self-disclose in a non-threatening manner. After this first round, continue to create contrasts for students to consider. Over time, the comparisons can become increasingly abstract. Here are a few ideas:

Are you more like...

a sitcom or a drama?	meatballs or spaghetti?	hardboiled eggs or scrambled eggs?
figure skater or speed skater?	pizza or ice cream?	a moon or a star?
a bicycle or a skateboard?	an apple or an orange?	field or a forest?
spring or fall?	winter or summer?	a wish or an idea?
a river or the ocean?	salt or sugar?	fireworks or a laser show
flashlight or candle?	oil or lotion?	museum or a circus?
a one-way or round trip?	morning or night?	story or a song?
down or up?	critic or a fan?	a canoe or a rowboat?

Debriefing Questions:
1. When you chose the location that you did, why did you choose it? [Have students "unpack" the values and attitudes that led to their choices.]
2. What new things did we learn about each other from this exercise?
3. Why are metaphors effective ways to describe thoughts, feelings, and interests?

[This activity is based on the book *Are You More Like? 1001 Colorful Quandaries for Quality Conversation* by Chris Cavert and Susana Acosta (2002) Oklahoma City, OK: Wood N Barnes Publishing. Portions reprinted with permission.]

PRACTICE

Facilitating Gatherings, Group Games, and Team Problem Solving

Moon Base

Materials: Markers; large news print or chart paper; Moon Base information cards

1. This is a jig-saw problem-solving activity. Cut up the information cards on the next page so that each student gets one information card. They are all different!!!
2. Divide students into groups of FOUR and pass out the information cards.
3. "You will be working on a problem in groups of FOUR. Each of you will receive a card with different information. You will need the information from all four cards to solve the problem. There is NO ONE RIGHT ANSWER and your group will need to create a solution that is 'good enough' to meet most of the criteria."
4. Here's what you need to do:
   • Decide who will take each role:

   FACILITATOR (gets group started; facilitates planning and discussion; ensures that every student's ideas are heard; gets agreement from the group about design decisions);

   ENCOURAGER/CHEERLEADER (encourages students to share ideas; makes supportive comments as people say and do things that help the group meet the goal or complete the product);

   DESIGNER (draws the Moon Base configuration using suggestions from the group);

   ACCURACY CHECKER (monitors progress; asks questions; and checks to see if the design meets the criteria specified in the information).

   • Share your information with each other so you can identify the problem.
   • Work together to solve the problem. Use scrap paper to keep track of your thinking and design process.
5. Give students about 20–30 minutes to work. After 5 minutes you may want to ask students how many pods they have (7) and how many tube connectors they have (22); which means they can use only 11 tubes to connect pods.

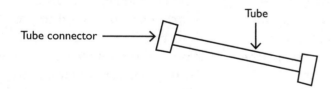

6. Draw your final design of Moon Base on large paper. Give your Moon Base a name and make sure everyone signs your design. Post final designs.
7. Debriefing: You might want to pair up groups and have each group share the highlights of their design and how it meets the criteria effectively. Ask groups to assess how they worked together using standard debriefing questions. (See pages 170–171.)

[This activity adapted and reprinted with permission from *United We Solve* by Tim Erickson (1996) Oakland, CA: Eeps Media.]

MOON BASE

Your group will design the moon base. Meet all the specifications and try to meet as many requests as you can. Try to be fair.

The moon base is made up of circular pods connected by tubes. You have only seven pods, though you were supposed to get ten.

The cook wants a Dining Pod connected to the Kitchen, the Commissary, the Bathroom, and the Dorm; and a Kitchen pod connected to Dining, Commissary, and the Office.

The original plans called for a Shower & Bathroom pod that also contained the water recycling equipment. That pod is essential.

MOON BASE

Your group will design the moon base.

Be sure to meet all the specifications. For example, no tubes may cross.

The Rec Director wants a Games Pod connected to the Dorm, the Library, the Dining pod, and the Commissary; and a Sports Pod (low-gravity handball, very fun) connected to the Showers and the Dorm.

The Commissary is the place where supplies such as food and oxygen tanks get stored.

A connector connects a pod to a tube. That's all it can do.

MOON BASE

Your group will design the moon base.

You only have 22 tube connectors (you were supposed to get 36). Each tube, of course, needs two connectors: one on each end.

The Science Director wants the Observatory connected to the Dining pod, the Dorm and the Library; and she wants the Games Pod far away (the lights from the video games interfere with the telescopes).

You will not be able to give everybody what they want.

A Dorm (Dormitory) is a room where people sleep.

MOON BASE

Your group will design the moon base.

Be sure to meet all the specifica-tions. For example, each tube must be straight.

The Personnel Director wants the Dorm Pod connected to the Office Pod, the Showers, and the Dining Pod; and the Office Pod connected to the Dorm, the Library, the Observatory, and the Dining Pod.

The Observatory is the whole point of the moon base. You have to give it its own pod. Since there aren't enough pods, other functions may have to be combined.

From: *United We Solve* ©1996. Eeps Media. Used with permission.

PRACTICE

Facilitating Gatherings, Group Games, and Team Problem Solving

Silent Square Puzzle Problem

Explain to the group that this is a PUZZLE PROBLEM that they will solve without speaking. Use the handout as a guide for making sets of puzzle pieces for each group.

1. Create an envelope for each group, each filled with all of the puzzle pieces. Give each group their envelope. Ask for a volunteer per group to give three pieces to each group member. When everyone has received their pieces, ask students to leave their pieces on the table without touching them.

2. Explain the goal of the activity: "At the end of this exercise, your group goal is to have 5 completed puzzles on your table. Each completed puzzle should be exactly the same size and each completed puzzle should have 3 pieces."

3. Here are the rules:
    *   You may not speak.
    *   You may only give pieces away to another member of your group.
    *   You may not take pieces from any member of the group.
    *   No finger pointing, grabbing, grunting, or groaning!

4. You will have about 7 minutes to solve the problem.

5. If groups get stuck, ask the group if they would like one clue. If they communicate a YES to you non-verbally, take one piece that is placed in the wrong puzzle and place it in the correct position in the puzzle where it fits.

Debriefing:

*   What did you notice about yourself and your group as you worked on this puzzle problem?

*   What feelings came up for you—at the beginning of the exercise, during the exercise, and at the end of the exercise? (This is a good opportunity to name the different comfort levels, experiences, and feelings we bring to specific learning experiences. Check out students' reactions when they heard the word PUZZLE or saw the puzzle pieces. Some students may have shut down immediately while others couldn't wait to begin. How we approach a new learning experience is often shaped by the feelings associated with prior similar experiences. Emotions drive our readiness and motivation to learn; we bring various kinds of comfort and competencies to different learning tasks.)

*   What are the tools, skills, and attitudes that helped you solve the puzzle? (Students will probably say things like: cooperation; trusting that if I gave you a piece, you would give me a piece; letting go of my original plan; observing what others were doing to see if one of my pieces fit in someone else's puzzle; give and take; negotiation; experimenting; patience and perseverance; thinking about the whole group and not just about me and what I needed.) Chart advisees' responses to use for the next two questions.

*   In what ways are these same skills and tools useful to you as a student, a friend, and a family member?

*   In what course or activities does it feel particularly important to apply and use these skills regularly?

Enlarge each square to 6 inches by 6 inches.

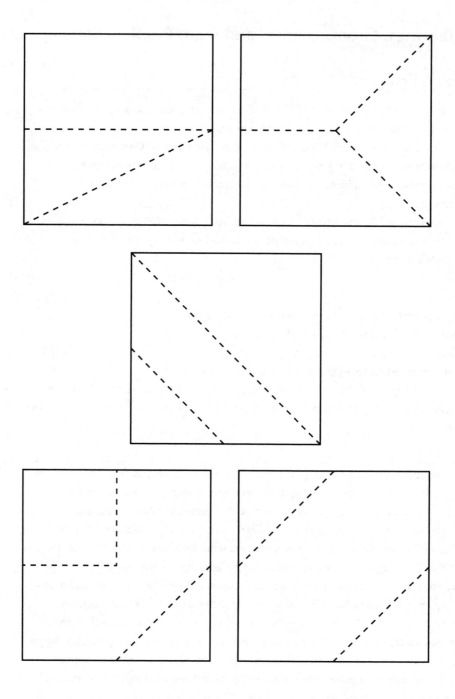

PRACTICE

Facilitating Gatherings, Group Games, and Team Problem Solving

Drawing a House

This activity surfaces issues about how to work cooperatively and how to negotiate and navigate relationships in school, at home, and with friends.

1. Cut easel paper sheets in half so that each pair of students has a large piece of paper. Each pair will also need two markers of contrasting colors.

   Divide students into pairs (random or self-selection) and say to the group, "We are going to do a drawing exercise to explore more about how people negotiate and work together. You and your partner will be drawing on the same piece of paper and each of you will use a different colored marker to draw. From this point on, everyone needs to participate in silence—no talking, whispering, or mumbling."

   "Now I'd like you to close your eyes and relax for a minute. In your mind's eye, imagine the house of your dreams." (You can also use the perfect room of your dreams and change what you say accordingly.) What does the outside of your house look like? What kinds of materials is your house built of? What does the roof line look like? What kinds of windows does it have? How many stories? What does the entrance look like? Now, walk out the front door. What do you see around you? What do you hear? Walk around to the back. What's there? You are really happy because you have always wanted to live in a place like this… Now open your eyes slowly and listen to the next set of instructions."

   "Let me explain what your task is. You and your partner will be drawing one house on your paper. You will need to remain silent until you finish drawing. Here is how you will draw your house. One of you will decide to be first and you will draw one stroke on the paper with your marker. Your partner will then take her/his marker and draw one stroke on the paper. You will continue taking turns drawing for 5 minutes."

2. Draw examples of what one stroke looks like:

   Draw examples of what one stroke is not:

3. Ask if there are any questions. (This is the one time students can speak.) Remind students that they may not talk or write any words on their papers. Set the timer for 5 minutes and let the drawing begin.

4. After 5 minutes, call time, and ask everyone to put their markers down.

5. Debriefing involves partners first, and then the whole group.

   • Give partners 3 minutes to talk to each other about what they drew, how they worked together, what they thought the other person was drawing, what was confusing or frustrating about the task.

   • Ask if there are any questions. (This is the one time students can speak.) Remind students that they may not talk or write any words on their papers. Set the timer for 5 minutes and let the drawing begin.

   • Now, in the whole group, invite students to discuss their observations and feelings during the activity. What made this activity feel fun, frustrating, satisfying, confusing, or interesting? What did you like or not like about the activity? For the pairs who felt satisfied with your houses, how would you describe your process? For the pairs who felt frustrated, how would you describe your process?

   • Chart their comments so you can refer to them for the next two questions. Expect these kinds of comments: I did one part and she did the other. I was more interested in the house and he worked more on the landscape. I had to let go of some things I wanted but I made sure that _____ was there on the paper. I stepped back and let her take the lead in the beginning. We had totally different ideas, but it worked out somehow. At first, I couldn't figure out where he was going at all, and then it started making sense to me. We totally misunderstood what each other was drawing. We were never in sync with each other. I thought we were looking down with aerial view and he thought we were looking at the house from straight in front of us. Sometimes we worked together and sometimes separately.

   • Now think about everything that you heard about what you and your partners experienced. What does this experience have to say about student-teacher relationships, parent-child relationships, and peer-to-peer relationships? Encourage insights about the art of negotiating. To realize a common goal everyone needs to have a voice in creating the vision and choices for how to get there—there's never only one form a goal can take, nor only one way to reach it. Students may also bring up that when you work together, there has to be some give and take—you don't necessarily get everything you want, but you do get need to get some things that are really important to you.

   • Students may be interested in trying this exercise again (soon or even months later) to see if they can improve their skills to negotiate.

PRACTICE

Facilitating Gatherings, Group Games, and Team Problem Solving

Plastic Cup Silent Towers

Materials: 100 large cups for each team

This activity is done in silence. Give each group of five to seven students about 100 paper or plastic cups. The goal? Make the tallest tower you can using all of your cups.

Rules:

1. Make the tallest tower you can.
2. You need to use all of your cups.
3. You can't have more than 12 cups on the bottom foundation of your tower.
4. Your group has to build your tower in silence.

By completing the product students are demonstrating a) strategic thinking skills; b) group cooperation; and c) leadership skills.

Debriefing/Closing/Feedback:

- What happened in your group? What was it like to do this collaborative challenge with your group?
- How did your group decide what strategy to use? How did you communicate your ideas without speaking? What did you teammates do that helped you solve the problem?
- How would you describe the role you played in your group?
- What can you take from this experience and apply to other learning experiences in the classroom?

Build the Tallest Tower

Your team will have twenty minutes to build the tallest tower you can using the following materials:
- 4 small paper plates
- 4 large pieces of chart paper
- 5 straws
- 4 paper or styrofoam cups
- 6 3"×5" note cards

You will share scissors, markers, and tape with other groups.

Here are the rules:

1. Before you begin building take a couple of minutes to plan and hear everyone's ideas.
2. Agree on a plan and start to build.
3. Be open to your team members' suggestions for adjustments and alterations as you build.
4. Your tower needs to stand alone with no other supports on the floor for at least one minute after building time is up
5. Your tower must reach a height of at least 5 feet.
6. You must attach 6 cards to your tower that describe: { Qualities of a good student **OR** Qualities of a safe, welcoming school **OR** Qualities of a high-performing group

APPENDIX C

Learning Protocols for Professional Development

Prereading Protocols

While-You-Read Protocols

Small and Large Group Protocols

Products / Presentations / Report Outs

Assessment / Feedback / Planning / Closings / Final Thoughts

Making Learning REAL and *Getting Classroom Management RIGHT* have both been designed to be used by:

- Individual teachers who choose to explore these books on their own

- University instructors who teach undergraduate, graduate, and professional development courses in *teaching and learning, adolescent development, assessment, methods and instructional practices,* and *classroom management*

- Professional development specialists, consultants, principals, and teacher leaders who facilitate district and school-based professional development

- Faculty and administrators who participate in study groups within a district or school

Thus, we have included an appendix of learning protocols that adult groups can use to explore key topics in both publications. We cannot overstate the importance of modeling learning protocols in education courses and professional development sessions that participants can take away and use immediately in their own classrooms. Every protocol cited in the appendix can be used with adolescent learners ("as is" or adapted for use with a particular group or with a specific course of study).

Key to Learning Protocols:

Protocol Description (Left Side of Page)   **Topic and Text Connections** (Right Side of Page)

(REAL, (X), p. xx) refers to protocol descriptions located by chapter (X) and page number in ***Making Learning REAL***	**REAL, [X], p. xx** refers to topics located by chapter [X] and page number in ***Making Learning REAL***
(RIGHT, (X), p. xx) refers to protocol descriptions located by chapter (X) and page number in ***Getting Classroom Management RIGHT***	**RIGHT, [X], p. xx** refers to topics located by chapter [X] and page number in ***Getting Classroom Management RIGHT***

Prereading Protocols	Topic and Text Connections
I. Webbing (*REAL*, (13), page 289) OR **2. Stick It Up** Give individuals or pairs a large post-it to record and post their first thoughts about a particular topic, issue, or concept. Use either of these exercises to get a quick "read" of the group's thinking about core concepts and principles. "When you hear the word _____, what words, images, or phrases come to mind?"	*REAL*, [I], pages 43–51, Readings 1–7: Personalization; Personalized Learning; Personalized Learning Environment; **pages 51–52, Reading 8:** Rigorous and Relevant Learning; **page 53, Reading 9:** Smaller Learning Community; **pages 54–55:** What Does a Personalized Learning Environment Feel Like? *REAL*, [2], pages 57–65, Readings 11–15: Learning Community; Community of Learners *REAL*, [3], pages 67–74, Readings 16–17: Adolescent Development; **pages 75–76, Reading 18:** Resilience; **pages 77–78, Reading 19:** Characteristics of Adolescent Learners; **pages 78–83, Reading 20:** Developmentally Appropriate Practice; **pages 83–84, Reading 21:** Expectations/Standards; **pages 85–88, Readings 22–24:** Personalized Support; **pages 89–92, Reading 25:** Motivation; **pages 92–93, Reading 26:** Different Supports for Students *REAL*, [4], pages 95–96, Reading 27: Diversity; **pages 96–99, Reading 28:** Identify Development; **pages 100–101, Reading 29:** Dominant Culture; **pages 101–107, Readings 30–31:** Privilege; **pages 108–109, Readings 32–33:** Culturally Responsive Teaching *REAL*, [5], pages 111–117, Readings 34–36: Life Skills; *REAL*, [7], pages 139–154: Assessment, Habits of Learning, Grading, and Progress Reports *REAL*, [8], pages 160–162: Teaching Stance
	RIGHT, [I], pages 26–27, Unwanted behaviors that get in the way learning OR three unwanted behaviors that you want to reduce in your classroom *RIGHT*, [I], pages 36–41, Frequently Used Terms that are used throughout the book, particularly: Discipline; Self-Discipline; Punishment; Consequences; Responsibility; Accountability
3. Personal Memory Share: With a partner share how you experienced a specific condition of schooling or a specific learning situation that is the focus of the text. What were you feeling? What were you doing? What was the teacher doing? Why does this memory stand out for you? How did this affect your experience of school or your learning? How has this experience been important in your life? Does this experience in any way impact what you do or don't do today?	Think about your own experience in school and share a learning experience… *REAL*, [I], pages 41–49, Readings 1–7: that you felt was *personalized* to fit your needs and interests. *REAL*, [I], pages 49–50, Reading 8: that you considered to be both *rigorous and relevant.* *REAL*, [2], pages 55–63, Readings 11–15: where you felt you experienced a genuine sense of community with other learners. *REAL*, [3], page 87, Reading 24: that was extremely negative for you.
	RIGHT, [6], pages 214–215: when you were struggling or discouraged and someone helped you turn around and get back on track

Prereading Protocols	**Topic and Text Connections**
4. Entry Tickets and Quick-Writes (*REAL*, (16), pages 381–383)	What do you do when students don't learn? *REAL, [3], pages 87–93; [16], pages 373–377; [16], pages 385–390* "Thinking about Discipline" question prompts
	RIGHT, [1], page 19 "Know Your Nos, Needs, and Nonnegotiables" question prompts *RIGHT, [3], page 71*
5. Where Do You Want Your Kids or School to Be? (*REAL*, Appendix B, page 437)	*REAL, [7], pages 139–154:* Grading practices and homework policies *REAL, [3], pages 80–82; [16], pages 364–373*
	RIGHT, [5], pages 161–165: Classroom learning supports and interventions for students who are struggling *RIGHT, [6], pages 209–219:* Student discipline and behavior
6. Quotes Café Select quotes related to a particular theme or issue. Cut typed quotes into separate sentence strips and ask participants to choose a quote that… • they believe and act on every day OR • they wish every adult in school believed and acted on every day Participants then share their selected quotes with three different partners in a "walk-about." • Why did you choose this quote? • How would school be different for students if every adult believed this statement?	*REAL, [1], page 46, Reading 3:* Personalization *REAL, [2], pages 60–61, Reading 12:* Teacher Behaviors that Support a Classroom Learning Community *REAL, [3], pages 67–74, Reading 16, 17:* Benchmarks and Facts about Adolescent Development *REAL, [3], pages 77–78, Reading 19:* How Adolescents Learn
7. Hopes and Hesitations (*REAL*, (9), pages 179–180) As we think and talk about _____, what are your hopes for this conversation? What are your hesitations (or fears)?	Use before reading and discussing any topics or issues that might be perceived as controversial, emotionally charged, or uncomfortable to confront. For example, discussion around common grading policies, diversity and cultural competency, or disciplinary expectations of teachers are likely to generate an array of opinions and some defensiveness.
8. Prior Knowledge: To get a read of the group's prior experience or familiarity with the topic, issue, or practice, ask the group to 1) pair up and share their prior experience or familiarity with the topic, issue, or practice; AND/OR 2) Ask the group to put up one to five fingers (a one if this is new/unfamiliar, to a five if this is something they're very familiar with or use regularly).	Use this whenever you don't know what experience and knowledge the group is bringing to the table about a specific topic and practice in *REAL* and *RIGHT*.
9. K-S-T-W (*REAL*, Appendix B, page 437)	Use this with any topics where you think that key concepts and principles may be unfamiliar to some of the group, or some participants may be bringing preconceived ideas or even misunderstandings to the topic that the selected reading may challenge. For example, this would be a useful entry point before examining the characteristics of adolescent learners.

Prereading Protocols	Topic and Text Connections
10. Carousel *(REAL, (13), page 284–285)*	***REAL, [4], pages 108–109, Readings 32 & 33:*** Question prompts about "Culturally Responsive Practice" ***REAL, [7], pages 139–140:*** Question prompts about "Assessment and Record Keeping"
	RIGHT, [6], [7], pages 178–192, 211–212: Post problematic student behaviors and ask pairs or trios to generate teacher responses that invite cooperation or self-correction or defuse, deflect, or de-escalate the provocation.
11. Point of View *(REAL, Appendix B, page 437)* In groups of five, share individually generated definitions and reach consensus on a group definition.	***REAL*** and ***RIGHT*** Use with any key term that is likely to generate an array of opinions.
12. By My Side: Create a snapshot of a real student you've taught (think specifically about a student who lives on the margins at school) and take that student with you while you read. After the reading, share with a partner or the group how the ideas and practices in the reading might change this student's experience of school.	***REAL*** This is especially useful for readings that focus on personalization, high expectations and high support, and culturally responsive teaching. ***[Readings 4–7, 10, 22–26, 28–32 and Practices 1, 2, 6, and 7]***
	RIGHT This is especially useful for readings in Step 3: Support Individuals and the Group ***[5]***, Step 4: Invite Student Engagement, Cooperation, and Self-Correction ***[6]***, and Step 5: Develop Accountable Consequences and Supportive Interventions ***[7]***
13. Opinion Continuum: *(REAL, (15), page 353–354)* Create normative statements around faculty practice, student expectations and outcomes, school discipline policies and practices, teacher roles and responsibilities that begin "All faculty should/should not…" OR, "All students should/should not…" OR, "The school should/should not…" OR, "The policy about _____ should/should not include…"	Use as an entry point with any readings and discussion related to discipline, grading and assessment, creating a academic culture of completion and quality, the role of independent learning, and the first week of school.
14. Why Doesn't It Change? *(REAL, Appendix B, page 437)*	Use when reading about specific practices that have obvious benefits but are rarely implemented widely or consistently. It's helpful to name what gets in the way in order to know what it will take and what faculty need to shift norms and practices.
15. The Wall of Resistance *(REAL, Appendix B, page 437)*	This is a useful exercise when addressing entrenched practices that haven't changed for decades. Resistance to… • changing assessment and grading practices • providing different kinds of time and support when some students don't learn • modeling, teaching, practicing, and assessing habits of learning and life skills • developing accountable consequences • academic and behavioral conferencing • offering great choice and differentiation of tasks and assessments

Prereading Protocols

Point of View

Topic or Issue

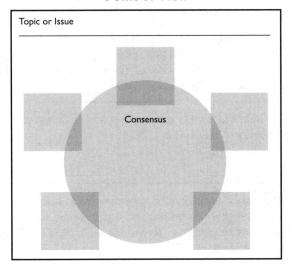

Consensus

Why Doesn't It Change?

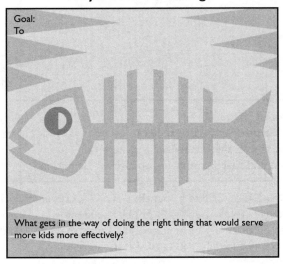

Goal:
To

What gets in the way of doing the right thing that would serve more kids more effectively?

K-S-T-W

I. What do you **know**?	2. What are your **sources** for what you know?
3. What do you **think** you know but you're not sure of?	4. What do you **want** to know more about?

The Wall of Resistance

What will it take to climb over the wall?

What factors build the wall of resistance?

Where Do You Want Your Kids or Your School to BE?

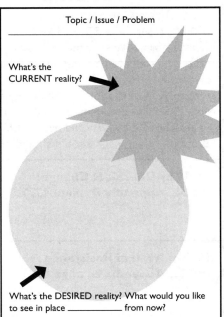

Topic / Issue / Problem

What's the CURRENT reality?

What's the DESIRED reality? What would you like to see in place _____ from now?

POINT OF VIEW

Topic or Issue

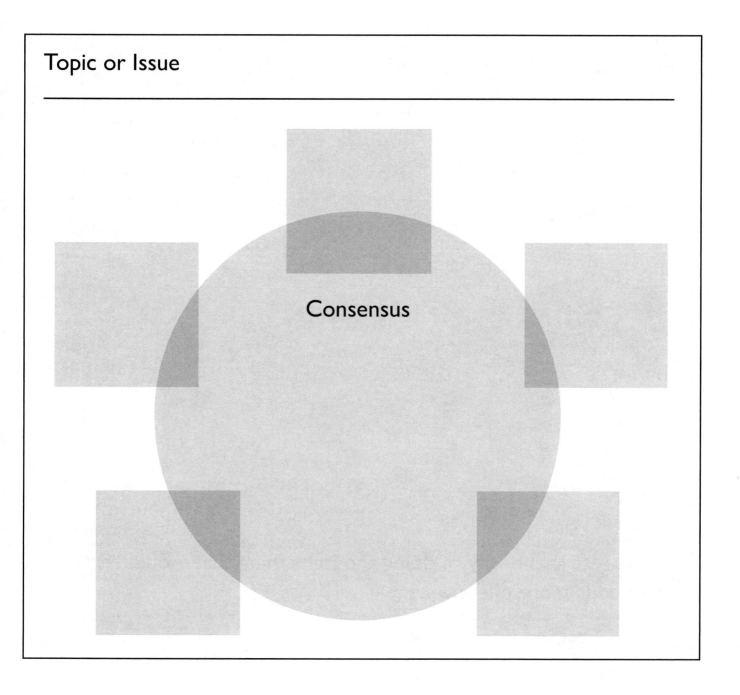

Consensus

WHY DOESN'T IT CHANGE?

Goal:
To

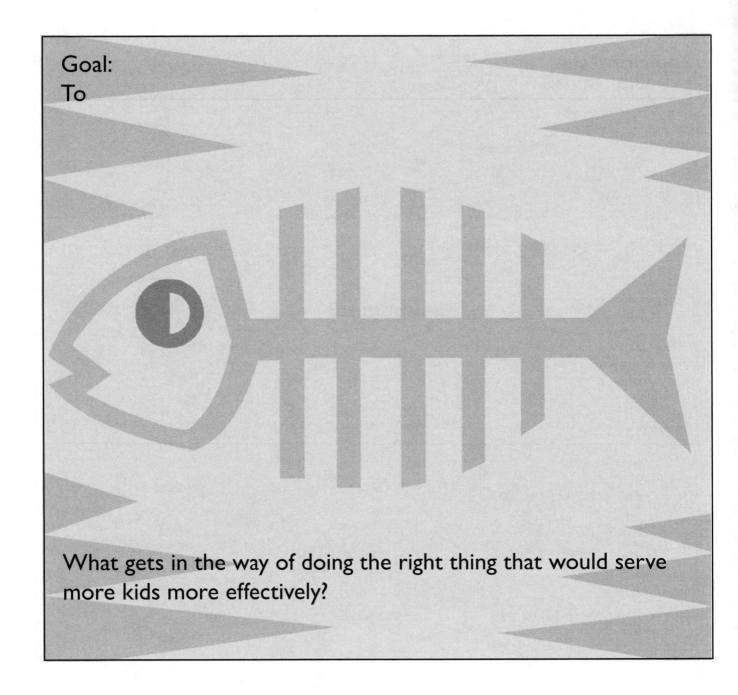

What gets in the way of doing the right thing that would serve more kids more effectively?

K - S - T - W

1. What do you *know*?	2. What are your *sources* for what you know?
3. What do you *think* you know but you're not sure of?	4. What do you *want* to know more about?

THE WALL OF RESISTANCE

What will it take to climb over the wall?

What factors build the wall of resistance?

WHERE DO YOU WANT YOUR KIDS OR YOUR SCHOOL TO BE?

Topic / Issue / Problem

_____

What's the
CURRENT reality?

What's the DESIRED reality? What would you like
to see in place _____ from now?

While-You-Read Protocols	Topic and Text Connections
16. Jigsaw Reading (*REAL*, (13), page 276) Be sure to give each person in a pair, trio, or foursome a focus question for their particular reading or suggest a protocol from this list for capturing what they read so they can bring what they learned back to their group.	*REAL* **Introduction, pages 23–25:** Juanita and Benita **[2], pages 57, 62, 63, 65, Readings 11, 13, 14, 15** **[6], pages 119–129:** A Tale of Two Classrooms
	RIGHT **[1], pages 19–23:** Three Approaches to Discipline **[2], pages 43–62:** Case Studies **[4], pages 116–134:** Procedures **[6], pages 177–186:** Invite Student Engagement, Cooperation, and Self-Correction
17. Double Entry Notes: Fold a piece of notebook paper in half and on the right side jot down and summarize important ideas you read in the text. On the left-hand side jot down your comments, reactions, questions, confusions, or reflections that help you make meaning of the text.	This is particularly useful for readings that introduce a new perspective or unfamiliar concept to the group or introduce material that may challenge the prevailing norms and practices of the group.
18. IT SAYS / I SAY / and SO... As people read, invite participants to pick three passages from the text that grab their attention and use this protocol to record and respond. IT SAYS (Write down the text that you've chosen) / I SAY (Jot down your reactions and comments) / and SO... (Jot down: a) questions you have or b) ways you might incorporate this idea or practice or c) what might be the implications or benefits of incorporating this idea into your classroom practice). Daniels, H., and Zemelman, S. (2004) *Subjects matter*, p. 122, Portsmouth, NH: Heinemann Press	*REAL*, **[11]–[17]** This is a good protocol to use with any of the core practices in Chapters 11–17
	RIGHT, **[3], pages 63–87:** This is a good protocol for readings in the "Know Yourself" section of Chapter 3, especially these topics: "Know how 'with-it' you are"; "Know how you define disrespect"; "Know how to depersonalize bad behavior"; "Know your communication style"; "Know how to recover."
19. Text Connect (*REAL*, Appendix B, page 440)	Use with any readings on any topics in *REAL* or *RIGHT.*
20. Paired Reading and **Trio Read and Respond** (*REAL*, (15), page 349)	These are good protocols for short readings where a) making meaning of the reading is critical to follow-up applications; b) the text introduces an unfamiliar idea or practice; or c) the text may be perceived as provocative.
21. Where Do I Stand (I) **Where Do I Stand (II)** **Where Do I Stand (III)** (*REAL*, Appendix B, page 450)	These protocols are especially useful for any readings that may generate a range of opinions or challenge prevailing norms of teaching and classroom practice. They require attentive reading and give participants permission to put their doubts and skepticism on the table.

While-You-Read Protocols	**Topic and Text Connections**
22. Question Pairs: Ask participants to read in pairs. The goal of this protocol is to jot down questions while you read. After you and your partner are finished reading, share the questions you crafted. Decide on two questions that you want to refine. Write your questions on newsprint or sentence strips. The questions will be used for later discussion. (Review the section in **REAL, (15), pages 355–356,** "Asking Good Questions," before you use this protocol.)	Use with any readings on any topics in **REAL** or **RIGHT.**
23. Text Coding and Underlining: Invite participants to create their own codes and symbols to use as they mark up the text while they read. OR you might develop a group code to try out (i.e., Underline _____; Circle _____; Put a _____ next to _____; etc.).	
24. Front and Back: On a note card use the front side to summarize important ideas in the text and use the back side for comments and questions you want to raise in the discussion.	
25. 3 Big Ideas: **(REAL, Appendix B, page 440)**	
26. Bookmarks: Literally create 2" × 8" paper bookmarks on the computer with the topic or issue printed on the top of the bookmark. Participants write their notes about the reading on the bookmark.	
27. Sticky Notes: Posting sticky notes on the text as you read is a great way to make your thinking transparent. You can suggest that participants do "free-range" sticky notes (comments, questions, reactions, connections, or yeah, buts), OR only use stickies for questions that emerge from your reading, OR use two colors of stickies and post on text where you agree (first color) or disagree or doubt (second color).	

While-You-Read Protocols

Where Do I Stand (I)

I agree			I'm not sure

Where Do I Stand (II)

Topic/Issue _____

A. (*Before you read*) Here's what I believe and do

B. (*While you read*) Here's what the text says

C. (*While you read*) This is where my beliefs and practice converge with the text.

D. (*After you read*) What do you want to try?

3 Big Ideas

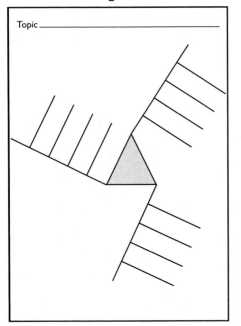

Topic _____

Where Do I Stand? (III)

What's new that I agree with?

What do I already believe?

What's provocative / off-putting / uncomfortable / out of the bounds of my experience?

Text Connect

_____

Ideas/Facts that matter	How would teaching and learning change if this informed what we do??

WHERE DO I STAND (I)

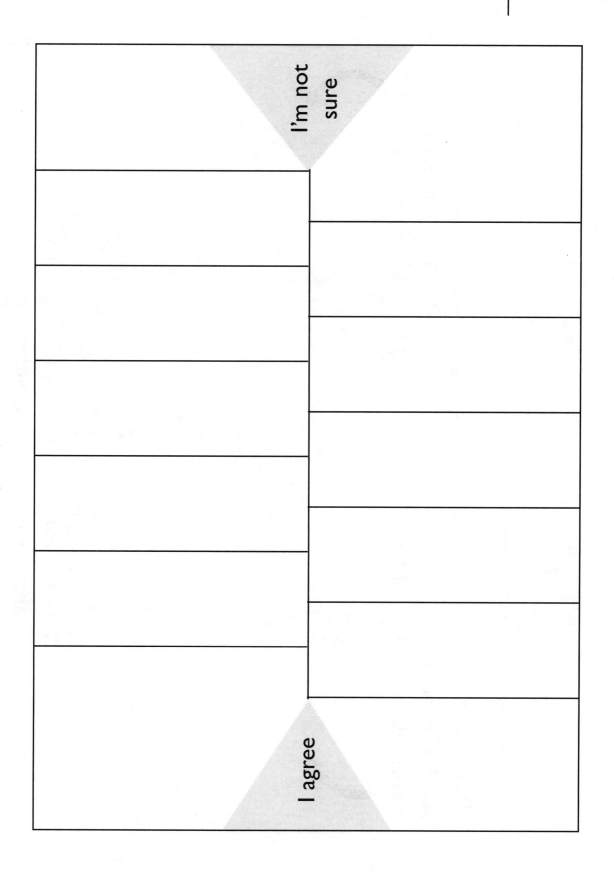

I'm not sure

I agree

WHERE DO I STAND (II)

Topic/Issue _____

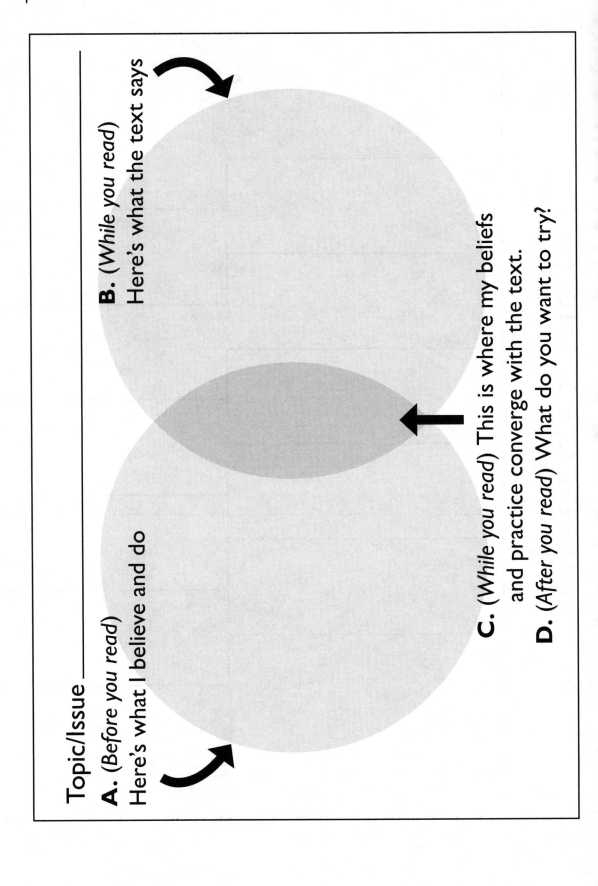

A. *(Before you read)*
Here's what I believe and do

B. *(While you read)*
Here's what the text says

C. *(While you read)* This is where my beliefs
and practice converge with the text.

D. *(After you read)* What do you want to try?

3 BIG IDEAS

Topic _____

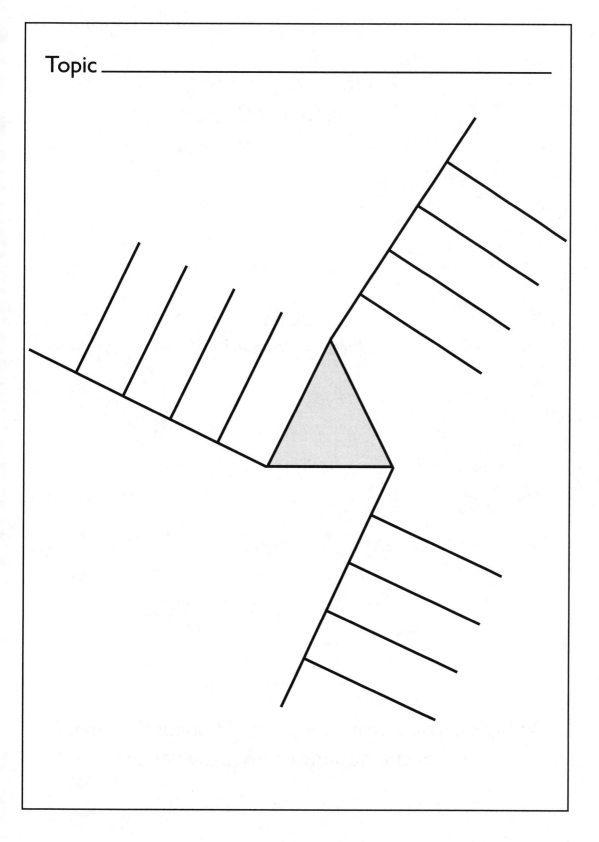

WHERE DO I STAND? (III)

What's new that
I agree with?

What do I
already believe?

What's provocative / off-putting / uncomfortable /
out of the bounds of my experience?

TEXT CONNECT

Ideas/Facts that matter	How would teaching and learning change if this informed what we do??

Small and Large Group Dialogue Protocols	Topic and Text Connections
28. Jigsaw Sharing: You have two choices after people finish their readings. OPTION A: Create "expert groups" by having all participants who read the same text meet for a focused discussion to clarify what they read, check for understanding, and raise questions and implications. Then "experts" return to their home groups and share what they learned. Other group members should take notes—every group member is responsible for understanding major ideas in all of the readings. OPTION B: After group members finish their readings they simply continue working in the same group, sharing what they read with each other.	**REAL** ***Introduction, pages 23–35:*** Juanita and Benita ***[2], pages 57, 62, 63, 65, Readings 11, 13, 14, 15*** ***[6], pages 117–127:*** A Tale of Two Classrooms **RIGHT** ***[1], pages 19–24:*** Three Approaches to Discipline ***[2], pages 43–62:*** Case Studies ***[4], pages 116–134:*** Procedures ***[6], pages 178–187:*** Invite Student Engagement, Cooperation, and Self-Correction
29. Case Study Analysis **(*RIGHT*, (2), pages 43–62)**	***RIGHT, [2], pages 43–62:*** Case Study Scenarios
30. Text-based Seminar **(*REAL*, (15), pages 355–358)** "Practicing and Assessing Good Talk"	Use with any readings on any topic that need to be read deliberatively with close attention to big ideas and the details.
31. Chalk Talk: Chalk Talk is a silent activity that requires a white board, chalk board, or butcher paper and chalk or markers. Pose a question that's relevant to the reading and write it in the center of the board or paper. Then pass out chalk or markers and invite participants to write down their thoughts and reactions to the question prompt when they are moved to do so. Participants are invited to write comments in response to what others have written; draw connections between their comments and the comments of others; write questions that spring from a comment; circle ideas they find compelling; etc. Don't be surprised if there are moments when no one is writing, as participants take in what they see. Take at least 15 minutes for this activity and take time afterwards to look for dominant themes/the range of opinions/clusters of similar ideas/anything that was a surprise to participants.	This is extremely helpful when the reading focuses on an issue that's emotionally charged or when the group is deeply divided in its opinion. Somehow the silence frees people to write what they're honestly thinking, without the fear of being judged. Here are some question prompts: ***REAL, [2], pages 55–59:*** "After the reading on community, what kinds of structures, activities, and opportunities would you like to see in your faculty learning community?" ***[4], pages 99–103:*** "After reading about dominant culture and privilege in high school, what are your thoughts about how your school supports equity and access for ALL students?" ***[7], pages 139–154:*** "After the reading on grading and assessment, what are you thinking, questioning, doubting, wondering?" OR "What thoughts do you want to share your school leadership team?" ***RIGHT, Introduction, [1], [2], [7]*** "After the reading on discipline what are you thinking about the current discipline practices in your school?"
32. Kid Talk Protocol **(*RIGHT*, (7), pages 254–256)**	***RIGHT, [7], page 255–256*** Practice using this protocol (choose a real student to discuss) in conjunction with readings about how to support struggling, angry, or discouraged students or students who engage in chronic unwanted behaviors.
33. Responsive Listening Protocols (*REAL* (15) All of these protocols enable participants to practice responsive listening. **Fish Bowl (page 354)** **Pair-Shares (page 350)** **Partner Paraphrasing (page 349)** **Paraphrasing Circles (page 353)** **Listening Lab (page 352)**	Generate your own questions for any topic, OR you might want to use questions that participants have generated from **Protocol 22. Question Pairs.**

Small and Large Group Dialogue Protocols	Topic and Text Connections
34. Role Chairs: This protocol is about defending your practice and what you believe. It's a powerful rehearsal for participants who are ready to try on classroom practices that may contradict the dominant teaching and learning norms in their school. Divide into groups of four. Ask one volunteer to become the defender of specific ideas, strategies, or practices you've read about and discussed. The other three group members take on the roles of a skeptical administrator, parent, and faculty colleague. They engage in a lively dialogue in which defenders share their reasons for introducing new practices in the classroom.	This protocol is especially useful when participants are rethinking and changing practices related to: ***REAL, [7], pages 139–154; [12], pages 228–237;* and *[16], pages 378–384:*** Assessment ***[12], pages 241–248:*** Well Paced, Student-Centered Lessons ***[12], pages 250–267:*** Independent and Project-Based Learning
	RIGHT, [4], pages 116–134: Procedures ***[5], pages 141–146:*** Teaching Life Skills ***[6], pages 184–186:*** Lesson Pacing and Engaging all Learners ***[7], pages 226–231:*** Accountable Consequences and Supportive Interventions
35. Save the Last Word: This works best in groups of three. 1) Each person first circles or underlines three passages in the reading that were particularly significant for them. 2) Person #1 reads one of her selected passages; 3) Persons #2 and #3 in the group share their thoughts and perspectives about that particular passage; 4) Person #1 gets the last word and shares why she chose this particular passage and the significance it has for her. 5) Repeat the protocol two more times so each person in the group has an opportunity to read their passage and have the "last word." (Daniels, H., and Zemelman, S. (2004) *Subjects matter*, p. 346, Portsmouth, NH: Heinemann Press.)	Any topics and readings in **REAL** or **RIGHT**
36. Written Conversation: Each participant receives a 5" × 8" note card and works with a partner. 1) Each person writes a first reaction to the reading; 2) Partners exchange cards and read them; 3) Partners write a response to what they read; 4) Partners exchange cards, then read and respond two more times. (Daniels, H., and Zemelman, S. (2004) *Subjects matter*, p. 130, Portsmouth, NH: Heinemann Press.)	
37. Author and Audience: In groups of five, ask a participant in each group to volunteer to serve in the role of author of the text. The other group members engage in a dialogue with the "author," asking clarifying questions, sharing their reactions, affirming what they agree with, and raising their cautions and concerns.	
38. Tools for Formative Assessment #2, 21, 22 (*REAL,* (13), page 381–384)	
39. Summary Points (*REAL,* (15), page 351)	Invite one group to end their discussion early and prepare summary points for the whole group.

Products / Presentations / Report Outs	Topic and Text Connections
40. What's the Difference? Use this protocol when a clear understanding of two related, but different terms is essential for discussion of the topic and application in the classroom. Give small groups two different colored large post-it notes. After completing the reading, the group discusses and reaches agreement on definitions or mantras that precisely capture the distinguishing characteristics of the two related terms or concepts.	*REAL* *[3], pages 83–84:* Expectations vs. Standards *[16], pages 378–380:* Formative vs. Summative Assessment *[12], pages 241–246:* Student-Centered vs. Teacher-Directed Instruction<hr>*RIGHT* *[1], pages 20–24:* Punishment, Do-Nothing vs. Guided Discipline *[1], pages 30, 229:* Punitive vs. Accountable Consequences *[1], page 39:* Responsibility vs. Accountability *[3], pages 66–67:* Authoritarian vs. Authoritative
41. MI3 Presentations: **(REAL, (13), pages 272–273)** Use three intelligences to present what you read to the rest of the group. Groups must post bullet points or a visual chart that highlights what the group agrees were the most significant ideas in the reading. Be sure to have plenty of props and materials around for the dramatically, artistically, and musically inclined.	This protocol is a good choice when different groups are responsible for sharing different readings on the same topic with the whole group.
42. Core Practice Trio Share **(REAL, Appendix, page 444)**	This is useful to do the following topics: the first day of school; the first week of school; grading and assessment; classroom discipline.
43. Dos and Don'ts: Generate a list of Dos and Don'ts that reflect your reading and discussion about a specific topic.	*REAL, [8], pages 159–169:* The First Day of School<hr>*RIGHT, [7], pages 196–203:* Responding to Provocative Speech
44. Elevator Speech Give participants ten minutes to write a one minute "elevator speech" that captures beliefs, rationale, and commitment that they associate with a specific practice. Present speeches to table group and solicit feedback and suggestions from table mates.	This is a useful protocol when participants perceive a change in practice as a risk that they need to confidently defend to other colleagues, an administrator, parents, or students.
45. Your Two Best Ideas: (REAL, Appendix, page 444)	These protocols provide a variety of ways to sum up and close small group discussions that follow any reading on any topic.
46. Golden Nuggets: (REAL, Appendix, page 444) After groups have mined their golden nuggets, do a quick whip around the room and invite each group to share one or two of their nuggets.	
47. A Text to Remember: A group chooses one sentence from the text that affirms the most important idea the group wants to take away from the reading. Write it on chart paper and post it.	
48. Going Further: (REAL, Appendix, page 444) Ask groups to generate questions that emerge from their discussion. Write questions on large sentence strips to post or chart further questions that the whole group generates together.	
49. Prioritizing Ideas: What Matters Most? **(REAL, Appendix, page 444)**	
50. Tools for Formative Assessment #1, 4, 8, 10, 11, 12, 14, 15, 17, 20 (REAL, (13) pages 381–385)	

Products / Presentations / Report Outs

Your Two Best Ideas

1 **What is it?**	2 **What is it?**
1. What are the benefits?	1. What are the benefits?
2. What do you need to make it happen?	2. What do you need to make it happen?
3. Who makes it happen?	3. Who makes it happen?
4. When?	4. When?

Prioritizing Ideas—What Matters Most?

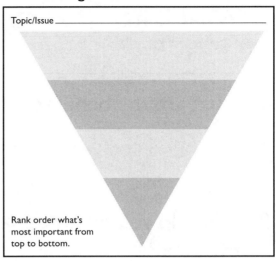

Topic/Issue _____

Rank order what's most important from top to bottom.

Core Practice Trio Share

Practice # _____

page _____ to page _____

Brief Description of Activities/Strategies

_____

Why and when would you use this?

What would be the benefits of using this with your students?

How might you modify or expand this activity for your groups?

Golden Nuggets

From your discussion what two or three "nuggets" feel most important to share with the whole group?

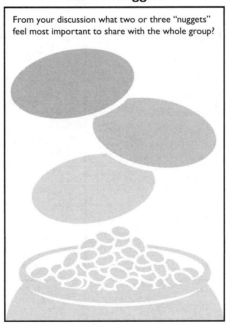

Going Further

I wonder…

What would it take to…?

If I couldn't fail I (we) would…

How come…?

Why do we…?

What if…?

Why couldn't we…?

What would happen if…?

I'm still puzzled by…

I'm curious about…

What if we tried…?

How could we…?

I'm still not sure about…

If _____ then _____

YOUR TWO BEST IDEAS

What is it?	**What is it?**
1. What are the benefits?	1. What are the benefits?
2. What do you need to make it happen?	2. What do you need to make it happen?
3. Who makes it happen?	3. Who makes it happen?
4. When?	4. When?

PRIORITIZING IDEAS— WHAT MATTERS MOST?

Topic/Issue _____

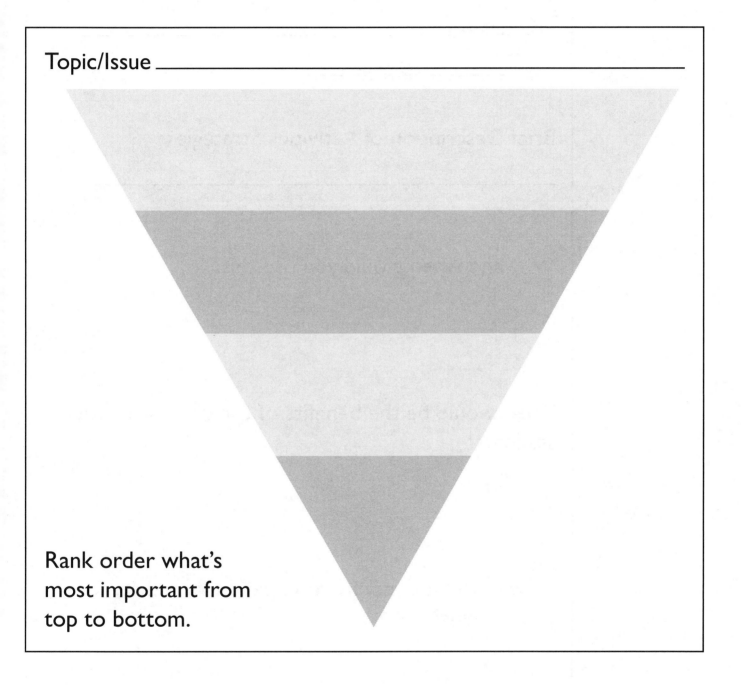

Rank order what's
most important from
top to bottom.

CORE PRACTICE TRIO SHARE

Practice # _____

page _____ to page _____

Brief Description of Activities/Strategies

_____

Why and when would you use this?

What would be the benefits of using this with your students?

How might you modify or expand this activity for your groups?

GOLDEN NUGGETS

From your discussion what two or three "nuggets" feel most important to share with the whole group?

GOING FURTHER

I wonder…

What would it take to…?

If I couldn't fail I (we) would…

How come…?

Why do we…?

What if…?

Why couldn't we…?

What would happen if…?

I'm still puzzled by…

I'm curious about…

What if we tried…?

How could we…?

I'm still not sure about…

If_____ then_____

Assessment / Feedback / Planning / Closings / Final Thoughts	Topic and Text Connections
51. Self-Assessment: **Question Prompts: (*REAL*, (12), pages 233–237)** **Exit Cards: (*REAL*, (15), pages 315–317)** **Ticket Out: (*REAL*, Appendix B, page 446)** **4–3–2–1: (*REAL*, Appendix B, page 446)** **Two Glows and a Grow: (*REAL*, (12), page 234)** **STOP Before You GO: (*REAL*, Appendix B, page 446)** **New Directions: (*REAL*, Appendix B, page 446)**	All of these protocols provide opportunities for self-reflection and feedback at the end of a PD session.
52. Learning Journey: Invite participants to use words, symbols, images, and other graphics to describe and map their learning journey during the course (Where you started / What you learned / What you gained / What you want to remember / Where you want to go)	This is a meaningful protocol to use at the end of a series of PDs or at the end of a course.
53. Group Assessment: **(*REAL*, (15), pages 276–277, 320–326)**	These protocols are useful when it's essential for participants to assess the performance and accomplishments of the whole group or small groups.
54. Letter to the Principal: Write letters to the principal in small groups that communicate: a) your experiences in this course or series of PD sessions; b) practices you would like to try out; c) issues and policies you would like to discuss with the leadership team; and/or d) the support you need to continue the work you started.	These protocols invite participants to think about how they want to continue their work as a group.
55. Next Steps: (*REAL*, Appendix B, page 446)	
56. Stick With It: Pass out large post-it notes and invite participants to write down: 1) practices they want to stick with and use regularly; or 2) issues they want to continue discussing within their team or professional learning community; or 3) consistent practices the group wants to establish across a team, grade level, or department.	
57. Banner Headlines: Share your big take-away from the PD session using seven words or less.	All of these closings invite participants to share their responses out loud at the end of a PD session.
58. Goodbye...Hello!!: Say "goodbye" to habits and practices you want to stop and say "hello" to practices you want to try out or do more often.	
59. I Can Do It!! I Can: Pass out note cards and invite people to write one thing that they can do in the next week to improve their practice and reach and support more students. Share them with the group.	
60. Connections: (*REAL*, (15), page 314)	
61. Appreciations: (*REAL*, (15), page 334)	

Assessment / Feedback / Planning / Closings / Final Thoughts

Ticket Out

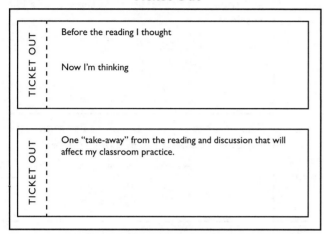

TICKET OUT | Before the reading I thought

Now I'm thinking

TICKET OUT | One "take-away" from the reading and discussion that will affect my classroom practice.

Next Steps

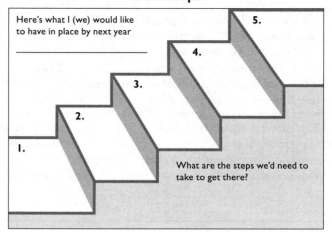

Here's what I (we) would like to have in place by next year

_____

5.

4.

3.

2.

1.

What are the steps we'd need to take to get there?

STOP Before You GO

What actions do you want to take or what practices do you want to try out?

What will you need to stop doing or do less often to make this happen?

What reminder will help you keep your commitment?

New Directions

In relation to the reading and the issue of

_____

Where are you now?

Where do you want to be?

What would you need to get there?

4–3–2–1

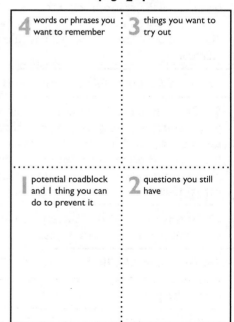

4 words or phrases you want to remember

3 things you want to try out

1 potential roadblock and 1 thing you can do to prevent it

2 questions you still have

TICKET OUT

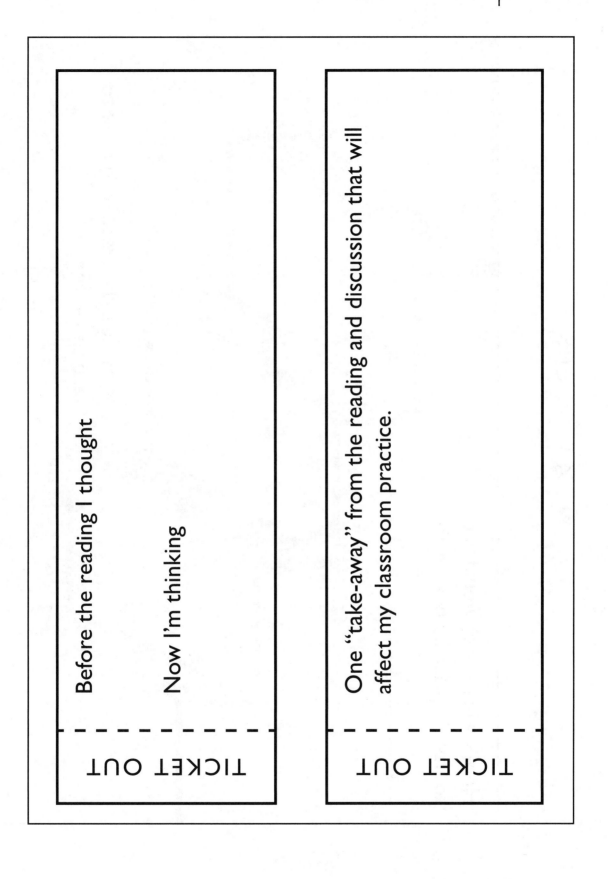

Before the reading I thought

Now I'm thinking

TICKET OUT

One "take-away" from the reading and discussion that will affect my classroom practice.

TICKET OUT

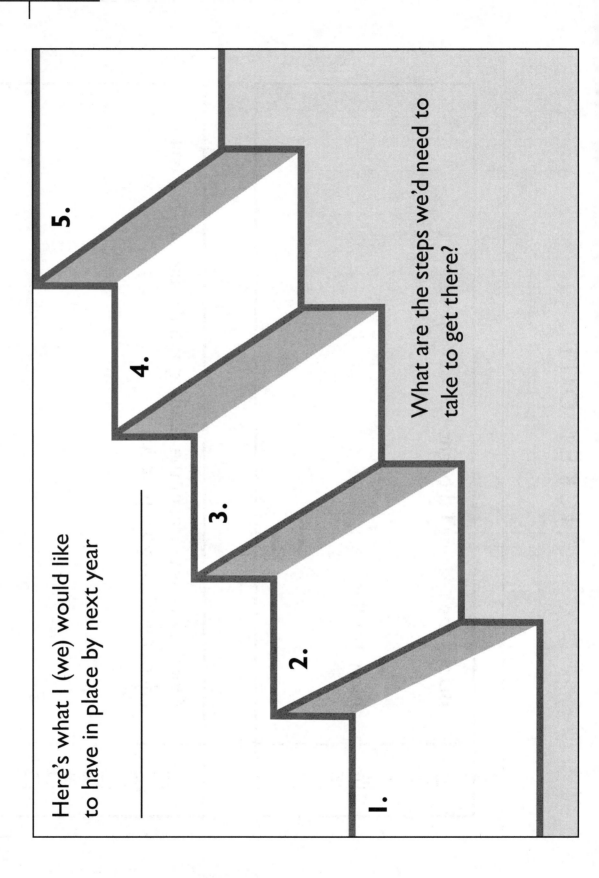

NEXT STEPS

Here's what I (we) would like to have in place by next year

What are the steps we'd need to take to get there?

1.

2.

3.

4.

5.

STOP BEFORE YOU GO

What actions do you want to take or what practices do you want to try out?

What will you need to stop doing or do less often to make this happen?

What reminder will help you keep your commitment?

NEW DIRECTIONS

In relation to the reading and the issue of

_____

Where are you now?

Where do you want to be?

What would you need to get there?

4 – 3 – 2 – 1

4 words or phrases you want to remember

3 things you want to try out

1 potential roadblock and 1 thing you can do to prevent it

2 questions you still have

INDEX

A

A, B, C, D, E problem solving, 137
absent students, 128
absent teachers, 129
academic accountable consequences, 297
Academic Assessment form, 248, 274
academic coaching, 163, 242
academic interventions, 297
Academic Learning Contract form, 248, 275
Academic Learning Gaps and Barriers to Learning (problem type)
    identification of, 25, 95
    management approaches, 47–49, 53–55
    responding to, 34
Acceptance, Attention, Appreciation, Affirmation, and Affection (five A's), 141, 158
accomplishments, 166–167, 172–173
accountability
    group, 101
    personal, 22
    responsibility vs., 39
    and self-correction, 67
    shared, 229
accountable consequences
    academic, 297
    behavioral, 22, 300–301
    defined, 36
    as guided discipline strategy, 22
    punitive consequences vs., 39, 229, 302–303
    refusal to carry out, 39

See also Develop Accountable Consequences and Supportive Interventions; Intensive Accountable Consequences and Interventions
acknowledging actions, 239
activity management, 177
administrators, 97–98, 251
admonishing communication style, 78
adolescents
    basic needs of, 146
    development of, 92–95
    mobility of, 1–2
aggression. See Student-to-Student Aggression; Student-to-Teacher Aggression
aggressive behavior, 151, 152, 154, 310–311
agreements, 101–104
Albert, Linda, 141, 148
allies, 249
alternative learning options, 251–252
anger
    conflict escalator, 82
    cues, 148, 150
    defusing, 211–213, 232
    expression of, 47
    and negative speech, 200
    reflections on, 284
    scenarios, 52
    triggers, 148, 150
anger iceberg, 313
anger management, 81, 148, 150, 211–212
"anger mountain," 148, 150
anxiety, 177

apologies, 236
appreciation notes, 174
Are You More Like...? activity, 326
arguing, 92, 194, 233
assertive speech, 151–154, 240, 310–311
assessments
    Academic Assessment form, 248, 274
    learning protocols, 363–369
    self-assessment documents, 129, 142
assignment notebooks, 127
assistant principals, 98, 255
attendance, 40, 97
attention, 240, 287
attitude, 146
authoritarian teaching, 67
authoritative teaching, 66–67
authority, 64–66
autonomy, 92, 93
avoidance, 21, 24

B

back-to-back drawings, 307
badgering questions, 77
baggage cards, 192
barriers to learning. See Academic Learning Gaps and Barriers to Learning
beginning class, 121, 188
behavioral accountable consequences and interventions, 300–301. See also Develop Accountable Consequences and Supportive Interventions

behavioral log, 115–116
behavioral supports, tiers of, 15, 16
behavior contracts, 61
Behavior/Learning Contract form, 248, 271
behavior report forms, 247–248
behavior(s)
    accountable consequences for, 22, 300–301
    aggressive, 151, 152, 154, 310–311
    desired, 37
    group talk, 136, 194
    high-impact, 32, 37, 55–61
    impulsive, 37, 147
    off-task, 30, 41, 72
    on-task, 38, 117
    passive, 151, 152, 154, 310–311
    problem, 242
    provocative, 195, 319
    replacement, 37
    self-regulated, 37
    target, 146, 239–240, 242
    teaching, 284
    unwanted (See unwanted behaviors)
body language, 182–183
books
    borrowing, 126
    and personalized support, 161–162
boredom, 184, 189, 205–206
Boundary Violations form, 247, 262

C
caring relationships, 94
case conferences, 14–16, 228
celebrations, 166, 172–173
character development, 96
Check-Ins and Conferences (response), 31
    academic learning gaps, 47–48, 53–54
    arrangement of, 97–98
    before beginning lessons, 191–192
    conferences for students who argue, 194
    daily conferencing, 241–246
    guide for conferencing, 321–322

implementing guided discipline, 215
    for improving public talk, 198
    lack of impulse control/self-management, 47–48, 56–58
    noncompletion, 62
    noncooperation and nonparticipation, 47–48, 56–58, 62
    one-minute check-ins, 158, 162
    procedural infractions, 38, 53–54
Chicken Soup for the Teenage Soul books, 162
choice, 78, 207–208
chronic unwanted behaviors
    consequences/interventions for, 55–61, 226
    defined, 36
    responding to, 32
    scaffolded consequences for, 40
    workout sessions for, 209
    See also Persistent unwanted behaviors
civil dialogue, 187
civility, 36
class-keeping, 123–124
class materials, 45–47, 50, 126, 240
class meetings, 136, 235–236
classroom discussion, 193–195
classroom environment procedures, 123–126
classroom management
    creating order with, 3
    goals of, 19
    ineffective, 86
    for Noncooperation and Nonparticipation, 62
    for Procedural Infractions, Noncompletion, and Noncompliance, 62
    reflections on, 283–284
    in RTI/PBS model, 13–16
    See also specific headings
classroom management and discipline plan, 286–301
    academic accountable consequences and interventions, 297

academic learning supports, 295–296
    behavioral accountable consequences and interventions, 300–301
    building cohesive group, 293
    essentials, 298–299
    expectations and norms, 288
    model, teach, practice, and assess behaviors, 289–292
    organizing your classroom, 286–287
    positive behavior supports, 293–294
Classroom Management That Works (Robert Marzano), 71
Classroom Referral and Request for Support form, 248, 276
classroom referrals, 40
classroom removal, 40
classroom rituals/routines, 172
classroom wager, 173–174
cleaning up materials, 123
closings, 170–171, 363–369
coaching, academic, 163, 242
cognitive development, 95
collaborative problem solving, 23, 82, 85
colleagues, 97–98, 251, 255–256
commands, 77
communication
    body language, 182–183
    of feelings, 148
    group participation, 171
    interpersonal, 142, 144
    with parents, 202, 253–254
    roadblocks in, 76–77
    styles of, 78–79
Community Contribution Cards, 125
Community Contribution Chart, 124
complaints, 208
conduct cards, 247, 254, 264
conferences, 65
    as accountable consequences, 36
    case, 14–16, 228
    defined, 40–41
    as guided discipline strategy, 23
    one-on-one, 216, 241–246

with parents, 254
Problem-Solving Conference form, 248, 270
re-entry, 256
student conference log, 115–116, 216, 218
See also Check-Ins and Conferences
confidence, 214–215
conflict
 group learning protocols for managing, 136–139
 handling, 81–83, 318
conflict escalator, 82, 83, 151, 312
conflict management styles, 315, 316
conflict resolution skills, 101, 171
conflict styles, 84–85, 285
confrontations, 232–234
confusion, 52
consensus process, 103
consequences
 acceptance of, 239
 accountable (*See* accountable consequences)
 and agreements, 104
 defined, 36
 logical, 36, 209–210
 procedural, 38
 punitive, 39, 229, 302–303
 reflective, 36
 restorative, 36
 scaffolded, 40
 schoolwide, 36, 40 (*See also* Immediate Enforcement, Intervention, and Follow-up of Schoolwide Consequences)
 tiers of, 13–16, 226, 228
 for unacceptable language, 197–199
consistent boundaries, 94
constructive speech, 197, 200, 202, 240, 308–309
contracts
 Academic Learning Contract form, 248, 275
 behavior, 61
 Behavior/Learning Contract form, 248, 271

Faculty Feedback for Student Contracts form, 248, 273
 learning, 159, 247–248
 Re-Entry Contract form, 248, 272
control, 94
cooperation, 78, 79, 142, 144, 146. *See also* Invite Student Engagement, Cooperation, and Self-Correction; Proximity, Prompts, and Invitations to Cooperate
cooperative learning protocols, 135
corrective consequences, 36
counselors, 98, 255
The Courage to Be Yourself (Al Desetta), 162
Create Group Norms, Procedures, and Learning Protocols (Step 2), 99–139
 approaches to discipline, 114–116
 checklist, 7
 classroom environment procedures, 123–126
 classroom management and discipline plan, 288
 enforcement of procedures, 117–119
 expectations, 100
 group learning protocols, 134–139
 group norms, 99–116
 group procedures, 116–134
 learning procedures, 126–127
 list of rights and responsibilities, 114
 managing conflict, 136–139
 negotiating learning, 136–139
 positive group guidelines and agreements, 101–104
 reasons for using procedures, 117–119
 research on, 8
 respect, 104–113
 student work procedures, 127–134
 transition procedures, 120–123
cues
 anger, 148, 150
 beginning class, 121
 physical, 182, 183

for transitioning, 179
cultural sharing, 285
culture disconnects, 87
curriculum, 66
cursing, 51, 196

D

Daily Conduct Card form, 247, 264
deadlines, 128
deans, 98, 255
debriefing, 170–171
demands, 77
depersonalizing bad behavior, 73–76
Desetta, Al, 162
desired behaviors, 37, 239–240, 242
detentions. *See* workout sessions
Develop Accountable Consequences and Supportive Interventions (Step 5), 221–256
 checklist, 11–12
 in classroom management and discipline plan, 297, 300–301
 communicating with parents, 253–254
 conferencing, 241–246
 defusing/de-escalating potential confrontations, 232–234
 desired target behaviors, 242
 diagnosing problem behaviors, 230–232
 dysfunctional classes, 249–252
 enforcement of accountable consequences, 251
 frequent fliers, 245–246
 for groups, 234–240
 levels of consequences and interventions, 226–228
 planning for, 221–232
 prioritizing problem behaviors, 223, 225
 problem solving with colleagues, 255–256
 protocols and learning contracts, 247–248
 punishment vs. accountable consequences, 229

research on, 12
scheduling time for, 241
unmotivated and resistant students, 244–245
upset students, 243–244
developed students, 95–96
dialogue, civil, 187
dignity, 239
discipline, 19–21
approaches to, 114–116
as common problem for teachers, xi, 19
defined, 37
do-nothing approach to, 21, 24
goals for, 69–71
guided discipline approach to, 21–25
punishment approach to, 20–21, 24
reflections on, 283–284
in RTI/PBS model, 13–16
self- (See self-discipline)
See also Guided Discipline and Personalized Support
discipline demeanor, 75–76, 183
discipline journals, 216
discipline policies, 96–97
discouragement, 47, 214
discussion, classroom, 193–195
disengagement, 52
disorganization, 45
disrespect, 72–73, 102, 104–107, 109
dissatisfied communication style, 78
documentation, 116, 202, 216–218
dominance (communication style), 78, 79
do-nothing approach, 21, 24
academic learning gaps, 47, 49, 53–55
lack of impulse control/self-management, 47, 56
noncompletion, 62
noncooperation and nonparticipation, 44, 47, 52, 56, 61, 62
procedural infractions, 46, 50, 53
student-to-student aggression, 51, 54–55, 59, 61

Do Now activity, 188, 216
"double or nothing" options, 209
Drawing a House activity, 331–332
drink policies, 123
dropout rates, x
dysfunctional classes, 249–252

E

effective teacher talk, 320
efforts, 94, 146, 164–166, 172–173
egregious offenses
defined, 37
and disrespect, 72
management approaches, 51–52
responding to, 33
emotional competencies, 13, 37, 38, 135
emotional development of students, 141–146, 314
emotional objectivity, 74
emotions
communication of, 76
managing, 135, 147–157
See also feelings; specific emotions
encouragement, 95, 158–159, 213
ending class, 121
energy, 189
engagement, 239. See also Invite Student Engagement, Cooperation, and Self-Correction
enthusiasm, 95
Evertson, C. M., 4, 99
exit referrals, 203
expectations, 100, 288
eye contact, 72, 180, 182, 183

F

facilitation skills, 88, 169–171
Faculty Feedback for Student Contracts form, 248, 273
failure rates, x
family relationships, 92
feedback, 158–159, 216, 242, 244
Faculty Feedback for Student Contracts form, 248, 273

Feedback and Suggestion form, 247, 265
learning protocols, 363–369
Feedback and Suggestion form, 247, 265
FEEL-ACT-THINK, 147
feeling-go-rounds, 192
feeling-learning connection, 314
feelings, 147–148, 242. See also emotions
feelings cards, 191
Feelings, Moods, and Attitudes (handout), 148, 149, 191
The Fifteen Minute Kid Talk Protocol form, 247, 268
final thoughts (learning protocols), 363–369
five A's (Acceptance, Attention, Appreciation, Affirmation, and Affection), 141, 158
focus, 52, 188–192, 240
folders, 217
follow-up of schoolwide consequences. See Immediate Enforcement, Intervention, and Follow-up of Schoolwide Consequences
food policies, 123
freedom, 78
"frequent fliers," 37, 245–246
Friday lottery tickets, 167
frustration, 47, 52, 211–213

G

games, 187, 323–333
gatherings, 192, 323–333
Ginsberg, M., 94
goals
for discipline and personalized support, 69–71
setting, 192
Gold Cards, 174–175
"Golden Rule," 104
go-rounds, 323
grades, 21, 133
group agreements, 101–104
group building tools, 187

group cohesiveness, 87
group efficacy, 142, 144
group facilitation, 169–171
group games, 323–333
group gatherings, 192
group learning protocols. *See* Create Group Norms, Procedures, and Learning Protocols
group norms. *See* Create Group Norms, Procedures, and Learning Protocols
group participation, 142, 144, 171
group procedures. *See* Create Group Norms, Procedures, and Learning Protocols
group recognition, 168–175
group talk behaviors, 136, 194
Guided Discipline and Personalized Support
    academic learning gaps, 47–49, 53–55
    lack of impulse control/self-management, 47–48, 56–58
    language of, 114
    noncompletion, 62
    noncooperation and nonparticipation, 45, 47–48, 52, 56–58, 61, 62
    and Positive Behavior Supports framework, 13–16
    procedural infractions, 46–47, 50, 53–54
    research supporting, 4–12
    and Response to Intervention framework, 13–16
    steps of, 3 (*See also specific steps*)
    student-to-student aggression, 51–52, 55, 59–61
guided discipline approach, 21–25
    defined, 37
    strategies in, 22–23
    supports and interventions, 215–218
    See also Guided Discipline and Personalized Support
gum policies, 123

H
habits of learning, 37, 94, 129, 130, 132. *See also* Life Skills
Habits of Learning Daily Checklist, 129, 132
Handbook of Classroom Management (C. M. Evertson and C. S. Weinstein), 4
harassment, 71, 197
helpful and friendly communication style, 78
HELP! signs, 128, 204
high-impact behaviors
    accountable consequences/interventions for, 55–61
    defined, 37
    responding to, 32
home groups, 124, 136
hope, 94
hostile freedom, 94
humor
    for deflating provocative behavior, 195
    as part of teaching stance, 68
    as source of power, 65

I
identity, adolescent, 92, 93
Immediate Enforcement, Intervention, and Follow-up of Schoolwide Consequences (response), 33, 51–52
Impulse Control, Self-management, and Personal Distress (problem type)
    conferencing to show concern, 243
    identification of, 25
    management approaches, 47–48, 56–58
    prioritizing behaviors, 225
    scenarios, 26
impulsive behaviors, 37, 147
incentives
    for following group procedures, 119
    for group support and recognition, 173–175
incomplete work, 128

independent work, 71, 127, 179, 222
individuals. *See* Support Individuals and the Group
in-school suspension, 256
instructions
    clarity of, 178, 180–181
    cues for giving, 121
    problems with, 87
instrumentation, 164
Intensive Accountable Consequences and Interventions (response), 32
    academic learning gaps, 55
    lack of impulse control/self-management, 56–58
    noncooperation/nonparticipation, 56–58, 61
    student-to-student aggression, 55
    student-to-teacher aggression, 59–60
intentionality, 168
interest, of students, 187
Interpersonal Classroom Conflicts form, 247, 261
interpersonal communication, 142, 144
interpersonal efficacy, 142, 144
interrupting others, 56
interventions
    academic, 297
    and agreements, 104
    behavioral, 300–301
    referrals for, 255
    scaffolded, 40, 223, 246
    student-to-student aggression, 51–52
    supportive, 41, 226–228
    tiers of, 14–16
    See also Develop Accountable Consequences and Supportive Interventions; *specific responses*
invitations to cooperate. *See* Proximity, Prompts, and Invitations to Cooperate
Invite Student Engagement, Cooperation, and Self-Correction (Step 4), 177–218
    anger and frustration, 211–213
    checklist, 10

cooperation, 204–207

discouragement, 214

engagement and cooperation, 178–187

getting ready to learn/focus, 188–192

guided discipline supports and interventions, 215–218

logical consequences, 209–210

negative speech/unacceptable language, 196–204

pitfalls that derail discussion, 193–195

problem solving, 207–208

research on, 11

self-correction, 200–201, 204–207

irrelevant questions, 210

J

Jensen, Eric, 189

Jones, Fred, 183

journals, discipline, 216

K

kid talk protocol, 247, 255, 268

Know Yourself, Know Your Students, Know Your School (Step 1), 63–98

adolescent development, 92–95

authoritarian vs. authoritative teaching, 66–67

colleagues and administrators, 97–98

communication roadblocks, 76–77

communication styles, 78–79

conflict styles, 84–85

depersonalizing bad behavior, 73–76

developed students, 95–96

diagnosing your own practice, 86–87

discipline and personalized support, 69–71

discipline policies, 96–97

disrespect, 72–73

handling conflict, 81–83

knowing your school, 96–98

knowing yourself, 63–88, 284–285

knowing your students, 89–96, 285

listening responsively, 80–81

managing your anger, 81

nos, needs, and nonnegotiables, 71

power/authority, 64–66

reasons for unwanted behaviors, 91

recovering, 85–86

referral policies, 96–97

strengthening your teacher roles, 87–88

teaching stance, 67–69

"with-it-ness," 71–72

Kounin, Jacob, 71, 177

L

labs, 127

large groups, 354–355

"lawyering up," 233

leadership, 78, 142, 144, 171

learning

barriers to (See Academic Learning Gaps and Barriers to Learning)

group learning protocols, 136–139

habits of, 37, 94, 129, 130, 132

learning carousel activity, 105–107

learning context, 222

learning contracts, 159, 247–248

learning gaps. See Academic Learning Gaps and Barriers to Learning

learning habits, 166

learning procedures. See Create Group Norms, Procedures, and Learning Protocols

learning protocols, 336–369

assessments/feedback/planning/closings/final thoughts, 363–369

cooperative, 135

prereading protocols, 337–345

products/presentations/report outs, 356–362

small and large group dialogue protocols, 354–355

while-you-read protocols, 346–353

See also Create Group Norms, Procedures, and Learning Protocols

learning supports, 14, 295–296

lecturing, 77

lesson plans, 216

lessons

pacing of, 184–187

student-centered, 184–187

Levine, Mel, 164

Life Skills, 23, 37, 141–146

assertive behavior, 151

assessing, 142–146

checklist of, 142

cooperation and self-correction, 204

defusing anger/frustration/discouragement, 211

defusing confrontations/power struggles, 232

derailed discussions, 193

feedback and encouragement, 158

getting ready to learn/focus, 188

group learning protocols, 134

group norms, 99

group problems, 234

group procedures, 116

group support and recognition, 168

improvement of, 166

in lesson plans, 216

linking personal effort and success, 164

logical consequences, 207

managing emotions, 147

personalized support, 161

problem solving, 207

recognizing individual accomplishments, 166

understanding feelings and behavior, 151

listening

conferencing, 242–245

responsive, 80–81, 239, 306

log book, 115–116

logical consequences, 36, 209–210

loss of focus, 52

lunch meetings, 161

M

Making It Right Between Us form, 247, 267
manners, 36
Manning, M., 93
Marzano, Robert, 66, 71
media, 105, 198
mediation, 138, 139, 251, 255
mediation protocol (S-T-A-R-T), 139
meetings, class, 235–236. See class meetings
Mendler, Allen, 94
mental health supports, 15
metacognitive development, 94
milestones, 166–167
missing work, 53, 126
M&Ms Game, 324
mobility, of adolescents, 1–2
model, teach, practice, and assess behaviors, 289–292
Moon Base activity, 327–328
moralizing, 77
Motivating Students Who Don't Care (Allen Mendler), 94
motivation, of students, 94–95, 146, 214, 244
music, 188

N

Name and Motion activity, 324
name calling, 54, 60
Name Card Match activity, 324
negative speech, 196–203
    ally behaviors for interrupting, 239
    constructive vs., 308–309
    interrupting, 198–202
    norms and consequences for, 197–199
    scenarios, 47
negotiation, 138, 208
neuroscience, 189
No Child Left Behind, x, xi
noncompletion. See Procedural Infractions, Noncompletion, and Noncompliance

noncompliance. See Procedural Infractions, Noncompletion, and Noncompliance
Noncooperation and Nonparticipation (problem type)
    disrespect vs., 72, 73
    identification of, 25
    management approaches, 44–45, 47–48, 52, 56–58, 62
    prioritizing behaviors, 225
    "sidebar" conversations, 44
"nos, needs, and nonnegotiables," 71
notebooks, assignment, 127

O

observation, 224, 250
offensive speech, 47, 59, 203
off-task behaviors, 30, 41, 72
"off the hook" classes, 249–252
one-on-one conferences, 216, 241–246
on-task behaviors, 38, 117
open-ended questions, 242
opposition, 79
optimism, 169
organization, 69, 87, 286–287
out-of-school suspension, 227, 256

P

pacing, 178, 184, 185
parent contact log, 216, 218
parent newsletters, 254
parents
    communication with, 202, 253–254
    relationships of adolescents and, 92
parent signatures, 254
parent-student homework, 254
participation
    as desired target behavior, 239
    in discussion, 193
    opportunities for, 94
partner walk-around, 190
passes, 121–122
passive behavior, 151, 152, 154, 310–311
PBS. See Positive Behavior Supports
PEARS (responsive listening), 81, 306

peers
    disrespectful interaction with, 54
    intimacy with, 92
pens and pencils, 126
persistent unwanted behaviors, 221–232
    consequences/interventions, 226–229
    diagnosing behaviors, 230–232
    planning for, 221–232
    prioritizing behaviors, 223, 225
    See also Chronic unwanted behaviors
personal accountability, 22
Personal Assets and Qualities of Character (handout), 160
personal conferences. See conferences
personal connections, 94, 158
personal distress. See also Impulse Control, Self-management, and Personal Distress
personal efficacy, 142, 143, 166
personal interest, 186, 187
Personalized Academic Supports and Interventions (response), 34
    academic learning gaps, 47–49
    goals for, 69–71
    guided discipline, 215–218
    struggling students, 161–163
personalized learning, x–xi
personalized recognition, 158–167
personalized support, 38. See also Personalized Academic Supports and Interventions
Personal Problem Solving Form, 247, 266
personal recognition notes, 167
personal relationships
    and authoritarian teachers, 66
    benefits of, 90
    lack of, 87
    quality of, 245
    as source of power, 65
phone calls, 202, 241, 253–254
planning (learning protocols), 363–369
Plastic Cup Silent Towers activity, 333
Polacco, Patricia, 161–162

portfolio organization, 129
Positive Behavior Supports (PBS), 13–16, 226, 293–294
"positive framing," 103
positive group guidelines and agreements, 101–104
posters, 118
power, 64–66
power reaches, 64, 65
power strengths, 64, 65
power struggles, 232–234
power vacuums, 64, 65
preparation for class, 240
prereading protocols, 337–345
presentations, 356–362
prevention
    importance of, 99
    as part of Guided Discipline and Personalized Support, 3
    in Positive Behavior Supports framework, 13
prevention initiatives, 38
principals, assistant, 98, 255
prioritizing problem behaviors, 223, 225
private conversation, 198
private spaces, 38–39
problem behavior calls, 253
problem behaviors, 242. See also unwanted behaviors; specific problem types
Problem Diagnosis worksheet, 230–232
problems
    diagnosis of, 37, 230–232
    discipline as, xi, 19
    factors in, 89–90
    identifying, 25
    responding to, 28–34
    types of, 26–27
problem solving, 207–208
    A, B, C, D, E, 137
    collaborative, 82, 85
    with colleagues, 255–256
    guide for, 317, 323–333
    as Life Skill, 144
    as part of resiliency, 93
    protocols for, 136–139, 247–248
    three-minute, 137

Problem-Solving Place Conference form, 248, 270
Problem-Solving Place Intake form, 247, 269
problem-solving reports, 215, 241
procedural consequences, 38
procedural infractions, 25, 29
Procedural Infractions form, 247, 259
Procedural Infractions, Noncompletion, and Noncompliance (problem type), 38
    classroom rule/norms/procedures, 45, 46, 50
    group procedures, 119
    management approaches, 45–47, 50, 53–54, 62
    noncompletion vs. disrespect, 72, 73
    prioritizing behaviors, 225
    procedural infractions scenarios, 26
    schoolwide procedural infractions, 40
Procedural Solutions (response), 29, 46–47, 50, 53–54
procedures, 38. See also Create Group Norms, Procedures, and Learning Protocols
products, 356–362
prompts. See Proximity, Prompts, and Invitations to Cooperate
protocol(s)
    kid talk, 247, 255, 268
    learning (See learning protocols)
    mediation, 139
    for problem solving, 136–139, 247–248
    re-entry, 40
    restorative justice, 40
provocative behavior/speech, 195, 319
Proximity, Prompts, and Invitations to Cooperate (response), 30
    academic learning gaps, 47–48
    lack of impulse control/self-management, 47–48
    noncooperation and nonparticipation, 45, 47–48, 52
    off-task students, 182–183

whole group instruction, 178
public apologies, 236
public conversation, 198
public spaces, 38–40
punishment approach, 20–21, 24
    academic learning gaps, 47, 48, 53, 54
    lack of impulse control/self-management, 47, 56
    noncompletion, 62
    noncooperation and nonparticipation, 44, 47, 52, 56, 60–62
    procedural infractions, 45, 50, 53
    student-to-student aggression, 51, 54, 59–61
punitive consequences (punishments), 39, 229, 302–303
purpose, 168
pushing/shoving, 51
put-downs, 54, 60, 77

Q

qualities of character, 160
quality of work, 240
Quarterly Learning Tasks and Progress Log, 129, 131
quizzes, 190

R

random reinforcement, 173
read-alouds, 136
recognition
    group, 168–175
    personalized, 158–167
record-keeping, 129
recovering, 85–86
reducers (anger), 148, 150
re-entry conferences, 256
Re-Entry Contract form, 248, 272
re-entry protocols, 40
referrals
    and conferencing, 244
    and double or nothing tactic, 209
    exit, 123, 203
    guide for, 305
    referral systems, 96–97
    submitting, 255

reflection documents, 129
reflections, 282–285
    about discipline, 283
    approaches to classroom management/discipline, 283–284
    building community of learners, 282
    urgent issues and questions, 283
reflective consequences, 36
refusal to carry out accountable consequences, 39
reinforcements, 173–175, 237, 251
relational development, 95
relationships
    caring, 94
    family, 92
    personal, 65, 66, 87, 90, 245
    student-teacher, x, 23, 24, 78
relay reviews, 190
relevant points, 194
remedial instruction, 163
repetitive unwanted behavior
    defined, 39
    scaffolded consequences for, 40
replacement behaviors, 37, 41
report cards, 117. See also grades
report outs, 356–362
resiliency, 93–94
resistant students, 244–245
Resnick, Lauren, 136
respect
    and authoritative teachers, 67
    as desired target behavior, 239
    as element in cohesive groups, 168
    and group norms, 102, 104–113
Response to Intervention (RTI), 13–16
responsibility(-ies), 114
    accountability vs., 39
    for behavior, 148
    and communication style, 78
    list of rights and, 209
    and student input, 101
responsive listening, 80–81, 239, 306
restorative consequences, 36
restorative justice protocols, 40
restrictions, 202
revisions/test corrections, 133
rewards, 173–175

ridicule, 197
rights and responsibilities list, 114
rituals, 172
role-plays, 109–110
routines, 172
RTI (Response to Intervention), 13–16
rudeness, 59
Rude, Uncivil, Disrespectful Speech form, 247, 263
rules
    classroom, 45, 46, 50
    establishing, 101
    schoolwide, 40, 104

S

safety officers, 98
Saphier, J. et al., 86, 98
sarcasm, 65, 77
scaffolded consequences/interventions, 40, 223, 246
scenarios, 43–62
    academic learning gaps, 47–49, 53–55
    lack of impulse control/self-management, 47–48, 56–58
    noncompletion, 62
    noncooperation and nonparticipation, 44–45, 47–48, 52, 56–58, 60–62
    procedural infractions, 45–47, 50, 53–54
    student-to-student aggression, 51–52, 54–55, 60–61
    student-to-teacher aggression, 59–60
Schindler, John, 146, 172
school, knowing. See Know Yourself, Know Your Students, Know Your School
school structures, ix–x
schoolwide consequences, 36, 40. See also Immediate Enforcement, Intervention, and Follow-up of Schoolwide Consequences
schoolwide procedural infractions, 40
schoolwide rules and discipline policies, 40, 104

scripts
    for managing emotions, 155–157
    for phone calls to parents, 253
seating arrangements, 251
security officers, 98, 123
self-actualization, 96
self-assessment documents, 129, 142
self-awareness, 142, 143
self-concept, of adolescents, 93
self-correction, 67. See also Invite Student Engagement, Cooperation, and Self-Correction
self-discipline
    defined, 22, 40
    as desired target behavior, 239
    as goal of classroom management, 19
self-esteem, of adolescents, 93
self-expression, 142, 143
self-grading, 133
self-management, 142, 143, 239. See also Impulse Control, Self-management, and Personal Distress
self-perpetuating routines, 187
self-regulated behavior, 37
self-talk, 37, 76, 213
sense of purpose, 93
Sergiovanni, Thomas, 168
shops, 127
"sidebar" conversation, 44, 56, 194
sign-in sheets, 128
silence, 126, 178, 181–182, 188
Silent Square Puzzle Problem, 329–330
situational interest, 186, 187
Sizer, Nancy, 81
Sizer, Ted, 81
The Skillful Teacher (J. Saphier et al.) 86, 98
small groups, 71, 127, 136, 222, 354–355
social competencies, 13, 37, 38, 93, 135
social development of students, 141–146
social workers, 98
standards movement, x
S-T-A-R-T mediation protocol, 139
stewardship tasks, 123–124

strict communication style, 78
struggling students, 161–163
student assistant programs, 255
student conference log, 115–116, 216, 218
student data cards, 217
Student Engagement. *See* Invite Student Engagement, Cooperation, and Self-Correction
Student Intervention/Support Team Referral form, 248, 277
student passes, 121–122
Student Perceptions of Teacher Respect, 108, 112
students
    absent, 128
    attention of, 187
    knowing (*See* Know Yourself, Know Your Students, Know Your School)
    personal connections with, 158
    social and emotional development of, 141–146
    struggling, 161–163
    voice of, 187
The Students Are Watching (Ted and Nancy Sizer), 81
Student Self-Reflection on Giving and Showing Respect, 107, 111
student support journals, 216
student-teacher relationships, x
    and approaches to discipline, 24
    communication styles, 78
    repairing, 23
Student-to-Student Aggression (problem type), 27
    identification of, 25
    management approaches, 51–52, 54–55
    prioritizing behaviors, 225
Student-to-Teacher Aggression (problem type), 27
    identification of, 25
    management approaches, 59–60
    prioritizing behaviors, 225
student work procedures, 127–134
studio classes, 127

submission, 79
success, 164–166
"sunshine calls," 215, 253
"sunshine notes," 253
Support Individuals and the Group (Step 3), 141–175
    accomplishments, 166–167
    assertive speech, 151–154
    building/maintaining cohesive group, 168–169
    checklist, 8–9
    classroom routines and rituals, 172
    conflict escalator, 151
    desired target behaviors, 239–240
    feedback and encouragement, 158–159
    group facilitation skills, 169–171
    group support and recognition, 168–175
    helping group get unstuck, 128, 235–236
    incentives, reinforcements and rewards, 173–175
    intervention plans, 237–238
    linking personal effort to success, 164–166
    managing emotions, 147–157
    monitoring/assessing group participation, 171
    personal connections with students, 158
    personalized support and recognition, 158–167
    recognizing efforts/accomplishments, 172–173
    research on, 9
    scripts, 155–157
    struggling students, 161–163
    students' social and emotional development, 141–146
supportive interventions, 13–16, 41. *See also* Develop Accountable Consequences and Supportive Interventions
support(s)
    behavioral, 15, 16
    communication of, 214–215

    guided discipline, 215–218
    learning, 14
    mental health, 15
    and motivation, 95
    personalized, 38 (*See also* Personalized Academic Supports and Interventions)
support team referrals, 255
suspension
    in-school, 256
    out-of-school, 227, 256

T

tardiness, 97, 120
target behaviors, 146, 239–240, 242
TAs. *See* teaching assistants
taunting, 54, 60, 197
teacher awareness, 3
Teacher Perceptions of Student Respect, 108, 113
teachers
    absent, 129
    as first responders, 24
    roles of, 87–88
"teacher talk," 177
teaching assistants (TAs), 123, 188
teaching behaviors, 284
teaching stance, 67–69
teaching toolbox, 186, 187
team conferencing, 254
teasing, 54, 60, 197
"tell me more" calls, 253
test corrections, 133
textbooks, 126
Thank You Mr. Falker (Patricia Polacco), 161–162
threats, 77
three-minute problem solving, 137
Tier 1 consequences and supportive interventions, 13–16, 226, 228
Tier 2 consequences and supportive interventions, 13–16, 226–228
Tier 3 consequences and supportive interventions, 13–16, 227, 228
Tools for Teaching (Fred Jones), 183
transition procedures, 120–123, 178, 179, 188

transparency, 217, 237
triggers (anger), 148, 150
trust, 168, 172
tutoring, 163

U

unacceptable language, 196–203
    interrupting, 198–202
    norms and consequences for,
      197–199
    See also negative speech
uncertain communication style, 78
Uncooperative, Off-Task Behaviors
      form, 247, 260
understanding communication style, 78
unmotivated students, 244–245
unwanted behaviors

chronic (*See* chronic unwanted
    behaviors)
    discipline for, 115
    persistent, 221–232
    repetitive, 39, 40
    scaffolded responses to, 223
    target behaviors to replace,
      239–240
    underlying reasons for, 91
upset students, 211, 213, 243–244

V

verbal instructions, 180
vision, 168
Vote with Your Feet exercise, 190

W

Warp Speed activity, 325

Weekly Habits of Learning Log, 129,
    130
Weinstein, C. S., 4, 99
When You Go Up Anger Mountain
    (handout), 148, 150
while-you-read protocols, 346–353
Whip activity, 324
whole group instruction, 121, 178
"why" questions, 77
"with-it-ness," 71–72, 177
Wlodkowski, R., 94
workout sessions, 41, 209, 224
write and post exercise, 190
written instructions, 180

Y

yelling, 51
You Like...I Like... activity, 325

About the Author

CAROL MILLER LIEBER got the call to teach as a teenager and never stopped. Exploration of the art, craft, and science of teaching and learning has been her driving passion for over forty years as an educator—in the roles of middle and high school teacher; school founder; principal; curriculum writer; clinical professor of teacher education; and professional development consultant, author, and program designer for Engaging Schools. Carol sup-ports principals, leadership teams, and faculty in large and small high schools in their efforts to embed the five Rs (rigor, relevance, relationships, responsibility, and readiness for college and career) into every aspect of schooling: school climate, culture, and student development initia-tives; classroom practice; professional learning communities; and schoolwide and classroom systems of discipline and student support.

She is the author of many books and articles, including, most recently, *Increasing College Access through School-Based Models of Postsecondary Preparation, Planning, and Support.* An unrepentant Deweyan, Carol holds two unwavering hopes for education in the 21st century: that schools will nurture the mind, heart, and spirit of every student within democratic learning communities and that teachers and learners will recapture the qualities of joy, meaning, and imagination in their classrooms. These are the things that make learning REAL.

About Engaging Schools

Engaging Schools is a nonprofit organization that collaborates with educators in middle and high schools to create school communities where each and every student develops the skills and mindsets needed to succeed and make positive contributions in school, work, and life. We help educators create a schoolwide community of learning that integrates academic, social, and emotional development. We offer professional development and resources with practical strategies that are grounded in the values of equity, community, and democracy. The result: educators who can better engage their students — and students who are prepared to make positive contributions in school, work, and life. Engaging Schools was founded in 1982 as Educators for Social Responsibility and changed its name to Engaging Schools in 2014.

Engaging Schools help middle and high schools create a positive climate and learning-focused culture. Educators adopt proven strategies for effectively teaching and communicating with students; supporting students academically, socially, and emotionally; and giving students the tools to learn, collaborate, and help one another thrive. We offer professional development services and products in three core areas: Engaged Classrooms, Schoolwide Discipline and Student Support, and Advisory Plus. We also feature additional programs and products for middle and high schools on bullying, peer mediation, conflict resolution, and diversity, as well as aligned programs and products for elementary schools.

Engaging Schools has a long history and a wealth of experience facilitating the change process and much practical expertise in how to create positive learning environments in today's schools. Our work with principals, school leadership teams, faculty members, students, and families is informed by current research and the best practices in educational leadership, instruction, discipline and student support, and youth development.

Visit us online at http://www.engagingschools.org for more information about additional Engaging Schools products and services, to sign up for our monthly e-newsletter, and to connect with us via social media.

We can be reached at:

Engaging Schools
23 Garden Street
Cambridge, MA 02138
phone: 617-492-1764
fax: 617-864-5164
info@engagingschools.org

Create, Relate, & Pop @ the Library

SERVICES & PROGRAMS FOR TEENS & TWEENS

ERIN HELMRICH AND ELIZABETH SCHNEIDER

Neal-Schuman Publishers, Inc.

New York   London

Published by Neal-Schuman Publishers, Inc.
100 William St., Suite 2004
New York, NY 10038

Printed and bound in the United States of America.

The paper used in this publication meets the minimum requirements of American National Standard for Information Sciences—Permanence of Paper for Printed Library Materials, ANSI Z39.48-1992.

Library of Congress Cataloging-in-Publication Data

Helmrich, Erin, 1972-
  Create, relate & pop @ the library : services & programs for teens & tweens / Erin Helmrich, Elizabeth Schneider.
    p. cm.
  Includes bibliographical references and index.
  ISBN 978-1-55570-722-4 (alk. paper)
  1. Young adults' libraries—Activity programs—United States. 2. Young adults' libraries—United States. 3. Libraries and teenagers—United States. I. Schneider, Elizabeth, 1980- II. Title. III. Title: Create, relate, and pop at the library.

Z718.5.H45 2011
027.62'6—dc22
                                                          2011004986

Contents

List of Figures vii

Preface ix

Acknowledgments xiii

Chapter 1. From "Dyn-O-*Mite!*" to "How *You* Doin'?": History of Teen/Tween Pop Culture 1

1950s 2
1960s 2
1970s 3
1980s 4
1990s 5
2000 to the Present 6
Library Services to Tweens 9
Library Services to Teens 9
References 9

Chapter 2. "Here It Is, Your Moment of Zen": Defining Create, Relate, & Pop 11

Create 11
Create Access 12
Relate 15
Pop 17
Conclusion 19
Reference 19

Chapter 3. "OMG!": Targeting Populations, Advertising, and Promotion 21

Introduction 21
Create: Branding Your Teen and Tween Services 22
Relate: Identifying Your Teens and Tweens 24
Pop: Types of Advertising and Promotion 32
Conclusion 37

References   38

Chapter 4. Make It Work: Collections   39
Create   39
Relate   40
Pop   42
Conclusion   43
Resources   44

Chapter 5. Keep 'Em Coming: Spaces   45
Create   45
Relate   47
Pop   48
Conclusion   49
Resources   49

Chapter 6. "I Want My MTV!": Programming   51
Foundations for Successful Teen/Tween Programming   51
Planning and Implementing Programs   52
Conclusion   52

Chapter 7. Programs: Art   55
Comic Book Academy   55
Comics Art Digital Coloring   58
Comics Artist Forum   60
Pinhole Photography   62

Chapter 8. Programs: Celebrity and Reality Television   65
Top Chef Season 4 Winner, Stephanie Izard, Appearance and Cooking Demo   65
MTV: *Made*   69
Project Runway Fashion Show or Challenge   72
Silent Library   79
Superhero Smashup   82

Chapter 9. Programs: Contests   85
Graffiti Contest   85
Photography Contest   88
LEGO Contest   90

Chapter 10. Programs: Cooking and Food, Food, Food   97
Food Tastings   97
Sushi Making   99
Vegetarian Cooking   101
Revolting Recipes   103
Smoothie Sensation   105

Bento Box Bonanza   108

Chapter 11. Programs: Crafts   113
Shrinky Dinks   113
Jean Pocket Purses   115
Duct Tape Crafts   117
T-shirt Remodel   120

Chapter 12. Programs: Gaming   123
Retro Octathlon   123
Pokémon Tournaments   126

Chapter 13. Programs: Japanese Popular Culture   129
Cosplay Contest   129
Amigurumi: Crochet Happy Fun   132

Chapter 14. Programs: Me—Beauty, Style, Body Modification, and Fashion   135
Nail Art   135
Kitchen Cosmetics   137
Tattoo History, Culture, and Safety   140

Chapter 15. Programs: Magic, Fantasy, and the Mystical World   143
Psychics, Astrology, and the Future Fair   143
Vampire Wreaths   145
Fairy Homes, Jewelry, Dolls, and More   148

Chapter 16. Programs: Music   153
High School Musical Karaoke   153

Chapter 17. Programs: Physical Activities   157
Dance Programs   157
Parkour and Freerunning   159
Double Dutch Program   160
EXPLODapalooza   162
Eggcellent Engineering   166
Cup Stack Attack   169

Chapter 18. Programs: Summer Reading   173
Teen Summer Reading Program   173
Tween Summer Reading Program   177

Chapter 19. Programs: Technology   181
Social Networking Programs   181
Library LEGO League   184
Technology Fashionistas   188

Library Makerspaces   191
Filmmaking 101   194
Game On! Envisioning Your Own Video Game   197

Chapter 20. "Where Do We Go from Here?": Conclusion   201

Index   203

About the Authors   217

List of Figures

Figure 2.1   Sample Policy: Restricted Temporary Library Cards for Teenagers
without Parental Signature. 13

Figure 3.1   Sno-Isle Libraries Teen Logo 25

Figure 3.2   Sno-Isle Teens Hat 25

Figure 3.3   AXIS Logo from the Ann Arbor District Library 26

Figure 3.4   Teen Patron Profile Survey. 28

Figure 3.5   Teen Patron Library Use Survey. 30

Figure 3.6   Vampire Wreath Program 33

Figure 8.1   Project Design: High School Fashion Show 75

Figure 8.2   Project Design: Submission Session Guidelines 76

Figure 8.3   Teen Drinking from a Shoe during a *Silent Library* Challenge
at the Monrovia (CA) Public Library. 81

Figure 9.1   Graffiti Contest at the Ann Arbor District Library 87

Figure 9.2   LEGO Contest Rules and Guidelines 92

Figure 9.3   LEGO Contest. 94

Figure 10.1   Healthy Bento Box Creation 109

Figure 10.2   Using Books to Inspire Bento Box Designs. 111

Figure 11.1   Creative Duct Tape Crafts 119

Figure 12.1   *Dance Dance Revolution* 124

Figure 14.1   Miss Moorpark Helping to Prepare a Natural Face Mask
at the Moorpark (CA) City Library 138

Figure 14.2   Tattoo Example 141

Figure 15.1   Vampire Wreath to Attract Vampires 146

Figure 15.2   Flower Fairy Clothes 150

Figure 15.3   Fairy Fashion in a Fairy Book 151

Figure 17.1   Eggcellent Engineering Rules and Regulations. 168

Figure 18.1   2009 Teen Summer Reading Program at Darien (CT) Library. . . 175

Figure 18.2   Tween Summer Reading Program Game Board at Kalamazoo
(MI) Public Library. 179

Figure 18.3   2007 Tween Summer Reading Program at Kalamazoo (MI)
Public Library. 180

Figure 19.1   LEGO Mindstorms History 186
Figure 19.2   Library LEGO League: The Rules 187
Figure 19.3   Technology Fashionista Program: Ear Buds, Flash Drive,
                LED Bracelet, and Lit-Up Figure. 190

Preface

Inspirational? Excitable? Adaptable? Informational? Yes! Traditional? No. As two librarians who bonded as coworkers over a shared obsession with pop culture, the authors are well aware that not all young adult librarians share their over-the-top interest in this arena.

Thus, *Create, Relate, & Pop @ the Library: Services & Programs for Teens & Tweens* is intended to make it easier for the youth specialist and generalist to keep up with the fast-paced world of tween and teen pop culture. This book presents a framework of philosophy for providing creative, relatable, and pop culture–relevant services and programs with practical tips and ideas for keeping up with the world of tweens and teens. Awesomely, there are also 47 detailed program descriptions divided into 13 different topic-based chapters!

Create, Relate, & Pop @ the Library explores how infusing pop culture into teen services with a focus on programming and events can engage the teens in your community in new and exciting ways. Learn how to become a facilitator and innovator of programming on topics you may have little to no interest in or no knowledge of. Turn your own particular obsessions, interests, and talents into potential service or programming opportunities. Find practical and detailed examples, instructions, and resources for providing tween and teen programming that uses pop culture as a jumping-off point. This approach will excite interest from reluctant library users and potentially engage devoted users in new ways. Learn how many of your younger teens may be better served by programs for tweens, as well as how to engage the older and edgier teens in your community.

The title *Create, Relate, & Pop @ the Library* came from trying to find a fun and catchy way to encapsulate the authors' philosophy of service to tweens and teens. Create, Relate, & Pop is a framework with which to plan, conduct, and evaluate library services and collections.

- **Create:** Library collections and services, like free access to information and services, create opportunities for young people to explore and try new things. Librarians live to provide opportunities to create: art, movies, jewelry, rockets, science experiments, food, music, clothes, gifts, etc. The *Create* part of the equation is where libraries and librarians are already doing a top-notch job. Libraries are more often filling the recreational, explorational, and inspirational roles that schools used to provide with after-school clubs and more extensive elective class selections.

- **Relate:** In order to grab the interest of teens and hold it, you need to be relevant to their lives. This of course happens using pop culture and being in tune with their lives and what's important and current, but it also has to do with creating opportunities for teens and tweens to become healthy, caring, responsible, and well-rounded people. Staying relevant is often the hardest part because the job never ends—as tween and teen interests and obsessions change and flow, so must librarians keep up with this change and flow.

- **Pop:** The *Pop* is the easy part. *Pop* is fun; *pop* is current; *pop* is what they want. *Pop* is also flexible. *Pop* does not just mean what's popular with the majority. Thanks to the Internet and its ability to digitally unite people from across the globe or across the street, there are many niche and cultlike communities based on interests about which the average American has never heard. In a country with more than 300 million people, an interest that attracts 500,000 or even 2 million is tiny enough to be obscure, but large enough that it shouldn't be ignored.

Using *Create, Relate, & Pop*

This book can be easily consumed by the on-demand reader who skips to the chapter describing a program that is needed next week as well as by the reader who prefers a cover-to-cover approach. The initial six chapters describe the why and how teens became so powerful and an entity unto themselves between the world of child and adulthood; next, dive into philosophies and how best to Create, Relate, & Pop in your library; and finish with 13 chapters packed with programming ideas, instructions, and resources, plus a final concluding chapter.

Chapter 1, "From 'Dyn-o-*Mite*' to 'How *You* Doin'?': History of Teen/Tween Pop Culture," outlines a brief timeline of teen and tween pop culture in the twentieth and twenty-first centuries. Take a trip down memory lane using pop culture touchstones or use it as a reference for infusing retro popular culture experiences into programs for today's teens.

The philosophy at the heart of *Create, Relate, & Pop* is explored and defined in Chapter 2, "'Here It Is, Your Moment of Zen': Defining Create, Relate, & Pop." Moving away from the traditional library model of serving teens and tweens can breathe life into programming. Learn to capitalize on the latest consumer trends by programming around them.

Determining different interest groups in a teen population is discussed in Chapter 3, "'OMG!': Targeting Populations, Advertising, and Promotion." Knowing your audience is very helpful when defining services at your library or school. Survey your teens/ tweens and find out who is living in your community. This chapter will help you match programs to your kids, whether they are socs, greasers, outsiders, goths, hippies, burn-outs, freaks, geeks, mean girls, emos, indies, or whatever the particular teen tribes are in your community. Once you have identified your audience and their interests, we will teach you how to market your program to them.

Programming using popular celebrities and trendy hobbies must be supported by the library collection. Chapter 4, "Make It Work: Collections," gives tips on how to keep the collection current, healthy, and, most important, relevant to the teen and tween interests of the moment.

Chapter 5, "Keep 'Em Coming: Spaces," gives ideas on how to make a teen or tween area in the library pop culture friendly. The chapter describes easy and creative ways to keep current with the latest trends using input from the young adults being served, producing a space defined by the popular interests of the moment.

More than anything else, this book is about programming. Programs are the best way to engage your users, get them into the library, and keep them coming back. Chapter 6, "'I Want My MTV!': Programming," explains the foundations for a successful teen/ tween library program.

The heart of *Create, Relate, & Pop @ the Library* is the 13 programming chapters, which include detailed information featuring 47 different program ideas. Chapters 7 through 19 are divided by topic: art, celebrities and reality television, contests, cooking and food, do-it-yourself crafts, gaming, Japanese popular culture, beauty and body modification, magic and mystical worlds, music, physical activities, summer reading programs, and technology. Each program description includes the following:

- General description
- *Pop*—how and in what specific way it relates to pop culture
- *Relate*—what opportunities for learning and experience this provides for the young person and the assets it may potentially provide
- Instructors/talent
- Audience—who is the best or potential audience
- Planning and supplies
- *Create*—detailed instructions on how to run the program
- Food, technology, and other mandatory extras
- Analysis—thoughts on the success of the program and other ideas for similar programs or things to try when you do it again

- Marketing tips
- Resources

Learn how to freshen up tried-and-true craft programs or how to use reality television, fandom, movies, and teen obsessions with food to offer dynamic and fun programs. Programs described include Comic Book Academy, Pinhole Photography, *Top Chef* Winner Appearance, Graffiti Contests, Sushi Making, Shrinky-Dink Crafts, Pokémon Tournaments, Amigurumi Crochet, Nail Art, Pyschic Fair, Parkour and Freerunning, Filmmaking 101, and more.

It's a New World! Let's Jump In!

One of the greatest opportunities that libraries and librarians have is to expose young people to the world around them—from meeting neighbors and community members to the world at large and everything in between. From culture and the arts to hands-on opportunities to learn skills, sciences, crafts, trades, and arts from people working in those fields, libraries offer young people opportunities that often cannot be found elsewhere—and certainly not for the library's "free of charge" level. It's a post–"give them what they want" world. There is no longer time to debate whether what's popular is "okay" and whether catering to their interests is "dumbing down" what librarians do. As institutions of the people, librarians must be relevant to the lives of our taxpayers. Embrace the change! From introducing the power of well-honed information-seeking skills in the real world to providing opportunities to create their own information and express themselves with art or culture, librarians are in a unique position to empower young people with their neutral and open position in the world. *Create, Relate, & Pop @ the Library* will do just that, demonstrating how you can relate to your tweens and teens in new ways and harness the enthusiasm they have for their obsessions in constructive and fun ways to create engaging programs. This new participatory, user-created world is a perfect fit for creating programs that teens and tweens want.

Acknowledgments

This book is a collaboration by many fabulous people who allowed us to include their innovative programming which captures the attention of teens and tweens all over the United States. Their dedication to the profession of librarianship makes us proud to call ourselves librarians. The library services and programs described in this book are walking advertisements for the importance of the public library in their communities.

Thank you to Meaghan Battle, Vicki Browne, Sharon Iverson, Eli Neiburger, and the staff at the Ann Arbor District Library in Ann Arbor, Michigan, for your support and commitment to consistently pushing the envelope in creating original programming for young adults.

Many of the photographs and programming ideas illustrating best practices in the profession were added to this book in collaboration with the Sno-Isle Libraries in Washington State, Moorpark (CA) City Library, Monrovia (CA) Public Library, Darien (CT) Library, Kalamazoo (MI) Public Library, Steve Teeri from the Detroit Public Library, Stewart Fritz from the Kalamazoo (MI) Public Library, and Justin Hoenke of the Portland (ME) Public Library. We thank them for their assistance in providing excellent examples of library services and programs supporting teens and tweens throughout the country.

We extend a heartfelt thank-you to our editor, Sandy Wood, who had so much patience with two librarians trying to traverse the landscape of the writing world. Thank you for holding our hands throughout this process, giving us ample feedback, and being honest when we seemed confused. We cannot thank you enough for your help.

Finally, thank you to our friends and family for your support and encouragement. E.H. would like to thank her parents, and her close friends who lent listening ears and support during the "OMG" moments of this amazing writing process. E.S. would like to personally thank her husband Curtis Schneider (you are the best!), her parents, and the staff at the Monrovia Public Library for listening to her think through ideas and complain only a little, and for encouraging her to indulge her hobby of incessantly reading blogs and magazines to know up-to-the-minute information on movie stars and celebrities.

Chapter 1

From "Dyn-O-*Mite*!" to "How *You* Doin'?": History of Teen/Tween Pop Culture

Defined by the *Oxford English Dictionary* (2010) as the cultural traditions of the ordinary people of a particular community, using popular culture is a unique and innovative technique to reach the interests and needs of teens and tweens in the library setting. This chapter leads you through a brief history of the highlights of teen/tween pop culture from the 1950s, which is usually considered the modern-day birthplace of teenage popular culture, to present day. Use this chapter as a reminder that the more things change, the more they stay the same—and to illustrate how easy it can be to develop programming for teens and tweens based on pop culture icons of today and yesteryear. Anastasia Goodstein, founder of the *YPulse* (http://www.ypulse.com) website, clearly makes the point in her book, *Totally Wired: What Teens and Tweens Are* Really *Doing Online*, that current technology is the modern-day equivalent of passing notes and staying obsessively in touch with your friends. Nothing has changed except the tools that teens use to fulfill their adolescent destinies (Goodstein, 2007). Since part of adolescence is the tendency to rediscover the past, opportunities may arise to interest teens in the library in innovative ways using retro pop culture.

Popular culture has always been and will always be about music, entertainment, food, clothes, sports, games, and generally the way people live, have fun, socialize, and bond in their free time. Whether they are discovering The Beatles as their own or wearing retread 1980s' clothes, without realizing it, popular culture is constantly recycled and co-opted by youth culture. By mining retro popular culture in new ways with teens and tweens, libraries can learn how to use the fads of the past to connect to youth in the present. Travel down memory lane with us, and discover the possibilities of using pop culture in the library.

1950s

America was in a prosperous time after World War II, with an emphasis on family values and building a secure and happy future. U.S. soldiers home from war started families, which resulted in the baby boom and the eventual development of suburbs. At the same time, teenagers were breaking out of the role of children and starting to show society that they would very quickly become voters and consumers.

American Bandstand became the first national TV show devoted to pop and rock music, creating a huge teen fan club following. Teen heartthrobs "Elvis the Pelvis" Presley and Pat Boone topped the music charts, though they could not have been more different visually or stylistically. Presley won over swooning girls with his gyrating dance moves, shocking adults. Ed Sullivan refused Presley an appearance on his show, calling him "unfit for a family audience" (Duden, 1989: 32). Meanwhile, the more parent-friendly, clean-cut Boone crooned in his white buckskin shoes.

RCA announced its first color television on March 29, 1950, the same month newspapers reported that "children spent as much time watching TV as they did going to school" (Duden, 1989: 6). Entertainment through technology started to move away from the typical trip to the movie theater. Drive-in theaters were the cool place to hang out, with the number of theaters around the country climbing to 2,200 in 1950—twice the number of 1949. The public donned 3-D glasses to watch lions jump into their laps in *Bwana Devil* in 1952, the first 3-D color movie.

Eating out was reinvented when fast-food hamburgers and fries became available from McDonald's in 1955, revolutionizing what teens would eat for lunch in future years; by 1959, more than 100 McDonald's restaurants were open for business. Wham-O began marketing Hula-hoops, selling 30 million in a few months in 1958. At the end of the decade, college students took on the challenge of fitting as many people as possible into a telephone booth; 34 people stuffed themselves into a telephone booth at Modesto Junior College in California, though the feat was met with controversy because the booth was on its side. Twenty-two students from the College of Saint Mary's in Moraga, California, filled a phone booth, and they were considered the most efficient group to meet the challenge at the time.

1960s

No longer interested in cramming people in phone booths, the teens of the 1960s entered into a time of social change and experimentation. With a driving need for individuality, teens dealt with the pressures of a tumultuous time, seeking meaning while the war in Vietnam escalated and civil rights protests raged.

Almost half of the population of the United States was under age 18 in 1960 (PBS, 2005), so the wants and needs of this growing segment of society grew more visible as well. Teens continued to rebel against 1950s' moral values and explored an alternative counterculture. Happenings, a form of performance art, took center stage as a form of artistic expression influenced by the Eastern philosophy of valuing the act of being. Yoko Ono staged a happening in 1966, during which members of the audience cut away pieces of her clothing for an hour as she knelt silently. Experimental theater groups formed all over the country, as an innovative way to express political viewpoints and educate the public on current issues, instead of using pamphlets or speeches. In 1967, poet Allen Ginsberg toured college campuses, speaking to sold-out audiences about the Summer of Love, a national hippie celebration of life and love. Ginsberg spoke of imagination and expanded consciousness through the use of drugs, meditation, and anything else that "turned people on" to loving oneself and humanity (Holland, 1999: 98).

The sixties was a groundbreaking time for dance and music. "The Twist," a song by R&B artist Hank Ballard, gained popularity after Chubby Checker's performance on *American Bandstand* in 1960. The associated dance became an international fad among teens, considered "one of the first connections of international youth culture" (Holland, 1999: 104). British rock bands like The Rolling Stones and The Who became popular, combining the black roots of American music with a British twist. By 1961, The Beatles had unexpectedly created a sensation called Beatlemania, becoming one of the first boy bands in the international music scene and playing to more than 70 million viewers on *The Ed Sullivan Show*. Political folksingers like Bob Dylan and Joan Baez took the stage to express their opinions on war, justice, civil rights, and "The Establishment." In 1961, when teens were starting to question war for the first time, The Kingston Trio released "Where Have All the Flowers Gone?," a song penned by Pete Seeger and Joe Hickerson. Creating the first successful black-owned record company in the nation, Berry Gordy Jr. started the Motown Company in 1960 and launched the careers of many famous soul music legends. The Jackson 5, Stevie Wonder, Diana Ross & the Supremes, and Smokey Robinson kept teens dancing in the aisles. Half a million people showed up to the music finale of the sixties, Woodstock, in the summer of 1969, to show their support of peacefully living and the end to war and racial injustice. Celebrated singers Janis Joplin and Jimi Hendrix played to a peaceful crowd, with Hendrix giving a preview of the new music genre acid rock that would become popular in the early seventies. To document all of these great movements in music, *Rolling Stone* magazine debuted in 1967, with John Lennon on its cover, and has since played a principal role in pop culture through its in-depth reporting on current music and politics (Carlson, 2006).

1970s

The political turmoil of the sixties continued into the seventies; two of the most important U.S. political events that occurred in this new decade were President Richard

Nixon's resignation following the Watergate scandal in 1974 and, only eight months later, the end of the Vietnam War. Throughout the decade, teens searched for ways to define their generation. They flocked to stores to purchase hot pants in the earliest years of the 1970s. Such notables as Jackie Kennedy Onassis, David Bowie, and Sammy Davis Jr. were known to have worn this fashion item (Stewart, 1999). Other fad items included pet rocks (an ideal self-sufficient pet), and mood rings, which changed color to supposedly reflect the wearer's mood. In 1974, streaking became the craze. Teens ran naked through public events to shock and amuse the public; the most famous incident occurred in that year at the Academy Awards, while host David Niven was introducing presenter Elizabeth Taylor (Stewart, 1999).

As The Beatles as a group began to break apart, the influence of their musical breadth was evident on new performers taking the stage. Glam rock, whose musicians wore showy, glittery clothing and often conveyed androgynous images, became very popular, with David Bowie as its front singer in the United Kingdom. Folksingers like James Taylor and Carole King also maintained a solid presence in the music scene. Heavy metal came into existence in the late 1960s and early 1970s, showcasing such legendary bands as Black Sabbath and Led Zeppelin. As a rebellion against rock musicians for "'selling out' by creating music that was pure sentimentalism," the punk movement began in New York in the mid-seventies (Stewart, 1999). Disco had been on the rise in popularity and finally hit the mainstream in 1974 with the Hues Corporation's hit, "Rock the Boat." Platform shoes and glittery clothes were a staple of this cultural phenomenon, which was captured on film in the 1977 movie *Saturday Night Fever*. Disco has continued to renew its hold on the generations, such as through the musical *Mamma Mia!*, a play based on the music of ABBA which has been continuously in production on Broadway since 2001.

Television and movies were reinvented in the seventies. The film industry focused on drawing in urban black audiences by creating movies with black heroes, such as private detective John Shaft (*Shaft*, 1971) and reluctant hero Sweetback (*Sweet Sweetback's Baadasssss Song*, 1971).

The comedy sketch show *Saturday Night Live* debuted in 1975, satirizing current culture and becoming a cultural icon itself. Blockbuster cult classics that premiered during this decade included *The Godfather*, *Jaws*, and *Star Wars*.

1980s

Though the 1980s saw the collapse of communism and the end of the Cold War, much of the decade was dedicated to materialistic pursuit. The superficiality of the decade was noted in the popular teen-centered films of John Hughes, including *The Breakfast Club* and *Some Kind of Wonderful*, which deftly addressed the social separations of classes in high school: the jocks, the geeks, the popular kids, the punks, and the rebels. Money and materialism were of interest to teens in this time of prosperity. The preppy collegiate look was made popular in part by editor Lisa Birnbach's book, *The Official Preppy Handbook*. The punk kids rocked shoulder pads, big hairsprayed hairdos, ripped jeans, and stiletto heels.

Music history was made in 1981 when the first music television station, MTV, debuted with "Video Killed the Radio Star," a music video by The Buggles. New genres of music, such as new wave and synthpop, entered the scene. These bands sang out against large corporations, similar to the antiestablishment lyrics commonly found in punk rock. Rock and roll topped the charts with bands like Van Halen and Aerosmith. A form of harder rock called thrash metal appeared in this decade from bands like Metallica and Slayer. Michael Jackson and Madonna became both music and fashion icons. Their fame was enhanced by their individuality and penchant for pushing the boundaries, wearing such signature items of clothing as one sequined glove or a leather bustier and showing their timelessness by reinventing themselves to interest teens through the decades. Concert charity events were very popular in the 1980s. The most memorable event, occurring in 1985, was USA for Africa, in which a group of popular entertainers recorded a single, "We Are the World," to raise money to fight disease and hunger in Africa, especially concentrating on Ethiopia, which was experiencing a famine at that time.

The 1980s were also the start of the computer age. Personal computing, as we know it now, was initiated by IBM's development of the first personal computer in 1981 and the invention of the World Wide Web by an English physicist named Tim Berners-Lee in 1989. Video game technology soared with the creation of arcade games *Pac-Man* in 1980, followed by *Ms. Pac-Man* in 1981. In the late eighties, teens started to leave the arcade to stay at home with personal gaming systems, especially the Nintendo Entertainment System (NES), which was released in the United States in 1985; and to play *Tetris*, the second-best game on IGN's Top 100 Games of All Time, after the 1989 launch of the handheld Nintendo Game Boy (IGN Entertainment, 2009). Listening to music became more portable with the Sony Walkman, and audiocassette tapes lost ground to compact discs (CDs), which were the music industry's first foray into digital music recordings.

1990s

The 1990s began in political and social turmoil with the Persian Gulf War and the AIDS epidemic in Africa. As the decade progressed, teens began to focus on technological advancements that helped to shape the world today. Cellular phones, pagers, fax machines, the personal computer, and the Internet suddenly allowed people many more forms of instant communication, creating the Digital Age. Instead of using the television as the sole entryway for entertainment and information, people started using the World Wide Web, launched to the public in 1991. Companies turned to the Internet for advertising and product placement, targeting teens because they were estimated to spend $122 billion of their own and their parents' money each year on media-related products such as CDs and movie theater tickets (Kallen, 1999). Entertainment such as television, music, movies, and sports were the primary focus for these technology-connected teens.

More television programming was targeted toward teen viewers than ever before. Teens watched *Sabrina the Teenage Witch*, *Boy Meets World*, *Dawson's Creek*, *Buffy the Vampire Slayer*, and *The Simpsons*. Merchandise based on hot television shows blanketed the market. Animated programs geared toward adults became a fad and would sometimes create huge controversy. For example, *Beavis and Butt-head*, a cartoon on MTV, was considered responsible by some critics for a boy burning down his family's mobile home (The People History, 2009). The movie *Titanic* was the highest grossing movie worldwide, and the sixth highest grossing movie, adjusted for ticket price inflation (Box Office Mojo, 2009a,b). Professional baseball and football enjoyed huge audiences. One of the decade's most popular star athletes was professional basketball player Michael Jordan, who was paid $30 million by the Chicago Bulls in 1997.

MTV reached 50 million American homes by 1990; in 1989 it had debuted the show *Unplugged*, where artists played songs acoustically. In 1993, Nirvana made an appearance on the show, which was one of the last public performances by lead singer Kurt Cobain before his unexpected death in April 1994. Nirvana is considered one of the groups that put grunge, the 1990s' biggest new rock trend, on the map. Pearl Jam and Soundgarden continued the grunge trend, with teen fans dressing in Doc Martens and flannel shirts. From grunge came alternative rock, with Smashing Pumpkins as one of the lead bands of the genre. All-female musical groups showed their popularity at Lilith Fair from 1997 through 1999, and hip-hop and rap music reached the top of record charts. Among the most famous rappers of the decade were Tupac Shakur, Dr. Dre, and Snoop Doggy Dogg.

2000 to the Present

The advent of tween popular culture can be roughly pinned down to the end of the 1990s, when Britney Spears, Justin Timberlake, and Christina Aguilera hit headliner status. The three pop and rock artists were Disney Mouseketeers only a few years before they became pop icons. In 1999, Spears won the American Music Award for best pop artist, changing the music scene, as well as fashion, for girls ages eight to 13. Tween girls began dressing in schoolgirl-plaid skirts and halter tops to match her style, practicing hip-hop dance moves, and looking to emulate other youthful and bold female icons.

Rolling Stone magazine called this "teen pop" time the "all Britney, all the time" era (Carlson, 2006).

Fast forward to today, where Disney-made icons are still cornering the tween market. A recent endeavor by Disney was *High School Musical*, a made-for-television movie that aired on January 20, 2006. The *High School Musical* phenomenon, a musical trilogy with two made-for-television movies and one feature-length film, has reinforced the buying power of tweens. The original CD was the biggest selling disc in the United States in 2006, with 3.72 million copies sold (Brock, 2007). The soundtrack went into the Guinness World Records in 2007 for having nine songs on the Billboard Singles Chart, the most from a single CD ever (Walt Disney Television, 2006). William Strauss and Neil Howe (2006), coauthors of *Millennials and the Pop Culture*, observed the effect of *High School Musical*, including a rebirth in youth theater around the world. YouTube videos have popped up with kids reenacting the dances and dialogue from the movies. Disney Theatricals licensed more than 800 amateur productions around the country (Brock, 2007). Karaoke and acting have seen a resurgence in popularity with younger kids, creating a great avenue for program development at the library.

Other tween pop sensations like Miley Cyrus and Raven-Symoné, one of the Cheetah Girls, have sprung from the "Disney tween machine." "Disney has written the blueprint for the tween market," says Billy Johnson Jr., senior program director at Yahoo! Music. "What is so genius about what Disney does is that they have a machine that maximizes the full extent of the talent of their stars. They can showcase their acting on their television shows. They can exploit their singing abilities on their radio stations and record labels. The Jonas Brothers are an even better success story" (Ollison, 2008). The tween pop culture scene seems to have very high turnover, though, so it is key for librarians to stay up on which youthful stars are currently ruling the Disney roost.

To go along with these pop stars and teen idols, marketing companies have targeted tweens in a big way, with everything from pillows to stickers to board games branded with the names and images of tweens' favorite musical artists. Research in 2006 showed that tweens spend between $38 billion and $59 billion a year of their own and their parents' money on consumer goods (Booth, 2006). Recent research shows that even in these tough economic times, tweens are spending $43 billion a year and have influence on such purchases as cell phones, vacations, and even cars (Research and Markets, 2009). "What's happened is there's now media outlets oriented to kids, like Nickelodeon and Radio Disney. In the old days, we maybe had a couple cable channels, MTV and no Internet," says Cliff Chenfeld, co-owner of KidzBop (Booth, 2006). Radio Disney is one company that has taken advantage of the fact that parents are the ones driving their kids around. Jennifer Kobashi, Radio Disney director of brand marketing, said, "We know that for every three kids listening to us, we've got about one mom. We let advertisers know our station is for moms and kids in a car as they're driving. We're the last medium and the last message they hear before they step out to make that purchase" (Booth, 2006). So the radio station has advertisements for DVDs and games but also for minivans and pharmaceuticals because "10-year-olds don't drive" (Booth, 2006).

While much of tween popular culture is family friendly and even enjoyed by parents, teens, as usual, are more interested in edgier content. Teen and tween popular culture in the 2000s was dominated by reality television and interactive video gaming, giving the average teen or youth a chance at fame and fortune. The idea that the typical teen can rise to stardom by showing up on a television show has become commonplace in U.S. society. Shows like MTV's *MADE*, *The Real World*, *Laguna Beach: The Real Orange County*, and *The Hills* have propelled participants into national fame. The Nintendo Wii video gaming console introduced active gaming in 2006, where the wireless controller can be used as a tennis racket, a baseball bat, a steering wheel, and in a host of other functions. *Guitar Hero* and *Rock Band* also joined the electronic market, allowing teens to "rock out" on video gaming controllers.

Tweens are also watching the more skill-based reality television shows, such as *Dancing with the Stars*, *American Idol*, and *America's Got Talent*, which focus more on showcasing talent. The Ninetendo Wii, *Guitar Hero*, and *Rock Band* are also favorites of tweens, but Pokémon on the handheld Nintendo DS console has also become a big hit. Based on the show and graphic novels, *Pokémon Red and Blue* came out in the United States for the Game Boy in September 1998. The franchise has grown over the years to create further generations of Pokémon and many more games. Learning and partaking in aspects of Japanese culture has become a fad for both teens and tweens, making anime, manga, and Japanese candy and toys very popular.

Literature has also had a profound effect on teens and tweens, and in the adult communities centered around entertainment. The *Harry Potter* series of books by J.K. Rowling held the top three slots of the *New York Times* adult best-seller list for a year (Smith, 2000). Finally in 2000, the *New York Times* created a children's best-seller list to separate them from—and remove them from competition with— books on the adult list. This change is an example of how much impact teen and tween interests are having on adult popular culture, as adults are fans of the series as well. The *Twilight* saga, a collection of four novels by Stephenie Meyer, is another phenomenon that has created popular interest in vampire books, movies, and television for all age groups. *Twilight*, the first novel of the series, was published as young adult literature in 2005; yet it was the top-selling title in 2008, with its first two sequels as the number-two and number-three best-selling titles (*USA Today*, 2009). Teens and tweens, as well as adults, have latched onto the *Harry Potter* and *Twilight* phenomena, showing how much literature can impact a society, similar to the way Harper Lee's *To Kill a Mockingbird* and Joseph Heller's *Catch-22* did in the 1960s.

Technology has become a given for communication. Most Americans own or have access to cellular phones and personal computers. Music is listened to on MP3 players. Social networking has become a way to stay connected to people in all aspects of one's life, through Facebook, MySpace, and Twitter. Information is available in an instant with iPhones and laptops, creating a more informed teen society, many of whom get their news through two popular satirical programs on Comedy Central: *The Daily Show with Jon Stewart* and *The Colbert Report*, starring Stephen Colbert.

Library Services to Tweens

What can we learn from this research to help create services and programs for tweens? Well, it is true that ten-year-olds cannot get themselves to the library on their own unless they can walk or bike. Library services and programs targeted to this age group must cater to and attract the interests of parents as well as kids. Fads and icons are heavily based on the entertainment industry's marketing efforts, so it's crucial to keep abreast of upcoming and new trends. Staying current on the most popular entertainers is very important but can be difficult to do, as their popularity seems to come and go overnight.

Library Services to Teens

As always, library services will become applicable to a teenager's life if he or she feels the establishment has his or her interests in mind. Just as a program on performance art would have appealed to teens in the 1960s, librarians should be aware of teen interests right now, such as using technology to alter photographs, creating vampire-themed book groups, or holding a "Library Idol" to discover the hidden talent among community teens.

References

Booth, William. 2006. "In the Concert Hall, It Smells Like Tween Spirit: Radio Disney Nurtures, and Taps Into, Emerging Fan Base." *Washington Post*, August 6. http://www.washingtonpost.com/wp-dyn/content/article/2006/08/04/AR2006080400223.html.

Box Office Mojo. 2009a. "All Time Box Office: Adjusted for Ticket Price Inflation." Box Office Mojo/IMDb.com. Accessed August 14. http://boxofficemojo.com/alltime/adjusted.htm.

Box Office Mojo. 2009b. "All Time Box Office: Worldwide Grosses." Box Office Mojo/IMDb.com. Accessed August 14. http://boxofficemojo.com/alltime/world/.

Brock, Wendell. 2007. "Tween Appeal and Geeky Clean: Disney's Cultural Phenomenon Stage Production 'High School Musical' Opens This Weekend at the Fox." *The Atlanta Journal-Constitution*, January 13: A1.

Carlson, Peter. 2006. "How Does It Feel?" *Washington Post*. May 4. http://www .washingtonpost.com/wp-dyn/content/article/2006/05/03/AR2006050302531 .html.

Duden, Jane. 1989. *1950s: Timelines*. New York: Crestwood House.

Goodstein, Anastasia. 2007. *Totally Wired: What Teens and Tweens Are* Really *Doing Online*. New York: St. Martin's Griffin.

Holland, Gini. 1999. *A Cultural History of the United States Through the Decades: The 1960s*. San Diego: Lucent Books.

IGN Entertainment. 2009. "IGN's Top 100 Games of All Time." IGN Entertainment. Accessed September 7. http://top100.ign.com/2007/ign_top_game_2.html.

Kallen, Stuart A. 1999. *A Cultural History of the United States Through the Decades: The 1990s*. San Diego: Lucent Books.

Ollison, Rashod D. 2008. "Disney Has Recipe for Tween Pop: As a Hot Act Cools, New One Warms Up." *Baltimore Sun*, July 20. http://articles.baltimoresun.com/ 2008-07-20/news/0807190096_1_jonas-brothers-hannah-montana-tween-pop.

Oxford English Dictionary. 2010. "Popular Culture." Oxford University Press, June. Accessed August 25. http://dictionary.oed.com.

PBS. 2005. "The Sixties: The Years That Shaped a Generation." Oregon Public Broadcasting. http://www.pbs.org/opb/thesixties/topics/culture/index.html.

The People History. 2009. "The People History: 1990s." The People History. Accessed September 7. http://www.thepeoplehistory.com/1990s.html.

Research and Markets. 2009. "Tween Spending and Influence." *Business Wire*. March 10. http://www.reuters.com/article/pressRelease/idUS145715+10-Mar-2009+BW20090310.

Smith, Dinitia. 2000. "The *Times* Plans a Children's Best-Seller List." *New York Times*, June 24. http://www.nytimes.com/2000/06/24/books/the-times-plans-a-children-s-best-seller-list.html.

Stewart, Gail B. 1999. *A Cultural History of the United States Through the Decades: The 1970s*. San Diego: Lucent Books.

Strauss, William and Neil Howe. 2006. *Millennials and the Pop Culture*. Great Falls, VA: LifeCourse Associates.

USA Today. 2009. "The Top 100 Books of 2008." USA Today, November 5. http:// www.usatoday.com/life/books/news/2009-01-14-top-100-titles_N.htm.

Walt Disney Television. 2006. "*High School Musical* Receives Its European Premiere in London." Walt Disney Television, September 10. http://www .waltdisneytelevision.com/cms_res/pressoffice/pressreleases/HSM_premiere_ 10092006.pdf.

Chapter 2

"Here It Is, Your Moment of Zen": Defining Create, Relate, & Pop

It's hoped that this book will provide new ways to view the programs you already offer, as well as inspiration to try a new approach. You may already have a cadre of great programming that could simply use a more hands-on or participatory element to make it fresh. Let's explore the three aspects of this approach: *Create*, *Relate*, and *Pop*.

Create

Create is at the heart of what Web 2.0 and participatory culture are all about. Tweens and teens of today are comfortable with technology, using message boards to express their opinions; maintaining personal profiles of themselves and their world on MySpace, Facebook, and other equivalent social networking sites; posting videos of themselves on YouTube; reading their friends' LiveJournal accounts; posting their artwork on deviantART.com; and adding tags everywhere! Tags allow users to define how they search for things and help identify what is important to them. The invitation to express themselves has been extended to today's young people, and they have answered the call. Present-day tweens and teens are so enmeshed in this culture that most cannot imagine a time when putting everything about yourself online for the world to see was not always an option.

Create has many meanings and in a library setting can be manifested in countless ways. You may recognize that this is simply a different way to frame youth participation. Youth participation is the core of the "create" part of this philosophy. *Create* is about users creating content; therefore, since tweens and teens are the users, their participation in hands-on experiences—from helping to plan programs to assisting younger children at programs—will result in investment and buy-in from the users and ultimately lead to a more successful and supported program or service.

Create Access

Does your library make it easy for a teen to get a library card? Do you offer "fine forgiveness" opportunities or the chance to work off fines? Do you have open and easy Internet access policies? Do you allow nonresidents to attend programs or participate in contests? Thinking about access and the various ways it manifests itself in your library is key.

Libraries as public places have many reasons to have policies in place, but when was the last time you took a look at those policies and thought about how they relate to open access for all users? Many teens may have gotten their first library card when they were very young, and over the years books were lost and fines mounted. Maybe a sibling or even a parent used the card and ran it up with lost materials. Now the cardholder is 13 and has $54 in fines and a parent that either cannot or will not help pay them off, creating one big whopping obstacle for the teen who might still be interested in checking out materials.

Maybe a teen has lost his or her card. Does your library require individuals to show their cards to get online? Do they have to have a card to attend programs? How easy is it to get a replacement card? Often you will find that a reluctance to use the library, or even open hostility toward it, is based on these barriers enforced in library policies. Think about the various ways you can make access easier for teens and consider changing access points like these.

- Allow young people to get a card without the signature of a parent or guardian. There are many fiscal reasons to require this step in a library registration process, but for many young people this is enough of an obstacle to prevent even the most basic entry into the library. The San Antonio Public Library has implemented this policy with great success and has consequently engaged many more youth by making it easier to use the library. The Moorpark City Library allows teens to acquire a library card with certain restrictions when a guardian is not present. Under Moorpark's policy, the teen can check out two books on a one-time-use card. The policy was put in place for teens that need research materials for school and do not have a parent with them to sign for the card. Once the teen has the one-time-use card, his or her guardian needs only to stop by the library, show a picture ID, and sign the library card application so the teen can have full access to library privileges. The process should take only a few minutes, making it easy on busy parents and getting the teen's foot in the door for a library card. The official policy verbiage is shown in Figure 2.1.
- Offer opportunities for young people to volunteer and "work off" overdue fines. Offer "fine forgiveness" coupons as incentives for summer programs or at events. Get creative about amnesty days, and have teens bring in canned goods

---

Figure 2.1. Sample Policy: Restricted Temporary Library Cards for Teenagers without Parental Signature

Patrons 12 years of age through 17 years of age are classified as teenagers in this policy. Teenagers do not need a parent's or legal guardian's signature to get a restricted, temporary, one-time-use card; however, a parent or legal guardian must sign the application in person, in the presence of Library staff, for the teenager to obtain their permanent card, which allows continued checkout of material, use of the public computers, and the ability to check out videos or DVDs. In order to obtain a temporary, one-time-use card, the teenager must be a Moorpark resident or attend a Moorpark School. To obtain their temporary card, the teenager must present a picture ID verifying residency or attendance at a Moorpark School. The temporary, one-time-use card allows teenagers to check out two written material items only. Library staff will provide the teenager with a letter for their parent or guardian which explains the temporary card.

Source: Moorpark City Council, 2010. City Council Policies Resolution 2010-1959.

---

for donation to local food banks in exchange for removing fines from their accounts. Whatever you end up doing, take the time to think about fines and how you can remove this barrier that keeps teens from coming through your doors.

- Remove the restriction of requiring a library card to use the computers, attend programs, or volunteer. Whatever the rationale for needing a library card for these activities, look at your policies and view them through the lens of providing open access to young people. Are the policies helping or hurting teen library patrons?

- Constantly and regularly advertise and remind teenagers that the library is a *free* service. Librarians know that libraries are free, but in the modern world this is a very difficult concept for people to grasp. When you hand out your program brochures or visit a school to promote summer reading, always be sure to emphasize the *free* aspect of the library. Culturally, some groups have no experience with free access in their home communities, so this message is an important part of educating users about what the library has to offer. Think about how often a teen runs home to describe all of the awesome stuff the library does— only to be met with parental skepticism about the hidden costs. Outreach is the only way to get the word out about the library's wealth of no-cost services.

Create Opportunities

Libraries are already very good at creating opportunities! Library missions revolve around providing education and recreational support. The fundamental role of libraries is usually to connect users with what they need; therefore, creating opportunities is the cornerstone of the library services model. That being said, take it a step further and think about how your programs and services can help expose young people to new ideas, cultures, philosophies, and experiences. Think about how to market or, if you already do, how to *continually* market your basic services to teens. Do you reinforce how much information they have access to and that it is free?

Whether you create an opportunity by providing programs on applying to college, getting a job, or obtaining financial aid for education, you must look at your programs as opportunities to expose teens to something new. Think about all of the different ways your programming exposes young people to ideas, careers, and ways of life that they never knew existed or considered exploring. Whether it is having a local chef discuss cooking and how to make it a career or a graphic novelist who opens the door for a teen to consider his or her art as a viable future, you are creating opportunities through education and validation. While you surely want to keep your community profile in mind, it is also good to consider exposing your community to something new.

Consider how video game tournaments can be used with this model. When a teen competes against other teens and wins a tournament due to his finely honed skills and obsession with, for example, an interactive game like *Rock Band*, you are creating an opportunity. You are creating an opportunity for that teen to feel good about himself and rewarded for something that is important to him. For some teens, this is a chance they may never before have encountered. School revolves around academics and sports, and there is rarely a year-end newsletter that will express how great Timmy is at *Rock Band*. However, *Rock Band* is important to Timmy, and the library video game tournament offers him something he's never had: an opportunity to feel good about a skill and enjoyable activity that is not necessarily "important" or noteworthy in the realm of real-world success.

Your collections create opportunities for teens to understand themselves better, as well as develop empathy for people whose lives are very different from their own. Your teen fiction collection creates the opportunity for teens to escape from their daily lives and peek into the lives of others. A nonfiction collection opens up the entire world to young people. They can learn how to repair a car, survive a shark attack, or plan a road trip. Audiovisual (AV) collections allow young people to see movies for free, listen to new music, or try out a new video game before spending their own hard-earned part-time job wages or allowance money.

Create Something

"*Create Something*" is the most basic and easy-to-apply aspect of *Create* in a library setting. Arts and crafts programs are often the cornerstone of library programs for young people, so this is an easy place to dive into the creation model.

Think about how structured most young people's lives are and how often their creativity is stifled or directed with such tight parameters that expression is rarely part of the goal. Libraries create access and opportunities for teens to create art, stories, videos, machines, fashion, and experiences in ways that are seldom encouraged in their day-to-day life.

Have you ever seen little kids who go nuts with glue and glitter because it is often the only time they are allowed to use these items with abandon? The same is often true for older kids. Programs that provide all of the supplies and allow the tweens or teens to make anything they want and take it home feeling good about the freedom of expression they experienced are one of the best gifts that libraries have to offer.

When a teen creates a Claymation puppet to take home or makes a gift for her mother or a pair of earrings for herself, it has value that cannot be measured. Think about teens who walk into the library and see 100 rolls of duct tape in 45 colors; come to a pizza-making program with tables covered in toppings; or attend a Halloween gingerbread event that has bowls filled with candy as far as the eye can see—and the only direction or expectation is that they can make anything they want. This is what *Create Something* is about: engaging curiosity, motivating self-expression, and building self-esteem.

Relate

Relate is often the hardest part of serving young people. Staying current on pop culture is the key to making relating easier. If you aren't familiar with the movies, TV, music, and websites that teens are into, it will make it impossible to plan relevant programs and harder to serve them as a whole.

Relate is when tweens come to the reference desk asking about Pokémon and, although you may not be able to spell it correctly, at least you know what they are talking about. Relating is when you are doing a book talk and can reference a currently popular movie or cartoon to make the connection for reluctant readers. Relating is when a cultural icon like Michael Jackson dies and you can talk to a tween who is asking for his music about how Jackson's music was a part of your own youth. Relating is about making connections and meeting young people where they are at, based on interests, maturity level, and location.

Relate Experiences

Whether it is an anecdote about your experience with Lego when you were a kid to kick off a Lego event or a conversation at the reference desk about soccer and how you used to play defense, relating experiences with young people should be a regular part of your job. Using pop culture as a reference point with young people makes it easier to meet their information needs and provide fun and relevant programs because you talk to your tweens and teens every day and know their interests.

Relating experiences is also one of the outcomes of offering diverse and experience-based programs. From the web-comic author to the martial arts enthusiast or the reality TV star, the presenters for these programs allow young people to learn about the experiences of other people and open them up to worlds that they may never have known existed. These real-life experiences teach teens empathy for others and also help form their views on lifestyle and freedom of choice. Some young people are not allowed much free choice in their lives, so learning about diverse experiences opens up options and opportunities that they may never have considered. By offering teens the opportunity to interact with your presenters and ask questions, you are empowering young people to be part of the world around them.

Make Connections

Look at using pop culture as an opportunity to connect with your tweens and teens in a meaningful way that will help you plan meaningful programs and services. At the reference desk, on the floor, or during a program, talk to young people and find out why Selena Gomez is so funny, why Pixar makes the best animated movies, or why Pokémon is so important to them. Chances are many tweens and teens have never been asked to explain their obsessions, and most will talk your ear off when given the chance.

Find out if the group of girls who sit and draw manga in your teen area all day would like to help teach a manga drawing class for younger kids. Ask the group of teens gathered around the Internet stations if there are any particular websites or software programs the library could teach classes about or have a program on that would be of interest to them.

The same tweens and teens you take the time to relate to may also end up being the ones who feel comfortable enough to ask for help finding books on GLBTQ (gay, lesbian, bisexual, transgender, questioning) topics or who have so enjoyed volunteering at the library that they feel comfortable enough to ask you to be a reference for their first job. Making connections is what youth services is all about.

Be Relevant

The relevance of libraries to young people, or lack thereof, is the most important issue facing youth services in libraries today. It is no longer acceptable to be passive about whether the library is relevant to users or continue to hold tried-and-true library programs without introducing new audiences to what the library has to offer. Are all members of your community being served by the library? If your library is quiet, you are doing it wrong. To be truly relevant to your community, the library should have permanent loud spaces, as well as regular, planned opportunities to be loud and involved. Silence is still a requirement in some areas of the library, but a library with 100 percent quiet at all times is an irrelevant library.

Some young people are lucky enough to have parents and families who embrace and participate in their interests. Some parents may want to engage on a topic but do not have enough information to get involved. The library can help both parents and children by offering collections and events to engage and educate both on different levels. Sometimes just having a conversation with parents about manga (or Justin Bieber, iCards, Silly Bandz, etc.) can help ease any worries they may have had about something foreign seeming or difficult to comprehend; sometimes that brief visit can give them perspective to allow them to talk to their children about their interests in new ways. The library is in a unique position to engage young people by providing collections and programs related to their recreational interests while also educating parents about the roles pop culture plays in their kids' lives from a neutral, nonprofit viewpoint. By using pop culture as an influence in different aspects of the library, the library can remain relevant to the young person and the parent at the same time.

Pop

Pop is the fun part of subscribing to this philosophy of programming and services. *Pop* is the flexible, the nimble, and the spontaneous approach to developing services, collections, and programs. *Pop* is now and what tweens and teens spend their lives obsessing about when they are not in school, involved in extracurriculars, or at home being a part of the family. "Popular" can mean "for the masses," but it can also apply to the underground, indie culture, fanzines, and more. "Popular" does not have to mean "for the majority." To truly engage the most teens in your community, you will need to go beyond the top 20 music video countdown. Look for the niche, fan, and cult interests in your community. Demonstrating relevance to more interests will keep teens coming back and looking for more of your offerings. With more than 300 million people in the United States, our "subgroups" are not small anymore and should not be ignored.

Be Current

Pop is what tweens and teens are interested in *now*. It means having books about the latest Pixar animated movie on the shelves before the movie hits theaters. *Pop* means that you weed your teen paperback series collection often enough that today's adult does not find their favorite TV shows among your collection. *Pop* means having a MySpace page for your library *before* teens start leaving in droves for a new social networking site. Your collections and your programs must reflect what your young people are into today, not yesterday, and not last year. It is true that trends can last over time and some things remain "in" for longer cycles. However, there should be a percentage of your collections and your programs that consistently reflect aspects of pop culture right now.

Staying current is either a chore or a delight, depending on your perspective, but staying current is a must. If you are a pop culture addict, you do not need any advice on how to keep up with what's hot. If you find it tough to keep up, track down the people in your life who consume pop culture (tweens, teens, co-workers, friends, etc.) and pick their brains! Getting the word from the fan's mouth is usually better than reading an article about it.

Some libraries have implemented "trend-spotting" committees that spend time identifying what the current hot topics and next best things may be, and then determining whether resources should be allocated in those directions. This system can be applied to collection development as well as programs and services. More important than the trend spotting itself is making sure that your policies and management allow for jumping on the bandwagon with certain interests. Bureaucracy may be your biggest obstacle to remaining current.

Be in Demand

With the recent economic downturn and the increased use of libraries in the past few years, libraries have not had to try hard to be in demand with patrons. With tighter budgets, many libraries are in demand without even trying because they have ordered only one copy of a new DVD instead of the ten copies they used to acquire. With tighter staffing levels, there may be fewer programs, which may cause you yourself to be in very high demand. We encourage you to think about your library services differently, and, ideally, by the time this book is in your hands libraries may be doing better budgetwise.

Think about being in demand as being the most popular kid in school. Be in demand because you are cool, your programs are fun, and you have a really popular graphic novel collection. Try to be in demand to the kids who think they are too cool for everything. To be in demand in this way is to anticipate the area where tweens and teens think you will get it wrong. Sometimes not having *Dance Dance Revolution* (*DDR*) is better than buying the cheapest pads around. If you are trying to get older teens involved, do not censor them at a poetry slam or have excessive rules about behavior at video game tournaments. Being in demand with teens means you are doing it right.

Having a low attendance at a certain program is to be expected in any library. Taking chances with your programs means that sometimes there will be a dud. Bad weather, a big school sports game at the same time, or a holiday you forgot about when you planned the event—all of these are reasons for occasional low attendance at a program. Nevertheless, working toward attracting a full group of kids should always be your goal. Sometimes this means not programming in certain areas if you consistently get low numbers. At the minimum you should be evaluating your low-attended events and thinking about what could be changed or how the marketing can be tweaked. Make it your goal to have at least a few events each season where you pack the house with lots of kids.

If you can get your tweens and teens to talk about your events and tell other kids about it, you know that you are in demand. Details on strategies for using word-of-mouth marketing and viral tricks are discussed in Chapter 3.

Have Fun

Being flexible and less rule oriented is at the heart of this attitude. Your staff should be having as much fun as the young people they serve. Staff at all levels should be on board with the idea of the library's need to serve tweens and teens.

Having fun means having a sense of humor about what you do and how you do it. Plan programs that are open-ended and can be adapted to the needs of all sorts of young people. Focus on providing structure and not creating obstacles. Do not worry about how the program turns out in the end, and ask yourself, *Did they have fun while they did it?* You often hear librarians trying to figure out how to get their teen advisory teens on task or struggle with the outcomes-based assessment of that type of program. As long as the teens are having fun and you are getting some useful feedback and involvement from them, that is usually all that should be expected.

Having fun means not worrying about whether the kids are reading everything they say they are during summer reading. The library is great at supporting the educational needs of its community, so having fun means focusing on recreation. Public libraries have the luxury of not being school. Use the freedom you have to embrace the full range of interests of your users.

Conclusion

Subscribing to the service model of using popular culture to create services and programs for teens and tweens allows librarians to relate more closely with their community and, therefore, make the library a more comfortable, relevant place to be. Be creative and bold with programming ideas, getting feedback from teens along the way. Trust your teens to tell you about their interests. Most of all, have fun while serving the informational and recreational needs of a community in this unique and fresh way.

Reference

Moorpark City Council. 2010. "Moorpark City Library Circulation Policy." Moorpark City Library, April 5. http://www.moorparklibrary.org/circulation.asp.

Chapter 3

"OMG!": Targeting Populations, Advertising, and Promotion

Introduction

Marketing is often the first term used to describe "getting the word out" about library events, but in actuality the correct term for this activity is *promotion*. Marketing in its purist form should happen at the highest levels of the library, from writing a mission statement to creating a strategic plan. True marketing involves a variety of facets, such as those explained in E. Jerome McCarthy's Product, Price, Promotion, and Place model (Perreault, Cannon, and McCarthy, 2010), which has become a standard for the marketing industry. In its simplest terms, this theory can be reduced to four questions:

- What product are we going to produce?
- What should we charge for the product?
- How will the product be distributed?
- How are we going to promote and sell this product?

This chapter does not include a formal description of marketing and promotion. Entire books have been written on marketing to libraries, such as Neal-Schuman's *Library Marketing That Works!* by Suzanne Walters (2004). Ideally, a true, robust marketing campaign will be initiated from the top of the organization and involve the entire library and all of its stakeholders, with marketing for young people one portion of the larger overall marketing plan. For this book's purposes, this chapter focuses solely on the "branding" of your tween or teen services (a small part of determining "what" your product is) and the promotion and advertising needed to let potential users know about your product (tween/teen collections, events at the library). The chapter explores various types of marketing: things that can be done very inexpensively or with some cash to spend. You may find that you are already doing some of these things but may need to tweak how you do them or find a more targeted approach. You will learn how to utilize the help of your teens to market your programs and techniques to market to specific niche populations.

Create: Branding Your Teen and Tween Services

It is not enough to just plan great programs and services for teens. Once you have done this work, it is imperative that you also work out how the services will be branded and promoted to the community. In its simplest form, a brand can be a name, a logo, a slogan, or a sign. A well-branded product makes it easy for users to refer to it by name and recommend it to others and also encourages users to become fans and followers of the brand. One of the biggest mistakes libraries make is assuming everyone knows how great the library is. Another mistake is thinking that simply advertising programs inside the library to those who already use it is enough to attract attendees. It is not. Being truly dedicated to changing the service model and reaching out to teens and tweens with these ideas means working to identify the population not being reached with current advertising and finding out how these potential users hear about things in the community and in the marketplace at large. The teen and tween audience is constantly targeted with advertising; therefore, promoting services to these age groups demands a more savvy and targeted plan. Using pop culture as your baseline means using mainstream for-profit tricks to promote your services. You want teens and tweens to align your programs within the framework in which they are used to consuming other cultural content. Part of any branding and promotion plan means meeting them where they are, using techniques and tricks with which they are familiar.

Let's get started! Start with branding your teen services first, and then think about how to separate your tween services from your regular children's services next. You are "selling" the library as a product, which is often difficult to stamp with any kind of "cool" factor. Coming up with a separate brand for teen services is a step toward changing the image of your services and creating the opportunity for your teens to feel a sense of ownership and investment in the library. A distinct and separate brand accomplishes several things:

- It lets the teens know that you are serious about serving them as a distinct and special group. Teens respond to things they perceive to be specifically designed for them. It lets them know that you recognize that they are not children, nor are they "stodgy" adults either.
- It acknowledges that your teens are different from other library patrons and should be treated differently and uniquely from others who use the library.

- Coming up with a brand separate from the general library brand makes it easier for teens to buy into it without feeling tainted with the potential uncool nature of being a "library teen."
- It creates a recognizable identity for your teens to look for once they know about the brand and want to start looking for the next program, event, or service that's designed just for them. Teens will be able to easily identify the events and services for them from within a webpage, a rack of brochures, or other marketing pieces that may contain multiple events and programs that target other members of your community. The brand allows them to cut through the clutter of your other services and quickly find the teen-centered items.
- Teens understand branding because it is modeled from the consumer culture that they know well. Teens are brand-conscious and therefore respond to direct marketing.
- It creates the opportunity to take the high-quality reputation that libraries have and combine it with a consumer-marketing model which teens respond to and which parents will be more likely to trust.

Once you are committed to creating a distinct teen brand it's important to *not* include the term *library* anywhere in the shorthand brand you're trying to create. Ask most any teen walking down the street or walking in the halls of school what the library means to them, and you will undoubtly hear responses like *uncool, frumpy, quiet, sshhh, mean librarians, no good books, I hate to read,* and surely some other choice comments. Consider the ways that movies, television shows, and the media in general portray libraries and librarians. In 2002's *Star Wars: Attack of the Clones,* future librarians have gray buns and a bad attitude. Sadly, even an episode of *Glee* featured an old lady librarian (even though she did have a sense of humor). Rare exceptions like Giles, the librarian on *Buffy the Vampire Slayer,* or the librarian cult favorite movie *Party Girl* can be found, but they are not necessarily geared toward teens, so the stereotypes remain.

A library that has worked hard to brand its teen services is the Ann Arbor District Library (AADL) in Ann Arbor, Michigan. AADL initially created AXIS as the name of its teen programming brochure, but it has become the shorthand reference to all teen services at the library. AXIS was chosen for several reasons:

- The alliteration of the name goes with Ann Arbor and AADL.
- It is short and evocative.
- It means the center of things or where things meet (like the library).
- AXIS sounds very similar to "access," and the ultimate goal of promoting to teens is to create more access.

The AXIS brochure does say "Stuff for Teens" and "Ann Arbor District Library" on the brochure itself, but the specially created marketing giveaways, like the popular rubber bracelets and custom containers of mints, have only "AXIS" with the axis.aadl.org website address printed on them. Teens knew that they received the item from the library, of course, but wearing the bracelet or otherwise referring to AXIS does not scream out "library teen!" If parents or others want to know what AXIS is and type in the website address, they would quickly realize it is part of the library.

In Washington, the Sno-Isle library system has branded their services as "Sno-Isle Teens: Infamous for Information" (see Figure 3.1). While this takes a slightly more traditional approach, it still does not include the word *library* in the branding and also has a great catch phrase attached to it for increased memorability. Hats and T-shirts have been made to promote the library in a covert way, without the word *library* stenciled on the item (see Figure 3.2).

Branding your services can be as simple as holding a contest and allowing teens to generate a name or even a logo for your brand. Then either pick one of their suggestions or vet the choices and then allow teens to vote. If there is funding, work with a graphic designer or graphic design firm to help brand your teen services. Coming up with an identifiable logo should be the minimum you do to create a brand. A logo can be used on print, digital, and ephemeral pieces, and even on signs within your teen space. If your logo is flexible enough it can be made to feel fresh with the use of different colors, themes, or seasons, depending on how you generally market the library. The AXIS logo incorporates spray paint designs which appear fresh and new, and can easily be redone with different colors each time a new brochure is created. This allows something relatively static to be dynamic in terms of the passage of time. Once your logo and brand are created, determine how you will use it on print materials (see Figure 3.3).

If you do not already do a program brochure or flyers for events, consider creating these pieces in order to showcase your services all in one place. Over time teens will begin to look for the brand and eagerly await the next brochure to find out about events.

Relate: Identifying Your Teens and Tweens

Before you embark on any new marketing campaign or services, you must identify who your teens are and what types of programs will be of interest to them. Determining audience is crucial in order to customize your promotion strategy. Pop culture is not "one size fits all," so determine the makeup of the teen crowds in your community and what slices of the cultural pie to focus on. The community may be full of country-music-loving NASCAR enthusiasts or hip-hop and R&B fans. Clearly, advertising and programs for these two audiences would be very different. Using teen input during the planning process of such a marketing campaign is crucial.

Figure 3.1. Sno-Isle Libraries Teen Logo

Source: © Sno-Isle Libraries.

Figure 3.2. Sno-Isle Teens Hat

Source: © Sno-Isle Libraries.

Figure 3.3. AXIS Logo from the Ann Arbor District Library

Maybe your library has already done community analysis, but did it include teens in the process? Seek out and use U.S. Census information and community data gathered by your local city hall or chamber of commerce. These numbers are a good starting point, but they will not give you everything you need to properly advertise and program for your teens. What you really want to determine is what your teens are interested in and what they like to do with their spare time. If your library has a Teen Advisory Board (TAB), that will also be a great help. But since most TAB teens are already "library teens" you will not necessarily gather the information you need to get the rest of your community's teens into the library. All librarians who serve teens know that on some level there are people on the library's staff who would not be upset if only quiet, studious library teens used the library. But we want the loud, jumping, excited teens too. We want all the teens!

The best and easiest way to get good information from teens about their interests is to create a comprehensive survey. Two example surveys can be found in this chapter (see Figure 3.4 and Figure 3.5). These surveys can easily be administered on paper as well as digitally. If you decide to create a digital version of your survey, there are many free survey services out there and reputable survey sites like SurveyMonkey (http://www.surveymonkey.com) that you can use to create it. These sites will do all of the software development for creating the survey and collecting the results. If you have programmers in your IT department, then a survey can be created in house to completely meet your needs. Digitally administered surveys can be added to your website for teens to fill out at their leisure or can be occasionally mailed to an e-mail list. Be sure you allow patrons to opt in to this list so you do not spam all your patrons. A digital survey will make compiling the results a bit easier if you are collecting lots of data.

Paper surveys are the easiest to use on the fly and are obviously the cheapest option available. Bring copies with you on routine school visits or ask teens at programs to fill them out. Also consider bringing them every time you visit outside the library where teens will be. With the cooperation of the schools, a larger-scale campaign could be conducted to survey as many of the teens as possible. Involving library media specialists (or library clerks or volunteers, where applicable) or English teachers are the most obvious choices, but you would certainly get more interesting and valuable information if you could ask art teachers or coaches to have their teens take the surveys, and therefore receive responses from different types of teens.

Surveys can be as long or short as you want them to be. If you want only to measure interest in one particular area, you might do a short survey targeted to teens interested in athletics. Ideally, with willing participants, it would be best to do a two-pronged questionnaire. The first portion would determine the teens' interests in movies, television, music, and recreation (see Figure 3.4). Be sure to ask about reading/watching/listening habits as well as questions about hair/style/identity. Use these results to establish the interests of your teens and inspire creative and unique programming ideas.

The second series of questions would measure the level of the teen interest in, involvement or lack thereof, and perceptions of the library (see Figure 3.5). This type of information is invaluable in determining what type of work you need to do in creating a advertising plan. Do you have a low number of teens with library cards? Do many of

Figure 3.4. Teen Patron Profile Survey

GRADE ___ 9 ___ 10 ___ 11 ___ 12   MALE ___   FEMALE ___
SCHOOL _____ TOWN where you live _____

Read for fun? YES ___   NO ___
If you read magazines, please list your favorites: _____
Prefer fiction or nonfiction? _____
Name the most recent book you read for pleasure and enjoyed: _____

Watch TV? YES ___   List your five favorite shows:

_____
_____
_____
_____
_____

            NO ___   Why not? _____

Own a cell phone? YES ___   NO ___   If yes, if you have a camera on your
phone, what do you do with the photos you take? _____

Listen to music?   YES ___   NO ___   If yes, name your five favorite bands/
performers:

_____
_____
_____
_____
_____

List up to five songs you recently downloaded or five CDs you are listening to right
now:

_____
_____
_____
_____
_____

Listen to radio?   YES ___   NO ___ If yes, then list your two favorite stations:

_____
_____

Have a job?   YES ___   If so, what do you do? _____
                 NO ___   If you don't have a job, what do you do for spending
                           money? _____

(Continued)

Figure 3.4 (Continued)

Other—if it's not listed above, tell us what you do in your free time!

Hang out with my friends	Spend time with family	Play paintball
Go to a movie	Volunteer	Go to the YMCA
Play a sport	Dance	Go to the Boys & Girls
Shop	Go to a museum	Club
Read a book of fiction	Read a nonfiction book	Go to a rec center
E-mail	Go to a club to see a live	Hang at a coffee shop
Listen to music	band/singer	Write fan fiction
Read online news	Sew/knit/needlepoint, etc.	Travel
Paint/draw/create	Dye/cut/braid my hair (or	Chat/IM
Go on a hike	someone else's hair)	Go to parties
Party	Talk on the phone	Collect things
Lift weights/work-out	Play video games	Text message
Read a magazine	Watch Japanese anime or	Watch TV
Play role-playing games	read manga	Read the newspaper
Eat in restaurants	Watch sports on TV	Do car-related activities

Describe your style:

punk	hip-hop	who cares
preppy	fashion-forward	black all the time, but not
sporty	retro	goth
goth	hippie	
clubber	T-shirt/jeans	

Other? _____

---

them have cards but also high fines? You might decide to do an amnesty day or offer "fine forgiveness" coupons at special events to get teens back into using the library. Maybe you will find out that most teens think the library does not offer anything for them. If this is the case, you will need to take a ground-up advertising approach to let parents and teens know that the library has special services for teens. In this case, consider asking the teens to get involved in more intense focus groups to gather information about how the library could better get the word out about teen services.

If you want more intensive results and have the staff time to devote to such an endeavor, you could do focus groups. Focus groups work best if you have the assistance of school counselors, local teen centers, or other youth-serving agencies to offer up the names of students who may be helpful and represent a diverse cross-section of the community of teens. Again, you want to find teens who are not already library users in order

Figure 3.5. Teen Patron Library Use Survey

GRADE   __ 9 __ 10 __ 11 __ 12   MALE __   FEMALE __
SCHOOL _____ TOWN where you live _____

Use your school library? YES __ How often? Daily Weekly Monthly Seasonally
                          NO __
Use the public library?   YES __ If yes, which location(s)?

How often do you use the library?
Daily   Weekly
Monthly   Seasonally
What do you use the library for?
Homework __   Go online __
Read magazines __   Hang out with friends__
Attend a program __   Kill time __   Study __
Other? _____
NO __   If you don't use the library, why not? _____
No library card __   High overdue fines __
I go online __   I buy books __
I use another library __
Other? _____

Ever attended a program or event at the library?   YES __   NO __
If yes, name the program(s): _____

How do you hear about events at the public library?

Friends   Parents   Flyer at store
Flyer at school   Teacher   I never hear about events
At the library   Newspaper ad   at AADL

Other: _____

Would you ever attend a program at the library? YES __   NO __

If you answered no, why not?
My friends won't come with me. __   I'm too cool for the library. __
I don't have any way to get to the library. __   My parents won't let me. __
I'm not interested in any of the programs offered. __
Other? _____

Do you know that all of the programs at the library are FREE?   YES __   NO __
Do you know that you usually don't have to sign up for a program (with a few
exceptions)? YES __   NO __

(Continued)

Figure 3.5 *(Continued)*

What kinds of programs would interest you? (Circle one.)

Arts and crafts	Dance	Hear an author talk
Music	How to get a job	Book discussion groups
Poetry	College help	See a TV personality or
Creative writing	Holiday-related events	other famous person
Video game events	Movies	talk about his or her
Comics/animation	Car repair/info	life/experiences
Food/cooking	Hair/makeup/fashion	Cultural events

Other? _____

Any ideas, questions, suggestions, or thoughts about the library?

_____

_____

_____

---

to accurately assess how your promotion is and is not penetrating the market. If you do only one or two focus groups, choose as broadly as possible in terms of gender, beliefs, culture, and socioeconomic levels of the participants. If you choose to facilitate several focus groups, you could gather together small groups of more like-minded teens to get a deeper picture of their interests. If you live in a community that is more homogeneous, you may find many teens who have similar interests. Dig deeper and find the secondary level that the teens might not necessarily self-identify with in a major way but, when pressed, admit to an interest in. For example, some teens may be fans of anime, manga, and Japanese culture, or role-playing games such as *Dungeons & Dragons*.

You may also find valuable demographic and interest information from other youth-serving agencies in the community. The local YMCA, Boys & Girls Club, and teen centers could share their program successes and failures to get you started in the right direction. Schools are also good places to gather this information. Teachers of physical education (PE) , art, and theater could offer crucial information about teen interests in your community. Looking at what clubs, sports, and after-school activities are offered is a perfect way to determine what you can complement. For example, cup stacking, also known as sport stacking or speed stacking, has been popular in elementary schools for years, with more than 20,000 schools worldwide offering cup stacking as part of their PE program. Its popularity soared in the early 2000s and was featured on commercials by McDonald's, Firefox, and the American Egg Board. Schools are a ripe source for community interests. If you wanted to do a cup-stacking event at your library, PE teachers would be able to help you advertise the event to the cup stackers in their schools.

Pop: Types of Advertising and Promotion

In order to keep up with what teens are interested in and properly market to them, you must also constantly be plugged in to teen pop culture or have figured out ways to keep up. Pay attention to how marketing is done for television shows, movies, and websites geared toward teens. In the mid-1990s, advertisers saw the potential of the teen demographic as consumers, and many great books have since been written on the subject. Peter Zollo's (1999) *Wise Up to Teens: Insights into Marketing and Advertising to Teenagers* is a great place to start when you are framing your marketing campaign or gathering information to convince administrators of this unique approach.

Blogs like *Ypulse* (http://ypulse.com) are excellent places to use as ground zero for staying abreast on what is happening with tween and teen pop culture. *Ypulse* will help you keep up with what is new, and you can also use it as an idea generator for how to market to teens in new and exciting ways. *Ypulse* keeps close track of teen social networking, mobile devices, and viral trends. Look at how many libraries created MySpace pages long after the bloom fell off the rose. Reading blogs will help you keep up with which trends have more lasting power and educate you on the entire landscape of teen media.

In order for libraries to be successful, pieces from the private sector's advertising model must be tweaked for use in the nonprofit world. As librarians we are selling a product: the library. The library's strategies for getting the teens to buy in to the product will not look much different from corporate advertising in the end. One advertising method is utilizing well-known pop culture references to market a product. The Moorpark City Library in Moorpark, California, used a photo of Edward, a character from the movie *Twilight*, on flyers to promote a Vampire Wreath program, attracting both vampire enthusiasts and fans of the movie star (Figure 3.6).

Be aware of various types of advertising and promotion, and utilize the best approaches for your community. Different methods of advertising include print materials, social networking, word of mouth by teens, guerrilla and viral marketing, paid advertisements, and going out into the community.

Print Advertising

The cheapest and easiest way to market your library is with print materials. Whether you do a full-fledged brochure, telephone pole posters, or postcard-sized flyers, this is the quickest way to get started with your marketing campaign.

Figure 3.6. Vampire Wreath Program

If you are looking to encourage hand selling of programs and want to take paper flyers to local businesses, schools, and hangouts, you must stick with a small size. Postcard size is standard; do not go any bigger if you expect people to take the flyers with them. In many cases, a business card–sized promo may be the perfect paper product. Multiple flyers can be made from a single sheet of paper, and more people are likely to take something small and portable that can easily go in a pocket. Also, if you plan to use teens to help hand out flyers, business card size is ideal. It is more discreet and easier for a teen to "sell" to the cool kids. If you look in any coffee shop, bookstore, or music store and find the freebies rack where music, art, and other events are advertised, everything is small and brightly colored. Small postcards can also be more easily used if you want to do stealth advertising in books or tucked into the book stacks. An example of this would be tucking a postcard with a list of local agencies and services for your lesbian/gay/bisexual/transgender/questioning (LGBTQ) community into your teen fiction titles about LGBTQ teens.

Social Networking Promotion

Keeping up with social networking as a marketing tool is a dynamic task that can never be viewed as being "done." If you still have a MySpace page, it is definitely time to delete it. Conversely, if you are not on Facebook yet, you'd better hurry. Word on the street is that it is on its way out. However, what is in or replacing it has not yet been determined. One of the best things currently about Facebook, though it may change tomorrow, is its advertising power. It is highly likely that an outside performer/speaker/author that is presenting a program at the library has his or her own Facebook page. Harness the power of the fan base and increase the exposure of the event by linking to the Facebook fan page. A good example of this phenomenon was when John and Hank Green went on their Nerdfighters tour in 2008. The Green brothers started with a strong blog presence, then became a huge video blog (vlog) sensation on YouTube, which naturally led to a robust following on Facebook. Attendance at their events in libraries was phenomenal because they did much of their own advertising online.

Currently Twitter is very hot for adults, but teens do not use the service much at all yet. Of course, by the time I finish typing this sentence, this could change. Alas, this is the nature of the social networking beast. If you are nimble enough and ambitious enough, you can easily and cheaply dip your toe into all sorts of social networking.

Perhaps you are doing a program on creative bento boxes (Japanese lunchboxes that have taken decorative food to new heights). You will want to target the Flickr (http://www.flickr.com) bento box group message boards. In addition to being a photo storage site, Flickr acts as a social site by allowing people to form groups based on common interests. This is one of the site's more popular features. There are several large bento box groups with hundreds and, in some cases, thousands of people as members. Obviously the members will not all be local. In fact, many will be from all over the world. Nevertheless, you will reach some new users, but in a place and a space that is unexpected and off the beaten path.

Targeted niche marketing is yet another way to utilize teen interests in creative ways. Other sites, such as the reviewing site Yelp (http://www.yelp.com) and the meet-new-people-around-common-interests site Meetup (http://www.meetup.com), are excellent choices for marketing your programs to 20- to 40-somethings. At the moment, these sites are not the best choices for targeting teens. Meetup is a great site to find instructors for programs and events that require some amount of "fandom," a cult-following fan base such as the passionate followers of *Harry Potter*. Do not forget to look to your staff for experts in specialized hobbies and interests to help with programs. It is necessary to note that websites may come and go very quickly, so keeping up is crucial.

Text messaging may not be the way to target new users, since libraries do not want to be in the spam text-messaging business, but it is a fantastic way to engage teens who have attended events and signed up to be on your text-messaging list. Send texts with reminders about events, teasers about upcoming events, and other select services you want to tell teens about. It is important that any text-messaging endeavor includes an "opt-in" feature from the user. Remember to consider the medium when crafting the message. Texting is by its nature short and concise so your messages should fit that model. For instance, "2nite@7 Downtown Library Mario Kart w/Prizes! Food! Free!" Cover the bases and keep it short. There are several software options for handling mass SMS text messaging. Companies like TextMarks (http://www.textmarks.com) or Club Texting (http://www.clubtexting.com) can be used to do this for the library, but they usually have advertisements attached to the messages. Any IT department worth its salt should be able to handle this type of service much more cheaply and without the ads. This can usually be done remotely and on a schedule so it does not actually require someone to type a text message into a phone.

Teens as Resource: Street Teams

Utilizing your teens as the library's street team is one of the best ways to encourage investment and ownership of your services by local teens and offer a level of credibility in marketing by having the message delivered by members of your audience. A street team by definition is a team of people that walks the streets, attends events, waits outside at movies or concerts for the crowds to emerge, and hands out promo bills for events that may be of interest to the targeted audience. For example, if Miley Cyrus is making an appearance at a mall or store near you, sending your team of teens to hand out flyers for programs would surely harness some new teen interest in the library. A street team could also help pass out flyers to local businesses and hangouts, and hang posters on telephone poles and in store windows, if local ordinances allow for this. Consider how unique it would be if one of your street-team teens handed out library postcards at a punk or metal show. This would surely change the perceptions that the attendees had about the library. The element of surprise cannot be underestimated as a marketing tool. Another way street teams can get the word out at their schools is putting flyers up in classrooms or hallways, or getting programs included in morning announcements. Again, teens tend to respond differently when they hear about events and programs from other teens.

Guerrilla, Viral, and Alternative Promotion

Guerrilla marketing is a term that was created by Jay Conrad Levinson (2010) in his now-popular series of books. Since his first use of the term in the mid-1980s, it has become mainstream and recognized as a distinct marketing tactic. Guerrilla marketing is defined as unconventional and potentially interactive, and often seeks to target its audience in surprising and unexpected places. The idea is to create a unique experience or concept to get the audience engaged and talking about whatever it is being advertised. Advertisers hope that this type of word-of-mouth approach will create buzz and then become viral.

Viral marketing is exactly what it sounds like: infecting consumers in quiet, intimate, face-to-face or computer-to-computer recommendations that pass from person to person, much like a virus spreads. The other benefit of these types of approaches is that they are often inexpensive to create and rely more on imagination than money.

The most infamous example of guerilla marketing was the 2007 Boston campaign for the *Aqua Teen Hunger Force* movie from the Cartoon Network Adult Swim animated TV show. Several lightboxes/machines were placed around the city and were intended to depict the characters in the movie. However, due to their flashing lights and other suspicious aspects of the devices, the campaign instead sparked a citywide bomb scare. Several freeways, subway stations, and bridges were closed while the devices were inspected. Clearly, the library does not want to model this scenario, but you get the idea. Think about how strategically placed billboards or a sign hanging from a tree with open-ended, vague, or even obtuse wording with a website listed could create interest and buzz about the library. The reality is that for teens, seeing the library running a tent at an outdoor street festival with *Dance Dance Revolution* or other video games is enough of a surprise to be considered guerrilla marketing and will very likely spark a viral word-of-mouth campaign.

Paid Advertising and Other Bells and Whistles

If you have a budget for more expensive advertising or perhaps have a Friends of the Library group who could put money toward promotion, there are many options. Paid ads in local papers, including school papers, can sometimes work depending on the topic. Paid ads on Facebook and other websites are also relatively inexpensive and can be targeted based on interest and location.

Movie theater advertising is another excellent option for grabbing teens' interest while they are a captive audience, waiting for a film to begin. Many theaters will offer a flat rate and show the ad before every showing of a particular movie. This is not cheap but certainly worth the bang you might get for a few select, high-profile events. Movie theaters are where many teens are, and choosing the right movie could provide maximum exposure for your event. Whether or not you have the ability to create an ad yourself, you surely could have teens themselves help with this process. You would be surprised at how easy it is to create a slick video with a very small budget—or even no budget at all.

Television advertising is also incredibly effective for reaching teens. It is possible to buy local airtime with the cable provider and then choose certain channels like MTV, Bravo, and Cartoon Network or other channels popular with teens. This is clearly an expensive proposition for many libraries, but even if it is something you only do once or twice a year the results may be dramatic. The market penetration would be quite deep using this medium.

Outreach Promotions

Taking your show on the road is the best and easiest way to meet teens where they are and advertise your programs and services in person. Classroom visits or having a table at open house or college/career nights that schools offer are obvious outreach marketing opportunities that you are most likely already doing in some form or another. Take a step further and think about all of the parades, street festivals, and fairs that the library could attend, and showcase programs or video game equipment by allowing teens to get hands on and learn more without ever having to enter the library. If your community has a teen center, consider holding events there once in a while. You will interest teens who probably would never respond to more traditional advertising models, as well as create connections between staff and teens. Your local YMCA or Boys & Girls Club may be interested in partnering with the library and allow you to bring your programs or services to them and share resources.

Price and Demand

Libraries often forget that for nonusers, it's not a well-known fact that library services are free or do not always require registration. The "freeness" of the library must be a constant part of all promotion the library does. For every person who asks, "What does it cost?" there are dozens more who assume the services are something they cannot afford and will never bother to ask. Teens are "sold" things so often that the *free* message is just as important for them to hear as well. Do not ever take for granted that the community knows how the library works.

Conclusion

More than anything else, be sure the advertising the library does for teens is fun, vibrant, and targeted. Start out with a plan and determine the most affordable option and what will get the most bang for the buck and the effort. Find out who the teens are, where they are, and what they are interested in. Stay on top of what kinds of advertising works in the for-profit sector, and copy what you can within your budget contraints. Use current social networking strategically and with discretion based on how the teens in the community use it and relate to it. Branding and advertising tween and teen services at the library is one of the most important ways to reach out to your teens with a pop culture focus and a mind toward being creative, relative, and popular.

All of these advertising, branding, and marketing tips will help you plan and promote the variety of programs we have laid out for you later in the book. Also, each of the programs listed in the book has specific tips for marketing that particular program in the most appropriate venues and to the right audience.

References

Levinson, Jay Conrad. 2010. *Guerrilla Marketing for Nonprofits*. New York: Entrepreneur Press.

Perreault Jr., William D., Joseph Cannon, and E. Jerome McCarthy. 2010. *Basic Marketing*. New York: McGraw-Hill Higher Education.

Walters, Suzanne. 2004. *Library Marketing That Works!* New York: Neal-Schuman.

Zollo, Peter. 1999. *Wise Up to Teens: Insights into Marketing and Advertising to Teenagers*. New York: New Strategist Publications.

Chapter 4

Make It Work: Collections

If you choose to follow the philosophy of using popular culture to create inventive programming for teens and tweens at your library, you should employ the same rules of thinking to your collection. Here are some tips on keeping your collection fresh and exciting, reflecting the current interests of teens.

Create

Maybe you are working on freshening up your teen collection to reflect the interests of your community, or maybe you are lucky enough to be creating an opening-day collection for a new building. Either way, it is important to keep your collection current with materials on popular trends and icons for teens and tweens to show that the library cares about their interests. Worried about knowing who is the popular teen idol of the month? You probably have a built-in focus group using your library every day. Let teens take part in creating your collection. Ask for feedback from teens at Teen Advisory Board meetings, put up a display in the teen section asking who or what is trendy and popular at the moment for teens, or post a survey on the library website asking teens their favorite singers, actors, television shows, and more.

In review journals, be on the lookout for biographies on musical groups and rappers, sports stars, movie celebrities, and reality show starlets. Fictionalized series and graphic novels based on popular television series are always being published, and teens and tweens love to read anything to do with their favorite show. The *Hannah Montana* and *High School Musical* book series for tweens were in high demand at the height of their popularity and enticed otherwise-reluctant readers to eat up these books like candy. Also, pay close attention to movie tie-in books, and try to have them in your collection while the movie is being marketed in time for the highest level of interest.

Create Access

Teens are a very diverse group with varied interests. Adding popular culture materials to your collection can be a way to attract many different types of teens to the library.

Make sure to search out materials that speak to the skateboarding population as well as reality television junkies. A biography on Paris Hilton will not likely appeal to a boy who is interested in the Woodstock music festival. Sometimes access to information on a pop culture reference can become educational, leading teens toward broader interests, such as how the advent of Japanese manga into mainstream U.S. society caused many teens to become interested in learning about Japanese culture through sushi making, learning to speak Japanese, and becoming involved with the fan culture of anime.

Create Opportunities

Adding popular culture materials to your collection is also a way to form opportunities for teens to find information on topics that they may be too shy or embarrassed to seek out on their own. For instance, adding biographies on prominent GLBTQ (gay, lesbian, bisexual, transgender, questioning) icons who have become successes in their own right is very important to share with those teens who are struggling with their own sexuality. This also goes for famous people of different races, cultures, and nationalities. While you may already make a conscious decision to include characters of different ethnicities in your fiction collection, make sure to carry over that philosophy into your nonfiction section. Teens need to read about people like themselves and be exposed to people that are not of their race or nationality to learn about other groups of people.

Create Something

Building a stellar popular culture collection does not just include books based on famous people and television shows. Materials on popular do-it-yourself activities and hobbies are also important in creating a well-rounded collection. Watch for hands-on books on fashionable crafts, sports, henna, jewelry, or cookbooks to support the latest crazes. For instance, the *Twilight* series has led to a teen obsession with vampires. There are tons of cookbooks and other kinds of books covering vampire culture that teens would enjoy; having those books in your collection encourages further reading on the topic.

Relate

Meet teens where they are at! A library collection should include materials to reflect the popular culture of the generation—or the collection will not be relevant to the community it is serving. A priority of a youth library collection is to have information for reports and projects, as well as materials to answer questions about life, health, and wellness. But another very important priority that sometimes gets overlooked is including materials that reflect the interests and famous people of the time. It is very important for that teen to find information on Greek mythology for his report, but we do not want him to walk away from the library thinking the only purpose of the library is to find factual information for school. One of the goals of a library is to serve the recreational needs of the community. If a teen sees that you have cookbooks based on the television show *Iron Chef*, then she may decide the library has her interests in mind and come back to check out materials for fun.

Relate Experiences

Trends do circle around to become popular again for different generations, but teens do not necessarily realize that trends recycle themselves. They are more in tune with the idea that they are the first to discover an exciting band or style of clothing. Use a short discussion about a book on how to repurpose a pair of old jeans into a purse as an opportunity to relate to teens that repurposing jeans into original creations to express your individuality was also very popular in the 1970s.

Make Connections

Being aware of the latest crazes is a great way to make connections with the teens that you serve. Owning materials on the topic acknowledges their interest, and being able to converse with them about it shows your intentional dedication to knowing about their passions. This does not mean spending every waking moment watching MTV. Flip through *J-14* magazine once in a while to discover the current heartthrobs for tweens. Pick up a *Rolling Stone* magazine to read the latest trends in music. If you cannot stomach some of the popular books series, at least read the first one so that you have some comprehension of who Bella and Edward are from the *Twilight* saga.

Making connections with teens now makes for future adult library users. Teens that feel comfortable at the library will eventually have families of their own. It is the hope of librarians everywhere that they bring their families to the library and passionately vote for the library in times of need.

Be Relevant

Include materials in your teen library collection that are of interest to the teen community. Introduce new teen audiences to your library through materials in your collection. Teens are using technology to gain and share information with friends. Instead of leaving their chair to look up the definition of a word while in a library, teens can text the services desk or a staff member who can then reply with the meaning of the word. Meet teens' needs by giving them access to audiobooks that can be downloaded to their iPods and other e-reading devices. Think about adding video games and Blu-ray movies to your collection. Highlight parts of the collection by blogging about the newest titles and allowing teens to leave comments. Instead of sending e-mails when books are due, send text messages. Be thinking of what new types of materials can be added to the collection that will better serve teens in the way they acquire information.

Pop

Staying up with trends in popular culture can become very expensive. If you have a small budget and can only purchase materials that will fill a need or receive the most use, you can still have a great collection that reflects current pop culture. At the very least, purchase books that go under the spotlight because movies and television shows come out based on them. Also spend a few dollars on books on popular hobbies and current kitschy trends. These materials can be highlighted at programs to increase visibility and circulation.

Be Current

Keep up with current popular culture materials in your collection. Teens will be your most honest customers, sometimes brutally so. Tweens may be more forgiving. While a television show or hobby can go out of style for fifth graders, the fourth graders coming up will discover this phenomenon like it is new. Therefore, there is less of a push to constantly weed the tween collection of outdated popular items.

Anticipate popularity. Publishers do this all the time. Look ahead to big events that are coming up, like the soccer World Cup or the Olympics. Purchase books on famous and well-known athletes in advance to be ready for the rush when the games begin.

Staying current means keeping up with books that are turned into movies; the release of the movie will spur interest in reading the original novel. Many times it is the reluctant readers that show the most interest in reading the books because they have such an interest in the movie. Making movies and television shows based on teen fiction and graphic novels is a huge trend in Hollywood right now. Take a look at the Youth Services Corner website and the GreenBeenTeenQueen blog for regular updates on the upcoming teen books being made into movies.

Be In Demand

Staying current with pop culture materials goes hand in hand with weeding your collection. Do not fall into the trap of keeping everything you purchase. A recent trip to a local library unearthed the find of a *Ghostwriter* book, based on the PBS children's series from the 1990s, prominently displayed on the endcap of a bookshelf. While tweens are more willing to overlook how out-of-date a book is, teens are not as forgiving! Regularly go through your biography section to weed out the fallen famous. Play close attention to entertainers and sports stars. While biographies on George Washington and Marie Curie will stand the test of time, a biography on 1990s' comedian Pauly Shore may not fly off your shelf any time soon.

Don't keep books for nostalgia's sake. Saving books because they may become popular again is a waste of shelf space. There is no point in keeping a book series on *Sabrina the Teenage Witch* in the hopes that it may become popular in the future. No one foresaw that the television shows *90210* and *Melrose Place* would be relaunched ten years later. At this point, teens are more interested in the actors in the new series than novelizations of the original characters of Brenda and Brandon Walsh. That said, beware of cult followings of what you feel is dated popular culture. If in doubt, check for fan sites or ask your teens to see what has fallen out of popularity.

Have Fun

So you have purchased the books, but how do you make sure teens know you have them in the collection? Most of the time, teens may not think to search out the Robert Pattinson biography in your collection. Create a display or face the books out in the shelving. Think about having programs to promote the new materials in your collection. The Ann Arbor District Library (AADL) had a Gundamfest, celebrating fandom for the Japanese anime series about giant robots called *Gundam*, which has franchised into video games, manga, and more. The AADL had purchased DVDs and manga, and to make the community aware of these materials the program included an anime showing, the opportunity to play *Gundam* video games, a craft component of making a *Gundam* model from a kit, and the opportunity to be the first to check out these new materials. Revive interest in cult classics to a new generation by holding trivia events on *Buffy the Vampire Slayer*, *Lord of the Rings*, and *Harry Potter*. These programs work best in conjunction with the release of a new movie, television show, or book—something that is getting attention in the media. Most of all, have fun showing off your great collection to teens and tweens.

Conclusion

There is a direct correlation between the library's collection and its programming. While this book focuses on using popular culture to create programs that will appeal to teens and tweens, there is little point in demonstrating to patrons the relevance of the library if the other services provided are not of high quality. The library is in a constant state of proving its worth to the community. If a teen comes in to participate in a comic-book-drawing event, there had better be materials in the collection to support the content of the workshop. Many times programs will pique teens' interests after they have attended a program, revealing to them that the library has further worth beyond homework and Internet access. High attendance to programs is great, but a large number of teens with library cards and high teen collection circulation is even better.

Alternatively, another purpose of the library is to serve the informational needs of the public. This is where staying up on the popular trends of youth is so important. The disappointment a teen feels when the librarian says the library does not have any Justin Bieber CDs and has no idea who that is can cause him or her to stop going to that library; that teen may never know about the programs that do interest him or her that are taking place at the library. From the teen's perspective, based on this one interaction, the library does not have his or her interests in mind, so why waste time going there? The bottom line is that the collection must support the programming that you do and the interests of the community.

Resources

GreenBeanTeenQueen [blog]. 2010. Accessed July 10. http://www.greenbeanteen queen.com/.

Youth Services Corner. 2010. Accessed July 10. http://www.youthservicescorner .com/.

Chapter 5

Keep 'Em Coming: Spaces

There have been many wonderful books, as well as regular columns in *VOYA*, dedicated to creating dynamic and wonderful teen spaces in libraries. Rather than replicate what these books have done or try to help plan the space of every teen's dreams, this chapter talks about simple ways to keep spaces responsive and related to pop culture without doing a complete makeover. Tween spaces are starting to crop up in some libraries and are definitely worth considering as an addition to a children's room. If money is no object or you are lucky enough to be getting ready to build a new library with a teen space, take the opportunity to expand "branding" teen services to the next level by branding the space. Signage with the logo on it is a simple and valuable way to expand the teen brand. It will remind the teens that said brand is all-encompassing. Taking branding to this next level of incorporating it into their own space completes the circle and connects all facets of teen services in the library.

Create

When planning to add or spruce up the presence of pop culture as part of a space in the library, think about it in terms of creating a space just for tweens or teens where their interests, obsessions, and passions are in the forefront, as well as engaging reluctant library users. From signage and furniture to displays and visuals, a space can be made more appealing with a big budget or even a small or nonexistent budget. The goal of spaces that incorporate pop culture materials is to let users know the library is up to the minute and responsive to what interests them.

Create Access

To hook a teen or tween visiting the library for the first time—or even for the hundredth time—having displays or posters that reflect what is happening now is an easy way to let the teen know that the library is not as out of it as he or she may have thought. The simplest way to have a constant visual presence of current pop culture is to maintain a robust magazine collection. A wall of current magazines on a variety of topics, including niche interests like skateboarding, manga, wrestling, music, and sports, is the cheapest and easiest way to keep a space looking new and current. Magazine subscriptions are one of the more inexpensive media types out there, so adding as many titles as possible is the way to go. If budgets are tight, consider asking your Friends of the Library group to pay for subscriptions, offer patrons the opportunity to "adopt" a subscription, or consider taking magazine donations. Teens who enjoy magazines are willing to overlook a missing issue since it is a recreational interest rather than a research need related to other, more studious periodical subscriptions in the library.

If the library has a graphic novel or a CliffsNotes collection, be sure the space and signage related to those collections is visible and prominent, since the goal is to alert even a casual visitor to your more unexpected collections. Teens visiting for the first time should be able to look around quickly and realize that the space is for them and identify the things that interest them most.

Create Opportunities

A teen space planned with pop culture in mind should also be responsive to teens with needs or interests that they may be too embarrassed or shy to ask for. Be sure that regular displays or posters reflect varied points of view, cultures, races, and ways of life. Prominently advertise programs that might be of interest to the GLBTQ (gay, lesbian, bisexual, transgender, questioning) community as well as those that discuss different cultures. Some users may never ask, so making it easy for them to stumble upon it should be part of the plan.

A well-planned space should also accommodate individual reading and study, as well as spaces for groups. A solo teen looking for a place to read should feel just as comfortable as a group that needs to find a place to hang out. Teens may also meet new people or be introduced to new things when given the room to explore.

Create Something

It is fairly commonplace to have manipulatives, art projects, or other hands-on activities for children in their spaces, but not as common in teen spaces. If the space is available, consider having constant hands-on crafts, puzzles, or brainteasers that encourage a teen who is killing time to want to hang out in the space. Some libraries have addressed this need by purchasing tables with chess, checkers, backgammon, or other game boards built into the tabletop. A magnetic tabletop or a whiteboard can encourage teens to hang out, leave messages, and be expressive. Of course, these "expressions" may also lead to profanity or gang tagging, but this is part of the teen landscape so learn to take the good with the bad and focus on the fact that some teens will appreciate the opportunity. Just remember to constantly monitor the space for inappropriate writing that needs to be taken down.

Relate

Offering teens a space that reflects the world they live in by acknowledging their interests is crucial. The quickest way to turn off a prospective user is to keep posters up that feature celebrities that are long past famous or irrelevant to the community. Encouraging reading is a large part of what libraries do, but clearly libraries also support other media and interests. Displays that focus only on reading for pleasure can easily turn off a new visitor who either does not know how or does not like to read. Posting images that portray music, sports, art, dance, or movies acknowledges the fact that not only does the library have collections that support these interests, but we're happy you're here! Yes, that potential user may eventually become a reader, but right now the goal is to make him or her feel welcome. Again, it is important to be mindful of whether displays or posters reflect diverse thoughts and life experiences.

Relate Experiences

One of the easiest ways to breathe life into your space with relevance in mind is to have displays that share reviews and opinions about books, movies, and magazines from the library staff, as well as other teens. It is important for teens to realize that the staff who work there are knowledgeable, interested in teen life, and able to offer recommendations. This can happen in the form of displays on a bulletin board or on the library's website, which is also a "space" for teens in the library. Give teens the opportunity to express themselves and relate their experiences with one another. Using a whiteboard or going "old school" with paper, consider having user polls on display in the teen area. Whether they are changed weekly, biweekly, or monthly, posting new polls (and the results of previous polls) keeps the space fresh and encourages teens to visit often. The poll questions could be anything, from asking teens about their favorite candy, food, drink, movie, or book to more involved questions about current events or "hot issues." Giving teens the opportunity to express themselves in the space encourages ownership of it and, therefore, of the library.

Make Connections

Having displays, signage, or activities in the space also creates the chance for staff to make connections with teens based on their interests. It also allows teens with similar interests to meet other teens or encourage connections among themselves. If there is a teen hanging out by the display of vampire-themed fiction, take the opportunity to talk to him or her and find out whether there is an interest in book recommendations and if he or she knows about the party the library is planning for the *Breaking Dawn* movie release. If the space is lively and inviting, these connections are that much easier to make.

Be Relevant

Having old series books in the collections is bad enough, but devoting a display to them is worse. This tells teens that the library does not know and does not care about what their interests are. Be sure that your most current items and displays are the first thing teens see when they enter the space. New books should be near the entrance, as should popular collections like graphic novels, music, and magazines.

Pop

Pop is where you can have fun and let the teens know that what they are into *now* is important! Having display cases in a teen room is a great way to accomplish a number of things. Perhaps local teens would enjoy putting their collections or artwork on display. Another idea for pop culture–oriented displays is to highlight interests like fairies, zombies, and unicorns, and include copies of book covers. Never take the most popular materials out of circulation! Include cool collectibles, toys, movies, or comics that are visually stimulating and get teens thinking about different ways to experience their interest. Also think about highlighting local events in the community that might interest teens. For example, include an advertisement for a local Renaissance festival in the fairy display, where teens are sure to pick up awesome glittery fairy wings and flower crowns. *Pop* is about visual appeal that works fast!

Be Current

Having collections that stay current is vital here, but continuously creating displays that feature the new materials or ongoing contests in the space takes it a step further. In anticipation of the next television show or movie being released based on a popular teen book or graphic novel, have a display highlighting what the library has related to that interest. Consider having "passive" contests, such as posters featuring the faces of celebrities with their eyes covered, and ask teens to guess their identities. This could be done with sports team logos, fonts from popular movies, or even lines of dialogue. These kinds of displays keep the space current and interesting and encourage teens to visit often.

Be In Demand

If budgets are tight, focus more money on what is most popular in the collections. The same is true for spaces. Consider displays or activities that highlight hidden gems that somehow relate to something currently popular. The passive displays and poll questions mentioned previously are a wonderful and simple way to make the teen space in demand. Teens are always looking for something new and interesting, and these types of efforts will make the teen space more popular and well used. Encouraging teens to create displays or help decorate the room will also create more demand and, again, increase the ownership that teens have of the space.

Have Fun

The goal of any changes or additions to a teen space should encourage fun. Let teens know that the library appreciates and encourages their recreational interests. Be sure that your purely recreational programming is prominently displayed and advertised in the space. Having teens involved in keeping the space current and popular is the best way to encourage fun!

Conclusion

Use popular culture as a muse for creating a teen-friendly environment in the library. Keep the space current using posters and displays that feature popular icons and trends of the moment. Enlist the help of teen advisory boards or teen library regulars to create displays based on topics they find interesting and appealing. But don't just think in two dimensions. The best bet in creating a teen-driven space is to have some sort of enclosed display space for teens to show off their collections. Some librarians that serve teens have collections of *Nightmare Before Christmas* figurines or Elvis memorabilia that teens may enjoy. Also, think of the teen space as a place to showcase events that may be happening in the library or elsewhere in the community, and create displays around these themes. Most important, think creatively!

Resources

Bernier, Anthony, ed. Forthcoming. *Making Space for Teens: Recognizing Young Adult Needs in Library Buildings*. Lanham, MD: The Scarecrow Press.

Bolan, Kimberly. 2008. "The Need for Teens Spaces in Public Libraries." Young Adult Library Services Association (YALSA) [white paper]. January. Accessed August 30. http://www.ala.org/ala/yalsa/profdev/whitepapers/teenspaces.cfm.

Bolan, Kimberly. 2009. *Teen Spaces: The Step-by-Step Library Makeover*. 2nd ed. Chicago: American Library Association.

"Teen Spaces 2nd Edition's Photostream." 2010. Flickr. Accessed August 30. http://www.flickr.com/ photos/kimbolan/. [Thousands of images of teen spaces are available through the Flickr website, including all of the images in Bolan's 2nd edition of Teen Spaces.]

Chapter 6

"I Want My MTV!": Programming

Foundations for Successful Teen/Tween Programming

The goals associated with offering programs at the library are many: attracting new patrons to use the library, enriching the lives of members of the community, and empowering the public by involving them in the creation and implementation of programming, to name only a few. Successful library programming is based on the interests of the community it serves. Many times, it can feel like you are programming in a vacuum, creatively coming up with fabulous ideas for programs that you believe teens and tweens will enjoy, only to have three people show up to the event. Many times, what is forgotten in the planning process is actually asking the members of your community what they want. More often than not, what happens instead is the event planners assume what teens will want to take part in based on successful programs at other libraries.

Involving your constituents is the first step in creating successful programs. This can be done through surveys either on the library website or on paper. If there is a teen advisory board, go to those teens for ideas on what they want to see happening at the library. Many times it works best to have a list of potential programming ideas for teens and tweens to pick from. Then, once the creative juices are flowing, ask them to come up with their own ideas for events. Empowering teens to help create programs will encourage higher attendance. Teens are being told what to do by many different adults, so the opportunity to make their own decisions is so important and satisfying that you may find you now have some very loyal library users.

Another important thing to keep in mind when programming with teens and tweens is to always follow through! If the teens come up with an idea, make it happen. If you offer up a suggestion that the teens take an interest in, make it happen. Trust can be lost very quickly. You want teens and tweens in your community to know that you will try very hard to not let them down. The library is a safe place to be, and honesty from and trust in the librarians and staff in the library is very important for building relationships with the youth community—for both creating lifelong library users and easing behavior problems. The teens that have the hardest time following the rules in the library but continually return consider the library a safe place whether or not they vocalize that feeling. Consider asking those teens to be involved with programming or helping around the library. They may be looking for an adult to pay attention to them. Plus, they may have great ideas for programs to engage reluctant readers.

Planning and Implementing Programs

Popular culture is a great muse for creating unique programming for teens and tweens. Teen and tween obsessions with singers, actors, video games, and toys can be very solitary activities. The library can design programs to make these obsessions social and introduce patrons to supporting resources available at the library about which they had been unaware.

Besides asking teens about their interests, keep up-to-date with what is popular and fresh by looking at magazines such as *J-14, Rolling Stone, US Weekly*, and *Game Informer*. Stay up on the trends by reading websites such as Ypulse.com (http://www .ypulse.com). Pay attention to which books are being checked out. Are they about vampires, werewolves, fairies, or dragons? Look to see what teens are doing at the library and what is on their clothes. Are teens playing chess? Is there a big group hanging out around the manga books? Do many tweens have *iCarly* on their backpacks? Is there a resurgence of Led Zeppelin T-shirts? All of these things can give you ideas for creating pop culture–centered library programs.

Once the idea for the program is in place, work on putting the program together based on the budgetary constraints of your library. Ask teens when is the best time to have the program, instead of assuming Saturdays are good days because they are not at school. Look throughout the community to make sure you are not duplicating a program. For instance, the teens may be keen on having a battle of the bands, but the local high school holds the event every spring. In that case, change the idea a little. Maybe the library battle of the bands is a warm-up to the big high school event, or maybe you can offer library teen volunteers to help with event or space at the library. Be creative with the idea. Be sure to advertise the event in places teens go, such as local coffee shops and arcades. But do not just stop with paper flyers. Advertise in electronic spaces, such as on the high school manga club website, Facebook, or community message boards. Again, ask teens where they get their information. You can ask tweens as well, but many times their parents are still finding out about events for them.

Conclusion

Chapters 7 through 19 contain ideas for teen and tween programs inspired by elements of popular culture. Each program write-up will include ideas on supplies, implementation, and advertising for the event. Take these ideas and make them work within the confines of your library's financial resources. These programs are meant to be suggestions to manipulate to work within your community. Strive to age-down the teen programs for your tween community as opposed to aging-up programs that were originally aimed at elementary school students. Many times, tweens are interested in the same things teens are, and they are also trying to pull away from being childish. It is hoped that the reader will find new ideas for programming in these chapters, as well as develop a mind-set for creating novel and unique programs created by and for teens and tweens, specific to your community using popular culture.

Chapter 7

Programs: Art

Various types of art and drawing go in and out of popularity with teens following media trends. The newest superhero movie creates interest in comic book art, and widespread interest in reading Japanese and Korean manga novels has piqued the interest of teens in drawing in that style. When a new Pixar movie hits theaters, cartooning as a hobby and profession become popular. The library can become the go-to place for learning the skills for creating these different forms of art through programs and resources. Learning the nuts and bolts of drawing is becoming harder for kids who cannot afford drawing classes, as art classes are often reduced in number and art electives are often the first to be cut from public school curricula during budget crunches.

Comic Book Academy

The Comic Book Academy program was written and contributed by Sharon Iverson, Teen Librarian at the Ann Arbor District Library.

General Description

The Comic Book Academy prepares teens interested in developing their graphic story-telling skills to create their own comic book or graphic novel. The class meets over a six-week period (two hours per class) to learn about the art of comic bookstorytelling, character design, writing dialogue, penciling the first draft, refining and completing the penciled pages, and inking or finishing the pages.

Pop

Movies based on superheroes, such as the *X-Men* and *Iron Man*, and cartoons like *Up* and *The Incredibles*, are very popular among the teen and tween crowd. Their box-of-fice successes signal a heightened interest in comics and graphic novels. Likewise, Japanese manga and anime also continues to hold high interest. While many teens like to create fan art, other teens are interested in bringing their original stories to life on paper.

Relate

Becoming a successful comics and graphic novel creator involves much more than becoming a good artist. Many teens come to the academy thinking they will spend most of their time improving and refining their drawing techniques. Instead, they learn how to elevate their storytelling skills both as a writer and as an artist. Besides creating the opportunity for teens interested in art and comic books to learn more, it is also a way for the library to support writing stories as a different art form.

Instructors/Talent

A local comics artist instructs the program. Motivated teens who are knowledgeable in the creation of comic books can help with big groups.

Audience

Teens in grades 6 through 12.

Planning and Supplies

The program was created based on the guidance and suggestions of the instructor. He recommended the number and length of sessions, suggesting that teens could best learn the information in a relaxed, no-pressure setting. He also provided "homework" handouts that reviewed what had been learned that day, as well as outlines of skills for each teen to practice at home.

Supply List
- No. 2 pencils
- Erasers
- Unlined paper
- Rulers
- Fine-tipped markers
- Smooth Bristol board

Create

The instructor kicks off each session (20 to 30 minutes) reviewing the past week's instruction and presenting a new element. Teens then work on their stories and practice what they have learned while the instructor moves about the room and interacts with each participant. As the weeks progress, teens begin to develop their visual stories. The hosting librarian keeps the teens supplied with the basics (sharpened pencils, paper, etc.) and also retrieves reference material (photographs of settings, characters, etc.) from the library shelves.

Food, Technology, and Other Mandatory Extras

- Laptop with weekly PowerPoint presentation downloaded
- Access to the Internet
- Projector to show slide show or websites on a large screen
- An over-the-shoulder "comics" camera set up so participants can watch on a large screen as the presenter demonstrates drawing techniques
- Whiteboard and markers

Analysis

Attendance is usually consistent from week one through week six. The teens interact with one another as well as the instructor, often staying past the end time of the program. A few teens completed a minicomic by the end of the six-week session, while most teens had a good start on their graphic stories to finish off at home.

Marketing Tips

Because the program is time intensive, it was held during the summer. Promotion of the program occurred during school visits in May and in library advertising materials, such as the teen brochure and the library website. The local newspaper was alerted to write a piece promoting the unique and free program. Do not forget to let middle and high school art instructors know about the event so they can pass along the information to their students and potentially offer some type of extra credit.

Resources

Abel, Jessica, and Matt Madden. 2008. *Drawing Words and Writing Pictures: Making Comics, Manga, Graphic Novels, and Beyond.* New York: First Second.

Art & Story. 2010. [Weekly podcast by cartoonists Jerzy Drozd, Mark Rudolph, and Kevin Cross, who share their experiences making comics and try to wrap their brains around the larger ideas behind their chosen art form.] Accessed August 31. http://www.cvcomics.com/artandstory/.

Hogarth, Burne. 1995. *Dynamic Wrinkles and Drapery: Solutions for Drawing the Clothed Figure.* New York: Watson-Guptill.

Hogarth, Burne. 2003. *Dynamic Anatomy.* New York: Watson-Guptill.

Janson, Klaus. 2002. *The DC Comics Guide to Penciling Comics.* New York: Watson-Guptill.

Lee, Stan, and John Buscema. 1978. *How to Draw Comics the Marvel Way.* New York: Simon and Schuster.

McCloud, Scott. 1993. *Understanding Comics.* Amherst, MA: Kitchen Sink Press.

McCloud, Scott. 2006. *Making Comics: Storytelling Secrets of Comics, Manga, and Graphic Novels.* New York: HarperPerennial.

Comics Art Digital Coloring

Information on the Comics Art Digital Coloring program was provided by Sharon Iverson, Teen Librarian at the Ann Arbor District Library.

General Description

In the two-hour Comics Art Digital Coloring workshop, participants learn how to use Adobe Photoshop Elements to clean up their art, fill in line work with colors and half-tones, create cool lettering, prep the finished page for printing, and more.

Pop

In recent years, comics heroes like Spider-Man, Batman, and Iron Man, along with Japanese manga heroes and heroines, have thrived on the big and small screen. Their popularity has increased demand for more creative works. The use of Adobe Photoshop software has enabled artists to move graphic works more quickly into the hands of adoring fans and also allows artists to animate their work.

Relate

Becoming a successful comics and graphic novel creator involves learning how to become an accomplished visual storyteller. Teens who want to make a career as a comics artist benefit if they can do their own writing and artwork. They also benefit from using a tool like Adobe Photoshop to finish their work in a more technical and professional way. The ability to use Adobe Photoshop opens doors to careers in web design, TV, film, and much more, making this a great program to offer at the library for teens interested in the comic book industry and who may not have any other way of obtaining this professional information.

Instructors/Talent

A local comics artist, experienced in creating his own comics and offering comics art instruction to kids, teens, and adults, presented the program. Local artists may be interested in talking about how they can create comics for free to get their name out in the community.

Audience

Teens in grades 6 through 12.

Planning and Supplies

This workshop is offered the week after the conclusion of the six-week Comic Book Academy program presented at the library. Participants of the academy are encouraged to learn and try out Adobe Photoshop Elements. Because of the small Apple lab (14 stations) and large enrollment of the academy (25 to 30 teens), two sessions are offered.

Create

The instructor, using one of his own scanned comics pages, explains the basics of Adobe Photoshop Elements and has participants experiment with the various tools. This takes up to an hour. A library staff person with knowledge of Adobe Photoshop Elements is available to assist. Then the remaining time belongs to the teens as they work on their own scanned work brought in on a USB drive or scanned by the librarian hosting the event.

Food, Technology, and Other Mandatory Extras

If not already purchased, the Adobe Photoshop Elements software will need to be purchased. This software exists for both Mac and PC computers. The program will run more smoothly if there is access to a computer lab, where a presentation by an instructor will not bother any other library users and teens can be a little bit louder as they work on their projects. An additional computer connected to a projector for the instructor to use is a great tool for showing steps on a large screen for the group.

Analysis

Historically, most of the teens enrolled in the academy follow up with this additional workshop. It is impressive how quickly the teens learn to become proficient with Adobe Photoshop Elements. Consideration is being given to opening the lab periodically for teens to continue their finishing work once the program is over. Whether staff time or the computer space can be devoted for extra time to work on the projects must be well thought out.

Marketing Tips

Occurring in the summer so that teens have more time to devote to their projects, this program is promoted via school visits in May, in the teen brochure, on the library website, and in the local newspaper. It could also be promoted to middle and high school art instructors to pass along to their students.

Resource

Art & Story. 2010. [Weekly podcast by cartoonists Jerzy Drozd, Mark Rudolph, and Kevin Cross, who share their experiences making comics and try to wrap their brains around the larger ideas behind their chosen art form.] Accessed August 31. http://www.cvcomics.com/artandstory/.

Comics Artist Forum

Information on the Comics Artist Forum program was provided by Sharon Iverson, Teen Librarian at the Ann Arbor District Library.

General Description

The monthly Comic Artists Forum offers participants who have interest in comics or graphic novel creation an opportunity to share their work with others, gather fresh ideas, and listen to other comics/graphic novel artists discuss their favorite techniques or latest trends in comics publications. Each month a guest comic artist offers an art or publishing tip.

Pop

Japanese manga and superhero comic books have stimulated an interest in drawing for teens. On a larger scale, people can meet up at conventions, where groups who share similar interests in manga, graphic novels, anime, and various cult followings such as Star Wars can gather when these annual events are held.

Relate

Most comics/graphic novel artists work in isolation. The monthly forum offers teens as well as adults the chance to share and pick one another's minds for ideas. Teens wanting to make comics creation a career can talk with adults who are publishing their work and learn about the realities of making a living as a comics artist. This program further supports the notion of libraries becoming a meeting place for special interest groups in the community. Putting up displays of supporting materials offered by the library may attract additional library card users.

Instructors/Talent

Invite guest comics artists to speak at the program.

Audience

Teens in grades 6 through 12 and adults.

Planning and Supplies

Two hours was determined to be a good length for the program, given that time is needed for a guest artist presentation, along with casual time to work and interact.
Basic drawing supplies are required:

- No. 2 pencils
- Erasers
- Unlined paper
- Rulers

- Fine-tipped markers

Create

These two-hour sessions are informal. The guest artist usually kicks the program off with a short presentation of about 20 to 30 minutes, depending on what he or she chooses to cover. The remainder of the time, the guest artist mingles with participants as they work and discuss the process. After the presentation, participants can get up and move about the room to check out what others are doing and chat.

Food, Technology, and Other Mandatory Extras

- Laptop with weekly PowerPoint presentation downloaded
- Access to the Internet
- Projector to show slide show or websites on a large screen
- An over-the-shoulder "comics" camera set up so participants can watch on a large screen as the presenter demonstrates drawing techniques
- Whiteboard and markers

Analysis

Attendance is consistently strong as participants get to know one another. Each session has newcomers checking out what the forum is all about. Most of the time some participants hang around after the end of the session and talk, using the library as a social meeting spot.

Marketing Tips

A five-by-eight-inch colorful postcard is created to advertise the inaugural round of six forums. This is in addition to the series being promoted in the teen brochure, on the library website, as well as on the websites of area comics artists.

Resource

Art & Story. 2010. Accessed August 31. http://www.cvcomics.com/artandstory/. [Weekly podcast by cartoonists Jerzy Drozd, Mark Rudolph, and Kevin Cross, who share their experiences making comics and try to wrap their brains around the larger ideas behind their chosen art form.]

Pinhole Photography

Information on the Pinhole Photography program was provided by Sharon Iverson, Teen Librarian at the Ann Arbor District Library.

General Description

Participants learn how pinhole photography works and then create their own pinhole camera and shoot several pictures. Their pinhole photographs are then exhibited in the library.

Pop

Pinhole photography is an old technology, but it still fascinates people both young and old. Using this simple camera, photographers can create pictures with "special effects," like ghosts lurking in the background, super large monsters, or speed blurs.

Relate

Besides being a lot of fun, pinhole photography requires the photographer to take time to think about the shot he or she wants to take, carefully set it up, and then take the shot. For teens used to instant gratification, having to wait several weeks for the pictures to be developed is both agonizing and rewarding.

Instructors/Talent

A local community member interested in this hobby presented the program.

Audience

Teens in grades 6 through 12.

Planning and Supplies

The presenter suggested a three-hour program to allow time to explain pinhole photography history and function, pinhole camera construction, and taking pictures. Each camera could shoot one picture at a time. A closet was set up as a darkroom for participants to exchange paper film negatives. To keep track of which pictures belonged to which photographer, each teen was assigned a number. A list containing each teen's name and number was compiled. Each teen received several white round stickers with his or her number. As pictures were taken, teens placed their number stickers on the back of the paper negative. This helped the presenter keep the developed pictures organized later.

Supplies

- Quart-sized paint can (to be made into a camera)
- Magnet tape roll
- Sharps
- Paper photo negatives
- White round sticker dots
- Black photo boxes
- High-gloss paper
- Pie pans
- Foam board

Create

The presenter talked about the history of photography and how early pinhole-style cameras worked. He showed pictures taken with a pinhole camera. Teens then learned how to build a camera and take pictures. Their cameras could hold just one negative; the teens entered the darkroom to "load" their cameras. They then took their pictures on library grounds and returned to the darkroom to unload the exposed negative and reload with a fresh negative. They tried a variety of angles and shots. The exposed negatives were developed by the presenter and placed on foam board for display. Months later, the photos were exhibited in the library. Teens, families, and friends were invited to a special opening night reception complete with refreshments.

Food, Technology, and Other Mandatory Extras

A laptop connected to the projector was needed for the history portion of the program and to show examples of pinhole photographs.

Analysis

The program was a big success. However, executing it was a logistical challenge. Once photographing began, the presenter spent all the time in the darkroom helping small groups of teens unload and load their cameras. If this part were botched, no pictures would turn out, because any light exposure could ruin both exposed and unexposed film. One library staff person needed to be outside to keep the eager teens from opening the darkroom door prematurely. Having another pinhole camera expert managing the darkroom would have freed the presenter to advise teens as they set up their shots. In the end, about 50 percent of the photos turned out, which is average for this primitive style of photography. The teens were pleased with the results and particularly with seeing their photos on display at the opening-night reception. A project like this one is also a great way to spruce up a part of the library with free artwork, and the fact that it is created by patrons of the library is a plus.

Marketing Tips

This was a summer program, so it was promoted via May school visits, in the teen brochure, on the library website, and in the local newspaper. It could also be promoted to middle and high school art instructors to pass along to their students.

Resource

Matt Callow Photography. http://mattcallow.com/.

Chapter 8

Programs: Celebrity and Reality Television

Reality television has become increasingly popular in the past decade and has been instrumental in making fame more possible for everyday teens and tweens. As *Star Search* did in the 1970s, today's television shows, like *American Idol*, *Project Runway*, and *Jersey Shore*, create opportunities for regular teens with talent (or not) to become famous on television. Many of the skill-based reality shows have highly creative premises, which can easily be translated to a fun program at the library. Plus, the already-instilled audience for these shows allows teens to meet other teens with the same passion for them.

Popular movies and television shows are also helpful in creating programs. Superhero movies are insanely popular, so put together a superhero drawing program or a costume contest. For tweens, *Wizards of Waverly Place* on the Disney Channel is a well-loved fantasy show; you could host a program on making wizard wands to celebrate the premiere of the new season. Get imaginative with creating programs using ideas from popular television and movies.

Top Chef Season 4 Winner, Stephanie Izard, Appearance and Cooking Demo

General Description

Stephanie Izard, a participant of the hit television show *Top Chef*, spoke to teens and adults about her experiences on the reality television show. It was a large-scale event due to the cost associated with securing the speaker and the cooking demo supplies, the large attendance (400), and the sheer number of details involved in the planning of the event. It was also an incredibly fun event on all levels. No matter where your library is located, there is surely someone from a popular reality television show who grew up, attended college, got married, or is otherwise associated with your town, region, or state. Assess what is popular on television with your teens to determine what would be best for your community. Doing a simple poll with your teens is a great way to find out what they are watching and chances are they know that "so-and-so who went to high school in town x was on *American Idol*." Use their interest as your guide.

Pop

Top Chef has been a popular reality television show on the cable channel Bravo since its debut in 2006. Teens are just as much in love with cooking and food television shows as the rest of America, so anytime you can combine cooking and food with a teen event, you are in good shape. Competition shows are also an incredibly popular subgenre of the reality television landscape. *Top Chef* has several cookbooks out now, and the show's hosts Padma Lakshmi and Tom Colicchio are now celebrities in their own right. The show has now morphed into *Top Chef Masters*, where established chefs compete for charity, and will soon debut a teen version of the show.

Relate

Every teen and youth librarian knows that anything relating to food will be popular with teens. An event like this serves several populations and interests at once. Teens interested in reality television will be drawn to a program like this, as will those interested in cooking shows or becoming a chef. In addition to being a popular television show, there are also now several books based on *Top Chef* that serve as supportive materials to the event. Titles include *How to Cook Like a Top Chef* (Miller, 2010), *Top Chef: The Quickfire Cookbook* (Miller, 2009), and *Top Chef: The Cookbook* (Martin, Krissoff, and Scheintaub, 2008). There is also a *Top Chef* Quickfire Challenge board game. In addition to these "official" *Top Chef* publications, there are many books written by former contestants and the show's hosts. For teens without access to cable television at home or those who have missed the previous season, DVDs are other materials to add to the library collection and support this event. Lastly, any program relating to a celebrity, especially when combined with a local angle, will resonate with a certain segment of your teen population. The incredible popularity of *Top Chef* is an easy way to justify any event of this nature.

Instructors/Talent

Locating your local reality television star is easier than you think. Ask your local teens and do research in local papers or websites to determine if anyone in your city, region, or state has ever been on a reality television show. Depending on their level of popularity and how far removed from the show they are, you should be prepared to pay speakers fees in the range of $200 to $2,000.

Audience

Grades 6 through 12 and adults. Parents with younger children were also able to attend because often the intense interest in the topic will usually keep the attention span of a younger person.

Planning and Supplies

During the booking phase of this event it was determined that another library in the area had also asked Stephanie Izard to speak. Working with another library is always a great way to pull off a more expensive event. In this case, the travel costs and arrangements were split between two library systems. When it came time to transport Izard between the two cities, the drivers met halfway; that way neither librarian had to do the longer drive and the library did not have to pay for transportation.

The planning aspect of this event was extensive. To find Izard's contact information, the television network Bravo was contacted, which gave the number for the public relations firm handling her public appearances. Depending on your speaker, you may be able to nail down many of the supplies and details early, but the nuts and bolts do not usually come together for an event like this until only a month or so before the engagement. Speakers are usually traveling constantly and can only concentrate on most any event about a month ahead of time.

Supplies

- Electric cooktops—the number depends on needs of the presenter
- Bowls
- Pans
- Knives
- Spatulas
- Whisk, serving utensils, etc. (Be prepared to supply whatever your presenter requests.)
- Food based on the shopping list of the presenter (Library staff took Izard to the grocery store and she picked out her ingredients.)
- Paper plates, napkins, and plastic forks for tastings
- Sous chef assistance (A couple of local culinary students and enthusiasts were asked to help Izard prepare the food before and during her presentation. These people were not compensated, as the thrill of meeting Izard was payment enough for them.)

Many of the preparation and cooking supplies were borrowed from a local deli, but you may have staff members who are willing to lend all of these supplies. While the library paid for the food used to cook at this event, you might also find a store willing to donate the food in exchange for a mention at the program or in publicity.

Create

The event itself was a traditional lecture environment with Izard speaking and doing a cooking demo and the audience sitting in chairs listening. She did a casual talk and took questions while she cooked three different recipes that she had created. Library staff handed out the samples to the audience as she spoke. In this case, the "creation" happened with Izard and the magic of her talk and Q&A. The attendees got to hear about her experiences on the show, behind-the-scenes secrets about the other contestants, and, most important, about her journey from being an undergrad at the University of Michigan to being a Top Chef. Many teens asked questions about her cooking and professional experiences in restaurants.

Food, Technology, and Other Mandatory Extras

The library conducted a podcast interview with Stephanie Izard, asking behind-the-scenes questions about *Top Chef*. The podcast is now archived on the library website for future listeners (http://www.aadl.org/video/feed/audio). The event was also taped and is available on the library website as video on demand (http://www.aadl.org/video). In addition, the event was broadcast on the local cable access channel. The technical services department at the library is already set up for taping, as they do this for many events, and has support staff to tape the event, edit, and produce the video. If you do not have this setup, look into purchasing a small camcorder for recording YouTube videos.

Analysis

This is one of the most popular events the library has ever hosted. More than 400 people attended the event, and of that audience about 80 of the attendees were teens. For many of those in the audience, this was the first time they had ever been to the library, and for others the first time they attended an event at the library. It was a great opportunity to change perceptions of the library. For many attendees, meeting Izard was a major highlight, so the association with the library was quite popular. Izard noted that she had a fun time visiting Ann Arbor and had a very changed perception of libraries as well.

Even though *Top Chef* may not always be as popular with teens, there will always be another reality television show that is popular. You could also spin off the idea of this event by having a "*Top Chef*-Style Competition" event for teens. Similarly, you could have chefs from popular restaurants in your community do a cooking demo and tasting. The possibilities for taking off from this program idea are endless.

Marketing Tips

This was an event with many bells and whistles. The library occasionally runs ads on local television channels for high-profile events or events whose audience, like *Top Chef*, warrant a television campaign. When the library runs an ad, it usually runs on Bravo, MTV, Comedy Central, and Cartoon Network. The channels were selected based on the targeted audience. For this event, an ad was run in the local newspaper advertising Stephanie Izard's scheduled appearance, and the event was put on the front page of the teen event brochure.

Resources

Check out these resources to create displays supporting this program:

Bravo Media. 2010. "Top Chef." Accessed September 2. http://www.bravotv.com/top-chef.

Martin, Brett, Liana Krissoff, and Leda Scheintaub. 2008. *Top Chef: The Cookbook*. San Francisco: Chronicle Books.

Miller, Emily Wise. 2009. *Top Chef: The Quickfire Cookbook*. San Francisco: Chronicle Books.

Miller, Emily Wise. 2010. *How to Cook Like a Top Chef*. San Francisco: Chronicle Books.

MTV: *Made*

General Description

This event model is applicable to any popular reality television show that features real tweens, teens, or young adults from your community or state. If a local young person has participated on a show that has an interesting, controversial, educational, or just plain fun plot with a competition or talent showcase, invite him or her to speak at the library. Dylan, a teen in Ann Arbor who appeared on MTV's *Made*, was a "class clown" in high school who wanted to become a fashion designer. Dylan and his clothes were also featured in the library *Project Runway* Fashion Show program discussed in a later section of this chapter.

Pop

Made is a show on MTV that allows a teen to realize a dream or goal in life. The show is described on the MTV website as "An ugly duckling transforms into a beautiful prom queen. An overweight couch potato becomes a model. A sci-fi nerd morphs into a hardcore rapper" (MTV Network, 2010). MTV, while slightly faded over the years, is still a helpful barometer for what is popular and compelling to some teens in your community. Simply using it as a reference point is a great advantage to marketing and gives you much potential to build a fun and compelling event. Since MTV is one of the main media sources that feature teens and showcases their talents on shows, it is a nice fit with the library model of enrichment and broadening horizons. MTV brings a diversity of faces and lifestyles into the living rooms of many teens who have never met teens "like that" before. Use MTV's riskiness to your advantage.

Relate

The best thing about this event is that it showcased a local teen to other area teens going out on a limb and not necessarily (by his own admission) succeeding. Many young people feel like "success" or doing something "big" comes when you are an adult, and the library is in a great position to expose them to opportunities they may not have known about previously. Fashion design is a very popular and competitive career path and it is a great opportunity to expose young people to the real work required to achieve that goal. An event like this is an occasion to market the fashion materials in your collection and let the audience know about the other resources your library can offer to further their interest. While there are no official MTV publications about the television show *Made*, there are plenty of fashion, sewing, and design books to purchase or put on display to support the program. More teen-friendly titles such as *Generation T: 108 Ways to Transform a T-Shirt* (Nicolay, 2006) or *AlterNation: Transform. Embellish. Customize* (Okey, 2007) are excellent additions to the library collection. Books that deal generally with teen creativity would also support the program, such as *Creative Expression Activities for Teens: Exploring Identity Through Art, Craft, and Journaling* (Thomas, 2010).

Instructors/Talent

This event comes down to access. Ideally, a teen in the general area or your state at large has appeared on a reality television show. MTV, Bravo, and the basic networks have some of the most popular reality television shows, but do not forget to check out athletic competitions, game shows, or poker events for potential local talent to invite a teen to present an event like this for the library. Locals are often more willing to speak gratis or for a smaller fee and won't require travel expenses. Also, even if they do use an agent or agency, you can potentially get in touch through a community connection. Of course, if you have a generous programming budget you can always hire anyone from a reality television show, local or not, to come and do a talk. Ex-reality television stars often make a nice living doing appearances and talking about their experiences. You can expect to pay anywhere from $500 to $10,000 (or more, depending) for a speaker from out of state, plus travel expenses. Be prepared to book through an agent, agency, or public relations firm in most cases.

Audience

This type of event can be targeted generally to a middle and high school audience and to young adults in their twenties and thirties. Also, as long as the content (your local star may have been on a show with drinking or sex, for example) is age appropriate—which, in the case of fashion design, it is—tweens can enjoy the event as well.

Planning and Supplies

Other than the items Dylan brought with him and coordination of his technology and display needs, there was not much to plan other than venue details.

Create

The event was a basic casual lecture, plus question and answer for the audience members. Dylan showed video clips from his episode, which were fun to watch and definitely enhanced by his accompanying commentary. He had slides and brought the clothes he made for the show for display during the event. Dylan's parents were also there, since they and other family members were on the show, and they answered some questions as well.

The beauty of this event is that the *Create* came from the young person showcased. Seeing a person their own age talk about his experiences and demonstrating confidence and creativity is important for other young people to see. Creating opportunities to learn something new and see things from a different viewpoint are important experiences to explore.

Food, Technology, and Other Mandatory Extras

A projector is required that can be hooked up to technology to access DVDs or stream the Internet in order to show the visual portions. Having the clothes on display was an added component that enhanced the program.

Analysis

This event attracted an enthusiastic and engaged variety of families: tweens, teens, and adults of various ages. The chance to showcase local talent is a great opportunity to put a face on something based in the mainstream media and provide your community access to how reality television "really" works.

Marketing Tips

Use MTV (or other channels for a similar event) to your advantage and employ a light and modern tone when writing the press releases and program descriptions. Take flyers or promos to local businesses, teen centers, and gathering spaces for teens and young adults. Do direct marketing to sewing stores, local sewing or fashion-interest groups, which you may be able to locate via Meetup.com, for example. Make sure middle and high school art teachers and counselors know so they might target teens that they know have a particular interest in fashion. Put flyers in the fashion magazines in your collection. If your marketing budget is generous, run an ad on cable to reach your potential audience where their attention is likely already focused.

Resources

Check out these books as supporting materials for the collection:

Nicolay, Megan. 2006. *Generation T: 108 Ways to Transform a T-Shirt*. New York: Workman.

Okey, Shannon. 2007. *AlterNation: Transform. Embellish. Customize*. Cincinnati, OH: North Light Books.

Thomas, Bonnie. 2010. *Creative Expression Activities for Teens: Exploring Identity Through Art, Craft, and Journaling*. Philadelphia: Jessica Kingsley Publishers.

Check out these websites for more information:

MTV Network. 2010. "Dylan Is *Made* into a Fashion Designer: Ep. 705." Accessed September 2. http://www.mtv.com/shows/made/episode.jhtml?episodeID= 106703.

MTV Network. 2010. "Made." Accessed September 2. http://www.mtv.com/ shows/made/series.jhtml.

Project Runway Fashion Show or Challenge

General Description

Project Runway is a popular fashion design television show on the cable station Lifetime. This event can take a variety of forms based on how simple, complicated, or involved you want it to be. The basic idea is to have teens apply to be in the fashion show with a portfolio, sketches, samples, etc. The teens would have several months to create their outfits (two to six is realistic for most teens) and would then show their creations during a runway show with models. Depending on the community, expect anywhere from a handful to 20 teens to try out for the show. Other options for an event like this would be to have local boutiques or department stores showcase local fashions at the library. A local college or university might have a fashion program and their students could also show at the library, with the instructor talking about careers in fashion. As an alternative, hold a simple event (competitive or not, although the television show is a competition) where clothing that can be altered is provided, such as donated prom dresses, cloth scraps, old clothes teens bring themselves, or other creative materials. This idea is modeled after the unusual challenges on the television show *Project Runway.* Teens would have a time limit on how long they would have during the "challenge" to create a new look.

Pop

Project Runway has been one of the most popular competition reality television shows among young people of all ages. The show is a fashion design competition where a group of adults ranging in age from twenties to fifties compete in a series of difficult challenges to design outfits. Each week a panel of judges composed of models, designers, and fashion experts sends one designer home. A final group of three or four designers creates a 12-piece fashion collection and competes to win money and the support to create a full clothing line, among other prizes. The show debuted on Bravo in 2004, and moved to the Lifetime channel in 2009. The show's colorful contests and judges continue to fuel its popularity. Fashion is always a popular topic to use with tween and teen programming because that is often when they are their most creative and uninhibited. Showcasing creativity and artistic expression is an excellent cultural touchstone.

Relate

This event was teen-driven. A teen brought the idea to the library and helped plan it. The teen was given the opportunity to plan, organize, and lead the event, and because it was teen-driven it was easy to generate peer interest. An event about fashion that celebrates teen talent and creative expression is a character-building experience and an opportunity to showcase the fashion-design materials in your collections and other resources that can assist teens interested in pursuing fashion as a career.

Instructors/Talent

It is possible to host this event entirely without hiring someone, but the program would be better if talent, fashion instructors, fashion designers, or models spoke or were otherwise involved with the event.

Audience

If the event includes a runway show featuring teen designs, plan on an audience of all ages. Family and friends of the teen, the designers, and the models will want to attend. If doing a hands-on design event or challenge, teens are your primary audience. Tweens and adults in their twenties, thirties, and forties might also be interested, so either make sure the competition is broken up by age group or consider doing separate programs for these different age groups.

Planning and Supplies

Planning is crucial for a runway show event.

- If you have teens apply to participate, you must create an application, guidelines, or criteria (see Figure 8.1).
- Create submission session guidelines for interviewing teens interested in showing their work in a fashion show (see Figure 8.2).
- Regular communication with the teens about progress, finding models, etc., is crucial.
- Live or recorded music will have to be coordinated.
- Consider having a committee of teens help with the planning.
- If only a handful of teens show clothing, the show could be over in five to ten minutes, so having other speakers or activities is crucial. A local teacher, designer, business owner, or enthusiast could speak about the fashion industry or fashion design as a career. A boutique or department store could display dresses, provide the models and clothing, or participate in the runway show if not enough teens participate. A local model or someone who works at a modeling agency could talk about that side of the business. If there is a fashion design college program in your area, ask if its students could show their designs.
- Models are a very important consideration. If teens show their own work, then have it be part of the commitment that they provide their own models. If you work with a boutique or department store, they will usually supply the models.
- If the library does not have a suitable space with good lighting or a sound system, consider partnering with a local teen center, community center, or school to see if the event could be held there. If local teens are spotlighted, it is easier to get other agencies serving those same teens to volunteer their space.

When doing a hands-on event or competition, supplies make the program more extensive.

- Clothing or dress donations will have to be sought, resale clothing purchased, fabric scraps purchased, or participants must bring clothing themselves.
- Hand sewing or hot gluing are the easiest and most affordable options.
- Borrowing sewing machines from staff or a local business is an option, although it will involve a lot more work and coordination. Consider liability issues as well, since something may happen to a machine while in the library's care.
- Beads, sequins, and other embellishments can be sewn or glued on as well.
- Fabric markers will allow teens to write text or create patterns on their creations.

Figure 8.1. Project Design: High School Fashion Show

The first ever [*your city/library name here*] fashion design event is a juried design exhibition. If you design and sew your own clothes, you are invited to submit your work for the fashion show. This is not a competition. This is a juried event and submitting your work does not guarantee you a spot in the runway show to be held on [*x date*].

Submission Panel Sessions

List dates and locations.

Submission Guidelines and Details

1. Eligibility: Students in grades 9 through 12.
2. You must attend a Submission Panel Session to enter your work into the exhibition.
3. You must bring the following to the submission panel sessions: Sketches/drawings of your designs and a written description of your fashion philosophy (not to exceed 500 words).
4. You will complete an entry form when you arrive for the panel session. You must also bring copies (not originals) of your philosophy statement and your sketches. These will be used by the panel to make their decisions and will not be returned to you.
5. You may bring (but are not required to bring) any of the following: photos of your designs, letters of recommendation or any awards you may have won, samples of clothes you have created and any other visuals or hands-on materials. You will not leave any of the items with the panel.
6. You will have five minutes to present your work to the panel. Be prepared to answer questions from the panel about your work and your fashion philosophy.
7. You will be notified by [*x date*] whether your work has been selected for the runway fashion show on [*x date*].

What Else You Need to Know (rules, judging details, etc.):

1. Teens must design and sew their clothing themselves. However, some assistance with construction is permitted.
2. Once you have been notified of your acceptance in the fashion show, you will have six weeks to create a minimum of two complete outfits (maximum six outfits). An outfit must be a head-to-toe look. Store-bought accessories are allowable.
3. You will be required to preview your completed work two weeks prior to the fashion show.
4. You must provide your own models for your creations.

The Project Design Runway Show will be held on [*x date*].

Figure 8.2. Project Design: Submission Session Guidelines

Questions/Information for Entrants:

1. Welcome the teens and ask them if they have any questions before you begin.
2. In general, we want to be sure that the skin/cloth ratio of the designs favors the cloth. No see-through shirts, blouses, no halter tops, tank tops/tube tops, undershirts, muscle shirts, or other tops that expose the midriff. Shorts and skirts must be size appropriate (arm extended straight down at sides, shorts or skirt bottom reaches fingertips); excessively tight-fitting designs are prohibited.
3. What about this opportunity excited you enough to come today?
4. Can you tell us about your sketches and about your designs?
5. What were your inspirations?
6. Do you have any designers that you admire?
7. Do you read about fashion? If so, what do you read?
8. Are there any movies or TV shows that have inspired your love of fashion?
9. Do you plan to pursue fashion after high school as a career?
10. Please tell us about your fashion philosophy.
11. Why do you think we should choose your designs for the show?

Judging Criteria

Please use the following areas to judge the submitted work. Use a 10-point range to assign points in each of the areas, 1 being the lowest score and 10 being the highest. Circle the score you have assigned for each area. Space is provided to take notes as needed. These notes will help remind you of your likes/dislikes and specific details.

Creativity/Originality

(The ability to transcend traditional ideas, rules, patterns, relationships, or the like, and to create meaningful new forms, interpretations, etc.; progressiveness, or imagination. Does the teen's design fulfill these expectations?)

1   2   3   4   5   6   7   8   9   10

Overall Look/Styling
(Does the presentation look like a complete outfit, ready to leave the house? Is the styling consistent and well done from head to toe? Does it look like care was given to all aspects of the design, including clothing and accessories? Do the accessories complement the designs with use of color/shape, etc.?)

1   2   3   4   5   6   7   8   9   10

(Continued)

Figure 8.2 *(Continued)*

Shape/Form/Line
(Does the design look pleasing to the eye and to the contours of the body? Are the lines complementary to the body? Do the shapes appear as though they complement each other?)

1   2   3   4   5   6   7   8   9   10

Sketches
(Did the sketches give you a good impression of what the clothing might look like? Were they presented in a fairly neat and organized fashion?)

1   2   3   4   5   6   7   8   9   10

Fashion Philosophy
(Do you get a sense of how the teen feels about fashion? Was it well written and presented? Did the philosophy reveal knowledge of fashion?)

1   2   3   4   5   6   7   8   9   10

TOTAL POINTS:

If tie-breaking is needed when you compile totals later on, we will use these additional categories to break those ties. Assign each area a score from 1 to 10.

Enthusiasm/Fashion Passion

1   2   3   4   5   6   7   8   9   10

Color
(Is the use of color complementary? Is it pleasing to the eye? Does the use of color attract your eye? Does the use of color evoke an emotional response in you?)

1   2   3   4   5   6   7   8   9   10

Create

If planning a runway show, arrange for a 30- to 45-minute event. If teens show their own work, it is important that family and friends and the other audience members enjoy a robust event with the teens as the centerpiece. Determine what and how many other elements to include at the event. It is best to save the exhibition of the teens' work for last so it is the final presentation that the audience sees. Whether you have other speakers, show excerpts from *Project Runway,* or boutique or department store model popular designs, the event should conclude with the teen-designed runway show.

- Music is crucial, so consider having a live DJ (perhaps a local teen or young adult) or teen-selected recorded music.
- If models must change into their outfits, a private changing area will be necessary.

If you do a hands-on event, leave it as open and unrestricted as possible. Allow the teens the freedom to make whatever they want. If the event is a competition, then clear and simple guidelines must be presented. If prizes are given out, the rules must be fair to all. Prizes could include gift certificates for a fabric store, or for a class at a store or school.

Food, Technology, and Other Mandatory Extras

For a runway event that celebrates teen work, consider having light refreshments before the event starts to offer a more "art opening" vibe and also to make it more special for the teens. Music and audio are important. While a CD player or MP3 player with speakers will work, ideally a sound system would make the event more professional. Lowered lighting and spotlights on the runway would also lend an air of authenticity to the event. Whatever can be done to replicate a runway environment will help.

Analysis

The runway event held at the library featured a total of nine designs by three teen girl designers. The girls located their own models and handled hair and makeup. A professor from a local university spoke about fashion as a career, and three of her students also showcased their work. Dylan from MTV's *Made* series (a program discussed earlier in this section) also showed his clothing designs. A local model who has been doing runway shows for many years spoke about her experiences at shows and shared humorous anecdotes. Ultimately, the program was a success with more than 100 attendees, but detailed pre-planning was required.

Marketing Tips

For a teen-centered runway show, ask the teens to help promote the event at their schools, in their neighborhoods, and to their family and friends. Promote the event directly to local schools with a focus on art teachers and counselors. Put up flyers or take brochures to boutiques that sell fashion-forward clothes and to schools who have fashion programs.

Resource

Check out this website to learn more about the television show:

My Lifetime. 2010. "*Project Runway.*" Accessed September 2. http://www.mylifetime .com/shows/project-runway.

Silent Library

General Description

Shhhh! The goal is to stay silent in the library! Teens participate in challenges but must stay silent while doing them. The last person with his or her lips sealed receives a prize.

Pop

Silent Library is a segment on a popular Japanese variety show called *Downtown no Gaki no Tsukai ya Arahende!!* and has been developed into a game show aired on MTV. Six players are seated around a study table in a library. Each player flips a card. Five of the cards are "safe" cards, while the last card has a skull and crossbones. The unlucky player to flip this card must do a bizarre challenge. To win the challenge, the noise level must stay below the red zone on the on-screen gauge. The unusual challenges include drinking a glass of grape juice freshly stomped by a woman with dirty feet or chewing through a pair of meat suspenders until the pants they are holding up fall down.

Relate

Obesity is an important topic in our society today. According to the American Heart Association, the number of overweight children between ages 12 and 19 increased from 6.1 percent in a 1971–1974 study, to 17.6 percent in a 2003–2006 study. Promoting physical activities in the library is a way to promote healthy living in the community. This program will not necessarily break teens into a sweat (though it could, depending on your programming space), but it is a step in the right direction for getting kids active.

Instructors/Talent

None needed.

Audience

Choosing either teens or tweens for this program would work very well. It will be much harder for the tweens to stay quiet.

Planning and Supplies

Most of the challenges actually done on the show are too painful or humiliating to do in a library setting, such as having people eat hot soup over the participant. Use the stunts from another show, *Fear Factor*, as inspiration for your challenges—for example, eating bugs and strange foods. Check with your library to see if you should have release forms signed for those challenges for liability reasons.

Minute to Win It games were used in this program. All the instructions for each game are on the website listed in the Resources section. Most of the supplies needed are things found around the library, such as toilet paper, rubber bands, or empty soda cans. If you are using *Minute to Win It* challenges, you will need a stopwatch as well, because each stunt must be completed in 60 seconds. Prizes for the quietest teen could range from gift cards, copying the television show which gives out cash prizes, or something as cheap and simple as coupons to local restaurants. The prizes need not be spectacular because the fun of the program is participating in the strange and unusual challenges.

Create

It is important to have a large programming room or space to do this program. Some of the challenges need space, plus everyone wants to watch the competitor do something silly and not make a sound. Set up your room with a few tables for tabletop stunts and chairs for the teens waiting for their turn to do a challenge. For large groups, you may have teens do the stunts in groups so that each person does not have to wait too long to do a challenge (see Figure 8.3). Most teens will act irritated when they receive the un-lucky card calling them out to participate in a challenge, but most of them secretly would like to do all of the challenges.

In this particular program, the large group was broken into groups of six. Each of the six stands around a table and receives a card. Everyone flips the card at the same time. The person with the joker has to complete a challenge. Challenges are chosen by picking a slip of paper out of a cup.

An example stunt that went over well is the "Face the Cookie" challenge listed on the *Minute to Win It* television show website. To complete the challenge, teens must move three Oreo cookies, one by one, from their foreheads to their mouths only using their faces. No hands are allowed. Those three cookies must be in their mouths in 60 seconds, and it is hysterical to watch! Only cookies are needed for this stunt.

The quiet component was self-monitored. Once a teen was out of the running for the prize, he or she stayed and laughed at the crazy stunts. The teens were also a great help with taking pictures while staff focused attention on setting up the stunts.

Food, Technology, and Other Mandatory Extras
None needed.

Analysis
An idea for keeping track of those who have not spoken is to have everyone wear a col-ored sticker. When a person talks or laughs, the sticker gets taken away. This gives you a way to visually see who is still in the game for the prize. This idea will probably not work if you have a very sensitive audience. Hurt feelings may be smoothed over by giv-

Figure 8.3. Teen Drinking from a Shoe during a *Silent Library* Challenge at the Monrovia (CA) Public Library

ing everyone a snack for participating and the silent winner a $5 gift certificate to a local store.

Marketing Tips

If it is possible to spend some money on commercial spots, it would be helpful to put up on ad on MTV to attract all those fans of the *Silent Library* game show. Also target anime clubs and fans of Japanese culture with flyers or post messages on their Facebook pages.

Resources

Check out these websites for ideas on challenges:

MTV Network. 2010. "*Silent Library*." Accessed September 2. http://www.mtv .com/shows/silent_library/series.jhtml.

NBC. 2010. "*Minute to Win It*." Accessed September 2. http://www.nbc.com/ minute-to-win-it/.

Superhero Smashup

General Description

In reaction to the superhero craze, a workshop was put together to teach patrons how to draw well-known superheroes and design their own superhero persona to create a comic strip.

Pop

Bringing superheroes to life from comic books to the big screen has become a popular trend in the 2000s. Fans are embroiled in the Marvel versus DC Comics battle, trying to choose who will win in a fight: Superman or Iron Man. The popular *X-Men* movie franchise has announced the *X-Men Origins* series, promising many movies to come, each focusing on a character from the popular superhero team. Remakes of such recognized characters as Batman, the Green Hornet, Wonder Woman, and the Green Lantern are also in the works, assuring the teen librarian profession many great years of material to utilize for programming.

Relate

Teens who enjoy superhero movies will enjoy this program, as will teens who like to draw. It is a great way for teens to show off their creative skills while creating their own characters and to highlight the library's graphic novel section, drawing books, and potentially the DVD collection.

Instructor/Talent

A local comic artist was asked to run a two-hour workshop, discussing how to develop a superhero character and how to effectively communicate story through a visual narrative. The program could be shortened and does not need to be so technical. It also does not necessarily need to be run by a professional if there is no local talent in your area or you need to save money. There are many books and websites to help you become a drawing expert.

Audience

Grades 6 through 12. The program could be done for younger tweens, but you must keep in mind the program involves a lot of sitting and listening to the instructor, so concentration skills and being able to sit still are needed.

Planning and Supplies

- White copy paper
- Pencils

- Colored pencils
- Rulers

Create

Strike a balance between teaching the skill of drawing and allowing time for drawing. Most teens do not want to sit and listen to a lecture, and you do not want your program to seem too much like school. It should be fun and enjoyable, keeping to the methodology that the library is for learning as well as for entertainment.

Start by asking the teens to brainstorm possible superhero powers and gadgets, and write the ideas where everyone can see them. This will help give them ideas for drawing their own superheroes later. Then lead the group in the basic drawing of one superhero of your choice, a popular character or one of your own creations.

Food, Technology, and Other Mandatory Extras

Having examples of superhero characters or ideas of potential superpowers and gadgets is always helpful for beginning drawers. Search your collection and the Internet for ideas.

Analysis

This program can be executed on many different levels. It can be an in-depth workshop on the technical aspects of cartooning, creating characters, and storyboarding; teaching how to create a comic from beginning to end. The program can also be as simple as explaining how to draw superheroes using examples from books and websites. Create the program according to how much your audience can handle. Another consideration that will help promote interest in the program is to plan to have the event near the premiere of a new superhero movie. Excitement will be in the air, and teens will be motivated to develop their own superheroes' personalities.

Marketing Tips

E-mail local middle school and high school art teachers about the program, and ask if they will give extra credit for participation. Also promote this program to anime and manga fans, as they are sometimes comic book and superhero enthusiasts as well. Make sure to let local comic book stores know about the program, and ask to leave small posters or flyers at the counter.

Resources

Use these books to help when designing the drawing program:

Amara, Philip. 2001. *So, You Wanna Be A Comic Book Artist?* Hillsboro, OR: Beyond Books.

Ames, Lee J. 1983. *Draw 50 Monsters, Creeps, Superheroes, Demons, Dragons, Nerds, Dirts, Ghouls, Giants, Vampires, Zombies, and Other Curiosa. . . .* New York: Random House Children's Books.

Chapter 9

Programs: Contests

Contests are healthy competition and a great way to freshen up a tried-and-true teen/tween programming model with elements of pop culture. Passive contests that include creation of materials outside the library can attract new users who may have been too shy to engage in library activities previously. Teens are probably creating their own YouTube videos, dabbling in photography, or recording their own beats and music using various types of technology. A contest would allow them to send in or drop off their creations for a chance at being validated with a big prize or at least recognition in the form of library display space or at a battle of the bands.

Graffiti Contest

The Graffiti Contest program was written and contributed by Vicki Browne, Teen Librarian at the Ann Arbor District Library.

General Description

During the Ann Arbor Art Fair, the library sponsors a Teen Graffiti Art Contest for area teens. Teens have 15 minutes to create a masterpiece using spray paint as their medium. Prizes are awarded at the end of the program to three winners, and the artwork is displayed in the library for a month.

Pop

The power of the spray can! A picture is displayed in minutes, empowering teens in their artistic creativity. Graffiti dates all the way back to when the Romans "tagged" their name on the buildings they conquered. New York City is where graffiti first became popular in the United States. It started on the sides of railway cars and quickly turned into a competition between artists to create works of self-expression. Starting as an underground art movement, it is found in many urban settings and became widespread in the 1980s as hip-hop culture extended across the country. While graffiti can be used to beautify otherwise grimy neighborhoods, it also has an association with gang activity, and the term has developed negative connotations over the years. Giving teens a productive place to develop their skills helps improve the perception of graffiti as an art form, as opposed to associating it with vandalism.

Relate

Rather than saying "Don't paint here" or Don't paint this," the library can encourage freedom of expression. This program may work very well in urban settings. Teens are also given a venue for showing their work if the library has room to create a display for the finished artwork. Many teens never have the opportunity to showcase their art, and it is another way to empower your local teen population.

Instructors/Talent

Often the contest's judge will talk about styles, techniques, and give feedback on the artists' works. Look into your community for local artists who specialize in graffiti as an art form, and ask them to serve as judges. Check with local art schools or art programs.

Audience

Grades 6 through 12.

Planning and Supplies

Supplies are purchased for the teens to use, which includes a variety of colored spray paint, nozzles, latex gloves, and paint masks. The tempered board, a thin, three-by-two-foot board, is purchased from a local lumber company and primed with white paint. The remaining supplies are all available from craft and art supply stores. The library was lucky enough to have talented staff in the facilities department make simple wooden easels to prop up the boards. The easels are reused every year.

Create

The program takes place in the library staff parking lot, and staff is asked to park elsewhere during the event (see Figure 9.1). Painter's plastic is put on any part of the library building that may get paint blown in its direction. Teens sign a registration form which allows us to exhibit their art at the library and also signifies that they understand that no "gang graffiti" artwork will be accepted. Volunteer staff members pass out supplies, and about a dozen teens can paint at once. While teens are waiting to paint, they can work on sketching out their ideas. Each teen has about 15 minutes to create his or her masterpiece. Allow two hours for the entire program.

Teens that finish their paintings early are encouraged to return at the end of the program and watch the judging. Finished boards are propped up around the library parking lot to dry and remain there so that they are available for judging. Prizes are gift

Figure 9.1. Graffiti Contest at the Ann Arbor District Library

certificates for art supplies at a local store. All canvases, labeled with the artist's name and grade, similar to a real art show, are displayed at the library for a month to share with the community. Then the teens can stop by and claim their works to keep.

Food, Technology, and Other Mandatory Extras

If this program happens during the summer, have a water cooler available for the teens.

Analysis

The program can be a stand-alone or a way for the library to contribute to a local festival or celebration. It is great outreach to show the community the caliber of program for teens that the library offers. Also, have big, old T-shirts available as smocks to protect the clothing of the teens participating in the event.

Marketing Tips

The library is able to schedule the contest during a citywide annual art fair so there is usually a sizable crowd, as it is advertised along with other art fair events. Advertise to local art programs and at art supply stores.

Resources

Check out these books to learn more about the history of graffiti and techniques:

Ganz, Nicholas. 2009. *Graffiti World: Street Art from Five Continents*. New York: Abrams.
Martinez, Scape. 2009. *GRAFF: The Art & Technique of Graffiti*. Cincinnati, OH: Impact.

Photography Contest

General Description

Pick a theme of some sort, like spring, summer, animals, or pets, and craft a basic photo contest for teens. Guidelines and rules will have to be formulated and a timeline planned. Then display the entries in the library and online if possible.

Pop

Teens see the world differently than adults and are always looking for ways to explore their point of view. Since it is increasingly popular for teens to have their own cell phones with cameras, you can use this angle in the photo contest. New cameras and apps with special effects are always coming out, and a photo contest is a way to play off that.

Relate

A photo contest is a great way to meet teens where they are at and showcase their talents and their points of view. Because entries for the photo contest are prepared at home, it just might reach some of the shyer or quiet teens who are looking for ways to be involved.

Instructors/Talent

No talent is required to run a photo contest, but you should consider finding photographers on the library staff or in the community to be judges for the contest.

Audience

A photo contest can be held for all ages, including teen categories such as grades 6 through 8 and 9 through 12, or it can be a contest just for teens.

Planning and Supplies

The planning for a photo contest will be all done up front. Come up with guidelines and rules for the contest, determine the date by which entries are due, and also the format in which those entries must be submitted. If the plan is to display the photos in the library, then it is best to require that entrants submit an actual photo and have it mounted on paper with their name. This way library staff will not have to spend time mounting photos and labeling the entries. Some photo contests are held online only to avoid dealing with the display of photos. Consider the following:

- How many entrants are allowed per person?
- What should the size of entries be?
- Will the photos be submitted in person at one location or by mail?
- Will there be an awards ceremony?
- What about prizes?

The contest can be as simple or as complicated as the planning allows for. In terms of supplies, they are minimal. If entrants are required to mount the entries, then staff will have only to locate a place to display them, provide pins for hanging the photos, and obtain prizes for the winners (if prizes are being given).

Create

This event is really all about the participants. The creation part happens with the teens and with the opportunity provided to them. Judging is an important component. Timing on judging can be difficult, so it is important to build in time between when entries are due, when judging happens, and when the display goes up. These dates and times should be stated into your contest guidelines. If the planning is done well, then the only "how" is perhaps an award ceremony. This can be very simple, with entrants gathering around the display and staff announcing the winners; or a reception atmosphere can work, with refreshments available, patterned after an art opening. Then, if there are winners to announce, this can be done at the end of the reception.

Food, Technology, and Other Mandatory Extras

Having photo entries available online on the library website is a nice addition to offer. These "galleries" can serve as publicity for future contests and are a lasting reminder to the teens about their participation. Having a reception with refreshments is also a nice touch.

Analysis

With any contest there will be a learning curve based on experience. There will always be a few things that come up due to participant questions or something that did not work that can be tweaked for the next year. Fairness and planning are the main things to focus on. As long as all involved feel that the judging was fair and enjoy seeing their photos on display, it is a successful event.

Marketing Tips

Market your theme well and get the word out to schools and art teachers. If the theme changes often to add freshness to the program, it will be something the teens look forward to year after year.

Resources

Check out these books for tips on photography:

Campbell, Mark. 2006. *Digital Photography for Teens*. Boston, MA: Course Technology.
Gaines, Thom. 2010. *Digital Photo Madness! 50 Weird and Wacky Things to Do with Your Digital Camera*. New York: Lark Books.
Wignall, Jeff. 2009. *Winning Digital Photo Contests*. New York: Lark Books.

LEGO Contest

General Description

This is a one-night-only LEGO contest that asks participants to create their projects at home and then bring them to the library for judging. The projects are available for viewing by the public on that day, and the contest ends with the awards ceremony. The event is in large part created by the users themselves. You will have to provide the venue, come up with rules, provide prizes, and then harness the enthusiasm. Summer is usually the best time to host an event like this since it is when kids and teens have the most free time on their hands to work on their projects. You will note that this contest does not include long-term display of the entries of winners. Without large, locking, and secure display cases it is not recommended to display the entries for longer periods of time when 100 percent staff presence cannot be guaranteed. Theft is an unfortunate reality considering how expensive LEGO sets are. Consider display issues carefully before making the decision.

Pop

LEGO has been a popular toy in the United States since its debut in its current form in the 1950s. Year after year, LEGO adds new themes and sets and now includes many popular TV and movie tie-ins, robots, and architecture sets. Aside from the toys, however, LEGO has further infiltrated popular culture with their popular video games, books, and of course the many stop-motion LEGO videos fans have uploaded to

YouTube. Further cementing their popularity have been their LEGO retail stores (over 30 in the United States alone) and their popular LEGO-Land theme parks.

Relate

Librarians often bemoan how difficult it is to get boys engaged in the library. LEGO is the single easiest way to engage and excite many boys in your community. While LEGO does appeal to both sexes, the most avid fans tend to be males, and holding a LEGO contest is a sure way to increase the number of boys your library reaches. LEGO enthusiasts are passionate about creating with LEGO and also enjoy looking at what others have created. A LEGO contest is an easy way to meet your users where they are at while rewarding their enthusiasm for LEGO with prizes!

Instructors/Talent

You surely have staff members or community members who are LEGO enthusiasts. Use these enthusiasts to conduct your judging. These people can help you determine the judging categories to use, guidelines, and other changes to the rules you might make for your community. (See Figure 9.2.) A local man who runs an annual educational LEGO event every year for families in the community was a judge for the event. Contacting local hobby and toy stores would also be another option for locating a LEGO hobbyist. However, in terms of conducting an event like thies, you do not need to be a LEGO fan yourself.

Audience

LEGO fans come in all ages and the library runs its contest for preschoolers through grade 12. While high school tends to be the smallest category in terms of the number of entrants, it is also the category that often has the most sophisticated entries, which everyone loves to look at. One high school entry included a replica of the family's ancestral castle in Europe.

Planning and Supplies

The bulk of the planning for an event like this is up front, when you create your rules and guidelines. Once your guidelines are released, you will need to work on getting prizes, getting medals (if you decide to give them out), and planning the details of the day of the event. Having a large enough space may be your biggest concern. The library's contest eventually outgrew its largest meeting room, so the event now uses an off-site location. Obviously, this is a budget consideration, if you go that route. In some communities it might work to trade with another organization or make other arrangements to have access to a larger space. If you do not have a large space then limit the maximum size that entries can be. However, the fewer limits the better, in order to fully encourage creativity.

Figure 9.2. LEGO Contest Rules and Guidelines

Your Library Presents: <u>Annual LEGO Contest Rules and Guidelines</u>
Awards Ceremony—When and Where: _____
Prizes will be awarded in five categories:
   Preschool, Grades K-2, Grades 3-5, Grades 6-8, and Grades 9-12

Prizes:
Within each category there will be three winners:
   1st Place, 1st Runner-Up, and 1st Honorable Mention

Winners will receive gift certificates for Toys 'R' Us in the amounts of $35.00, $25.00, and $15.00, respectively. Winners will also receive prize ribbons.

Prize ribbons will also be awarded in each category for the following:
   Best Motorized Project; Best Architectural/Engineering Project; Coolest Robot; Best Vehicle; Most Creative; Most Sophisticated, and [Your Library] LEGO Master Builder

Every entrant will receive a certificate of participation.

Rules:
1. Use your own LEGO, Duplo, Mega blocks, or other LEGO-compatible plastic bricks.
2. Entries must be your own creation, not a LEGO-designed kit, project found online, in a magazine, etc.
3. One entry per participant or team, where applicable.
4. Your creation must fit within a space of 24 inches by 24 inches. Your completed project may be no taller than four feet.
5. Team projects will be placed in the category of the oldest participant in the team. Individual entries will not be permitted for team participants. Please note that while all members of a team will receive a certificate and a prize ribbon (if applicable) for participation, a team will compete for a single prize.
6. Include a label/sign that explains the idea/inspiration for your creation to help the judges make their determinations.
7. Please provide a sign/label with your project with your name(s), grade(s), and phone number(s).
8. Completed projects must be delivered to _____ on _____ between 9 a.m. and 4 p.m.
9. Judging will be conducted the evening of _____ at _____ by a team of adult LEGO enthusiasts.
10. The doors will open at 7 p.m. to allow for the entries to be viewed by the public.
11. The awards ceremony will begin at _____.
12. Completed entries *must* be taken home on the evening of _____.

For more information, please contact _____.

PARENTS: If you authorize that your child's work or image may be considered for display and/or promotion of [Your Library] programming and services, please also complete the talent release form.

Disclaimer: LEGO is a trademark of the LEGO Group of companies which does not sponsor, authorize, or endorse this contest.

For the day of the event you will need the following:

- Tables, enough to cover the number of entrants you either anticipate or can estimate based on past events. With almost 100 entries, the library started with ten six-foot tables.
- Signage labeling each table and category
- Signs telling the public "do not touch" the entries
- Entry forms (this is helpful in keeping a tally of all attendees too)
- Amplification system to read out the winners

Create

On the day of the LEGO contest, the actual event takes four forms:

- Drop-off time: This is an excellent time for staff to meet and greet users as they drop off their projects, talk up other events, and have more one-on-one time with the young people than will be available later in the day. Have staff stationed during the entire drop-off period, and handle the intake of projects as they are dropped off. When you are planning your drop-off time, consider offering the evening before the event, say from 5 to 9 p.m. This allows daytime working families a chance to participate. Doing this will mean more staff time and that your room will be further occupied, so it might not always be possible, but it is something to consider.
- Judging/photography: Once the doors are closed, the judges can work together to make their decisions. Having your judges involved during the planning of the contest will help make the judging process go more smoothly. Allowing your judges the freedom to come up with their own method for determining the winners is the best thing you can do. Try not to micromanage your judges. The library allows three hours to conduct the judging. With well over 100 entries at this point, time is of the essence. During the judging, staff can take pictures of the entries. Two people will be needed to take pictures. Use the photographer's trick of holding up two white pieces of foam core to put around the entry as you take the photo to create a neutral background.
- Viewing: From 7 to 8 p.m. the library allows the public to come and view all of the entries. Many people who didn't enter the contest will come to view the entries, but the room is mostly filled with the families of the entrants. Be prepared for a large crowd! Take every entry and multiply it by at least three to guess how many people will attend the event (see Figure 9.3).
- Award ceremony: Starting at 8 p.m., library staff take to the microphone and welcome the attendees, announce other library events, and then begin the award

ceremony. Experience has taught us to ask the attendees to wait until the *end* of the ceremony to take their projects home with them, if possible. This will avoid the rudeness and disruption of winners trying to leave while you are still announcing winners in other categories. As winners are announced the medals and gift certificates are handed out. Consider how crowded the front of the room will get when planning the event and looking at your space. It is easy to lose control during this phase without enough planning.

In this case, again, it is the users themselves who get the opportunity to create. The library's role is mainly in creating the platform and the opportunity. When a tween or teen is awarded for excellence in LEGO building, it may often trump other more traditional awards because it acknowledges a love and interest that he or she is not often rewarded for. Any opportunity to reward a young person for creativity is a good thing. The library's role here is coming up with fun and exciting categories and great prizes.

Figure 9.3. LEGO Contest

Food, Technology, and Other Mandatory Extras

Taking photos of the entries is a wonderful added extra that your contest can offer. You can create a visual display of the event on a bulletin board or library website so patrons can continue to enjoy the event long after it is over for this year.

Analysis

LEGO events have continued to be popular in libraries year after year. At the library, the annual LEGO contest has grown in size every year and has become one of the most eagerly anticipated events. There is not much in libraries teens wait for with baited breath! You will find that the bang for the buck in engagement and new users that a successfully run LEGO event will garner is worth every penny. If you have a limited budget, hold a LEGO event.

Marketing Tips

The program is advertised in the summer reading program flyer, with directions to stop by the library or visit the library website for a copy of the rules and guidelines. The program is also promoted by a local LEGO enthusiast who runs another family LEGO event in town. Look for local groups or message boards online to post details about the event.

Resources

Check out these resources for help with a LEGO program:

Bedford, Allan. 2005. *The Unofficial LEGO Builders Guide.* San Francisco: No Starch Press.

Bulger, Aaron. 2010. "LEGO Contests." Accessed March 8. http://legocontests .blogspot.com/.

Lipkowitz, Daniel. 2009. *The LEGO Book.* London: DK Publishing.

Chapter 10

Programs: Cooking and Food, Food, Food

Food is always popular with teens and tweens. Specific types of food go in and out of style and can be fun to highlight at library programs, where it might be the only place a teen has a chance to try that type of food. Pick an exotic type of food for your community such as sushi, vegetarian dishes, or a Tofurky Thanksgiving, and create a program where teens develop their cooking skills and try new dishes that they may enjoy.

Food Tastings

General Description

Tastings of any type of food are highly popular because the one thing most teens love to do is eat. Collectively, we have tried chocolate, cheese, gelato, bacon, soda, and pizza tastings. The tastings can be a game where participants guess the brand of a certain type of food, such as a chocolate candy bar tasting. Another angle for a tasting is to try different types of a certain category of food for the sake of awareness or just plain fun.

Pop

A *foodie* is defined as a person who is devoted to good food and drink. The term was coined in *New York Magazine* by food critic Gael Greene in the early 1980s. There are tons of websites dedicated to listing the best types of food in certain areas. Through Yelp (http://www.yelp.com), people can find others' opinions on restaurants and join meetups to tour cities for the best hot dogs in town.

Relate

The pizza-tasting program was used as a tool to make teens aware of the different local pizza places in the area. It helped the pizza restaurants out by giving them publicity, and it was a great day of eating pizza for the teens. We hoped it also opened the teens' eyes to other possibilities for ordering pizza besides the big chains.

Instructors/Talent

The cheese, gelato, and bacon tastings were coordinated by a local gourmet deli. The programs were run presentation style, where representatives from the deli gave a PowerPoint on the history of the food, while different types of cheese, for instance, were passed around the seated crowd. Adults also attended this speaker-audience program.

Audience

Both teens and tweens were invited to the pizza program. The teens took the tasting very seriously, but the tweens spent a lot of time giggling. It worked out fine to have the groups together, but it may be better to hold the program separately for each group. The teens seemed to appreciate the processes of choosing their favorite pizza. It was more of a party atmosphere for the tweens, which is great too, and more about just eating lots of pizza.

Planning and Supplies

Talk to area pizza restaurants for donations. You can offer promotion of their restaurant to the attendees and send out press releases to local newspapers for potential articles. Even one pizza from each place is fine because it can be cut it into small pieces. The event included pizza from six different places, so having small tastes of each was best to limit the upchuck possibilities. Create worksheets for the teens to write down notes as they try each pizza.

Create

As the teens taste each pizza, have them rate the pizzas for the best sauce, the best cheese, the best crust, and the best overall pizza. Everyone tries each pizza once while taking notes, then go through the pizzas again in order, asking if anyone needs a second tasting to make up their minds. Then take a group vote, discovering the best pizza in every category. Many of the pizza places gave coupons to pass onto the teens. The soda tasting was very similar, where bottles of colas from around the world were purchased from a local specialty soda shop. Small paper cups were used so that teens could have small tastes of ten different colas.

Food, Technology, and Other Mandatory Extras

Food is the point of the program, so food is definitely needed! A computer and projector are needed if you are doing a PowerPoint presentation.

Analysis

These are great programs because everyone loves to try different types of food. Choose a type of food that teens are into, like cookies or ice cream. Beware of feeding the teens too much food. There is potential for upchuck. If local businesses are kind enough to donate food, send a letter to each restaurant or business, thanking them with a picture of the teens enjoying the food.

Marketing Tips

If you are partnered with a local deli, ask them to promote the program at their establishment.

Resources

Check Yelp (http://www.yelp.com) for ideas on local establishments with interesting food that you want to showcase to your teens.

Sushi Making

General Description

Hire a local sushi restaurant to come and teach a hands-on sushi-making class or, if staff is feeling ambitious, try teaching the class without the experts. With a sushi chef the program can include some demonstrations of fancy knife work and show the teens the technique. Avoiding raw fish is easy as there are tons of vegetarian sushi rolls. Also consider making California rolls with imitation crab meat since that is a processed meat and not raw.

Pop

Anything having to do with the Japanese culture has been hot for teens for years, and sushi continues to be popular. Japanese culture and aesthetics are fascinating to American teens and exposing them to the how-to of sushi is a great way to engage teens who also like anime and manga.

Relate

This program has crossover appeal. Teens interested in anime, manga, and other aspects of Japanese culture will enjoy this event, as will teens who enjoy food programming and want to try something new. This is also a slightly exotic program and requires some special supplies, so it is a great way to expose teens to something they might not otherwise experience at home. Include this program in your repertoire to reach other cultures as well as for cultural awareness.

Instructors/Talent

Unless staff is feeling really ambitious and also feels versed in teaching some of the traditions of sushi, it is recommended to hire a restaurant to facilitate this program. A restaurant will already have all supplies and expertise on hand, and it is a great way for them to market their business to a new clientele. Depending on the restaurant, this event could be free to the library or an agreement can be made for a low-cost price.

Audience

This is definitely an event for teens and adults. Teens will love getting their hands dirty making sushi rolls and trying something new.

Planning and Supplies

Planning and supplies all depends on if the program is taught by a restaurant or library staff. If library staff conducts the program, this is just a sampling of the supplies that will be needed:

- Sushi rolling mats
- Saran wrap
- Rice cookers
- Sushi rice vinegar
- Gloves
- Nori (seaweed)
- A variety of Japanese vegetables
- Sharp knives for cutting
- Coverings to keep rice off the floor and tables

If a restaurant conducts the program, all of these supplies will be provided, and it is recommended that "kits" for each teen are created with nori and vegetables already portioned out. Since the rice needs to stay slightly warm so it does not stick together, the restaurant can handle this easily. Work closely with the restaurant and this will be a fun and smooth event.

Create

This event should start with a talk about the history or significance of sushi in Japanese culture, and this can be done while the sushi chef demonstrates and prepares some special rolls. Then the instructor will tell the teens what they will be making and how to make it. Ideally this event will go off better if the setup allows for a camera to be over the shoulder of the chef, then projected on a screen so the participants can follow along. If this is not possible, be sure to have several staff on hand (versed in the basics if they are not restaurant staff) that can walk around and assist the teens. After that, it is all about rolling and eating!

Food, Technology, and Other Mandatory Extras

As mentioned, a setup that allows for a cooking show atmosphere is ideal. If a camera can project what the chef is doing on a screen, then the participants can watch the chef demonstrate his or her impressive skills and follow along. If this is not possible, then having several staff on hand is important.

Analysis

This event must be hands on if the audience is primarily teens. If, however, it was more of a lecture-and-listen event with a sushi tasting, then this format is more ideal for older teens and adults. This has consistently been one of the most popular food events at the library and, depending on your community, you should be prepared for a large attendance. Running out of food is not an option.

Marketing Tips

Market this event in a way that will appeal to all teens, with a focus on teens interested in anime, manga, and Japanese culture. Be sure to emphasize that no raw fish will be used.

Resources

Check out these books for tips on sushi making:

Kariya, Tetsu. 2009. *Oishinbo: Fish, Sushi & Sashimi: A La Carte.* San Francisco: Viz Media.
Strada, Judi, and Mineko Takane Moreno. 2004. *Sushi for Dummies.* Hoboken, NJ: Wiley Publishing.

Vegetarian Cooking

General Description

Vegetarianism and all the various subsets, such as veganism, ovo, lacto, fruit vegetarianism and more, have been rising in popularity and commonality for more than 30 years now. It is often during the teen years that many people try it for the first time. Teens need good information about eating healthy while learning to make vegetarian food. This event can happen any time of the year and takes several forms, but consider offering it near Thanksgiving or Easter or any event that often centers around meat as the focus of a family meal.

Pop

Many people first explore vegetarianism during their teen years. Vegetarianism is trendy in certain circles of teens and is often the first time a teen takes control over something significant in his or her life. This can create challenges for the family in some cases. Many parents have concerns about proper nutrition for this diet, so information is important for teens. The various ethical, religious, environmental, and health reasons people become vegetarian is an important part of the movement. Millions of people around the world, the largest concentration in India, are vegetarians. Organizations like PETA are often in the news with their provocative and often controversial tactics and advertising.

Relate

Teaching vegetarian cooking to teens is an important educational life skill and will provide valuable information to teens looking to become vegetarians. Teens will not only learn new cooking techniques but may also meet other vegetarians.

Instructors/Talent

Hire a vegetarian chef, caterer, or talented local enthusiast to present a vegetarian cooking class. This event can be mostly demonstration wherein the chef cooks and talks about the food, cooking tips, and offers the audience samples (library staff or the chef's helpers will do this). Alternately, offer a hands-on cooking opportunity that allows participants to make items themselves. This can be done either with individuals making items like a single-serve salad or a group of teens cooking one recipe that allows everyone to try some when it is done. If you or other library staff are enthusiastic vegetarian cooks, it may not be necessary to hire someone to run this event.

Audience

Teens and also adults are the main audience for this type of event. Depending on the approach, it would also appeal to some tweens.

Planning and Supplies

If outside presenters are hired, they should ideally provide all of the supplies and materials. In that case, it will be necessary to determine electrical and setup needs for your space. Determine whether they will also provide plates, utensils, and napkins for sampling, or if the library will provide these. Participants will want copies of the recipes, so plan handouts for this part of the presentation.

Create

This event depends largely on the enthusiasm of the presenter. Determine if you want to stick with strictly vegetable products or if you want to introduce meat replacements as well. If you do the event near Thanksgiving, be sure to include a Tofurky since it is such an infamous meat replacement.

Food, Technology, and Other Mandatory Extras

If you are doing a cooking demo and have access to cameras or a projector, consider replicating the "over the shoulder" cooking camera seen on cooking shows so that participants can see the hands of the demonstrator.

Analysis

This is a popular event that can surely be offered every year to appeal to a new crop of teens each time. Since there are endless recipes out there, it is not possible to run out of new dishes to demonstrate. Some participants may be reluctant to try certain items. This is normal and a good reason not to focus exclusively on meat replacement options, since that is often what some people find odd to eat.

Marketing Tips

Take flyers and promos to health food stores, vegetarian restaurants, and other places where holistic services are offered. Promote the event to the schools, emphasizing the "hands-on" aspect of the program.

Resource

Check out this book for recipes:

Pierson, Stephanie. 1999. *Vegetables Rock! A Complete Guide for Teenage Vegetarians*. New York: Bantam Books.

Revolting Recipes

General Description

By blending cooking and the witty imagination of Roald Dahl, tweens can get creative with candy and re-create aspects from our favorite stories such as *Charlie and the Chocolate Factory* and *The Twits*. This program can be in honor of Roald Dahl Day, September 13, in celebration of another book turned to movie, or just because Dahl is one of the coolest authors ever.

Pop

One of children's literature's best-loved authors, Roald Dahl has captured the interest of everyone from book lovers to reluctant readers with his revolting humor. Many of his books have been made into movies, with *Charlie and the Chocolate Factory* made into two versions so far. Who cannot get a kick out of children smelling of dog droppings in *The Witches*, and a boy climbing into a giant peach and making friends with a bunch of insects in *James and the Giant Peach*? The most recent adaptation of a Dahl book to hit the big screen is *Fantastic Mr. Fox*.

Relate

Libraries are well-known for their book clubs and book-based programming. What better way to make a lasting impression than to make a book come alive with fun activities based on the magical elements of the stories?

Instructors/Talent

No instructors needed.

Audience

Tweens, grades 3 through 6.

Planning and Supplies

- Fruit Roll-Ups
- Frosting
- Candy
- Instant mashed potatoes
- Paper plates, plastic flatware, plastic wrap to take home creations
- Tarp

Create

The programming room was set up with three stations: Lickable Wallpaper, Mr. Twit's Beard, and a cookie frosting table. Staff members monitored the food tables throughout the room so that the candy was dispersed evenly.

Everyone has wondered what snozzberry wallpaper would really taste like because "Who ever heard of a snozzberry?" Well, you have, and you get to come up with your own lickable wallpaper. Each participant received a Fruit Roll-Up, frosting, and an assortment of candy and Pull-and-Peel Licorice to create sweet designs.

In honor of Mr. Twit and his scrumptious beard, kids were given their color choice of instant mashed potatoes dyed with food coloring. Using the mashed potatoes as their canvas, they added food pieces that would collect in Mr. Twit's beard as he ate, such as chow mein noodles, raisins, Maraschino cherries, and candy.

Finally, to use up the leftover candy, kids decorated cookies with frosting and candy. The program was topped off with fizzy lifting drinks: lemon-lime soda with a touch of sherbet to make it foamy.

Food, Technology, and Other Mandatory Extras

No extra food is needed for this event, as there will be enough candy to snack on while making delectable Dahl creations.

Analysis

This program is sure to cause a sugar rush and would be great paired with a book discussion, but the candy activities should probably happen at the end of the program to maintain concentration. It is also really important to put tarps on the floor because mashed potatoes and frosting will get everywhere. Another possible addition to this program could be to show one of the movies based on a Roald Dahl book. The kids can make their own snacks for the showing of the movie. Put up a display of Dahl books, so that those who are interested can pick out a new title to read.

Marketing Tips

Promote this program to fourth- and fifth-grade teachers, as well as homeschool groups, as a supplemental program to books they may be reading in class. Try some guerrilla advertising tactics by leaving flyers in the Roald Dahl books on the shelf or posting small posters in the shelving next to targeted books and the cookbook section.

Resources

Use these resources to add more activities to this program:

Dahl, Roald. 1997. *Roald Dahl's Revolting Recipes.* New York: Viking.
Roald Dahl Day. http://www.roalddahlday.info/.
Roald Dahl: The Official Web site. http://www.roalddahl.com/.

Smoothie Sensation

General Description

Smoothies are a blended, chilled, sometimes sweetened beverage made from fresh fruit or vegetables. The drink sometimes includes ice, frozen fruit, honey, yogurt, or ice cream, with 100 percent fruit as the healthiest option. This event could take many forms in terms of approach, but in its simplest terms you provide some recipes, some food, and blenders, and let the teens have a great time making smoothies! You could also hire a local smoothie store or stand to come and do this event if you have a budget to use.

Pop

With the increasing epidemic of childhood obesity, any opportunity to expose young people to healthy choices like fruit-based snacks is a good thing. Smoothies have been around in popular culture for years, going back to Orange Julius, which rose to popularity in the 1960s. The current smoothie house of choice for the popular sweet treat is Jamba Juice, which can be found at a mall near you.

Relate

Giving teens the chance to make their own snacks and explore their taste preferences is a great way to give teens a fun time at the library. Healthy eating is an important skill for teens to learn and this type of program lets them try new foods, find out how easy they are to make themselves, and leave with a variety of recipes to take home.

Instructors/Talent

This is an easy enough program for staff to conquer themselves, but hire an instructor if you have the budget to spend and do not want to fuss with the complications of collecting blenders and shopping for food. In addition to the franchises that serve smoothies, there are also many small neighborhood smoothie shops that may be interested in helping you with your event. Sometimes you may not need to pay them if they feel that they get enough marketing and publicity to offset the cost of the event.

Audience

Grades 6 through 12.

Planning and Supplies

It is very easy to track down a wide variety of smoothie recipes. Just using an Internet search engine will bring up a myriad of options. See the Resources section for more ideas.

- Kitchen
- Recipes: Laminate several copies of each recipe to keep them dry.
- Blenders
- Measuring cups and spoons, several sets
- Fruit
- Table covers

- Paper cups

Create

It is important to have several staff members on hand for an event like this. If you think you will get more than 20 teens, then two to three staff members are recommended. If you do not control the ingredients or have enough of everything, it is very easy for this to become a wild and insanely messy event. Too much planning is not possible. Ideally, you would like to have one staff member stationed in the kitchen or at a food station to hand out the supplies recipe by recipe, and to rinse out the blenders and measuring utensils in between uses. You will want to offer three to seven recipes for a more varied experience for the teens. Have the teens work in groups to make the recipes. This event is relatively fast moving so be prepared for the participants to prepare each recipe a minimum of four times.

Food, Technology, and Other Mandatory Extras

Use this event as an opportunity to expose the teens to some unusual fruits or textures. You do not have to go too weird in case they will not eat it, but be creative.

Analysis

Do this year after year with new recipes and it never gets old. The tweens and teens always have a blast when they are given permission to make a mess and do things themselves. Some teens never get the chance to explore or be inventive with food. Teens will have a great time at this event and leave with a variety of recipes to take home to their family to try again or adjust to their liking.

Marketing Tips

It is usually not difficult to attact tweens and teens to a program about food. In addition to the traditional library advertising, spread the word by putting flyers up in food establishments where teens hang out, such as coffee shops, pizza places, and fast-food joints. If the local schools have any type of home economics program, consider letting those teachers know and also ask if flyers can be posted in the cafeteria.

Resources

Check out these books for ideas for smoothie recipes:

Barber, Mary. 1997. *Smoothies: 50 Recipes for High-Energy Refreshment*. San Francisco: Chronicle Books.

Chace, Daniella. 1998. *Smoothies for Life! Yummy, Fun and Nutritious*. Rocklin, CA: Prima Publishing.

Constans, Gabriel. 1997. *Great American Smoothies: The Ultimate Blending Guide for Shakes, Slushes, Desserts, and Thirst Quenchers.* New York: Avery.

Bento Box Bonanza

General Description

The bento box event is a combination of fun, food, and cultural exposure. Bento boxes are a traditional Japanese way of holding lunch, but there is also an art to packing a nice bento. In recent years it has become an art form, making carrots look like anime characters or friendly animals. It is also a fun way to entice young people to try healthy foods in a new way. The library will provide the box, the food, and the inspiration, while the attendees will enjoy making their own decorative bento boxes. This event can also include inviting members of the Japanese culture to come and talk about bento.

The women who spoke at the library about bento took a video at a local Saturday Japanese school to show children eating their bento. They also did a cooking demonstration to show how a piece of hot dog can be cut and then cooked to look like an octopus. The cooking process makes the "tentacles" curl. Bento also usually includes molded rice that has nori (seaweed) or other things mixed in for color, texture, and details. Hard-boiled eggs at the right temperature can be molded in a special mold in the shape of a bunny or with other face details. Fruits, vegetables, processed meats, seeds, eggs, and more can be cut and arranged in decorative and clever ways.

Pop

Bento has a long history in Japan, but its popularity in the United States is just beginning. With the focus on getting young people to eat healthier, bento is a perfect Japanese tradition to become popular in the United States where obesity in children has become a concern. Like much in Japanese culture, the aesthetics and the *kawaii* (cute) aspect of bento are very aesthetically appealing. In Japan, there are bento contests, and parents often make bento lunches that look like Hello Kitty, Totoro, or video game characters. Over 400 photo groups on the popular photo-sharing website Flickr.com are devoted to bento boxes. Looking at photos of decorative bento boxes is an excellent way to get ideas. In September 2009, the *New York Times* published an article about the rise of bento boxes in United States homes (Storey, 2009).

Relate

Japanese pop culture has continued to be a popular interest for many tweens and teens. From Pokémon to Hello Kitty, sushi, and manga, in between there is a segment of every population with an interest in Japanese pop culture. This is a great way to engage your users who read manga or check out your anime collection. It is also an excellent educational event to explore the traditions and origins of bento culture in Japan. Involve teens who may want to share their culture with others and help out at the program. Many books can be added to your collection to complement the event as well. This is an excellent hands-on opportunity that gives tweens and teens a creative outlet while exposing them to another way to try healthy foods (see Figure 10.1).

Instructors/Talent

In order to fully conduct the program, you do not need to hire any experts, but it would be a far better event if you had volunteers from the Japanese community or staff from a local Japanese restaurant come to talk and do a demonstration of traditional bento boxes. This portion of the event could include a talk, a video, photo boards, bento samples, examples of rice molds, egg molds, food picks, and bento boxes.

Audience

Grades 4 through 8.

Planning and Supplies

You will have to locate boxes for each participant to use for their bento boxes. Whether you use real bento boxes which can be pricey, ranging from $1.50 to $3.00 each in bulk,

Figure 10.1. Healthy Bento Box Creation

Gladware, or even ask participants to bring their own containers, you can easily pull off this event. Locate any local Japanese cultural groups to find volunteers or contact Japanese restaurants in your area to see if they would be able to help do a bento box presentation.

Stick with the more traditional U.S. foods that are in bento boxes instead of Japanese specialty foods, unless you have a very large budget. Offering traditional ginger or pickled plums would be very costly but very cool. So use your budget to guide you. Use strawberries, grapes, tomatoes, leaf lettuce, processed cheeses and meats, broccoli, sunflower seeds, poppy seeds, sesame seeds, nori, asparagus, peppers, green beans, and snow peas, which are all easily acquired and make for a lovely bento box.

Supplies include:

- Kitchen
- Bento boxes or equivalent
- Plastic cookie cutters, e.g., letters, animals, foods, or shapes to cut shapes in the processed cheese and meat
- Food, including mostly fruits and vegetables like grapes, strawberries, lettuce, processed turkey (avoiding ham is good for dietary and religious reasons), processed cheeses, seeds, nori
- Scissors, sanitized, used to cut the nori
- Plastic knives to cut the food
- Napkins
- Trash bags, large quantity

Create

This is a very supply-and-setup-heavy event that will require several staff members. Ideally you will want someone in the kitchen or at a food station to hand out the food and be sure that the public does not touch the food. It is important for staff to wear gloves and use utensils to hand out the food. Scissors and the cookie cutters can be put out on the tables before the event. If you have a large crowd, it's best to release the participants to pick up their food table by table. It is a good idea to have paper and pencils or markers on hand, so that while participants are waiting to get their food, they can plan out how they want their bento box to look. Participants can think about characters or look at the display the volunteers or restaurant brought to give them ideas.

Food, Technology, and Other Mandatory Extras

One relatively easy way to add something extra to the program is to create an image slide show in PowerPoint of images of bento boxes from Flickr.com. Include a computer, projector, and screen to your list of supplies if this is feasible for you. A slide show was created with 40 images ranging from traditional aesthetic bento boxes to a variety of anime, manga, and character bentos in many colors. People looked to the images as inspiration for their drawings as they planned, and it also served as a pleasant diversion while the participants waited for food. Also, be sure to have a selection of books on hand for participants to check out after the event (see Figure 10.2).

Analysis

This event is one that seems to make everyone happy! Who doesn't enjoy using good ingredients to create cute characters in adorable little plastic boxes? Participants learn something new and are inspired to try new things. As an anecdote, at the end of the program a mother mentioned that her daughter started munching on a raw piece of asparagus for the first time ever! It is a great way to encourage healthy eating and smaller portion size.

Marketing Tips

Reaching out to Japanese nationals and to enthusiasts of Japanese culture is the best way to get the word out about this event. See if local sushi restaurants or Asian/Japanese markets will put up a flyer in their businesses. Many schools have anime/manga clubs, so seek out the teachers and students who run these groups and let them know about

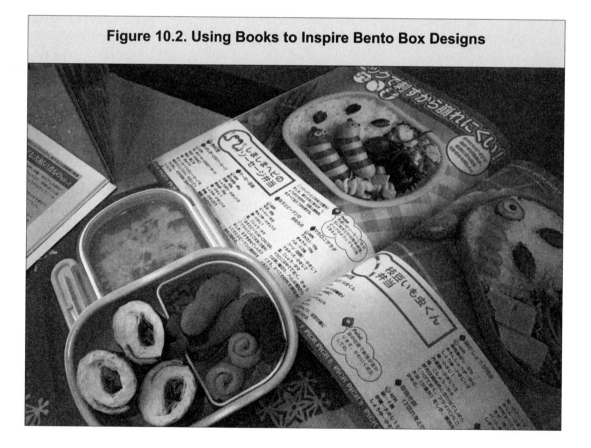

Figure 10.2. Using Books to Inspire Bento Box Designs

the program. If there is a local comic book store or other business that sells manga and other Japanese pop culture items, be sure they get a stack of flyers too.

Resources

Check out these books for recipes and ideas:

Ishihara, Yoko. 2007. *The Manga Cookbook*. Japan: Manga University Culinary Institute.

Salyers, Christopher. 2008. *Face Food: The Visual Creativity of Japanese Bento Boxes*. New York: Mark Batty Publishers.

Staff, Joie. 2006. *Kawaii Bento Boxes: Cute and Convenient Japanese Meals on the Go*. New York: Kodansha.

Storey, Samantha. 2009. "Bento Boxes Win Lunch Fans." *New York Times*. September 8. http://www.nytimes.com/2009/09/09/dining/09bentohtml.

Chapter 11

Programs: Crafts

Libraries are very good at providing craft programs for everyone from preschool age through mature adulthood. Think about ways to add spice to your craft programs with the inspiration of pop culture. Bring back the pet rock from the 1970s. Use popular craft books to build programs that will teach a fun new skill as well as encourage use of the craft collection at the library.

Shrinky Dinks

General Description

This is a wonderfully versatile craft program that will appeal to boys and girls equally. Using Shrinky Dink plastic, the teens can make jewelry, key chains, pins, pet tags, and more. This is a workshop that is open-ended and does not have to be project based.

Pop

Shrinky Dinks appeal to the nostalgia factor for many adults and are still fun and weird enough for teens to get into it. The fact that it is something that many of their parents remember will be a fun aspect for teens to share.

Relate

Any teen who enjoys creating and making things will enjoy this workshop. The flexibility and open-ended nature of working with Shrinky Dinks is an appealing aspect for any teen. Also, Shrinky Dinks are incredibly easy to make, so the sense of success for the teen will be high.

Instructors/Talent

This is an easy program to conduct; no talent is needed.

Audience

Shrinky Dinks appeal to children, teens, and adults. Adults who recall Shrinky Dinks from their youth will love it, and it is easy enough for children as young as age five to participate. As long as the oven is an adult-only zone, this activity can safely appeal to many ages.

Planning and Supplies

This program involves providing all of the supplies and letting the teens do the rest. The shrinking plastic can be purchased at most craft stores and online. You will need to provide the following:

- Shrinky Dink plastic in a variety of colors (white, black, brown, etc.) but mostly the "rough and ready" clear plastic. Preroughened plastic allows for ink to stick to the plastic. Otherwise, it must first be sanded. Several other companies make this material, not just Shrinky Dink.
- Scissors
- Hole punches (any holes must be punched *before* the creation goes in the oven)
- Sharpie markers in a variety of colors
- Rubber stamps
- Stamp pads in a variety of colors
- Jewelry supplies like jump rings, hemp, string
- Key chains, pin backs, and jump rings to make pet tags
- Brown paper bags cut into pieces to put the Shrinky Dinks on when they go in the oven.
- An oven, preferably one with a glass door and light so you can see inside. Watching the plastic cook is the best part!

Create

Provide the supplies, then give the teens the basic rundown on how Shrinky Dinks work and what the various options are with the supplies available. Then let them go to it! Once teens have completed some projects, start putting the pieces in the oven. If it is possible, and there is enough adult supervision, teens will enjoy watching them shrink too.

Food, Technology, and Other Mandatory Extras

None needed.

Analysis

This is an event that will become part of your staple craft programs. Because the possibilities are endless and the teens can make whatever they want, they will not tire of the program. This event can be tailored to a specific project (for example, making pins for Mother's Day) and is as versatile as you make it.

Marketing Tips

When marketing to teens who may not know what Shrinky Dinks are, it might be necessary to briefly describe how it works. But be sure to mention the wide variety of things that can be made, particularly if an audience of both boys and girls is desired. Also, put up examples around the teen area to get teens interested.

Resources

Check out these books for ideas on how to be creative with Shrinky Dinks:

Phillips, Karen. 2007. *Shrink Art Jewelry*. Palo Alto, CA: Klutz.
Roulston, Jane. 2002. *Shrink Art 101*. Fort Worth, TX: Design Originals.

Jean Pocket Purses

General Description

Reworking and redesigning clothes is a popular hobby for teens and adults. Using the pockets of old jeans, teens can make tiny purses to accessorize their outfits, give as gifts, or use to put small gifts inside.

Pop

Personalizing jeans became very popular in the 1970s. Teens adorned their bellbottom jeans with bells, patchwork, embroidery, appliqués, and antiwar graffiti. Recycling jeans into cutoffs and miniskirts was a fashion commonly worn by flower children during the hippie revolution.

Relate

Creating a space for teens to make their own clothes to illustrate their original and unique fashion sense is very important. It is also great modeling to show teens you do not need to purchase new clothes all the time; instead, you can rework and repurpose what you already have in your closet to create a new look. It is "going green" for clothes. Highlight your clothing craft books and fashion materials, as well as your decade books, on a display near the project area. This program might prompt a teen to find out more about what the hippie culture was really like.

Instructors/Talent

No instructor is needed.

Audience

This is a great project for both tweens and teens. Crafty adults might want to sneak into this program too. Depending on how well your different-aged library groups get along, it might be best to have separate programs for tweens and teens. Tweens will need more attention and help with glue guns.

Planning and Supplies

What a great excuse to clean out your closet! Collect gently used jeans from staff or purchase jeans from a used clothing store as a last resort. Cut the pockets out of the jeans, but save the rest of the denim for another craft project later.

- Ribbons for handle
- Beads
- Fabric paint (if the audience can handle it)
- Fabric pens
- Jewels
- Buttons
- Craft glue
- Hot-glue guns
- Sharp scissors
- Needle and thread

Create

Make up a sample to inspire teens with ideas, and then throw all the supplies out on tables for teens to get creative. Craft glue worked very well to keep small embellishments attached to the pocket. The glue guns were broken out to secure the ribbon handles and kept in a corner for safety purposes, so staff could watch over them. Every teen was asked to take a pledge by putting the two "Scout's honor" fingers in the air and saying, "I will not burn myself." It was hokey, but it at least got everyone in the room remembering that the glue guns are hot.

Food, Technology, and Other Mandatory Extras

No treats are needed for the event.

Analysis

The program was scheduled for the week before Christmas. Teens came in to make last-minute gifts. Present this program before Mother's Day as well for all those kids who want to make their mothers a present. A lot of boys were attracted to this program, which was surprising, but they seemed to be in desperation mode for presents for loved ones.

Marketing Tips

Contact local home education classes and fashion clubs to spread the word about this program. Put flyers in the shelving next to the clothing craft books in the library.

Resource

Check out this book for other ideas of how to repurpose denim:

Blakeney Faith, Justina Blakeney, and Ellen Schultz. 2007. *99 Ways to Cut, Sew, & Deck Out Your Denim*. New York: Potter Craft.

Duct Tape Crafts

General Description

Duct tape events are fairly ubiquitous in libraries, but do not let that fool you into thinking it is not cool anymore. Duct tape craft events are a surefire way to bring in a consistently unisex audience. The library has been doing duct tape events for more than five years and there is still heavy attendance each time. Basically, all you need to do is provide tape, cutting surfaces, cutting implements, and some patterns. Voila! Instant program.

Pop

Duct tape has been a staple of library programming for years but not without good reason. Duct tape manages to be squeaky clean and tough at the same time, and it cuts across gender lines in a way few other hands-on projects do. Duct tape prom contests have been the rage for several years. Teens make the entire prom dress and suit from duct tape in schools across the country. Duck Brand tape sponsored its 10th Annual Stuck at the Prom Contest in 2010 with prizes of scholarships for the winners. Also in 2009 a teen whose home was rebuilt on *Extreme Makeover: Home Edition* got a bedroom decked out in duct tape creations and a work table and supply of duct tape to last him for years.

Relate

Offering duct tape seasonally or even monthly in some cases is a great way to engage a steady group of teens in library events. There will always be a group of teens who enjoy making things out of duct tape, and you want to be sure to offer a place in your library for their interests.

Instructors/Talent

The great thing about duct tape is that you do not need an expert. If you have a local teen who is really talented and enthusiastic, you might have him or her teach a workshop, but most teens can teach themselves how to make something out of duct tape using instructions and templates. You can also make an assortment of samples to keep on hand so that participants can have a tangible sample.

Audience

Grades 6 through 12.

Planning and Supplies

Purchase an inventory of a wide selection of duct tape, inexpensive scrap wood to make cutting boards that can be used again and again, a supply of X-Acto knives for cutting, and a wide assortment of project descriptions that you can laminate and keep on hand:

- Duct tape: primary colors, pastels, fluorescent, black, camouflage, caution, tie-dye, clear, plaid, glow-in-the-dark
- Cutting boards: 20 to 70 pieces, depending on attendance
- X-Acto knives: 20 to 70
- Instructions for duct tape projects like wallets, ties, flip-flops, purses, roses, etc., that have been laminated for repeated use
- Scissors
- Rulers
- Sharpie markers in a variety of colors
- Velcro in a variety of sizes and shapes

Create

This program is all about creating opportunities. How many teens would ever be able to have all of the colors of duct tape that the library can provide at a program? Give the teens the opportunity and the access, and the possibilities are endless. Provide all the supplies and the laminated directions, and other than being there to offer support, it is a self-running event (see Figure 11.1).

Figure 11.1. Creative Duct Tape Crafts

Food, Technology, and Other Mandatory Extras

As a frill-free event, if you felt so inclined you could create a slide show of duct tape prom images to show during the event for fun. PowerPoint, a laptop, projector, and screen would be required. As an alternative, you could have a laptop with a slide show set up for teens to take turns viewing during the event.

Analysis

The cost-benefit for this event is difficult to argue with. At how many events do you get equal numbers of boys and girls in high numbers? Not many. This is a solid creative event that will offer a continual positive perception of the library.

Marketing Tips

Promote this program to local Boys & Girls Clubs and teen centers looking for easy, entertaining events to refer their teens to during the summer. Put up displays of original and unique duct tape creations designed by staff or, even better, by teens to both showcase artwork and advertise the program.

Resources

Learn the art of creating things with duct tape and get some fun ideas of crafts to make:

Bonaddio, T.L. 2009. *Stick It!: 99 Duct Tape Projects.* Philadelphia, PA: Running Press Kids.

Duck. 2010. "Stuck at Prom Scholarship Contest." Accessed September 2. http://www.duckbrand.com/Promotions/stuck-at-prom.aspx.

Duct Tape Fashion. http://www.ducttapefashion.com/.

Schiedermayer, Ellie. 2002. *Got Tape? Roll Out the Fun with Duct Tape.* Lola, WI: Krause Publications.

Tape Brothers. http://www.tapebrothers.com/.

Wilson, Joe. 2006. *Ductigami: The Art of the Tape.* Ontario, Canada: Boston Mills Press.

T-shirt Remodel

General Description

In this project, teens rework old T-shirts to create funky and stylish new fashion designs.

Pop

Teens have their own sense of style, different from the clothing styles popular with adults, because teens use their clothes to express who they are and their own subculture within the hierarchy of high school. Clothing is a symbol for which clique or group they belong to: goth, preppy, sporty, nerd-chic?

Relate

If clothing is a great way for teens to express themselves, why not help them discover their style while at the library? It is a great way to showcase your DIY craft books.

Instructors/Talent

No instructor is needed.

Audience

Grades 6 through 12. The enormous decision of whether to use fabric paint might help you decide which audience to focus on.

Planning and Supplies

- T-shirts: Take donations from staff for the just-in-case scenario that a teen forgets to bring his or her own shirt.
- Ribbons
- Beads
- Fabric paint (if the audience can handle it)
- Jewels
- Hot-glue guns
- Sharp scissors
- Needle and thread

Create

Depending on the skills of the participants, this program can get as creative as you would like. As led by a scissors-and-hot-glue-gun kind of girl, the program was not heavy on sewing, though needles and thread were available for those more talented. If you can sew, you could even bring in a sewing machine for the teens to use. The *Generation T* books listed in the Resources section have good instructions for creating cool T-shirts with no sewing required (Nicolay, 2006).

Food, Technology, and Other Mandatory Extras

No extras are needed, but food is always appreciated by the participants.

Analysis

Boys also participated in this event, even though it seems more like a girl-centric program, because there were a lot of boy-friendly T-shirts available to remodel, including old shirts with name brands boys associate with, like Fear Street and Mossimo. Plus, having fabric paint allowed boys to add sayings to their shirts instead of ribbons and jewels, though they were more than welcome to use all supplies provided.

Marketing Tips

This program can be marketed as a T-shirt remodeling program or can be structured around a theme such as Valentine's Day or school spirit for football games.

Resources

Check out these books for ideas of how to rework T-shirts:

Marshall, Carmia. 2006. *T-Shirt Makeovers: 20 Transformations for Fabulous Fashions*. New York: Gliteratti Inc.

Nicolay, Megan. 2006. *Generation T: 108 Ways to Transform a T-Shirt*. New York: Workman Publishing Company.

Nicolay, Megan. 2009. *Generation T: Beyond Fashion, 110 T-Shirt Transformations for Pets, Babies, Friends, Your Home, Car, and You*. New York: Workman Publishing Company.

Chapter 12

Programs: Gaming

Video games have become increasing popular since their inception and have become a large part of our culture. The tough part now is staying up on the most trendy games of the moment. Take an extremely solitary activity and make it a social event where the library is the hangout. Look to different formats such as computer, handheld (PSP or Nintendo DS), or console games (Nintendo Wii, Sony Playstation 3, or Microsoft Xbox 360). Ask teens and tweens what their favorite titles are (see Figure 12.1).

Retro Octathlon

General Description

Showcase those older video games that you loved so much as a kid and introduce them to a newer generation. Go through that closet and pull out the Atari or your original Nintendo Entertainment System (NES), or play the new releases of older games on newer game consoles. (Note to whippersnappers: "retro" means pre-1990.)

Pop

Video games began their creation as hobbies for smart techies. The games were available only on large computers. In the 1970s, video games diversified into arcade, handheld, and home computers. *Pong*, based on table tennis, was a big hit for its revolutionary technology in 1972 and was played on the Atari, one of the first widely successful gaming consoles in the United States. Innovation in video gaming technology in the 1980s brought about such classic gems as *Street Fighter, Pac-Man*, and *Mario Bros.*, many of which could be played on the NES. These games are oldies but goodies; they have been reimaged again and again during the past 30 years.

Relate

This can be an intergenerational program, bringing together teens and twentysomethings in friendly competition. Young adults can introduce the teens to the enjoyment of these older video game titles.

Figure 12.1. *Dance Dance Revolution*

Instructors/Talent

No instructors are needed for this program.

Audience

Plan for teens, but expect young adults in their twenties and parents showing up and asking to play. Young adults are always the hardest age group to get into the library, and their interests usually straddle those of teens and older adults. If you are looking for a program to bring in young adults, especially men who stopped using the library after high school, this is the program to try out.

Planning and Supplies

Choose any older games that you enjoyed and want to share with others. If you decide on eight games, you have the "octathlon." And you can change the title of the program if you find fewer games to share; you can make it a "Retro Pentathlon." Some examples are original *Super Mario Bros.*, *Breakout*, *Marble Madness*, *Pole Position*, *Pac-Man*, and *Donkey Kong*. Several older games have been released on the newer consoles, including the Wii, Xbox 360, and Playstation 3. So do not worry about trying to dig up an old Nintendo. This program can be done very cheaply. Look to your staff to borrow older video games and consoles.

Decide whether you would like to run the program as a tournament or as an exhibition, where everyone cycles through the games and tries them out. An optimal situation would be to have multiple televisions, so people can play different games at one time, and cycle through the room. If that's not possible, using one television is also fine. In that situation, each person has a turn on a game and then the game is switched out for another.

Create

Depending on whether you are having a tournament or a retro video gaming petting zoo, have the teens write down their score for each game. Compare the scores on each game, having the high scorers on the most games win prizes. Give out gift cards to local video game stores, or dig up swag for retro games, such as *Mario Bros.* stuffed animals. These can be found most times at comic book stores.

Food, Technology, and Other Mandatory Extras

Food is a must! Especially if you have the teens play eight games. That means they will be playing for a couple of hours, and those teens do get hungry. Snacks like pretzels and Goldfish are great. Make sure there is water available too.

Analysis

This is a low-key program. It is a fun activity to do during school breaks when teens are looking for something to do and can spend the afternoon at the library. Also think about having the program in the evening to attract college students.

Marketing Tips

Promote this program in arcades, local video gaming centers, and comic book stores. Ask to put flyers next to the cash registers. Put up flyers in student unions of local colleges. Blog about this program on Facebook to get the word out to the gaming community.

Resource

Check out this book for the history of gaming:

Kent, Steven L. 2001. *The Ultimate History of Video Games.* New York: Three Rivers Press.

Pokémon Tournaments

General Description

Tweens and teens bring a Nintendo DS or other handheld console to battle their *Pokémon* characters against others.

Pop

Pokémon is a huge phenomenon that has branched out from manga graphic novels to anime, video games, card games, books, toys, and more. Parents to preschoolers know who Pikachu is, one of the best-known *Pokémon* characters. Created in Japan, *Pokémon* means "Pocket Monsters," which accurately explains the concept. The basic idea is that when a trainer comes upon a wild Pokémon, to capture it he or she must throw out the Poke Ball. If the trainer can catch the Pokémon in the ball, then it is his or hers to keep. Hence, the collection of the Pokémon.

Relate

Video gaming has become a major part of teen and tween culture for this current generation. Though at first glance, it does not seem educational, many reluctant readers are reading the text in the game, getting interested in the story line, and searching for books and graphic novels to read based on the characters from the game. This type of program can attract teens who are new to the library, so make sure you put out displays of materials that might interest them and show the value of using the library. Plus, these teens will be adults, having children in no time, and showing the library is interested in their interests now will help create future lifelong library users.

Instructors/Talent

Running gaming programs can be difficult if you have no interest or knowledge in this area. Check around with your staff for video game lovers who can help set up and facilitate the program. Members of the IT department are always good targets. Otherwise, the older kids who participate in the program can be very helpful with answering detailed questions about the game and manning the tournament. Plus, it is great to empower your participants, encouraging their input in the running of the program.

Audience

Plan for grades 3 through 6, but this program will attract younger kids and even middle schoolers.

Planning and Supplies

Based on your budget, this program can cost as little as the price of food. So starting small, the modern versions of the video game *Pokémon* are played on handheld video game systems such as the Nintendo DS, Nintendo DS Lite, and Nintendo DSi. If you have a Wii, buying the game *Pokémon Battle Revolution* for Wii will enable your players to link their DS systems up to the Wii and battle it out on the big screen.

Create

When teens enter the programming room, give them a piece of paper to keep track of their wins and losses during battles. Teens will play ten games with players around the programming room with their DS systems connecting to each other wirelessly. Everyone must have a character enter a certain room in the game ("The Union Room"), where they will pair off for battle. (This is a virtual room in the game, not a real room in your library, which causes confusion every time.) When all players have completed their battles, tally up the sheets, identifying the players with the most wins. Those players will go on to the next round. Everyone else is out of the tournament but can still hang out and keep playing for fun. Let the players in the tournament do battle, using a bracket system: one loss and you're out. The prize to the winner can be a gift certificate to a local video game store or the satisfaction of having the most awesome Pokémon that day and a paper crown with different Pokémon on it. Make the program work for your budget.

An option to consider is to ask that players do not use legendary Pokémon characters. Allowing players to use "Legendaries" gives advantage to the most experienced players and makes it harder for new players to have a chance. Also, if you have players that may have bought their copy of *Pokémon* in Europe or Asia, you can't guarantee that they'll be able to link up with players using the North American version of the DS or Wii games. Foreign copies might work, but they might not, and either way there's nothing you as a tournament organizer can do about it other than set the expectations at the beginning of the event to minimize disappointment.

Food, Technology, and Other Mandatory Extras

Snacks are very important. Make the program have a party atmosphere. Promote healthy eating by putting out fruits and carrots. Teens will pretty much eat anything put out on a table. Be sure to have treats too, like cookies or crackers. Some kids do not get to eat those things at home, so give those kids a little decadence with a root beer float.

Also think about putting the final battles on the big screen! Attach the Wii to a projector so that everyone in the room can watch the action.

Analysis

If you find some kids get finished with their ten games way before the rest of the group, you might have another activity available for them. Many times this program can turn into a family affair because older siblings bring younger ones. The younger kids tend to get bored quickly. There are quite a few craft projects centered around *Pokémon* characters on the Internet. Leave out craft foam, markers, and googly eyes for kids to make their favorite characters. Use all those leftover weeded CDs to create characters as well.

Marketing Tips

Be sure to target anime and manga groups, as well as any comic book or specialty manga stores, with flyers promoting the program. Also, stop by local arcades and check to see if you can leave flyers on a bulletin board or next to the register.

Resources

Check out these books to learn more about *Pokémon* and view the website for craft ideas:

DTLK's Crafts for Kids. 2010. "Chansey Pokémon Craft." Accessed September 6. http://www.dltk-kids .com/pokemon/mchansey.html.

Mylonas, Eric. 2006. *Pokémon: 10th Anniversary Pokédex.* Roseville, CA: Prima Games.

Ryan, Michael G. 2010. *Pokémon Heartgold Version, Soulsilver Version: The Official Pokemon Johto Guide & Pokédex.* Bellevue, WA: Pokémon Company International.

Chapter 13

Programs: Japanese Popular Culture

Japanese popular culture has moved to the United States. Teens and tweens heartily enjoy manga and anime and, because of this interest, have become very attracted to learning about Japanese culture. Teens want to learn the language and experience the food, the crafts, and various popular activities, such as Cosplay.

Cosplay Contest

General Description

Cosplay is short for "costume play" and is popular with enthusiasts of Japanese anime, manga, video games and pop culture. Cosplayers create highly detailed costumes and accessories to look like, and often act like, the character they are playing. A cosplay contest would appeal to teens and adults. Contestants will compete for prizes such as gift certificates for stores who sell Japanese merchandise or to fabric stores where they can buy the supplies they need for more costumes.

Pop

The term *cosplay* originated in Japan at a science fiction convention in the mid 1980s and is generally based around the comics and manga conventions in Japan and around the world. Cosplay is closely tied with *Otaku*, Japanese fan culture, and Tokyo's Harajuku district is the center of the scene in Japan. There are also "cosplay cafés" in Japan, where staff are dressed in cosplay. With the increased popularity of Japanese pop culture in the United States, cosplay has also risen in popularity and is mostly centered around anime and science fiction conventions. U.S. cosplay is varied and often includes more science fiction (*Star Wars*) and fantasy (*Lord of the Rings*) costumes, in addition to Japanese characters.

Relate

This event will appeal to a special portion of your community of teens. Depending on the community, this may be a small or large group of teens. Regardless of size, the enthusiasm that *Otaku* fans and cosplayers have will fill any room. If you have a popular manga and graphic novel collection, this event will appeal to some of those users. This event is a perfect opportunity to reach out to enthusiasts in the community who may not currently use the library. The contest celebrates creativity and individuality, and it also creates an opportunity for enthusiasts to meet new people. *Otaku* fans are passionate, dedicated, and once introduced to the library, may become some of its most dedicated users.

Instructors/Talent

There may be local adult fans willing to help plan this event or help judge the contest. There may be library staff that are manga and anime fans who could also help plan or judge. Perhaps someone at the local comic shop or Japanese market would be interested in helping as well. Knowledge of manga, anime, video games, science fiction, or fantasy is greatly beneficial and will make the contest better.

Audience

Teens and young adults are the main audience for cosplay. Due to the time and resources involved, the more intense enthusiasts are often older teens and adults. However, middle schoolers will enjoy themselves, so breaking the contest competition into age categories is important.

Planning and Supplies

This is an incredibly easy event to plan and set up.

- Rules and guidelines will need to be determined. For example: Judging will be based on a combination of enthusiasm for and knowledge of your character, costume quality, and execution.
- Determine what age categories are needed, such as grades 6 through 8, grades 9 through 12, and/or adult. Determine whether original characters are also allowed.
- Create a sign-in sheet.
- Set up the room to allow the participants to line up and walk in front of the judges' table.
- Make sure the judges have a table with chairs, tally sheets, and a laptop to look up images of characters to check authenticity of costume.

- Have something else for the teens to do, like *Dance Dance Revolution (DDR)*, screening anime, crafts, or all of the above.
- Display manga, graphic novels, and applicable magazines.
- Provide drinks and Japanese snacks like Pocky or gummy candies to add to a festive atmosphere.
- Purchase prizes such as gift certificates to Japanese stores, markets, or to a fabric store to support the cosplay habit. Provide prizes for all age categories.

Create

Having refreshments and video games set up, preferably *DDR* with Japanese pop playing loudly, is a great way to get participants in the mood for the contest. Have participants sign in when they arrive and let everyone know when judging will take place. Depending on how many entries there are, the judging could take 15 to 30 minutes or more if many people are participating. When it is time to start judging, have all participants line up. Each will approach the judges' table one at a time to tell the judges the character's name, why that character was chosen or created if it is original, and the process of creating the costume.

After everyone has had a turn, the judges will deliberate. During this process, the participants can take part in the other activities you have set up. Have fun awarding the prizes once the judges are done. Consider inviting other teens to come and watch and play *DDR* since that will help create more excitement with more attendees. Many teens may not create costumes themselves but will enjoy seeing what others have created.

Food, Technology, and Other Mandatory Extras

- Having something to drink and Japanese snacks makes the event more festive.
- Setting up *DDR* or other Japanese video games, screening anime, and putting out a selection of manga, graphic novels, magazines, and DVDs will expose new users to your materials and showcase what is new in the collection to current users.
- Having a laptop on hand to look up characters is very helpful in judging. Even someone who really knows manga, anime, and video games will come across an obscure character he or she has never seen. This resource will also help with judging costume quality and authenticity.

Analysis

Cosplay contests may not be popular in all communities, so use your collections, requests, and observation as guidelines for determining the desire for this event. Be prepared to start out slow and take time to build an audience. If the event is successful consider having contests several times a year.

Marketing Tips

Reaching out to the online cosplay community using message boards is the best way to get the word out about a cosplay contest. If there is a Japanese store or market in the area, take publicity there. Comic book stores, toy stores, and other places enthusiasts hang out are other places to advertise. Put flyers in manga, graphic novels, sci-fi, and fantasy materials in your collection. Costume and fabric stores are also places cosplayers might see an ad.

Resources

Check out these articles for more information on cosplay:

Brehm-Heeger, Paula, Ann Conway, and Carrie Vale. 2007. "Cosplay, Gaming and Conventions: Amazing Unexpected Places an Anime Club Can Lead Unsuspecting Librarians." *Young Adult Library Services* 5, no. 2 (Winter): 14–16.

Knight, Meribah. 2010. "A Thriving Business Built on Geeks' Backs." *Chicago News Cooperative.* May 14. http://www.chicagonewscoop.org/a-thriving-business-built-on-geeks%E2%80%99-backs/.

Amigurumi: Crochet Happy Fun

General Description

Patrons are invited to learn how to crochet small creatures, food items, and dolls inspired by the Japanese *amigurumi* tradition.

Pop

Amigurumi—literally translated as "knitted stuffed toy"—is the Japanese art of knitting or crocheting small stuffed animals and anthropomorphic creatures. *Amigurumi* are typically cute animals (such as bears, rabbits, cats, dogs) but can include inanimate objects endowed with anthropomorphism. *Amigurumi* can be either knitted or crocheted. In recent years, crocheted *amigurumi* are more popular and more commonly seen. This activity is another craze born from the Japanese obsession with "cute" things, commonly called *kawaii*.

Relate

Teens interested in *Otaku* of Japanese fan culture, manga, anime, or Japanese fashions, like those into the Gothic Lolita scene, will respond to a program like this. However, it also exposes teens who enjoy crafts and DIY culture to an interest they may not yet know about.

Instructors/Talent

When teaching a group of people something detailed, it is key to either have several people to assist or use technology to follow one person. Have a camera film a close-up of the instructor's hands while simultaneously projecting this image on a large screen. The instructor can talk the group through the techniques while demonstrating it in a way so that all can see. After this technique was utilized during a sushi instruction class, it was dubbed the "sushi cam" whenever this setup is requested for a program.

Audience

Teens in grades 6 through 12 and adults.

Planning and Supplies

Luckily, crochet is a relatively easy craft in terms of supplies. Supplies included a quantity of crochet hooks that ranged from G, H, I, to J sizes, based on the recommendation of the instructor, and an assortment of worsted weight 100 acrylic yarn in bright colors. The instructor came up with several designs of her own, but if you need patterns there are a multitude of *amigurumi* books to consult. The instructor also created visual handouts for the participants to take home.

Create

A local crochet instructor was located by posting on a local Meetup.com message board. In the message, the program was described, as were the skills the library was interested in. An instructor was hired who had experience working with young people and in teaching. Although she was not familiar with *amigurumi*, she was more than willing to learn. You may find an instructor in the opposite fashion—someone who is an *amigurumi* fan and took up crochet to fuel this interest. Some library staff who knit have helped with past programs, but in this case no staff was interested in learning the new craft. If you have in-house talent, use them.

Food, Technology, and Other Mandatory Extras

Food is not necessary for this program, and the technology mentioned under instructors/talent is very helpful but not mandatory if you have enough people to do hands-on instruction.

Analysis

This program can be very difficult for some people, so be prepared for some frustration and even some tears. Having an instructor who is patient and willing to show people the same thing over and over again is very important. Some people will be persistent enough to keep trying and others will not. Crochet is not easy to learn, but it is possible.

Marketing Tips

Advertise the program to anime and manga clubs at the local middle school and high schools. Consider introducing this new craft during a knitting program for creating scarves, mittens, and blankets. It might create some interest that could spread by word of mouth.

Resources

Take a look at these materials for techniques and patterns:

Haden, Christen. 2008. *Creepy Cute Crochet: Zombies, Ninjas, Robots, and More!* Philadelphia, PA: Quirk Books.

Obaachan, Annie. 2008. *Amigurumi Animals: 15 Patterns and Dozens of Techniques for Creating Cute Crochet Creatures.* New York: St. Martin's Griffin.

Rimoli, Ana Paula. 2008. *Amigurumi World: Seriously Cute Crochet.* Bothell, WA: Martingale & Co Inc.

Yee, Jou Ling. 2010. "Amigurumi Kingdom." Accessed September 2. http://www.amigurumikingdom.com/.

Chapter 14

Programs: Me—Beauty, Style, Body Modification, and Fashion

The tween and teen years are the time when youth start to become individuals, developing their own opinions and styles. Design programs to encourage self-discovery of beauty and fashion, as well as to provide good information about such big decisions as tattoos and piercings.

Nail Art

Information on the Nail Art program was provided by Meaghan Battle, Youth Services Librarian at the Ann Arbor District Library.

General Description

This project is a nail decoration extravaganza that encourages self-expression through the use of nail polishes, decals, and rhinestones.

Pop

This program takes advantage of the whole DIY craze and combines tween and teen creativity with fun!

Relate

Painting fingernails is a very solitary activity. Why not make it social and have a group of teens do it all together at the library?

Instructors/Talent

No instructors were used for this program, but it might be fun to invite a few airbrush technicians for an airbrushed nail station.

Audience

Grades 4 through 8.

Planning and Supplies

- Large selection of nail polish colors; nail rhinestones, which are much cheaper in large quantities when ordering online
- Nail decals
- Nail art brushes
- Emery boards
- Little plastic cups
- Palmolive (for soaking nails and cuticles)
- Paper towels
- Orangewood sticks
- Access to water

Create

Attendees are told where materials and design ideas are located and encouraged to ask questions for anything they need throughout the activity. Nail polishes, decals, and rhinestones can be distributed to each table before the program, or all such materials can be placed at a larger central table. A pitcher of water, small plastic cups, and Palmolive dishwashing liquid should be centrally located for those who want to soak their nails before they begin.

Each table should have a supply of emery boards, nail art brushes, cotton swabs, paper towels, nail polish remover, orangewood sticks, and top coat. This allows tweens to experiment with body art as a form of self-expression without the permanence of tattoos. Emery boards, orangewood sticks, and cotton swabs used by individuals become their property and should not be shared with others for hygienic reasons.

Food, Technology, and Other Mandatory Extras

No food is needed for this event, but fun, popular music playing in the background is a huge plus. It keeps the atmosphere lively.

Analysis

An hour is a great time frame for this program. Any longer and tweens may start to get bored. Be sure to put up a display showcasing books on sleepover activities. The Kitchen Cosmetics program in this chapter is also fun for tweens to try at home in a group.

Marketing Tips

Invite local Girl Scout groups. Put up flyers at nail and beauty salons.

Resource

Check out this helpful book for explicit instructions on trendy and simple nail designs:

Haab, Sherri. 2009. *Nail Art*. Palo Alto, CA: Klutz Publishing.

Kitchen Cosmetics

The Kitchen Cosmetics program was written and contributed by Meaghan Battle, Youth Services Librarian at the Ann Arbor District Library.

General Description

Use food and other kitchen items to make skin care products. Create samples at the library and take some home with you. Example recipes are cucumber honey toner, refreshing orange scrub, and strawberry hand and foot exfoliant.

Pop

The movement toward green personal products fits perfectly with this environmentally conscious program. The ingredients for all of the products are natural and widely available at local markets.

Relate

All libraries are making a conscious effort to "go green" by using less paper in all aspects of operation. Some summer reading programs are only available online; fewer flyers are being distributed for promotion; amd websites and televisions placed throughout the physical library space instead does the promotion with electronic advertisements. Library programming should also model environmentally aware alternatives to common activities.

Instructors/Talent

If there is a spa or salon in town that specializes in all-natural treatments, consider inviting a technician. This is not a requirement. You can run this program very successfully if you have no training in making homemade beauty products. Miss Moorpark and Miss Simi Valley came to help in one iteration of this program (see Figure 14.1). Many times local beauty pageant winners are looking for opportunities to volunteer in their communities. Their presenace added an element of elegance to the program, and they even wore their crowns!

Figure 14.1. Miss Moorpark Helping to Prepare a Natural Face Mask at the Moorpark (CA) City Library

Audience

Grades 4 through 8.

Planning and Supplies

Simple recipes for making different beauty supplies can be found in many spa books or online. Favorite blogs include *Kitchen, Crafts, & More*, and the All Natural Beauty website. Below is a list of supplies needed for the program:

- Blenders
- Small tins or jars (Ziploc bags or small Tupperware containers will work too)
- Small labels
- Rubber spatulas
- Measuring spoons and cups
- Recipe sheets (with instructions for participants to re-create recipes at home)
- Necessary groceries
- Mixing bowls

- Mixing spoons
- Tablecloths

Create

- Set up a blender station or two at the front of the room. If a large crowd is expected, consider having more than one station to improved traffic flow. Make sure that you have enough staff to operate the blenders.
- The room can be arranged into stations, with ingredients for each recipe placed on tables around the room.
- Set up tables for seating with tablecloths, recipe sheets, mixing bowls and spoons, and storage tins. Encourage kids to choose recipes and go about mixing up their cosmetics. With a smaller crowd, it might be more convenient for everyone to work together to make each recipe and then divide it among the group to take home.

Food, Technology, and Other Mandatory Extras

Fun, popular music playing in the background is a huge plus. It keeps the atmosphere lively. Consider easy access to sinks for hand washing. Cosmetic creations can and will get messy.

Analysis

Remind participants that these ingredients are perishable, so any cosmetics taken home should be refrigerated and used within a few days of the program. Whatever supplies you purchase will be used up, so buy way more ingredients than you think you will need. Kids will want to make all of the recipes at least once and take home many of them. If you have a very limited number of tins or jars, set a limit from the beginning. This program is a messy proposition due to the mixing, so be ready to spend time cleaning up the room after the program.

Marketing Tips

Leave flyers at local beauty salons. Parents will pass along information about different and interesting programs to their teens.

Resources

Check out these books and websites for help with finding recipes:

All Natural Beauty. http://allnaturalbeauty.us/hbr_ingredients.htm.
Bonnell, Jennifer. 2003. *D.I.Y. Girl: The Real Girl's Guide to Making Everything from Lip Gloss to Lamps*. New York: Puffin Books.

Kitchen, Crafts & More (blog). http://www.kitchencraftsnmore.net/bath3.html.

Tattoo History, Culture, and Safety

General Description

While teens cannot get a tattoo until they are 18 in most states, the desire to get one often starts much earlier. This program should cover the historical and cultural significance of tattooing, as well as information about tattoo safety and health. For teens who may be tempted to have a friend do the tattoo, the health information is important.

Pop

Tattoos are now a very common and popular form of personal expression. At one time, only sailors or bikers had tattoos, but that has obviously changed considerably. In fact, a 2007 Pew Research Center poll found that one-third of "Generation Next," young adults ages 18 to 25, had tattoos (The Pew Research Center for the People & the Press, 2007). The popularity of reality television shows like *Miami Ink* and *LA Ink* have only made the art seem more appealing. Tattoos are now almost ubiquitous on sports players and celebrities—not to mention quite a few librarians.

Relate

Rather than taking a negative stand against tattoos or being precautionary about them, it is much wiser to give teens and their parents the information they need to make informed choices about whether getting a tattoo is something they might want to do. Tattoos are such a lightning rod of interest for many teens that it is a perfect way to show relevance to the teens in the community.

Instructors/Talent

This type of program should be conducted by a licensed and trained tattoo artist. Search around for tattoo artists that perhaps have experience teaching classes or otherwise have enough knowledge and enthusiasm for the topic. Ask library staff, family, or friends who have tattoos if they have a local shop or an artist that they really like. Ideally, the instructor would bring along some of the tattoo supplies to show to the group.

Audience

Teens, their parents, and adults are the best audience for this type of program. Younger children might also be interested, but in that case it would be best if their parents came along.

Planning and Supplies

The bulk of the planning for this event is up front in locating a tattoo artist who is up to the challenge. Beyond that, encouraging the artist to do a PowerPoint slide show or other visual presentation is recommended, since it is a visual art. Have the artist bring tattoo instruments and supplies so attendees can see them up close and ask questions. Be sure to have some books and magazines on tattooing available for checkout after the program.

Create

A knowledgeable and enthusiastic artist is all you need to create a unique and interesting program. Discuss the content of the presentation with the artist so you can anticipate questions from the audience. Be sure the artist emphasizes the lifelong commitment involved in getting a tattoo and encourages young people to think and plan long and hard before they make a decision (see Figure 14.2).

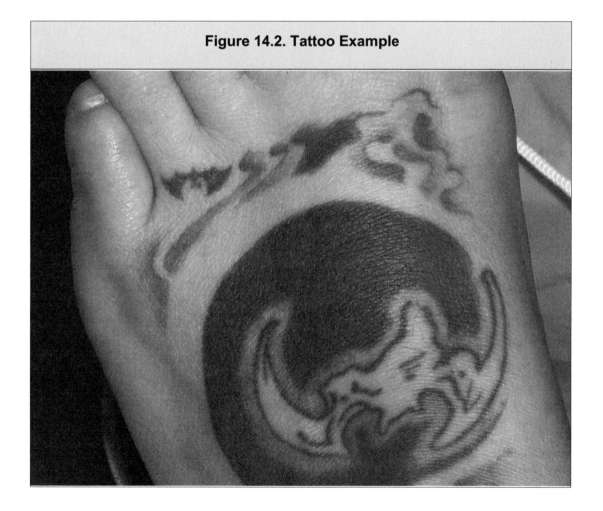

Figure 14.2. Tattoo Example

Food, Technology, and Other Mandatory Extras

If the instructor does a visual presentation, having a projector that can hook up to a laptop is key.

Analysis

Do not let fear of community outrage or potential bad apples keep this program from being planned. The intent is to educate and inform the public about tattooing and dispel myths and confusion. A well-planned program is the best strategy. Tattoo artists are in the business of staying in business, so they have an investment in making sure people are safe and responsible.

Marketing Tips

Target art teachers and coaches at the high schools to get the word out, since some teens who enjoy these activities may be the most inclined to be interested. Since tattoos are so prevalent in sports today, teens who play sports may be eager to learn more. If there are any tattooing interest groups on Flickr.com or Meetup.com postings, posting the activity on their message boards is also a good idea.

Resources

Check out these books for more information on tattoos:

Hesselt van Dinter, Maarten, 2007. *The World of Tattoo: An Illustrated History.* Amsterdam: KIT Publishers.

The Pew Research Center for the People & the Press. 2007. "How Young People View Their Lives, Futures and Politics: A Portrait of 'Generation Next.'" January 9. http://people-press.org/reports/pdf/ 300.pdf.

Von D, Kat. 2009. *High Voltage Tattoo.* New York: Collins Design.

Chapter 15

Programs: Magic, Fantasy, and the Mystical World

The mystical is always in style in one form or another. From *Dungeons & Dragons* role-playing games to fascination with vampires, teens are always interested in the mystical world. Create programs that engage teens with the most popular mystical creatures of the day: dragons, vampires, werewolves, fairies, or unicorns to name a few. The most popular books and movies are the best indicators to the current teen obsession. Think creatively about modifying typical craft programs to encompass these creatures simply by using different supplies. For example, what was once a house for a fairy last year is now a vampire shrine using bubble-gum eyeballs and red paint for blood.

Psychics, Astrology, and the Future Fair

General Description

Invite teens to get the chance to have readings from psychics, astrologers, palm readers, tarot card readers, aura readers, dream analyzers, runestone readers, and more. With a number of professional readers on hand, teens can get several readings.

Pop

Being fascinated with ghosts, astrology, past lives, the future, tarot cards, and palm reading are often part of adolescence. The recent popularity of television shows like *Psychic Kids: Children of the Paranormal* and *John Edward Cross Country*, and movies like *Paranormal Activity*, have only made teen fascination with the unknown more popular.

Relate

Giving teens the opportunity to explore their world and try out new things implies trust. This type of program is a great way to let teens try something new that normally is fairly cost-prohibitive since using the services of psychics and other mediums can be expensive.

Instructors/Talent

Having a variety and quantity of six to eight readers is important to the success of this program. Depending on how popular the event is, some teens may need to wait, but with that many readers, teens should get several readings. Finding the readers will vary in difficulty depending on the location and size of the community. A fairly large metropolitan area should have some sort of guide or free weekly newspaper that features a directory of local practitioners. There are many national magazines that may be helpful in finding readers too. When contacting potential readers, be sure to ask if they have ever participated in an event like this for young people. Some may have been hired to work at birthday or high school graduation parties. Readers with that type of experience are what to look for. Negotiating the fees is very important, so be sure to look for someone who will charge for the block of time rather than the number of readings given. This way as many teens as possible can get a reading and the charge will not be based on the number of teens in attendance.

Audience

Teens and adults would be interested in such a program, but if space and resources are limited, then restricting the event to just teens is recommended. Adults looking for free readings could easily overwhelm the event and take chances away from the teens.

Planning and Supplies

The bulk of the planning will be up front and in organizing the space properly. When locating and booking readers, determine how much space each of them will need and ask about privacy considerations. During the readings, it is important that each teen has privacy. With an aura reader they will need space to set up a screen and possibly a printer if they are going to provide the teens with a printout of their aura. Most readers, other than aura, will not have much in the way of supplies, so setup is fairly easy.

Create

The most important thing to do is to be sure you have a system for determining how many readings each teen will get and getting them signed up in an orderly fashion. Depending on the number of attendees, this could get fairly complicated. Be sure to plan some alternate activities so that teens do not get bored waiting for their turn. Have a hands-on craft area available or set up some displays in the waiting area for teens who have time to kill.

Food, Technology, and Other Mandatory Extras

Some teens may want to record their readings so they can go back and listen to them later. Consider allowing teens to bring their own recording devices or, if you have access to several portable podcast devices, the files could be saved and sent to the teens via e-mail. This technology is constantly changing, but devices can usually be purchased for less than $100. In some cases, the readers may have these types of devices and could do the same thing for teens.

Analysis

This type of event is sure to be popular and will likely bring in some teens who have never before attended a library event. It is important to note that some people object to the notion of psychics and astrologers, usually due to religious reasons and sometimes because it is believed that there is something evil about the practice. As long as the library's mission statement is clear about serving people of all interests and beliefs, these types of complaints can be handled easily. Of course there are some communities and parts of the country where this may be a harder sell; nevertheless, it does not mean the program would not be popular or serve a need among the community's teens.

Marketing Tips

This type of event should be promoted at teen hangouts including coffee shops and other casual businesses where the hip teens hang out. It would also be a good idea to take flyers to places like the YMCA or Boys & Girls Clubs.

Resources

Check out these books for further information about the psychic realm:

Abadie, M.J. 2003. *Teen Dream Power: Unlock the Meaning of Your Dreams.* Rochester, VT: Bindu Books.
Abadie, M.J. 2003. *Teen Psychic: Exploring Your Intuitive Spiritual Powers.* Rochester, VT: Bindu Books.
Thompson, Alicia, Joost Elffers, and Gary Goldschneider. 2010. *Secret Language of Birthdays,* Teen Ed. New York: Razorbill.

Vampire Wreaths

General Description

Do you consider yourself a true authority on vampire lore? Are you interested in the undead? Or maybe you just love the *Twilight* series? Teens were invited to stop by the library and make wreaths to decorate their rooms to attract (or distract) vampires (see Figure 15.1).

Figure 15.1. Vampire Wreath to Attract Vampires

Pop

Stephenie Meyer's *Twilight* series is a teen phenomenon that began in 2005. A mix of vampires and forbidden loves, with an extra love interest thrown in for good measure, *Twilight* has become a favorite for girls, boys, and many adults. In current popular culture, everyone is forced to choose a side: Team Edward or Team Jacob. Vampire lovers are on the lookout for new books, television shows, graphic novels, and anything else they can sink their teeth into.

Relate

Teens are interested in reading anything with vampires. Spotlight other vampire materials in your collection, encouraging teens who are stuck on *Twilight* to branch out and potentially discover werewolves, ghosts, zombies, and other strange paranormals involved in love triangles.

Instructors/Talent

No instructors are needed.

Audience

Grades 6 through 12.

Planning and Supplies

To Keep Vampires Away

- Small wreaths (12-inch grapevine wreaths)
- Craft glue
- Hot-glue gun and glue sticks
- Red and black glass garden beads
- Red and black ribbon
- Craft wood to make wooden stakes and crosses
- Dried garlic
- Silver ribbon to simulate silver chains

To Attract Vampires

- Silver spray glitter
- Lavender
- Craft foam to create signs: "Welcome Vampires. Please come in."
- Red and black craft paint (for fake blood)
- Red ribbon roses
- Plastic eyeballs

Create

Place tables and chairs around the room; supply each station with glue, scissors, and wreaths. Fill another table with all of the craft supplies, separating the supplies into two areas: "Keeping Vampires Away" and "Attracting Vampires." Teens will be asked to choose which type of wreath they would like to make. Put the glue guns and glue sticks in one area so that use of the hot guns can be monitored.

Food, Technology, and Other Mandatory Extras

If the program is during Halloween, serve candy. Otherwise, serve vampire-inspired food such as Red Hots (for "red hot vampire love") or red velvet cupcakes with black chocolate frosting.

Analysis

This program works very well near Halloween. There are lots of great supplies to purchase, like plastic severed fingers, which would definitely attract vampires. The program would also be great paired with another activity, like watching a *Twilight* movie while doing the project or having a *Twilight* trivia tournament after the craft.

Marketing Tips

Make sure the librarians at the middle schools and high schools are aware of the program so they can promote it to the known *Twilight* fans.

Resources

Check out these books for fun facts about vampires:

Gray, Amy Tipton. *How to Be a Vampire: A Fangs-On Guide for the Newly Undead.* Somerville, MA: Candlewick Press.

Karg, Barb. *The Girl's Guide to Vampires: All You Need to Know about the Original Bad Boys.* Avon, MA: Adams Media.

Fairy Homes, Jewelry, Dolls, and More

General Description

Many different types of programs can be designed with fairies in mind: creating fairy homes out of natural materials, designing a mosaic fairy wand, making fairy clothes, sewing a fairy-attracting satchet or even making fairy food.

Pop

Fairies became part of the public consciousness with the popularization of Tinkerbell, the fairy from *Peter Pan*. Disney continues to keep Tinkerbell popular with her own books and movies. Mattel added to the craze by introducing Fairytopia dolls and all of their various incarnations. *Fairy Tale: A True Story*, a movie which came out in 1998, heralded the craze that has not abated since. Cicely Mary Barker's fairies have also been remade with a modern audience in mind, with books similar to the *Dragonology* titles. Of course, books for teens like *Wicked Lovely* by Melissa Marr have made fairies that much more popular too.

Relate

The fantasy and beauty associated with fairies is very magnetic to teens, and they enjoy the "darker" side of fairies with their mischievous tricks. Teens can indulge their love of fairies in a creative and hands-on manner with this activity.

Instructors/Talent

No instructors are required, but finding someone creative with a passion for fairies is a bonus. Florists or others who make their living creating fairy crafts or dolls would be good options to explore when looking for a potential instructor. However, many good fairy craft books are available now. An enthusiastic library staff person can easily conduct these workshops with a little planning and creativity.

Audience

Children, teens, and adults all love fairies, so it is up to the librarian and presenters to determine the audience's age range for any particular program.

Planning and Supplies

Fairy Houses or Gardens

- Shoebox to hold the house or garden
- A small dish for water
- Twigs, bark, small pine cones
- Flowers, real and silk
- Sand or gravel
- Moss (live or spanish)
- Hot-glue guns to attach twigs together to make structures

Fairy Sachet

- Loose dried lavender, chamomile, or other fragrant dried herbs
- Small pieces of colorful fabric to hold the herbs
- Ribbon to tie the sachet closed
- Silk cord to string it and wear as a necklace

Fairy Clothes

- Thick white paper to glue designs down to
- Dried flowers from potpourri or silk flowers cut up
- Dried leaves, grass, etc.
- Colored pencils
- Glue (See Figure 15.2.)

Create

The wonderful thing about a fairy program is that because it is fantasy, there are no rules. Having an abundance of supply options is always important, so that participants

Figure 15.2. Flower Fairy Clothes

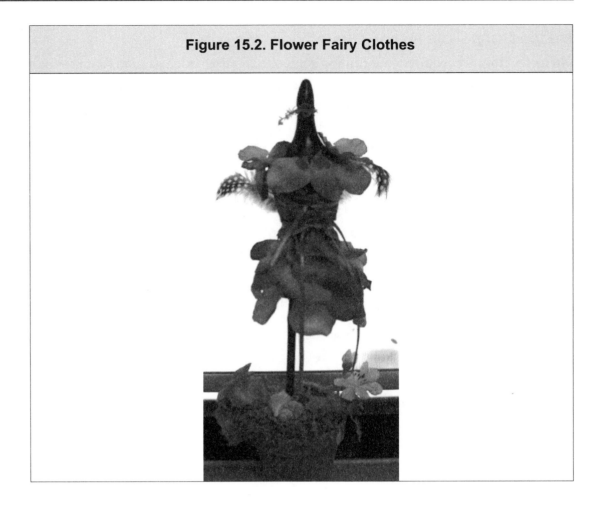

can be as free as they like. If the fairy house is going to be constructed out of twigs and less about the natural setting, then use hot glue to make something sturdier. Collecting things outside is ideal, but supplies can be purchased at craft stores too. For a fairy clothing or "fashion" event (see Figure 15.3), be sure to use the book *Fairie-ality: The Fashion Collection from the House of Ellwand* (Shields, 2002). The book has wonderful photos and ideas for inspiration.

Food, Technology, and Other Mandatory Extras

For a more festive fairy party vibe, considering offering special fairy cupcakes, fairy lavender punch, and fairy rings with mushrooms and fruit. Have fresh-cut flowers out to add to the ambiance.

Analysis

This type of program can go in any direction and lends itself to being altered and changed with new ideas. Supplies can easily be saved for another event or recycled in new ways.

Figure 15.3. Fairy Fashion in a Fairy Book

Marketing Tips

Advertise through craft stores, florist shops, English teachers at the schools, or to any businesses in the area that sell whimsical or fairy-related gift items.

Resources

Barker, Cicely Mary. 2004. *How to Host a Flower Fairy Tea-Party*. London: Frederick Warne.

Beery, Barbara. 2007. *Fairies Cookbook*. Layton, UT: Gibbs-Smith Publishers.

Kane, Barry. 2008. *Fairy House and Beyond!* Lee, NH: Light-Beams.

Mullaney, Colleen. 2010. *Fairy Parties: Recipes, Crafts, and Games for Enchanting Celebrations*. San Francisco: Chronicle Books.

Ross, Kathy. 2008. *Fairy World Crafts*. North Minneapolis, MN: First Avenue.

Shields, Genie. 2002. *Fairie-ality: The Fashion Collection from the House of Ellwand*. Somerville, MA: Candlewick.

Chapter 16

Programs: Music

Music is such a big part of teens' and tweens' lives. Musicals have become particularly popular lately, creating great fan bases and such movie and television phenomena as *High School Musical* and *Glee*. Think about modeling programs after popular musical-oriented television shows or movies, such as *American Idol* or *The Singing Bee*. But do not forget about using music teens listen to as inspiration for programs as well. Try a battle of the bands using video game technology or with actual band equipment. Let teens use the computer lab to create beats on GarageBand software or have a music video contest using YouTube.

High School Musical Karaoke

General Description

A twist on classic karaoke, *High School Musical* karaoke is a niche program, designed for fans of the movies and those interested in trying something new. Teens take turns going up to the laptop and picking their favorite songs to sing from the movies. While waiting their turn, other teens can design tote bags and picture frames with the *High School Musical* logos and pictures of the characters. Though a passing craze, this program can be used as a model for the next musical phenomenon, such as the Emmy award-winning television show *Glee*.

Pop

High School Musical (HSM) began as a made-for-television movie, which aired on the Disney Channel in 2006. Since then, two more movies have come out, including one in theaters. The movie phenomenon has created a resurgence in musicals for teens and tweens, and it has participated in the "tween marketing machine," with a diverse product line featuring everything from board games to books to bedspreads. Stage productions of the musical have popped up all over the country, and the Troy and Gabriella love story can even be enjoyed in video games and ice-skating shows.

Relate

Besides being a major entertainment interest for tweens and some teens, the movie also sends out a positive message about respecting your friends for having interests and skills that might not be considered popular. Many books about the movie and further adventures of the characters have been published, which can be promoted at your program. It would also be a great time to highlight your library's DVD and CD collections by introducing other musicals the kids might enjoy.

Instructors/Talent

No instructors needed.

Audience

Grades 4 through 8. *HSM* is hugely popular with grades 2 and 3 as well, so you could open the program up to younger kids.

Planning and Supplies

- Laptop
- *High School Musical* karaoke CD
- Craft supplies and decorations purchased from a party store

Create

Teens take turns picking their favorite *HSM* songs and singing them in the front of the room. Besides watching the others perform and singing along to the music, teens are engaged with crafts. Your local party store may have decorations and other items that sport the *HSM* characters and logo. Stickers of *HSM* characters, including the beloved Troy and Gabriella, can be used to decorate inexpensive acrylic picture frames, which can be purchased in bulk on the Internet. White cotton tote bags, also purchased in bulk, can be decorated with fabric markers, the school's mascot, the cougar; and basketballs, which are all aspects popular in the first movie.

Food, Technology, and Other Mandatory Extras

Your laptop can be plugged into the programming room's sound system, but using the laptop speakers in a small room may be sufficient. The laptop can be hooked into a projector so that the audience can sing along to the words. The preferred karaoke CD to purchase is a CD+G, which is an audio CD that contains embedded graphics, including the words to the songs that cross the screen as you sing. When purchasing a karaoke CD, check to see if it is only instrumental background music, or if you can sing along with the original movie's singers. Your tweens might be particular, so it is something to keep in mind. Decorate the room with posters from the movie and crepe paper to create a party ambiance. Place light snacks at each table.

Analysis

Though Troy and Gabriella have graduated from high school and moved on, there are many movie/musical acts from Disney and Nickelodeon to create karaoke programs around for tweens. Try a Jonas Brothers program or Justin Bieber karaoke. For an older audience, pick up the CD of songs performed on the television show *Glee* or the *Buffy the Vampire Slayer* musical episode. Even if a karaoke CD is not available, with a little extra legwork you can create a sing-along by printing off the words to the songs and passing them around. Another addition to the program could be a trivia component, quizzing the fans on the idiosyncrasies of the musicals.

Marketing Tips

Post the event on the library's Facebook page, and you might attract teens and tweens that do not normally attend library programs. Be sure to post details for the program in the teen and tween spaces of the library too.

Resource

Disney Channel. 2010. "*High School Musical* Official Website." Accessed September 2. http://tv.disney.go.com/disneychannel/originalmovies/highschoolmusical/index.html.

Chapter 17

Programs: Physical Activities

Popular physical activities can be inspired by musicians, movies, television, and famous sports stars. Also look to making programs hands-on involving science experiments, which have been promoted through television shows like *MythBusters* on the Discovery Channel. Reading is a stationary activity, so anything the library can do to promote activity is a plus.

Dance Programs

General Description

Teens are invited to attend one-time workshops on different types of dance, including a demonstration and instruction. Pick a type of dance that is popular at the moment: ballroom dancing, capoeira mandinga, breakdancing, bellydancing, krumping, and more.

Pop

Dancing is huge with teens, and dance sequences are currently big in movies marketed to teens and tweens. Popular reality television shows *So You Think You Can Dance* and *Dancing with the Stars* demonstrate that regular people can get their chance to become professional dancers. Dances like the tango are given a rebirth from movies such as *Mad Hot Ballroom*. Video games are created to teach the dance moves shown in such movies as *High School Musical*. Media interest in different types of dance creates fascination by teens to try out these dances.

Relate

Promoting health activity is always a plus for libraries, and dancing is a very energetic hobby. It is also a great way to highlight the library's music collection, whether it be CDs or music downloads.

Instructors/Talent

Unless you are an expert in a certain type of dance or feel comfortable learning a dance sequence and teaching it to a group, find a local instructor. Check with dance studios, dance groups at local colleges, or instructors for community recreation classes.

Audience

Grades 6 through 12.

Planning and Supplies

All that is needed is a large room. If the talent plans on doing a demonstration, make sure there is room for a stage or performance area. Use colored masking tape to designate the stage area so that participants will not sit in it if they are sitting on the floor. Collect CDs, dance instruction DVDs, and books, and create a display for participants who want to learn more about the dance. For ambiance, play appropriate music through a sound system or boombox as participants enter the room.

Create

Let the teens dance. The program should probably be 60 to 90 minutes at the most. Those that are dedicated will want to dance longer, but an hour and a half is probably long enough for teens to get a taste of the new dance.

Food, Technology, and Other Mandatory Extras

Water is a must because participants will be working up a sweat.

Analysis

Do not forget to look to musical groups who may have popular dance sequences or have made a certain type of music popular. Learning how to swing dance was a big deal in the late 1990s. The "swing revival" was supported by bands like the Squirrel Nut Zippers and Big Bad Voodoo Daddy. Plan to hold the event near school dances or proms. If a dance is particularly popular, partygoers will want to show off their dance skills in front of their classmates.

Marketing Tips

Ask to have the program promoted over the morning announcements at middle schools and high schools before a dance.

Resources

Resources are based on the type of dance chosen for the program.

Parkour and Freerunning

The Parkour and Freerunning program was written and contributed by Vicki Browne, Teen Librarian at the Ann Arbor District Library.

General Description

Parkour is the art of moving through your environment using only your body and whatever is in your surroundings to propel yourself along. It can include but is not limited to running, crawling, leaping, and climbing. Think the beginning chase scene in the movie *Casino Royale*. The local university's parkour running club members were asked to do a demo off-site at a local park and fitness center, and also talk about technique and training for parkour. A ready-made obstacle course right in your urban landscape is waiting to be explored!

Pop

Many films, like James Bond classics or *The Bourne Ultimatum*, have amazing freerunning scenes. The hobby is highly appealing for teens: to try maneuvering pathways that are easy to reproduce wherever their urban landscape is. Parkour was highlighted in the television show *American Ninja Warrior* shown on G4, the video gaming television channel, where participants raced to complete obstacle courses with the fastest time.

Relate

Encouraging fitness and healthy living in programs for teens is a great goal. Holding events outside out of the library is also a beneficial form of outreach, to illustrate to community members who do not frequent the library what the library can offer them.

Instructors/Talent

One of our freerunning events was led by Levi Meeuwenberg, of *American Ninja Warrior* fame, who happened to be a local contact. The leader of the local college club did a live demo at a local county park as well.

Audience

Grades 6 to adult. This program may also appeal to the skateboarding crowd.

Planning and Supplies

Planning involves seeking out those in your area who are currently involved in the parkour and freerunning hobby. Look to local colleges to see if they have a club.

Create

Offer an informational meeting with discussion of background and the "how-to" of the activities; then hold a demo. At the demo, the leader and his guest performers were able to practice techniques of safe jumping and landing positions, talk about how to participate safely in the hobby, and how to work with the community to make this "sport" happen.

Food, Technology, and Other Mandatory Extras

The local county park facility had an indoor gym in which the informational discussion part of the program could take place, as well as an outdoor park with wooden play structures and benches perfect for an outdoor demonstration.

Analysis

This is a great program that highlights a little-known physical hobby and involves a partnership with a local organization. If an AV system is available, showing clips of parkour scenes from movies and television shows would be a great addition to the program.

Marketing Tips

Market this program at BMX, skateboarding, and snowboarding shops. Teens who are attracted to extreme lifestyle sports would be interesting in attending this program.

Resource

Check out this book to learn more about parkour:

Edwardes, Dan. 2009. *The Parkour and Freerunning Handbook*. New York: It Books.

Double Dutch Program

Information on the Double Dutch program was provided by Vicki Browne, Teen Librarian at the Ann Arbor District Library.

General Description

Incorporate physical activity into a fun and easy program for teens and tweens. Create a space for participants to jump rope and break a sweat while having a great time.

Pop

Double Dutch started on the sidewalks of New York City, and was brought over by Dutch settlers. It became particularly popular in urban areas, where kids and teens would sing along to rhymes while turning and jumping rope. The game became a sport when the first Double Dutch tournament was held in the 1970s and attracted almost 600 middle schoolers. Now a form of performance art, the combination of simple moves to music have become national and international pastimes, where people can join the International Double Dutch Federation, the National Double Dutch League, and the Dynamic Diplomats of Double Dutch team.

Relate

Jumping rope is healthy and fun. It is a sport where no one has to worry about being first string, nor does it take years of training. While being a physical activity, jumping rope does not take any special skill. Use this program to promote overall health in teens.

Instructors/Talent

A local jump rope team called the Heartbeats was invited to perform tricks and demos as a team for the program participants. The group stayed for the duration of the program and was available to instruct the finer points of Double Dutch. While enhancing the program and bringing something extra for the patrons, the group benefited from free advertisement to the community.

Audience

The program was offered to grades 4 through 12, but expect adults to attend the program. Lots of grown-ups are drawn in remembering when they jumped rope way back when.

Planning and Supplies

Purchase assorted jump ropes, including standard single-size ropes, Double Dutch ropes, and Chinese jump ropes. If purchasing jump ropes is not an option, try borrowing them from local schools or gyms like the YMCA. Block off a portion of your parking lot with orange cones. If the weather is very warm, set up a table with a water cooler, and you may even have on hand some spray bottles with water.

Create

If possible, have an experienced group perform for the first part of the program. Then throw the ropes out and let everyone have a good time. The participants will need to share the ropes.

Food, Technology, and Other Mandatory Extras

Nothing extra is needed for this event. If there is room in the budget, give the crowd a little summer treat like popsicles or small ice cream cups. No fancy sound system is needed. With a simple boombox you can add music to the mix, which is a great motivator.

Analysis

This is a simple, fun, low-budget program. The programming room of the library was reserved in case of rain. You may also request guest athletes from your local sports teams (university or high school) to join in and speak about the importance of incorporating physical activity into everyday life.

Marketing Tips

Some jump rope groups or organizations may exist in your community. Check with area schools and then make sure to invite them. Also, let physical education teachers know about the program. Maybe they can offer extra credit for attendance to the program.

Resources

For music, the *Jump In* soundtrack is a must:

Various Artists. 2007. *Jump In*. Walt Disney Records. CD.

Collect good jump rope rhymes:

Boardman, Bob. 1993. *Red Hot Peppers: The Skookum Book of Jump Rope Games, Rhymes, and Fancy Footwork*. Seattle, WA: Sasquatch Books.
Cole, Joanna. 1989. *Anna Banana: 101 Jump Rope Rhymes*. New York: HarperCollins.

EXPLODapalooza

General Description

Teens blow up things in the name of science! Different scientific concepts are illustrated in fun, hands-on experiments where liquids tend to erupt.

Pop

Most people, teens and tweens included, would love to be able to make things explode without hurting themselves or others or ruining anything. The hosts on the television show *MythBusters* allow the viewers at home to live vicariously through their large-scale science experiments, verifying and disproving myths while blowing stuff up. From rumors to myths, from classic movie scenes to news stories, the validity of each of these elements of popular culture is tested by professionals using the basic elements of the scientific method in hands-on experiments.

Relate

Library programming usually heavily supports reading and writing. Science and math are professions that not many kids are drawn to and, besides having resources for science fair projects and books on how things work, offering science programs in your library might spike the interest of some teens who never realized they might want to be chemists or other kinds of scientists someday.

Instructors/Talent

Do not be intimidated by science. All of the explanations of how things work can be found in books or on the Internet. If you do not feel comfortable explaining what happens chemically when baking soda mixes with vinegar to make a foamy, bubbly mixture, create a poster with the explanation or ask a local science teacher to come in and give some context to the experiments.

Audience

Grades 4 through 8.

Planning and Supplies

Alka-Seltzer Rockets

- Film canisters
- Soda water
- Alka-Seltzer
- Bowls
- Safety glasses
- Tarp

Volcanic Eruptions

- Baking soda
- Vinegar
- Food coloring
- Longnecked bottles

Air Cannons
- Plastic soda bottles
- Saran Wrap or Ziploc baggies
- Rubber bands
- Things to blow across the room, like pieces of paper, Ping-Pong balls, balloons

Balloon Station
- Long skinny balloons
- Balloon pumps

Mentos Fountains
- 2-liter Diet Coke
- Mentos

Create

The room was divided into stations, with one staff member or teen volunteer manning each table. The stations included Alka-Seltzer Rockets, Volcanic Eruptions, Balloons, and Air Cannons. A staff member talked for about five minutes showing the group each experiment, explaining a little of the science and asking them to hypothesize what might happen. The details of the science of how the experiments work should be posted at each station. The teens cycled through the stations at their own speed and then came together at the end for the finale: Mentos Fountains.

Alka-Seltzer Rockets

This is a wet station. If you have room, you can do it outside. This project was done inside, with a "splash zone" around the table created with a painter's tarp and masking tape. Only small amounts of soda water escaped from the experiments, and there was no element of danger, but the "splash zone" and the wearing of the goggles enforced the importance of safety when performing science experiments.

Four teens at a time put on safety goggles. They put about one-fourth of a tablet of Alka-Seltzer in a film canister filled with soda water, put the top on the canister and shook it as much as they could, putting the canister into a plastic bowl to minimize the amount of water flying around. Once the pressure is too great, the top of the canister flies off, along with the water, creating a wet explosion!

Volcanic Eruptions

Everyone has made the volcano before, but the most fun about this experiment is the teens got to mix food coloring to create great colors for the lava, plus try different sizes of bottles to see what would happen.

Two longneck, cleaned-out glass soda bottles were placed in a plastic tub to minimize mess and help with cleanup. Each teen received a paper cup of vinegar. They added any color of food coloring to the vinegar. A tablespoon of baking soda was put at the bottom of the bottle. When the vinegar was poured into the bottle, colorful lava flowed everywhere. Try using different sizes of bottles to compare the outcomes or race the bottles.

Balloons

Balloons will explode without too much effort. Long skinny balloons and plastic balloon pumps were set out, with different instructions for making dogs, flowers, and other balloon animals. The goal was not to explode the balloons on purpose, but it definitely happened.

Air Cannons

Make your own air cannon and see how powerful it can be. Cut the bottom off a plastic soda bottle, and fold Saran Wrap or a plastic Ziploc baggie over the end. Seal the end with a rubber band. Aim the open end (the end where the cap would go) at a pile of small pieces of paper, and then tap the plastic wrap with your finger. Paper should fly. Try moving Ping-Pong balls or air-filled balloons.

Mentos Fountains

For the last experiment, everyone went outside and circled around 2-liter bottles of Diet Coke. A few volunteers were picked to drop Mentos candies into the bottles and jump out of the way as the Diet Coke spurted up into a fountain.

Food, Technology, and Other Mandatory Extras

At the end of the program, everyone has a little exploding treat. One year the group enjoyed sparkling punch with lemon-lime soda and sherbet. Another year the treat was Fizzies drink tablets which when dropped into a glass of water create an instant sugary soda beverage. Eating Pop Rocks would also be a fun addition to this program.

Analysis

Beware! This can be a messy program. Take this time to try out different science experiments like making slime or acid-base chemistry. Choose experiments where teens can explore and guess what the outcome may be. Then try it out! If the experiment does not work the way you thought it would, allow the teens to try to figure it out. No matter what happens, it is a learning experience for everyone.

Marketing Tips

This might be a great program to have at the beginning of science fair season. It will get the kids in the mood for thinking about the scientific method. The program could be done in conjunction with a presentation on the resources the library can offer for creating science fair experiments. Promote the program to local science teachers.

Resources

Check out these websites for more details on the experiments:

Instructables. 2010. "Shockwave Air Cannon." Accessed September 3. http://www .instructables.com/id/Shockwave-Air-Cannon/.

Steve Spangler Science. 2010. "Alka-Seltzer Rocket." Accessed September 3. http:// www.stevespanglerscience.com/experiment/00000068.

Steve Spangler Science. 2010. "Mentos Diet Coke Geyser." Accessed September 3. http://www.stevespanglerscience.com/experiment/00000109.

Eggcellent Engineering

General Description

Teens have a half hour to design a container around an egg, which is then dropped off a ladder. The goal is for the egg to not break.

Pop

This is a classic science exercise performed in physics classics for upper elementary kids all the way through college.

Relate

Science does not show up in library programming that often, and it is a really important topic to expose teens to while they are thinking about career paths or hobbies. Create a dynamic display to highlight your science experiment and physics books.

Instructors/Talent

No instructor is needed, but inviting a teacher to talk about the physics of dropping an egg off a building might be interesting.

Audience

Grades 4 through 8.

Planning and Supplies

- Painter's tarps
- Tall ladder
- Eggs
- Recycled materials like rubber bands, toothpicks, small strips of windbreak material, straws
- Mini marshmallows: Limit marshmallows used per teen since they could be packed around the egg to make a sugary pillow

Create

At the beginning of the program, teens found a list of rules on each table. A staff member explained the rules too to make sure no one had any questions about how the program was going to work. (See Figure 17.1 for example rules and regulations.) Then the building began. Teens were able to build their creations from recycled materials collected around the library and at a local reuse supply center.

At the end of the allotted time, a staff member stood on an eight-foot ladder in the middle of the programming room and dropped the eggs. The entire room was covered in painter's tarps. Try to do this outside if you can. Another staff member stood at the bottom of the ladder and checked to see if the eggs had cracked.

The eggs that do not crack move on to the second round. The egg container and egg were weighed on a mail scale which could measure very small incremental differences in weight. The three lightest creations, meaning the egg-drop designs that used the least amount of materials to protect the egg, won. Prizes for this program were Eggcellent Engineer crowns.

Food, Technology, and Other Mandatory Extras

No food or extras are needed.

Analysis

This is a super-fun program for everyone involved. The teens get to be really creative, trying to use materials that are as far from pillows as they can be, and create a container that will keep an egg safe during an eight-foot fall. The best part is when the eggs splat all over. It is a good idea to create a splash zone so that only the staff members end up "egged," not the participants. Also, think about the amount of time to allow for building. Younger tweens may get done really quickly, but older middle schoolers will want more time to design. One of the best designs at a program so far was when a teen created a hang glider for his egg using straws and strips of windbreaker material!

Figure 17.1. Eggcellent Engineering Rules and Regulations

Rules:
- Kids must work individually.
- Each kid will get one egg. Eggs are supplied by the library (Grade A, Large).
- Containers for the egg must be made out of the materials provided.
- Only use eight marshmallows in the egg container.
- The egg must be easily placed into and removed from the container.
- Individuals are eliminated once the egg breaks.
- Balloons are not allowed.

Preliminaries:
All eggs are dropped during the preliminary trials. Eggs that survive (do not crack) will move on to the finals.

Finals:
Each egg within its container will be weighed. The lightest survivor is the winner, with the second and third lightest as runners-up.

Marketing Tips

This is a project commonly done in school science classes or in Boy Scouts. To increase the number of participants, it might be possible to coordinate your program with these other groups to have a major egg-drop event. Talk to local physics departments at universities to show off some really creative designs.

Resources

You can make up your own rules for the competition, but here are some examples where the winners can be based on nonbreakage and weight or dimensions of the container around the egg:

Columbia College. 2007. "Columbia University Egg Drop." Accessed September 3. http://www.columbiasc.edu/academics/math/Egg_Drop_Rules.pdf.
MMU Egg Drop. http://www.angelfire.com/vt2/eggdrop/.
Montshire Museum of Science. 2010. "Guidelines for the Montshire Egg Drop." Accessed September 3. http://www.montshire.org/eggdrop/rules.html.

Cup Stack Attack

General Description

How fast can you stack? Tweens and teens competed for the fastest time to stack cups in different configurations. The fastest three stackers in the beginner bracket and the advanced bracket received prizes.

Pop

Sport stacking, or cup stacking, is a sports phenomenon that started in the late 1980s and has become a competitive sport played all over the world. The sport involves individuals or teams stacking specialized plastic cups into prescribed sequences as fast as they possibly can. Rules are created and enforced by the WSSA (World Sport Stacking Association). Many schools have purchased the cups to help with development of hand-eye coordination and focus, as well as self-confidence and teamwork.

Relate

Sports programs can sometimes be difficult to create when having to stay within the library parameters. There usually is not enough in or near the library for a flag football event, plus there are liability issues to think about. Sport stacking is a great program to promote sporty activities and competition, and will fit right in your programming room.

Instructors/Talent

There is no need for an instructor. You can easily become the expert for this program, but find out if there are any schools in your area that have stacking teams. Empower older teens to teach younger ones how to stack and give demonstrations to get everyone excited to stack as fast as they can. It takes some of the pressure off you to get your skills up to speed before the big tournament. Speak with physical education teachers or school psychologists that implement speed stacking in their programs to identify teens/tweens that may want to help with the program and/or show off their skills.

Audience

Grades 3 through 8. Younger kids can have a tough time remembering the specific stacking sequences and learning the exact rules. It is nice to have a few extra sets for kids to mess around with and get a feel playing with the cups.

Planning and Supplies

- Speed Stacks Stackpack—12 plastic cups, one StackMat, and competitive timer
- Stopwatches

Sets of cups can be sold individually or with the mat and timer. Two stackpacks and extra sets of cups were purchased for this program. The sets are usually $39.99 and the cups on their own are $17.99. Two people could be competing and timing themselves on the mat, while others practiced with the cups around the room and had friends time them on the stopwatches.

This program can be as fancy or as laid-back as you and your budget would like it to be. The library can purchase the special cups as supplies to keep at the library, ask teens to bring their own if the cups are being used widely in the area, or ask a local school if you can borrow their sets for an afternoon.

Create

Teens chose an area in the room to practice stacking and took turns using the two StackMat and timer stations. As they practiced, they signed up for the tournament in either the beginner bracket or the advanced bracket for the competitive stackers.

First the teens were led in practice drills and activities in preparation for the tournament. Cups are stacked in pyramids with a certain amount of cups and can be stacked in patterns. For instance, the three-stack and the six-stack are commom formations and can be stacked in patterns like 3-6-3, 6-6, or 3-3-3. For the first activity, a staff member picked a stack like 3-3-3 and asked all participants to try to stack as fast as they could. When they were finished, they had to complete another task, such as raising their hands, do three jumping-jacks, or jogging in place until everyone completed the stack. Other warm-up activities included stacking certain patterns with their eyes closed, stacking to music and stopping only when the music stopped, or working in teams of two where one person stacks the cups on one side of the room and crabwalks back, and the partner crabwalks up to downstack the pyramid in the quickest amount of time.

Once everyone is warmed up, the tournament begins. A certain pattern of stacks must be picked so that everyone competes at the same thing. For beginners, choose the 3-6-3 stack; for the advanced teens, choose the cycle. The cycle stack is a pattern of a 3-6-3 stack, a 6-6 stack, and a 1-10-1 stack, ending in a downstacked 3-6-3. All participants get three tries to stack the formation as fast as they can, and the fastest time is selected. The winners from each bracket were given $5 gift certificates to a local bookstore, but a cheaper prize could be a Cup Stack Attack crown or ribbon.

Food, Technology, and Other Mandatory Extras

If possible, show an exciting clip from YouTube video on a television or projector to get the group ready for some stacking while watching some talented teens performing this activity.

Analysis

This is a great rainy-day program and fun for promoting healthy living. If sport stacking is not popular in your community, you might want to purchase one or two sets of cups and see if it catches on. In a pinch, regular party cups can be used, but they do not have the same weight as the special cups.

Resources

Check out these websites for more information on cup stacking:

Speed Stacks. http://www.speedstacks.com/.
World Sports Stacking Association. http://www.thewssa.com.

Chapter 18

Programs: Summer Reading

Summer reading programs for teens are not as rare as they used to be, but they are certainly not ubiquitous either. That being said, it is fairly common to have a summer program that focuses almost exclusively on reading and rarely offers opportunities to participate with other formats. Focusing solely on reading is a mistake and a lost opportunity for the library.

On the other hand, summer reading programs exclusively designed for tweens are few and far between. The normal model followed is to develop a program for toddlers and preschoolers all the way up to grade five. The needs and interests of fifth graders are extremely different from preschoolers. Start thinking about the graphics on the children's summer reading program materials. Are they targeted toward preschoolers? Are tweens that are trying to pull away from being treated as a child going to be excited to join that summer reading program?

Teen Summer Reading Program

General Description

Summertime is a school-free time for teens and should be flexible and relaxed. Libraries long ago started offering other formats and services in addition to books in their collections, so it does not make sense that a summer program should focus solely on books. While reading books should be a part of any summer program, it should not be the sole focus. A summer program should embrace the various formats available in the library as well as the variety of venues and media teens use to read, learn, listen, and otherwise spend their recreational time during the summer.

Pop

Teens who are avid readers rarely need encouragement to read, but teens who are not readers almost always need incentives. The main challenge for a teen librarian in the summer is figuring out ways to get teens into the library and engaged in the programs and services that the library offers. Offering a summer program that not only allows but encourages teens to listen to music, watch DVDs, read magazines, or better yet something unexpected, like teach an adult to play a video game, will change the way a teen views the library. An open and fun summer program demonstrates to teens that the library is not just an extension of learning and school but is also a place to have fun and try new things.

Relate

This type of open program, which does not focus only on reading books, is the simplest and best way to connect with the reluctant readers, the nonreaders, and the apathetic readers in your community. Teens who consume any content other than books will be able to join and feel active in the library in a different way. Relating to the multiformat world that teens live in is key to providing them with up-to-the-minute services. This type of program can also be tweaked and added to every year to reflect the newest interest or gadget.

Instructors/Talent

No instructors are needed for this program.

Audience

Teens in grades 6 through 12, with a focus on flexibility and fun for the full variety of teens in the community. This means that bookworms and reluctant readers are both welcome and invited to participate in the program.

Planning and Supplies

When planning the details and rules of a program, you should base it on what your library and your staff can support and what it cannot. If you are in a smaller library and you, as the teen librarian, are probably going to be the only one handling things, you might be able to get away with a more complicated and involved program. If you are in a larger system or depend on many other staff members to help teens with the program, then simple is best. Let's focus on the basic idea and leave it to you to decide how much further you want to take it.

Create

The Ann Arbor District Library (AADL) calls its summer program the Teen Game, and each year it has a different theme based on the overarching theme collectively picked for the youth, teen, and adult reading programs. The visuals of the larger theme are adapted to suit the teen audience. For example, in 2008 the overarching theme was "Under Construction." For the teens, this simply meant that the Teen Game visual was an image of an orange construction cone: evocative but not youthful or cluttered. Another year, the larger theme was "Figure It Out," so the Teen Game had a close-up photo of the locally infamous "gum wall," which is appropriately gross and cool at the same time. Think about using pop culture references that teens can relate to, such as "I Love DL," a teen summer reading program theme used by the Darien Library, that plays off the well-known slogan, "I Love NY" (see Figure 18.1).

In order to finish the Teen Game, teens must complete a minimum of ten activities listed on the game card. The library does not dictate which activities the teens choose or how many times they choose to do a certain activity. The activities are divided up into categories: Read, Watch, Listen, and Do. Each choice counts toward one of the ten activities the teens must do to complete the game.

Figure 18.1. 2009 Teen Summer Reading Program at Darien (CT) Library

Source: Courtesy of Darien Library.

Options you might use underneath the main headings:

- READ options: a book of poetry; a collection of short stories; two magazines cover to cover; a newspaper online for one hour; a classic; a biography; a book from the teen collection; an old favorite; or anything you want for one hour.
- WATCH options: a documentary; an anime film; a movie based on a book; a how-to video; YouTube for one hour; streaming video online for one hour.
- LISTEN options: to your MP3 player for one hour; to your mom and dad's favorite CD; a podcast or podcasts for one hour; to a book on CD.
- DO options: attend a library event; post to the library blog; teach an adult how to play a video game; read to a child or senior citizen; spend an entire day without electronics or television; encourage a friend or family member to sign up for the summer game; volunteer your time for an hour.

You get the idea! Every year the options are tweaked a little bit by adding whatever may be the newest website, format, or media teens are using.

Food, Technology, and Other Mandatory Extras

In the case of a summer program, the extras that are most needed are prizes. Whether you offer a large grand prize like an iPod or a generous gift certificate to a popular store, prizes are the easiest way to encourage reluctant library users to join your program. It is always fun to announce the prizes to an auditorium full of teens during a promotional school visit. A loud response of happiness is usually heard. What prizes you offer is dependent on your budget, whether you have a Friends of the Library group who will fund prizes or whether you are savvy enough to solicit prizes from not just local businesses but also corporations who have locations in your neighborhood. Soliciting prizes is rarely fun, but asking for corporate donations is usually a more straightforward process, not as fraught with the often-uncomfortable action of begging a cash-strapped local business owner for something. Most corporations have a person or a department on staff whose job it is to field such requests.

AADL also offers smaller incentives that are just as important. Every teen who completes the program gets to choose a free book to keep from an assortment chosen by librarians and funded by the Friends of the Library. The past couple of years we have also offered every teen who completes the program a special two-sided coupon. Side one, and the most popular choice by far, is the "$5 Off Overdue Fines" choice. Anyone who works with teens knows that accumulated fines or losing one item can prevent a teen from being able to check out books in the future. Any opportunity to reduce these fines is crucial. For teens who do not have overdue fines, the other side of the coupon offers "One Free Zoom Lends DVD Rental." This allows the teen to check out one of the newer DVDs we own, from our special "Zoom" collection that normally costs $1 for a week. You surely have things in your collection that you can give as rewards without any real up-front cost to the library.

Another extra element to add to your program is a mechanism to give avid readers additional opportunities to win prizes for their efforts. You will find that sometimes your most avid readers forgo a summer program because it is not challenging enough. You may also find that the parents of avid readers are more open to the nonreading options and less resistant (certainly when you explain the goal of attracting all teens and not just some teens) when they see an opportunity for their overachiever to overachieve. The separate incentive program is called Bibliomaniacs, wherein teens can fill out slips that equal additional entries into the grand prize drawing for every 300 pages they read. Staff will not have to expend much energy on this incentive, aside from providing the slips and storing them as they come in. This is a self-directed way for prodigious readers to get credit for the reading without making the other teens feel like they are doing less.

Analysis

You will find that an entire new base of teens will be engaged in your library during the summer. When this model was first proposed at the library, a coworker commented, "Well, this will be the first time I can get my son to sign up!" Bingo! This is entirely the point.

Marketing Tips

May and June are good times to get the word out about the summer reading program. Ask school librarians, English teachers, and principals to give short presentations at the schools to get teens excited about participating in the program.

Tween Summer Reading Program

Expertise on creating a summer reading program for tweens was provided by the Kalamazoo Public Library in Kalamazoo, MI.

General Description

Tweens, grades 5 through 7, participate in a summer reading program designed just for them at the Kalamazoo Public Library (KPL) in Kalamazoo, Michigan.

Pop

Tweens have become a defined group by the consumer market and the media, which cannot be overlooked by the library.

Relate

Tweens are a consistently forgotten group when the summer reading program is created. The graphics on the reading log are usually geared toward preschoolers, even though upper elementary children are very active participants in the reading program. Attract even more participants with a program dedicated to this age group, with their interests in mind, including age-appropriate graphics.

Instructors/Talent

No instructor is needed.

Audience

For the specific program detailed in this section, the summer reading program was created for grades 5 through 7. How do you define your tween population?

Planning and Supplies

Using the developmental attributes of tweens, the program was developed into a game to foster interaction, instead of a reading log where only the titles of books read would be listed. The goal of the game is to complete all four corner boxes on the game board (see Figure 18.2). When each box is filled in, the tween receives a prize and a certain number of raffle tickets. Any type of material goes: books, magazines, and more. Reading extra pages earns the participant bonuses and rewards those who love to read. The page bonus square in the center of the board allows the tween to roll a die to earn extra raffle tickets.

In many summer reading programs, the participant can only participate once due to the amount of prizes available. In the KPL Tween Summer Reading Game, tweens are encouraged to ask for another game board when they complete their first one. They may not receive more prizes, but they can accrue more raffle tickets. This encourages more reading in the summer. Additional raffle tickets can also be earned by attending tween programs at the library.

Create

Prizes include small things like a wristband, a pen, a T-shirt, or a book. The raffle prizes are bigger ticket items either purchased by the library or donated by local businesses. The summer is divided into three reading periods, ending July 1, August 1, and September 1. The program goes all summer, right up to when school starts. A drawing is held at the end of each reading period and then the raffle tickets are discarded, so it is in the best interest of the tween to read all summer to continue adding his or her name to the next drawings.

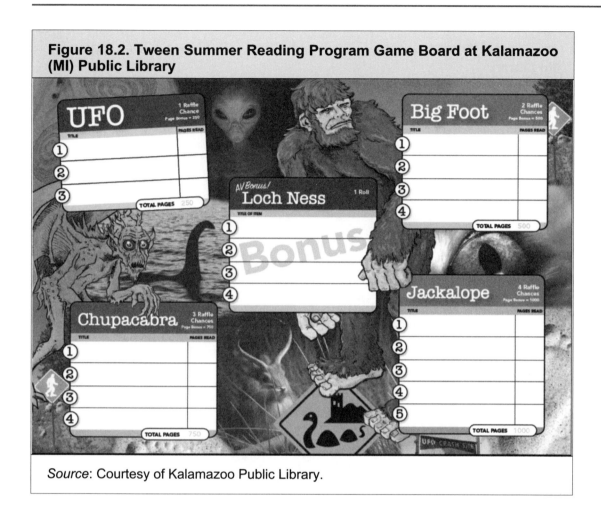

Figure 18.2. Tween Summer Reading Program Game Board at Kalamazoo (MI) Public Library

Source: Courtesy of Kalamazoo Public Library.

The graphics on the brochure and game piece are very important and should be age appropriate. In this case the theme, You Never Know!, integrated aliens, Big Foot, and other supernatural beings, an area of interest to tweens (see Figure 18.3).

Food, Technology, and Other Mandatory Extras

No food or technology is needed, but consider moving the program online. The participants are already technology savvy and can handle entering their completed books into a database. Another benefit of putting the summer reading program online is less money spent printing flyers, brochures, reading logs, and game boards. If you do not have a technology department that can build such a program, many companies have created templates that can be altered to fit what the library needs for such a summer reading program.

Analysis

Make this program as easy as possible. You probably already have a children's reading program, a teen program, and an adult program. Librarians tend to organize and cate-

Figure 18.3. 2007 Tween Summer Reading Program at Kalamazoo (MI) Public Library

Source: Courtesy of Kalamazoo Public Library.

gorize things to death, to the point of making their summer programs extremely confusing. Break down the programs in the best way possible so that they will not confuse staff and the participants.

Marketing Tips

Take the promotion of the summer reading program on the road. Promote the program at schools and summer camps, such as Boys & Girls Club, YMCA, and the city recreation camp. These large groups can participate but possibly in a modified version. Allow on-site sign-up for the program at city fairs, attracting participants that may never have entered the library. Create a YouTube video encouraging participation, and post it on your library website and Facebook. This video would be even better if tweens act in it, as well as create the video. Then it is tween approved!

Chapter 19

Programs: Technology

In just a few short years, technology has become a big part of young people's lives and has changed quite dramatically from days of the Rubik's Cube and the ghetto blaster. In some situations, kids are more tech-savvy than adults at downloading music to their iPods, creating videos for YouTube, and using Flash to create animations on their blogs or websites.

Though using technology can seem like a solo activity, you can create programs centered on these popular gadgets and turn a solo event to a social event. In some cases these programs can be a large expense to the organization because technology is expensive, but with a little creativity these programs can be put together for a low cost.

Social Networking Programs

General Description

Teens are given space in a computer lab or computer area to work on designing their own webpages, uploading pictures to their Facebook page, or editing videos to put on YouTube.

Pop

Using the Internet, people have discovered that they can find more than information; they can also find people. Websites like Classmates.com allow people to rekindle friendships with school friends they have not seen for many years. The concept of social networking websites has grown tenfold, allowing people to find long-lost girlfriends, boyfriends, and classmates; to link with business professionals on LinkedIn; to promote bands on MySpace; market businesses on Facebook; and catch up on the minute-to-minute activities of your friend of a friend on Twitter. Social networking sites bring complete strangers together to play games and are a major pastime for both teens and adults.

Relate

Connecting with friends on social networking websites like Facebook, MySpace, and YouTube is a common activity for teens. Teens go to the library to use the computers for homework but also to chat with friends, check out other people's photos and videos, and design their own virtual spaces. They want to comment to their friends about what they are looking at, and stand four around a computer. Most libraries do not have large enough computer areas to accommodate crowding around computers. If there is not a specific teen computing area, most of the time teens are sharing the space with adults, creating a war over quiet versus social space.

This program allows teens to have an environment where they can laugh and comment to one another while updating their Facebook pages. It also allows you, as the librarian, to talk a little about the security issues that come up with using social networking sites and point them in the right direction to find more information about using the technology, such as learning HTML to program graphics on a MySpace page.

Instructors/Talent

No instructor is needed for this program. It is helpful to have someone from IT on hand for complex computing questions, but you may already be well versed in all things computer. Make yourself a resource on using social technology for teens who may not otherwise have access to someone who can help them benefit the most from these popular websites. Especially in urban areas where the library is one of the only access points for teens to the Internet, there are not many opportunities for them to learn all of the technological ins and outs of the Internet, especially in situations where they do not have tech-savvy adults at home.

Audience

Grades 8 through 12. Policies from both Facebook and MySpace state that a child must be age 13 or older to register.

Planning and Supplies

- Computers (lab area or meeting room where laptops can be set up)
- Handouts with tips or suggestions for additions to MySpace/Facebook pages
- Video camera for making videos to upload to YouTube

Create

This program can range from being as simple as providing the space and time for teens to work on their MySpace/Facebook pages with the ability to socialize with their friends and keep the volume level a little higher than normal computer-area level. If you want to get a little more creative, teach teens how to write their own HTML code to design. Create a handout with fun tips on games and applications that can be added to a Facebook page. You can even lead the group in the creation of a short library promotional video and ask the teens to edit it to post on YouTube.

Creation of a YouTube video involves creating a script, for which the teens can brainstorm and help with the writing. Making a summer reading promotional video is a great project. Once the writing is completed and props have been prepared, have the teens film the video. Then show them how to edit the film on MovieMaker and upload it to YouTube. This project will probably take multiple times of meeting together. An alternative is to have a YouTube watching night, where you create a list of teen-appropriate videos to watch as a group. Each video is only about three to four minutes long, so choose 15 videos. It will likely be a fun time filled with laughter.

Food, Technology, and Other Mandatory Extras

Food is not needed, especially if your library does not allow food in the computer area.

Analysis

Make this program fun, not like school. Find passive ways to talk about privacy and security settings on these websites, such as telling anecdotes about the potential consequences of posting your phone number and address on your Facebook page. Some teens may not even realize what information they are putting out there for the world to see or even that the whole world can see it or that anything bad could happen to them.

Marketing Tips

Advertise this program to the teens that frequent your computer area. Word of mouth is the best approach to gaining interest in this program.

Resources

Check out these resources for ideas on how to put some more pizzazz into an online profile:

Facebook. 2010. "Facebook Application Directory." Accessed August 8. http://www.facebook.com/apps/directory.php.

Gunter, Sherry Kinkoph. 2010. *Sams Teach Yourself Facebook in 10 Minutes*. Indianapolis: Sams Publishing.

Hepner, Ryan. 2008. *MySpace for Dummies*. Hoboken, NJ: Wiley.

Windows Live. 2010. *Windows Live Movie Maker 2011*. [Software download for movies and slide shows from photos and videos.] Accessed August 8. http://explore.live.com/windows-live-movie-maker.

Library LEGO League

General Description

Library LEGO League is a program where kids design, build, and program a LEGO Mindstorms NXT robot that will complete in challenges against other teams. It was created as a joint effort by our Youth Department and Information Technology Department. Kids in grades four through eight form teams of two to four people, and spend one day, from 10 a.m. to 4 p.m., building their robots for the challenge held at the end of the program. The program was repeated for three days, with different challenges for each day, so that many kids could participate, as the supplies limited the participation in the program. Details on the winners of the challenge and discussion of challenge were posted on the L3 blog at http://www.aadl.org/l3. The challenges are designed for beginners, with minimal to no knowledge of using the equipment. The robot must complete a certain goal, such as going through a maze built of tables, circling around a garbage can and returning to a designated spot, or finding a ball using a motion sensor, picking it up, and taking it to a designated area.

Pop

Library LEGO League (L3) is a robotics program using a LEGO Mindstorms NXT robot, a commercial line from LEGO. This LEGO set combines electric motors, sensors, and LEGO bricks, as well as LEGO Technic pieces, which include gears, axles, and beams, to create motorized vehicles. Robots have received popular culture recognition through many avenues including the television show *BattleBots*. On that series, teams would design and build "combat robots" to be put in an arena to battle other robots, with the purpose of dominating or disabling other robots.

Relate

The L3 program was created to appeal to kids interested in robotics and computer programming, and to expose kids who may enjoy the concept of the television series *BattleBots* to the technical side of robots.

Instructors/Talent

This program can be run using staff within the library. Collaboration between youth/teen staff and technology specialists works well, unless youth/teen staff are tech savvy. A nice touch to this program is to invite local robotics organizations to do demonstrations or help the kids with building and programming during the program. The program was loosely formatted after the FIRST LEGO League (FLL), a global program which utilizes theme-based challenges to excite kids in science and technology.

Audience

Grades 4 through 8. The program would obviously work for older teens as well. Third graders were invited the first year of the program, but the kids did not have the attention span to last the whole day. If you are defining your tween set as a little younger crowd, then it is advisable to shorten the program or have a different activity in the middle of the event to break up the day.

Planning and Supplies

- LEGO Mindstorms NXT set
- Computer
- Internet access
- Work space
- Prizes: For example, gift certificates can be given to the winning team of the competition.
- Participatory ribbons for all attendees of the program

Six LEGO Mindstorms NXT sets should be purchased so that six teams of four kids can build robots at the same time. Depending on the size of the expected audience and the computers available, fewer sets could be purchased, or more sessions could be planned so that more kids have a chance to use the sets. Another cost-saving alternative would be to borrow Mindstorm kits or ask kids to bring their kits from home. Currently, the LEGO Mindstorms NXT 2.0 set is out on the market for $279.99 each (see Figure 19.1).

Create

1. Each team has a workstation that includes a LEGO Mindstorms NXT set, a computer, and Internet access.
2. The challenge for the day, determined beforehand, is announced at the start of the session, so that no team has an advantage.
3. A quick tutorial is presented on the sensors and motors in the LEGO set and how to use the programming software.
4. Equipment is passed out to the teams, and they have until 3 p.m. to build and program a robot that will best complete the day's challenge. (See Figure 19.2 for rules.) Two to three staff members should stay in the room to help teams with any design or computer programming problems.
5. At 3 p.m., friends and family are invited to return and watch the robots compete in the challenge.

Figure 19.1. LEGO Mindstorms History

The LEGO MINDSTORMS NXT robotics toolkit comes with building instructions for 4 main models ranging in building complexity, going from the Quick Start model that you can assemble and program in 30 minutes, to the ultimate Humanoid—all models are designed for easy battery change.

6 building and programming challenges are included on the software CD, complete with step-by-step building instructions and programming guide for all models.

Shooterbot is a moving vehicle robot that can guard your room and will shoot balls at intruders!

Color Sorter is a robotic sorting machine that can sort different colored objects and dispense them as you please. It can easily be modified with a catapult mechanism that can precisely shoot the different colors where you like.

Alpha Rex is the ultimate robot. It is a humanoid robot, easy to assemble and with multiple functions; it walks and turns, dances, talks, can see and avoid obstacles, can grab and distinguish between different colored objects.

Robogator is the animal robot that moves like an alligator. It will protect its area and jump forward and snap at anything that comes too near. Watch out!

Source: http://mindstorms.lego.com/en-us/history/default.aspx.

6. When all teams have presented their robots, the fastest four teams at completing the challenge have 20 more minutes to fix up their robots. These teams have one more chance to show off their robots.

7. Prizes are given to the three teams to complete the challenge in the fastest time. Prizes are not mandatory for the program to be successful. The opportunity to build the robots and compete in the challenge can be reward enough. Knowing your audience and budget can help determine whether prizes are considered necessary.

Food, Technology, and Other Mandatory Extras

Lunch and snacks should be served because the program as presented is a full day long. Costs can be cut by asking kids to bring their own lunches.

Analysis

The Library LEGO League program is a marriage of technology, robotics, and physics, and fills the tween need for secure guidelines with room for creative expression. Each robot kit comes with specific instructions to make the basic robot. Each challenge is designed to be completed by the basic robot. If a team chooses to be more curious and cre-

---

Figure 19.2. Library LEGO League: The Rules

LEGO League Rules

1. No outside Lego is allowed. Robot must be built using only the Lego provided.
2. Teams may bring their own laptops, but programs can only be transferred to their robot from the teams' provided computer.
3. Teams may work elsewhere in the library, but Lego parts must remain in the multipurpose room.
4. Teams must be on time and should plan to stay through 4:00 p.m. This is not a walk-in event. Teams failing to appear by 10:30 a.m. on the day of the competition will be disqualified.

---

ative, they can experiment with the use of different sensors or design a completely new robot to complete the task more efficiently.

Marketing Tips

Let local science and physics teachers know about the event so they can encourage their students to attend. Look in your community for groups participating in engineering projects, such as children's science museums, that may be able to spread the word to interested parties. The video gaming community might enjoy this program as well.

Resources

Check out these books and websites on robotics, and specifically the NXT robot:

Ferrari, Mario, and Giulio Ferarri. 2002. *Building Robots with LEGO Mindstorms: The Ultimate Tool for Mindstorms Maniacs!* Burlington, MA: Syngress.

FIRST. 2010. "For Inspiration and Recognition of Science and Technology." Accessed August 8. http://www.usfirst.org/.

FLL. 2010. "FIRST LEGO League." Accessed August 8. http://www.firstLEGOleague.org/.

LEGO. 2010. "Mindstorms Official Web site." Accessed August 8. http://mindstorms.LEGO.com/en-us/Default.aspx.

Perdue, David J. 2008. *The Unofficial Lego Mindstorms NXT Inventor's Guide.* San Francisco: No Starch Press.

Perdue, David J. 2010. "The Unofficial LEGO Mindstorms NXT Inventor's Guide." Accessed August 8. http://nxtguide.davidjperdue.com/.

Technology Fashionistas

General Description

Crafts meet technology! Teens can jazz up their ear buds and flash drives, making them unique to their personalities and making accessories out of technology toys. They can also make bracelets that light up with LED (light-emitting diode) lights.

Pop

We live in a tech culture. While the Internet gave us anonymity, it also spurred on a great desire to carve out a unique space for ourselves on our websites, blogs, and Facebook pages so we could show the world who we are. This philosophy spilled over onto our tech toy culture, where teens and tweens own their own cell phones, iPods, laptops, and countless other toys, creating another avenue to proudly demonstrate individualism. We cover our laptops in designer stickers, coat our cell phone cases with jewels, and purchase iPods in many bright colors, all to show uniqueness in a technology-driven society.

Relate

This is a very involved program but worth it because physics is not often highlighted in youth and teen programming. Besides promoting your technical and crafty books, it might spur some interest in the physics and electrical books in your collection.

Instructors/Talent

Look into your staff and community to see if you can find someone who has experience working with LED lights. The books listed in the Resources section can teach you step by step how to build circuits, but if you do not feel comfortable building circuits with copper wire and batteries, try to find someone who is. Check with electrician or fashion programs at local community colleges for possible help with this program.

Audience

Grades 6 through 12. This is a very detail-oriented program, so it will appeal only to teens that can concentrate and not get frustrated easily. If the right decorative supplies are purchased, it is a great program for both girls and boys.

Planning and Supplies

Three activities were chosen: dressing up ear buds, accessorizing flash drives, and creating LED bracelets. If you are teaching yourself how to build the circuit for the bracelet, make sure you give yourself enough time for trial and error. Teens were asked to bring their own ear buds and flash drives, but the library could also provide them. They might be great giveaways for Teen Tech Week. Over-the-ear buds leave more room for adding decorations.

Ear Buds Activity

- Ear buds—over-the-ear or regular ear buds
- Craft felt
- Beads
- Glitter pens
- Thread
- Needles

Flash Drives Activity

- Flash drives
- Craft felt
- Army guys/action figures
- Ribbon
- Hot-glue gun, with glue sticks
- Scissors
- Permanent markers

LED Bracelets Activity

Most of the supplies for the bracelets were purchased at an electronics store. For information on specific types of batteries, LED lights, and the best materials to use for conductors, check out the books listed in the Resources section. The craft book *Fashioning Technology* has templates and instructions for the bracelet (see Figure 19.3).

Create

The supplies and decorations were laid out on the tables, along with example designs of ear buds and flash drives. The design of the LED bracelet was modified to be simpler than explained in the book because of my physics knowledge and sewing ability. The final product did not turn out as professional looking as the bracelet detailed in the book, so it is up to you how creative and high quality you want to be with the design. Instead of conductive wire, craft copper wire and electrical tape were used to connect the battery to the LED lights to create a circuit. The wire was scraped with a rough sponge to remove any oxidization on the copper and make it a better conductor of energy. A soldering iron would be a better, more permanent approach to connect the battery to the copper wire, instead of electrical tape, but the tool and solder may be tough to get your hands on. Black electrical tape was an easy and cheaper solution.

Figure 19.3. Technology Fashionista Program: Ear Buds, Flash Drive, LED Bracelet, and Lit-Up Figure

Food, Technology, and Other Mandatory Extras

The creations the teens can come up with are limitless. Make examples to give a starting point and to show some of the possibilities of mixing DIY crafts with technology. Be sure to create a display of the great technology craft books in the library collection to help the creative juices flow. Food is always appreciated, especially if it is an after-school event, but none is needed for this event to be a success.

Analysis

This can be a pricey program depending on the number of participants and if ear buds and flash drives are going to be given away. The cost for fabric, batteries, LED lights, copper wire, and decorations comes to around $100 for 40 participants.

Marketing Tips

This program was advertised during Teen Tech Week. It would be great to be publicized to any home economics classes, fashion clubs, or sewing groups. Because some boys aren't likely to attend a workshop that seems to be centered around crafts, you can play down the crafts aspect and put a technology slant on the flyer and blurb wordage; this is a good way to promote the program to computer and technology classes, which can often be male dominated.

Resources

Check out these books for templates and more techno-craft ideas:

Eng, Diana. 2007. *Fashion Geek: Clothing Accessories Tech*. Cincinnati, OH: North Light Books.

Lewis, Alison with Fang-Yu Lin. 2008. *Switch Craft: Battery-Powered Crafts to Make and Sew*. New York: Potter Craft.

Pakhchyan, Syuzi. 2008. *Fashioning Technology: A DIY Intro to Smart Crafting*. San Jose, CA: O'Reilly Media.

Library Makerspaces

The Library Makerspaces program was written and contributed by Steve Teeri of the Detroit Public Library.

General Description

Library makerspaces provides access for teens to design and fabrication technologies and the freedom to explore them. Through these interactions, teens can become more comfortable with concepts related to mathematics, engineering, and science. Of equal importance, the teens will feel a sense of accomplishment and an empowerment to create the world around them.

Teens today are technologically savvy. A library makerspace serves as a bridge to take their knowledge into the fields of design and manufacturing. By empowering teens with the ability to create and build their own objects and devices, a whole new world is opened to them. Instilling this Do-It-Yourself (DIY) attitude at a young age will pay dividends in the future of adults who are more knowledgeable and willing to explore.

Pop

The hackerspace or makerspace movement has caught on all over the world for people who are tired of paying to repair electronics and gadgets and have decided to create their own inventions incorporating technology and computers. The spaces are community labs where people can come together to share equipment and resources and create homemade technology (Saini, 2009). To showcase this ingenuity maker faires, which originated in San Francisco, are now taking place across the United States. These faires bring together makers from a wide variety of disciplines,and allow the public to see the innovation taking place within their communities. A trip to a maker faire, if feasible, would provide an excellent real-world demonstration of what can be accomplished through library makerspaces.

Relate

Work in a library makerspace is a collaborative process, allowing teens to learn together in mastering the technologies at their disposal. As cheap mass-produced goods have entered our markets, the concept of making your own things has dwindled. While it is easy to go to the store and buy something, you do not gain the same knowledge, enrichment, and satisfaction from making it yourself. Similarly, as the U.S. economy has evolved from a manufacturing-based economy to one based on service, fewer people in our society have the knowledge and ability to make things.

Instructors/Talent

Makerspaces have appeared throughout the United States and, indeed, throughout the world in recent years. These existing collectives offer a wealth of expertise into which libraries can tap, establishing their own makerspaces. Magazines such as *Make* offer articles on projects that can take place within libraries (*Make*, 2010). In addition, many websites offer current information on the maker movement at little or no cost. Library staff members and volunteers can be trained in the use of the equipment and technologies. As some of the maker equipment has the potential to cause physical damage if used improperly, it is imperative to have a disciplined and safe environment. Mitch Altman, inventor of the TV B Gone, is an expert in hosting a mobile soldering beginners' class (TV B Gone, 2010). Traveling around the United States and the world, Mitch is an evangelist for the maker spirit to young people.

Audience

Grades 8 through 12, with parental or guardian permission.

Planning and Supplies

1. Space where equipment will be set up (well ventilated, nonflammable)
2. Handouts with tips or suggestions on using equipment
3. Materials such as vinyl, plastic, wood, and metal that will be raw material for projects
4. Video camera for making videos to upload to a website, Twitter, YouTube, etc.

Create

Soldering irons are a good first step in learning the tools in a makerspace. Users can learn the basics of electricity while turning kits into useful electronic gadgets. A by-product of these programs will be teens gaining a greater familiarity with the multitude of electronics they come in contact with daily.

The Makerbot Cupcake CNC (Computer Numerical Controller) 3-D printer is another technology that would benefit a library makerspace. This printer allows users to design objects, from replacement machine parts to art sculptures, and transform them into real-life items made through the milling of plastic or other materials.

Shopbot offers a full-size CNC machine for creating life-sized objects, such as furniture. Once teens have mastered the art and science of creating small objects on the Cupcake CNC, they can then progress to larger and more complex projects.

Laser cutters, such as the Epilog Mini 24, allow precise cutting and engraving of materials. This ability makes them one of the most useful tools in a makerspace. High-tolerance parts engraving will allow teens to create things on level with professional goods in the market.

Vinyl cutters, such as the Roland CAMM-1 Servo GX-24, allow users to cut out detailed patterns, which can then be applied to clothing and objects. These devices allow users to express their artistic creativity on a computer and then receive a usable copy for application in the real world.

Food, Technology, and Other Mandatory Extras

Prizes and incentives can be offered in competitions to challenge young adults in building their skill sets as makers.

Analysis

Teens are smart, creative, and able people. Once the makerspace is assembled, give the teens required training and then let them explore the technology. Staff or volunteer experts should be made available to answer questions as the teens run across them. An environment fostering creativity and imagination should permeate the library makerspace.

Note that the term *makerspace* is interchangeable with *hackerspace*. The reason *makerspace* has been chosen for use in libraries is to avoid the unfortunate negative connotation the term *hacker* has become associated with over the years, and possible backlash from members of the community who do not understand its etymology.

Marketing Tips

Advertise this program to the teens that frequent your library locations. Word of mouth is the best approach to gaining interest in this program. Facebook, Twitter, and YouTube offer additional online avenues for marketing your library makerspace.

Resources

Check out these resources for more information on makerspaces:

A2 MechShop. http://www.a2mechshop.com.

Frauenfelder, Mark. 2010. *Made by Hand: Searching for Meaning in a Throwaway World*. New York: Portfolio Hardcover.

Hack Pittsburgh. http://www.hackpittsburgh.org.

I3 Detroit: Metro Detroit's Art & Technology Collective. http://www.i3detroit.com.

Make: Technology on Your Time. http://www.makezine.com.

Maker Faire. http://makerfaire.com.

Maker SHED: DIY Kits + Tools + Books + Fun. http://www.makershed.com.

Massachusetts Institute of Technology. 2010. "Mobile Fab Lab Hits the Road." Accessed October 25. http://web.mit.edu/spotlight/mobile-fablab.

Noise Bridge Makerspace. http://www.noisebridge.net.

Saini, Angela. 2009. "DIY Gadgetry." *BBC News,* June 19. Available: http://news.bbc.co.uk/2/hi/uk_news/magazine/8107803.stm.

The Hacktory. http://thehacktory.org.

TV B Gone. http://www.tvbgone.com.

Check out these supply websites:

Epilog Mini 24 Laser Cutter. http://www.epiloglaser.com.

MakerBot Store. 2010. "Cupcake CNC." Accessed October 25. http://store.makerbot.com/3d-printers/cupcake-cnc.html.

Roland CAMM-1 Servo GX-24 Vinyl Cutter. http://www.rolanddga.com.

Shopbot. http://www.shopbottools.com.

Filmmaking 101

Information on the Filmmaking 101 program was provided by Stewart Fritz, Kalamazoo Public Library.

General Description

Great filmmakers are not born, they're made. Filmmaking 101 teaches teens the basics of filmmaking, from drawing up storyboards and planning a shot list to operating a camera and digitally editing a short film masterpiece. Instructors brought cameras, tripods, and laptops with digital editing software, and teens and tweens brought their imaginations! No previous filmmaking experience necessary. Besides, as even the cheapest cell phones, laptops, and handheld gaming devices come standard with built-in video cameras these days, the number of tweens and teens who have never used a camera continues to shrink.

Pop

How many of your teen patrons come into the library and plop down in front of the computer, fire up YouTube, and spend the afternoon passively watching? Did you ever wonder if you could persuade them to actively create instead of just mindlessly consume? Now you can! Running a teen filmmaking program is not nearly as difficult as you might imagine, and the end results are well worth the effort.

Relate

If your library has a strong focus on reading, listening, and viewing for pleasure, especially with youth audiences, this is a great way to introduce them to your collection of DIY film books and materials. Also, budding filmmakers need inspiration and a well-stocked AV collection is a natural place for them to look.

If your city has a public access TV station or a college or university with film courses, it is definitely worth asking if they will partner with you to actually run the program. You get the expertise of a professional, and they get free exposure and the chance to do some outreach of their own. Plus, having someone else there to run the show gives you a chance to interact with your teen patrons in a new way. Library staff often get pulled in for supporting roles (with permission, of course) by teens shooting their magnum opus in the library.

Instructors/Talent

Obviously, pulling off a program like this requires at least a working knowledge of how to make movies. While a degree in film studies is not a prerequisite, at the very least if library staff members are going to run this program themselves they should know some filmmaking fundamentals. On the technical side, knowing how to set up and operate a variety of average consumer-grade video cameras is essential. If you cannot figure out how to turn it on or load a tape, you probably won't be able to teach someone else effectively.

Familiarity with editing software, even the free applications that come bundled with most computers, is also good to know. More important than just knowing hardware and software, however, are the fundamentals of good filmmaking: making a storyboard, planning a list of shots, and developing at least a bare-bones script so the director and actors are all on the same page before they begin shooting anything.

Audience

Any tween or teen with an interest in making their own movies should be able to handle this program. Chances are, they will catch on immediately and crank out a great film by the end of the program. Do not limit programs to camera geeks. A great film needs a script, and kids interested in comics can get involved with drawing up the storyboards as well.

Planning and Supplies

The one thing you absolutely cannot have too much of with this program is time. Even though the scripting and storyboarding phase of the film project can seem less exciting than breaking the camera out and filming away, it is an essential step in the process that can admittedly take a while. Shooting the footage for just a three-to-five-minute film can take at least an hour, and that's with no retakes. As much time as it takes to script and shoot the footage, plan to give your participants at least double that for editing and tweaking. If you can plan this program so that it takes place over two or even three days, it will be that much better. The final product will be well worth the time investment.

Aside from time, you will also need space to shoot scenes (if you don't want to let teens shoot in the stacks, that is), and you will need a meeting space to regroup and show rough footage. An ideal space is a computer lab or meeting room where videos can be played without disturbing other patrons; it's even better if the room is equipped with a projector or large monitor so everyone can see without having to crowd in.

Finally, and there is no way around it, you will need some equipment. This is filmmaking we're talking about here, and that means cameras. The good news is that you do not need to spend a bundle. You can get some fairly high-quality footage from digital video cameras that cost under $100 on the low end. You will also need a computer to edit the footage, but fortunately there is no need to spend money on editing software. Both Apple and Windows machines have free editing tools, and there are several open-source alternatives as well. The bad news is that you will need to take some time beforehand and learn how to use the software, but most of the packages are fairly easy to learn.

Create

The best part of the Filmmaking 101 program is that at the end of the day, your teens have something tangible they can take away with them and show off to the world. Beyond simply posting to YouTube or Facebook, the films the teens create can be the gateway into something even bigger. There are literally dozens of film festivals that promote works by young film directors, and local cable access stations are often willing to showcase student films. Teens interested in pursuing a film career can use the films they create in this program as part of their demo reels as well.

Food, Technology, and Other Mandatory Extras

Your teens will probably want to keep making films, and there are lots of resources available that can help put the polish on their productions. There are more books on low-budget filmmaking than you can possibly imagine, and tons of great DIY tips on the web for making movies on the cheap. Tons of tutorials can be found online, from how to make fake blood to making a camera crane out of PVC tubing. Instructables (http://www.instructables.com) and *Make* (http://www.makezine.com) are two great places to find all sorts of DIY tips and tricks. Other follow-up resources include the local cable access center (especially if they helped produce your program), community college, or high school film and video classes.

Analysis

When given direction and resources, the teens made highly creative films, way beyond what was imagined when this program was being put together. Hold a movie premiere night, complete with a red carpet and Hollywood stars on the floor, to show off the teens' finished products. Make the films available on the library website or teen space to highlight the fabulous works teens have done in your community.

Marketing Tips

Get the word out to schools, in particular any film or editing instructors, and also post advertisements at local movie theaters and places teens who pursue creative activities spend their time.

Resources

Check out these websites for DIY tips and tricks for creating films:

Instructables. http://www.instructables.com.
Make: Technology on Your Time. http://www.makezine.com.

Game On! Envisioning Your Own Video Game

The Game On! Envisioning Your Own Video Game program was written and contributed by Justin Hoenke of the Portland Public Library, Portland, Maine.

General Description

Have you ever had an idea for your own video game? In this workshop, teens will brainstorm, flesh out our ideas, create storyboards, and draft up a proposal to make their own video game.

Pop

Video games are now a staple in households with teens and tweens. Many families have more than one gaming console connected to their televisions. Young people are usually the consumers of video games instead of the creators. When given the opportunity to create their own video game, those passionate about the digital art form are sure to generate a unique creation.

Relate

When the Portland Public Library started lending out video games, the staff noticed new types of patrons coming to the library. The first was the avid video game player who before did not have much of a reason to come to the library. The other was the avid reader and casual video game fan that was mostly interested in video games for their story and characters. To best serve these two populations, the library partnered with a local writing organization in Portland, Maine, called The Telling Room (http://tellingroom.org), and together developed this program with the goal of showing just how important excellent writing, story, and characters are to successful video games.

Instructors/Talent

This program works best when done in collaboration with another organization, be it either a writing organization or a group related to video games.

Audience

The program was opened up to teens ages 12 to 18. A total of 12 teens signed up, all of whom were teenage boys between the ages of 12 and 16.

Planning and Supplies

- Laptop
- Projector
- Easel and paper
- Markers, crayons, and pens
- Cameras

Create

Scratch is a simple programming language that teens can use to actually build their ideas (http://scratch.mit.edu/). While they may not be able to create the exact game they are envisioning, using this program will show them how essential programming and planning is to game development. The program was broken up into six sessions, each lasting one hour, leading the participants step by step through the video game creation process.

Session One

- Ice breaker: Name, school, favorite video game character and why
- Introduction about the workshop
- Brainstorm characters lists: Name, place, etc.
- Share with the group
- Slide presentation: Classic video game characters
- 20 questions on your character (include special powers)
- Slides on supporting characters
- Create more characters

Session Two: World and Objective

- Discuss what a hero is and describe different types.
- Go out into the community with cameras and find images.
- Slide presentation: Different video game objectives and settings.

Session Three: Genre

- Brainstorm different genres of video games.
- Group work: Have teens combine their ideas to make one solid game; emphasize communication and collaboration as a way to accomplish goals.

Session Four: Continue Group Work

- Merging worlds, characters, objectives: Teens begin to collaborate on building their games.
- Storyboarding begins.

Session Five: Storyboarding

- Teens establish a beginning, middle, and end to their video game.

Session Six: Presentations and Ideas

- Teens pitch their ideas to staff as if they are looking to sell their title to a video game company.

Food, Technology, and Other Mandatory Extras

No other technology is needed unless demonstrations were held with various video games. If that is the case, have a Nintendo Wii or Xbox 360 and favorite games. Food is also a fun addition but not mandatory.

Analysis

This program is a surefire way to invite and engage teen boys in the library.

Marketing Tips

Marketing was handled mostly in house by the Portland Public Library and The Telling Room. The program was promoted through various local outlets (schools, workshops, homeschooling, and unschooling families) as well as media outlets. The program was also heavily advertised on the TV information boards at the Portland Public Library.

Resources

Check out these game development tools:

Game Star Mechanic. http://gamestarmechanic.com/.
Learn Scratch. http://learnscratch.org/.
Scratch: Imagine. Program. Share. http://scratch.mit.edu/.
YoYo Games. http://www.yoyogames.com/make.

Chapter 20

"Where Do We Go from Here?": Conclusion

Show your teen and tween communities that the library is in tune with pop culture. The original concept of a library was a quiet place to hold books, meant for studying and contemplation. However, libraries have had to change with the times and transform into something that can better serve the current communities. Libraries are now community centers, places for people to meet up and take part in common activities such as story time, lectures, and hands-on events. They are still a place for research and learning, but libraries have taken an active role in offering free opportunities for community members to discover new things through programs and events. For teens and tweens to be interested and take part in these experiences, the programs and services must be relevant. That is where popular culture plays an important part.

It is hoped that after reading this book, readers feel comfortable exploring the various aspects of popular culture and integrating it into their programming style. This integration takes something that teens and tweens are already interested in and shows them that the library can create opportunities for them to share in their passion or obsession. It also creates opportunities for teens and tweens to experience different aspects of pop culture that they might not have otherwise been exposed to because of where they live. If the library is about establishing access to information for all and creating recreational opportunities, then combining those two mission statements together will naturally generate popular culture–driven programs and services for teens and tweens.

Decisions made at the library to create spaces for teens and tweens, purchase teen-centered materials, and create appropriately themed events and programs should be driven by teen and tween interest. Ask them what they want to see and do instead of deciding for them. You will create lifelong users of the library who feel invested in what goes on there, further building community around the library.

Index

A

A2 MechShop, 194
AADL. *See* Ann Arbor District Library
Abadie, M. J., 145
ABBA (band), 4
Abel, Jessica, 57
Academy Awards, 4
Access
    to collection, 39–40
    creating, 12–13
    to teen/tween spaces, 45–46
Adobe Photoshop Elements, 58–59
Advertising
    guerrilla, viral, alternative promotion, 36
    outreach promotions, 37
    paid, 36–37
    print, 32–34
    of programs, 52
    social networking promotion, 34–35
    street teams, 35
    See also Marketing; Marketing tips; Promotion
Aerosmith (band), 5
Aguilera, Christina, 6
Air Cannons, 164, 165
"Alka-Seltzer Rocket" (Steve Spangler Science),
    166
Alka-Seltzer Rockets, 163, 164–165
All Natural Beauty website, 138, 139
AlterNation: Transform. Embellish. Customize
    (Okey), 70, 72
Alternative rock, 6
Altman, Mitch, 192
Amara, Philip, 83
American Bandstand (television show), 2, 3
American Idol (television show), 153
American Ninja Warrior (television show), 159
Ames, Lee J., 84
Amigurumi Animals: 15 Patterns and Dozens of
    Techniques for Creating Cute Crochet
    Creatures (Obaachan), 134
Amigurumi: Crochet Happy Fun, 132–134

"Amigurumi Kingdom" (Yee), 134
Amigurumi World: Seriously Cute Crochet
    (Rimoli), 134
Anime
    Bento Box Bonanza and, 108, 111
    Comic Book Academy, 55–57
    Cosplay Contest, 129–132
    Gundam, 43
    Pokémon Tournaments, 126–128
    Superhero Smashup and, 83
    Sushi Making and, 99
Ann Arbor District Library (AADL)
    AXIS logo, 26
    branding, 23–24
    Comic Book Academy, 55–57
    Comics Art Digital Coloring, 58–59
    Double Dutch Program, 160–162
    Graffiti Contest, 85–88
    Gundamfest, 43
    Kitchen Cosmetics, 137–140
    Library LEGO League, 184
    Nail Art program, 135–137
    Parkour and Freerunning, 159–160
    Pinhole Photography, 62–64
    Teen Game, 174–177
Anna Banana: 101 Jump Rope Rhymes (Cole), 162
Apparel. *See* Clothing; Fashion design
Aqua Teen Hunger Force (movie), 36
Art & Story podcast, 57, 59, 61
Art programs
    Comic Book Academy, 55–57
    Comics Art Digital Coloring, 58–59
    Comics Artist Forum, 60–61
    Graffiti Contest, 85–88
    Photography Contest, 88–90
    Pinhole Photography, 62–64
    Superhero Smashup, 82–84
Astrology program, 143–145
Atari, 123
Attendance
    at library programs, 18–19
    teen involvement in programming and, 51

Attitude, 19
Aura reader, 144
Award ceremony, 93–94
Awards. *See* Prizes
AXIS logo (Ann Arbor District Library), 23–24, 26

B
Baez, Joan, 3
Ballard, Hank, 3
Balloon Station, 164, 165
Barber, Mary, 107
Barker, Cicely Mary, 148, 151
Battle, Meaghan
     Kitchen Cosmetics, 137–140
     Nail Art, 135–137
BattleBots (television show), 184
Beatles, 3, 4
Beauty, style, body modification, fashion programs
     Kitchen Cosmetics, 137–140
     Nail Art, 135–137
     Tattoo History, Culture, and Safety, 140–142
Beavis and Butt-head (MTV cartoon), 6
Bedford, Allan, 95
Beery, Barbara, 151
Bento Box Bonanza, 108–112
"Bento Boxes Win Lunch Fans" (Storey), 112
Berners-Lee, Tim, 5
Bibliomaniacs program, 177
Birnbach, Lisa, 5
Black Sabbath (band), 4
Blakeney, Faith, 117
Blakeney, Justina, 117
Blogs
     for cosmetics recipes, 138
     GreenBeanTeenQueen blog, 42
     Kitchen, Crafts, & More, 140
     Library LEGO League, 184
     Ypulse, 1, 32, 52
Boardman, Bob, 162
Body modification program, 140–142
Bonnadio, T. L., 120
Bonnell, Jennifer, 139
Books
     based on *Top Chef*, 66
     in summer reading program, 173
     See also Collections; Resources
Boone, Pat, 2
Booth, William, 7, 8
Bowie, David, 4
Box Office Mojo, 6
Bracelets, LED, 188–191
Branding
     AXIS logo from Ann Arbor District Library, 26
     Sno-Isle Libraries Teen logo, 25
     of teen/tween space, 45
     of tween/teen services, 21, 22–24
Bravo Media, 66, 69

Breakfast Club, The (movie), 4–5
Brehm-Heeger, Paula, 132
Brochure, 23–24
Brock, Wendell, 7
Browne, Vicki
     Double Dutch Program, 160–162
     Graffiti Contest, 85–88
     Parkour and Freerunning, 159–160
Budget
     cost of Technology Fashionistas, 190
     for library advertising, 37–38
     library collection and, 42
Buffy the Vampire Slayer (movie), 23
Buggles, The, 5
*Building Robots with LEGO Mindstorms: The
     Ultimate Tool for Mindstorms Maniacs!*
     (Ferrari & Ferrari), 187
Bulger, Aaron, 95
Buscema, John, 57
Bwana Devil (movie), 2

C
Callow, Matt, 64
Camera
     for Filmmaking 101, 194–197
     for Vegetarian Cooking demo, 103
     See also Video camera
Campbell, Mark, 90
Carlson, Peter, 3, 6
Catch-22 (Heller), 8
CD
     dance, 158
     karaoke, 154
Celebrity and reality television programs
     MTV: *Made*, 69–72
     Project Runway fashion show or challenge, 72–78
     Silent Library, 79–81
     Superhero Smashup, 82–84
     Top Chef Season 4 winner, Stephanie Izard,
          appearance/cooking demo, 65–69
Chace, Daniella, 107
"Chansey Pokémon Craft" (DTLK's Crafts for
     Kids), 128
Charlie and the Chocolate Factory (Dahl), 103, 104
Checker, Chubby, 3
Chef, 102
Chemistry, EXPLODapalooza, 162–166
Chenfeld, Cliff, 7
Chicago Bulls, 6
Classmates.com, 181
CliffsNotes collection, 46
Clothing
     Cosplay Contest, 129–132
     fairy, 149, 150, 151
     Jean Pocket Purses, 115–117
     T-shirt Remodel, 120–122
     See also Fashion design

Club Texting, 35
Cobain, Kurt, 6
Colbert Report, The (television show), 9
Cole, Joanna, 162
Collections
    conclusion about, 43–44
    create, 39–40
    create opportunities for teens, 14
    display of current materials, 48
    keeping current, 17–18, 39
    pop, 42–43
    relate, 40–42
College of Saint Mary's, California, 2
Columbia College, 168
"Columbia University Egg Drop" (Columbia
        College), 168
Comedy Central, 9
Comic Book Academy, 55–57
Comic books
    Cosplay Contest, 129–132
    Pokémon Tournaments, 126–128
    Superhero Smashup, 82–84
Comics Art Digital Coloring, 58–59
Comics Artist Forum, 60–61
Computer
    for Bento Box Bonanza, 110
    for Comics Art Digital Coloring, 59
    for Filmmaking 101, 196
    in 1980s, 5
    in 1990s, 5–6
    for Social Networking Programs, 182
    video game history, 123
    See also Technology programs
Concert charity events, 5
Connections
    library collection for making, 41
    making in teen space, 47
    making with tweens/teens, 16
Constans, Gabriel, 108
Contests
    Cosplay Contest, 129–132
    Cup Stack Attack, 169–171
    duct tape prom contest, 117
    Graffiti Contest, 85–88
    LEGO Contest, 90–95
    Photography Contest, 88–90
Conway, Ann, 132
Cooking/food programs
    Bento Box Bonanza, 108–112
    Food Tastings, 97–99
    Revolting Recipes, 103–105
    Smoothie Sensation, 105–108
    Sushi Making, 99–101
    Top Chef Season 4 winner, Stephanie Izard,
        appearance/cooking demo, 65–69
    Vegetarian Cooking, 101–103
Cosmetics, Kitchen, 137–140

"Cosplay, Gaming and Conventions: Amazing
        Unexpected Places an Anime Club Can
        Lead Unsuspecting Librarians"
        (Brehm-Heeger, Conway, & Vale), 132
Cosplay Contest, 129–132
Costumes contest, 129–132
Coupon, 12, 176–177
Crafts, materials in collection on, 40
Crafts programs
    Amigurumi: Crochet Happy Fun, 132–134
    Duct Tape Crafts, 117–120
    Jean Pocket Purses, 115–117
    Shrinky Dinks, 113–115
    Technology Fashionistas, 188–191
    T-shirt Remodel, 120–122
Create
    access, 12–13
    branding your teen/tween services, 22–24
    collections, 39–40
    description of, 11
    opportunities, 13–14
    something, 14–15
    spaces for teens/tweens, 45–46
Create, Relate, & Pop approach
    Create, 11–15
    Pop, 17–19
    Relate, 15–17
Create something
    with library, 14–15
    materials for in library collection, 40
    in teen spaces, 46
*Creative Expression Activities for Teens: Exploring
        Identity through Art, Craft, and
        Journaling* (Thomas), 70, 72
*Creepy Cute Crochet: Zombies, Ninjas, Robots,
        and More!* (Haden), 134
Crochet program, 132–134
Cross, Kevin, 57, 59, 61
Culture. *See* Japanese culture; Pop culture;
        Teen/tween pop culture, history of
Cup Stack Attack, 169–171
Cup stacking, 31–32
Current
    elements of being, 17–18
    library collection, 42
    programs, planning/implementing, 52
    teen space as, 48
Cyrus, Miley, 7

D

Dahl, Roald, 103–105
Daily Show with Jon Stewart, The (television
        show), 9
Dance
    in 1960s, 3
    programs, 157–158
Dance Dance Revolution (*DDR*), 131

Dancing with the Stars (television show), 157
Darien Library, 175
Davis, Sammy, Jr., 4
DC Comics Guide to Penciling Comics, The (Janson), 57
Demand
    library collection in, 42–43
    library in, 18–19
    spaces in, 48–49
Detroit Public Library, 191–194
Digital Age, 5–6
Digital Photo Madness! 50 Weird and Wacky Things to Do with Your Digital Camera (Gaines), 90
Digital Photography for Teens (Campbell), 90
Digital survey, 27
Disco, 4
Disney Channel, 155
Display case
    for LEGO Contest, 90
    for teen space, 48, 49
Displays, in teen space, 45, 47, 48–49
"DIY Gadgetry" (Saini), 194
D.I.Y. Girl: The Real Girl's Guide to Making Everything from Lip Gloss to Lamps (Bonnell), 139
Double Dutch Program, 160–162
Dr. Dre, 6
Draw 50 Monsters, Creeps, Superheroes, Demons, Dragons, Nerds, Dirts, Ghouls, Giants, Vampires, Zombies, and Other Curiosa . . . (Ames), 84
Drawing Words and Writing Pictures: Making Comics, Manga, Graphic Novels, and Beyond (Abel & Madden), 57
Drive-in theaters, 2
Drop-off time, 93
Drozd, Jerzy, 57, 59, 61
DTLK's Crafts for Kids, 128
Duckbrand.com, 120
Duct Tape Crafts, 117–120
Ductigami: The Art of the Tape (Wilson), 120
Ducttapefashion.com, 120
Duden, Jane, 2
DVDs
    coupon for free, 176–177
    dance, 158
    of musicals, 154
    for *Top Chef* program, 66
Dylan, Bob, 3
Dynamic Anatomy (Hogarth), 57
Dynamic Wrinkles and Drapery: Solutions for Drawing the Clothed Figure (Hogarth), 57

E

Ear buds, dressing up, 188–191
Ed Sullivan Show, The (television show), 3

Editing software, 195, 196
Edwardes, Dan, 160
Eggcellent Engineering, 166–168
Elffers, Joost, 145
Eng, Diana, 191
Epilog Mini 24 (laser cutter), 192, 193
Exercise. *See* Physical activities programs
Experience-based programs, 16
Experiences
    relating, 15–16
    relating in teen space, 47
    relating recycling of trends, 41
EXPLODapalooza, 162–166
Extreme Makeover: Home Edition (television show), 117

F

Face Food: The Visual Creativity of Japanese Bento Boxes (Salyers), 112
"Face the Cookie" challenge, 80
Facebook
    paid ads on, 36
    promotion with, 34
    Social Networking Programs, 181–183
"Facebook Application Directory" (Facebook), 183
Fairie-ality: The Fashion Collection from the House of Ellwand (Shields), 150, 151
Fairies Cookbook (Beery), 151
Fairy Homes, Jewelry, Dolls, and More program, 148–151
Fairy House and Beyond! (Kane), 151
Fairy Parties: Recipes, Crafts, and Games for Enchanting Celebrations (Mullaney), 151
Fairy Tale: A True Story (movie), 148
Fairy World Crafts (Ross), 151
Fantastic Mr. Fox (Dahl), 104
Fantasy programs. *See* Magic, fantasy, mystical world programs
Fashion design
    MTV: *Made* program and, 70
    Project Runway fashion show or challenge, 72–78
    Technology Fashionistas, 188–191
    See also Clothing
Fashion Geek: Clothing Accessories Tech (Eng), 191
Fashioning Technology: A DIY Intro to Smart Crafting (Pakhchyan), 191
Ferrari, Giulio, 187
Ferrari, Mario, 187
Filmmaking 101, 194–197
Fines
    coupon for, 12, 176
    opportunities to work off, 12–13
First LEGO League, 184, 187
Flash drives, dressing up, 188–191
Flickr.com
    bento box images from, 108, 110
    promotion with, 34

Flyers, 32–34
Focus groups, 29, 31
Follow through, with programming, 51
Food, 65–69. *See also* Cooking/food programs
Food, technology, other mandatory extras
　　for *Amigurumi: Crochet Happy Fun*, 133
　　for Bento Box Bonanza, 110–111
　　for Comic Book Academy, 57
　　for Comics Art Digital Coloring, 59
　　for Comics Artist Forum, 61
　　for Cosplay Contest, 131
　　for Cup Stack Attack, 170
　　for Double Dutch Program, 162
　　for Duct Tape Crafts, 119
　　for EXPLODapalooza, 165
　　for fairy program, 150
　　for Filmmaking 101, 197
　　for Food Tastings, 98
　　for Graffiti Contest, 87
　　for *High School Musical* Karaoke, 154–155
　　for LEGO Contest, 95
　　for Library LEGO League, 186
　　for MTV: *Made*, 71
　　for Parkour and Freerunning, 160
　　for Photography Contest, 89
　　for Pinhole Photography, 63
　　for Pokémon Tournaments, 127
　　for *Project Runway* fashion show or challenge, 78
　　for Psychics, Astrology, and the Future Fair, 145
　　for Retro Octathlon, 125
　　for Smoothie Sensation, 107
　　for Superhero Smashup, 83
　　for Sushi Making, 101
　　for Technology Fashionistas, 190
　　for Teen Summer Reading Program, 176–177
　　for *Top Chef* winner, appearance/cooking demo, 68
　　for Tween Summer Reading Program, 179
　　for Vampire Wreaths, 147
　　for Vegetarian Cooking, 103
Food Tastings, 97–99
Foodie, 97
"For Inspiration and Recognition of Science and Technology" (FIRST), 187
Frauenfelder, Mark, 194
Free, library as, 13–14, 37
Freerunning, Parkour and, 159–160
Fritz, Stewart, 192
Fun, 19, 49

G
Gaines, Thom, 90
Game Informer magazine, 52
Game On! Envisioning Your Own Video Game, 197–200
Game Star Mechanic (website), 200

Gaming programs
　　Game On! Envisioning Your Own Video Game, 197–200
　　Pokémon Tournaments, 126–128
　　Retro Octathlon, 123–125
　　See also Video games
Ganz, Nicholas, 88
GarageBand software, 153
Garden, fairy, 149
Generation T: 108 Ways to Transform a T-Shirt (Nicolay), 70, 72, 121, 122
Generation T: Beyond Fashion, 110 T-Shirt Transformations for Pets, Babies, Friends, Your Home, Car, and You (Nicolay), 122
Ginsberg, Allen, 3
Girl's Guide to Vampires: All You Need to Know about the Original Bad Boys, The (Karg), 148
GLBTQ (gay, lesbian, bisexual, transgender, questioning) community, 46
Glee (television show), 23, 153
Godfather, The (movie), 4
Goldschneider, Gary, 145
Goodstein, Anastasia, 1
Gordy, Berry, Jr., 3
Got Tape? Roll Out the Fun with Duct Tape (Schiedermayer), 120
GRAFF: The Art & Technique of Graffiti (Martinez), 88
Graffiti Contest, 85–88
Graffiti World: Street Art from Five Continents (Ganz), 88
Graphic novels
　　collection, space/signage related to, 46
　　Comic Book Academy, 55–57
　　Comics Artist Forum, 60–61
Gray, Amy Tipton, 148
Great American Smoothies: The Ultimate Blending Guide for Shakes, Slushes, Desserts, and Thirst Quenchers (Constans), 108
Green, John and Hank, 34
GreenBeanTeenQueen blog, 42
Greene, Gael, 97
Grunge (music genre), 6
Guerrilla marketing, 36
"Guidelines for the Montshire Egg Drop" (Montshire Museum of Science), 168
Guinness World Records, 7
Guitar Hero (video game), 8
Gundam (Japanese anime series), 43
Gunter, Sherry Kinkoph, 183

H
Haab, Sherri, 137
Hack Pittsburgh (website), 194
Hackerspace, 191, 193
Hacktory, The (website), 194

Haden, Christen, 134
Halloween, 147–148
Hannah Montana book series, 39
Happenings, 3
Harry Potter series (Rowling), 8
Heartbeats (jump rope team), 161
Heavy metal, 4
Heller, Joseph, 8
Hendrix, Jimi, 3
Hepner, Ryan, 183
Hesselt van Dinter, Maarten, 142
Hickerson, Joe, 3
High school fashion show, project design, 75
High School Musical (made-for-television movie), 7, 153, 155
High School Musical book series, 39
High School Musical Karaoke, 153–155
Hobbies, materials in collection on, 40
Hoenke, Justin, 197–200
Hogarth, Burne, 57
Holland, Gini, 3
Hot pants, 4
House, fairy, 149, 150
How to Be a Vampire: A Fangs-On Guide for the Newly Undead (Gray), 148
How to Cook Like a Top Chef (Miller), 66, 69
How to Draw Comics the Marvel Way (Lee & Buscema), 57
How to Host a Flower Fairy Tea-Party (Barker), 151
"How Young People View Their Lives, Futures and Politics: A Portrait of 'Generation Next'" (Pew Research Center for the People & the Press), 142
Howe, Neil, 7
Hughes, John, 4–5

I

I3 Detroit: Metro Detroit's Art & Technology Collective, 194
IBM, 5
Identification
    of library audience, 22
    of your teens/tweens, 24–32
IGN Entertainment, 5
Implementation, of programs, 52
Instructables.com, 166, 197
Instructors/talent
    for *Amigurumi*: Crochet Happy Fun, 133
    for Bento Box Bonanza, 109
    for Comic Book Academy, 56
    for Comics Art Digital Coloring, 58
    for Comics Artist Forum, 60
    for Cosplay Contest, 130
    for Cup Stack Attack, 169
    for Dance Programs, 158
    for Double Dutch Program, 161
    for Duct Tape Crafts, 118
    for Eggcellent Engineering, 166
    for EXPLODapalooza, 163
    for fairy program, 149
    for Filmmaking 101, 195
    for Food Tastings, 98
    for Game On! Envisioning Your Own Video Game, 198
    for Graffiti Contest, 86
    for Kitchen Cosmetics, 137
    for LEGO Contest, 91
    for Library LEGO League, 184
    for Library Makerspaces, 192
    for MTV: *Made*, 70
    for Parkour and Freerunning, 159
    for Photography Contest, 88
    for Pinhole Photography, 62
    for Pokémon Tournaments, 126
    for *Project Runway* fashion show or challenge, 73, 74, 78
    for Psychics, Astrology, and the Future Fair, 144
    for Smoothie Sensation, 106
    for Social Networking Programs, 182
    for Superhero Smashup, 82
    for Sushi Making, 99–100
    for Tattoo History, Culture, and Safety, 140
    for Technology Fashionistas, 188
    for *Top Chef* winner, appearance/cooking demo, 66
    for Vegetarian Cooking, 102
Interests
    focus groups for identification of, 29, 31
    programming based on, 51
    spaces for teens/tweens and, 46, 47, 48
    survey for identification of, 27–29
Internet
    in 1990s, 6
    in 2000s, 9
    Social Networking Programs, 181–183
Ishihara, Yoko, 112
Iverson, Sharon
    Comic Book Academy, 55–57
    Comics Art Digital Coloring, 58–59
    Pinhole Photography, 62–64
Izard, Stephanie, 65–69

J

J-14 magazine, 41, 52
Jackson, Michael, 5
James and the Giant Peach (Dahl), 104
Janson, Klaus, 57
Japanese culture
    Amigurumi: Crochet Happy Fun, 132–134
    Bento Box Bonanza, 108–112
    Cosplay Contest, 129–132
    manga, interest in Japanese culture from, 40
    Pokémon Tournaments, 126–128
    Sushi Making, 99–101

Jaws (movie), 4
Jean Pocket Purses, 115–117
Jeans, repurposing, 41
Jewelry, LED bracelets, 188–191
John Edward Cross Country (television show), 143
Johnson, Billy, Jr., 7
Jonas Brothers, 7
Joplin, Janis, 3
Jordan, Michael, 6
Judging
    for Cosplay Contest, 130, 131
    in LEGO Contest, 93
Jump rope program, 160–162

K
Kalamazoo Public Library
    Filmmaking 101, 194–197
    Tween Summer Reading Program, 177–180
Kallen, Stuart A., 6
Kane, Barry, 151
Karaoke, *High School Musical*, 153–155
Karg, Barb, 148
Kariya, Tetsu, 101
Kawaii (cute things), 132
Kawaii Bento Boxes: Cute and Convenient Japanese Meals on the Go (Staff), 112
Kent, Steven L., 125
KidzBop, 7
King, Carole, 4
Kingston Trio, 3
Kitchen, Crafts, & More (blog), 138, 140
Kitchen Cosmetics, 137–140
Knight, Maribeth, 132
Kobashi, Jennifer, 7–8
Krissoff, Liana, 66, 69

L
LA Ink (television show), 140
Laptop, 153, 154
Laser cutters, 192, 193
Learn Scratch (website), 200
LED bracelets, 188–191
Led Zeppelin (band), 4
Lee, Harper, 8
Lee, Stan, 57
LEGO
    LEGO Contest, 90–95
    LEGO Contest Rules and Guidelines, 92
    Library LEGO League, 184–187
    "Mindstorms Official Web site," 187
LEGO Book, The (Lipkowitz), 95
"LEGO Contests" (Bulger), 95
LEGO Mindstorms NXT robot, 184–187
Lennon, John, 3
Levinson, Jay Conrad, 36
Lewis, Alison, 191

Librarians, stereotypes of, 23
Library
    access to, 12–13
    as community center, 201
Library card, 12–13
Library LEGO League, 184–187
Library Makerspaces, 191–194
Library Marketing That Works! (Walters), 21
Library programs
    attendance at, 18–19
    create something, 14–15
    as fun, 19
    for tweens/teens, 9
    See also Programs
Lifetime channel, 72, 73, 78
Lilith Fair, 6
Lin, Fang-Yu, 191
Lipkowitz, Daniel, 95
Literature, 8
Logo
    AXIS logo from Ann Arbor District Library, 26
    for branding teen/tween services, 24
    on signage for teen/tween space, 45
    Sno-Isle Libraries Teen logo, 25

M
Mad Hot Ballroom (movie), 157
Madden, Matt, 57
Made by Hand: Searching for Meaning in a Throwaway World (Frauenfelder), 194
Madonna, 5
Magazine collection, 45–46
Magic, fantasy, mystical world programs
    Fairy Homes, Jewelry, Dolls, and More, 148–151
    Psychics, Astrology, and the Future Fair, 143–145
    Vampire Wreaths, 145–148
Make magazine, 192
Make: Technology on Your Time (website), 194, 197
Maker Faire (website), 194
Maker faires, 191–192
Maker SHED: DIY Kits + Tools + Books + Fun, 194
Makerbot Cupcake CNC (Computer Numerical Controller) 3-D printer, 193
MakerBot Store, 192
Makerspaces, Library, 191–194
Making Comings: Storytelling Secrets of Comics, Manga, and Graphic Novels (McCloud), 57
Mamma Mia! (movie), 4
Manga
    Bento Box Bonanza and, 108, 111, 112
    Comic Book Academy, 55–57
    Cosplay Contest, 129–132
    Gundam, 43
    interest in Japanese culture from, 40
    parents and, 17
    Pokémon Tournaments, 126–128
    popularity of, 58, 60

Manga (continued)
    Superhero Smashup and, 83
    Sushi Making and, 99
Manga Cookbook, The (Ishihara), 112
Mario Bros. (video game), 123, 125
Marketing
    for Comic Book Academy, 57
    elements of, 21–22
    of library services, 13–14
    of programs, 52
    for Silent Library, 81
    See also Promotion
Marketing tips
    for Amigurumi: Crochet Happy Fun, 134
    for Bento Box Bonanza, 111–112
    for Comic Book Academy, 57
    for Comics Art Digital Coloring, 59
    for Comics Artist Forum, 61
    for Cosplay Contest, 132
    for Dance Programs, 158
    for Double Dutch Program, 162
    for Duct Tape Crafts, 119
    for Eggcellent Engineering, 168
    for EXPLODapalooza, 166
    for fairy program, 151
    for Filmmaking 101, 197
    for Food Tastings, 99
    for Game On! Envisioning Your Own Video
        Game, 200
    for Graffiti Contest, 87
    for High School Musical Karaoke, 155
    for Jean Pocket Purses, 117
    for Kitchen Cosmetics, 139
    for LEGO Contest, 95
    for Library LEGO League, 187
    for Library Makerspaces, 193
    for MTV: Made, 71–72
    for Nail Art, 137
    for Parkour and Freerunning, 160
    for Photography Contest, 90
    for Pinhole Photography, 64
    for Pokémon Tournaments, 128
    for Project Runway fashion show or challenge,
        78
    for Psychics, Astrology, and the Future Fair, 145
    for Retro Octathlon, 125
    for Revolting Recipes, 105
    for Shrinky Dinks, 115
    for Smoothie Sensation, 107
    for Social Networking Programs, 183
    for Superhero Smashup, 83
    for Sushi Making, 101
    for Tattoo History, Culture, and Safety, 142
    for Technology Fashionistas, 190–191
    for Teen Summer Reading Program, 177
    for Top Chef winner, appearance/cooking
        demo, 69

    for T-shirt Remodel, 121
    for Tween Summer Reading Program, 180
    for Vampire Wreaths, 148
    for Vegetarian Cooking, 103
Marr, Melissa, 148
Marshall, Carmia, 121
Martin, Brett, 66, 69
Martinez, Scape, 88
Massachusetts Institute of Technology, 194
Mattel, 148
McCarthy, E. Jerome, 21
McCloud, Scott, 57
McDonald's, 2
Meetup.com, 34–35, 133
Meeuwenberg, Levi, 159
"Mentos Diet Coke Geyser" (Steve Spangler
    Science), 166
Mentos Fountains, 164, 165
Message boards, 132, 133
Metallica (band), 5
Meyer, Stephenie, 8, 146
Miami Ink (television show), 140
Millennials and the Pop Culture (Strauss &
    Howe), 7
Miller, Emily Wise, 66, 69
"Mindstorms Official Web site" (LEGO), 187
Minute to Win It games, 80
Minute to Win It (NBC), 81
MMU Egg Drop, 168
"Mobile Fab Lab Hits the Road" (MIT), 194
Models, 74
Modesto Junior College, California, 2
Monrovia (CA) Public Library, 81
Montshire Museum of Science, 168
Mood rings, 4
Moorpark City Library
    library card policy at, 12, 13
    Vampire Wreath program flier, 32, 33
Moreno, Mineko Takane, 101
Motown Company, 3
Movie theater advertising, 36–37
Movies
    adaptation of Roald Dahl's books, 104
    books made into, 42
    Filmmaking 101, 194–197
    librarian stereotypes in, 23
    musicals, 153
    of 1970s, 4
    of 1980s, 4–5
    of 1990s, 6
    superheroes in, 82
Ms. Pac-Man (video game), 5
MTV: Made, 69–72
MTV Network
    debut of, 5
    in 1990s, 6
    Silent Library, 81

website, 72
Mullaney, Colleen, 151
Music
    in 1950s, 2
    in 1960s, 3
    in 1970s, 4
    in 1980s, 5
    in 2000s, 7
    for Double Dutch Program, 162
    High School Musical Karaoke program, 153–155
    for Kitchen Cosmetics, 139
    for Nail Art program, 136
    for *Project Runway* fashion show or challenge, 78
Mylonas, Eric, 128
MySpace
    library page on, 34
    Social Networking Programs, 181–183
MySpace for Dummies (Hepner), 183
Mystical world programs. *See* Magic, fantasy, mystical world programs
MythBusters (television show), 162–163

N
Nail Art, 135–137
Nail Art (Haab), 137
NBC, 81
NES. *See* Nintendo Entertainment System
New York Magazine, 97
New York Times, 8, 108
Niche marketing, 34
Nicolay, Megan
    books by, 122
    Generation T: 108 Ways to Transform a T-Shirt, 70, 72, 121
99 Ways to Cut, Sew, & Deck Out Your Denim (Blakeney, Blakeney, & Schultz), 117
Nintendo DS, 126, 127
Nintendo Entertainment System (NES)
    release of, 5
    Retro Octathlon, 123–125
    Wii video gaming console, 8, 127
Nirvana (band), 6
Niven, David, 4
Nixon, Richard, 3–4
Noise, in library, 16–17
Noise Bridge Makerspace, 194

O
Obaachan, Annie, 134
Obesity, 79–81, 108
Official Preppy Handbook, The (Birnbach), 5
Oishinbo: Fish, Sushi & Sashimi: A La Carte (Kariya), 101
Okey, Shannon, 70, 72
Ollison, Rashod D., 7

Onassis, Jackie Kennedy, 4
One-time-use card, 12
Ono, Yoko, 3
Opportunities
    creating with teen space, 46
    libraries for creating, 13–14
    with pop culture materials in collection, 40
"Opt-in" feature, for text messaging, 35
Otaku (Japanese fan culture), 129, 130, 132
Outreach
    for library, 13–14
    promotions, 37
Oxford English Dictionary, 1

P
Pac-Man (video game), 5, 123
Paid advertising, 36–37
Pakhchyan, Syuzi, 191
Paper survey, 27
Paranormal Activity (movie), 143
Parents, library help for, 17
Parkour and Freerunning, 159–160
Parkour and Freerunning Handbook, The (Edwardes), 160
Party Girl (movie), 23
"Passive" contests, 48
PBS, 2
Pearl Jam (band), 6
People History, The, 6
Perdue, David J., 187
Personal computing, 5
Pet rocks, 4
Pew Research Center for the People & the Press, 140, 142
Phillips, Karen, 115
Photography
    in LEGO Contest, 93
    Photography Contest, 88–90
    Pinhole Photography, 62–64
Physical activities programs
    Cup Stack Attack, 169–171
    Dance Programs, 157–158
    Double Dutch Program, 160–162
    Eggcellent Engineering, 166–168
    EXPLODapalooza, 162–166
    Parkour and Freerunning, 159–160
Pierson, Stephanie, 103
Pinhole Photography, 62–64
Pizza-tasting program, 97, 98
Planning, of programs, 52
Planning/supplies
    for *Amigurumi*: Crochet Happy Fun, 133
    for Bento Box Bonanza, 109–110
    for Comic Book Academy, 56
    for Comics Art Digital Coloring, 58–59
    for Comics Artist Forum, 60–61
    for Cosplay Contest, 130–131

Planning/supplies *(continued)*
    for Cup Stack Attack, 169–170
    for Dance Programs, 158
    for Double Dutch Program, 161
    for Duct Tape Crafts, 118
    for Eggcellent Engineering, 167
    for EXPLODapalooza, 163–164
    for fairy program, 149
    for Filmmaking 101, 196
    for Food Tastings, 98
    for Game On! Envisioning Your Own Video
        Game, 198
    for Graffiti Contest, 86
    for *High School Musical* Karaoke, 154
    for Jean Pocket Purses, 116
    for Kitchen Cosmetics, 138–139
    for LEGO Contest, 91, 93
    for Library LEGO League, 185
    for Library Makerspaces, 192
    for MTV: *Made*, 71
    for Nail Art, 136
    for Parkour and Freerunning, 159
    for Photography Contest, 88–89
    for Pinhole Photography, 62–63
    for Pokémon Tournaments, 127
    for *Project Runway* fashion show or challenge,
        74–77
    for Psychics, Astrology, and the Future Fair, 144
    for Retro Octathlon, 124–125
    for Revolting Recipes, 104
    for Shrinky Dinks, 114
    for Silent Library, 79–80
    for Smoothie Sensation, 106–107
    for Social Networking Programs, 182
    for Superhero Smashup, 82–83
    for Sushi Making, 100
    for Tattoo History, Culture, and Safety, 141
    for Technology Fashionistas, 188–189
    for Teen Summer Reading Program, 174
    for *Top Chef* winner, appearance/cooking
        demo, 67–68
    for T-shirt Remodel, 121
    for Tween Summer Reading Program, 178
    for Vampire Wreaths, 147
    for Vegetarian Cooking, 102
Podcast
    Art & Story podcast, 57, 59, 61
    interview with Stephanie Izard, 68
    portable podcast device, 145
Pokémon: 10th Anniversary Pokédex (Mylonas), 128
Pokémon Battle Revolution (video game), 127
Pokémon Heartgold Version, Soulsilver Version:
    The Official Pokémon Johto Guide &
    Pokédex (Ryan), 128
Pokémon Red and Blue (video game), 8
Pokémon Tournaments, 126–128
Polls, for teen space, 47

Pong (video game), 123
Pop
    be current, 17–18
    be in demand, 18–19
    description of, 17
    have fun, 19
    for library collection, 42–43
    spaces for teens/tweens, 48–49
Pop culture
    advertising/promotion of library to
        teens/tweens, 32
    definition of, 1
    library and, 201
    library collection and, 39–40, 42–43
    library relevancy and, 17
    for making connections, 16
    programs, planning/implementing, 52
    for relating to teens/tweens, 15–16
    spaces that incorporate, 45
    teen space and, 49
    See also Teen/tween pop culture, history of
Portland Public Library, 197–200
Postcards, 33–34
Posters, 45, 47
Presley, Elvis, 2
Print advertising, 32–34
Prizes
    for Cosplay Contest, 129, 131
    for Cup Stack Attack, 170
    for Eggcellent Engineering, 167
    for Graffiti Contest, 85, 86–87
    for LEGO Contest, 91, 92, 94
    for Library LEGO League, 185, 186
    for Library Makerspaces, 193
    for Photography Contest, 89
    for Pokémon Tournaments, 127
    for *Project Runway* fashion show or challenge,
        73, 78
    for Retro Octathlon, 125
    for Silent Library, 80
    for Teen Summer Reading Program, 176–177
    for Tween Summer Reading Program, 178
Product, Price, Promotion, and Place model, 21
Programs
    art, 55–64
    celebrity and reality television, 65–84
    conclusion about, 52–53
    contests, 85–95
    cooking and food, 97–112
    foundations for successful, 51–52
    gaming, 123–128
    Japanese popular culture, 129–134
    magic, fantasy, mystical world, 143–151
    me-beauty/fashion, 135–142
    music, 153–155
    physical activities, 157–171
    planning/implementing, 52–53

summer reading, 173–180
technology, 181–200
See also Library programs
Project Runway fashion show or challenge, 72–78
Projector
for Bento Box Bonanza, 110–111
for Comics Art Digital Coloring, 59
for MTV: *Made*, 71
for Pinhole Photography, 63
Promotion
AXIS logo from Ann Arbor District Library, 26
branding your teen/tween services, 22–24
conclusion about, 37–38
elements of, 21–22
guerrilla, viral, alternative, 36
identifying your teens/tweens, 24–32
outreach promotions, 37
paid advertising, 36–37
print advertising, 32–34
of programs, 52
Sno-Isle Libraries Teen logo, 25
social networking promotion, 34–35
street teams, 35
Teen Patron Library Use Survey, 30–31
Teen Patron Profile Survey, 28–29
Psychic Kids: Children of the Paranormal
(television show), 143
Psychics, Astrology, and the Future Fair, 143–145
Punk movement, 4

Q
Quiet, in library, 16–17

R
Radio Disney, 7–8
Raffle tickets, 178
Raven-Symoné, 7
RCA, 2
Readers, 144
Reading
Teen Summer Reading Program, 173–177
Tween Summer Reading Program, 177–180
Reality television, 157. *See also* Celebrity and
reality television programs
*Red Hot Peppers: The Skookum Book of Jump
Rope Games, Rhymes, and Fancy
Footwork* (Boardman), 162
Relate
connections, making, 16
description of, 15
experiences, 15–16
identification of teens/tweens, 24–32
library collection, 40–42
relevancy, 16–17
teen spaces, 47–48

Relevancy
of libraries, 16–17
of library collection, 41–42
of teen space, 48
Research and Markets, 7
Resources
for *Amigurumi*: Crochet Happy Fun, 134
for Bento Box Bonanza, 112
for Comic Book Academy, 57
for Comics Art Digital Coloring, 59
for Comics Artist Forum, 61
for Cosplay Contest, 132
for Cup Stack Attack, 171
for Double Dutch Program, 162
for Duct Tape Crafts, 120
for Eggcellent Engineering, 168
for EXPLODapalooza, 166
for fairy program, 151
for Filmmaking 101, 197
for Food Tastings, 99
for Game On! Envisioning Your Own Video
Game, 200
for Graffiti Contest, 88
for *High School Musical* Karaoke, 155
for Jean Pocket Purses, 117
for Kitchen Cosmetics, 139
for LEGO Contest, 95
for Library LEGO League, 187
for Library Makerspaces, 194
for MTV: *Made*, 72
for Nail Art, 137
for Parkour and Freerunning, 160
for Photography Contest, 90
for Pinhole Photography, 64
for Pokémon Tournaments, 128
for Psychics, Astrology, and the Future Fair, 145
for Retro Octathlon, 125
for Revolting Recipes, 105
for Shrinky Dinks, 115
for Silent Library, 81
for Smoothie Sensation, 107
for Social Networking Programs, 183
for Superhero Smashup, 83–84
for Sushi Making, 101
for Tattoo History, Culture, and Safety, 142
for Technology Fashionistas, 191
for *Top Chef* program, 69
for T-shirt Remodel, 121–122
for Vampire Wreaths, 148
for Vegetarian Cooking, 103
Retro Octathlon, 123–125
Revolting Recipes, 103–105
Rimoli, Ana Paula, 134
Roald Dahl's Revolting Recipes (Dahl), 105
Robot, LEGO Mindstorms NXT, 184–187
Rock Band (video game), 8, 14
Roland CAMM-1 Servo GX-24 (vinyl cutter),
192, 193

Rolling Stone magazine
    debut of, 3
    for latest trends in music, 41, 52
    on teen pop, 6
Rolling Stones, The (band), 3
Ross, Kathy, 151
Roulston, Jane, 115
Rowling, J. K., 8
Rudolph, Mark, 57, 59, 61
Runway show, 72–78
Ryan, Michael G., 128

S
Saini, Angela, 191, 194
Salyers, Christopher, 112
Sams Teach Yourself Facebook in 10 Minutes
    (Gunter), 183
San Antonio Public Library, 12
Sachet, fairy, 149
Saturday Night Fever (movie), 4
Saturday Night Live (television show), 4
Schedule, for teen/tween program, 52
Scheintaub, Leda, 66, 69
Schiedermayer, Ellie, 120
Schultz, Ellen, 117
Science
    Eggcellent Engineering, 166–168
    EXPLODapalooza, 162–166
Scratch (programming language), 198–199, 200
Scratch: Imagine. Program. Share. (website), 200
Secret Language of Birthdays (Thompson, Elffers,
    & Goldschneider), 145
Seeger, Pete, 3
Shaft (movie), 4
Shakur, Tupac, 6
Shields, Genie, 150, 151
Shobpot, 193
"Shockwave Air Cannon" (Instructables.com), 166
Shopbot (website), 192
Shrink Art 101 (Roulston), 115
Shrink Art Jewelry (Phillips), 115
Shrinky Dinks, 113–115
Signage, 45
Silent Library, 79–81
"Silent Library" (MTV Network), 81
Singing Bee, The (television show), 153
Slayer (band), 5
Slide show
    for Bento Box Bonanza, 110–111
    of duct tape prom images, 119
Smashing Pumpkins, 6
Smith, Diana, 8
Smoothie Sensation, 105–108
*Smoothies: 50 Recipes for High-Energy
    Refreshment* (Barber), 107
Smoothies for Life! Yummy, Fun and Nutritious
    (Chace), 107

Sno-Isle Libraries Teen logo, 24, 25
Snoop Doggy Dogg, 6
So You Think You Can Dance (television show), 157
So, You Wanna Be a Comic Book Artist? (Amara), 83
Social networking
    library page for, 17
    popularity of, 9
    programs, 181–183
    promotion with, 34–35
Soldering irons, 192–193
Some Kind of Wonderful (movie), 4–5
Soundgarden (band), 6
Space
    for Filmmaking 101, 196
    for LEGO Contest, 90
    for Parkour and Freerunning, 160
    for Psychics, Astrology, and the Future Fair, 144
    for Silent Library, 80
Spaces for teens/tweens
    creating, 45–46
    pop, 48–49
    relate, 47–48
Spangler, Steve, 166
Spears, Britney, 6–7
Sspeedstacks.com, 171
Staff, Joie, 112
Star Wars (movie), 4
Star Wars: Attack of the Clones (movie), 23
Stevespanglerscience.com, 166
Stewart, Gail B., 4
Stick It! 99 Duct Tape Projects (Bonnadio), 120
Storey, Samantha, 108, 112
Strada, Judi, 101
Strauss, William, 7
Street Fighter (video game), 123
Street teams, 35
"Stuck at Prom Scholarship Contest"
    (Duckbrand.com), 120
Stuck at the Prom Contest, 117
Submission session guidelines, project design, 76–77
Sullivan, Ed, 2
Summer reading programs
    Teen Summer Reading Program, 173–177
    Tween Summer Reading Program, 177–180
Superhero Smashup, 82–84
Supplies. See Planning/supplies
Survey
    for interests of teens, 27–29
    for programming ideas, 51
    Teen Patron Library Use Survey, 30–31
    Teen Patron Profile Survey, 28–29
SurveyMonkey, 27
Sushi for Dummies (Strada & Moreno), 101
Sushi Making, 99–101
Sweet Sweetback's Baadasssss Song (movie), 4
*Switch Craft: Battery-Powered Crafts to Make and
    Sew* (Lewis & Lin), 191

T

Tapebrothers.com, 120
Tastings, Food, 97–99
Tattoo artist, 140–142
Tattoo History, Culture, and Safety, 140–142
Taylor, Elizabeth, 4
Taylor, James, 4
Technology
    in 1980s, 5
    in 1990s, 5–6
    in 2000s, 9
    for Comic Book Academy, 57
    See also Food, technology, other mandatory
        extras
Technology Fashionistas, 188–191
Technology programs
    Filmmaking 101, 194–197
    Game On! Envisioning Your Own Video
        Game, 197–200
    Library LEGO League, 184–187
    Library Makerspaces, 191–194
    Social Networking Programs, 181–183
    Technology Fashionistas, 188–191
Teen Advisory Board
    for identification of audience, 27
    for programming ideas, 51
*Teen Dream Power: Unlock the Meaning of Your
    Dreams* (Abadie), 145
Teen Game (summer reading program),
    174–176
Teen Patron Library Use Survey, 30–31
Teen Patron Profile Survey, 28–29
*Teen Psychic: Exploring Your Intuitive Spiritual
    Powers* (Abadie), 145
Teen Summer Reading Program, 173–177
Teenagers
    audience, identification of, 22, 24–32
    library programming for, 201
    library services to, 9
    programming ideas from, 51–52
    as resource, street teams, 35
Teen/tween pop culture, history of
    in 1950s, 2
    in 1960s, 2–3
    in 1970s, 3–4
    in 1980s, 4–5
    in 1990s, 5–6
    in 2000 to present, 6–9
    library services to tweens/teens, 9
    recycling of, 1
Teen/tween services
    branding, 22–24
    identification of teens/tweens, 24–32
    library collection and, 43–44
    See also Programs
Teeri, Steve, 191–194

Television
    in 1950s, 2
    in 1970s, 4
    in 1990s, 6
    in 2000s, 8
    advertising for library programs, 37
    Comedy Central, 9
    dance shows, 157
    library advertising on, 69
    musicals, 153
    tattoo shows, 140
    Top Chef Season 4 winner, Stephanie Izard,
        appearance/cooking demo, 65–69
    See also Celebrity and reality television
        programs
Telling Room, The, 198
Tetris (video game), 5
Text messaging, 35
TextMarks, 35
Thomas, Bonnie, 70, 72
Thompson, Alicia, 145
"Thriving Business Built on Geeks' Backs, A"
    (Knight), 132
Timberlake, Justin, 6
Tinkerbell (fairy from *Peter Pan*), 148
Titanic (movie), 6
To Kill a Mockingbird (Lee), 8
Top Chef Season 4 winner, Stephanie Izard,
    appearance/cooking demo, 65–69
Top Chef: The Cookbook (Martin, Krissoff, &
    Scheintaub), 66, 69
Top Chef: The Quickfire Cookbook (Miller), 66, 69
*Totally Wired: What Teens and Tweens Are
    Really Doing Online* (Goodstein), 1
Trends, recycling of, 41
"Trend-spotting" committees, 18
*T-Shirt Makeovers: 20 Transformations for
    Fabulous Fashions* (Marshall), 121
T-shirt Remodel, 120–122
TV B Gone, 192, 194
Tween Summer Reading Program, 177–180
Tweens
    audience, identification of, 22, 24–32
    library services to, 9
    programming for, 52–53, 201
    programming ideas from, 51–52
    spending by, 7
    summer reading programs for, 173, 177–180
    See also Teen/tween pop culture, history of;
        Teen/tween services
Twilight saga (Meyer)
    familiarity with, 41
    materials in collection on vampires, 40
    popularity of, 8
    Vampire Wreath program flier, 32, 33
Twits, The (Dahl), 103, 104–105
Twitter, 34

U

Ultimate History of Video Games, The (Kent), 125
Understanding Comics (McCloud), 57
Unofficial LEGO Builders Guide, The (Bedford), 95
Unofficial Lego Mindstorms NXT Inventor's Guide, The (Perdue), 187
US Weekly magazine, 52

V

Vale, Carrie, 132
Vampire Wreaths, 145–148
Van Halen (band), 5
Vegetables Rock! A Complete Guide for Teenage Vegetarians (Pierson), 103
Vegetarian Cooking, 101–103
Video camera
    for event with Stephanie Izard, 68
    Filmmaking 101, 194–197
    for Library Makerspaces, 192
    for Social Networking Programs, 182
Video games
    in 1980s, 5
    in 2000s, 8
    for Cosplay Contest, 131
    Game On! Envisioning Your Own Video Game, 197–200
    Pokémon Tournaments, 126–128
    Retro Octathlon, 123–125
    to teach dance moves, 157
    tournaments, creating opportunity with, 14
Vietnam War, 4
Vinyl cutters, 192, 193
Viral marketing, 36
Volcanic Eruptions, 163

W

Walt Disney Company
    "*High School Musical* Official Website," 155
    Tinkerbell (fairy from *Peter Pan*), 148
    in tween market, 6–8
Walters, Suzanne, 21
Watergate scandal, 3–4
Web 2.0, 11

Website, library
    online summer reading program, 179
    photo entries on, 89
Websites. *See* Resources
Weeding, of library collection, 42–43
Who, The (band), 3
Wicked Lovely (Marr), 148
Wignall, Jeff, 90
Wii video gaming console, 8, 127
Wilson, Joe, 120
Windows Live Movie Maker, 183
Windows Live Movie Maker 2011 (Windows Live), 183
Winning Digital Photo Contests (Wignall), 90
Wise Up to Teens: Insights into Marketing and Advertising to Teenagers (Zollo), 32
Witches, The (Dahl), 104
Woodstock, 3
World of Tattoo: An Illustrated History, The (Hesselt van Dinter), 142
World Sport Stacking Association (WSSA), 169, 171
World War II, 2
World Wide Web, 5
Wreaths, Vampire, 145–148

Y

Yee, Jou Ling, 134
Yelp
    for Food Tastings, 99
    for opinions on restaurants, 97
    promotion of library programs with, 34
Youth participation, 11
Youth Services Corner website, 42
YouTube
    cup stacking clip, 170
    music video contest, 153
    Social Networking Programs, 181–183
    video for Tween Summer Reading Program, 180
YoYo Games (website), 200
Ypulse (blog), 1, 32, 52

Z

Zollo, Peter, 32

About the Authors

Erin Helmrich is a teen services librarian at the Ann Arbor District Library in Ann Arbor, Michigan. She has worked as a youth and teen librarian since 1996. She has been writing the popular Voice of Youth Advocates (VOYA) "Teen Pop-Culture Quizzes" since 1999. Erin is the chair of the 2012 Young Adult Library Services Association (YALSA) Printz Award Committee and served on the YALSA Board of Directors from 2006 to 2009. Erin is the recipient of two Michigan Library Association awards: she won the Loleta D. Fyan award (for imaginative and unique service) in 2002 and the Frances H. Pletz award (excellence in teen services) in 2008, both for providing excellent teen services. She has presented on teen collection development, programming and marketing for teens, video gaming, and teen popular culture around the country. Erin received her master's in library science at Wayne State University in Detroit, Michigan, and has an undergraduate degree in film studies. Originally from San Francisco, Erin lives to travel and try new things. A lover of animals, plants, and the outdoors, she is also a media junkie who loves news and gossip more than she should. Erin lives in Ann Arbor and is loving that the recent film incentives offered by the state of Michigan means regular celeb sightings are possible! Erin and Elizabeth became friends over a shared love of cats and pop culture, and they used to share a cubicle wall at the Ann Arbor District Library in Michigan.

Elizabeth Schneider is a youth services librarian at the Monrovia Public Library in Monrovia, California. She has been a librarian since 2006, focusing on services to teens and tweens. Elizabeth has also worked closely on video gaming events and special projects such as Library Lego League and podcasting at the Ann Arbor District Library in Ann Arbor, Michigan. She has been very active at the state level, presenting innovative tween programming at the Michigan Library Association Summer Reading Workshop in 2006 and serving on the 2008 Youth/Teen Spring Institute Conference planning committee. Elizabeth is currently serving on the Popular Paperbacks for Young Adults committee for YALSA. She received her master's in information at the University of

Michigan, Ann Arbor, and her bachelor's of science in chemistry from Washington State University. Elizabeth is a dedicated cat lover, constantly saving kittens from the wild, and enjoys hiking, college football, and looking out for movie star sightings in Los Angeles.